Who's Who
IN CONTEMPORARY
WORLD THEATRE

WHO'S WHO SERIES

*Available in USA from Oxford University Press

Who's Who
IN CONTEMPORARY
WORLD THEATRE

Edited by Daniel
Meyer-Dinkgräfe

London and New York

First published 2000
by Routledge
11 New Fetter Lane, London EC4P 4EE

Simultaneously published in the USA and Canada
by Routledge
29 West 35th Street, New York, NY 10001

Routledge is an imprint of the Taylor & Francis Group

Typeset in Sabon by Taylor & Francis Books Ltd
Printed and bound in Great Britain by TJ International Ltd,
Padstow, Cornwall

British Library Cataloguing in Publication Data
A catalogue record for this book is available from the British Library

Library of Congress Cataloging-in-Publication Data
Who's who in contemporary world theatre / editor, Daniel Meyer-Dinkgräfe.
p. cm.
1. Theater–Biography–Dictionaries. 2. Dramatists–Biography–Dictionaries.
I. Meyer-Dinkgräfe, Daniel.
PN2035.W485 2000
792'.092'2–dc21
[B] 99-047437

ISBN 0–415–14161–3

Contents

Contributors

Sayed Jamil Ahmed Chairman, Department of Theatre and Music, University of Dhaka, Dhaka; *Bangladesh*

Peter Antonissen Theatre critic of *De Morgen*; *Belgium*

Sudeshree Bannerjee *Seagull Theatre Quarterly*, Calcutta; *India*

Chittali Basu *Seagull Theatre Quarterly*, Calcutta; *India*

Reinhard Bösing Formerly dramaturg with Peter Stein's Schaubühne, Berlin; *Germany* (additional material for Achternbusch, Berndl, Buhre, Clever, Dorn, Tina Engel, Freyer, Froboess, Glittenberg, Grashof, Gudzuhn, Hoger, Holtz, Karge, Kirchhoff, Manzel, Marthaler, Mattes, Matthes, Samel, Sander, Schade, Elisabeth Schwarz)

Dwayne Brenna Assistant Professor, Department of Drama, University of Saskatchewan; *Canada*

Natalia Chechel Assistant Professor, Department of Theatre Studies, Karpenko Kary Institute for the Art of the Theatre, Kiev; *Ukraine*

Necla Cikigil Associate Professor, Instructor of English, Drama and History of Theatre, Department of Modern Languages, Middle East Technical University, Ankara; *Turkey*

Margaret Coldiron
Assistant Professor, Department of Theatre and Dance, Hamilton College, USA; *Indonesia*

Adrienne Darvay Nagy Freelance researcher and theatre historian, Hungary; *Hungary*

Maria M. Delgado Lecturer in Drama, Queen Mary and Westfield College, University of London, UK; *France* (Chéreau, Lavelli), *Spain* (Amat, Belbel, Diosdado, Espert, Gas, Molina, Pasqual, Nieva, Pedrero)

Sita Dickson-Littlewood University of the West Indies and Roehampton

Institute, London, UK; *French Caribbean* (Jenny Alpha, Michèle Césaire, Exelis, Germain, Justin-Joseph, Laou, Leal, Salibur)

Gabriella Giannachi Lecturer, Department of Theatre Studies, Lancaster University, UK; *Italy*

Won-Jae Jang *Monthly Korean Theatre Review* and Royal Holloway College, University of London, UK; *Korea*

Bridget Jones Senior Research Fellow, Department of Modern Languages, Roehampton Institute, London, UK; *French Caribbean*

Anjum Katyal *Seagull Theatre Quarterly*, Calcutta; *India*

Nick Kaye Professor, Department of Drama, University of Manchester, UK; *China*

Rob Klinkenberg Editor, Amsterdam; The Netherlands

Marina Litavrina Professor, Russian Academy of Theatre Art, Moscow; *Russia*

John London Hebrew University of Jerusalem; *Spain* (Flotats, Font, Boadella)

Xiao Cun Liu Editor of *Drama*, Beijing; *China* (Xi Mei Juan)

Robin Loon Seong Yun Senior Tutor, Theatre Studies Programme, National University of Singapore; *Singapore*

Ken McCoy Assistant Professor, Communication Studies and Theatre Arts, Stetson University, DeLand, Florida, USA; *Puerto Rico*

Kristel Marcoen Vlaams Theater Instituut; *Belgium*

Daniel Meyer-Dinkgräfe Lecturer, Department of Theatre, Film and Television Studies, University of Wales Aberystwyth, UK; *General Editor* (contributions for USA (with Riedel), Germany, Austria and Switzerland (with Bösing), Great Britain (with Rankin) and Canada (with Brenna); on the basis of material provided by the countries' ITI: Brazil, Bulgaria, Croatia, Cyprus, Denmark, Finland, Greece, Hungary, Jamaica, Jordan, Latvia, Mexico, Norway, Poland, Romania, Slovenia and Sweden)

Mara Negrón Associate Professor, Department of Comparative Literature, University of Puerto Rico; *France* (Azencot, Barriera, Bigot, Caubère, Cixous, Derenne, Guy-Claude François, Hardy, Mnouchkine, Nityanandam)

Athipet Nirmala Reader, Department of English, Madurai Kamaraj University, Madurai; *India* (Alekar, Allana, Bharati, Kambar, Karnad, Parthasarathy, Ramaswamy, Shah)

Osita Okagbue Lecturer, Department of Theatre and Performance Studies, University of Plymouth, Plymouth, UK; *African nations*

David Ian Rabey Reader, Department of Theatre, Film and Television Studies, University of Wales, Aberystwyth, UK; *Great Britain* (Barker, Rudkin)

Parasuram Ramamoorthi Reader and Chairman, Department of Theatre Arts, Madurai Kamaraj University, Madurai; *India* (Bajaj, Chowdhry, Govind Deshpande, Sulaba Deshpande, Dubey, Jalan, Kaul, Lagoo, Maharishi, Muthusamy, Pathak, Pillai, Ramanujam, Roy, Sircar, Subbanna, Tanvir, Tendulkar, Thambiran)

Charles Rankin Freelance writer, lecturer and trainer, UK; *Great Britain* (additional material for Bill Alexander, Barton, Beale, Bogdanov, Branagh, Brook, Bury, Cox, Edgar, Finney, Gambon, Griffiths, Hands, Jacobi, McCowen, McKellen, Pinter, Poliakoff, Rickman, Sher, Stevenson, Stoppard, Warner)

Mala Renganathan Lecturer, Department of English, Assam University, Silchar; *India* (Arambam, Deboo, Dossa, Krishnamoorthy, Raju, Thiyam)

Leslie Riedel Professor at the Department of Theatre Arts, University of Delaware; *USA*

Freddie Rokem Professor, Department of Theatre Arts, University of Tel Aviv; *Israel*

Laura Rota I Roca Denmark; *Cuba*

Amitav Roy Professor of Shakespeare Studies, Rabindra Nharati University, Calcutta; *India* (Bandopadhyay, Mitra, Sen)

Mercè Saumell Lecturer in Theatre History and Practice, University of Gerona and Institut del Teatre, Barcelona; *Spain* (Cabal, Cantó, Gómez, Heras, Hipólito, Homar, Lizaran, Marsillach, Paredes, Pellicena, Plaza, Puicorbé, Salvat, Sánchesz-Gijón, Sanchis Sinisterra, Távora)

Elizabeth Schafer Senior Lecturer, Department of Drama and Theatre Studies, Royal Holloway College, University of London, UK; *Australia*

Eric Schneider Freelance writer, actor and director, London and Luxembourg; *Luxembourg*

Lin Shen Deputy Director, Research Institute of the Central Academy of Drama; *China* (Gao Xing Jian, Meng Jin Hui, Mo Sen, Lin Sao Hua)

Brian Singleton Lecturer, Samuel Beckett Centre for Drama and Theatre Studies, Trinity College, Dublin; *Ireland*

Renganathan Sudha Lecturer, Department of French, Madurai Kamaraj University, Madurai; *India* (Karanth, Panikar, Prasanna, Raina, Ramamoorthi, Viswanathan)

Berni Sweeney Samuel Beckett Centre for Drama and Theatre Studies, Trinity College, Dublin; *Ireland*

John Thomson Reader, Department of English, Victoria University of Wellington; *New Zealand*

Ken Wong Department of Drama, Theatre and Media Arts, Royal Holloway College, University of London, UK; *Hong Kong*

Huang Yi Librarian, Central Academy of Drama; *China*

Masako Yuasa Lecturer in Japanese and Japanese Theatre, Department of East Asian Studies, University of Leeds, UK; *Japan*

Gergely Zöldi Theatre journalist and translator; *Hungary*

Preface

Who's Who in Contemporary World Theatre provides 1,400 entries on currently active theatre artists from 68 countries worldwide. 'Theatre artists' means just that: people who work in the theatre today as actors, directors, designers and dramatists. The book thus expressly excludes artists who work predominantly in the distinct and separate genres of performance art, musical, operetta, opera and dance. The reason for this exclusion is the mere availability of space in view of the fact that each of these genres would merit an independent *Who's Who*. Some, mainly non-western theatre artists covered in this book cross the boundaries between genres; special attention is drawn to this in the relevant entries.

The contributors for each country have selected artists who are alive and active today. Those artists 'have made it': they are well-known, at least nationally and in many cases internationally, to a wide audience, not only to their peers in the theatre world. Their work has been acclaimed, in many cases praised, in some also controversially discussed. They are regarded as important to the theatre practice at least of their own country, and in many cases have influenced the theatre beyond.

The entries provide factual information on the artists selected: year of birth, nationality, professional training and major achievements of the artists' careers. Some artists decline to reveal their year of birth, accounting for omissions in this category. In some cases, artists have moved between different countries. They are listed under the country in which they spent most of their active careers, with brief indication to their country of birth. Reference to the professional training helps to position and place the artists within their countries. Cross-references to the work of other theatre artists who have a separate entry in the *Who's Who* are indicated in SMALL CAPITALS. Titles of plays originally written in languages other than English are presented in the original language, followed by an English translation. In some cases, however, the original titles are untranslatable.

In addition to factual information, each entry provides the reader with an insight into the special characteristics of the individual artists: what sets them apart from the rest? What has gained them their status among peers, audiences and critics? In some entries, contributors have quoted from other sources in their characterization, clearly indicating this by using quotation marks. In order not to complicate reading, acknowledgements for these quotations are summarized in the acknowledgement section following this preface.

Who's Who in Contemporary World Theatre places much emphasis on being up to date. Information here is as accurate as possible at the time of going to print. Any changes that may have taken place since then only serve to emphasize how rapidly contemporary theatre changes.

Acknowledgements

I would like to thank all those who helped in making this book possible: colleagues who suggested contributors, colleagues who read initial lists for countries, and whose comments were very valuable, the contributors, who are listed separately; and the staff at the International Theatre Institute, who provided me or other contributors with names and addresses of theatre artists of their countries, or provided me with rich material which I used to write the entries. They are: Brazil, Bulgaria, Croatia, Cuba, Cyprus, Denmark, Finland, Greece, Hungary, Jamaica, Jordan, Latvia, Mexico, Norway, Poland, Romania, Slovenia, Sweden and Venezuela.

I would like to thank the publishers for permission to use quotes for the following entries:

Theater Heute
Anne Bennent (2/1993, p. 7), Ritter (Jahrbuch 1985, p. 138), Tukur (Jahrbuch 1986, p. 19), Wuttke (Jahrbuch 1995, pp. 114–21).

Die Deutsche Bühne
Ciulli, Engel, Griem, Grüber, Haußmann, Hürlimann, Jelinek, Langhoff, Dieter Mann, Morgenroth, Mouchtar-Samorai, Müller, Niermeyer, Pohl, Schwab, Turrini, Watanabe.

The Cambridge Guide to Theatre, edited by Martin Banham, Cambridge: Cambridge University Press, 1995.
Cartwright, Rabe, Wilson.

The Cambridge Guide to American Theatre, edited by Don B. Wilmeth and Tice L. Miller, Cambridge: Cambridge University Press, 1993.
Beatty, Channing, Fornés, Gotanda, Harris, Herrmann, Landesmann, Lobel, Malkovich, McNally, Tsypin.

Canadian Theatre Encyclopedia, http://www.canadiantheatre.com.
Burroughs, Gélinas, Fiona Reid, Stratton.

The *Guardian*
Hands, Mitchell.

The Oxford Companion to Canadian Theatre, edited by Eugene Benton and
L.W. Connolly, Oxford, Ont., 1990.
Eagan, Silver, Thompson, Walker.

The World Encyclopedia of Contemporary Theatre, edited by Don Rubin, vol. 2,
'The Americas', London and New York: Routledge, 1996.
Chang, Foreman, Geiogamah, Henley, Norman, Robert Wilson.

Theatrical Designers, edited by Thomas J. Mikotowicz, reproduced with
permission of Greenwood Publishing Group, Inc., Westport, CT.
Bury, Conklin, Koltai, Loquasto.

Theatrical Directors: A Biographical Dictionary, edited by John W. Frick and
Stephen M. Vallillo, reproduced with permission of Greenwood Publishing
Group, Inc., Westport, CT.
Donnellan, Flimm, Glassco, LeCompte, Emily Mann, Meadow, Noble, Nunn,
Sellars, Zaks.

Theaterlexikon. Autoren, Regisseure, Schauspieler, Dramaturgen, Bühnenbild-
ner, Kritiker, herausgegeben von C. Bernd Sucher, München: Deutscher
Taschenbuch Verlag, 1994.
Bickel, Bondy, Domröse, Gotscheff, Hollmann, Lampe, Minks, Neuenfels,
Rose, Gisela Stein, Voss, Wonder, Zadek.

Contemporary Dramatists, edited by K.A. Berney, 5th edn, London: St James
Press, 1993.
Howe, Hwang, Kopit, Arthur Miller.

International Dictionary of the Theatre, vol. 2, 'Playwrights', edited by Mark
Hawkins-Dady, London: St James Press, 1994.
Blessing.

A

Abraham, F. Murray (1939–) Actor, USA. Abraham is best known for his portrayal of Salieri in the film of SHAFFER's *Amadeus* (1985). He studied drama at the University of Texas at El Paso and acting with Uta Hagen at the Herbert Berghof Studio, New York City. His debut on the stage was in 1965, and he first appeared on Broadway in 1968. After many parts in new and experimental work in the earlier years of his career, the beginning of the 1980s marked a change when he appeared as Dorn in Chekhov's *Cajka* (*The Seagull*, 1980), and Creon in Sophocles' *Antigone* (1982). Following *Amadeus* he played Malvolio in *Twelfth Night* (1986) and the title roles in *Macbeth* (1987) and *King Lear* (1991), as well as Pozzo in Beckett's *Waiting for Godot* (1988). He is a professor at Brooklyn College of the City University of New York. His more recent work has been mostly devoted to film, apart from a star turn as Roy Cohn in Kushner's *Angels in America* (1995). He is best known for playing dark, psychologically complex characters.

Abujamra, Antonio (1932–) Director, Brazil. Abujamra studied journalism at Pontificia Universidade Católica in São Paulo, and worked with Roger Planchon, Jean Villar, the Berliner Ensemble in Germany and Joan Littlewood in Britain. He is currently theatre reviewer for two Porto Alegre newspapers, and teaches performance at the University of São Paulo, and the Fundação Armando Alvares, Penteado. Major productions include Racine's *Phèdre*, *Waiting for Godot* by Beckett, Strindberg's *Pelikanen* (*The Pelican*), Ionesco's *Les chaises* (*The Chairs*) and Molière's *Tartuffe*.

Achternbusch, Herbert (1938–) Dramatist, director and actor, Germany. Achternbusch studied at the Nuremberg Academy of Art under Gerhard Wendland. He has directed and produced numerous films, and written plays for the theatre such as *Susn* (1980), *Sintflut* (*Primordial Flood*, 1984), *An der Donau* (*At the Danube*, 1987), *Der Stiefel und sein Socken* (*The Boot and its Sock*, 1993), *Der letzte Gast* (*The Last Guest*, 1996), *Meine Grabinschrift* (*My Epitaph*, 1996) and *Neue Freiheit. Keine Jobs. Schönes München. Stillstand* (*New Freedom. No Jobs. Beautiful Munich. Standstill*, 1998). His material is predominantly autobiographical, taking up his roots in Bavarian mentality. His characters are nonconformist people: swimming against the current, they get drained of their energies and substance.

Adamová, Jaroslava (1925–) Actor, Czech Republic. After graduating from the Prague Conservatory, Adamová first found success in comic roles, but soon moved on to internally complex and abnormal characters of modern drama at the Prague Municipal Theatre, where she has worked since the 1950s. Roles include Claire Zachanassian in Dürrenmatt's *Der Besuch der alten Dame* (*The Visit*, 1959), Electre in Sartre's *Les mouches* (*The Flies*, 1968), Carol in Williams's *Orpheus Descending* (1963), the title role in Ibsen's *Hedda Gabler* (1965), and Alice in Dürrenmatt's *Play Strindberg* (1970). She is most famous from Cocteau's *La voix humaine* (*The Human Voice*), in which she acted for several years. In Czech theatre, she is the leading representative of the *femme fatale*. Her acting is noted for its powerful tension, balancing between tragedy and a fascinating female diabolism, and supported by an explosive temperament and proud nobility. The peak role of her mature work is La Baboulenka in Pavel Kohout's adaptation of Dostoyevsky's *Hrác* (*The Player*, 1993).

Adejobi, Oyin Actor-manager, Nigeria. Adejobi is the founder, manager, director and lead actor of Oyin Adejobi Theatre Company. He is one of the successful and enduring actor-managers of the popular Yoruba Travelling Theatre and operatic tradition (others are the late Hubert Ogunde, the pioneer of the genre, and also Moses ADEJUMO (Baba Sala), Isola OGUNSOLA, Ade AFOLAYAN and Lere PAIMO). Adejobi is a fine example of the creative eclecticism of the travelling theatre tradition in his appropriation of modern technology and other sophisticated performance media such as television and film. He makes use of the popular *juju* bands to provide accompanying entertainment for his shows, thereby ensuring a very wide audience. His major plays include *Ono Ola* and *Ekuro Oloja*. Like the other practitioners of the genre, most of Adejobi's plays are improvized (evidence of their origin and influences from the traditional Yoruba *Alarinjo* theatre) and hardly ever scripted. The companies have managed to get round this problem

through recording the performances on film and video.

Adejumo, Moses Olaiya (Baba Sala) (1936–) Actor-manager, Nigeria. Adejumo is one of the very few non-university educated Nigerian theatre artists. He belongs to a vanishing breed of actor-managers of the popular Yoruba Travelling Theatre and operatic tradition (those still active include Ade AFOLAYAN, Isola OGUNSOLA and Oyin ADEJOBI). Adejumo, founder-owner of the Alawada Theatre, is popularly and better known throughout Nigeria and along the Yoruba-speaking West African coast as Baba Sala, the delightfully roguish stage character which he plays in all his productions. He is essentially a comedian who performs in his native Yoruba language, and is noted for his bold experiments with Yoruba traditional theatre forms and techniques, especially the *yeye* style. All his plays centre around the hilarious misadventures and antics of Lamidi Sani, a part played by Adejumo himself with consummate comic skill and gusto. The plays are usually improvized, are very witty and always popular with stage and television audiences.

Adelugba, Dapo Actor and director, Nigeria. Adelugba was a leading member of the Orisun Theatre Company (he actually kept the company going in defiance of the military regime of Yakubu Gowon during Wole SOYINKA's detention between 1967–9). One of his earliest roles was that of the Blind Beggar in Soyinka's *The Swamp Dwellers*, directed by Ken Post in 1959. His other roles include that of Murano in *The Road*, performed in Nigeria and in the United Kingdom (1965), and Daodu in *Kongi's Harvest* (1965). His directing credits include numerous Soyinka plays such as *The Lion and the Jewel* (1965, with choreography by Betty OKOTIE), *The Trial of Brother Jero* in 1966, with good performances from Bettie Okotie as Amope and Wale

OGUNYEMI as Chume, and Ganesh Bagchi's *The Deviant* (with Ogunyemi as Dibu in 1971). Ogunyemi's epic *Langbodo*, which he directed, was Nigeria's entry for FESTAC 1977. He has also written many seminal and influential essays on Nigerian and African theatre.

Admiraal, Joop (1937–) Actor, The Netherlands. Joop Admiraal graduated from the Drama School in Amsterdam in 1959. He spent a year with the Nederlandse Comedie, the leading theatre company of the time, then decided to try his luck in the Italian film industry, without success. A rich career followed, at first with experimental companies like Studio and then from 1968 with the legendary Werkteater collective, of which he was one of the founder members. With his dog Kino, he developed his solo show *You Are My Mother*. The production toured Germany and other countries and was awarded the Louis d'Or. Admiraal is renowned for the sensitive way in which he plays women: 'they allow me to show more of myself', he says. Since 1987 Admiraal has acted with Gerardjan RIJNDERS's company Toneelgroep Amsterdam, playing a memorable role as a bag lady in *Nadien* (Edelenbos) and as a general in Thomas Bernhard's *Die Jagdgesellschaft* (*The Hunting Party*).

Adwan, Mamdouh (1941–) Dramatist and poet, Syria. Following his studies of English, Adwan worked in journalism for thirty years. His first play *Al-Makhad* (*The Parturition*, 1967), written in verse, is about a popular legendary freedom fighter. Later plays are in prose and focus on current issues, beginning with the politically daring *Muhakamatu 'l-Rajol' Lazi Lam Yuhareb* (*The Trial of a Man who Did Not Fight*, 1970). *Kaifa Tarakta 'l-Saif* (*Why did you Leave the Sword*, 1972) and *Laylu 'l-Abeed* (*The Night of Slaves*, 1977) were banned by censorship because they projected the conflicts encountered by religious, historical figures

during the prime of Islam onto the contemporary political situation. Other plays take their inspiration from world drama, such as *Hamlet Yastayqez Muta'akheran* (*Hamlet Wakes up too Late*, 1977), and *Don Quixote* (1979, directed by Mahmoud KHADOUR), from local history, as in *Sadar Barlek* (1994) and *Al-Ghoul* (*The Monster*, 1996), and from the Arabic literary heritage, such as *Haki'l-Saraya* (*The Chat of Concubines*, 1992). His one-act play *The Mask* (1992) was a double bill in English and Arabic, directed by Penny Black and Riad Asmat. His four one-man shows, beginning with *Ahwalu'l-Dunya* (*How Life Is*) and ending with *Akalatu Luhumi'l-Bashar* (*The Cannibals*), were performed and directed by Zeinati Oudseya.

Afolayan, Ade Actor-manager and dramatist, Nigeria. Like the late Hubert Ogunde, Moses ADEJUMO, Isola OGUNSOLA and Oyin ADEJOBI, Ade Afolayan is a successful actor-manager and playwright of the Yoruba Travelling Theatre and operatic tradition. His plays are mainly historical dramas that sought to use the rich history and culture of the Yoruba people of Nigeria as both metaphor and context for exploring and articulating social issues facing the contemporary Yoruba. Afolayan is credited with moving the travelling theatre into its most revolutionary phase, that of film. Moving into film and video meant that the punishing schedule of tours that the companies have had to undertake to cover a country as extensive as Nigeria and their West African audiences in Togo, Benin and Ghana were no longer necessary, as the films are now screened in hotels and other venues for paying audiences, and the videos hit the market after a year or two in cinemas.

Ağaoğlu, Adalet (1929–) Dramatist, novelist and short story writer, Turkey. Between 1951–70 Agaoglu worked as a radio programmer and a dramaturg for the Ankara Radio and for the Turkish Radio and Television Institution. In 1980, she received the best play award of the Turkish Language Institution for her play *Üç Oyun* (*Three Plays*). Some of her famous plays are *Bir Piyes Yazalim* (*Let's Write a Play*, 1953), *Tombala Bingo* (1963), *Çatıdaki Çatlak* (*The Crack in the Roof*, 1964), *Sınırlarda* (*At the Borders*, 1966), *Kendini Yazan Şarkı* (*The Self-Written Song*, 1970), *Bir Kahramanin Ölümü* (*The Death of a Hero*, 1968), *Kozalar* (*The Cocoons*, 1971), and *Çıkış* (*The Exit*, 1970). Some of her novels have been translated into German, Bulgarian and Czech, and some of her stories have been translated into English. In her writings she usually explores the problems of the Turkish Republican Period in Turkish history, and she discusses family relationships under social pressures.

Agashe, Mohan (1947–) Actor, India. Agashe is a founder member of the Theatre Academy, Pune, and currently serves as director of the Film and Television Institute of India, and Honorary Director of DATE (Developing Awareness Through Entertainment). The role of Nana Phadnavis in Vijay TENDULKAR's folk musical *Ghasiram Kotwal* (1972) brought him national and international recognition. Other important productions include Tendulkar's *Ashi Pakhare Yeti* (1970), P.L. Deshpande's *Teen Paishacha Tamasha* (1978) and Satish ALEKAR's *Begum Barve* (1979). In addition to theatre, his name is synonymous with villainy in Hindi cinema. For the last ten years he has been developing and promoting Gripps Theatre, the children's theatre of Berlin, in India. Agashe, a practising psychiatrist, says, 'The best of the performances I have seen have been in my ward. It became a school of acting for me. When a patient in acute excitement walked in, in a state of schizophrenic or manic excitement, or a paranoid patient – I learned from him what the character of Othello is.'

Ahmad, Sayeed (1931–) Dramatist, Bangladesh. Sayeed Ahmad trained to play sitar under Ustad Alauddin Khan. A playwright of immense repute, Sayeed Ahmad created a sensation during the 1960s with his plays *The Thing* (1961), *Milepost* (1964) and *Survival* (1967), originally in English but subsequently rendered into Bengali by himself and then translated into various other languages. A playwright who has 'caused a fusion of western compactness of form with eastern sensibilities', Sayeed Ahmad's works 'always have a dominant ringing note of all-powerful Nature and man's ability to take on challenge'. A retired government servant, he has extensively lectured abroad. He has also won a number of national and international awards, including the Legion d'Honneur conferred by the French government (1993).

Ahmed, Sheikh Mansuruddin (1957–) Designer, Bangladesh. A graphic designer by profession, his career as a set designer began in 1972, and today he has thirty-four designs to his credit. Those which have been highly acclaimed for their artistic merit are adaptations of Zuckmayer's *Der Hauptmann von Köpenick* (*The Captain of Köpenick*, directed by Aly ZAKER, 1981), *Hamlet* (directed by Aly Zaker, 1990), a translation of Brecht's *Leben des Galilei* (*Life of Galileo*, directed by Ataur RAHMAN, 1988), Tagore's *Muktadhara* (*The Liberated Stream*, 1989), and Syed Huq's *Nooraldeener Sarajeeban* (*Noraldeen: A Life*, directed by Aly Zaker, 1981). Ahmed's designs can be described best as a visual reworking of the horizontal plane of the performance space to which sometimes he adds a touch of realism. He is an active member of Nagorik Natya Sampradaya (a leading theatre group in Bangladesh).

Ahmed, Mamtazuddin (1935–) Dramatist, actor and director, Bangladesh. His successful plays include *Spartacus Bishayak Jatilata* (*Complications Regarding Spartacus*,

1973), *Phalaphal Nimnachap* (*Sum Total Result: Depression*, 1974), *Harin Chita Cheel* (*The Deer, the Leopard, the Eagle*, 1974), *Raja Anushwarer Pala* (*The Episode of King Anushwar*, 1988) and *Shat Ghater Kana-kadi* (1991). He has also adapted plays such as Chekhov's *Lebedinaya pesnya* (*The Swan Song*), *Predlozenie* (*The Proposal*) and *Medved* (*The Bear*, 1977), and novels such as Tagore's *Dui Bon* (*The Two Sisters*, directed by Ferdausi MAJUMDAR, 1978) and Meer Mosharraf Hosain's *Jamidar Darpan* (*The Mirror of the Landlord*, 1983). Mamtazuddin's plays are often constructed with 'episodic plots, elegant language and events brought about by outside forces and struck by coincidence'. The recipient of many national awards, Mamtazuddin is a teacher by profession, currently working with the Department of Theatre and Music, University of Dhaka.

Ahmed, Syed Jamil (1955–) Director and designer, Bangladesh. Trained at the National School of Drama, New Delhi (1975–8), Jamil Ahmed's set designs created great impact for their compositional richness, expansive power and poetic visualisation. Important among his designs are Salim AL-DEEN's *Kittan Khola* (*The Fair of Kittan Khola*, directed by Nasiruddin YOUSUFF, 1981), translations of Sophocles's *Oidipus Tyrannos* (*King Oedipus*, directed by Kamaluddin NILU, 1981), *The Tempest* (directed by Deborah WARNER, 1986), and an adaptation of Brecht's *Der Gute Mensch von Sezuan* (*The Good Person of Sezuan*, directed by Rudraprasad Sengupta, Calcutta, 1989). His directorial work includes Al-Deen's *Chaka* (*The Wheel*, 1991, the set of which he also designed) and an adaptation of Meer Mosharraf Hosain's *Bishad Sindhu* (*Ocean of Trogos: The Legend of Karbala*), Parts I and II (with Habib, 1991 and 1992, the sets of which he also designed). These productions received artistic acclaim for their visual poetry and for integration of indigenous theatrical elements with Euro-American technique. Jamil Ahmed teaches at the Department of Theatre and Music, University of Dhaka, and has a number of publications to his credit. He has designed, directed and taught abroad, attended seminars and given workshops.

Aidoo, Ama Ata (1942–) Dramatist, Ghana. Aidoo was educated at the University of Ghana, Legon and at Stanford University, California. She was writer-in-residence at the University of Richmond, Virginia. Her reputation as a playwright rests mainly on her two published and widely popular and often performed plays, *The Dilemma of a Ghost* and *Anowa*. Her themes range from the clash of cultures and the inability of some people to make the transition from one to the other (in *The Dilemma of a Ghost*) to the decimation and still traumatic legacy of trans-Atlantic slavery. One of her greatest strengths as a playwright is the linguistic sophistication of her plays in which levels and layers of language deployment are actually part of the characterization achieved through a domestication/indigenization of English.

Akalaitis, JoAnne (1937–) Director, USA. She studied at the Actors Workshop in San Francisco, and briefly with Herbert Berghof, Bill Hickey, Joyce Aaron, Spalding GRAY and Jerzy Grotowski. Akalaitis has created her own performance pieces, such as *Dressed Like an Egg* (1977), exploring what it means to be female, and *Dead End Kids* (1980) on the relationship of alchemy, science and the threat of nuclear holocaust. Her production of KROETZ's *Wunschkonzert* (*Request Concert*, 1980) showed her skill in extreme realism. Her main characteriztic in directing is, however, often termed 'postmodern', highlighting the fragmentary nature of human existence. Sometimes controversial but often creating beautiful images, this technique is geared to provoke the audience into thinking for themselves.

She served as Artistic Director of the New York Shakespeare Festival from 1991-3, and is currently at Chicago's Court Theatre with projects scheduled through the year 2000 season. More recent work includes Euripides *Troades* (*The Trojan Women*, 1999).

Akimoto Matsuyo (1911–) Dramatist, Japan. She joined Gikyoku Kenkyû Kai (the Society of Drama Study) led by Jyûrô Miyoshi, one of the leading playwrights of the time, and published her first play *Keijin* (*The Light Dust*) in the journal *Gekisaku* in 1946. In her play *Reifuku* (*The Formal Clothes*), Akimoto discussed the family system of Japan, and in *Muraoka Iheiji Den* (*The Biography of Iheiji Muraoka*, 1964) she discussed Japanese colonialism; both plays are in the style of comedy. Her *Hitachibo* (*Kaison, The Priest of Hitachi*, 1964) and *Kasabutashikibu Kô* (*Lady Kasabuta* 1966) criticized the structure of Japanese industrialism from the viewpoint of the bottom of society. She started writing for commercial theatres with *Chikamatsu Shinjû Monogatari* (*Chikamatsu Love Suicide Story*) in 1989, followed by *Nanboku Koi Monogatari* (*Nanboku Love Story*), both directed by NINAGAWA. Akimoto's strength lies in adding some comical element to serious plays. Her theatrical language is fluent and rich, informed by her reading Japanese classics when young.

Albee, Edward (1928–) Dramatist, USA. His four one-act plays, *The Zoo Story* (1958), *The Death of Bernie Smith* (1959), *The Sandbox* (1959) and *The American Dream* (1960), written in an absurdist style about the disillusionment of the 1950s, made Albee famous. His name was linked to Tennessee Williams, Arthur MILLER and even Eugene O'Neill. The realistic *Who's Afraid of Virginia Woolf?* (1962) proved a popular success, and in 1966 he won the Pulitzer Prize for *A Delicate Balance*. In *Seascape* (1975), he combined experiment with social commentary. His fame decreased considerably over the years, but despite all claims that he had nothing more to say, Albee re-emerged in the 1990s with the Pulitzer Prize-winning *Three Tall Women* (with Maggie SMITH and Frances DE LA TOUR in the London production). In 1996 he received the National Medal of the Arts and was a Kennedy Centre Honoree.

Albertazzi, Giorgio (1925–) Actor, director and dramatist, Italy. After graduating in architecture, Giorgio Albertazzi made his theatrical debut in Giuseppe Giacosa's *Come le foglie* (*Like the Leaves*, 1942). In 1949 he worked with Luchino Visconti in *Troilus and Cressida*, from which he emerged as one of Italy's leading stage actors. He then worked at the Teatro Nazionale between 1950-2, and with the Ricci-Magni-Proclemer-Albertazzi-Buazzelli theatre company after 1955. Albertazzi has produced plays by classical as well as contemporary authors, such as Gabriele D'Annunzio, William Faulkner, Albert Camus, Henrik Ibsen and Jean-Paul Sartre. Known internationally through his television and film appearances, such as Alain Resnai's *L'anno scorso a Marienbad* (*Last Year at Marienbad*, 1961), Albertazzi is a strong lead player with an impressive stage presence. Among his most notable performances are *Hamlet* (1964, directed by Franco Zeffirelli), Schiller's *Maria Stuart* (1965), Marguerite Yourcenar's *Le memorie di Adriano* (*Mémoires d'Hadrien*, 1989, directed by Maurizio Scaparro), and Arnold Wesker's *Letter to a Daughter* (1993). Since 1965 Albertazzi, who has also written and directed a number of plays, has been artistic director of the festival Taormina Arte.

Al-Deen, Salim (1948–) Dramatist, Bangladesh. His major achievements as a playwright include *Kittan Khola* (*The Fair of Kittan Khola*, with Shimul YOUSUFF, Shubarna MUSTAFA, Humayan FARIDI and Raisul ASAD in the cast, designed by Jamil

AHMED and directed by Nasiruddin YOU-SUFF, 1981); *Keramat Mangal* (*The Epic of Keramat*, with Shimul Yousuff and Faridi in the cast, designed by Jamil Ahmed and directed by Nasiruddin You-suff, 1985); *Hat Hadai* (*The Seven Voyages*, with Shimul Yousuff as Chhuk-kuni, Asad as Anarbhandari and directed by Nasiruddin Yousuff, 1989); *Chaka* (*The Wheel*, with Asad as the Ox-cart Driver and Shimul Yousuff as the Narra-tor, directed and designed by Jamil Ahmed, 1991); and *Jaibati Kanyar Mon* (*The Soul of the Virtuous Maiden*, with Shimul Yousuff as Kalindi, Shubarna Mustafa as Paree, directed by Nasiruddin Yousuff, 1993). A translation of *Chaka* has also been directed by Steve Friedman in New York (1994). From *Kittan Khola* onwards, Al-Deen has attempted to incor-porate indigenous theatrical elements (in-cluding the narrative form) in his plays and evolve a language capable of reflect-ing the traditional heritage of Bangladesh, imbibed with contemporary relevance. A poet in the truest sense, Al-Deen's plays are literally woven with gossamer which capture the essence with briefest strokes and subvert reality, revealing the fathom-less depths which lie beyond.

Alekar, Satish (1949–) Dramatist and actor, India. The major influences on Alekar are Satyajit Ray, Jabbar Patel, Vijay TENDULKAR and P.L. Deshpande. He writes in a satirical style with a dead-pan expression. His first full-length play was *Mikie Ani Memsaheb. Begum Barve* is a controversial play about a female impersonator which was a sensation on the Bombay stage, and *Mahanirvan*, a play about death, has had more than 250 performances. It was translated into sev-eral Indian languages and into English. Other plays include *Shaniwar Raviwar Atirekee* and *Doosra Samna*. He has also written screen plays for films, and acted with Jabbar Patel and Mohan AGASHE. Alekar is currently working as Professor in the Department of Performing Arts at the University of Pune.

Aleksandrovych-Dochevs'ky, **Andrii** (1958–) Designer, Ukraine. Aleksandro-vych-Dochevs'ky graduated from the Taras Shevchenko Kiev State Institute for Arts, the Faculty of Painting, Theatrical Department (the workshop of Daniil LI-DER, 1983), and has been chief designer of the Ivan Franko Ukrainian Drama Thea-tre, Kiev, since 1993. He has designed above forty productions and has partici-pated in twenty exhibitions, including the Prague Quadrennial Scenography Exhibi-tion. His work include sets for Shake-speare's plays: *Hamlet* (1991), *The Taming of the Shrew* (Poland, 1995 and Kiev, 1996, directed by Serhii DANCHENKO), *King Lear* (Kiev, 1997, directed by Dan-chenko), as well as Lorca's *La casa de Bernarda Alba* (*The House of Bernarda Alba*, Luts'k, 1987), Byron's *Cain* (L'viv, directed by Iaroslav FEDORYSHYN, 1993), Mykola Kulish's *Patetychna sonata* (*The Passionate Sonata*, Kiev, directed by Dan-chenko, 1993), and Ibsen's *Gengangere* (*Ghosts*, Kiev, 1996). His sets, structurally complex, are characterized by aristocratic refinement, stylistic perfection and a cer-tain coldness of tonality.

Alexander, Bill (1948–) Director, Great Britain. Trained at the Bristol Old Vic, he began his professional career as a director at the Royal Court in 1973. From 1978–91 he worked with the Royal Shakespeare Company, first as assistant director (1978–80), then resident director (1980–4), and associate director (1984–91). Pro-ductions with the Royal Shakespeare Company include Barry Keefe's *Bastard Angel* (1980), Bulwer-Lytton's *Money* (1982, with Juliet STEVENSON), Molière's *Tartuffe* (1983, with Anthony SHER and Mark RYLANCE), and many Shakespeare revivals (*Richard III*, 1985; *Twelfth Night*, 1988; *Much Ado About Nothing*, 1991). Alexander's approach to *Richard III* was characterized by the stark visual contrast between William DUDLEY's austere Gothic perpendicular set with the 'bottled spider' of Anthony Sher's Richard. Alexander emphasized the mythic aspects of the play: Richard became a reincarnation of the vice figure of medieval morality, and the three queens were a Greek Tragic chorus. In his *Cymbeline* (The Other Place, 1988), the actors were like fairytale characters, performing in a tiny space, in extreme close-up: one was able to appreciate the full power of the language, and the effect was paradoxically to create a world of huge space. Since 1992 he has been artistic director of the Birmingham Repertory Theatre, where more recent productions include Ben Jonson's *The Alchemist* (1996), *The Merchant of Venice* (1997) and Bryony Lavery's *Frozen* (1998).

Alexander, Jane (1939–) Actor, USA. She played Kattrin in Brecht's *Mutter Courage und ihre Kinder* (*Mother Courage and her Children*, 1970), the title role in Shaw's *Major Barbara* (1971), Gertrude in *Hamlet* (1975), Hilde in Ibsen's *Bygmester Solness* (*The Master Builder*, 1977), the title role in *Hedda Gabler* (1981), Anna in PINTER's *Old Times* (1983), Joy Gresham in William Nicholson's *Shadowlands* (1990) and Clare Zachanassian in Dürrenmatt's *Der Besuch der Alten Dame* (*The Visit*, 1992). In 1993 she was appointed as first artist to head the National Endowment for the Arts, where she proved an outspoken, liberal advocate for the arts. Serving until 1997, she returned to the stage in 1998 in Joanna MURRAY-SMITH's *Honour*.

Alexander, Susana Actor, Mexico. Trained at the Actor's Studio of Mexico under Dimitros Sarras, she later pursued postgraduate work in drama at the University of Wales, UK. She has had an equally distinguished career in television and on stage, where major roles include Ophelia, Puck, the title role in Euripides's *Electra*, roles in Genet's *Les bonnes* (*The Maids*),

Wesker's *The Four Seasons* and Marsha NORMAN's *'night Mother*, and Stephanie in Tom Kempinski's *Duet for One*. She has also devised and performed several one-woman shows both in Mexico and abroad. In 1982 she performed in Venezuela, and in 1985 she represented Mexico at the New York Shakespeare Festival's Latino Festival. In 1987 she visited Cuba and Brazil as Mexico's official representative.

Alit, Ida Bagus (1956–) Performer and designer, Indonesia. From the priest-scholar Brahmana caste, Alit learned woodcarving from the age of ten from his father and grandfather. This was later augmented by a period of time working with the master carver Ida Bagus ANOM. Alit creates Topeng masks of startling vitality as well as imaginative original designs for actors and companies in Europe and the United States. In addition, he is an active performer of the traditional, sacred Topeng Pajegan, particularly powerful in the roles of the Strong Prime Minister and the High Priest. Although he began dancing only fairly recently, he quickly won acclaim as a master storyteller. He has made a comprehensive study of the ancient chronicles upon which the Topeng scenarios are based, and has a deep understanding of their ritual significance. He feels that carving and dancing are complementary, each art enhancing and developing the other.

Alkazi, Ebrahim (1925–) Director, India. Alkazi trained at the Royal Academy of Dramatic Art, London, and won the BBC Broadcasting Award in 1950. Alkazi ranges amongst the most influential directors of India who relate India to the Western theatre. His productions are known for their spectacular scale, and include the plays of Girish KARNAD, Shakespeare, Chekhov and some Greek plays such as Sophocles's *Electra*. He was director of the National School of Drama, New Delhi, for a decade, and was also the editor of *Theatre Unit Bulletin*.

Allana, Amal (1947–) Director and designer, India. The daughter of Ebrahim ALKAZI, Allana graduated from the National School of Drama, New Delhi and received training at the Berliner Ensemble and the National Theatre, Weimar. She has been directing plays and designing costumes and sets since 1968. She has a special interest in Brecht and epic theatre and directed *Die Dreigroschenoper* (*The Threepenny Opera*), *Mann ist Mann* (*A Man's a Man*), *Der Gute Mensch von Sezuan* (*The Good Person of Sezuan*) and many Indian plays. Her productions of Girish KARNAD's *Hayavadana*, *Tughlag*, *Ashad Ka Ek Din* and *Bhagawad Ajjukiem* set a trend in Indian theatre of reading Indian plays with a modern sensibility. Amal Allana's production of *King Lear* is considered a milestone in Indian theatre for its costumes. She designed the costumes for Richard Attenborough film *Gandhi*.

Almagor, Gila (1939–) Actor and dramatist, Israel. Trained at the Habima studio in Tel Aviv and with Lee Strasberg in New York, Almagor began her professional stage career at the age of seventeen as Anna Frank at the Habima national theatre. She joined the Cameri Tel Aviv municipal theatre playing roles like Olivia (*Twelfth Night*) and Virginia (Brecht's *Leben des Galilei* (*Life of Galileo*)) and later the independent Bimot theatre, playing major roles in many newly written Israeli plays. She has also played roles like Cassandra (Euripides's *Troades* (*The Trojan Women*)), the title role in Shaw's *St Joan* and Mrs Alving (Ibsen's *Gengangere* (*Ghosts*)). Her own play *Aviva's Summer*, about the daughter of a Holocaust survivor, with herself as the only actor, has also been filmed. She has appeared in more than fifty films, and often appears publicly in peace activities.

Al-Mamun, Abdullah (1942–) Dramatist, actor and director, Bangladesh. Al-Mamun trained for television in The Nether-

lands (1969) and Malaysia (1976, 1981 and 1991). Since 1974 he has written a number of plays, directed their productions and performed in them. He played the Boss (with Ferdausi MAJUMDAR as Ranu) in *Subochan Nirbasane* (*Virtue in Exile*), Bepari in *Ekhon Duhshomoy* (*Its Bad Times Now*, 1976, with Ferdausi Majumdar as Marjina), *Ekhono Kritodas* (*Still a Slave*, 1980, with Ferdausi Majumdar as Kandoni and Ramendu MAJUMDAR as Talebali) and Gada Fakir in *Meraj Fakirer Ma* (*The Mother of Meraj Fakir*, 1996, with Ferdausi Majumdar as the mother and Ramendu Majumdar as Kazi Tobarak). His prime concern as a playwright is for the 'decadence of social values'. He writes primarily for the urban middle class, 'with the anguish, pain and criticism of a committed artist'.

Alpha, Jenny Actor, singer and dancer, France and Martinique. Leaving Martinique to continue her education at the Sorbonne, Jenny Alpha-Villard's stage career was launched in the 1939 Cabaret *La Canne à Sucre* (*Sugar Cane*). She founded her own band (1950), with which she toured widely until 1966. Having accepted parts such as a prostitute and a savage on provincial tours, the role of Neige in Les Griots (The African Story-Tellers) production of Genet's *Les nègres* (*The Blacks*, 1958) placed her in the midst of an emerging theatre offering significant roles to black actors. In the next decade she worked in plays as diverse as CÉSAIRE's *La Tragédie du roi Christophe* (*King Christophe*), and Corneille's *Rodugune*. Reviews praise her natural and precise style of inhabiting her characters as in her portrayal of Amélie's madness in Julius Amédée LAOU's much revived *Folie ordinaire d'une fille de Cham* (*Ordinary Madness of a Daughter of Ham*). With over a hundred radio plays and many television roles to her name, she entered the 1990s starring simultaneously in festivals of theatre, with *Brûle rivière brûle* (*Burn River Burn*), and film, in the title role of Laou – MESGUICH's award-winning film *La Vieille Quimboiseuse et le majordome* (*The Old Sorceress and the Valet*).

Alpha, José (1952–) Actor, director and author, France and Martinique. Beginning as a young singer-impresario (*Hair*, 1971) and as an actor with Henri Melon's Théâtre Populaire Martiniquais, Alpha then formed his own small group, Existence, performing eloquently symbolical pieces on frustration and the quest for freedom such as *L'étau* (The Vice, 1978). With the founding in 1983 of a new company, Teat Lari (Creole for 'street theatre'), he moved into creating a Caribbean popular theatre, adapting folktales (*Lajan Diab.* (Devil Money); *Madlo missié Li Wa* (The King's Pond); *Ti Mano et le Fromap-er* (Little Mano and the Cotton-Tree)), staging novels (*L'Affaire Solibo* (The Solibo Case) by Patrick Chamoiseau), and with a particular interest in historical material such as his script *1902*, on the volcanic eruption. A compact, dynamic performer of great vitality on stage, Alpha has a strong sense of social purpose, has run workshops in prison and worked with alcoholics, and gives a high priority to plays for young people. Over a long period his independent group has co-operated with many local writers and artists, developing worthwhile entertainment in a theatrical language which appeals to a wide public.

Al-Sheikh, Jibreel Ahmad (1949–) Dramatist, Jordan. Al-Sheikh studied arts in Palestine, and linguistics and medicine in Czechoslovakia. He is a folklore expert and consultant, and many of his plays for the stage and scripts for television combine a documentational folkloric and a contemporary line. His plays are based on two methodologies, analytical and constructive. He looks at the details of folklore, anthropology, history and archaeology with a magnifying glass. From the resultant mosaic, he constructs a new

overall image. In recent years, Al-Sheikh has shifted his interest to a revival of the Kana'an Legends in Palestine, basing his research on a critical assessment of new archaeological findings and old documentations. The outcome is amazingly interesting and stimulates fresh questions that lead to new plays and scripts.

Al-Tal Batayneh, Lina (1960–) Actor, Jordan. Al-Tal trained at the Webber Douglas Academy of Dramatic Art. Appearances as an experienced actor in mainstream theatre and on Jordanian television include Chekhov's *Visnevyi Sad* (*The Cherry Orchard*), Ibsen's *En Folkefiende* (*An Enemy of the People*) and *Love's Labour's Lost*. In performance, her method of acting is more or less traditional in the Stanislavskian sense: she does not get involved with her roles to the extent where she can remain fairly detached, always very conscious of the emotional state of the character. Her strengths are in roles which require body technique or mime. Over the years, Theatre in Education has become her main area of activity; she trained for it at Bretton Hall, UK, and obtained an MA in Theatre in Education from the University of Wales. Since 1987 she has been director of the Theatre and Drama in Education Programme at the Noor Al-Hussein Foundation, attending conferences and receiving major awards for her work.

Amagatsu Ushio (1949–) Butoh dancer, Japan. Amagatsu first studied classical ballet and Graham method dance. He became one of the founder members of MARO Akaji's Dai-Rakuda-kan (1972). He then founded Sankai-juku in 1975 and presented *Kinkan Shônen* (*The Conquant Seeds*) in 1977. Amagatsu works with four dancers trained under him. The dancers of Sankai-juku are skin-headed and wear white mask make-up. Their performances in Paris in 1980, as part of their European tour, were successful and the company was given a contract to perform every two years at the Théâtre de la Ville, Paris, resulting in *Netsu no Katachi* (*The Shape of Heat*, 1984), *Unetsu* (*The Passion for a Bird Egg*, 1986), *Shijima* (*The Dark and Quiet*, 1988) and *Omote* (*The Grazed Surface*, 1991). The positioning of five dancers in the design is always their prime concern for the productions of the Sankai-juku.

Amat, Frederic (1952–) Designer, Spain. He studied at Barcelona's School of Architecture and the Centre d'Estudis d'Expressió, where his tutor in stage design was Fabià Puigserver. He is now regarded as one of the foremost artists in Spain. His first work in theatre design involved collaborating with Puigserver on PASQUAL's production of *El público* (*The Public*, 1986). He has since gone on to work with Pasqual on four other projects including the Odéon Théâtre de l'Europe's production of *Tirano Banderas* (*Banderas the Tyrant*), but has also worked with director Lluís HOMAR and choreographers Víctor Ullate and Cesc Gelabert. His bold designs are fervently anti-naturalistic and often dominated by a strong metaphoric image, as with the merry-go-round in *Tirano Banderas* or the crane in the 1996 adaptation of Lorca's *Bodas de sangre* (*Blood Wedding*) staged by Pasqual as *Haciendo Lorca* (*Making Lorca*). Amat's exhuberant sense of colour and space is also a feature of his work as a poster artist where his commissions have included theatre productions, film logos, festivals, CD covers and charitable organizations. His first film, *Viaje a la luna* (*Journey to the Moon*), a realisation of Lorca's only screenplay, was released in 1998.

Ambush, Benny Sato (1951–) Director, USA. Ambush obtained an MFA in directing from the University of California, San Diego (1977). Subsequently, he was an assistant director in residence at the Arena Stage in Washington, and in the 1980–1 season Ambush was an National Endowment of the Arts Directing Fellow at the Pittsburgh Theatre. From 1982–90 he was artistic director at the Oakland Ensemble Theatre, and is currently an associate artistic director with the American Conservatory Theatre in San Francisco. Ambush is one of the leading representatives in theory and practice of African-American and multicultural theatre. He also works regularly on the classics at Shakespeare Festivals throughout the USA.

Amos, Janet (1945–) Actor, director and dramatist, Canada. In 1968, Amos made her professional debut as an actor while still studying at the University of Toronto. From 1972–6 she worked on collective productions for Théâtre Passe Muraille, and later returned to direct there. She was artistic director of the Blyth festival (1980–4), and Theatre New Brunswick (1984–8). In both positions she concentrated on new plays by Canadian dramatists such as Anne CHISLETT. Amos returned to the post of artistic director at the Blyth Festival between 1993–7. She has also written plays, including *Alligator Pie* (adapted from Dennis Lee's poems), *Down North* (1981) and *My Wild Irish Rose*.

Anderson, Axel (1929–) Director and actor, Puerto Rico. Born in Berlin, Axel Anderson was active in the professional theatres of Europe, Argentina and other countries of the Americas before settling in Puerto Rico. With no formal university education, Anderson has become one of Puerto Rico's most prominent dramatic actor-directors. He is particularly noted for his bold choices as an experimental and conceptual director in the European avante-garde tradition. He founded the group Teatro la Máscara with Helena Montalbán in 1960, where he has directed over half of the company's productions, including Coward's *Private Lives* (1977), Moliere's *Le malade imaginaire* (*The Imaginary Invalid*, 1977) and

Cocteau's *L'aigle a deux têtes* (*Two Headed Eagle*, (1973). Anderson has also played leading roles in Wilder's *Our Town*, and the farce *Run for Your Wife* by Ray Cooney, and appeared in the films *Assassins* (1995) with Sylvester Stallone and Antonio Banderas, and *Desvío al paraíso* (*Shortcut to Paradise*, 1994).

Anom, Ida Bagus (1952–) Designer and performer, Indonesia. Well-known and highly respected as one of Bali's foremost mask makers, Anom is also a performer of traditional Balinese Topeng. He began carving and dancing as a child under the instruction of his father, and by the time he reached his twenties was dancing in temple ceremonies. He continues to perform in temples, particularly in his own village of Mas, Gianyar, but he also gives occasional specially commissioned performances for tourists. However, he is principally known as a master carver of theatrical masks and is frequently called upon to execute commissions for theatre companies in Europe, Asia and America. He is also very much in demand as a teacher and maintains an active studio at his home in Mas.

Antal, Csaba (1950–) Designer, Hungary. Antal studied at the Budapest Technical University's Faculty of Architecture and took a course in theatre architecture and set design with Czech designer-professor Joseph SVOBODA at the Prague Applied Arts College. He has worked at the Szolnok Szigligeti Theatre (1980–7), the Budapest Katona József Theatre (1987–94), and since 1994 at the Új Theatre, but has also been a guest in other theatres in the country and abroad. He has taught at the Justus Liebig University Giessen, Germany (since 1988) and at the Academy of Theatre and Film Art (since 1990). Major set designs include MROZEK's *Emigranci* (*Emigrants*), Brecht's *Die Dreigroschenoper* (*The Threepenny Opera*), Büchner's *Woyzeck*, HARE's *The Secret Rapture*, Molière's *Dom Juan*, Chekhov's *Platonov*

and *Ivanov*, and DORST's *Merlin, oder Das Wüste Land* (*Merlin, or The Waste Land*). Although specializing in set design, in some cases he also designed costumes (ALBEE's *The American Dream*, Pirandello's *Enrico IV* (*Henry IV*), Kleist's *Prinz Friedrich von Homburg*, Euripides's *Medeia*) and so on. His work is characterized by exact construction of space, conscious composition of naturalistic and metaphorical elements and interesting use of lighting effects.

Arambam, Lokendra (1939–) Director and dramatist, India. He is the co-ordinator for the Audio-Visual Research Centre, Manipur University, Imphal, and director of the Forum Theatre Laboratory at Imphal. Arambam gained recognition with his first play, *Karbar* (1969), a production which used Manipuri folk music and dances. His productions of his plays *Irabot, Yotpak Yotlei Ama* (an adaptation of Louise Beach's *The Clod*), *Khuman Chakha Moireng Ngamaba* (1981), and *Numit Kappa* also highlighted the use of folk theatre forms in contemporary Indian theatre. Arambam is involved in many theatre projects examining aspects of Manipur theatre, ethno–dramaturgy, clown–actor development and martial arts.

Archer, Robyn (1948–) Director, singer, composer and dramatist, Australia. After several years as director of the National Festival of Australian Theatre (Canberra 1993–5), Archer has now taken up the position of artistic director of the prestigious Adelaide Festival. Archer is possibly still best known internationally for her Brecht–Weill recitals and political – especially feminist – cabarets, such as *A Star is Torn* (1979). She has collaborated on many internationally successful writing projects such as *The Pack of Women* (1981) and the aboriginal one-woman show *Ningali* (1994); her satire based on *fin de siècle* Vienna, *Cafe Fledermaus*, has been published, as has *The Robyn Archer Songbook* (1980). Archer is still primarily associated with feminist, satirical, politically committed, anti-establishment theatre.

Arkhurt, Sandy (1941–) Director and theatre activist, Ghana. Sandy Arkhurt holds a diploma in Drama from the University of Ghana at Legon and a certificate in Drama and Theatre from Birmingham University. He has practiced and taught theatre both in Ghana and in Nigeria where he has been at the forefront of the theatre-for-development movement. He has been artistic director of the Ghana Drama Studio for two spells (1967–71 and 1980–93). The drama studio has been associated with and produced notable Ghanaian theatre artists such as Efua Sutherland, Martin OWUSU, Joe de Graft, Ama Ata AIDOO and Mary YIRENKYI. He has also been the artistic director for The Studio Players as well as being the founder-director of the Popular Theatre Collective, which is responsible for promoting theatre-for-development in Ghana.

Armfield, Neil (1955–) Director, Australia. Armfield's first professional production was David Allen's *Upside Down at the Bottom of the World* in 1979 for Nimrod, Sydney. Armfield went on to direct extensively at Nimrod and the Lighthouse, Adelaide, but he is best known for directing at Belvoir Street, Sydney, where, as artistic director of Company B, he has established a strong ensemble. He ranges widely in his work, but particular strengths are modern Australian plays, the plays of Patrick White, most of which Armfield has directed, Ben Jonson (Armfield started postgraduate research on 'The Theatre of Ben Jonson' but decided that Jonson 'has to be *done*'), and Shakespeare, productions of which include *Hamlet* (1994&5), *The Tempest* (1990&5) and an extremely successful production of *Twelfth Night* (1983) which was filmed. Armfield's 1989 production of Gogol's *Zapiski Sumasshed-*

shego (*The Diary of a Madman*) won many awards and in 1992 toured Russia and Georgia. Armfield's direction is always intelligently provocative and often upsets accepted notions about canonical plays.

Arye, Yevgeny (1932–) Director, Israel. Born in Moscow, he directed in Moscow and Leningrad before his emigration to Israel in 1990. In Tel Aviv, Arye established the bilingual (Russian and Hebrew) Gesher ('Bridge', in Hebrew) theatre together with a group of Russian actors and theatre artists. The first Gesher production was STOPPARD's *Rosencrantz and Guildenstern are Dead*, which was followed by productions of Russian materials like Bulgakov's *Molière*, Dostoyevsky's *Idiot* (*The Idiot*), Babel's *The City* (1997), and Chekhov's *Tri sestry* (*Three Sisters*, 1997). Arie has also worked with Israeli materials in *Adam Ben Kelev* (*Adam Resurrected*, 1994), based on a novel by Yoram Kaniuk, SOBOL's play *K'far* (*Village*, 1996), and Shabtai's *Ochlim* (*Eating*, 1999). Within a decade, the Gesher theatre led by Arye has become one of the leading theatres in Israel. It has also toured to numerous festivals outside the country.

Arzoglou, Costas (1947–) Actor and director, Greece. Arzoglou trained at the Drama School of the National Theatre of Greece. Between 1969–79 he was a leading member of Free Theatre, a group which has been credited with establishing a contemporary theatre language through its thorough research and involvement with political theatre. Arzoglou directed and played leading roles in many more productions after 1979, including David Henry HWANG's *M. Butterfly*, Arthur MILLER's *All my Sons, The Taming of the Shrew* and *A Midsummer Night's Dream*. He also has a distinguished career on television to his credit.

Asad, Raisul Islam (1954–) Actor, Bangladesh. Appearing on stage for the first time in 1972, Asad made name for himself with his performance of Vishwamitra in *Shakuntala* by Salim AL-DEEN (with Shurbarna MUSTAFA in the title role and Humayun FARIDI as Takkhak, directed by Nasiruddin YOUSUFF, 1978). Other important parts include Bayati in Al-Deen's *Kittan Khola* (*The Fair of Kittan Khola*, with Shurbarna Mustafa as Banasribala, Faridi as Chhaya-ranjan and Shimul YOUSUFF as Dalimon, set design by Jamil AHMED, directed by Nasiruddin Yousuff, 1981), Anarbhandari in Al-Deen's *Hat Hadai* (with Shimul Yousuff as Chhukkuni, directed by Nasiruddin Yousuff, 1989) and the Ox-cart Driver in Al-Deen's *Chaka* (with Shimul Yousuff as the Narrator, directed and designed by Jamil Ahmed, 1991). The most striking feature about his performance is his unique dynamism charged with explosive power which radiates physically. Asad's performances on film and television have also been highly acclaimed for artistic merit. He is an active member of Dhaka Theatre (a leading theatre group in Bangladesh).

Asakura Setsu (1922–) Designer, Japan. Asakura began her career as an artist. In 1970, she went to the USA to study stage art by an invitation of the Rockefeller Foundation. She has designed the stage for NINAGAWA's production of Euripides's *Medeia* (1978), AKIMOTO Matsuyo's *Chikamatsu Shinjû Monogatari* (*Chikamatsu Love Suicide Story*, 1979), Ennosuke's *Coq d'or* in Paris (1984) and Takeshi Umchara's *Yamato Takeru* (*Tarkeru Yamato*, 1986). In 1988 an exhibition of her scenography was held in New York and Los Angeles. Asakura has also worked closely with KARA Jûrô, who was the leader, playwright and director of the Jôkyô Gekijô (the Situation Theatre Company) since 1960s. Her stage design varies from the detailed period stage to very spectacular large-scale stage. Her designs

for *Medeia* and NODA's *Yume no Yûminsha* well represent the wide scope of her design.

Ascher, Tamás (1949–) Director, Hungary. After attending the Academy of Theatre and Film Art, where he received his director's degree in 1973, he joined the Csiky Gergely Theatre in Kaposvár. In 1978 ZSÁMBÉKI brought him and several members of the company to the National Theatre of Budapest, but he kept on working in Kaposvár as well. In 1981 he returned to Kaposvár and has been a leading director there ever since. Since 1989 he has also been a member of the Budapest Katona József Theatre and the Paris European Theatre Council. He represented Hungary in the board of directors at the Central European Theatre Festival in Cividale since 1991. Major productions (some of which toured worldwide) include Ödön von Horváth's *Geschichten aus dem Wiener Wald* (*Tales from the Vienna Wood*) and *Kazimir und Karoline*, Beckett's *Waiting for Godot*, Bulgakov's *Master i Margarita* (*The Master and Margarita*), *Hamlet*, Chekhov's *Tri sestry* (*Three Sisters*) and *Platonov*, Howard BARKER's *Scenes from an Execution*, Arden's *Live Like Pigs* and Dürrenmatt's *Der Besuch der Alten Dame* (*The Visit*). Ascher's productions present everyday problems in a clear artistic form, and are characterized by vivid stage life, pace and concentrated acting.

Asti, Adriana (1936–) Actor, Italy. After a period of training at Fantasio Piccoli's Compagnia del Carrozzone and at the Piccolo Teatro in Milan, Adriana Asti made her first important theatrical appearance in Arthur MILLER's *The Crucible* (1955), directed by Luchino Visconti. She also worked with Visconti in Natalia Ginsburg's *Ti ho sposato per allegria* (*I Married you just for Cheerfulness*, 1966), which Ginsburg wrote specifically for her, Harold PINTER's *Old Times* (1973), more recently, *Ashes to Ashes* (1998), written and directed by Pinter. Asti also worked, among others, with Luca RONCONI on his acclaimed production of *Orlando Furioso* (1969), Luigi SQUARZINA on *Rosa Luxemburg* (1976) and Susan Sontag on Luigi Pirandello's *Come tu mi vuoi* (*As You Desire Me*, 1980). As a film actor, Asti worked with Pier Paolo Pasolini in *Accattone* (1961), Bernardo Bertolucci in *Prima della rivoluzione* (*Before the Revolution*, 1964), Visconti in *Rocco e I suoi Fratelli* (*Rocco and his Brothers*) and Vittorio de Sica in *Una breve vacanza* (*A Short Holiday*, 1973). Asti, one of Italy's most popular stage, television and film actors, is a strong lead player who has time and again enchanted her audiences with her passionate and charismatic acting style.

Atanasov, Atanas Gueorguiev (1955–) Actor, Bulgaria. He trained at the National Academy for Theatre and Film Arts 'Krastjo Sarafov', Sofia. As an actor, he worked for the National Theatre 'Ivan Vazov', the Bulgarian Army Theatre, Theatre 199, Youth Theatre and as an instructor of acting at the National Academy for Theatre and Film Arts 'Krastjo Sarafov', Sofia. Major parts include Pozzo in Beckett's *Waiting for Godot*, Touchstone in *As You Like It*, Frick in Arthur MILLER's *Last Yankee* and Deeley in Harold PINTER's *Old Times*.

Autran, Paulo (1922–) Actor and director, Brazil. During his long and distinguished career as a stage, television and film actor, critics have been unanimous in their praise for his creativity, enthusiasm and love for his art. Major parts include title roles in *Othello*, *Macbeth*, *Coriolanus* and *King Lear*, Molière's *Tartuffe*, Brecht's *Leben des Galilei* (*Life of Galileo*), the Father in Pirandello's *Sei personaggi in cerca d'autore* (*Six Characters in Search of an Author*), Willy Loman in Arthur MILLER's *Death of a Salesman*, Solness in *Bygmester Solness* (*The Master Builder*) by Ibsen, and the husband and the lover by turns in PINTER's *Betrayal*.

Apart from his work as an actor, Autran has translated and directed plays.

Ayckbourn, Alan (1939–) Dramatist and director, Great Britain. Ayckbourn first worked in the theatre as stage manager and actor in Donald Wolfit's company. From 1962–4 he acted and directed at Stephen Joseph's Theatre in Scarborough, the town he has since made his residence. Since his first major success as a dramatist (*Relatively Speaking*, 1967), Ayckbourn's dramatic output has been considerable, with at least one new play per year, usually first performed in the author's own production in Scarborough. Ayckbourn's plays are comedies in the broadest sense. Their subjects vary from contemporary middle-class life to futuristic settings (*Henceforward*, 1987), and plays for children (*Mr A's Amazing Maze Plays*, 1993). His earlier works are at times hilariously funny, in recent years the emphasis seems to have shifted to darker aspects of human nature. The plots are often intricate, making use of devices as hallucinatory states induced by an accident (*Woman in Mind*, 1983), or time travel (*Communicating Doors*, 1994). Whereas Ayckbourn's commercial success is beyond doubt, the literary value of his 'well-made plays' is occasionally questioned. However, an increasing number of serious publications not only in Britain demonstrates Ayckbourn's growing importance in contemporary British drama.

Azcarate, Leonor (1955–) Dramatist, Mexico. During the 1970s, she started writing plays while participating in the drama workshops of Vicente Leñero, Hector Azar, Hugo Argüelles and Ricardo Gariba. The vision of Mexico as cruel and terrible, the complete portrait of social fatality which causes great tragedies in everyday life, the vision that unveils the cultural mask which hides moral intolerance, and the description of a dubious reality where good and evil may be confused and innocence and crime are not separated constitute the main concerns of her plays, which include *The Midnight Passenger*, *Fauna Rock*, *Regina 52* and *Dirty Work*.

Azencot, Myriam (1945–) Actor, France. Born in Oran, Algeria, Azencot entered the Théâtre du Soleil in 1981, where she has played major roles in several works directed by Ariane MNOUCHKINE, including the Duchess of Gloucester in *Richard II* (1981), Madame Khieu Samnol, the vegetable seller in Hélène CIXOUS's *The Terrible but Unfinished Story of Norodom Sihanouk, King of Cambodia* (1985), Sarojini Naïdu in *The Indiad or the India of Their Dreams* (1987), Aeschylus in *La ville parjure ou le réveil des Erinyes* (*The Perjury City or the Awakening of the Furies*, 1994), and Mme Pernelle in Molière's *Tartuffe* (1995). Formed in the tradition of the Italian comedy, her acting expresses itself mainly in the body.

B

Bacci, Roberto (1949–) Director, Italy. After graduating in Italian Literature with a thesis on Eugenio BARBA and the Odin Teatret, Roberto Bacci started working at the Piccolo Teatro di Pontedera in 1973. In 1974 he founded the Centro per la Sperimentazione e la Ricerca Teatrale in Pontedera, which hosts a number of alternative theatre festivals, performances, seminars and workshops and is home to Jerzy Grotowski's internationally acclaimed research centre. Throughout the last thirty years Bacci, who is very much at the centre of Pontedera's activities, has provided practitioners from all over the world with a lively and exciting forum for debate and exchange of artistic practices. Among his most notable productions at Pontedera are the devised pieces *Tosca* (1980), *Il giardino* (*The Garden*, 1982), *Zeitnot* (1984), *In carne ed ossa* (*Flesh and Blood*, 1989), *Danza di legno* (*Wodden Dance*, 1994) and *Nostos* (1995). Bacci has also directed the Festival Internazionale di Teatro in Piazza in Santarcangelo (1978–80 and 1984–7), the festival Passaggio in Pontedera (1985–8) and the festival Volterrateatro in Volterra (1990–6).

Baik Soung-Hee (1925–) Actor, Korea. Baik trained with the Victor Musical Company and the Hyundai Theatre Company. Her flexibility both in body and voice enabled her to take on a wide variety of contrasting roles. Her major works in the apprentice era were *Baekya* (*White Night*, 1945, by Ham Se-Deok), and *Wonsool-Rang* (1950, written and directed by Yoo Chi-Jin). Since the 1960s, she has been particularly praised when taking roles of elderly women, for example, the Wife in *Pokpoongjooeuibo* (*A Storm Warning*, 1957, directed by Lee Jin-Soon) and Mrs Goon-Po in *Manseon* (*Full Catch*, 1964). During the same period, Baik also performed a young woman role, that of the Princess in Tieck's *Der Gestiefelte Kater* (*Puss in Boots*, 1982). As a member of the Korean National Theatre, Baik still makes regular stage appearances, including *Sijipganun Nal* (*The Wedding Day*, 1997, by Oh Young-Jin), *Mokpoeui Noonmool* (*Tears of Mokpo City*, 1998, by Jang Woo-Je) and *Three Independant Women* (1995), by I. Manchel, a performance in celebration of the fiftieth anniversary of Baik's debut.

Bajaj, RamGopal (1940–) Actor and director, India. He trained at the National School of Drama, New Delhi. Currently he is professor of acting and director of the National School of Drama, New Delhi. RamGopal Bajaj has acted in more than fifty plays, and some of his memorable roles are Lucky in Beckett's *Waiting for Godot*, Old Man in Sophocles's *Electra*, Nana in TENDULKAR's *Ghashiram*

Kotwal, Yuyutsu in BHARATI's *Andhayug*, Barani in KARNAD's *Tughlag* and Amal in SIRCAR's *Evam Indrajit* (*I am Indrajit*). There is a poetic sensibility in his acting: he is a great master of *The Natyashastra*. Bajaj has also directed more than twenty plays and has translated many Western and Indian plays into Hindi.

Bakar, Abu (1944–) Director, Indonesia. Founder-director of Teater Poliklinik, the most prominent contemporary theatre group in Bali, Bakar has directed plays by Chekhov, Arifin C. Noer, Putu Wijaya, IKRANAGARA and others. His work integrates traditional themes within the context of a contemporary sensibility. More recently, he has collaborated with Ida Bagus Nyoman MAS in the creation of a new Kecak production for the 1997 Singapore Arts Festival. He also writes fiction, poetry and screenplays for television.

Bakhri, Muhammad (1953–) Actor, Israel/Palestine. Bajhri studied acting at Tel Aviv University and has played leading roles in the Israeli theatre in plays like Lorca's *Bodas de sangre* (*Blood Wedding*), Sophocles's *Oidipus*, and in both Arabic and Hebrew in the stage version of the story *The Opsimist* (a title combining 'optimist' and 'pessimist') by the Israeli Palestinian writer Emil Habibi, performed more than 800 times. In this production, the combination of his strong stage personality and his political commitment received their fullest expression. His most famous film role is in *Meachorei Hasoragim* (*Beyond the Walls*).

Bălănuță, Leopoldina (1934–) Actor, Romania. Balanuta graduated from the Bucharest Theatre and Film Institute in 1957. After a year at the Teatrul Tineretului (Youth Theatre) in Piatra Neamtz, she joined the Teatrul Mic (Little Theatre) in Bucharest (1959), with guest appearances at the National Theatre. She has played major parts under the direction of outstanding directors, such as Andrei

SERBAN, Cătălina BUZOIANU and Silviu PURCĂRETE. These include Arkadina in Chekhov's *Cajka* (*The Seagull*), the title role in *Antigone* by Sophocles, Giraudoux's *La folle de Chaillot* (*The Madwoman of Chaillot*), and the title role in Dario FO's *Elizabeth, Accidentally a Woman*. She created a much acclaimed one-woman show with poetry by Mihai Eminescu, Nichita Stănescu, Ion Barbu, Rainer Maria Rilke and folk poetry. A versatile actor on television and film, she won several prizes and awards. 'Poetry is my prayer', she says. Her emotional intensity is always under critical control and uttered with refined articulation.

Banai, Yossi (1932–) Actor, Israel. After participation in an army entertainment group, Banai had problems joining the Habima theatre because of his oriental Hebrew accent, and together with dramatist Nissim Aloni he established 'Teatron Ha-Onot' (The Theatre of Seasons) in 1962. Even if this theatre closed after two seasons it has left a lasting impression, mainly because of its absurdist style and Banai's achievements. When later accepted at Habima he played roles such as the title role in Ibsen's *Peer Gynt*, Iago in *Othello* and Azdak in Brecht's *Der Kaukasische Kreidekreis* (*The Caucasian Chalk Circle*) and in many of Nissim Aloni's plays. Banai is also a popular singer and entertainer, and is one of the few people in Israeli theatre with this kind of range.

Banda, Victor Hugo Rascon Dramatist, Mexico. Banda studied law at the Law College of the National Autonomous University of Mexico, obtaining both his masters degree and doctorate. Most of his plays are influenced by his second profession as a lawyer: they are based upon real events in Mexico which have become well-known judicial prosecution cases. His theatre has been considered social theatre. Banda writes for theatre, television and cinema. Among his plays, those which have been produced most frequently are *The Illegals*, *White Arms*, *Hands Up*, *Close the Doors* and *Hallucinated*.

Bandele-Thomas, Biyi (1967–) Dramatist, Nigeria. Bandele-Thomas is among a new group of African artists, such as Tess ONWUEME, Gabriel GBADAMOSI, Ngugi wa THIONG'O and Wole SOYINKA, who live and work abroad. Bandele-Thomas lives in London, where several of his plays have been performed, including the award-winning *Resurrections* which was presented at the Cochrane Theatre by the Talawa Theatre company, directed by Yvonne Brewster, and *Two Horsemen*, which played at the Bush Theatre directed by Roxana Silbert (the latter play won the main prize at the 1994 London New Play Festival). Although he lives abroad, Bandele-Thomas's theatre is still preoccupied with the theme of the Nigerian nation, its problematic politics and the effects of this on the Nigerian people, as in *Marching for Fausa* (1993).

Bandem, I Made (1945–) Performer and director, Indonesia. He trained at ASTI (Akademi Seni Tinggi Indonesia), and obtained an MA in dance from the University of California in Los Angeles, and a PhD in ethnomusicology from Wesleyan University. An accomplished performer of traditional Balinese Topeng, Dr Bandem is especially renowned for his rendering of Dalem, the Refined King in Topeng Pajegan. His Dalem is at once refined and commanding, his movement articulate and precise. Since the late 1970s, he has emerged as one of the foremost scholars and performers of traditional Balinese dance drama, and has been instrumental in bringing Balinese performance to world attention. Until recently he was director of STSI (the Academy of Performing Arts) in Denpasar, Bali, and he continues to perform both in Bali and internationally.

Bandô Tamasaburô V (1950–) Kabuki actor and director, Japan. Tamasaburô took kabuki dance lessons under Kanshie Fujima since his childhood, and he became the step-son of Morita Kanya XIV. He succeeded to the present stage name in 1964. He played Shiragikumaru in Namboku Tsuruya's *Sakurahime Azumabunsho* (*The Scarlet Princess of Edo*, 1967) and the Prince Shirotae in Mishima Yukio's Chinsetsu *Yumiharizuki* (*The Crescent*, 1969) at the National Theatre, and began to attract public attention by his exceptionally beautiful appearance and skilled performances as an *onnagata* (a female impersonator) actor. He plays roles such as the Princess Taema in *Narukami Fudo Kitayama Zakura* (*Saint Narukami and the God Fudo*) by Hanjuro Tsuuchi, Abun Yasada and Mansuke Nakada; Shizuka in *Yoshitsune Senbon Zakura* (*Yoshitsune Thousand Cherry Trees*) by Izumo Takeda, Shoraku Miyoshi and Senryu Namiki; and O-some in *Osome Hisamatsu Ukina no Yomiuri* (*Seven Appearances of O-some*) by Namboku Tsuruya. He also acted the leading female parts in the plays by Izumi Kyôka and Mishima's *Madam de Sade* for Shinpa (New Kabuki) Theatre company. He danced *Sagi Musume* for the centennial of the New York Metropolitan Opera House in 1984, and joined a kabuki overseas tour to the USA and Europe in 1985 and 1986. He has directed plays, including *Romeo and Juliet* (1986), Michio Kato's *Nayotake* and Mishima's *Kuro Tokage* (*The Black Lizard*, 1990).

Bang-Hansen, Kjetil (1940–) Director and actor, Norway. Bang-Hansen attended the Norwegian State Drama School, and pursued studies in literature at Oslo University and studies in ballet and choreography in London and Stockholm. Between 1962–7 he worked as an actor, adding directing to his credits in 1967. Since 1970 he has held posts as artistic and resident director at several companies throughout Norway, in Oslo, Stavanger and Bergen, with over 100 productions to his credit both in Norway and abroad, including plays by Sophocles, Shakespeare, Molière, Ibsen, Chekhov and Brecht and contemporary plays from every genre, including musicals. Tom Remlov, artistic director of Norsk Film, writes: 'Strikingly evident in Kjetil Bang-Hansen's productions is his primary commitment to the unique life and laws of the stage, with an emphasis on the creation of images and on employing the expressiveness of the actor. This has led to Mr. Bang-Hansen being labelled theatrical, expressive, poetic – terms which really only serve to distinguish his work from current trends of social realism and dialectical theatre post-Brecht. Rather, Mr. Bang-Hansen's work should be characterized as a theatre of counterpoint – constantly and consciously juxtaposing the actor and his character, music and spoken word, image and action, and with humour and delicate use of comedy as important elements.'

Barba, Eugenio (1936–) Director, Italy. After a period of training at the directors' school in Warsaw, Eugenio Barba joined Jerzy Grotowski's Laboratory Theatre as an observer in 1961. He then founded the Odin Teatret, with which he worked first in Oslo (1964) and then in Holsterbrö in Denmark. Throughout the years, Barba has come to represent not only one of the most innovative and challenging directors working in Europe, but also one of the most interesting theorists of contemporary theatre practice. With Odin, Barba has been exploring the boundaries of performance from an anthropological and physiological point of view, organizing workshops, conferences and 'barters', cross-cultural exchanges between practices from different traditions. In 1979 Barba founded the International School of Theatre Anthropology, which works with practitioners from various cultural traditions to study the principles of performers' techniques. Some of his more memorable writings have been collected in *The Float-*

ing Islands (1979), *The Dilated Body* (1985) and *Beyond the Floating Islands* (1986). Important productions include *Ferai* (1969), *Min Fars Hus* (*My Father's House*, 1972), *Come! and the Day Will Be Ours* (1976), *Brechts Aske* (*Brecht's Ashes*, 1982), *The Gospel According to Oxyrhincus* (1985), *Talabot* (1988) and *The Castle of Holstebro* (1990).

Barbareschi, Luca (1956–) Actor and director, Italy. After training with Lee Strasberg, Stella Adler, Nicholas Ray and at the Studio Fersen in Rome, Luca Barbareschi started working as a theatre, film and television actor with Gabriele Lavia and Gabriele Salvatores. An eclectic and versatile actor who has contributed substantially to introducing a number of contemporary European and North American authors to the Italian theatre scene, Barbareschi is a popular lead player with a strong stage presence. Among his most notable productions are Sam SHEPARD's *True West* (1985) and David MAMET's *American Buffalo* (1984) and *Oleanna* (1993).

Barbeau, Jean (1945–) Dramatist, Canada. Barbeau began writing plays while at university. In 1970–1, eight of his plays were produced within sixteen months, including *Le Chémin de Lacroix* (*The Way of Lacross*) and *Joualez – moi d'amour* (*Speak to Me of Love*). Up to 1976, Barbeau's plays reflect the political situation in francophone Québec. Since the Parti Québecois was elected in 1976, Barbeau has written less and shifted his emphasis to more universal themes. In 1989, his play *L'Abominable Hommes de Sables* (*The Abominable Sandman*) was produced at the Théâtre de La Poudrière.

Barberio Corsetti, Giorgio (1951–) Director, dramatist and performer, Italy. After graduating from the National Academy of Dramatic Art in 1975, Barberio Corsetti founded with Marco Solari and Alessandra Vanzi the company Gaia Scienza

(1976), which he left in 1984 to found his own group, the Compagnia Teatrale di Barberio Corsetti. Amongst his most notable devised productions are *Blu oltremare* (*Overseas Blue*, 1978), *Il ladro d'anime* (*The Souls' Thief*, 1984), *La camera astratta* (*The Abstract Room*, 1987), *Frammenti di una battaglia* (*Fragments of a Battle*, 1988), *Il legno dei violini* (*Wood for Violins*, 1990) and *I cinque corpi regolari* (*Five Regular Bodies*, 1992). Barberio Corsetti also co-directed a number of site specific performances with Stephane Braunschweig (1993), Mario MARTONE and Claudio Morganti (1995), Robert WILSON and the designer Giorgio Armani (1996). Barberio Corsetti was one of the first Italian practitioners to explore the application of new technologies to the theatre. His highly formalist practice is centred around the objectification of the body in performance and experimentation with the pictorial and lyrical components constructing theatrical space. In his latest works, he has been exploring the intimate and subjective space of the human mind.

Barker, Howard (1946–) Dramatist, Great Britain. History (which Barker read at the University of Sussex in Brighton) dominates his dramatic output, not for its own sake but used as a metaphor, as in *Love of a Good Man* (Almeida Theatre, 1978) set during the First World War, or *The Europeans*, set in the aftermath of the liberation of Vienna from Islamic forces, written in 1984 and first performed in 1993. In *Uncle Vanya* (1995), Barker offers a new version of Chekhov's famous original, emphasizing the individual's freedom of choice. Barker plays never fail to be complex and provocative. Many are written in a densely poetic style, often focusing on the transforming character of desire and the exploration of acts conventionally perceived as cruel, but considered in a morally re-evaluative context of the catastrophic will to new identity.

Barnes, Ben (1956–) Director, Ireland. Barnes trained as a theatre director with the assistance of many prestigious bursaries and scholarships. He was Resident Director at the Abbey Theatre, Dublin (1982–6), Director of the National Youth Theatre (1984–8), Director of the Gaiety Theatre, Dublin (1993–6), founding Artistic Director of Opera Theatre Company and Director of the independent Groundwork company (1987–96). In 1987 he won a Harveys' award for Best Director for his Gate Theatre, Dublin production of HAMPTON's *Les Liaisons Dangereuses* and his Abbey Theatre production of *The Field* by John B. KEANE, with whose popular rural dramas he has been closely associated, having recently directed *Sive* and *Sharon's Grave*. He is noted as a director of new Irish writing, including six plays by Bernard Farrell, most recently *Kevin's Bed* (Abbey Theatre, 1998). He has directed Beckett's *Rockaby*, *Footfalls* and *Rough for Theatre I* for the Gate Theatre's Beckett Festival (Dublin and New York, 1996), and PINTER's *No Man's Land* as part of the Pinter Festival also at the Gate in 1997. In 1998 he directed *The Salvage Shop* by Jim Nolan for Red Kettle Theatre Company, Waterford, and Brian Friel's version of Chekhov's *Djadja Vanja* (*Uncle Vanya*) for the Gate Theatre, both staged as part of the Dublin Theatre Festival.

Barriera, Jean-Claude (1939–) Designer, France. Barriera trained as a dancer and has worked with the Ballet of Madrid. He has not studied costume designing, which has allowed him much freedom in choosing fabrics for his often unconventional costumes. He prefers not to incorporate historical references into his costume conceptions, but rather to transpose ideas from the Oriental tradition. He first came to Ariane MNOUCHKINE's Théâtre du Soleil during the preparation of *1789*; he worked also on *1783*, *1793* and *L'Age d'or*. However, he is mostly known for the creation of the colorful and marvelous costumes of *The Shakespeare Cycle* (1981–4). Some of these weighed as much as 50 kg, but they did not look heavy and the actors' movements on stage suggested lightness. Later, he designed the costumes for Hélène CIXOUS's *The Terrible but Unfinished Story of Norodom Sihanouk, King of Cambodia* (1985) and *The Indiad or the India of their Dreams* (1987). During forty-one years of designing he has had the opportunity to work with many other directors, including an Indian play, *Nil-Shada-Lal* (*Blue, White, Red*, 1989) directed by Uptal Dutt; *Poussière d'ange* (1991) by Fatima Gallaire, directed by Mustaphah Aoun; and *Quichotte et Sancho* and *The Wizard of Oz* directed by Gille Galliot (1997).

Barry, Sebastian (1955–) Dramatist, Ireland. Barry's work is characterized by an extraordinarily lyrical use of language. By exploring and expanding aspects of his own family history, Barry has addressed wider issues while engaging with the fates of indivuals. His plays include *Boss Grady's Boys* (1988), *Prayers of Sherkin* (1989) and *White Woman Street* (1992), all directed by Caroline Fitzgerald, and *The Only True History of Lizzie Finn* (1995), directed by Patrick MASON for the Abbey Theatre, Dublin. In 1995 *The Stewart of Christendom* (featuring Donal McCann) was produced at London's Royal Court Theatre Upstairs by Out of Joint and directed by Max STAFFORD-CLARK. It won a number of major prizes. In 1998 his most recent play, *Our Lady of Sligo*, featuring Sinéad Cusack and directed by Max Stafford-Clark, was first staged as a Royal National–Out of Joint production in London. Barry is a member of Aosdána (affiliation of Irish artists, writers and composers) and a recipient of numerous awards.

Bar-Shavit, Shlomo (1928–) Actor and director, Israel. Bar-Shavit is one of the first actors trained at the Habima studio and later joined the company, serving as its artistic director in the late 1970s. He has played a large number of major roles such as the title role in *Richard III* and the old man in Ionesco's *Les chaises* (*The Chairs*). He has also directed a large number of productions in different contexts, for film and radio and has worked in education for the theatre.

Barth, Susanne (1944–) Actor, Germany. Born in Hungary, Barth trained for the stage in Hannover. Following six years in Frankfurt (1968–74), where she played in productions of Peter Palitzsch and Hans NEUENFELS, she has been working freelance since 1974, appearing in Stuttgart, Köln, Munich and Frankfurt. Parts include Martha in Edward ALBEE's *Who's Afraid of Virginia Woolf?* (1983), Inès in Sartre's *Huis clos* (*In Camera*, 1988), and Hippolita in John Ford's *T'is Pity She's a Whore* (1992, directed by Michael BOGDANOV). More recently she appeared in Shaw's *Heartbreak House* in Düsseldorf and in Ariane MNOCHKINE's adaptation of Klaus Mann's novel *Mephisto* in Köln (both 1997).

Barton, John (1928–) Director, Great Britain. Barton studied at King's College, Cambridge and went on to teach English at Cambridge University, where he directed plays and influenced the young Peter HALL. When Hall set up the Royal Shakespeare Company in 1960, he invited Barton, Peter BROOK and Michel St Denis to join him at Stratford, and Barton became an Associate Director of the RSC in 1964. One of his first major projects was to adapt and co-direct, with Peter Hall and Clifford Williams, *The Wars of the Roses*, a three-part adaptation of Shakespeare's *Henry VI Parts I–III* and *Richard III*. Apart from numerous productions of Shakespeare, he created the three-part *The Greeks* (1980), an adaptation of nine plays by Aeschylus, Sophocles and Euripides with a play written by himself based on material from Homer's *Iliad*. Other productions include Strindberg's *Ett Drömspel* (*A Dream Play*, 1985), Chekhov's *Tri sestry* (*Three Sisters*, 1988) and Byron's *Cain* (1995). Barton seminally influenced the Royal Shakespeare Company's style of speaking Shakespeare's verse. In 1990 he directed Ibsen's *Peer Gynt* at The Nationalteatret in Oslo. Although the production was in Norwegian, a language which Barton does not speak himself, critics praised the verse-speaking as the best for that play in their memory.

Bartoška, Jiří (1947–) Actor, Czech Republic. After studying in the Brno Academy of Performing Arts, Bartoška acted in the experimental group Goose on a String – Husa na provázku. In 1972, he moved to the Činoherní studio in Ústí n.L., where he worked his way up over four years into an actor with enormous personal charisma and a wide range of expression. His most important role was that of Mister in Kundera's adaptation of Diderot's *Jacques the Fatalist* (1975, directed by Ivan RAJMONT), which he played for eighteen years. From 1978–91 he was a leading light of the Theatre on the Balustrade/Na zábradlí. Here he created, among other roles, the lead in Molière's *Dom Juan* (1989) and Leopold, the main part in HAVEL's *Largo Desolato* (1990). Since 1992 he has been working in the independent Theatre Without a Balustrade/Divadlo bez zábradlí, which he co-founded. At present he is also the president of the Karlovy Vary Film Festival Foundation, and a leading personality in this international festival.

Bašić, Relja (1930–) Actor and director, Croatia. Bašić graduated from the Academy of Dramatic Art in Zagreb in 1959. At HNK in Zagreb (Croatian National Theatre) he played the title roles in Brezovački's *Diogeneš* and Krleža's *Aretej* (*Areteus*). In 1962 he portrayed Aurel in Krleža's *Leda*, and created George in Edward ALBEE's *Who's Afraid of Virginia Woolf?* (1965). Since 1967 he has worked

as a freelance artist. In 1973 he founded the travelling troupe Teatar u gostima (Theatre in Visit), where he works as an actor and director. The group has performed in more than 300 places all over Croatia. In 1998 it celebrated its twenty-fifth anniversary with Yasmine Reza's play *Art* (starring Basic and Vanya DRACH). In addition to acting, Basic has directed around twenty Croatian first productions of Anglo-Saxon writers. He has acted in 120 movies by Croatian and foreign directors (including Ustinov, Welles, Schlöndorf and Guanaco), and is perhaps best-known as Mr Fulir in Golik's film *Tko pjeva, zlo ne misli* (*The One Who Sings No Evil Brings*). In 1995 he celebrated forty years of his acting career at the HNK in a dramatisation of Šenoa's novel *Kletva* (*The Curse*).

Básti, Juli (1957–) Actor, Hungary. Básti trained at the Academy of Theatre and Film Art. In 1980 she joined the Cisky Gergely Theatre of Kaposvár, and since 1984 she has been a member of the Katona József Theatre in Budapest. Major roles include Helena in *A Midsummer Night's Dream*, Olivia in *Twelfth Night*, The Mayor's Wife in Gogol's *Revizor* (*The Government Inspector*), Masha in Chekhov's *Tri sestry* (*Three Sisters*), Anna Petrovna in Chekhov's *Platonov* and Katherine Glass in David HARE's *The Secret Rapture*. Básti is an extremely gifted actor who can impersonate exquisite heroines, tragic queens and ordinary, distorted or grotesque figures with the same depth and credibility.

Bates, Alan (1934–) Actor, Great Britain. Bates trained at the Royal Academy of Dramatic Art. One of his first major successes was as Cliff Lewis in the original production of Osborne's *Look Back in Anger* at the Royal Court in 1956. In 1960 he created the part of Mick in Harold PINTER's *The Caretaker*. Over the next twenty years Bates became associated especially with plays by David

STOREY and Simon GRAY, most recently in Gray's *Life Support* (1997, directed by Pinter). He also played the title role in Peter SHAFFER's *Yonadab* (1985) at the National Theatre, London, directed by Peter HALL, who invited him to play Solness in his revival of Ibsen's *Bygmester Solness* (*The Master Builder*, 1995).

Bates, Kathy (1948–) Actor, USA. Kathy Bates is today best known from her film career, notably as Annie Wilkes in *Misery* (1990). She graduated from Southern Methodist University with a BFA in 1969. In 1983 she received several awards for her portrayal of Jessie Cates in Marsha NORMAN's *Night Mother*, and in 1988 she played Elsa Barlow in Fugard's *The Road to Mecca*, a part she later repeated in the film version (1991). Recent films like *Titanic* (1997) and *Primary Colors* (1998) demonstrate her great skill in comic and dramatic roles.

Bauer, Wolfgang Maria (1963–) Actor and dramatist, Germany. Bauer trained for two years at the Hochschule für Darstellende Kunst in Stuttgart. Between 1990–3 he was an actor with the Bayerisches Staatsschauspiel in Munich, where his roles include Arnold in Hauptmann's *Michael Kramer* (directed by Peter Palitzsch), and Mercutio in Leander HAUßMANN's production of *Romeo and Juliet*. In 1998 he played St Just in Robert WILSON's production of Büchner's *Danton's Tod* (*Danton's Death*), a co-production of the Salzburg festival and Berliner Ensemble. In 1995 he joined Peter Brook's company in Paris. In 1996 he appeared in Hebbel's *Judith* in Düsseldorf and in Schnitzler's *La Ronde* in Munich. As an actor, he commands a strong physical stage presence. Bauer's first play was *Der Zikadenzüchter* (*The Cicada Breeder*, 1992), followed by *In den Augen eines Fremden* (*In the Eyes of a Stranger*, 1993). With Tarkovsky as favourite film director and Peter Handke, Koltès and Pirandello as favourite playwrights, his

plays show ritualistic and theatrically existential situations.

Baydur, Mehmet (1951–) Dramatist and director, Turkey. Mehmet Baydur lived in London and Paris for a long period after first going to those cities for his university education. Between 1980–94 he wrote plays such as *Limon* (*Lemon*), *Gun Gecel Oyun Ölüm* (*Day Night/Play Death*), *Kadın İstasyonu* (*The Station for Women*), *Yangın Yerinde Orkideler* (*The Orchids in the Fire Location*), *Maskeli Süvari* (*The Masked Brigadier*), *Kamyon* (*The Lorry*), *Menekse Korsanlari* (*The Pirates of Violets*) and *Ask* (*Love*). *Kadın İstasyonu* (*The Station for Women*) was staged by himself at Richard Martin-Toursky Theatre in Marseilles. *Doğum* (*Birth*) and *Çin Kelebeği* (*The Chinese Butterfly*) were staged at Théâtre de Folles Pensée and directed by Roland Fichet, first in St Brieuc and later at the Avignon Theatre Festival. His plays have been widely translated into English, French and Spanish. Baydur is not writing only about Turkish issues, but explores the case of individuals constantly encountering problems that continue haunting them. His plays ask questions, challenging the spectator by never providing precise and definitive answers.

Beale, Simon Russell Actor, Great Britain. Beale first attracted attention in a small comic role as the Young Shepherd in *The Winter's Tale*. He went on to play a number of comic parts for the Royal Shakespeare Company, including four out of five of the fops in a season of Restoration Comedies at the Swan: this allowed him to create a series of comic grotesques played with enormous zest and relish. At the same time, he was also able to encompass evil in Nick Dear's *The Art of Success*, and he continued to extend his range as *Richard III* (1992), as Osvald in Ibsen's *Gengangere* (*Ghosts*) and as Edgar in *King Lear* (1994). He made his debut at the Royal National Theatre in 1995 as

Mosca in Ben Jonson's *Volpone*, returning in 1997 to play Iago in *Othello* and joining Trevor NUNN's 1999 ensemble.

Beatty, John Lee (1948–) Designer, USA. Beatty received an MFA from Yale in 1973. He designed numerous productions, among them Brecht's *Baal* (1974), FRIEL's *Faith Healer* (1979), Simon GRAY's *Close of Play* (1981), Arthur MILLER's *After the Fall* (1984), Lanford WILSON's *Burn This* (1987), Terence MCNALLY's *Lips Together, Teeth Apart* (1991), Lillian Hellman's *The Little Foxes* (1997, with Stockard CHANNING in the cast), Neil SIMON's *Proposals* (1997) and Alfred Uhry's *The Last Night of Ballyhoo* (1997). He has been called a 'master of poetic or lyric realism'.

Bedford, Brian (1935–) Actor, USA. Bedford was born in Britain and trained at the Royal Academy of Dramatic Art. Since his New York debut in 1959 as Clive in SHAFFER's *Five Finger Exercise*, Bedford has mainly worked in the USA and Canada. His roles include Alceste in Molière's *Le misanthrope* (*The Misanthropist*, 1968), George Moore in STOPPARD's *Jumpers* (1974), the title role in Molière's *Tartuffe* (1982), Vladimir in Beckett's *Waiting for Godot* (1984) and Arnolphe in Molière's *L'école des femmes* (*School for Wives*, 1991), as well as many Shakespeare parts: Richard II, Macbeth, Hamlet, Richard III, Shylock and a one-man show which he toured between 1989–93. In 1995 he played Salieri in SHAFFER's *Amadeus*, and starred in Boucicoult's *London Assurance* in 1997. He is highly regarded as a gifted specialist in classic plays. In 1996 he was inducted into the Theatre Hall of Fame.

Beier, Karin Director, Germany. While studying Drama and English at Köln University, Beier founded a Shakespeare company and directed nine of Shakespeare's plays in various locations inspired by the plays, such as churches, castle gardens and factories. The managing director of the theatre in Düsseldorf saw one of these productions and invited her to work as an assistant director at his theatre; later she went on to her own independent work. In 1993 her production of *Romeo and Juliet* opened the theatre season of the Schauspielhaus in Düsseldorf, and since then she has directed there regularly as well as in Hamburg and Bonn. Company work has been described as her strength: with an international group of actors from nine European countries, she presented *A Midsummer Night's Dream* (1995), and she plans further international collaborations. More recent productions include Ionesco's *Les chaises* (*The Chairs*, Düsseldorf, 1996), *Twelfth Night* (Hamburg, 1996) and *Measure for Measure* (Hamburg, 1998).

Belbel, Sergi (1963–) Dramatist, director and translator, Spain. His first play, *A.G/ V.W., Calidoscopios y faros de hoy* (*A.G./ V.W., Kaleidoscopes and Lighthouses of Today*, begun in Catalan and completed in Spanish) was written while he was still at Barcelona's Autonomous University. Produced at Madrid's Centro Nacional de Nuevas Tendencias Escénicas, it immediately established him as a dynamic anti-realist playfully interrogating the nature of textuality and providing a new model for Catalan drama in the 1980s. His plays, which include *En companyia d' abisme* (*Deep Down*, 1989), *Caricies* (*Caresses*, 1992) and *Després de la pluja* (*After the Rain*, 1993, written first in Catalan and then translated by the dramatist into Spanish) have been seen in both Barcelona and Madrid's most adventurous venues. In recent years Belbel has also directed the plays of Catalan contemporaries including Josep Benet i Jornet's *Testament* (1997), as well as classical pieces by Shakespeare, Molière and Goldoni for Barcelona's major theatres. His many translations into Spanish and Catalan include works by Bernard-Marie Koltès, Beckett, Racine and Perec. As well as producing various scripts for television and working with Ventura Pons on an adaptation of *Caricies* for film, Belbel teaches Dramatic Literature at Barcelona's Institut del Teatre.

Beligan, Radu (1918–) Actor, Romania. He trained at the Royal Academy of Music and Drama in Bucharest and soon afterwards made his debut with the company Muncă şi Voie Bună (Work and Mirth), immediately noted as a peculiar and highly personal actor of comedy. However, he also played Tuzenbach in Chekhov's *Tri sestry* (*Three Sisters*), with a lyrical, reflexive touch added to his personal sense of humour, and created the role of Bérenger in Ionesco's *Rhinocéros*. In 1969 he became Director General of the National Theatre, again playing a wide range of main parts, such as George in *Who's Afraid of Virginia Woolf?* by Edward ALBEE, the title roles in Dürrenmatt's *Romulus der Große* (*Romulus the Great*) and *Richard III*, the one-man show *Der Kontrabaß* (*The Double Bass*) by Patrick Süskind, and Salieri in Peter SHAFFER's *Amadeus*. He published volumes of essays about theatre inspired by his rich experience and high culture, and has played in many films and appeared on television and radio.

Bell, John (1940–) Director and actor, Australia. Now known primarily for reviving the classics, especially Shakespeare, Bell has also vigorously promoted new Australian playwriting. Bell first acted professionally with The Old Tote, Sydney, in 1963. In 1965 he studied at the Bristol Old Vic and worked with the Royal Shakespeare Company. On returning to Australia he produced *The Legend of King O'Malley* (1970), an iconoclastic musical revue which helped to make a brash, non-realistic approach to theatre very popular. Bell co-founded the Nimrod Theatre, Sydney, where he directed and acted in several classics alongside a large number of Australian plays, most of them new, such as David WILLIAMSON's *The*

Removalists. In 1990 he founded the Bell Shakespeare Company, which tours much of Australia with the aim of making Shakespeare more relevant to its Australian audiences; Bell Shakespeare editions, which include stage histories of the individual plays in Australia, are also being published. Bell has always promoted a larrikin, vagabond and knockabout idea of theatre. His current position of actor-manager seems particularly appropriate to an actor who relishes self-evident theatricality.

Bemba, Sylvain (1934–) Dramatist, Congo. Bemba was trained as a journalist in Strasbourg under the name of Michel Belavin, where he wrote and produced a short feature film and also a pageant on the colonial experience in his native Congo. He wrote his first play, *L'enfer c'est Orfeo* (*Hell is Orfeo*) in 1966. His other published plays are: *L'Homme qui tua le crocodile* (*The Man Who Killed the Crocodile*, 1973), *Une Eau dormante* (*Sleepy Waters*, 1975), *Tarentelle noire et diable blanc* (*Black Tarantula and White Devil*, 1976) and *Un Foutu de monde pour un blanchisseur trop honête* (*A Rotten World for an Over-Honest Laundryman*, 1979). Bemba's theatre focuses on political and economic themes, and relies on satire and fantasy for its stage images.

Bene, Carmelo (1937–) Director, actor and dramatist, Italy. Carmelo Bene made his debut in 1959 with a stage production of Albert Camus's *Caligula*. Bene gradually developed a highly sophisticated and provocative acting style centred around the exploration of a diversity of physical and vocal skills and focused on the distortion and deconstruction of theatrical signs. Inspired by Antonin Artaud, Bene has been practising a baroque and iconoclastic form of total theatre. In Bene's work, words are in fact often interpreted at the level of phonemes; in the articulation of language, he experiments in terms of space and time. His refusal to work in conventional theatrical spaces and the exploration of the most decadent, dark and anguishing aspects of the human mind have inspired various theorists and performers alike, such as Gilles Deleuze in *Per Carmelo Bene* (*For Carmelo Bene*, 1995). Bene's most memorable stage works, which are often controversial adaptations from classical texts, are *Pinocchio* (1962), *S.a.d.e.* (1974), *Hamlet* (1974), *Romeo and Juliet* (1976), *Lectura Dantis per voce solista* (*Lectura Dantis for solo voice*, 1981), *Hommelette for Hamlet* (1987) and *Macbeth – Horror Suite* (1996). Bene also directed and acted in a number of films including Pier Paolo Pasolini's *Edipo Re* (*Oedipus Rex*, 1967).

Benigni, Roberto (1952–) Actor, director, dramatist and singer, Italy. After a period of work in the experimental theatre scene, Roberto Benigni rose to international fame in the film industry with Giuseppe Bertolucci's *Berlinguer ti voglio bene* (*Berlinguer I Love You*, 1976), Jim Jarmusch's *Down by Law* (1986), Federico Fellini's *La voce della luna* (*The Voice of the Moon*, 1989) and Jarmusch's *Night on Earth* (1991). Benigni, who is known for the creation of roles of down-to-earth urban survivors, has a formidable stage presence, characterized by his capacity to be at the same time politically ironic and introspectively lyrical. For his own *Life is Beautiful* (1998) he received an Academy Award.

Bennent, Anne (1963–) Actor, Germany. Daughter of Heinz BENNENT and sister of David BENNENT, she began her acting career at the age of ten. After work in Berlin, Munich, and Stuttgart, she joined the Burgtheater in Vienna (1991–3), where her parts included title roles in Kleist's *Penthesilea* (directed by the late Ruth Berghaus) and *Das Käthchen von Heilbronn* (directed by Hans NEUENFELS). At the Deutsches Schauspielhaus in Hamburg she played Cressida in Leander

HAUSSMANN's production of *Troilus and Cressida* (1993). In 1994 she played Masha in Chekhov's *Tri sestry* (*Three Sisters*), directed by Haußmann, appeared in Handke's *Zurüstungen für die Unsterblichkeit* (*Preparing for Immortality*, Burgtheater, Vienna, directed by Claus PEYMANN, 1997), and played the title role in Lessing's *Minna von Barnhelm* (Vienna, directed by Jens Daniel HERZOG, 1998). 'She often combines a childlike innocence with fierce determination.'

Bennent, David (1966–) Actor, Germany. Son of Heinz BENNENT and brother of Anne BENNENT, he made his debut at the age of twelve, creating the role of Oskar Matzerath in Volker Schlöndorff's film adaptation of *Die Blechtrommel* (*The Tin Drum*) by Günther Grass. In 1985 he played at the Comédie Française, and in 1986 he was the Fool in Klaus Michael GRÜBER's production of *King Lear* at the Schaubühne in Berlin. Following more work with Grüber, as well as Robert WILSON and Einar SCHLEEF, Bennent joined Peter BROOK's company in Paris in 1990. There he scored a major success as Caliban in *The Tempest*. He also played several parts in Brook's production of *The Man Who*. Small of stature, he frequently brings out impish qualities in the characters he portrays.

Bennent, Heinz (1921–) Actor, Germany. Father of Anne BENNENT and David BENNENT, he took private acting lessons after the Second World War, and has worked as a freelance actor since 1947, appearing on all major stages in Germany and Austria as well as in France. He played Jerry in PINTER's *Betrayal* (1979), the actor Maximilian Steinberg in Botho STRAUSS's *Besucher* (*Visitors*, 1988, directed by Dieter DORN), and the Fool in *King Lear* (1992, also directed by Dorn). Bennent is regarded as a highly professional performer, energetic both in quiet and explosive moments on the stage.

Bennett, Alan (1934–) Dramatist, actor and director, Great Britain. Bennett began his acting career in 1959 while still a student at Exeter College, Oxford. His first play, *40 Years On*, was produced in 1968 at the Apollo Theatre in London with John GIELGUD in the cast. In 1973, *Habeas Corpus* starred Alec Guiness, and *An Englishman Abroad* (1983) provided a vehicle for Alan BATES. Following *Kafka's Dick*, a play inspired by German writer Franz Kafka at the Royal Court in 1986, *The Madness of George III* with Nigel HAWTHORNE became an instant success at the Royal National Theatre in 1991, and was later adapted into an equally successful film version, both directed by Nicholas HYTNER.

Benning, Achim (1935–) Director and actor, Germany. Benning trained at the Max Reinhardt Seminar in Vienna. In 1959 he joined the Burgtheater in Vienna, initially as an actor, later as a director. Between 1976–86 he was artistic director there, and from 1987–92 in Zürich. He has also directed in Hamburg and Munich, and returned to direct in Vienna under the artistic directorship of Claus PEYMANN. Recent productions include Chekhov's *Djadja Vanja* (*Uncle Vanya*, 1992, Vienna), Nestroy's *Der Talismann* (Vienna, 1993), *Einen Jux will er sich machen* (the basis for STOPPARD's *On The Razzle* and Thornton Wilder's *The Matchmaker*, 1996, Vienna), Ostrovsky's *Volki I Ovcy* (*Wolves and Sheep*, 1997, Zürich), and Schnitzler's *Das Weite Land* (*Undiscovered Country*, 1999).

Bensasson, Lucia (1941–) Actor, Tunisia and France. Benasson studied theatre at the University of Paris until 1966. In 1968, she joined Ariane MNOUCHKINE's Théâtre du Soleil, playing a series of major parts including Salouha in *L'Age d'Or* (collective creation, 1975); the lead role Carola Martin in Klaus Mann's novel *Méphisto* (1979–80); the Marquise Thérèse Duparc in *Molière* (1976–7), the film

written and directed by Mnouchkine; and the Duchess of Gloucester in *Richard II* (1982–3). In 1983 she created the part of Pandala in Hélène CIXOUS's *The Conquest of the School of Madhubaï,*, directed by Michelle Marquais at Odéon Theatre. She directed workshops in France, China, Spain and Italy. With Claire Duhamel, she took part in 1989 in the founding of ARTA (Association de Recherche des Traditions de l'Acteur) located at the Cartoucherie de Vincennes, where she now works. Each year, the ARTA invites great masters of the Oriental tradition in order to initiate young artists to the sources of theatre.

Berkoff, Steven (1937–) Actor, dramatist and director, Great Britain. Berkoff trained for the stage at Webber Douglas Academy in London and at the École Jacques Lecoq in Paris. Mime and non-verbal elements consequently dominate Berkoff's work as actor and director, as in his one-man show *One Man* in 1993, his production of *Hamlet* which he toured worldwide (1979), and his adaptation and production of Franz Kafka's *The Trial* at the National Theatre. His own plays, such as *East 1975*, *Kvetch* (1986) and *Brighton Beach Scumbags* (1994), offended many by their violent images and their harsh attacks on the establishment. Critical response to all of Berkoff's work tends to be highly controversial.

Bernabé, Joby (1945–) Performer and dramatic poet, France and Martinique. After obtaining a degree in Spanish at Paris-Nanterre, he spent two years in Africa and then was active in student theatre in Paris, especially the collective creation, *Kimafoutiésa* (*What Kind of Craziness*, 1975), a satirical protest play mainly in Creole attacking official policies of sponsored migration to France. Since returning to the Caribbean, he has worked on recitals of his compositions in Creole. He aims to explore a wide range of moods and topics, love poems, sarcastic mimicry of the slavish imitation of things French, respect for the natural environment, and topical issues. An active member of the 'Corps musical' group, renewing traditional musical forms, his recitals combine poetry and music with a virtuoso use of his own wide range of vocal timbre (illustrated in the wake scene in Palcy's film *La rue Cases-Nègres/Black Shack Alley* (1983), where he played the role of Saint-Louis).

Berndl, Christa (1932–) Actor, Germany. She began her career at the age of seven in ballet. At the age of fifteen she played Gretchen in Goethe's *Urfaust*. In her long and distinguished career she has worked with the theatre companies in Stuttgart, Augsburg, Kiel, Essen, Nürnberg, Bochum, Köln, Münchner Kammerspiele, and Bayerisches Staatsschauspiel, Munich, Düsseldorfer Schauspielhaus and Deutsches Schauspielhaus Hamburg. Equally able of successfully portraying eccentric or shy characters, she has worked with important directors such as Wilfried MINKS, Peter Palitzsch, Peter ZADEK, Michael BOGDANOV, Jürgen FLIMM and Luc BONDY. Major parts include Arkadina in Chekhov's *Cajka* (*The Seagull*), Winnie in Beckett's *Happy Days*, Hedda in *Bekannte Gesichter, Gemischte Gefühle* (*Known Faces, Mixed Feelings*) by Botho STRAUSS, Juno in O'Casey's *Juno and the Paycock*, and Mrs Loman in Arthur MILLER's *Death of a Salesman*. Since 1993 she has presented her own evenings of *chansons*. Whether she plays elegant ladies, quietly suffering house wives or resolute lower-class characters, Berndl masters all roles in the genres of comedy, tragedy, farce or operetta.

Betancourt, Marcos (*c*. 1925–) Actor, Puerto Rico. Marcos Betancourt is one of Puerto Rico's most prolific and versatile actors, performing both comic and dramatic roles in plays from modern Europe as well as Puerto Rico. Notable roles include Werner in Sartre's *Les séquestrés d'Altona* (*Prisoners of Altona*, Alta Escena/El Cemí, 1974), the father in Pirandello's *Sei personaggi in cerca d'autore* (*Six Characters in Search of an Author*, Teatro Epidaurus, 1975); the mayor in Victoria ESPINOSA's production of Juan González's *La plena murió en Mayagüez* (*The Plena Died in Mayagüez*, 1979), with Lucy BOSCANA as Marcela; and Vidal in Jaime Carrero's *La caja de caudales FM* (*FM Safe*, 1979). Betancourt has also enjoyed a coincidental partnership with the comic actor Ernesto CONCEPCIÓN in works which include Ghelderode's *The Dump* (1976), Herrero's *La Balada de los tres inocentes* (*Ballad of the Three Innocents*, 1978), and Luis Torres Nadal's *Maten a Borges* (*They are Killing Borges*, 1984) and *La Santa Noche del Sábado* (*Holy Saturday Night*, 1986). He is also a founder of the theatre group El Cemí.

Betsuyaku Minoru (1937–) Dramatist, fantasy writer and essayist, Japan. Over the years, Betsuyaku has co-founded several companies, including the Gekidan Jiyû Butai (the Freedom Stage Theatre Company) with SUZUKI Tadashi and others, the Te no Kai (The Hand Theatre Company) with YAMAZAKI Masakazu and SUEKI Toshifumi in 1972, and Katatsumuri no Kai (the Snail Theatre Company) with MURAI Shimako and his wife and actor, KUSUNOKI Yûko, in 1978. Major plays include *Zô* (*The Elephant*, 1962, called the first Japanese play in the style of anti-theatre in Japan), *Mattchi Uri no Shôjo* (*The Match Girl*, 1967), *Nishimuku Samurai* (*Small Months*, 1977), *Ashi no Aru Shitai* (*A Corpse with Feet*, 1982), and *Haru Natsu Aki Fuyu* (*Spring Summer Autumn and Winter*, 1993). Betsuyaku was initially influenced by Kafka, Beckett and Ionesco and introduced the Theatre of the Absurd to contemporary Japanese theatre. His distinctive style of absurdist theatre is extremely funny and at the same time very true.

Betti, Paulo (1952–) Actor, Brazil. Initially, Betti worked in non-professional theatre. In 1975 he co-founded the Pessoal do Victor group; he became President of the Casa da Gáeva in 1991, held a Brazilian distinguished Artist Fellowship (Fulbright) in 1993, and was involved in organizing the curriculum of the theatre studies course at the Campinas University, São Paulo. He participated in Peter Brook's *The Ik* at Atum, and played Klestakov in Gogol's *Revizor* (*The Government Inspector*), Juliano in Mauro Rasi's *Viagem Forli* and Sigismund in Calderón's *La vida es sueño* (*Life is a Dream*).

Bharati, Dharamvir (1926–) Dramatist, India. *Andha Yug* (*The Blind Age*, based on an episode from *The Mahabharata*), his first play in verse, is a trendsetter which began a series of rediscoveries of the epic and has been translated into many Indian languages. First produced by Satyadev DUBEY in 1962, who calls it 'one of the ten best plays in the world', and since then by almost every major Indian director, it is one of the first contemporary plays to raise questions about the ethics in *The Mahabharata*. In a recent Tamil production by Mu RAMA-SWAMY, it became an anti-nuclear war play. Bharati's fame rests on this single play.

Biaggi, Julio (ca. 1950–) Designer, Puerto Rico. Educated in Madrid, Julio Biaggi is Puerto Rico's premier scene designer for theatre as well as television. In addition to his regular position at San Juan's Channel 2, he has worked with numerous theatre groups including El Cemí, El Otro Grupo and Proscenio. His work includes designs entered in several Festivals of Puerto Rican Theatre, including Manuel Méndez Ballester's *La invasión* (*The Invasion*, 1971), Roberto Rodríguez's *El Casorio* (*The Wedding*, 1969) and Jaime Carrero's *La caja de caudales FM* (*FM Safe*, 1979). Biaggi has also designed in a wide range of styles for plays from the world theatre, including Williams's *A Streetcar Named Desire* (1977) and Jason Miller's *That Championship Season* (1976), both directed by Dean ZAYAS, and also Beckett's *Waiting for Godot* (1974), for which he created an innovative, medieval-esque, stained glass cathedral design.

Bibič, Polde (1933–) Actor, Slovenia. Bibič trained at the Academy for Theatre Arts in Ljubljana. Major parts in his distinguished career include Mephistopheles in Goethe's *Faust*, Lopakhin in Chekhov's *Visnevyi sad* (*The Cherry Orchard*), Pozzo in Beckett's *Waiting for Godot* and Davis in Pinter's *The Caretaker*. According to the statement accompanying the award of lifetime contributions to the arts in Slovenia, Bibič has proved to be an actor who most personifies those qualities of Slovenian acting which are in accordance with both Slovenian and European theatrical tradition and at the same time represent a new quest for the undiscovered and modern in their positive sense. He has created unforgettable characters within the classic and modern repertory, thoughtful, temperamental and deeply moving in tragedy, thrillingly funny in comedy and thus very much at ease in folk plays.

Bickel, Moidele (1937–) Designer, Germany. Bickel has designed costumes both for classics such as Aeschylus' *Oresteia*, *Hamlet* and *The Winter's Tale*, and contemporary plays including *Kalldewey Farce* (by Botho STRAUSS) and Peter HANDKE's *Ritt über den Bodensee* (*Ride across Lake Constance*), working with directors Claus PEYMANN, Peter STEIN, Luc BONDY and Klaus Michael GRÜBER. According to critic Georg Hensel, Bickel's costumes 'are elementary. She narrates through fabrics, cuts and colours, and her realism is that of the fairy tale. She uses her comprehensive knowledge of all stylistic epochs with classical elegance and refinement.'

Bieito, Calixto (1963–) Director, Spain. Bieito studied at the University of Barcelona, Tarragona's Drama School and the Institut del Teatre (Barcelona). Between 1979–85 he was associated with the Instituto de Bahillerato of Villanova y la Geltrú and the town's municipal theatre. Since 1989 he has worked regularly at Barcelona's Grec Festival and at all major theatres in Barcelona, as well as at Madrid's Centro Dramático Nacional. As a radical innovator, he is comfortable working within musical theatre (Sondheim, Barbieri, Schönberg), and with more contemporary writers (Shaw, Plath, Lorca, Bernhard). In addition, he has demonstrated a veritable ability to reinvent the classics, stripping them of the legacy of past productions and imagining them for contemporary audiences both in his native Catalonia and beyond. His production of Calderón's *La vida es sueño* (*Life is a Dream*) for The Royal Lyceum Company as part of the 1998 Edinburgh Festival was widely praised for its delicate interrogation of the ever-shifting relationship between illusion and reality, its wry humour and its dynamic urgency. Catalan designer Carles Pujol's grey sandy set overlooked by a giant suspended mirror provided a dazzling image of an elusive world which can never be controlled and of which the audience are as much a part as the performers. Bieito is currently an associate director of the National Theatre of Catalonia.

Bigot, Georges (1955–) Actor, France. He joined Ariane MNOUCHKINE's Théâtre du Soleil in 1981 and played a series of major parts; during the *Shakespeare Cycle* (1981–4) he played the title role in *Richard II*, Count Orsino and Fabien in *Twelth Night* and Prince Henry in *Henry IV*. He was King Sihanouk in the eight-hour epic tragedy written by Hélène CIXOUS, *The Terrible but Unfinished Story of Norodom Sihanouk, King of Cambodia* (1985). For this role, he was awarded the prize of best actor of the year

by the Syndicat de la Critique Dramatique. He also played the lead role, Pandit Nehru, in *The Indiad or the India of their Dreams* by Cixous (1987). Bigot is forceful actor, whose acting style is very physical and whose diction is musical. He gives body expression to the internal emotions. He has worked with other theatre directors, including Jean-Paul Wenzel (Horvath's *Figaro läßt sich scheiden* (*Figaro's Divorce*), 1992), and Stuart Seide (*Le grain et la balle* by Samuel Beckett). In 1993, he co-directed *Kalo* with the author of the play, Maurice Durozier, and in 1994 he directed Marivaux's *La dispute* (*The Dispute*) at the Festival of Blaye. Since 1996 he has been artistic director of the Theatre Festival 'Les Chantiers de Blaye' in France.

Bil'chenko, Valerii (1959–) Director, Ukraine. He trained at the workshop of the Russian director Anatoly VASSILYEV at the Russian State Academy for Theatre Art (GITIS), Moscow, and attended a special course at the Moscow Theatre School of Dramatic Art. He took part in the famous production of Pirandello's *Sei personaggi in cerca d'autore* (*Six Characters in Search of an Author*), directed by Vassilyev. The director's popularity results from his experimental–destructive productions – *Arkheolohiia* (*Archaeology*, 1989), and *...I skazav B...* (*...And has said B...*, 1991) by Shypenko at Kiev Molodizhnyi (Youth) Theatre – as well as with the peak of the studio movement in the period of the national self-consciousness and creation of the state. In 1992 he founded the Kiev Experimental Theatre, a non-repertory theatre–laboratory for the study of the nature of the art of actor and director with the actors Veronika Avdieienko, Anatolii Petrov and Vladislav Chornen'kyi. In 1995 he was awarded the prize Kievs'ka Pektoral' for his radical interpretation of Chekhov's *Visnevyi sad* (*The Cherry Orchard*), staged under the title *Vystrel v sadu* (*The Shot in the Autumn Orchard*, 1993). He also directed productions of street theatre including *Opys chudovys'ka* (*The Description of the Monster*, Sevastopol, 1993) and *Skhidnyi marsh* (*The Oriental March*, Kiev, 1995).

Blais, Marie-Claire (1939–) Dramatist, Canada. Blais became internationally renowned as a novelist, having been awarded Guggenheim Fellowships in 1963 and 1964. She has written many plays for radio and television as well as some stage plays. Her theatrical work includes *L'exécution: pièce en deux actes* (*The Execution*, 1968), a play which adopts 'an almost Greek-tragic tone to tell the story' about two boys who plot to commit murder. One critic labelled it as 'another journey into the dark mind of this openly Lesbian writer'. More recent work includes *Sommeil d'Hiver* (*Wintersleep*, 1985).

Blakemore, Michael (1928–) Director, Great Britain. Trained at the Royal Academy of Dramatic Art, London, Blakemore began as an actor in repertory companies, and in 1967 he was very successful as a director at the Glasgow Citizen's Theatre with a production of Peter Nichols's *A Day in the Death of Joe Egg*. He is considered one of the most influential directors in Britain and has directed a wide range of new plays, notably by Michael FRAYN (such as *Copenhagen*, 1998, at the Royal National Theatre, London). In 1990 he directed a revival of MILLER's *After the Fall* and cast a black actor, Josette Simon, as Maggie, the character traditionally believed to be based on Marilyn Monroe, thus giving the play a new dimension.

Blanchett, Cate (1969–) Actor, Australia. Blanchett graduated from the National Institute of Dramatic Art, Sydney in 1992. She is carving out a successful film and television career (most recently she played the title role in *Elizabeth*) as well as producing highly acclaimed work in

the theatre. Blanchett's most striking characteristic as a performer is her ability to transform from role to role, to inhabit a character completely. As Nina, in Neil ARMFIELD's production of Chekhov's *Cajka* (*The Seagull*), Blanchett was impulsive and vulnerable but also completely compelling, and at the very end of the play this Nina was full of determination as well as defeat. The relationship with Richard ROXBURGH's Trigorin was played as genuinely, even tremulously hopeful for both Nina and Trigorin in its initial stages. Blanchett has played several roles for Armfield's Belvoir Street ensemble, including Ophelia in *Hamlet*, the seductress Rose Draper in *The Blind Giant is Dancing* by Stephen SEWELL and Miranda in *The Tempest*. Blanchett also won several awards for her performance in the Sydney Theatre Company's production of MAMET's *Oleanna* (opposite Geoffrey RUSH) in 1993.

Blankers, Anne-Wil (1940–) Actor, The Netherlands. Anne-Wil Blankers was originally a secretary who took up acting and went to the Maastricht Drama Academy, from which she graduated in 1963. She was immediately employed by the Haagse Comedie, playing Desdemona in *Othello*. Remarkably, Blankers stayed on with this company until its demise in 1983, after which she played in non-subsidized productions and with the successor to the The Hague company, Het Nationale Toneel. Her acting is typical of the The Hague style: elegant, technically perfect, but quite conventional. Blankers, a very popular actor, considers the title role in Sophocles's *Electra* (1976) as her best part, but she has played in a wide range of repertory plays: comedies by Molière, Feydeau, AYCKBOURN and Coward, but also serious plays, such as Schiller's *Maria Stuart* (1991), Norén's *Hebriana* (1989) and Bernhard's *Heldenplatz* (1991). Blankers frequently appears on television and is the current bearer of the Theo Mann-Bouwmeester Ring, a ring passed on from one generation of actors to the next and awarded the most distinguished actor of the era.

Blei, Dina (1958–) Actor, Israel. Blei trained at the Kibbutz Seminar and began her career at the Haifa municipal theatre. She then worked with Rina YERUSHALMI, playing Ophelia and the Doctor in Büchner's *Woyzeck*. At the Habima theatre she has played leading parts in Hanoch LEVIN's *Hayeled Cholem* (*A Child Dreams*) and *Kritat Rosh* (*Beheading*). With her slim figure, Blei is frequently cast in roles with metaphysical overtones, which makes her distinct and interesting as an actor on the Israeli stage.

Blessing, Lee (1949–) Dramatist, USA. Blessing obtained an MFA in Speech/ Theatre from the University of Iowa. His major plays include *Nice People Dancing to Good Country Music* (1982), *Riches* (1985), *A Walk in the Woods* (1987, his most popular success, which transferred to London and New York) and *Lake Street Extension*. According to critical opinion, 'style and subject matter are eclectic, though Blessing is characterized by an interest in characters whose past interferes with their future. Cyclical structures coupled with non-traditional plots create a unique style in which character and language are pivotal dramatic elements, and unique observations about relationships create impassioned moments on stage.'

Blythe, Domini (1947–) Actor, Canada. Born in Britain, Domini Blythe studied at the Central School of Speech and Drama in London. Before moving to Canada in 1972, she played with the Birmingham Repertory Theatre and the Royal Shakespeare Company (1968–70). In Canada, she gained national acclaim in many leading roles, such as Viola (*Twelfth Night*), Juliet (1972–6), Rosaline in *Love's Labour's Lost* (1977), the title role in Strindberg's *Fröken Julie* (*Miss Julie*,

1977), Margery in Wycherley's *The Country Wife* (1983) and Elmire in Molière's *Tartuffe* (1984). From 1981–3 she returned to the Royal Shakespeare Company to play Queen Elizabeth in *Richard III* and Helen in C.P. Taylor's *Good*. Her acting is characterized by its quiet intensity and its disarming vulnerability.

Boadella, Albert (1943–) Director and actor, Spain. Boadella was a founding member (in 1962) and, from 1966, the director of the Catalan performance group Els Joglars (meaning minstrels, jongleurs or jugglers). To start with, the company worked within the realm of pure mime, influenced by Etienne Marcel Decroux and Marcel Marceau. However, they later began to incorporate songs and words into shows which increasingly emphasised their Catalan identity and protested against aspects of the Francoist dictatorship (1939–75) such as torture. Brecht and Jacques Lecoq provided other important sources of inspiration. Boadella develops his work through improvization and video recordings during long rehearsal periods. In earlier shows such as *Mary d'ous* (*Egg Mary*, 1972), there was experimentation with repeated, sometimes banal, gestures, whereas latterly Els Joglars have used *in situ* observation in hospitals and religious communities as part of their research, for performances such as *Teledeum* (1983). Many productions by Els Joglars have been strongly political, amongst them the account of a seventeenth-century Catalan bandit *Alias Serrallonga* (1974) and *La torna* (*Left-overs*, 1977), a homage to a Catalan anarchist, for which Boadella was twice imprisoned and had to spend a year in exile in France. Other important productions include *Laetius* (1980), *Olympic Man Movement* (1981), *Virtuosos de Fontainebleau* (*Virtuosi of Fontainebleau*, 1985) and *Yo tengo un tío en América* (*I Have an Uncle in America*, 1991). Els Joglars have also made television programmes and regularly tour abroad.

Boermans, Theu (1950–) Director and actor, The Netherlands. After his training as an actor at the Maastricht Drama Academy (1968–72), Boermans played a few smaller roles. He came into his own after joining the Globe company in Eindhoven in 1975, possibly because of its location in the south, the region where he was brought up. Boermans was one of the first to use his regional dialect unashamedly, bringing energy to the Globe as well as a fluffy charm and a rapid, mumbling kind of speech. He paired well with Hans Hoes in Diderot's *Le neveu de Rameau* (*Rameau's Nephew*) and Beckett's *Waiting for Godot*, and starred in *Pericles* and *Troilus and Cressida*, a remarkable production by RIJNDERS. While still at the Globe he took up directing (1982), abandoning acting except for some film appearances. As a director, Boermans founded The Trust in 1986, a new company of young actors. He championed the work of Austrian playwrights like Gustav Ernst and Werner Schwab, and The Trust is presently a success story. Boermans also directs films, with the Trust actors in the main parts.

Bogart, Anne (1951–) Director, USA. Bogart's stage work is mainly experimental, combining spoken word, movement, gesture and song. Some of her productions are site-specific, while in others, showing the influence of Richard Schechner, spectators have to become participants. Bogart has also re-written more traditional texts, such as Wedekind's *Frühlings Erwachen* (*Spring Awakening*, 1984), and the musical *South Pacific*, which in her version is set in a rehabilitation clinic for war veterans, and critically assesses the issues of patriotism and racism inherent in the original. Her work has been called highly imagistic in style. She has recently become a force in training young performers in her methods, strongly influenced by her collaboration with Japanese director SUZUKI Tadashi.

She currently teaches at Columbia University.

Bogdanov, Michael (1938–) Director, Great Britain. A man of many nations, he studied in Ireland, Munich and Paris, and has worked in Britain and Germany, where, from 1989–93, he served as artistic director (Intendant) at the Schauspielhaus in Hamburg. From 1978–80 he was director of the Young Vic in London, and became an associate director at the National Theatre in 1980. Bogdanov's barnstorming, populist approach is well illustrated in his adaptation of *The Three Musketeers* in the early 1980s, which combined high good humour, ingenious visual and physical gags and audience participation. His version of the Christopher Sly prologue in *The Taming of the Shrew* (Royal Shakespeare Company, 1976) remains an indelible memory: a tramp invades the auditorium, argues with the usherettes, starts fighting with the staff, then jumps onto the stage and in a frenzy demolishes the set. In 1986 Bogdanov founded the English Shakespeare Company together with actor-director Michael PENNINGTON. Their emphasis was to show Shakespeare as a writer of present and future times. The company toured altogether seventeen productions in Britain and worldwide, and closed due to lack of funding between 1994–7. In 1995, Bogdanov directed a widely acclaimed version by Howard BRENTON of Goethe's *Faust* for the Royal Shakespeare Company.

Bohdalová, Jiřina (1931–) Actor, Czech Republic. A graduate of the Prague Academy of Performing Arts, her comic talent allowed her success in the lead role of Achard's *A Shot in the Dark* (1963, Prague Municipal Theatre, with more than 600 performances). Her acting links up with the tradition of entertaining city theatre, and shows many signs of typical Czech popular humour (a plebian ribaldry and panache, a directness and lack of constraint). She is probably the most popular contemporary Czech actor (she is even discussed in HAVEL's *Audience*). She has been a member of the leading Prague Vinohrady theatre since 1970, and has often demonstrated her talents outside the comedy genre as well, playing Mrs Wahl in Schnitzler's *Das Weite Land* (*Undiscovered Country*, 1992), but her preferred domain remains the comic: Frosina in Molière's *L'avare* (*The Miser*, 1971), Dolly in Wilder's *The Matchmaker* (1990) and the Nurse in *Romeo and Juliet* (1992), which she tries to bring closer to the Czech mentality. More recently she played the role of Erzhi in Orkény's *Cat Game* (1995).

Bokma, Pierre (1955–) Actor, The Netherlands. Pierre Bokma received his training as an actor at the Maastricht Drama Academy. Even there he was recognized as a major talent, and immediately after his graduation in 1982 he was chosen by Gerardjan RIJNDERS to play the innocent Cardenio in Gerrit Komrij's neoclassical verse drama *Het Chemisch Huwelijk* (*The Chemical Wedlock*). Energetic, clever and awesome in his ability to transform himself, Bokma is a prototypical actor, perhaps the best-known stage personality in The Netherlands. Although he did much freelance and film work, he is best known for his work with Rijnders, whose Toneelgroep Amsterdam he joined in 1987. He has stayed on with the company, starring in *Hamlet*, *Richard III*, Chekhov's *Ivanov* and PINTER's *Ashes to Ashes*, but also appearing in many smaller roles. Bokma has received numerous distinctions and awards.

Bond, Edward (1934–) Dramatist and director, Great Britain. Bond left school at the age of fourteen, and achieved notoriety in the theatre with his play *Saved* (Royal Court, 1965), especially the scene in which a group of adolescents stone a baby to death in its pram. Bond then turned away from drastic portrayals

of contemporary life, writing rather about the past as a mirror of the present, as in *Early Morning* (1968) and *Lear* (1971), a version of Shakespeare's *King Lear*. As a result, Bond's status in the theatre became less controversial, and his plays were taken up by the National Theatre (*Summer*, 1982) and the Royal Shakespeare Company (*The War Plays*, 1985). Although Bond has continued to write new plays, many have not been performed in Britain for some years (*Coffee* in 1997 was an exception). Revivals of his plays, though, are produced worldwide.

Bondy, Luc (1948–) Director, Switzerland. Bondy trained as an actor at Jacques Lecoq's school in Paris. In 1969 he was an assistant director at the Thalia Theatre, Hamburg, and has directed his own productions from 1971 onwards, in Göttingen, Wuppertal, Darmstadt, Frankfurt Hamburg, Berlin and Köln. He is particularly associated with the Schaubühne in Berlin, whose joint artistic director he was between 1985–8. Important productions include plays by Ibsen (*Gengangere* (*Ghosts*), *John Gabriel Borkman*), Shakespeare (*The Winter's Tale*, *Macbeth*), as well as contemporary plays by Edward BOND, Peter HANDKE and Botho STRAUSS. The eminent German theatre critic Friedrich Luft wrote of Bondy's production of *Ghosts*: 'Luc Bondy only reveals the wonder of this dramatic construction. He allows the piece to play itself. He allows the parts to develop themselves. He directs Ibsen. He only serves the purpose.'

Bortnowski, Paul (1922–) Designer and architect, Romania. A graduate of the Architecture Institute in Bucharest, his work covers a large area of concerns in architecture, design, theatre scenography and most of the environmental arts. He was the set designer (scenographer) of the Bulandra Theatre and The National Theatre in Bucharest, also working with other theatres in Romania and with major directors such as Liviu Ciulei. Major productions include Shakespeare (*The Winter's Tale, Hamlet*), Chekhov (*Visnevyi sad* (*The Cherry Orchard*)), Gogol (*Revizor* (*The Government Inspector*), *Zenit'ba* (*The Wedding*)), Shaw (*Mrs Warren's Profession, Caesar and Cleopatra, Pygmalion*), O'Neill (*Mourning Becomes Electra*) and Samuel Beckett (*Waiting for Godot*) as well as with Romanian plays by D.R. POPESCU and Iosif NAGHIU. Bortnowski held a professorship in set design at the Fine Arts Institute of Bucharest. As well as his work in theatre, he has contributed to exhibitions and studies about Romanian architecture and published a study about new theatre spaces and new stage techniques (Avignon 1974). His scenography combines the architect's precision with a metaphorical vision and reflection.

Boscana, Lucy (1924–) Actor, Puerto Rico. Born in Mayagüez, Lucy Boscana earned a BA in French and Theatre from Oberlin College in 1945 and afterwards pursued several months of postgraduate studies at the University of Puerto Rico under don Leopoldo Santiago LAVANDERO. Boscana first gained critical attention as Sandra in the world premiere of Francisco Arriví's *María Soledad* (*Maria Solitude*, Tinglado Puertorriqueño, 1947). She also created roles in other works by some of Puerto Rico's major playwrights of the mid-twentieth century, including Gabriela in René Marqué's *La Carreta* (*The Oxcart*, 1953); she recreated the latter role in the 1966 English-language production off-Broadway with Raúl Julia and Miriam Colón. She has also appeared as Martha in Edward ALBEE's *Who's Afraid of Virginia Woolf?*, as Mary in O'Neill's *Long Day's Journey into Night*, and as Beatrice in Paul Zindel's *Effect of Gamma Rays on Man-in-the-Moon Marigolds* (Teatro de Sesenta, 1971). Boscana is noted for her passion, intensity and total commitment to her roles. She has been frequently honoured at theatre festivals in Puerto Rico and has served as

Director of the theatre group Tablado Puertorriqueño since 1971.

Boukman, Daniel (1936–) Author, France and Martinique. Boukman took an arts degree at Paris University, but refused to do his national service and moved to North Africa, where he worked for nineteen years as a teacher and radical journalist, beginning to write with a strongly anti-colonial fervour although influenced by the poetic rhetoric of Aimé Césaire. After three shorter dramatic poems, of which *Orphée nègre* (*Black Orpheus*), deriding Négritude, is the best known, he wrote *Les négriers* (*The Slave Traders*, published 1971), which satirizes French policies of recruiting cheap labour in the Caribbean by making parallels with the slave trade. In a broader perspective, *Ventres pleins, ventres creux* (*Full Bellies, Empty Bellies*) attacks worldwide capitalism, as does the pro-Palestinian *Et jusqu'à la dernière pulsation de nos veines* (*To the Last Throb of our Veins*, 1976). Boukman returned to France, working in independent radio and joining the pro-Creole movement with poetry and a new play, *Délivrans* (1995). His drama appeals to activist groups by snappy sequences of sketches, strong views and dialogue in a clear French which has reworked readily into Cuban Spanish, Arabic or Creole.

Bourek, Zlatko (1929–) Designer, puppeteer and director, Croatia. In 1955 Bourek graduated in sculpture from the Academy of Fine Arts in Zagreb. His debut as a set and costume designer came in 1959 at the Zagreb Theatre Gavella with the medieval farce *Maître Pathelin*. In 1977 he designed the puppets and directed Isaac's farce *Orlando Maleroso* by merging the tradition of Dubrovnik with the Japanese puppet theatre. In 1982 he again turned to the Japanese puppet play when directing the puppet version of *Hamlet*, in turn based on STOPPARD's version of Shakespeare's play, which was performed at the most important theatre festivals in

Croatia and abroad and won him two theatre awards. As a set designer, he has worked in Wuppertal, Dortmund, New York, Munich and Turin. To show the world of distorted reality, he often uses the grotesque in his designs. His set designs have appeared in about forty cartoon films of distinguished representatives of the Zagreb School. Since 1961 he has been active as an independent author of cartoon and short feature films. For his own film *Kapetan Marko Arbanas* (*Captain Marko Arbanas*, 1967), he received an award at the Film Festival in Oberhausen. He is a recognized painter and sculptor. In 1969 his drawings were exhibited in the Museum of Contemporary Art in New York.

Boyce, Raymond (1928–) Designer, New Zealand. Boyce trained at the Old Vic Theatre School, coming to New Zealand soon after as resident designer for the New Zealand Players Company, 1953–7. After a period of freelance work he became associate director, design, at the Downstage Theatre, Wellington, from 1976–87. He had already been a regular designer there for the previous decade, and designed the purpose-built Hannah Playhouse (1973) for the company. Throughout his career he has been the country's most influential and outstanding stage designer, working on over 250 productions (a figure which includes many highly acclaimed operatic designs). Especially admired dramatic work includes Edward BOND's *Bingo* (1978), Brecht's *Leben des Galilei* (*Life of Galileo*, 1985) and Vincent O'Sullivan's *Jones & Jones* (1988), all at the Downstage. He is at his best, according to Bruce Mason, in productions which aim for 'ravishment and intricate enchantment'.

Branagh, Kenneth (1960–) Actor and director, Great Britain. Trained at the Royal Academy of Dramatic Art, Branagh made his debut in *Another Country* by Adrian Mitchell. After seasons with the Royal Shakespeare Company (playing Laertes in *Hamlet*, 1985), he founded the Renaissance Theatre Company (1987), for which he played Hamlet in 1988 and Edgar in *King Lear* in 1990, and directed *Twelfth Night*, *A Midsummer Night's Dream* and *King Lear* in 1989–90. He returned to the RSC in 1992 to play the title role in Adrian NOBLE's production of *Hamlet*. He wrote his autobiography when he was twenty-eight, and shifted his emphasis to film; *Henry V* in 1989 was later followed by *Much Ado About Nothing*, *Othello* and *Hamlet*. Perhaps his most engaging film is *In the Bleak Midwinter*, a funny and moving tribute to the whole process of 'doing Shakespeare'.

Brandauer, Klaus Maria (1944–) Actor and director, Austria. Brandauer trained at the Academy of Music and Dramatic Arts in Stuttgart, Germany. He is a lifetime member of the Burgtheater in Vienna, where he has played Hamlet, Romeo, Petrucchio, Schiller's Don Carlos and Molière's Tartuffe. He also appeared in the title role of *Jedermann* (*Everyman*) by Hugo von Hofmannsthal at the Salzburg Festival for several years running. More recently, he played George in ALBEE's *Who's Afraid of Virginia Woolf?* (Vienna, 1991, directed by Hans NEUENFELS), emphasizing the character's fragile nature. In 1999 he took his own production of Ester Vilar's *Speer* to London's Almeida Theatre, playing the charismatic title character Albert Speer, Hitler's Minister of Armaments. His portrayal of actor Henrik Höfgen in the film of *Mephisto* (1982) launched his international film career.

Breathnach, Paraic (1956–) Devisor and director, Ireland. Breathnach, who describes himself as a freelance creature counsel, was a founder member of the Galway-based company Macnas in 1986. Influenced by the English company Footsbarn and the Catalan Els Comediants, Macnas became known for its stunning outdoor spectaculars, including *The Big Game* at the Connaught Football Final, Castlebar (1987), *Gulliver* for the Dublin Millenium (1988) and *Tír Faoi Thonn* for the Galway Arts Festival (1989). When Macnas also began to work indoors (while maintaining the scope and vision of their work) Breathnach devised and scripted versions of *Alice in Wonderland*, co-directed with Peter Sammon (1989), and *Treasure Island*, directed by Rod Goodall (1990). The company's work took on a new direction in 1992 with *The Celtic Trilogy*, a series of plays which explored the stage languages of image, music, percussion and movement, and using sound rather than words. *Taín*, directed by Rod Goodall, was first performed at Expo92 in Seville and at the Galway Arts Festival, *Buile Shuibhne/Sweeney* at the Galway Arts festival (1993) and *Balor* in Bogota (1996). Also in 1996 Breathnach explored the potentials of percussion, a strong element of his earlier work, in *The Power Tool Orchestra* for the Temple Bar Festival, Dublin.

Brennan, Bríd (1955–) Actor, Ireland. Brennan began her acting career in Dublin, where she appeared in most of the major theatres (Gate, Peacock, Gaiety) as well as touring community centres with Moving Theatre. She received great acclaim for her tough portrayal of Lorna in Graham Reid's successful *Billy* trilogy for television (1982) acting alongside Kenneth BRANAGH, and played the eponymous heroine in the 1987 sequel *Lorna*. Other Irish roles include Josie in Anne DEVLIN's *Ourselves Alone* (1985) at the Royal Court Theatre, London, directed by Simon Curtis; Pegeen Mike in Druid Theatre Company's production of Synge's *The Playboy of the Western World* in Galway and on tour; and Agnes in Brian FRIEL's *Dancing at Lughnasa*, Abbey Theatre, Dublin, the National and Phoenix Theatre, London, and the Plymouth Theatre, New York. Her successful television and film career is matched by her

many stage performances, mostly in England, including roles at the Royal National Theatre and the Royal Shakespeare Company, playing Lady Macbeth in Tim Albery's production of *Macbeth* in 1996, and Mary in Tom MURPHY's *Bailegangaire* in James MacDonald's production at the Royal Court in 1997.

Brenton, Howard (1942–) Dramatist, Great Britain. Brenton is associated with socialist writing at the Royal Court theatre in London. In 1969 his play *Revenge* was produced at the Royal Court Upstairs, and toured by David HARE's company Portable Theatre. The Royal Court also presented Brenton's *Magnificence* (1973). A homosexual rape scene in *The Romans in Britain* caused a scandal at the National Theatre, London in 1980, culminating in an unsuccessful law case against Brenton and director Michael BOGDANOV. *Bloody Poetry* (1984) deals with poets Byron and Shelley. *Pravda* (National Theatre, 1985), written with David HARE, about contemporary newspaper politics, starred Anthony HOPKINS and proved a popular success. In *Berlin Bertie* (Royal Court, 1992), the action of the characters is psychologically motivated, which marks a departure from Brenton's issue plays in an epic style. Apart from original plays, Brenton has also made a name with adaptations and translations such as Brecht's *Galileo* and Goethe's *Faust* (Royal Shakespeare Company, 1995).

Brešan, Ivo (1936–) Dramatist, Croatia. For twenty-three years Brešan worked as a teacher of Croatian language and literature at the grammar school in Šibenik. Since 1983 he has been an art manager of the Cultural Centre and International Children's Festival in Šibenik. His breakthrough as a playwright came in 1971 when the &TD Theatre (ETC Theatre) staged his grotesque tragedy *Predstava Hamleta u selu Mrduša Donja* (*The Performance of Hamlet in Central Dalmatia*).

The production was an immediate hit and the play was soon translated and staged in Austria, Poland, Germany, the Soviet Union, Bulgaria and Sweden. He has written around twenty grotesque tragedies in which political primitivism is disclosed and satirized. Some of them are modernizations of the well-known dramatic models such as *Hamlet*, Goethe's *Faust*, Gogol's *Revizor* (*The Government Inspector*), and both Racine's *Phèdre* and Molière's *Tartuffe* in *Hidrocentrala u Suhom dolu* (*The Hydroelectric Station in Suhi Dol*, 1985). Together with the film director Krsto Papiæ he worked on the screenplays for three movies: *The Performance of Hamlet in Central Dalmatia* (1973), *Izbavitelj* (*The Redeemer*, 1977) and *Tajna Nikole Tesle* (*The Secret of Nikola Tesla*, 1980). In 1996 he and his son Vinko (screenwriter and director) achieved a great success with the movie *Kako je poïeo rat na mome otoku* (*The Way the War Broke Out on My Island*).

Breth, Andrea (1952–) Director, Germany. Breth began as an assistant director in Heidelberg, moving on to her own productions in Zürich, Freiburg and, from 1986–9, Bochum. Since then she has mainly directed at the Schaubühne am Lehniner Platz in Berlin and at the Burgtheater in Vienna. Important productions include Kaiser's *Von Morgens bis Mitternachts* (*From Morn to Midnight*), Ibsen's *Hedda Gabler* (1994, which caused controversy among critics), *Orestes* by Euripides (1995), Kleist's *Die Familie Schroffenstein* (*The Schroffenstein Family*, 1997), Chekhov's *Djadja Vanja* (*Uncle Vanya*, 1998, with Corina KIRCHOFF as Elena) and Goethe's *Stella* (1999, with Kirchhoff as Stella and Jutta LAMPE as Cäcilie). Her style has been described as magical realism fathoming the depths of human psychology.

Breuer, Lee (1937–) Director, actor and dramatist, USA. Breuer began his career as an actor and director in experimental work at the San Francisco Actor's Workshop. Between 1965–70 Breuer and his wife, actor Ruth Maleczech, travelled in Europe, studying with the Berliner Ensemble and with Grotowski's Theatre Lab, and directing in Paris. In 1970 he co-founded Mabou Mines (together with JoAnne AKALAITIS, Philip Glass and David Warrilow). Breuer's approach is intercultural, using material from Japanese kabuki, nô and bunraku as well as Indian performance techniques. In addition to theatre work, Breuer writes poetry and criticism and teaches at universities.

Bringsværd, Tor Åge (1939–) Dramatist, Norway. Following studies of folklore and mythology at the University of Oslo, Bringsværd has been working as a full-time writer and playwright since 1967. He divides his time equally between writing for children and adults. Besides eleven novels, ten collections of short stories, three collections of essays and over forty children's books, he has written some forty-five plays for the stage, radio and television. His work has been translated into eighteen languages, and his plays have been performed in fourteen countries besides Norway. His play *Nesegrevet* (*The Girl who Had a Nose as Long as a Hoe*) was part of the cultural programme in the Olympic Winter Games 1994 in Lillehammer. He believes that fairy tales, myths and modern science fiction are our best tools for understanding the so-called reality of our daily life.

Brisbane, Katharine (1932–) Critic and publisher, Australia. Along with her husband Philip Parsons, Brisbane founded Currency Press (Sydney) in 1971. Currency was then pioneering the publishing of Australian authored playscripts and it is still the major outlet for Australian plays and books on Australian theatre. The Currency National Theatre series has a particular commitment to publishing nineteenth century plays in order to establish a historical context for more recent developments in Australian theatre. As a theatre critic for twenty-one years, Brisbane championed the cause of Australian playwriting during the Renaissance years of the late 1960s and early 1970s and encouraged many writers; for example, she was one of the very first to identify the importance of David WILLIAMSON's writing. Brisbane has written extensively on the subject of Australian drama and theatre, and her influence in fostering Australian drama and theatre is incalculable.

Brook, Peter (1925–) Director, Great Britain. Brook initially directed in mainstream theatre in Britain, including the Royal Shakespeare Company, where he became a co-director in 1961, as well as opera and film. Major influences have been Kott, Artaud, Grotowski and non-Western theatre. Brook's aim is to create theatre that is living and organic, not dead. The sheer power of his attention is a catalyst in rehearsal; he allows full rein to the actors' creativity and edits the results later. Notable productions include *King Lear* (1962) with Paul SCOFIELD, Peter Weiss's *Marat/Sade* (RSC, 1964) and *A Midsummer Night's Dream* (RSC, 1970). In 1970 Brook left Britain and founded the Centre International de Récherche Théâtrale in Paris, from where he has since conducted his theatre research, including journeys to Africa, the USA and India, and projects including *Orghast*, *Conference of the Birds*, *The Tragedy of Carmen* (1983), *The Mahabharata* (1985) and *The Tempest* (1989). With *The Man Who* (1994), Brook returned to London on tour (Royal National Theatre), followed by *Happy Days* by Beckett, (Riverside Studios, 1997). Throughout his work in Paris, Brook has been following a quest to discover a universal language of the theatre. Admired by many as a genius, he is also subject to much controversy, especially regarding accusations of cultural appropriation in *The Mahabharata* (1985).

Brophy, Geraldine (1961–) Actor, New Zealand. Brophy never sought training at a drama school, beginning her professional career in 1983 at the Centrepoint Theatre, Palmerston North. After a year at the Fortune Theatre, Dunedin, she became for many years especially associated with the Court Theatre in Christchurch, where, developing under Elric HOOPER's guidance, she played many major roles, outstanding among them Elizabeth Proctor in Arthur MILLER's *The Crucible* (1988) and the title roles in Shaw's *St Joan* (1991) and Euripides's *Medeia* (1995). In 1993 she toured New Zealand, playing opposite Cathy DOWNES in the centennial women's suffrage play *Farewell Speech* (adapted by Downes from the novel by Rachel McAlpine, directed by Stuart DEVENIE). She now appears mainly in Wellington and Auckland, and won an award for her role in *Tzigane* by John Vakidis at the Downstage (1996).

Brunning, Nancy (1971–) Actor, New Zealand. Of Ngai Tuhoe and Ngati Raukawa descent, Brunning trained at the New Zealand Drama School, where she was among the first substantial group of Maori students to be enrolled. She quickly became well-known on television, and has developed into one of the country's best young actors. In 1992 she won Wellington's most promising newcomer award. She has been especially associated with the plays of Hone KOUKA, appearing in *Hide 'n' Seek* (1992), *Waiora* (1996), and most notably in the Colin MCCOLL production of *Nga Tangata Toa* (1994) at the Taki Rua Theatre, Wellington, where her remarkable ability to convey a sense of fiery yet contained emotional force was strikingly evident.

Buano, Avi Yona (1955–) Designer, Israel. After working in Israel and England for rock concerts and operas until the mid-1980s he worked for Mike Alfreds in London. After returning to Israel he has become one of the most sought for light-ing designers for theatre as well as dance performances. He has designed the light-ing for classical plays as well as newly written ones and is known for his original use of lighting technologies.

Buhre, Traugott (1929–) Actor, Germany. After attending drama school in Han-nover, Buhre gave his professional debut in 1952. From 1968–72 he was a member of the ensemble of Peter Palitzsch in Stuttgart and Frankfurt. Since then he has performed in Bochum, Hamburg and Vienna. His wide repertory ranges from unscrupulous villains to crafty rogues, and is especially valuable in portraying char-acters in Thomas Bernhard's plays. Major parts include the title roles in Goethe's *Faust* (Hamburg, 1979), Lessing's *Nathan der Weise* (*Nathan the Sage*, Bochum, 1981), as well as major parts in Thomas Bernard's *Der Theatermacher* (*The Thea-tremaker* 1986-7), Kleist's *Der Zerbro-chene Krug* (*The Broken Jug*, Vienna, 1990), *Waiting for Godot* (Vienna, 1991), TURRINI's *Alpenglühen* (*Glowing Alps*, Vienna, 1992), JELINEK's *Raststätte oder Sie Machens Alle*, (*Inn, or They All Do It*, Burgtheater, 1994, with sets by Karl-Ernst HERRMANN and starring Kirsten DENE and Martin SCHWAB), Turrini's *Die Schlacht um Vienna* (*The Battle for Vienna*, Burgtheater, 1995, directed by Claus PEY-MANN), and Bernhard's *Vor dem Ruhe-stand* (*Before Retirement*, 1999, with Kirsten Dene in the cast, directed by Peymann).

Bury, John (1925–) Designer, Great Brit-ain. From 1954–62 Bury worked with Joan Littlewood at the Theatre Work-shop. Between 1973–85 he was head of design at the National Theatre under Peter HALL. His style has been described as 'unfussy and modern'; he went against the prevalent semi-naturalistic style in the 1950s, and his use of highly textured natural materials, such as wood and metal, was an attempt to impart a sensory

experience of an object. This is perhaps best exemplified in his monumental, me-tallic set for The *Wars of the Roses* (Royal Shakespeare Company, 1964). Other im-portant productions for the stage include Marlowe's *Edward II* (1956), Dürren-matt's *Die Physiker* (*The Physicists*, 1963), PINTER's *Old Times* (1971) and Hall's productions of SHAFFER's *Amadeus* (1979) *Coriolanus* (1985), and *The Home-coming* (1991).

Bulbul, Farhan (1937–) Dramatist and director, Syria. Bulbul studied Arabic lit-erature and taught it at schools for many years. He launched a number of amateur groups in his city, Homs, especially The Workers' Theatre, to which he contribu-ted as a manager and director, as well as playwright. His breakthrough came with *Al-Mumathloun Yatarashaqun'l-Hijara* (*The Actors Throw Stones at Each Other*, 1974). Other major works include *Al-Ushaaw La Yafshaloun* (*Lovers do not Fail*, 1977), *La Tanzur Min Thuqbi'l-Bab* (*Do not Look through the Keyhole*, 1978), and *Al-Qura Tasaad Ila'l-Qamar* (*The Villages Mount up to the Moon*, 1980), an adaptation of Brecht's *Der Kaukasische Kreidekreis* (*The Caucasian Chalk Circle*). His latest play is *La Tarhab Hada'l-Saif* (*Do Not Fear the Edge of the Sword*, 1984). Bulbul's plays focus on class conflicts, but when he aimed at social realism with strong messages, he ended up merely with well-made melo-dramas with moral didacticism. In addi-tion to some productions of plays by other dramatists, he directed all the pre-mieres of his plays in his hometown; only one was revived by another director for the Damascus National Theatre. Bulbul once directed for a commercial troupe in Aleppo. More recently, he has dedicated himself to writing educational and docu-mentation books on theatre history in Syria and the Arab world.

Burroughs, Jackie (1941–) Actor, Canada. Born in Britain, Burroughs trained with

Uta Hagen in New York. In Canada, she has appeared with Crest Theatre, Manitoba Theatre Centre and the Stratford Festival. In 1996 she starred as Georgina O'Keefe in John MURRELL's *The Faraway Nearby* at the Saidye Bronfman Centre in Toronto. Some of Burroughs's most provocative and emotionally daring stage work has been showcased in Toronto's alternative theatres, notably the Toronto Free Theatre. In addition, she has a very successful film (*Winter Tan*, 1988) and television (*Road to Avonlea*) career. 'At one time a mannered actor (often compared to Katherine Hepburn or Maggie SMITH) she has, with age, become a vivacious, fearless and focused performer, delighting audiences and pulling in critics even when the vehicle in which she is starring is deeply flawed'.

Buzoianu, Cătălina (1938–) Director, Romania. Buzoianu began directing while still a student at the Bucharest Theatre and Film Institute, soon becoming one of the most praised young directors with Molière's *Le malade imaginaire* (*The Imaginary Invalid*) and Romanian plays such as Chitic's *Marele drum al încrederii* (*The Large Way of Confidence*). Working in Bucharest since 1975, she gained much praise for her outstanding productions for The Mic Theatre, among them *The Effect of Gamma Rays...* by Paul Zindel, and Romanian plays such as Ecaterina Oproiu's *Nu sunt Turnuc Eiffel* (*I'm Not the Eiffel Tower*). She often directed her own adaptations of novels, such as Dinu Sararu's *Niste Tirani* (*Some Peasants*). at the Bulandra Theatre, she achieved other successful productions such as Tankred DORST's *Merlin* and Sam SHEPARD's *Buried Child*. Winner of many prizes, her style has been called visual and poetical. In addition to theatre, she has directed opera and has worked in Israel, Poland, Italy, Spain, France and other countries. She is Professor at the Academy of Theatre and Film in Bucharest, teaching the art of directing. In 1992 she founded the Romanian Centre of Research and Theatre Anthropology.

Byrne, Catherine (1954–) Actor, Ireland. Having trained at the Abbey School of Acting, Byrne spent two years at the Gate Theatre Dublin before joining the Irish Theatre Company. As an actor, she is particularly noted for her work in Brian FRIEL's recent plays, which have given her an international profile. Roles include Chris in *Dancing at Lughnasa* (1990), which toured to London and Broadway, Angela in *Wonderful Tennessee* (1993), which also travelled to Broadway (both produced at the Abbey Theatre, Dublin) and the title role in *Molly Sweeney* at the Gate Theatre, Dublin (1995) directed by Friel. In 1997 Byrne played Daisy in the Abbey Theatre production of *Give Me Your Answer, Do!*, again directed by Friel. Other roles include Natalya in Turgenev's *Mesjac v derevne* (*A Month in the Country*, 1992), and Trassie Conlee in *Sharon's Grave* by John B. KEANE (1995), directed by Ben BARNES for the Gate Theatre, Dublin. In 1987 Byrne won a Harveys award for best actor for her performance of the title role of Lorca's *Yerma* in a version by Frank MCGUINNESS, staged at the Peacock Theatre for the Dublin Theatre Festival. Her television work includes the RTE (Radio Telefis Eireann) series *Upwardly Mobile* and BBC's *Ballykissangel*.

C

Cabal, Fermín (1948–) Dramatist and director. Spain. Cabal is regarded as one of the leading figures of Madrid's alternative theatre movement of the 1980s. Born and educated in Madrid, at the age of twenty-three he became associated with the fringe movement known as Teatro Independiente (Independent Theatre). As a member of some of its most prominent companies, such as Los Goliardos and Tábano, he founded a number of the city's most important alternative theatre spaces (Sala Independiente Cadarso and Sala Independiente Gayo Vallecano). In 1978 he wrote and directed his first successful production, *Tú estas loco, Briones* (*You Are Mad, Briones*). The premiere at the Centro Dramático Nacional of *Vade retro* (*Get Thee Behind Me*) in 1982 consolidated his status as an innovative writer capable of infusing realism with topical touches. *Esta noche gran velada* (*Tonight's Big Soiree*, 1983) was awarded the Critic's Award for that year. His plays are comedies mostly inhabited by recognizable archetypes and are characterized by the contemporary colloquial tone of his dialogues. It is perhaps not surprising, for a dramatist whose work has strong filmic resonances, that Cabal has chosen increasingly to work in television and film. *Farmacia de guardia* (*24 Hour Pharmacy*) proved one of the most popular television series of the mid-1990s.

Caird, John (1948–) Director, Great Britain. In 1980, Caird co-directed the highly successful adaptation by David EDGAR of *Nicholas Nickleby* for the Royal Shakespeare Company, together with Trevor NUNN. He continued with the RSC throughout the 1980s and into the 1990s, directing among others Ben Jonson's *Every Man in his Humour*, Shaw's *Misalliance* (both 1986), *A Midsummer Night's Dream* (1989), *As You Like It* (1990) and *Anthony and Cleopatra* (1993). Gorki's *Philistines* (1985) and *A Question of Geography* by John Berger and Nella Bielski (1987) were outstanding for their emotional power and truth. In 1994 he made his debut at the Royal National Theatre with Arthur Wing Pinero's *Trelawney of the Wells*, followed by Chekhov's *Cajka* (*The Seagull*) in 1994 and Pam GEMS's *Stanley* (1996), with Anthony SHER. In 1998, Caird and Nunn renewed their partnership at the Royal National Theatre when Nunn took over as its artistic director. Apart from productions for mainstream theatre, Caird has also directed and co-directed very successful musicals such as *Les Miserables* (with Trevor Nunn) and *Peter Pan* (Royal National Theatre, 1997).

Caldwell, Zoe (1934–) Actor and director, USA. Born in Australia, in 1953 she played the title role in Shaw's *Major Barbara* in Melbourne. From 1958–61 she pursued her career in Britain and performed with the Royal Shakespeare Company (Cordelia in *King Lear*, 1961) and the Royal Court (Isabella in Middleton's *The Changeling*). Following a season in Canada, Caldwell moved to the USA where she continued her distinguished career, adding directing to her credits. More recently she created the character of Maria Callas in *Master Class* by Terence MCNALLY (1995).

Calenda, Antonio (1939–) Director, Italy. After graduating in Law, Antonio Calenda co-founded with Virginio Gazzolo and Luigi Proietti the experimental theatre company Teatro dei Centouno, which introduced new writing to the Italian theatre scene. Amongst its most interesting productions are Boris Vian's *Il Rumore* (*The Empire Builders*, 1965), interpreted by Virginio Gazzolo and Piera Degli ESPOSTI; Pablo Picasso's *Il Desiderio Preso per la Coda* (*Desire Caught by the Tale*, 1967); Sophocles's *Oidipus epi Kolono* (*Oedipus at Colonus*, 1997); and Achille Campanile's *Un'indimenticabile serata* (*An Unforgettable Evening*, 1997), also interpreted by Degli Esposti. Calenda subsequently founded the Compagnia Teatro d'Arte in 1982 and worked both in Italy and abroad as a theatre, opera, radio, television and film director. Known internationally for the film *Il giorno del furore* (*Days of Fury: One Russian Summer*, 1973), co-written with Edward BOND, Calenda has directed some of the most interesting Italian practitioners in a repertoire of over a hundred classical and contemporary plays. His commitment to new writing, which over the years brought him to explore a wide range of dramatic forms, has contributed to his reputation as one of Italy's most eclectic and adventurous theatre directors.

Callow, Simon (1949–) Actor and director, Great Britain. Trained at the Drama Centre, London, Callow worked with the Joint Stock Company for a few years

before playing Orlando in *As You Like It* at the National Theatre (1979), where he also created the part of Mozart in Peter SHAFFER's *Amadeus*, directed by Peter HALL and starring Paul SCOFIELD and Felicity KENDAL (1979). Major parts in the 1980s include Edward BOND's *Restoration* at the Royal Court (1981), Manuel Puig's *Kiss of the Spiderwoman* with Mark RYLANCE, and the title part in Goethe's *Faust*, directed by David Freeman. More recently, he played Oscar Wilde in *The Importance of Being Oscar* (1997). Since the end of the 1980s Callow has directed several plays, including Willy Russell's *Shirley Valentine* (1988), the musical *Carmen Jones* and Sharman MacDonald's *Shades*. Callow has also made a reputation in films, and has written books about acting and biographies of Orson Welles and Charles Laughton.

Campbell, Cheryl (1951–) Actor, Great Britain. Campbell trained at the London Academy of Music and Dramatic Arts, and achieved a major success playing strong women characters of the classical repertory, such as Nora in Ibsen's *Et Dukkehjem* (*A Doll's House*) for the Royal Shakespeare Company in 1981. Her portrayal of the title role in Strindberg's *Fröken Julie* (*Miss Julie*) in 1983 was equally memorable. In 1985 she played Asta in Ibsen's *Lille Eyolf* (*Little Eyolf*), and in 1991 Emma in a revival of PINTER's *Betrayal* at the Almeida Theatre, London. For the 1993–4 season she once again joined the Royal Shakespeare Company to play Lady Macbeth opposite Derek JACOBI, as well as major parts in Middleton's *The Changeling* and Richard Nelson and Alexander Gelman's *Misha's Party*.

Campos, Rosi (1954–) Actor, Brazil. Campos studied journalism at the School of Communication and Arts, University of São Paulo. Major stages in her career are work with the theatre company Mambembe with C.A. Soffredini, at Teatro do

Ornitorrinco with Cacá Rosset, and at Circo Grafitti. Major stage credits include Mother Ubu in Jarry's *Ubu Roi* (*King Ubu*), Amandla Amanda in Soffredini's *Vem Buscar–me que ainda sou Teu*, and several characters in Noemi Marinho's *Almanaque Brazil*. She organizes world literature research groups to study it's more interesting theatrical aspects. In the theatre she has specialized in musicals, and finds teamwork essential to her profession.

Canto, Toni (1965–) Actor, Spain. Canto took acting lessons at the Academy of William Layton and studied with the well-established director José Carlos PLAZA in Madrid. During the 1990s, while Plaza was artistic director of Madrid's Centro Dramático Nacional, he enjoyed prominent roles in a number of high-profile productions. His tall physique and dark classic good looks placed him in much demand as an attractive lead actor. He gained critical and commercial success in a range of productions including Aeschylus's *Oresteia* (1990), the 1991 production of Valle-Inclán's *Comedias bárbaras* (*Savage Plays*) and *The Merchant of Venice* (1992). Other successful productions include Robert WILSON's acclaimed *Don Juan Ultimo* (*The Last Don Juan*), based on a play by novelist Vicente Molina Foix (1992), and more recently Mario GAS's production of Tennessee Williams's *Cat on a Hot Tin Roof* (1995). The very popular television series of *Los Ochenta son nuestros* (*The Eighties are Ours*), written and directed by Ana DIOS-DADO in 1988, catapulted him to success within the media spectrum and he has gone on to work regularly in film and television.

Caramitru, Ion (1942–) Actor and director, Romania. In 1964, Caramitru made his professional debut as an actor at the National Theatre in Bucharest with the title role in *Emineseu* (by Mircea Stefǎnescu) while still a student at the Theatre

and Film Institute in Bucharest. After graduating he joined the Bulandra Theatre in Bucharest, becoming one of its main actors until he was appointed its director general (1990–3). A notorious figure in the Romanian Revolution of December 1989, Ion Caramitru was elected President of the Theatre-Union of Romania (UNITER), created in 1990, which he led until 1996 when he became Minister of Culture. As a theatre actor, he appeared in more then sixty roles in plays by Shakespeare (Romeo, Hamlet, Octavius and Ferdinand), Chekhov, Pirandello (*I giganti della montagna* (*The Mountain Giants*)), Büchner (*Leonce und Lena*), Shaw (Eugene Marchbanks in *Candida*), Rolf Hochhuth (*Der Stellvertreter* (*The Deputy*)), Sütö András, Marin Sorescu and others. Caramitru also directed many productions, including Sorescu's *Third Stake* and Howard BARKER's *The Shape of the Table* for the theatre, as well as opera. He created acclaimed one-man shows with poetry by Eminescu and Shakespeare. He is an actor with a specific charm and with a unique power to communicate the emotions through a strong cerebral control.

Carballido, Emilio (1925–) Dramatist and director, Mexico. Carballido studied French at the National University and has become one of the foremost dramatists in Mexico. In addition, he writes for the screen and directs and teaches at university level. His many plays cover a wide range of styles. *The Strand of Gold* edges towards surrealism, and *I Also Speak of the Rose* is a comedy that takes place in the space between reality and fiction. At the heart of this work there is often a national question: what reality governs Mexican people? Is it one propagated by legend or advertising, or is it everyday reality? In the 1980s, he turned his attention to a simpler, more direct type of theatre in such works as *Mimi and Fifi on the Orinoco* and *Rose of Two Aromas*.

Cardinal, Tantoo (1950–) Actor, Canada. Cardinal learned the craft of acting at theatres in Western Canada, including 25th Street Theatre and Persephone Theatre. She played the title role in *Jessica* at Toronto's Théâtre Passe Muraille. Cardinal was nominated for a Genie award for her role as Roseanne in Anne Wheeler's 1986 feature film *Loyalties*. Her other films include *Dances With Wolves* (1990), *Black Robe* (1991) and *Legends of the Fall* (1993). Although her stage acting has offered evidence of strong comedic gifts, Cardinal tends to be typecast as a proud, stoical aboriginal woman in her film roles.

Cariou, Len (1939–) Actor and director, Canada. Cariou studied singing as a child and voice with Kristin Linklater in New York. His professional debut was in 1959. Between 1962–5 he appeared at the Stratford Festival. In 1965 he moved to the USA, where he established himself as a leading actor in repertory and on Broadway. In 1975 Cariou returned to Canada, appearing as Dysart in SHAFFER's *Equus*, Macbeth (1979), Coriolanus and Petruchio (1981), and King Lear (1983). He is a versatile performer, capable of quiet intensity (particularly in his television and film roles) and also of great vocal and physical power.

Carmon, Yosef (1934–) Actor, Israel. Carmon started his career at the Haifa municipal theatre with parts like Orlando in *As You Like It* and Andri in Frisch's *Andorra*. Carmon joined the Cameri Tel Aviv municipal theatre playing roles like Brutus in *Julius Caesar* and the title roles in *Macbeth* and an adaptation of Kleist's *Michael Kohlhaas*. There he also played major roles in many of Hanoch LEVIN's plays such as *Yesurei Iov* (*Job's Sufferings*), *Hazona Hagedola mi-Bavel* (*The Great Whore of Babylon*) and *Heffetz*, showing his virtuosity and versatility as an actor.

Carr, Marina (1964–) Dramatist, Ireland. Carr's early work includes *Ullaloo* (1991), *Low In The Dark* (1989) and *This Love Thing* (1991). *The Mai* (1994), directed for the Peacock Theatre by Brian Brady, weaves together language, image and folklore into a strongly theatrical work. Drawing on her own Irish Midlands background, Carr lends her work a particular sense of place, as evident in *Portia Coughlan*, directed by Garry HYNES for the Peacock Theatre (1996), which toured to The Royal Court Theatre, London. Commissioned by the National Maternity Hospital, Dublin, and written entirely in Midlands dialect, *Portia Coughlan* is peopled by damaged, grotesque characters. *By the Bog of Cats* (1998) marked Carr's move to the main stage of the Abbey Theatre, directed by Patrick MASON as part of the Dublin Theatre Festival. It combines myth and literary allusion to explore the fate of Hester Swayne, played by Olwen Fouere, as she struggles to deal with rejection and betrayal, and singles out Carr as Ireland's leading woman dramatist.

Carrero, Tonia (1922–) Actor, Brazil. Carrero took a performance course in Paris and studied in Brazil with Zbigniev Zienbinsky, Eugenio Kusnet and Adolfo Celli. She became famous for her beauty, which she herself regarded as a precious gift but not essential for her career, which was informed by pursuit of perfection and social awareness. Major parts include Estelle in Sartre's *Huis clos* (*In Camera*), Desdemona in *Othello*, Lady Macbeth, Nora in Ibsen's *Et Dukkehjem* (*A Doll's House*) and Claire in Marguerite Duras' *L'Amante Anglaise*.

Carroll, Peter (1944–) Actor, Australia. Trained at Central School of Speech and Drama (London), Carroll began his professional career in 1974 when he joined the Nimrod Theatre, Sydney. As a boy soprano he had hoped for a career in opera, but he has worked mainly in musicals such as *Les Miserables* and *Evita*. For the Melbourne Theatre Company, Carroll starred in *Sweeney Todd* in a performance which combined comedy, tragedy and horror very precisely. Carroll won a Green Room award for his performance as Stalin in David Pownall's *Masterclass* and received much acclaim for his solo performance in Ron Blair's *The Christian Brothers* (1975), which toured Australia and overseas. He created major roles in David WILLIAMSON's *Emerald City*, *The Perfectionist* and *Money and Friends*. Carroll also teaches voice at the National Institute of Dramatic Art, Sydney, and does a great deal of radio work, especially poetry reading, and voiceovers in film and television.

Cartwright, Jim (1958–) Dramatist, Great Britain. Cartwright attended the Royal Academy of Dramatic Art and was a writer in residence with Octagon Theatre, Bolton, between 1989–91. 'Claiming to have read only four books in his life, Cartwright shows intuitive skill at poetic realism in portraying his borderline characters': the unemployed in a housing estate in *Road* (1989), old age in *Bed* (1989) and the dream of stardom in *The Rise and Fall of Little Voice* (1992, Royal National Theatre).

Carver, Brent (1951–) Actor, Canada. Carver has acted in almost every major theatre in Canada, including the Stratford Festival and the Citadel Theatre. Early in his career, he played leading musical roles (Pirate King in Gilbert and Sullivan's *The Pirates of Penzance*). Other roles include Ariel in *The Tempest*, Hamlet, Horst in Martin Sherman's *Bent* (1982) and the Master of Ceremonies in *Cabaret* (1987). Carver made his Broadway debut in the musical of *Kiss of the Spiderwoman* (1993), for which he received a Theatre World Award. He was a member of the new Toronto repertory company, Soulpepper, in 1998. Carver is equally at home in emotional dramatic roles and in glitzy musical performances.

Casas, Myrna (1934–) Dramatist, director, producer, actor and designer, Puerto Rico. In addition to being a director and producer, Myrna Casas is one of Puerto Rico's principal contemporary dramatists. In 1963 she founded the group Producciones Cisne, where she continues to direct her efforts as producer and dramatist. Her major plays include *Cristal roto en el tiempo* (*Window Broken in Time*, 1960), *Absurdos en soledad* (*Absurdists in Solitude*, 1964), and *El gran circo Eukranio* (*The Great Ukranian Circus*, 1988). Her later plays are renowned for their post-absurdist critiques of the social and political structures of Puerto Rican art and society. Since 1985, her company has been a member of the organization Productores Internacional de Teatro (International Producers of Theatre) and has toured productions throughout the Americas. Casas's work as director includes the Antonio Buero Vallejo translation of *Hamlet* (1993). Casas has also worked as a costume designer and actor, originating the role of Hortensia in Rene Marques's classic of the Puerto Rican drama *Los Soles Truncos* (*The Fanlights*), directed by Victoria ESPINOSA in 1958.

Cassiers, Guy (1960–) Director and actor, Belgium. Cassiers trained at the Royal Academy of Fine Arts in Antwerp, but afterwards found himself working in the theatre, first as an actor and then as a director. From 1987–92 he led Oud Huis Stekelbees in Ghent, which broke through its traditional barriers as a young people's theatre to influence Flemish and Dutch theatre as a whole. For the Kaaitheater in Brussels, he directed *Het Liegen in Ontbinding* (*Lying in Decay*, 1993), a montage of Samuel Beckett and Julian Barnes, as well as *De Pijl van de Tijd* (1994, after Martin Amis's novel *Time's Arrow*). He is also active in The Netherlands, where he directed the Dutch-language premiere of

Tony Kushner's *Angels in America* (1995) at the RO Theatre in Rotterdam. Cassiers's work reads as a plea for human imagination, urging its audience to take a fresh look at reality. An important ingredient in his productions is the interaction with visual arts and video.

Castellucci, Romeo (1960–) Director, Italy. Romeo Castellucci, together with Claudia Castellucci, Chiara Guidi and Paolo Guidi, founded the Societas Raffaello Sanzio in 1981, which held a number of exhibitions and multimedia installations in Rome (1983, 1984 and 1987), at the Biennale in Venice (1984), at Documenta 8 in Kassel (1987) and in Milan (1984 and 1988). Among Castellucci's most notable productions for Raffaello Sanzio are *Santa Sofia, teatro khmer* (*Saint Sophia, Khmer Theatre*, 1985), *Alla bellezza tanto antica* (*For Such Ancient Beauty*, 1988), *Gilgamesh* (1990) and *Hamlet* (1992). Castellucci has been exploring, together with his company, the boundaries and excesses of the use of the body in performance, the creation of artificial and non-verbal languages, the use of iconoclastic theatre in opposition to verbal theatre, the simultaneous use of a plurality of performance spaces and the application of ritual and myth to the performing arts.

Castorf, Frank (1951–) Director, Germany. In 1976 he became director of the Theater der Bergarbeiter in Senftenberg. Between 1981–5 he was Schauspieldirektor (head of drama) in Anklam, since 1992 he has been Intendant of the Volksbühne Berlin. His productions, mainly of standard classical texts, are anything but standard: they are highly iconoclastic, fragmentary, irritating and thus controversial, intending to achieve a new view of contemporary life. Among his important productions are Goethe's *Clavigo* (1986), *Hamlet* (Köln, 1989), Goethe's *Stella* (1990), Schiller's *Wilhelm Tell* (1991), Hebbel's *Die Nibelungen* (1995), JELINEK's

Die Raststätte oder Sie machen's alle (*Inn, or The all do it*, 1995), Heiner Müller's *Der Auftrag* (*The Request*, 1996, Berliner Ensemble), *Trainspotting* (Volksbühne, 1997) and Sartre's *Les mains sales* (*The Dirty Hands*, 1998, Volksbühne).

Castri, Massimo (1943–) Director and actor, Italy. After a period of training with amateur theatre companies, Castri co-founded the theatre company Cab 65 in 1965, which introduced Italian audiences to a variety of contemporary European plays. He then worked with a number of directors, including Carlo QUARTUCCI and Antonio CALENDA. After graduating with a thesis on political theatre in 1971 Castri started directing his own projects, producing among others three visually striking and dramaturgically adventurous interpretations of Luigi Pirandello's *Vestire gli ignudi* (*To Dress the Naked*, 1976), *La vita che ti diedi* (*The Life I Gave You*, 1978) and *Così è (se vi pare)* (*It Is So, If You Think So*, 1979), as well as new interpretations of Gabriele D'Annunzio's *Fedra* (*Phèdre*, 1988) and Euripides's *Orestes* (1997). Castri also appeared in a number of films, such as *Sotto il segno dello scorpione* (*Under the Sign of the Scorpio*, 1969), directed by Paolo and Vittorio Taviani. Starting from an experimentation with Artaudian and Brechtian theatrical forms, Castri developed a particular style of theatre which focused on the oneiric, often reminiscent of Freudian and Lacanian theories, while at the same time politically and socially engaged. This form of nocturnal, meta-theatrical theatre, usually dealing with texts representing bourgeoisie crisis, has come to represent one of the most sought after styles of the contemporary Italian theatre scene.

Catra, I Nyoman (1954–) Performer, Indonesia. Catra trained at ASTI (Akademi Seni Tinggi Indonesia), Denpasar, and obtained an MA from Wesleyan University. From a family of musicians, Catra began performing as a drummer with gamelan ensembles. He joined his village Barong group at age thirteen and soon developed into a gifted comedian. He began his acting career playing Anoman in the *Ramayana* for tourist shows in Kuta, but is now acknowledged as a master of the comic Bondres masks. He has performed with a number of different ensembles in Topeng Panca and Prembon, as well as in the newer genres of Wayang Listrik and Bondres. He also performs Barong for temple ceremonies, teaches at STSI (the Academy of Performing Arts) in Denpasar and leads workshops in Balinese theatre and music in the United States and Europe.

Caubère, Philippe (1950–) Actor and director, France. Caubère worked with Théâtre du Soleil between 1971–6, where he played leading parts in *1789*, *1793* and *L'âge d'or* (*The Golden Age*). He also played the lead role in the the film version of *Molière*, written and directed by MNOUCHKINE. In 1978 he directed and played in Molière's *Dom Juan* at the Théâtre du Soleil. After leaving the company he created a series of performances, all of which are improvized scripts based on his life experience as an actor in the Théâtre du Soleil: *La danse du diable* (*The Devil's Dance*, 1981) directed by J.P. Tailhade and C. Massart; *Le roman d'un acteur* (*The Novel of an Actor*, 1983–5, also performed at Avignon Festival of 1993); *Ariane ou l'âge d'or* (*Ariane or The Golden Age*, 1986); *Les enfants du soleil* (*Children of the Sun*); *La fête de l'amour* (*Festival of Love*); and *Le triomphe de la jalousie* (*Triumph of Jealousy*, 1988–9). In 1996 he directed a film inspired by these performances, *Les enfants du soleil* (*Children of the Sun*). He also worked as a film actor, appearing in *La gloire de mon père* (*My Father's Glory*) and *Le château de ma mère* (*My Mother's Castle*) directed by Yves Robert and based on Marcel Pagnol's novels.

Cecchi, Carlo (1942–) Director and actor, Italy. After a period of training at the Accademia d'Arte Drammatica in Rome, Carlo Cecchi made his debut in the theatre in 1968 in Dacia MARAINI's *Il Ricatto a Teatro* (*Blackmail in the Theatre*). In 1969 he founded the alternative theatre company Granteatro, for which he directed both classical and contemporary plays. Among his most notable productions with Granteatro are Bertold Brecht's *Trommeln in der Nacht* (*Drums in the Night*, 1972), Georg Büchner's *Woyzeck* (1973), Luigi Pirandello's *L'uomo, la bestia e la virtù* (*The Man, the Beast and Virtue*, 1980) and Samuel Beckett's *Endgame* (1995). Cecchi's productions are a fascinating synthesis of Italian popular theatre and styles drawn from the historical avant-gardes. His strong stage presence and his innovatory directing and acting styles have made him one of the most interesting and influential experimental directors and performers of the Italian theatre scene. Cecchi has also appeared in a number of films, such as Mario MARTONE's *Morte di un Matematico Napoletano* (*Death of a Neapolitan Mathematician*, 1991), Ricky Tognazzi's *La Scorta* (*The Escort*, 1993) and Bernardo Bertolucci's *Io Ballo da Sola* (*Dancing Alone*, 1995).

Cenean, Stefania (1958–) Designer, Romania. A graduate (1982) of the Fine Arts Institute Nicolae Grigorescu, Bucharest, Cenean created the set and costume design for more than thirty theatre productions in Bucharest, Craiova (where she is based), Sibiu and Târgu-Mures. She participated in the Trienniale of Scenography in Bucharest and the Prague Quadriennale of Scenography in 1992, and organized a personal exhibition of set and costume design at the Institut Français of Bucharest, 1995. Major productions include Chekhov's *Djadja Vanja* (*Uncle Vanya*) at the National Theatre in Craiova, and WERTENBAKER's *Our Country's Good* at the National Theatre Bucharest, directed by Andrei SERBAN. She designed Silviu PURCĂRETE's productions of, among others, D.R. POPESCU's *Piticul în grădina de vară* (*The Dwarf in the Summer Garden*) and *Titus Andronicus*. Cenean was awarded many prizes for her creative contribution to the suggestive and poetical visual image of theatrical events.

Césaire, Ina (1942–) Author, France and Martinique. A former lecturer at Paris university, with a doctorate for research in ethnology at the Ecole des Languages Orientales, Ina Césaire (eldest daughter of the poet-politician of Négritude) found in Peter BROOK's work the inspiration for transmitting the tales and oral history she was collecting to a wider audience. Her first play, *Mémoires d'Isles: Maman N. et Maman F* (*Island Memories*, 1983), interweaves the life histories of two elderly grandmothers (based in part on her own family lore), and toured widely in a production by Jean-Claude Penchenat. *L'Enfant des passages ou La geste de Ti Jean* (*Child of the Crossings or The Epic of Little John*, 1987) recreates the initiatory journey of the dauntless folk hero, whose origins lie in West African tales. In *Rosanie Soleil* (1992), an uprising in the South of Martinique in 1870 is reflected through three women's lives. Ina Césaire continues to explore drama, fiction and documentary film in her recreation and transmission of the traditions and social history of Martinique.

Césaire, Michèle (1951–) Writer and director, France and Martinique. Niece of Négritude writer-politician Aimé Césaire, she holds a masters degree in history from the University of Paris. Working in both France and Martinique from 1982–6, she divided her energies between the promotion of French West Indian culture in France and developing her skills as a writer-director. Her *Conte du monde d'en bas* (*Tales of the Netherworld*, 1986) was a natural outcome of her deep interest in folktales, but she has drawn from sources

as divergent as James Baldwin and Cesar Pavese for her stage adaptations. *La Nef* (*The Ship*), first produced for the 1992 Festival de Fort-de-France, is an allegory of Caribbean identity; her dramatic comedy *Bal d'éventails* (*Fan-dancing*, 1994) evokes postwar Martinican racial tension; and *L'Année de tous les saints* (*The Year of All Saints*, 1998) builds on the traditional rituals commemorating the dead on 1 November. She founded Racines in 1982 to support original artistic creation in theatre, literature and the arts.

Chae Hi-Wan (1948–) Director and dramatist, Korea. Chae graduated from Seoul National University, where he was known as an underground artist who believed theatre to be a weapon. He sharply confronted Korea's political problems with his group, Handoore, through unpublicized open air performances and illegal private performances. For the dramaturgy, he reconstructed elements of traditional Korean mask dancing. He dramatized the hardship of the labour movement in *Jinogui Goot* (1973), *Agoo* (1974, with KIM Suk-Man), *Gumgwaneui Yesoo* (*Life of Jesus*, 1978), *Gongjangeui Boolbit* (*Light of a Factory*, by Kim Min-Gi), *Nodongjaeui Hwatbool* (*A Torch of Labour*, 1980), *Jeo Hanuleui Byeocheoreom* (*Like a Star in the Sky*, 1981), *Duidui Bangbang* (*Rush Rush Driver*, 1985), *Minjoo Gotsinbaram* (*Wind of Democratic Flower Shoes*, 1989) and *Kalnorae Kalchoom* (*Sword Song Sword Dance*, 1994). All his productions are based on fact in order to gain the sympathy of the audience. Since 1990, Chae has extended the scale of his works, and directed carnival-like productions such as *Welcome to History – Festival for the Memory of Goboo Rebelion* (1994) and the *Consolation Festival for the Spirit of Death by False Charge* (1996), which was performed over several days.

Chaikin, Joseph (1935–) Director and actor, USA. Chaikin graduated in drama and philosophy from Drake University, studied method acting with Herbert Berghof, Mira Rostova and Nola CHILTON, and made his acting debut in 1958. He was a member of The Living Theatre for several years before co-founding the Open Theatre, which 'broke with Stanislavskian character-based performance and enabled actors' bodies to transform elastically from character to object to metaphor, and [...] enabled actors to play roles outside their character "type". What began as a laboratory developed into a collective producing theatre.' In 1984 Chaikin suffered a stroke resulting in aphasia, and in 1991 he appeared in plays co-authored with Sam SHEPARD (*The War in Heaven*) and van Itallie (*Struck Dumb*) that reflected his experience. Along with Julian Beck and Judith Malina, he is regarded as one of the most influential theatre avant-gardists of the last thirty years.

Chan, Anthony (1953–) Dramatist, director, set and costume designer, China (Hong Kong SAR). Chan is considered to be a versatile dramatist who has written, directed and designed sets and costumes for more than fifty productions. Chan's *Hong Kong Heartbeat*, an ensemble work with mime and dance, was staged as part of the Hong Kong Festival in London (1992) and Calgary (1993). *Nuwa Mends the Sky* (1992) won the award for best script and toured in Tarascon and Bordeaux (France). In 1994 Chan translated, directed and designed the set for *You Can't Take It with You* (by Moss Hart and George Kaufman) for the Hong Kong Repertory Theatre, which then went on to win the top ten best production award of the year. His other major directions cover Ronald Harwood's *The Dresser* (1997), and his own farcical Chinese opera *Love's Labour's Won*, starring Hollywood film actor Chow Yun-Fat (1998). Chan has also received much acclaim for his set and costume design the 1996 production of Mark Medoff's *Children of a Lesser God* (Hong Kong and Beijing).

Chang, Tisa (1945–) Director, USA. Born in China, Chang grew up in the USA, studied ballet and traditional Chinese dance, received a scholarship from the Martha Graham Dance Company, and studied acting with Uta Hagen. In 1977 she founded Pan Asian Repertory Theatre, to 'produce the work of Asian-American playwrights as well as to translate Asian masterpieces into English and innovatively adapt Western classics'. For her, the commercial theatre is no longer a yardstick of American theatre. The impact of American theatre is now more far-reaching and meaningful.

Channing, Stockard (1944–) Actor, USA. Channing made her stage debut in 1966. Among her roles are Alice in Dürrenmatt's *Play Strindberg* (1972), Jane in AYCKBOURN's *Absurd Person Singular* (1978), Sheila in Peter Nichols's *A Day in the Death of Joe Egg* (1982, 1985) for which she received an Antoinette Perry Award, Susan in Ayckbourn's *Woman in Mind* (1988, Drama Desk Award), GUARE's *Six Degrees of Separation* (New York, 1990 and London, 1992) and Tom STOPPARD's *Hapgood* (1994). In 1997 she appeared in *The Little Foxes* by Lillian Hellman. 'She has the ability to combine a sense of comedy with a sense of pathos to get at the ache underneath.'

Charalambous, Nicos (1941–) Actor and director, Greece. Born in Cyprus, he trained at the Karolos Koun Drama School, and took courses in directing, dramaturgy and movement at the University of Erlangen, Germany. From 1964–9 and again in 1975–6 he was actor and assistant director at Karolos Koun Art Theatre, where he participated in acclaimed productions of Aeschylus's *Persai* (*The Persians*), as well as in Aristophanes's *Ornithes* (*The Birds*) and *Batrachoi* (*The Frogs*), which toured to London, Paris, Munich, Berlin, Venice, Moscow, Warsaw and Tel Aviv. From 1970–4 he was an actor with RIK Theatre, Cyprus, and 1975–80 actor and director at Thessaloniki Theatre and Theatre of Cyprus. From 1980 onwards he has been an actor at the Amphi Theatre and a director with Theatre of Cyprus. He played leading roles in plays by Weiss, O'Neill, PINTER, Dürrenmatt, Anouilh, Molière, Beckett, Brecht and Strindberg as well as many Greek playwrights. His directing credits include many Greek classics as well as Lorca's *La casa de Bernarda Alba* (*The House of Bernarda Alba*), Peter Weiss's *Marat/Sade*, Brecht's *Die Dreigroschenoper* (*The Threepenny Opera*) and several plays by Tennessee Williams and Shakespeare.

Chen Ming Zheng (1932–) Director, China. Chen trained as an actor at the Shanghai Academy of Drama and has become a professor in its acting department. His major productions from the 1980s to the 1990s include *Hamlet*, Luo Jian Fan's *Hei Jun Ma* (*Black Stallion*), Cao Lu Sheng's *Bai Niang Niang* (*White Snake Lady*), *The Big Bridge*, Zhao Hua Nan's *OK Gu Piao* (*OK, Stocks*), Zhang Xian's *Mei Guo Lai De Qi Zi* (*The America-Returned Wife*), Cao Lu Sheng's *Da Pi Guan* (*The Cleaving of the Coffin*) and *Cang Tiang Zai Shang* (*Heavens Above*). He is known in the Chinese theatre as a 'poetical director' with a theoretical interest in the 'sub-conscious'.

Chen Rong (1929–) Director, China. Chen studied at the Central Academy of Drama and Moscow Lunarcharski School of Drama 1950–9, and has been a major director at the China Youth Theatre. Her pre-Cultural Revolution productions include Ren De Yao's *Malan Hua* (*Malan Flower*), Chekhov's *Tri sestry* (*Three Sisters*), and Beaumarchais's *Le mariage de Figaro* (*The Marriage of Figaro*, designed by Mao Jin Gang). Her works after the Cultural Revolution include Brecht's *Leben des Galilei* (*Life of Galileo*, designed by XUE Dian Jie), Wang Zheng's *Chi Kai De Hua Duo* (*Late Bloom*), *Jie Shang Liu*

Xing Hong Qun Zi (*Red Skirts Are now Fashion*) by Ma Zhong Jun and Jia Hong Yuan, Wang Cheng Gang's *Ben Bao Xing Qi Si Di Si Ban* (*The Forth Page of Our Newspaper Last Thursday*), Brecht's *Der Kaukasische Kreidekreis* (*The Caucasian Chalk Circle*) and Dürrenmatt's *Ein Engel kommt nach Babylon* (*An Angel comes to Babylon*). Her most recent work is Brecht's *Die Dreigroschenoper* (*The Threepenny Opera*, 1998). Chen Rong has always been a passionate director. Believing in a 'people's theatre', she is interested in comparative studies between Chinese theatrical heritage and contemporary trends in theatre outside China.

Chen Xin Ying (also Chen Ping) (1938–) Director, China. Her major productions include *Othello* (1986), Zhao Qi Yang's *Hong Yan* (*Red Cliff*, 1989), *Bai Ju Yi Zai Chang An* (*Bai Ju Yi in Changan*, 1990) by Li Min Sheng and Yang Zhi Ping, Xu Fen's *Xin Hai Chao* (*1911 Revolution*, 1991), Su Lei's *Fu Qin De Che Zhan* (*My Father's Station*, 1992), Sun De Min's *Di Shi San Shi Da Lai La Ma* (*The Thirteenth Dalai Lama*, 1993), Qin Bei Chun's *Bai Ma Fei-Fei* (*White Horse Fei-Fei*, 1995) and *Shangyang* (1996, designed by HUANG Hai Wei). She favors grand stage presentation. Her productions often manifest ingenious use of space. She holds it as her principle to repeat neither herself nor others.

Chéreau, Patrice (1944–) Director and actor, France. While studying at the Sorbonne Chéreau staged his first production, Victor Hugo's *L'intervention* at Louis-le-Grand. He gained early recognition for a lively production of Labiche's *L'affaire de la rue de Lourcine* (*The Lourcine Street Affair*, 1966) and Rossini's *L'italiana in Algeri* (*The Italian Girl in Algiers*, 1969), his first opera staging. Working with Roger PLANCHON as artistic director of the Théâtre National Populaire in Villeurbanne, he directed a number of controversial high-profile production which quickly gained him an international profile. Equally at home with opera, classics and more modern pieces, Chéreau has often attracted controversy for the daring, visually audacious nature of his productions. He is perhaps best known for his work in opera, especially the notorious Marxist Bayreuth centennial production of *Der Ring des Nibelungen* (*The Ring Cycle*, 1976). As artistic director of the Théâtre des Amandiers at Nanterre, Chéreau championed a number of young actors and playwrights including Bernard-Marie Koltès, whose visceral uncompromising plays were brilliantly realized by Chéreau and his long-time designer Richard Peduzzi. Chéreau's performances include the role of the Dealer in two of his productions of Koltès' *Dans la solitude des champs de coton* (*In the Solitude of the Cotton Fields*, 1987 and 1995). His five films as director include *Hôtel de France* (1987) and *La Reine Margot* (1994).

Chifunyise, Stephen J. (1948–) Dramatist, Zimbabwe. Stephen Chifunyise is a product of the Chikwakwa Theatre, an open air theatre established by the University of Zambia in 1971 as a means of taking theatre to the people in the manner of the University of Ibadan Travelling Theatre in Nigeria (1961) and the Makerere Travelling Theatre in Uganda (1964). Chikwakwa is in principle a commitment to making theatre out of traditional and folk forms of the country. All these are clearly reflected in Chifunyise's theatre practice, especially in his theatre-for-development/community-based theatre projects, in which he has collaborated with Ngugi WA MIRII and Kimani Gecau, the two Kenyans who were part of the Kamiriithu community projects with Ngugi WA THIONG'O. Most of Chifunyise's plays are very short dance-dramas. Some of these have now been published in a collection, *Medicine for Love* (1984). His other plays are *The District Governor Visits a Village* (1973), which toured the Northern

Province in Zambia with Chikwakwa Theatre, *Mabusisi and Blood* (1975) and *I Resign* (1975).

Chilton, Nola (1926–) Director, Israel. Born in New York and trained by Lee Strasberg, Chilton played in several productions on Broadway and off-Broadway before joining theatre laboratory work in New York and San Fransisco. In 1963 Chilton emigrated to Israel where she has become a leading director, with plays like Beckett's *Endgame* and O'Neill's *The Iceman Cometh*. She is mostly renowned for her collective forms of documentary theatre dealing with controversial subjects, like the Arab–Israeli conflict, the situation of battered women, old people, immigrants and prisoners. These productions serve as a landmark for the development of the distinct Israeli version of documentary theatre, most prominently in SOBOL, whose early plays Chilton directed. She teaches at the Theatre Department at Tel Aviv University.

Chislett, Anne (1942–) Dramatist, Canada. Chislett studied theatre at the University of British Columbia. Until 1980 she taught theatre at high schools in Ontario. Together with her husband, James Roy, she founded the Blyth Festival, where all her plays have been performed. Many of Chislett's plays deal with the conflict between tradition and innovation in the farm communities of southern Ontario. Plays include *The Tomorrow Box* (1980), *Quiet in the Land* (1981, set in an Amish community during the First World War), *Another Season's Promise* (1986), *Yankee Notions* (1990) and *Glengarry School Days* (1994). *Quiet in the Land* won the Governor General's Award for English drama.

Chitty, Alison (1948–) Designer, Great Britain. Chitty was an assistant designer (1971–4) and head of design (1974–7) at the Victoria Theatre, Stoke-on-Trent. Since then she has worked freelance all over the UK, and is especially associated with productions directed by Peter GILL, such as *Measure for Measure* and *Julius Caesar* (Riverside Studios, 1979), and at the National Theatre, Turgenev's *Mesjac v derevne* (*A Month in the County*), Molière's *Dom Juan* and *Much Ado About Nothing* (all 1981), and most recently Gill's *Cardiff East* (1997).

Choi Hyung-In (1949–) Actor and director, Korea. Choi trained at Saint Joseph's University, Philadelphia (BA in French), the American University, Washington (BA in Performing Arts), and New York University (MFA in Acting). Soon after returning to Korea, she gained fame as a teacher of acting who could extract the full potential from actors. As an actor herself, Choi performed the leading roles in *Nicht Fisch, Nicht Fleisch* (*Neither Fish Nor Meat*, 1988, by Franz Xaver KROETZ, directed by KIM Kwang-Lim), *The Constant Wife* (by Somerset Maugham) and *Miss Readon Drinks a Little* (by Zindel). As a director, she founded the Hanyang Repertory Company and directed Brecht's *Der Gute Mensch von Sezuan* (*The Good Person of Sezuan*, 1988), *A Midsummer Night's Dream*, Ibsen's *Gengangere* (*Ghosts*), OH Tae-Seok's *Choon-Poong's Wife* and Kim Ji-Won's *Gooreongi Sinranggwa Gueui Sinboo* (*The Serpent Bridegroom and His Wife*, 1996).

Choi In-Hoon (1936–) Novelist and dramatist, Korea. Choi's career as a dramatist began in 1970 with his first play, *Eodiseo Mooeosi Doieo Dasi Mannarya* (*When, Where to meet Again as What*, with PARK Jung-Ja in the cast). Choi published a series of plays which dramatise Korean legends and tales using the shape of poetic drama, not only in the lines of the characters but also in the stage directions. His imaginative scripts, *Yennal Yetjeoge Hwei Hwei* (*Shoo Shoo Once upon a Time*, 1976), *Bomi Omyeon Sane Dule* (*When Spring Comes to Hill and Dales*, 1977), *Doong Doong Nakrang Dong*

(*Dom Dom the Drumrall of Nangrang*, 1978), *Dala Dala Balgun Dala* (*Moon Moon Bright Full Moon*, 1978) and *Hanswa Gretel* (*Hans and Gretel* 1981), have proved to be a challenging source of motivation for Korean directors. In 1996, all of his plays were performed at the specially organized Choi In-Hoon Theatre Festival in Seoul using various directors.

Chowdhry, Neelam Mansingh (1950–) Director, India. Chowdhry trained at the National School of Drama, New Delhi, and has worked with B.V. KARANTH in Bhopal, has produced plays at the Prithvi Theatre Bombay and is now settled in Chandigarh with her group called The Company. At the London International Festival of Theatre, she has presented her productions of Lorca's *Yerma* and Girish KARNAD's *Naga-Mandala*. Consciously using Indian body language and the folk theatre forms, hers is not the theatre of realism: she believes in the exoticism of Indian theatre. Her production of Jean Giraudoux's *La folle de Chaillot* (*The Madwoman of Chaillot*) was a notable success in Bombay, and her group performed at the Festival d' Avignon in 1996. She is one of the few Indian women directors and believes that 'to be in theatre, male and female principles have to go together'.

Chowdhury, Qamruzzaman Runu (1952–) Designer and director, Bangladesh. Qamruzzaman Runu Chowdhury trained in theatre at the National School of Drama in New Delhi from 1978–81. Important among his design credits are Syed HUQ's *Juddha Ebang Juddha*, directed by Tariq KHAN (1986), and translations of Anouilh's *Antigone* (1992), Taufique Al-Hakim's *Sultan's Dilemma* (directed by Kamaluddin NILU, 1991) Brecht's *Mann ist Mann* (*A Man's a Man*, directed by Fritz Bennewitz, 1993) and Wole SOYINKA's *The Lion and the Jewel* (directed by himself, 1994). Equally adept in formalism and realism, Chowdhury has earned a reputation as a designer who can skillfully handle complex demands of a text to meet its functional requirements. He has also directed a number of adaptations of indigenous performance texts, the most popular of which was *Mahua*. Chowdhury is a well-reputed art director of the movies.

Christodoulides, Andreas (1951–) Director, Cyprus. Christodoulides trained at the Academy of Live and Recorded Arts, London, and took a postgraduate course in theatre studies at University College Cardiff, Wales. He also trained at the theatres in Linköping and Norköping, Sweden. Major productions include Wilde's *Salome*, Williams's *The Glass Menagerie* and *A Streetcar Named Desire*, Strindberg's *Fadren* (*The Father*), Christopher HAMPTON's *Les Liaisons Dangereuses*, Tony Kushner's *Angels in America*, David Henry HWANG's *M. Butterfly* and Rina Katselli's *Trelli Yiayia* (*Crazy Granny*). He is a resident director of Theatro Ena. His directorial approach is rather realistic, and he pays special attention to effective lighting as well as detailed props.

Chung King-fai (1937–) Director and actor, China (Hong Kong SAR). Chung worked extensively in Hong Kong's television and stage industries after receiving his MFA degree at Yale University in 1965. Chung was the first person to promote the theatre of the absurd and the Broadway musical in Cantonese. His collaboration with local theatre practitioners led to the establishment of the Hong Kong Repertory Theatre in 1977. Since the 1970s he has directed many successful productions, including *Becket* by Jean Anouilh (1990), David Henry HWANG's *M. Butterfly* (1992, revived in 1993) and Michael Cristofer's *The Shadow Box* (1996). More recently he directed the Cantonese drama *Sentimental Journey* (1999, by Raymond TO) for the Springtime Stage Productions. Acting

credits include Shaw's *Pygmalion* (1997) and Ronald Harwood's *The Dresser* (1998, Hong Kong Arts Festival). Chung won the Hong Kong Drama Awards for best director in 1996 and 1997, and is currently the Dean of Drama at the Hong Kong Academy for Performing Arts.

Chung Kyung-Soon (1963–) Actor, Korea. Chung graduated from Seongshin Women's University and trained at the London Theatre School and London Academy of Music and Dramatic Art. She started her professional career in 1991 as a European specialist for the Korean stage. She performed Lady Macbeth in *Macbeth* (1991), Catharina in *Taming of the Shrew* (1991), Irena in Chekhov's *Tri sestry* (*Three Sisters*, 1992), General in *King Lear* (1993, adapted by OH Oun-Hee), Eva in Brecht's *Herr Puntila und sein Knecht Matti* (*Mr Puntila and his Servant Matti*, 1993, with YOON Ju-Sang in the cast) and Grucheka in an adaptation of Dostoyevsky's *Brat'ia Karamazovy* (*The Karamazov Brothers*, 1996). In addition, she performed as Hi-Ju in the Korean original LEE Man-Hee's *Dolaseoseo Deonara* (*Don't Look Back When You Leave*, 1996, with HAN Myeong-Gu in the cast). Chung has the ability to respond to both the director's instructions and the writer's intentions naturally and expressively. She has received substantial praise for her performance in both the theatre and films since the mid-1990s.

Churchill, Caryl (1938–) Dramatist, Great Britain. One of Churchill's first plays to be performed was *Owners*, in 1972. *Cloud Nine* was a popular and critical success, as was *Top Girls* (1982), about successful women throughout history. *Fen* (1983) focuses on the plight of rural workers. *Serious Money* (1987) is about life on the stock exchange. *The Skriker*, presented at the Royal National Theatre in 1994, puzzled critics because of the fairytale motifs and particularly intricate poetic language.

Ciulli, Roberto (1934–) Director, Germany. Born in Italy, Ciulli worked as an assistant director and then director with the Deutsches Theater in Göttingen (1965–72). From 1972–9 he was director at Schauspielhaus Köln, and from 1979–80 at the Düsseldorfer Schauspielhaus. Since 1980 he has been artistic director of Theater an der Ruhr in Mülheim, where he has become known for his unpredictably innovative approach, which tends to be controversial. In his 1991 production of Chekhov's *Tri sestry* (*Three Sisters*), for example, Act IV is cut. 'Instead, the aged three sisters remember their past. Reality was thus not brought close to the spectator, but sealed off in art.' More recently he directed *Bericht für eine Akademie* (*Report to an Academy*, 1997) after Kafka in Mülheim, and Lorca's *Dona Rosita la soltera* (*Donna Rosita Remains Single*, 1998) in Munich.

Cixous, Hélène (1937–) Writer, France. Born in Oran, Algeria, Cixous's mother's family was of Ashkenazic Germanic and Austro-Czechoslovakian descent while her father's family was of Sephardic Spanish origin. She arrived in France in 1955. First known in the 1960s as a university scholar, over the years she has increasingly written for the theatre, although she has not abandoned poetic fiction. Certain theatrical texts incarnate important contemporary women figures such as her feminist rereading of Freud's well-known case study, in *Portrait of Dora* (1976); the staging of the story of Phoolan Devi, the rebellious Indian outlaw who has since become an important political leader, *The Conquest of the School at Madhubaï* (1984); and that of the Russian poetess and victim of Stalinist repression Anna Akhmatova, in *Black Sail White Sail* (1994). However, her theatrical work took truly epic and legendary dimensions when she began to write for Ariane MNOUCHKINE's renowned Théâtre du Soleil, creating three major historical plays set in the twentieth century: *The Terrible but Unfinished Story of Norodom Sihanouk, King of Cambodia* (1985), *The Indiad or the India of their Dreams* (1987) and *La Ville parjure ou le réveil des Erinyes* (*The Perjury City, or the Awakening of the Furies*, 1994). She has also worked with Daniel MESGUICH, with *On ne part pas, on ne revient pas* (1991) and *L'Histoire qu'on ne connaître jamais* (1994). She won the prize of the Syndicat de la Critique Dramatique in 1994 for the best theatrical work of the year.

Clark-Bekederemo, John Pepper (1935–) Dramatist, Nigeria. A contemporary of Wole SOYINKA and Ola ROTIMI, Clark has published numerous plays which have also been performed both in Nigeria and abroad. His earliest plays appeared in a collection which includes *Song of a Goat*, *Masquerade* and *The Raft*. These were followed by major theatrical pieces such as *Ozidi* (*The Ozidi Saga*), a documentation of the traditional theatre of his Ijo culture. His most recent plays are *The Wives' Revolt* and *The Bikoroa Plays* (consisting of *The Boat*, *The Return* and *Full Circle*). Clark's writing has moved from the strong influences of classical Greek drama (in *Song of a Goat*) to the prosaic but still powerfully moving dialogue of the Bikoroa trilogy. His charcters have also moved from the almost mythical and tragic powerlessness of Ebiere, Zifa and Tufa to the ordinary assertiveness of the key characters in the trilogy.

Claus, Hugo (1929–) Dramatist, poet, novelist, painter, cineast and director, Belgium. Claus is a self-educated man. He is the *éminence grise* of Flemish literature and has written a voluminous oeuvre of novels, poetry and plays, for which he has received numerous literary prizes. His work has also been received well abroad, and has been translated into several languages. He is considered to be Flanders's most important dramatist. After a few one-act plays, Claus came out with his first full-length play, *Een bruid in de morgen* (*A Bride in the Morning*), in 1953. Since then he produced around forty 'original' plays and just as many adaptations and translations. Because of its tremendous diversity, his oeuvre cannot possibly be categorized. Some of his best known works are *Suiker* (*Sugar*, 1958), *Vrijdag* (*Friday*, 1969), *Thyestes* (After Seneca, 1966), *Thuis* (*Home*, 1975), *Het Haar van de hond* (*The Dog's Hair*, 1982), *Het schommelpaard* (*The Rocking Horse*, 1988) and *Onder de torens* (*Under the Towers*, 1993). In his plays, Claus not only composes the dialogue but also designs the set, music and so on. As a director, Claus has worked in Flanders and The Netherlands, mostly staging his own plays.

Clees, Michèle (1954–) Actor, Luxembourg. After her training at the Schauspielakademie Zürich, Clees worked as a resident actor in several theatres, the Théâtre Populaire Romand (1982, Switzerland), the Staatstheater Saarbrücken (1984–90), and in Luxembourg at the Théâtre des Capucins and the Théâtre du Centaure, with internationally recognized theatre artists such as Andrea BRETH, Wolfgang ENGEL, Pavel Mikulastik and Holk Freytag. Clees is a trained breathing therapist and her in-depth research on the subject, which she teaches at the Conservatoire de Luxembourg and at the Hochschule für Musik und Theater in Saarbrücken, was published. In 1997, she played one of the leading roles in the acclaimed production of Werner Schwab's *Die Präsidentinnen* (*The Presidents*, Théâtre du Centaure, directed by Jean FLAMMANG). She has also appeared in a number of films in Luxembourg and the USA.

Clever, Edith (1940–) Actor and director, Germany. Clever trained at the Otto-Falckenberg-Schule in Munich. After seasons in Kassel she joined the theatre in Bremen, where she first worked with

Peter STEIN; later she went with Stein to the Schaubühne in Berlin, becoming one of the most prominent actors of that company. Mainly seen in tragedy, she is the contemporary German actor with the most comprehensive range of expression through voice and gestures. Apart from Stein, she has worked with Claus PEYMANN, Klaus Michael GRÜBER, Peter ZADEK and Wilfried MINKS. Major roles include Luise in Schiller's *Kabale und Liebe* (*Intrigue and Love*), Isabella in *Measure for Measure*, Gertrude in *Hamlet* and more recently Cleopatra in *Anthony and Cleopatra* (Salzburg Festival. 1994). In 1992 she added directing to her credits, including Euripides's *Medeia* (1996, in which she also played the title role), Botho STRAUSS's *Jeffers-Akt I und II* (1998, with Bruno GANZ in the cast) and Hofmannsthal's *Elektra* (1999, in which she also played the title role).

Close, Glenn (1947–) Actor, USA. Widely known for her prestigious film career, including commercial successes such as *Fatal Attraction* and *Les Liaisons Dangereuses*, Close has an equally impressive record as a stage actor. She obtained a BA in theatre from the College of William and Mary (1974) and made her stage debut as Angelica in Congreve's *Love for Love* (1974). Further parts have included Annie in STOPPARD's *The Real Thing* (1984), Jane in FRAYN's *Benefactors* (1985–6) and Paulina in Dorfman's *Death and the Maiden* (1992). In 1993–4 she played Norma Desmond in Lloyd-Webber's musical *Sunset Boulevard*. Her great skill is to bring to life women who are possessed of great passion and intelligence.

Concepción, Ernesto (1943–) Actor and producer, Puerto Rico. Ernesto Concepción founded the company Bohio Puertotrriqueño. As one of Puerto Rico's most beloved comic actors, Concepción has worked with nearly everyone in the Puerto Rican theatre, television and film, including Elsie Moreau (his wife), José Luis MARRERO, Miguel Ángel SUÁREZ, Victoria ESPINOSA and Dean ZAYAS. Concepción has won the highly esteemed Critics Circle Award for acting on several occasions, and he is noted for his energetic physical comedy as well as for his dramatic ability. Concepción has also enjoyed a coincidental partnership with Marcos BETANCOURT in works by Ghelderode, Pedro Mario Herrero and the Puerto Rican dramatist Luis Torres Nadal. Other notable roles include Berenger in Ionesco's *Rhinocéros* (1974) and *Exit the King* (1976); Cook in Brecht's *Mutter Courage und ihre Kinder* (*Mother Courage and her Children*, 1978); Captain Horster in Ibsen's *En folkefiende* (*An Enemy of the People*, 1978), and Don Pepón in Francisco Arriví's *Club de Solteros* (*Lonely Hearts' Club*, 1986).

Condé, Maryse (1937–) Author, France and Guadeloupe. Although better known as a best-selling novelist, Condé has taken an active interest in theatre. Her earlier work has a more political and existential resonance, dealing in *Le Morne de Massabielle* (*The Hill of Massabielle*, 1970) with the search for personal and national identity of a young man of mixed race. *Mort d'Oluwémi d'Ajumako* (*The Death of Oluwémi d'Ajumako*, 1973), based on a real incident in Nigeria, shows a chief regaining his sense of honour after trying to cheat tradition. All Condé's plays give an important place to the search for a loving tenderness which is not tainted with exploitation, especially *Pension les Alizés* (*The Tropical Breeze Hotel*, 1988), a two-hander composed for Sonia Emmanuel, showing the fragile illusions of an ageing Guadeloupean 'exotic' dancer and the Haitian doctor she takes into her home. Emmanuel directed Condé's ambitious open-air work to commemorate the Bicentenary, *An Tan Revolisyon* (*Revolution Time*, 1989), reminiscent of MNOUCHKINE's *1789* in giving a voice to the people in the march of history. *Comédie d'Amour* (*The Comedy of Love*, 1993) is a family drama, featuring two sisters.

Conklin, John (1937–) Designer and director, USA. Conklin began his prolific career in the late 1950s. Designing initially for regional and repertory theatres such as Hartford Stage Company, he added directing opera in the 1980s, gaining international acclaim. He has worked extensively with Robert WILSON, Mark LAMOS, Jonathan MILLER and Robert FALLS. 'In designing a work, Conklin seeks the aspects that resonate most completely with the present. His style ranges from his heavily detailed naturalism of [Chekhov's] *Tri sestry* (*Three Sisters*, 1984) to his minimalistic and highly eclectic style for Sam SHEPARD's *The Tooth of Crime* (1986). Conklin emphasises that a scenic design must move an audience emotionally, and he attempts to illuminate the psychological and social state of a play as well.'

Conte, Tonino (1935–) Director and dramatist, Italy. Tonino Conte started working in the theatre with Aldo Trionfo and Carmelo BENE. He began directing in 1968 with a production of Alfred Jarry's *Ubu Roi* (*King Ubu*), which marked the beginning of his collaboration with scenographer Emanuele LUZZATI. He then worked at the Piccolo Teatro and the Teatri Stabili of Turin, and in Trieste and Genoa. In 1975 he founded, together with Luzzati, the Teatro della Tosse. Conte, who has directed over 150 productions, has specialized in the area of musical theatre and since 1981 has produced a number of large-scale site-specific performances. Among his most successful productions are *Recitarcantando* (*Acting-singing*, 1978), *Molo magico* (*Magic Pier*, 1988) and *Storie di santi, di diavoli, di vergini e di arcangeli* (*Stories of Saints, Devils, Virgins and Archangels*, 1995).

Cortez, Raul (1931–) Actor, Brazil. Cortez trained at the Facultade de Direito at the University of Campinas. He worked with Teatro Paulista do Estudante, Teatro de Arena, Teatro Brasileiro de Comedia, and Teatro Oficina. His theatre credits include numerous parts in Brazilian plays, as well as Salieri in Peter SHAFFER's *Amadeus*, the Bishop in Genet's *Le balcon* (*The Balcony*) and George in ALBEE's *Who's Afraid of Virginia Woolf?*, serving for three periods of office as President of *Associação Paulista de Empresarios Teatrais do Estado de São Paulo*. Cortez has, throughout his career, closely and critically followed the political events in Brazil.

Courbois, Kitty (1937–) Actor, The Netherlands. Kitty Courbois started in cabaret shows and then went to drama school. After graduating in 1960, she was immediately taken on by the leading company, De Nederlandse Comedie, where she stayed for eleven years. Courbois was one of the few actors to survive the 'tomato-revolt', in which a new generation of theatre-makers literally pelted their predecessors off the stage. She made a fresh start with the Baal company, performing remarkably in *Leedvermaak* (*The Wedding Party*) by Judith HERZBERG, Sartre's *Nekrassov* and Brecht's *Mutter Courage und ihre Kinder* (*Mother Courage and her Children*). Courbois's husky, sensual but tough qualities also came out well in film. In 1987 she moved to Toneelgroep Amsterdam, where she starred as Medea and played a wonderful Duchess of York in *Richard III* (next to Pierre BOKMA).

Cox, Brian (1946–) Actor, Great Britain. Cox trained for the stage at the London Academy of Music and Dramatic Art. In 1966, he played Orlando in *As You Like It* at Birmingham Repertory and London. In Birmingham he also played the title role in Ibsen's *Peer Gynt* (1967). Cox appers vocally and physically craggy, which provides an even stronger contrast when his controversial charcters crumble and reveal their vulnerability. Major roles include Lövborg in Ibsen's *Hedda Gabler* (Royal Court, 1972), Brutus (*Julius Caesar*, National Theatre, 1977), a memorable Petruccio in Jonathan MILLER's production of *The Taming of The Shrew* (Old Vic, 1987, with Fiona SHAW as Katherine), King Lear (National Theatre, 1990) and, more recently, a theatre critic in Conor MCPHERSON's *St Nicholas* (Bush Theatre, 1997).

Cracknell, Ruth (1925–) Actor, Australia. Cracknell trained at the Independent Drama School, Sydney. Since her stage debut in 1947, Cracknell has had a very varied and immensely successful career. In the late 1950s and 1960s Cracknell was best known for her appearances in the Phillip Street Revues, Sydney. Later career highlights include roles as diverse as Mrs Rafi in Edward BOND's *The Sea*, and Jocasta for Tyrone Guthrie in Sophocles's *Oidipus tyrannos* (*King Oedipus*) at the Old Tote (1970). In 1977 Cracknell appeared in a solo show *Just Ruth*, and in 1991 she played Winnie in Beckett's *Happy Days*. Cracknell has played many strong women roles but prefers high comedy, and her comic timing is legendary. Cracknell is now best-known for an ABC television comedy series, *Mother and Son*, in which she plays an elderly and idiosyncratic mother. Cracknell's career continues to flourish as a performer; in 1991 she appeared in Wilde's *The Importance of Being Earnest*, in 1996 she featured in the film *Lilian's Story* and in 1997 she appeared in a smash hit production of *A Little Night Music*. After many years on the board of the Sydney Theatre Company (1979–95), Cracknell is now the company's first Patron and was specially honoured at a command performance marking the twentieth anniversary of the Sydney Opera House.

Crippa, Maddalena (1957–) Actor, Italy. After a period of training with small amateur theatre companies, Maddalena Crippa made her theatrical debut in Carlo Goldoni's *Il Campiello* (*The Campiello*, 1975), directed by Giorgio Strehler. Among her most notable performances are Goldoni's *I Due Gemelli Veneziani* (*The Venetian Twins*, 1978, directed by Luigi SQUARZINA), Arthur Schnitzler's *Liebelei* (*The Game of Love*, 1985, directed by Luca RONCONI), Natalia Ginsburg's *Ti ho sposato per allegria* (*I Married You Just for Cheerfulness*, 1987, directed by Antonio CALENDA), Gabriele D'Annunzio's *Fedra* (1988, directed by Massimo CASTRI), *Titus Andronicus* (1990) and Anton Chekhov's *Djadja Vanja* (*Uncle Vanya*, 1996), both directed by Peter STEIN. Crippa, who is one of Italy's most versatile and talented actors, has also made a number of television and film appearances, such as Francesco Rosi's *Tre fratelli* (*Three Brothers*, 1980) and Sergio Sollima's *Berlino 39* (1992). In both her theatre and in her film and television work, Crippa has time and again demonstrated her capacity to deal with classical as well as contemporary texts in an innovative and an original way.

Crowley, Bob (1952–) Designer, Ireland. Crowley studied at the Crawford Municipal School of Art, Cork, and the Bristol Old Vic Theatre School. Currently one of the leading designers working in Britain, Crowley is known for the clarity and deceptive simplicity of his work. He has worked extensively for the Royal Shakespeare Company, where his productions include HAMPTON's *Les Liaisons Dangereuses*, *A Midsummer Night's Dream* and *Hamlet* (1992). Design for the Royal National Theatre, London, includes *Macbeth* (1992), Victor Hugo's *The Prince's Play* (1996) and Shawn Wallace's *The Designated Mourner* (1996). Crowley has also designed for the English National Opera, the Royal Exchange, Manchester, the Gate Theatre, Dublin, and the Châtelet, Paris, among others. For Field Day Theatre Company, Derry, Crowley designed Terry Eagleton's *Saint Oscar* (1989) and developed this association by designing and co-directing (with Stephen REA) *The Cure at Troy* by Seamus Heaney (1990). His film credits include costume design for Arthur MILLER's *The Crucible*. His recent work includes design for the Cottesloe Theatre production of Martin McDonagh's *Cripple of Inishmann* (1997), and the Field Dat/Tinderbox production of Stewart Parker's *Northern Star*, directed by Stephen Rea (1998). Crowley is an Associate Artist of the Royal Shakespeare Company and the Royal National Theatre.

Crowley, John (1969–) Director, Ireland. A graduate of University College Cork, Crowley directed *John Hughdy – Tom John* by Vincent Woods for Druid Theatre, Galway (1991), *One For The Road* by Harold PINTER for the Gate Theatre, Dublin (1994), and devised *True Lines* for Bickerstaffe Theatre Company, for the 1994 Dublin Theatre Festival. *True Lines* and its sequel *Double Helix* established Crowley's reputation as a challenging director, who could work in collaboration with actors to devise work based on a series of motifs, but also handle a given text with assurance and creativity. Further productions include MILLER's *The Crucible* (1995) and Thomas KILROY's version of *Six Characters in Search of an Author* (1996) for the Abbey Theatre, Dublin, and Derek Mahon's interpretation of Racine's *Phèdre* for the Gate Theatre, Dublin, also in 1996. Recent work includes Peter Oswald's *Fair Ladies at a Game of Poem Cards* for the Royal National Theatre, London (1997), Genet's *Les bonnes* (*The Maids*) at the Donmar Warehouse, London (1997), and *Shadows*, a presentation of work by Synge and Yeats for the RSC (1998).

Curino, Laura (1956–) Actor and dramatist, Italy. Laura Curino founded with

Gabriele VACIS, Mariella Fabbris, Roberto Tarasco and others the Cooperativa Teatro Settimo (1979). She has taken part in some of Teatro Settimo's most memorable performances, such as *Esercizi sulla tavola di Mendeleev* (*Exercises on the Mendeleyev Table*, 1984), *Elementi di struttura del sentimento* (*Structural Elements of Feeling*, 1985), *Stabat Mater* (1989) and *La storia di Romeo e Giulietta* (*The Story of Romeo and Juliet*, 1991), which she devised together with the company. Recently she has also devised a number of solo performances, displaying witty and provocative writing skills, most interestingly *Passione* (*Passion*, 1992) and *Olivetti* (1996), which launched her as one of Italy's leading actors and dramatists. Curino has a singularly powerful stage presence, characterized by eclecticism and adventurousness.

Curtis, Stephen (1957–) Designer, Australia. Curtis graduated from the National Institute of Dramatic Art in 1978. Early work for Nimrod, Sydney, and Light-house, Adelaide was followed by a long association with Neil ARMFIELD. Curtis's designs are always intelligent, provocative and often humorous; for example his designs for Etheridge's *The Country Wife* wittily mixed Restoration, 1950s Teddy Boy styles, baroque and punk; his seedy, decadent set for Jonson's *The Alchemist* (1996) mixed Jacobean with mock Tudor-bethan, house interior with exterior, and the set was boobytrapped with jokes such as the doorbell that appropriately played 'The Sting' among other tunes. Curtis also designed the first production of the phenomenally successful musical *The Venetian Twins* by Nick ENRIGHT at Nimrod, Sydney (1979); this was ideally suited to Curtis's design style, being a pastiche musical with a wide mixture of literary, musical and visual styles. Currently Curtis also teaches as Head of Design at the Australian Film, Television and Radio School.

D

Dadie, Bernard Binlin (1916–) Dramatist, Ivory Coast. Dadie was educated at Ecole William Ponty in Senegal, and it was here that he received his theatre apprenticeship. Dadie, often seen as the father and old man of Ivorian theatre, is a poet, novelist, dramatist and politician. His plays, both written and performed at Ponty, include *Les Villes* (*The Towns*, 1933) and *Assemein Dehyle* (1934), five sketches which he wrote for the Folklore Cultural Circle of the Ivory Coast, an organization of which he was a co-founder. However, it is for his later plays that Dadie is best known: *Beatrice du Congo* (*Beatrice of the Congo*, 1970), *Les Voix dans le Vent* (*The Voice in the Wind*, 1970), *Monsieur Thogo-Ghini* (1970), *Papassidi maitre escroc* (1975) and *Mhoi-Ceul* (1979). A central theme which runs through most of Dadie's plays is the preoccupation of his central characters with the pursuit and exercise of political power.

Daldry, Stephen (1947–) Director, Great Britain. One of Daldry's earlier productions was Robert Tressell's *The Ragged Trousered Philanthropists* at Theatre Royal in Stratford East, London, in 1988. In 1989 he directed Horvath's *Der Jüngste Tag* (*Judgment Day*) at the Old Red Lion. In 1990 he first directed at the Royal Court, and he later took over the Gate Theatre where he directed, among others, Marie Luise Fleissner's *Pioniere in Ingolstadt* (*Pioneers in Ingolstadt*) and *Fegefeuer in Ingolstadt* (*Purgatory in Ingolstadt*), and a season of plays from the Spanish Golden Age. His expressionistic production of Priestley's *An Inspector Calls* for the National Theatre was a major success, as was Sophie Treadwell's *Machinal*, also for the National Theatre, in 1994 with Fiona SHAW. From 1994–8 Daldry, who ranges among the most talented directors since Peter Brook, was artistic director of the Royal Court Theatre, where he began by directing a revival of Wesker's *The Kitchen*, and where most recently he directed David HARE's *Via Dolorosa* (1998).

Dalmat, Aurélie (1958–) Actor and director, France and Martinique. From childhood, Dalmat was fascinated by the stage, and she took part in one of the earliest theatre workshops organized by the municipality of Fort-de-France. In France she studied acting with Alain Knapp, and worked professionally at the Théâtre du Quartier d'lvry, the Théâtre Populaire des Cevennes and several summer festivals. Among her productions were *Madame de Sade* by Mishima Yukio, but she especially favoured one-woman shows, as she resisted the tendency to stereotyping for black actors. In 1986 she resettled in Martinique, putting on *Les Mains Négatives* (*Handprints*, 1987) by Marguérite

Duras with Annick JUSTIN-JOSEPH, and she has continued to work with the Centre Dramatique Régional on a wide variety of plays. This essentially classical tragic actor, with great stage presence even in repose (*Britannicus*, 1993; Orville's *Romance*, 1995; *Othello*, 1998), has equally directed and played in the broadest Creole comedies, such as Régina's marital farce *Bakannal o Tribinal* (*Trouble in the Divorce Court*, 1991) based on a Cervantes interlude, and tried her hand at street theatre.

Dambury, Gerty (1957–) Author, actor and director, France and Guadeloupe. With degree qualifications in languages (English and Arabic) from Paris-Vincennes, Dambury has worked in educational development and teaches English. After some training courses in drama, she directed and acted in most of her own plays including the role of Sylvia, a Barbadian woman in *Carfax* (1986), a love story reflecting her pan-Caribbean sympathies; *Bâton Maréchal* (*Marshal's Baton*, 1987), giving the women's view of the Vichy occupation of Guadeloupe; and a poetic personal odyssey, *Rabordaille* (Avignon, 1988). A residency at the Festival International des Francophonies in Limoges (1992) assisted publication of *Lettres indiennes*, set on a sugar plantation in La Réunion and produced at Avignon in 1996 and the Guadeloupe Artchipel. *Madjaka ou la fin du bal* (*The Party's Over*, 1996) deals with male bonding and AIDS. *Carêmes* (*Dry Seasons*, 1998) relives a lynching, seeking renewal for arid hearts. Combative in defence of cultural independence for Guadeloupe, Dambury is a lithe and vital performer on stage and screen, who has plenty of ideas for future productions.

Damidov, Alexander (1958–) Actor, Israel. Damidov trained as an engineer before studying theatre in Moscow, where he worked as an actor before emigrating to Israel in 1990. In Tel Aviv he joined Yevgeny ARYE in establishing the Gesher Theatre, where he has played leading parts in all of the company's productions. Among his more memorable roles are the Nazi officer in *Adam Ben Kelev* (*Adam, Son of a B*), Mishkin in a stage adaptation of Dostoyevsky's *Idiot* (*The Idiot*) and the young boy Yossi in the production of SOBOL's *Kfar* (*Village*). He has also played in several film roles and television series since his arrival in Israel and has become a very popular actor, representing the positive sides of the recent Russian immigration.

Danchenko, Serhii (1937–) Director, Ukraine. In 1965 Danchenko received his degree from Karpenko-Kary Institute for the Art of the Theatre, Kiev. From 1970–8 he was a chief director of Maria Zan'kovets'ka Ukrainian Drama Theatre, Lviv. Since 1978 he has been artistic director at the Ivan Franko Ukrainian Drama Theatre, Kiev. He has staged over fifty plays. After the years of Stalin's prohibitions and repressions, he staged Mykola Kulish's *Maklena Grasa* (1967). Danchenko developed a new interpretation of Ukrainian theatre and drama, integrating it into the context of European theatre. Inclined to an academic manner, he is fond of large-scale productions and prefers classical dramaturgy: in Ukrainian, *Kam'ianyi hospodar* (*The Stone Host*, by Lesia Ukrainka, L'viv, 1971 and Kiev, 1988), *Ukradene shchastia* (*A Stolen Happiness*, by Ivan Franko, L'viv, 1977 and Kiev, 1979) and *Eneida* (*Aeneid*, by Ivan Kotliarevs'ky, 1986); in Russian, Chekhov's *Djadja Vanja* (*Uncle Vanya*, 1985) and *Visnevyi sad* (*The Cherry Orchard*, Maxim Gorky Art Theatre, Moskow, 1988); and from Europe, *Richard III* (1974), Dürrenmatt's *Der Besuch der Alten Dame* (*The Visit*, Kiev, 1983 and Krakow, Poland, 1989) and Ibsen's *Rosmersholm*, 1994). Danchenko's productions are independent and original without becoming offensive or defiant.

Dar, Ruth (1941–) Designer, Israel. Dar trained at Sadler's Wells in London. She has designed both scenography and costumes for numerous productions of major classics like Chekhov's *Visnevyi sad* (*The Cherry Orchard*) and *The Merchant of Venice*, and has become a close collaborator with Hanoch LEVIN, designing several of his productions. Her work usually stresses the textures of the materials, in costumes as well as in the set, creating different forms of correspondence between them rather than trying to establish a sense of a given location. This stylistic characteristic has made her a very sought-after designer for several directors. She designs up to five productions for the Israeli theatre every year.

Darvas, Iván (1925–) Actor and director, Hungary. Darvas trained at the Academy of Theatre and Film Art. In 1946 he became a member of the Mûvész Theatre, and between 1949 and 1956 was a member of Madách Theatre, both based in Budapest. Because of his involvement in the revolution in 1956, he spent two years in prison and was removed from the stage. In 1963 he worked for one season in the country (Miskolc), and later for another season at the József Attila Theatre in Budapest. Between 1965 and 1989 he was a member of the Vígszínház. Since 1990 he has worked freelance, apart from a season with the Mûvész Theatre. He also served as a Member of Parliament. Major roles include Orpheus (Anouilh, *Eurydike*), Romeo (*Romeo and Juliet*), Ruy Blas (Hugo, *Ruy Blas*), von Berg (MILLER, *Incident at Vichy*), Beutler-Newton (Dürrenmatt, *Die Physiker* (*The Physicists*)), Astrov (Chekhov, *Djadja Vanja* (*Uncle Vanya*)), Firs (Chekhov, *Visnevyi sad* (*The Cherry Orchard*)), Tuzenbach, Vershinin (Checkhov, *Tri sestry* (*Three Sisters*)), Trigorin (Chekhov, *Cajka* (*The Seagull*)), Martin Dysart (SHAFFER, *Equus*), Stomil (MROZEK, *Tango*) and Tobias (ALBEE, *Delicate Balance*). Darvas has also acted in films, and has directed

for the theatre. As an actor, he has been described as a charmeur, an elegant, intellectual actor with delicate irony.

Darwaza, Sawsan (1962–) Director and dramatist, Jordan. Darwaza is currently executive director and partner of Mir'at Media Production Company and president of the Jordanian centre of the International Theatre Institute. She has directed Beckett's *Waiting for Godot* (with Nasser OMAR as Vladimir), SHAFFER's *Five Finger Exercise* and several plays by Jordanian authors, including *The Lights of Jericho* by Haya HUSSEINI. Darwaza, who has also adapted and co-written plays, is the only female theatre director in Jordan who has established a certain continuity and uniqueness in her theatre projects. Her works are a combination of Arabic cultural stylistic plays within a modern (more or less) western vision. This shows best in her adaptation of *Waiting for Godot*: she transferred the play into an Arabic atmosphere, but kept the absurd spirit and philosophical connotations of Beckett.

Davies, Howard (1945–) Director, Great Britain. Davies began his career in the theatre in 1968 as assistant stage manager at the Birmingham Repertory Company. From 1972–4 he was associate director at Bristol Old Vic. Since 1976 he has been associated with the Royal Shakespeare Company, where he directed Edward BOND's *Bingo* (1976), *Piaf* by Pam GEMS (1978, with Jane LAPOTAIRE) and Christopher HAMPTON's adaptation of *Les Liaisons Dangereuses* (1985, with Alan RICKMAN and Juliet STEVENSON). Since 1988 Davies has also been associated with the National Theatre, where his productions include Ibsen's *Hedda Gabler* with Juliet Stevenson (1989), David HARE's *The Secret Rapture* (1989), Arthur MILLER's *The Crucible* (1990) and Schiller's *Maria Stuart* (1996). More recent work includes a revival of ALBEE's *Who's Afraid of Virginia Woolf?* at the Almeida with

Diana RIGG, Richard Nelson's *The General from America* (1997) and *Wassa* after Gorky (1999), both at the Royal National Theatre. Throughout his career, Davies has placed much emphasis on structural and conceptual clarity, allowing his actors to go beyond intellectual understanding in developing deeply felt emotions.

Davis, Jack (1917–) Dramatist, actor and poet, Australia. Davis's plays focus on the experiences of the Aboriginal peoples of Western Australia and so inevitably deal with oppression and tragedy, but they also offer humour and a strong sense of survival against the odds. Davis wrote his first play at sixty-one, *Kullark*, which focused on the violent displacement of Aboriginals and offered an alternative statement to the 1979 sesquicentenary of Western Australia celebrations. Davis's plays *The Dreamers* (1982), *No Sugar* (1985, World Theatre Festival and 1986, Vancouver) and *Barungin* (1988) were performed as *The First-Born* trilogy in 1988, the Australian Bicentennial year, with several of Davis's family taking part. The production, in the imposing Fitzroy Town Hall, Melbourne, was semi-promenade; the audience had to get up and follow the Wallitch family when they were moved from their homes to the reserve. At the end of *Barungin*, there is a roll call of names of Aboriginals who have died in police custody. That the actors then made peace signs to the audience is symptomatic of how Davis's plays tell stories that need to be told but also seek to move beyond violence.

De Berardinis, Leo (1940–) Director and actor, Italy. After training at the Piccolo Teatro in Milan, Leo de Berardinis made his acting debut in 1962 in Samuel Beckett's *Endgame* directed by Carlo QUARTUCCI. In 1965 he founded, together with Perla Peragallo, his own theatre company for whom he directed and acted in the memorable devised pieces *La faticosa messinscena dell'Amleto di Shakespeare*

(The Tiresome Production of Shakespeare's Hamlet, 1967) and *Sir and Lady Macbeth* (1968). De Berardinis and Peragallo then founded the Teatro di Marigliano (1970) and produced *King lacreme Lear napulitane* (1973) and *Sudd* (1974). After 1981 De Berardinis discontinued his collaboration with Peragallo and worked with Carmelo BENE, on Miguel Cervantes's *Don Chisciotte* (1968), with the Cooperativa Nuova Scena (1983–7) and with his own company Teatro di Leo (from 1987), which also functions as a research centre. De Berardinis, who since 1994 has also been the artistic director of the Festival Santarcangelo di Romagna, is a versatile actor with an impressive stage presence. His ongoing research into performance skills and his capacity to investigate classical roles in the light of alternative theatre practices have made him one of the most challenging, original and entertaining artists of the Italian theatre scene.

Deboo, Astad (1947–) Performer, India. Astad Aderbad Deboo received training in Kathak under Guru Prahlad Das in Calcutta and in Kathakali under Guru E.K. Pannicker. At the London School of Contemporary Dance he learnt Martha Graham's modern dance technique; in New York, he was influenced by Jose Limon and attended workshops at the Pilobolus Dance Company. Deboo has created a dance–theatre style which assimilates Indian and Western techniques. He has experimented with a variety of forms, themes, concepts and performance spaces. His dance–theatre represents an important segment of Indian theatre, with his direction of *Shakuntala* as a classic example of the East–West fusion.

De Capitani, Elio (1954–) Director, dramatist and actor, Italy. After training as an administrator and actor, Elio de Capitani started working at the Teatro dell'Elfo in 1973, mostly in collaboration with Gabriele Salvatores. The Italian premiere of Nigel Williams's *Class Enemy* (1982) marked de Capitani's directorial debut at the Teatro dell'Elfo. Since then de Capitani has introduced a number of contemporary European authors to the Italian theatre scene, focusing his practice on the exploration of dramaturgically controversial texts and the encouragement of social and political awareness. Among de Capitani's most interesting productions with the Teatro dell'Elfo are Botho STRAUSS's *Trilogie des Wiedersehens* (*Three Acts of Recognition*, 1984), Athol Fugard's *The Island* (1984), which he directed with Ferdinando Bruni, Rainer Werner Fassbinder's *Die Bitteren Tränen der Petra von Kant* (*The Bitter Tears of Petra von Kant*, 1988), and Copi's *Tango barbaro* (*Barbaric Tango*, 1997).

Decleir, Jan (1946–) Actor, Belgium. Decleir trained at the Royal Academy of Fine Arts and the Studio Herman Teirlinck in Antwerp, then founded the socially engaged Internationale Nieuwe Scène, of which he was a member till 1979, with productions such as Majakovskij's *Misterium Buffo*. Since 1988 he has regularly played parts for the Blauwe Maandag Compagnie, such as Mark Anthony in John Dryden's *All for Love* (1993), directed by Luk PERCEVAL. Decleir has also made a reputation in films. He is an actor of immense stage presence, embodying both physical strength and emotional fragility, a combination which has been labeled as 'typically Flemish'.

Degli Esposti, Piera (1938–) Actor and dramatist, Italy. Piera degli Esposti started working in the theatre with Teatro Centouno and made her theatrical debut in 1964 with Gruppo 63. She then worked at the Teatro Stabile dell'Aquila and, after a short break, was freelance from 1979. Her book *Storia di Piera* (*Piera's Story*, 1983) was made into a film, for which she and Dacia MARAINI wrote the script. The film was directed by Marco Ferreri and featured Marcello Mastroianni and

Hannah Schygulla as the protagonists. Degli Esposti and Maraini also co-wrote *Futuro è donna* (*The Future is Female*, 1984), again directed by Ferreri and with Schygulla in the lead role. Among degli Esposti's most interesting theatre productions are Witold Gombrowicz's *Operetta* (1970), directed by Antonio CALENDA, *Molly cara* (*Dear Molly*, 1979), directed by Ida Bassignano, Ibsen's *Rosmersholm* (1981–2), directed by Massimo CASTRI, and Bertold Brecht's *Mutter Courage und ihre Kinder* (*Mother Courage and her Children*, 1991), directed by Calenda. Degli Esposti's unique capacity to reinvent herself as a performer and her wide repertoire, both as a performer and a dramatist, together with her commitment to political and feminist causes, make her one of the most interesting and provocative artists working in contemporary Italian theatre.

De Graaf, Rob (1952–) Dramatist, The Netherlands. Rob de Graaf, who trained as a librarian, was born in 'New West', a postwar housing development in Amsterdam. It gave its name to the three-man theatre company Nieuw-West, for which de Graaf wrote many texts. Nieuw-West started in 1978 and was disbanded in the mid-1990s. Some highlights were *Rinus* (1987), *Pygmalion* (1989), *Lever* (*Liver*, 1990, with Cas ENKLAAR), and *A Hard Day's Night* (1991). De Graaf writes his plays (texts is a better word) straight into the veins of his actors. They are tough, centred on language rather than plot, often about 'a man's world', and they always question the truthfulness of acting. After the dissolution of Nieuw-West, de Graaf started writing for the young Dood Paard company. They produced his award-winning play *2Skin* (1996). He has been an editor of magazines on architecture and theatre, and from 1991–6 he was director of the Mime Department at the Drama School in Amsterdam. Some of his plays have been translated into German.

De Groen, Alma (1941–) Dramatist, Australia. De Groen was brought up in New Zealand but became a naturalized Australian. She is a feminist playwright who writes in widely disparate dramatic forms with a forceful self-consciousness about her artistry. In *The Rivers of China* (1987), de Groen interweaves the last days of Katherine Mansfield with a science fiction narrative set in a world where women rule and oppress men. In *Vocations* (1981), Joy, a woman science fiction writer, and Vicki, an actor, struggle to maintain their integrity in the face of demands from men in relationships and careers. *The Girl Who Saw Everything* (1991), which looks at different generations of women's reactions to feminism, proved controversial. De Groen's plays often show characters, especially women, becoming trapped or marginalized and resorting to bizarre, even dangerous behaviour. De Groen has also written for television, film and radio: radio plays include *Available Light* (1993), *Stories in the Dark* (with Ian D. Mackenzie) and *Invisible Sun* (1997).

De Jong, Trudy (1948–) Actor, The Netherlands. Trudy de Jong went to the Amsterdam Drama School, from which she graduated in 1972. She made her debut with De Appel in The Hague and made a one-off appearance in the *Rocky Horror Show*, before joining the Baal company where she worked from 1975–85. She starred in Judith HERZBERG's hit play *Leedvermaak* (*The Wedding Party*, 1982), Botho STRAUSS's *Die Hypochonder* (*The Hypochondriacs*) and plays by Peter HANDKE including *Kaspar Hauser*. De Jong, a stocky, emotional actor whose enormous presence always rings true, also worked with Gerardjan RIJNDERS in his montage plays *Bakeliet* and *Ballet*, and has recently performed regularly in Frans STRIJARDS's company Art & Pro, with a magnificent interpretation of Gina Ekdal in Ibsen's *Vildanden* (*The Wild Duck*) and a revival of *Kaspar Hauser* (1997).

de la Tour, Frances (1944–) Actor, Great Britain. De la Tour trained at Drama Centre, and played Helena in the famous production of *A Midsummer Night's Dream* by Peter BROOK for the Royal Shakespeare Company (1970). She took on the title part in *Hamlet* (1979), and achieved a major success as Stephanie in Kempinski's *Duet for One* (1980, subsequently also on television). At the National Theatre she played the title role in Shaw's *St Joan* (1984) and Leonie in Cocteau's in *Les parents terribles* (*The Terrible Parents*, 1995), and appeared in Ostrovsky's *Les* (*The Forest*, 1999). Striking features and a dark voice help de la Tour in her portrayal of women whose strength is undergoing severe tests. When those women lose control, de la Tour provides shattering insights into the human psyche.

Demidova, Alla (1936–) Actor, Russia. Demidova trained at Schukin Theatre College (Moscow Vakhtangov Theatre School) and has been an actor of the Taganka Drama Theatre since 1964. Her most important parts include Gertrude in *Hamlet* (1970), directed by Yuri LIUBIMOV, Ranevskaya in Chekhov's *Visnevyi sad* (*The Cherry Orchard*, 1975), directed by Anatoly Efros, and the title role in Racine's *Phèdre*, directed by Viktiouk (1988). Demidova is an intellectual actor, an acclaimed performer of tragic parts on the modern stage. After 1988 she organized her own theatre company (Theatre A) and toured successfully in Greece. Greek director TERZOPOULOS staged *Quartett* by Heiner Müller for her (1993), in a highly stylized, modernistic production. Her beauty and intelligence brought her success in film roles in the 1960–1970s, including Tarkovsky's *Mirror* and the Dutchess Marlborough in *Le verre d'eau* (*A Glass of Water*) by Scribe. A winner of several awards and prizes, she has written several books about theatre and about her colleagues.

De Muynck, Viviane (1946–) Actor, Belgium. De Muynck trained at the Royal Conservatory of Brussels, then started acting with De Mannen van den Dam in 1980. In 1987 she played the award-winning part of Martha in Edward AL-BEE's *Who's Afraid of Virginia Woolf?*, directed by Sam Bogaerts at Het Gezelschap van de Witte Kraai (White Crow Company). In the late 1980s and early 1990s she worked in Amsterdam, first with Maatschappij Discordia, then with Toneelgroep Amsterdam in Gerardjan RIJNDERS's *Count your Blessings* (1992). In 1994 she starred in two productions at the Brussels Kaaitheater: *Philoctetes Variations*, by Jan Ritsema, with Dirk ROOF-THOOFT, and *De Pijl van de Tijd* (*Time's Arrow*), by Guy CASSIERS. Since 1993 she has been working regularly with director Jan LAUWERS and Needcompany.

Dench, Judi (1934–) Actor, Great Britain. After training at the Central School for Speech Training and Dramatic Art, Judi Dench began her career in the theatre as Ophelia opposite John Neville's Hamlet at the Old Vic (1957). She soon joined the Royal Shakespeare Company, where she played Titania in *A Midsummer Night's Dream* and Isabella in *Measure for Measure*. Following seasons in Nottingham and Oxford, Dench returned to the RSC in 1969. Since the 1970s Judi Dench has established herself as one of the leading actors in Britain. In 1976 she played Lady Macbeth in a memorable production of *Macbeth* with Ian MCKELLEN, the title role in Brecht's *Mutter Courage und ihre Kinder* (*Mother Courage and her Children*) in 1984, and the female lead in Peter SHAFFER's *The Gift of the Gorgon*, directed by Peter HALL, in 1992. For the National Theatre, she has appeared as Lady Bracknell in Wilde's *The Importance of Being Earnest* (1982), Cleopatra in *Anthony and Cleopatra*, directed by Peter Hall and with Anthony HOPKINS as Anthony, Chekhov's *Cajka* (*The Seagull*,

1994), and David HARE's *Amy's View* (1997, directed by Richard EYRE).

Dene, Kirsten (1943–) Actor, Germany. Dene trained at the Hamburg Academy of Music and Dramatic Arts. Her career began in Essen (1961–3), and developed via Frankfurt (1963–70), Berlin (1970–2), Stuttgart (1972–9) and Bochum (1980–6) to the Burgtheater in Vienna, where she is still a member of the company. Major roles include Rosalind in *As You Like It*, Lena in Büchner's *Leonce und Lena*, and the title roles in Goethe's *Iphigenie auf Tauris* and Brecht's *Mutter Courage und ihre Kinder* (*Mother Courage and her Children*). In 1994 she appeared in JELI-NEK's *Raststätte oder Sie Machens Alle* (*Inn, or, They All Do It*), in 1995 in TURRINI's *Die Schlacht um Vienna* (*The Battle for Vienna*), in 1996 in Strindberg's *Dödsdansen* (*Dance of Death*), in 1998 in Turrini's *Die Liebe in Madagaskar* (*Love in Madagascar*) and in 1999 in Claus PEYMANN's production of Bernhard's *Vor dem Ruhestand* (*Before Retirement*), all at the Burgtheater, Vienna. Thanks to her expressive abilities, she is able to fathom and reveal the characteristics of a role with one gesture or one glance.

De Pauw, Josse (1952–) Actor, dramatist and director, Belgium. Following studies at the Royal Conservatory in Brussels, de Pauw joined Radeis (1977–84), which specialized in visual comedy. He then concentrated on his writing, resulting in the two Kaaitheater productions, *Ward Comblez. He do the life in different voices*, 1988 and *Het Kind van de Smid* (*The Blacksmith's Child*, 1990), written and directed together with Peter van Kraaij. In 1992 de Pauw and van Kraaij completed their first feature film, *Vinaya*. At the Kaaitheater, de Pauw played the part of Richard Rowan in James Joyce's *Exiles* (1993), directed by van Kraaij, and starred in Chantal Akerman's *De Verhuizing* (*The Removal*, 1995), directed by Jürgen GOSCH. In 1995 he created

Laagland, a small production unit, with Dutch actor and director Tom Jansen. De Pauw also made a reputation in films. He is a remarkably intense actor, whose work balances on the border between theatre and real life.

Derenne, Josephine (1939–) Actor, France. Derenne was a member of Ariane MNOUCHKINE's Théâtre du Soleil between 1965–83, appearing in Gorky's *Mescane (The Petty Bourgeoisie*, 1964–5), Théophile Gautier's *Capitaine Fracasse* (1965–6), Arnold Wesker's *The Kitchen* (1967), *A Midsummer Night's Dream* (1968), *1789* (1970–1), *1793* (1972–3), Klaus Mann's *Méphisto, The Novel of a Career* (1979–80) and *Twelfth Night* (1982). In 1976–7 she played the part of Madelaine Béjart in *Molière*, the film written and directed by Mnouchkine. She has worked with many theatre directors, including the part of Kunti in Peter BROOK's *Mahabaratha* (1983), as Gerturde in *Hamlet* (1983) and with Christian Schiaretti in Alain Badiou's *Des citrouilles (Pumpkins,* 1997). Her acting style is inspired by the *commedia dell'arte*, which gives her an immense stage presence and intensity of feeling.

Deshpande, Govind Purushottam (1938–) Dramatist, India. Deshpande is a leading Marxist intellectual, and this ideological position informs his Marathi plays in which he confronts the problem of the individual enmeshed and struggling in dark times. His first play, *Uddhwasta Dharmashala (A Man In Dark Times,* 1975), was directed by Shreeram LAGOO, and many other Indian directors have acclaimed it as important political theatre. *Ek Vajoon Gela Ahe (Past One o' Clock)* draws its title from a poem found in Mayakovsky's pocket after his suicide in 1930. *Andhar Yatra (Inner Journey,* 1987) completes the political trilogy. He says: 'I would submit that in my plays there is an organic and symbiotic relationship between human beings and ideas.' *Chanakya*

Vishnugupta, a play set at the time of Alexander the Great's Indian campaign, examines relationships between individual, society and government. His most recent play, *Satyashodak (The Seeker of Truth)*, is again a political commentary.

Deshpande, Sulaba (1937–) Actor, India. Deshpande joined professional theatre groups in the 1950s and has appeared in more than seventy-five plays on the Marathi and Hindi stage. Among many roles that have received acclaim are Miss Benare in Vijay TENDULKAR's *Shantata Court Chalu Ahe, (Silence! The Court is in Session)* and Champa in Tendulkar's *Sakhram Binder*. Together with her husband, Arvind Deshpande, she founded the theatre group Awishkar, through which she has made a significant contribution to children's theatre, representing India in many international forums. She has also played notable roles in a number of films and television productions.

Devenie, Stuart (1951–) Actor and director, New Zealand. Rather than attend the New Zealand Drama School, Devenie studied at Victoria University of Wellington and Canterbury University. He had, however, already accumulated considerable acting experience on radio, television and the stage, and in 1977 he won Wellington's best actor award for his Henry Law in Tom STOPPARD's *Travesties* at the Downstage, where his controlled presence, deft movements and chiselled voice also contributed to his Aubrey Tanqueray in Pinero's *The Second Mrs Tanqueray* (1979). His abilities have also made him successful in roles which are at first sight very different, such as that of Dr Frank N Furter in Richard O'Brien's *The New Rocky Horror Show* (1995). After three years acting and directing at the Court Theatre, Christchurch, where his performance of Molière's miser Harpagon was outstanding, he became Artistic Director at the Centrepoint Theatre, Palmerston North, for a year in 1984 before returning to freelance acting and directing, especially in Auckland and Christchurch. He also teaches acting and directing.

Devi, Mahasweta (1926–) Novelist, social activist and dramatist, India. Mahasweta Devi is a Bengali writer who has worked extensively for and with tribal and marginalized communities. Intense commitment, thorough empirical research into customs and language patterns, and varied and imaginative use of register characterize her work; she has adapted five of her best-known stories for the stage (*Five Plays*), and these display a wide variety of forms while focusing on the marginalized or oppressed. *Mother of 1084*, dealing with anti-'terrorist' measures in Bengal, uses a split stage and multiple flashback; *Urvashi and Johnny* presents a commentary on Mrs Gandhi's Emergency Powers law via the figure of a ventriloquist with throat cancer and is structured around popular film songs; *Water* (about corruption and exploitation by officials and landowners) and *Bayen* (on the outcasting of a woman whose job is to watch over the dead) make use of rural dance and music. Another of her stories, *Rudali*, was reworked as a play in Hindi by the well-known Calcutta director Usha Ganguli in 1992.

Devlin, Anne (1951–) Dramatist, Ireland. Born and raised in Northern Ireland, Devlin's first play *Ourselves Alone* explored the experience of women living within the patriarchies of nationalism. The play was first produced at the Liverpool Playhouse and the Royal Court, London in 1985 and was directed by Simon Curtis. Since then she has written plays for BBC radio and television, including *A Woman Calling* and *The Long March*. She adapted *Wuthering Heights* for Paramount Pictures in 1991. *After Easter* was first produced by the Royal Shakespeare Company at the Other Place, Stratford in 1994, directed by Michael

Attenborough. This play was in many ways a more recent reaction to political events in Northern Ireland, but like *Ourselves Alone* it took a very personal perspective and was a development of the earlier work.

Dibia, I Wayan (1948–) Performer and director, Indonesia. Dibia trained at the National Dance Academy of Indonesia, and obtained an MA in dance and a PhD in Interdisciplinary Studies in Southeast Asian Performing Arts, both from the University of California, Los Angeles. He is now director of STSI (the Academy of Performing Arts) in Denpasar, Bali. Pak Dibia studied traditional Balinese traditional dance drama from childhood with his parents, who were both dancers, and his later formal studies at institutions were always augmented by private study with master performers in his village. He is particularly renowned as a Barong dancer, but also performs Topeng Pajegan and various roles in Chalonarang (traditional exorcistic dance-drama featuring the widow-witch Rangda), including both the Prime Minister and Rangda. As a director, he has choreographed a number of new Kecak productions in Indonesia, the United States and Europe. He has led international tours of troupes from the village of Singapadu and from STSI. A scholar, teacher, director and performer of international stature, Pak Dibia also continues to perform regularly in his village temples. His performances of masked characters, including the Jauk demon and refined characters of Topeng, show precision and musicality, and his comic Bondres characters are brilliantly executed. As a director, his innovative work with performers has produced startlingly powerful productions of both traditional Balinese material and adaptations of Western classics.

Diosdado, Ana (1938–) Dramatist and actor, Spain. Born in Buenos Aires where her father, a prominent Spanish actor, was then working, she made her stage debut at age four with Margarita Xirgu in a production of Lorca's *Mariana Pineda*. She abandoned her studies in philosophy and literature at Madrid's Complutense University in 1959 to concentrate full-time on writing. First published as a novelist in 1965, she turned to playwriting in 1970 when her first work *Olvida los tambores (Forget the Drums)* was staged. Since then she has worked prolifically both as an actor, adaptor and dramatist whose works, like *Los ochenta son nuestros (The Eighties are Ours*, 1988) and *Tresceintos veintiuno, trescientos veintidós (Three Hundred and Twenty-One, Three Hundred and Twenty-Two*, 1991), the latter directed by her husband Carlos Larrañaga, have sought to examine gender, sexual, ideological and generational conflicts in the new democratic Spain. As a popular television actor and screenwriter and award-winning novelist, Diosdado has enjoyed a strong visibility within the cultural scene of Spain over the past twenty years.

Djimat, I Made (1948–) Performer, Indonesia. The son of dancers, Djimat studied traditional Balinese dance with his father from the age of five, and by the age of ten had already made a name for himself with Baris and the masked dance, Jauk. At thirteen he began to study the ancient Gambuh dance form with Agung Raka in Batuan, and later went on to master Topeng Pajegan. Since 1974 he has had his own company based in Batuan, which has performed and given workshops all over the world. Djimat himself is very much in demand as a dancer and musician in Bali and elsewhere, and has collaborated with Eugenio BARBA on projects for the International School of Theatre Anthropology (ISTA). In Bali, he is held to be one of the finest dancers who demonstrates the brilliance of technique which was the hallmark of performers of the previous generation. His children are all dancers with his company, and he has

many other students in Europe, America, Australia and Japan. He also participates in Cristina WISTARI's Gambuh Preservation Project as a teacher, and gives regular performances of Gambuh in Batuan.

Dodin, Lev (1944–) Director, Russia. Dodin graduated from the Leningrad State Institute for Drama, Music and Cinematography, and joined the Leningrad Children's Theatre in 1967 where, in 1972, he directed Ostrovsky's *Bankrot (The Bankrupt)*. Everyday situations were treated as theatre, as a market show, underscored by a subtle lyrical mood, even melancholy. Dodin's production of Dostoyevsky's *Krotkaya (The Meek One)* in St Petersburg revealed his outstanding capacity for inner concentration. At the Moscow Art Theatre, Dodin directed Saltykov-Shedrin's *Gospoda Golovlyov (Messieurs Golovlyovs)*, and revived *The Meek One*. His breakthrough came with *Bratya & Sestri (Brothers and Sisters*, 1978, revived 1985), adapted from the novel by Fyodor Abramov. Critics stated that it was not merely an outspoken production about Russian village life, but an overwhelming event in current culture which awakened Russians' interest in themselves as historical personalities. Later work includes adaptations of William Golding's *Lord of the Flies* (1986), of Dostoyevsky's *Besy (The Possessed*, 1991) and of Chekhov's *Platonov* (1998).

Domröse, Angelica (1941–) Actor, Germany. Domröse attended the Babelsberg Film Academy (1958–61). Between 1961 and 1996 she was a member of the Berliner Ensemble, and in 1966 she joined the Berliner Volksbühne (GDR). In 1980 she first appeared in West Germany, playing Helena in Goethe's *Faust II*. Important productions since then include the title role in Wedekind's *Lulu*, Cäcilie in Goethe's *Stella*, Charlotte in Lars Norén's *Nachtwache* and Maria Callas in Terrence MCNALLY's *Master Class (1999)* Critics praised her 'strong ability to present different nuances of tone, movement and gesture'.

Donnellan, Declan (1953–) Director, Great Britain. Donnellan began his career in the theatre as a freelance director with the Activists at the Royal Court. Since 1980 he has been working with the designer Nick Ormerod, with whom he founded the company Cheek by Jowl, aiming to make classics relevant to a late twentieth-century audience. In 1988 Donnellan and Ormerod directed Lope de Vega's *Fuente Ovejuna* at the National Theatre, followed by Ibsen's *Peer Gynt* (1990) and Kushner's *Angels in America* (1992). 'Rather than strict adherence to the formalistic structure of the language, Donnellan's style places a priority on the clear expression of the text through the creation of a specific and detailed physical life for the characters.'

Donutil, Miroslav (1951–) Actor, Czech Republic. Donutil trained at the Brno Academy of Performing Arts, and worked with the Brno experimental group Goose on a String (Husa na provázku) from 1973. Here he played the main part in *Ballad for a Bandit* (a musical by Milan Uhde and Miloš Štedron, based on the novel by Ivan Olbracht, 1975), then Brighella in the *Commedie dell arte* (1974), Fyodor Karamazov in Dostoyevsky's *Brat'ia Karamazovy* (*The Karamazov Brothers*, 1981) and Creon in Sophocles's *Antigone* (1989). In 1990 he became a member of the National Theatre in Prague where, in addition to his comic roles – the Fool in *As You Like It*, (1991), the Old Man in Ionesco's *Les chaises* (*The Chairs*, 1992, directed by Jan KAČER), Truffaldino in Goldoni's *Il Servitore di due padroni* (*The Servant of Two Masters*, 1994) – he has also taken on internally contradictory characters such as Hjalmar in Ibsen's *Vildanden* (*The Wild Duck*, 1993) and the title role in Chekhov's *Djadja Vanja* (*Uncle Vanya*, 1990, directed by Ivan RAJMONT). In his roles he

mixes physical and conversational expression, the serious with the comic, the large gesture with the minor detail. He does not 'mould' with the character but maintains a certain distance, and one component of his acting is his perspective on the character as if seen from outside. This oscillation results in certain important elements and comic effects.

Dorn, Dieter (1935–) Director and actor, Germany. Dorn studied drama at the Theaterschule in Leipzig, and trained as an actor with Hilde Körber and Lucie Höflich at the Max Reinhardt Schule in Berlin. From 1958–68 he worked as actor, director and dramaturg in Hannover. After some seasons as director in Essen, Oberhausen and Berlin, he joined the Münchner Kammerspiele in 1976, becoming its artistic director and manager from 1983–99. Recent productions include *King Lear* (1992, with Heinz BENNENT as Fool), *The Tempest* (1994, with Jürgen HOLTZMANN as Prospero and Gisela STEIN as Ariel) and *Ithaka* by Botho STRAUSS. His productions are characterized by poetic realism, deriving all his insights solely from the dramatic texts.

Dorst, Tankred (1925–) Dramatist, Germany. Dorst wrote his first full-length stage play, *Die Mohrin* (*The Mooress*) in 1954, and won a major award for his 1960 play *Gesellschaft im Herbst* (*Society in Autumn*). Further plays include *Toller: Szenen einer Deutschen Revolution* (*Toller: Scenes from a German Revolution*, 1968) and *Eiszeit* (*Ice Age*, 1973). In *Merlin oder das Wüste Land* (*Merlin, or The Waste Land*, 1981), Dorst takes up the myth of King Arthur and Merlin to tell a story of our own time, that of the failure of utopias. Later plays include *Ich, Feuerbach* (1986), *Korbes* (1988), *Karlos* (1990) *Fernando Krapp hat mir diesen Brief geschrieben* (*Fernando Krapp Wrote This Letter to Me*, 1991), and *Wegen Rechtum Geschlossen* (*Closed Because of Wealth*, 1998). Dorst, who usually writes with his wife Ursula Ehler, has also been successful writing plays for children as well as prose fiction.

Dossa, Pragji (1907–) Dramatist, India. Dossa is a dramatist specializing in plays in Gujarati for children. Most of his plays have been translated into other Indian languages. *Chhoru Kachhoru* (*Spoilt Child*) was produced in Russia by the Gorky Theatre and had a run of 300 performances at Tashkent and Moscow. It was also staged in Britain, Sri Lanka and East Africa. His other popular plays include *Mangal Mandir, Poonam ni Raat* and *Agantuk Ek Andheri Raat*, which have been popular with schools and colleges. Dossa received many awards for his work in children's theatre.

Dowling, Joe (1948–) Director, Ireland. Dowling became a member of the Abbey acting company while still a student at University College Dublin. In 1970 he founded Young Abbey, a theatre-in-education company. He was director of the Peacock Theatre (1973–6), artistic director of the Irish Theatre Company until 1978, and at twenty-nine he became the youngest ever artistic director of the Abbey (1978–85). Dowling directed the first production of a number of Brian FRIEL's plays including *Aristocrats* for the Abbey Theatre (1979). In 1986 Dowling became the managing director of the Gaiety Theatre, Dublin and founded the Gaiety School of Acting. He directed many acclaimed productions in Dublin, including Brian Friel's *Faith Healer* for the Abbey Theatre (1980) and Timberlake WERTENBAKER's *Our Country's Good* for the Gate Theatre (1991). Dowling's work in the USA has included *Othello* with Raul Julia and Christopher Walken for the New York Shakespeare Festival, Central Park (1991). Dowling is currently the artistic director of the Guthrie Theatre, Minneapolis. By combining his creative and business skills once again, Dowling has developed a wider audience base and a greater appreciation of Irish drama outside Ireland.

Downes, Cathy (1950–) Actor and director, New Zealand. Downes graduated from Nola Millar's New Zealand Drama School in Wellington in 1973. Her accomplishment was recognized after 1978 when her solo performance in her own *The Case of Katherine Mansfield*, compiled from that author's writings, began to win recognition in many countries throughout the world, as well as two awards at the 1979 Edinburgh Festival. The piece has had continued success, including a full New Zealand tour in the Mansfield centenary year of 1988. Other notable roles have been Blanche in Tennessee Williams's *A Streetcar Named Desire* (Court Theatre, Christchurch, 1989) and Isobel Glass in *The Secret Rapture* by David HARE (Circa Theatre, Wellington, 1990). In recent years she has made a name for direction, especially of modern American plays, including Edward ALBEE's *Three Tall Women* at the Circa in 1996, but also of Australian and New Zealand plays such as *Good Works* by Nick ENRIGHT (Downstage, 1995), and *Tzigane* by John Vakidis (Downstage, 1996) which won Wellington's best director and best production awards.

Drach, Oleg (1959–) Actor, Ukraine. Drach graduated from the Karpenko-Kary Institute for the Art of the Theatre, Kiev in 1981. As an actor at the Maria Zan'kovets'ka Ukrainian Drama Theatre, Lviv (1981–7) he appeared in more than thirty parts, including D'Artagnan in *Three Musketeers* by Dumas (1987). In 1988 he joined the Les Kurbas Theatre, L'viv with a series of major parts, including Panas in Vynnychenko's *Mizh dvokh syl* (*Between Two Powers*, 1990); Dostoyevsky's *Prestuplenie I nakazanie* (*Crime and Punishment*), directed by Volodymyr KUCHYNS'KY; Raskol'nikov in *Sny* (*Dreams*, 1991); Svidrigailov in *Zabavy dlia Fausta* (*Games for Faust*, 1994);

and Lopakhin in Chekhov's *Visnevyi sad* (*The Cherry Orchard*, 1996). Drach also starred as Lukash in the New York (La MaMa) production of *Lisova pisnia* (*Yara Forest Song*) after Lesia Ukrainka, directed by Virliana Tkach (1994). The bright appearance of the blond, handsome actor is supplemented by deep emotional and psychological energy, and expressive plasticity and articulation.

Drach, Vanya (1932–) Actor, Croatia. Drach trained at the Academy of Dramatic Art in Zagreb. For most of his career he has worked with the HNK in Zagreb (Croatian National Theatre). Since his breakthrough in 1958, when he played the title role in Matković's *Heraklo* (*Heracles*), he has been praised for his control of the stage speech. On the one hand, he completely identifies himself with the character, while on the other he follows closely the writer's idea, thus staying truthful to both writer's and director's conception. His stage credits include strong and seemingly rough but in fact deeply eroded characters, such as Edmund Tyrone in O'Neill's *A Long Day's Journey into Night* (1958), Franz in Sartre's *Les séquestrés d'Altona* (*The Condemned of Altona*, 1962), Jason in Euripides's *Medeia* (1965) and the title role in Ibsen's *John Gabriel Borkman* (1972). Among the Croatian repertory, he excelled especially in Krleza's plays. Drach is also a notable interpreter of Shakespeare's characters, such as Angelo in *Measure for Measure* (1974), and the title role in *Cymbeline* (1986). In 1998 he crowned the forty years of his acting career by playing Lear.

Dubé, Marcel (1930–) Dramatist, Canada. While studying at the Université de Montréal, Dubé co-founded his own theatre company, La Jeune Scène. His first critical acclaim came with *Zone* (1953), which was equally successful on television. *Un simple soldat* (*A Simple Soldier*, 1958) continues to be his most produced play. During the late 1950s and early 1960s, he wrote prolifically for radio and television. He also worked as a speechwriter for Québec Liberal Leader Jean Lesage. In 1965 he returned to the stage with his play *Les Beaux Dimanches* (*Beautiful Sundays*), which is heavily influenced by Edward ALBEE, and wrote thirteen stage plays in the next ten years. His plays initially dealt with 'characters from the urban working classes', while the second phase of Dubé's writing focuses on middle-class characters. He is also known as an essayist, novelist and poet.

Dubey, Satyadev (1936–) Director and dramatist, India. Dubey, who began his career in 1965, has directed the plays of most of the prominent Indian playwrights, including Girish KARNAD's *Hayavadana*, Mohan Rakesh's *Adhe Adhure* and Dharmvir BHARATI's *Andha Yug*. His production of Badal SIRCAR's *Evam Indrajit* is an example of truly modern Indian theatre, capturing the mood of the Indian middle class. Recently he has written and directed his own play, *Insha Allah*, a strong political drama which received excellent reviews. Dubey has also directed some of the New Wave Hindi films.

Dudley, William (1947–) Designer, Great Britain. Dudley trained and studied at St Martins and the Slade School of Art. He worked for Nottingham Playhouse (*Hamlet*, 1970), Newcastle, the Royal Shakespeare Company and the National Theatre, where he has been a resident designer since 1981. His designs include an imaginative *Don Quixote* with Paul SCOFIELD (1982), the promenade productions of Bill Bryden's *The Mysteries* and David EDGAR's *Entertaining Strangers* (1987), Beckett's *Waiting for Godot* with Alec MCCOWEN (1988), and Dylan Thomas's *Under Milk Wood* (1995). The over-elaborate sets for Shaw's *Pygmalion* in Howard DAVIES's production in 1992 were considered one of Dudley's few failures, upstaging the actors. For the Royal Court, his designs include Richard EYRE's 1980 production of *Hamlet* with Jonathan Pryce. Dudley has also worked in opera, including Peter HALL's controversial production of Wagner's *Ring* cycle in Bayreuth. More recent work includes a revival of Harold PINTER's *The Homecoming* at the Royal National Theatre, Peter Hall's production of *A Streetcar Named Desire* in the West End, and Terry JOHNSON's *Cleo, Camping, Emanuelle and Dick* (starring Anthony SHER, Royal National Theatre, 1998).

Dueñas Gonzalez, Miriam (1944–) Designer, Cuba. Since her graduation as a costume designer from the Escuela de Artes Dramaticas, Dueñas has worked in more than seventy theatre, dance and musical productions as well as film. Until 1991 she was a costume design teacher at the Escuela Nacional de Arte and at the Instituto Superior de Diseño Industrial in Havana. Among her most representative works are Lorca's *Doña Rosita la Soltera* (*Dona Rosita the Spinster* 1968), Vazquez's *Para un Príncipe Enano* (*For a Dwarf Prince*, 1979), Molière's *Dom Juan* (1982), Montes y Chico Buarque's *Gota D'agua* (*Drop of Water* 1986), Muñoz Seca's *La Venganza de Don Mendo* (*Don Mendo's Revenge*, 1989), *Antología del Bolero* (*An Anthology of Boleros*, Madrid, 1993) and *La Noche* (*The Night*, 1995).

Dukakis, Olympia (1931–) Actor and director, USA. Dukakis graduated with an MFA from Boston University. She has enjoyed a very successful career in the theatre, in film and on television. Major parts for the stage were Widow Leocadia Begbick in Brecht's *Mann ist Mann* (*A Man's a Man*, 1963), the title role in Brecht's *Mutter Courage und ihre Kinder* (*Mother Courage and her Children*, 1967), Ranevskaya in Chekhov's *Visnevyi*

sad (*The Cherry Orchard*, 1981), Mrs Alving in Ibsen's *Gengangere* (*Ghosts*) and Arkadina in Chekhov's *Cajka* (*The Seagull*, 1986). From 1976–90 she was artistic director of the New Jersey Whole Theatre Company. Equally adept at comic and dramatic parts, her primary work now is in major supporting roles in motion pictures, averaging three films a year through the last decade. In 1999 she made her British debut in Martin Sherman's *Rose* at the Royal National Theatre. She describes herself as a strong feminist, and teaches at New York and Yale universities.

Dündar, Hakan (1967–) Designer, Turkey. Dündar graduated from the Department of Stage Design, Dokuz Eylül University, İzmir in 1989. Between 1989–91 he worked as Culture and Arts Advisor for İzmir Buca Municipality. In Buca, he restored a 170-year old English Protestant church and transformed it into a Culture and Arts Centre. In 1991 he started to work as a stage designer for the Turkish State Theatres. He also functioned as an artistic director for the cinema and television series and programmes, preparing various puppets for numerous children's programmes on television. He contributed to the designs of various theatre projects of Turkish-English and Turkish-Austrian productions, and worked with Swiss, German, Austrian and English directors. Also, using deserted stone quarries and historical sites dating back to ancient periods, he promoted 'happenings' and 'installations'. As a professional designer, he created costume and set designs and puppet designs for more than sixty plays and modern ballets, including *Macbeth*, *The Merchant of Venice*, *Twelfth Night*, Peter SHAFFER's *Equus* and Molière's *Tartuffe*. Currently, he is involved in experimental design research, claiming that twenty-first century theatre will depend more on design, paving the way for a Theatre of Design.

Duruaku, Toni (1957–) Actor, dramatist and director, Nigeria. Duruaku was a member of the Oak Theatre at Nsukka founded by Ossie ENEKWE and Kalu Uka. He is a very powerful performer whose stage presence and a talent for effective delivery, both for comic and tragic roles, make him compelling. Stage credits include Okereke in Sonny Oti's *The Old Masters* (1977), Ajala in Zulu Sofola's *The Sweet Trap* (1978–9), Macbeth in Oak Theatre production of *Macbeth* (1979–80 under the direction of Ossie Enekwe and featuring among others, Esiaba IROBI as Duncan), Chima in Emman Owums's *Too Late, My Son* (1979) and Captain Bluntschli in Bernard Shaw's *Arms and the Man* (1980). His published works include *Silhouettes* (1993) and *A Question of Choice* (1995), both of which he directed and appeared in as an actor.

Dušek, Jan (1942–) Designer, Czech Republic. After studying at the Prague Academy of Performing Arts, in the 1970s Dušek became one of the representatives of so-called 'action scenography'. He makes use of the meanings and spatial variability of the stage object, and deliberately works with simple means to release the stage for the play of the actors. In *Coriolanus* (1979, Tyl Theatre, Plzeò), he defined the space with thin strips of white canvas, which were raised, torn down and so on. The costume is a prop for him, which may metamorphose in meaning: the long coat in Anouilh's *L'Alouette* (*The Lark*, 1970 Bezruè theatre, Ostrava) changes into a tent. In O'Neill's *A Long Day's Journey into Night* (1983, South Bohemian Theatre, České Budijovice), he assembled authentic objects (boxes, strings, paper) into 'situation scenarios' according to the course of the action and movement of the actor. He is a scenographer in great demand, working with almost all Czech theatres, including opera, where he has disrupted the traditional conception with his unpretentious designs (Smetana's *Prodana nevesta* (*The Bartered Bride*), 1992 at the National Theatre Prague). He has been teaching at the Prague Academy of Performing Arts since 1977, and has been the head of its Scenography Department since 1991.

E

Eagan, Michael (1942–) Designer, Canada. Having trained in theatre design at the National Theatre School, Eagan has since worked in many of Canada's major theatres, including the Stratford Festival, the Shaw Festival and the Canadian Stage Company, as well as in New York. In his designs, he rejects fragmentation in favour of classical forms, combining built and painted reliefs 'to provide an elaborately detailed environment that is never without a light, fantastic element'. Eagan is equally well at home in realism, expressionism, lyricism and parody.

Edgar, David (1948–) Dramatist, Great Britain. Early in his career, Edgar worked as a journalist and wrote numerous agit-prop plays, at great speed, for the fringe. An early success in mainstream theatre was *Destiny* for the Royal Shakespeare Company in 1976, an attempt to understand the roots of extreme right-wing parties. Edgar's historical-political awareness informed his adaptation of Dickens's novel *Nicholas Nickleby* for the RSC (1980, directed by Trevor NUNN and John CAIRD). For the RSC he also adapted *The Strange Case of Dr Jekyll and Mr Hyde* (1991, with Simon Russell BEALE in the title role), and wrote *Pentecost* in 1994. The National Theatre staged Edgar's *Maydays* (1983). *Entertaining Strangers* was commissioned by Ann Jellicoe's company for community theatre; later, the National Theatre revived the play in professional production, (1987, designed by William DUDLEY), adopting a promenade style to maintain some of the interaction between audience and performers characteristic of the original community theatre set-up. For the National Theatre, Edgar also wrote *The Shape of the Table* (1990). He teaches a postgraduate course in playwrighting at Birmingham University, modelled on the postgraduate course in fiction writing created by Malcolm Bradbury at the University of East Anglia.

Edwards, Gale (1954–) Director, Australia. Edwards studied at Flinders University Drama Centre (Adelaide), the University of Adelaide, the Mime Centre, London and the National Institute of Dramatic Art, Sydney. She began mainstage directing in collaboration with John GADEN at the South Australia Theatre Company, Adelaide and has since then also directed several productions for the Melbourne Theatre Company and the Sydney Theatre Company. Edwards's success as Associate Director on Trevor NUNN's *Les Misérables* (1987) led to more work on musicals and she has directed several Andrew Lloyd Webber musicals, her 1992 production of *Aspects of Love* being particularly praised. Edwards now works largely in the UK; she has directed classics for the Royal Shakespeare Company (*The Taming of the Shrew* and Webster's *The White*

Devil) and her West End production of Shaw's *St Joan* was later restaged in Sydney. In 1998 she directed the British premiere of Andrew Lloyd Webber's musical *Whistle Down the Wind*. Highly acclaimed productions in Australia include *Coriolanus* (for STC) starring John HOWARD, Aphra Behn's *The Rover* (for the State Theatre Company of South Australia) starring Pamela RABE, and Ibsen's *Et Dukkehjem* (*A Doll's House*) at Belvoir Street, Sydney. Edwards has a bold approach to directing and often opens productions with a strong visual statement signalling her interpretation of the piece. She is known for her skill in exploiting big theatre spaces.

Ekmanner, Agneta (1938–) Actor, Sweden. Ekmanner trained at Malmö School of Drama as well as at Stockholm City Theatre. Early roles include Helena in *All's Well that Ends Well* and Celimène in Molière's *Le misanthrope* (*The Misanthropist*). Since 1989 she has been a member of the Royal Dramatic Theatre in Stockholm, where she played in Mishima's *Madame de Sade* and in *The Misanthropist*, both directed by Ingmar BERGMAN, as well as several plays by Scandinavian playwrights. In addition to her stage career, Ekmanner appeared on film and television, playing Rebecca West in Ibsen's *Rosmersholm* and Mrs Alving in *Gengangere* (*Ghosts*).

Enekwe, Ossie Onuora Director, dramatist and poet, Nigeria. During his undergraduate days at Nsukka, Enekwe helped found the Oak Theatre, an amateur theatre company that has produced many of the very fine actors and theatre artists from the eastern part of the country. Enekwe's production of *Macbeth* toured the Eastern states of Nigeria between 1979–81 with a cast that included Toni DURUAKU as Macbeth and Esiaba IROBI as Duncan (and later Macbeth when Duruaku left); in 1983 he directed Ngugi WA THIONG'O and Micere MUGO's *The Trial*

of Dedan Kimathi, with Irobi as Henderson. One quality of Enekwe's direction is a certain thoroughness and attention to detail which he brings to bear on all his productions, and to this he adds his fondness for spectacle, colourful movement and high energy in the dramatic action. Enekwe has one published play to his credit, *The Betrayal* (1992).

Engel, Tina (1950–) Actor, Germany. Engel trained for the stage at the Staatliche Hochschule für Musik und Theater in Hannover. After seasons in Rendsburg, Bielefeld and Zürich, she joined the Schaubühne am Halleschen Ufer in Berlin in 1976. She is a powerful actor, radiating strong physical presence. Thus she is often cast as a character who is actively and decisively striving for power. Major roles include Celia in *As You Like It* (directed by Peter STEIN) and Irene Herms in Schnitzler's *Der Einsame Weg* (*Lonely Road*, directed by Andrea BRETH). In 1996 she appeared in Mishima's *Madame de Sade*, and in 1998 in Eduardo de Filippo's *Sabato, domenica e lunedi* (*Saturday, Sunday, Monday*).

Engel, Wolfgang (1943–) Director and actor, Germany. Engel trained as an actor at the Mecklenburgisches Staatstheater Schwerin, where he also began his career as an actor, adding directing to his credits in 1973. After working as a director in Radebeul and Berlin, he taught at the Hochschule für Schauspielkunst 'Ernst Busch' in Berlin. Drom 1980–91 he was resident director in Dresden, and began working in West Germany in the mid-1980s. After several seasons as resident director in Frankfurt, Engel became artistic director and manager of the theatre in Leipzig in 1995. Recent productions include *The Merchant of Venice*, Schiller's *Don Carlos*, *Titus Andronicus*, Goethe's *Clavigo*, *Richard III*, Woody Allen's *Bullets over Broadway* and Marlowe's *Edward II*. He regards the theatre as 'the place where it has to be beautiful, no matter how horribly'.

Englert, Jan (1943–) Actor and director, Poland. Englert trained at the State Theatre Academy of Warsaw and subsequently joined the staff, serving as dean of the Acting Department (1981–7) and as president (1987–93, re-elected in 1996). His acting credits include over 100 theatre roles in plays by Mickiewicz, Wyspianski, Gombrowicz and four world premieres of plays by MROZEK (*Krawiec* (*The Tailor*, 1977), *Letni Dzien* (*A Summer Day*, 1978), *Kontrakt* (*Contract*, 1985) and *Portret* (*Portrait*, 1986). From the classical repertory he played Hamlet, Dom Juan (Molière), Richard II, Richard III and Mark Anthony in *Julius Caesar*. He also appeared in more than seventy films and directed twenty-six productions, mainly for television theatre. After an early career playing heroic lovers, in his later years he developed specifically sarcastic and ironic qualities, leading to major success in characterizing people who face their internal conflicts or weaknesses, or hypocrites and tyrants.

Enklaar, Cas (1943–) Actor, The Netherlands. Cas Enklaar was a student at the Drama School in Amsterdam from 1965–8. He first appeared with Toneelgroep Centrum, but is best known for his work with the Werkteater, which he joined in 1971. This collective, which included Joop ADMIRAAL and – initially – Jan Joris LAMERS, attained great fame with their improvisational plays about social themes and everyday people. A movie addict, Enklaar devised a one-man show in which he played Joan Crawford (later taken up in Germany by television). After the collapse of the Werkteater in the 1980s, Enklaar did some freelance work (for example, *Silicone* with Marlies HEUER), briefly joined Toneelgroep Amsterdam, and then went his own way again. He has since been at the centre of various productions, working with director Matin

van VELDHUIZEN (as Blanche in Williams's *A Streetcar Named Desire* and an adaptation of Wilde's *The Portrait of Dorian Grey*), playing in Bernhard's *Minetti* and a dramatization of Kafka's *Letter to Father* (1994). Lanky, tough but with an almost feminine elegance, Enklaar has played in many films. He is a typical example of the Dutch 'actor-dramatist', creating his own work.

Enright, Nick (1950–) Dramatist, actor, director and translator, Australia. Enright was artistic director of the State Theatre of South Australia 1979–81 and head of acting at the National Institute of Dramatic Art, Sydney 1982–4. He is currently enjoying great commercial success as a playwright, but he is also an actor, a writer of musicals (such as his smash hit adaptation of *The Venetian Twins*) and has done much work with youth theatre. Enright's plays include a community theatre piece on the Australian Great Depression, *On the Wallaby*; a prize-winning, jetsetting farce, *Daylight Saving* (1989); an exploration of theatre personalities and their rivalries, *Mongrels* (1991, revised 1997); the depiction of a community in shock after a terrible crime has been committed, *Black Rock* (filmed 1997); an exploration of ethnicity and growing up in 1960s Australia, in *Playgrounds* (1996); and *Good Works*, which juxtaposes different time sequences as it unfolds the stories of two mothers and their sons. Enright also co-scripted the film *Lorenzo's Oil* with George Miller. Growing up and sexuality are subjects often treated in detail in Enright's plays.

Erkal, Genco (1938–) Actor and director, Turkey. In 1958, Erkal joined the amateur Young Players group. Between 1959–63 he worked as a professional actor. In 1963 he won an award for his successful acting in Jaroslav Hacek's *Aslan Asker Şvayk* (*The Heroic Soldier Şvayk*), staged by Arena Theatre. He worked with the Southern Germany Radio Orchestra to narrate Stravinsky's *Bir Askerin Öyküsü* (*A Soldier's Tale*). In the 1967–8 season he visited Rome, Paris, Berlin, Prague and London to explore theatre schools, regional theatres and people's theatres. In 1969 he founded Dostlar Theatre in Istanbul to stage and act in plays by Weiss, Gorky, Steinbeck, Brecht, Mehmet Akan, Macit Koper and Aziz Nesin. He also featured in films like *At* (*Horse*) in 1982, and *Faize Hücum* (*Rush for the Interest Rates*). His most famous acting was seen in Gogol's *Zapiski Sumasshedshego* (*The Diary of a Madman*), a one-man play that has been staged again and again since 1966. He also appeared in *The Alchemist* (*Simyacı*), written by Paul Coelho and adapted for the stage by Mehmet Ulusoy. This play was staged on 7 October 1996 in Paris at Théâtre de Liberté.

Erten, Yücel (1945–) Director, actor and designer, Turkey. Yücel Erten completed his theatrical training at the Ankara State Conservatory (Theatre Department) in 1969. In 1974, he graduated from the Folkwang Schule in Essen (Germany). As well as training to become a director, he specialized in stage and costume design. He has directed at most important theatres in Turkey and the self-styled Turkish Republic of North Cyprus, at the People's Theatre in Skopje, Macedonia, at the Yej Guardia State Theatre in Taskent, Uzbekistan, and at the Tiyatrom in Berlin. Between 1992–4 he was the General Director of the Turkish State Theatres. Some of his notable productions are Aristophanes's *Ekklesiazusai* (*Women in Parliament*, 1974, Germany), Brecht's *Der Aufhaltsame Aufstieg des Arturo Ui* (*The Resistable Rise of Arturo Ui*, 1979), Peter SHAFFER's *Amadeus* (1983), *The Taming of the Shrew* (1985), Chekhov's *Cajka* (*The Seagull*, 1986), Brecht's *Der Kaukasische Kreidekreis* (*The Caucasian Chalk Circle*, 1988, Yugoslavia), *A Midsummer Night's Dream* (1991, 1993) and Brecht's *Happy End* (1998). His awareness of space is obvious when he uses different playhouses for staging plays. Through his use of the stage, sound and light effects, costume and make-up, he highlights the plays' crucial points. His performers do not just 'enter' and 'exit': they become the characters.

Escobar, Ruth (1935–) Actor, Brazil. Trained at Schola Cantorum, École Superieure de Musique, Escobar owns a theatre building with three auditoria in São Paulo where more than forty plays and several international festivals were staged, events that were crucial for her development as a theatre woman. Her major stage credits as an actor include Irma in Genet's *Le balcon* (*The Balcony*), Jenny in Brecht's *Die Dreigroschenoper* (*The Threepenny Opera*) and Mme Merteuil in Heiner Müller's *Quartett*. Apart from acting and producing, Escobar is a political activist for human rights. She founded Women's Precinct and was twice elected for congress.

Espert, Nuria (1935–) Actor and director, Spain. Espert began performing professionally in the theatre at the age of twelve. Key roles came early with Juliet at sixteen and the title role in Euripides *Medeia* at nineteen. She founded the Compañia Nuria Espert with her husband Armando Moreno in 1959, and the company has since been producing plays almost continuously. She gained international recognition for her work with the Argentinian director Víctor García on a series of productions including the visually audacious *Yerma*, by Lorca (1971), set on a trampoline, and Genet's *Les bonnes* (*The Maids*, 1969) which toured extensively throughout Europe. More recently she has worked with García's contemporary Jorge LAVELLI on Lorca's *Doña Rosita la soltera* (*Dona Rosita the Spinster*, 1980) and Catalan directors Lluís PASQUAL and Mario GAS on Euripides's *Medeia* (1981), Wilde's *Salomé* (1985), *Haciendo Lorca* (*Making Lorca*, 1996) and Terrence MCNALLY's *Master Class* (1998). Her dark angular features and compelling intensity made her a leading tragic actor of her generation. Her directorial debut, a high profile production of Lorca's *La casa de Bernarda Alba* (*The House of Bernarda Alba*, 1986) with Glenda Jackson and Joan Plowright opened up other directing opportunities in Britain, where she has gone on to direct a number of operas including *Madama Butterfly* for Scottish Opera (1987) and *Rigoletto* for The Royal Opera House (1988).

Espinosa, Victoria (1926–) Director and actor, Puerto Rico. The 'grand dame' of Puerto Rican theatre, Victoria Espinosa has been active as a theatre director for over fifty years, directing more than 200 productions and working with nearly every theatre practitioner of note. She studied under don Leopoldo Santiago Lavandero at the University of Puerto Rico (BA, 1949). As a member of the faculty at the University of Puerto Rico, she has managed its Children's Theatre programme, as well as that of the Institute of Puerto Rican Culture (1984–8). As a director, Espinosa is known for her spectacular stagings of such works as Teresa Marichal's *La Isla Antilla* (*The Antillean Island*, 1992), which toured to Washington, DC and New York in 1996. Espinosa also has the distinction of directing the premier production of René Marqués' classic Puerto Rican drama *Los Soles Truncos* (*The Fanlights*, 1958). She is a recipient of numerous awards, including the Lifetime Achievement Award of the XII International Hispanic Theatre Festival in Miami (1997).

Estorino, Abellardo (1925–) Dramatist and director, Cuba. Abellardo started his career as a dramatist in 1956 with the publication of his play *El Peine y el Espejo* (*The Comb and the Mirror*, first produced in 1958). With his next play, *El Robo del Cochino* (*The Theft of the Pig*), he received the Casa de las Americas award. In 1962 he wrote a musical comedy, *Las Vacas Gordas* (*The Fat Cows*). He has written several other plays such as *La Casa Vieja* (*The Old House*, 1964, directed by Berta MARTÍNEZ), *Los Mangos the Cain* (*Cain's Mangoes*, 1965), and *La Dolorosa Historia del Amor Secreto de Jose Jacinto Milanes* (*The Painful Secret Love Story of Jose Jacinto Milanes*, 1973). He has successfully directed some of his own plays, such as *Ni un Si Ni un No* (*Neither Yes nor No*, 1980) and *Que el Diablo te Acompane* (*The Devil Will Be With You*, 1987). Estorino has also staged national and international plays such as Lope de Vega's *La Discreta Enamorada* (*The Discreet Woman in Love*), Ibsen's *Et Dukkehjem* (*A Doll's House*), Gambaro's *La Malasangre* (*Bad Blood*) and Luares's *Aristodemo*.

Eszenyi, Eniko (1961–) Actor and director, Hungary. She trained at the Academy of Theatre and Film Art. In 1983 she joined the Vígszínház company. Since 1990 she has also directed. Major roles include Ala in MROZEK's *Tango*, Mme de Tourvel in Christopher HAMPTON's *Les Liaisons Dangereuses*, Alison in Osborne's *Look Back in Anger*, Rosalind in *As You Like It* and the title role in Shaw's *Saint Joan*. Major directing credits include Büchner's *Leonce und Lena*, Kleist's *Das Käthchen von Heilbronn* and Brecht's *Baal*. With her ingenue looks and characteristic voice and articulation, she adapts the roles of tragic heroines or modern girls to herself. She is not simply an actor-director, but is capable of creating a unique world on stage, dominated by visual effects.

Euba, Femi Actor and director, Nigeria. His first credits as an actor include his gawky but appealing Lakunle in Athol Fugard's 1966 London production of Wole SOYINKA's *The Lion and the Jewel*. Before then he had also featured in another Soyinka play, *A Dance of the Forests*, in which he played Dirgeman, Slave Dealer and Forest Crier in 1960. In 1977 he played very convincingly the role of Colonel Moses, who was invited to berate Professor Bamgbapo (equally well played by Kole OMOTOSO). Productions directed include Akin Isola's *Madam Tinubu* in 1979; he was also part of the production team for Soyinka's *Requiem for a Futurologist*, which featured Jimi SOLANKE in the lead role.

Evangelatos, Spyros (1940–) Director, Greece. Trained at the Drama School of the National Theatre of Greece, Evangelatos currently serves as professor of drama at the University of Athens. He has directed more than 140 works of Greek and foreign classic and contemporary writers, as well as opera both in Greece and abroad (in the USA, Germany, Austria, Switzerland and Spain). He was general director of the State Theatre of Northern Greece (1977–80) and the Greek National Opera (1984–7). Since October 1992 he has been the president of the Greek centre of the International Theatre Institute. He has published widely, mainly on the theatre in Crete and the Ionian islands.

Evron, Gilead (1955–) Dramatist, Israel. Evron began studies at the Bezalel Art Academy but left after a students' rebellion, there taking up a job as an art teacher in a development town. His play *Geshem* (*Rain*, 1988) and the script to the television film *Lechem* (*Bread*), which received the Prix Italia, reflect his strong social involvement. His later plays, *Yehu* (1991) and *Har lo zaz* (*A Mountain Doesn't Move*, 1996), reacting to the murder of Rabin with a play about 16th century Japan, and *Lev Tov* (*A Good Heart*, 1999) all directed by Hanan SNIR at the Habima theatre, focus on issues of power and corruption.

Exelis, José (1961–) Actor, dramatist and director, France and Martinique. A product of the Théâtre de la Soif Nouvelle, Exelis played in many of their productions for the annual Festival of Fort-de-

France, including SOYINKA's *The Trials of Brother Jéro* (1986). A strong agile performer who has acted with a wide range of directors, most extensively with José ALPHA, he founded the company Derivaj in 1992. Music and movement are integral to his plays, as in the Chaplinesque two-hander on emigration, *Endeviran* (*On the Way Back*, 1986), in which the fantastic often figures largely, and also *Balade Overdose* (*Overdose Wandering*, 1988) and *Bagnia Terria* (*Land of Hard Labour*, 1990). In 1995 he won an award for his direction of Sylvestre's musical, *H.L.M. Story* (1995), staged in a four-storey building, while 1996 saw him orchestrating an outreach theatrical experience, *Paroles et gestes de vous, de nous* (*Words and Gestures from You, from Us*). With *Voyages* (1996) and *Wopso* (*Wicked*, 1997), he continues to explore the integration of text and music.

Eyre, Richard (1943–) Director, Great Britain. While artistic director at Nottingham Playhouse, Eyre encouraged new writing by Trevor GRIFFITHS, David HARE and Howard BRENTON. In 1980 he was invited to direct a classic at the Royal Court, and chose *Hamlet*. Eyre's concept of making the classic come to life for a contemporary audience worked well, assisted by a virtuoso performance in the title role by Jonathan Pryce. Since 1980, he has also directed at the National Theatre, whose artistic director he was between 1988–97, succeeding Peter HALL. Productions there include the musical *Guys and Dolls* (1982), *Hamlet* (1989), Jonson's *Bartholomew Fair* (1988), *The Night of the Iguana* (Tennessee Williams, 1992), *Richard III* (1992, with Ian MCKELLEN), *Macbeth* (1993) and a trilogy of plays by David HARE, *Racing Demon*, *Murmuring Judges* and *The Absence of War* (1990–4). Under his leadership, the Royal National Theatre has been very successful commercially and artistically.

F

Fabbri, Marisa (1931–) Actor, Italy. After training at the Scuola di Recitazione di Firenze, Marisa Fabbri started working at the Teatro Universitario in Florence and achieved national recognition while working at the Teatro Stabile of Trieste in the 1960s. Her major theatrical roles have been Thomas Middleton's *The Changeling* (1965), Luigi Pirandello's *I giganti della montagna* (*The Mountain Giants*, 1966), directed by Giorgio Strehler, Aeschylus's *Oresteia* (1972), directed by Luca RON-CONI, Sophocles's *Electra* (1975) and, more recently, Eugene O'Neill's *Mourning Becomes Elektra* (1997). Politically engaged (she worked with Strehler at the Gruppo Teatro Azione), Fabbri, who has also made a number of film appearances, has been offering innovative and challenging interpretations of a number of classical and contemporary female roles.

Fabre, Jan (1958–) Director, choreographer, dramatist and visual artist, Belgium. Following studies at the Royal Academy of Fine Arts and a number of exhibitions and small performances in his native Antwerp, Fabre startled theatre audiences with the eight-hour long *Het is theater zoals te verwachten en te voorzien was* (*It's Theatre as was to be Expected and Foreseen*, 1982), followed by the equally monumental *De macht der theaterlijke dwaasheden* (*The Power of Theatrical Follies*, 1984). In the late 1980s he moved

towards opera and dance, followed by a trilogy for the theatre, *Sweet Temptations* (1991) and *Universal Copyrights 1 and 9* (1995). Gradually, Fabre also started staging the monologues he wrote, including *Het interview dat sterft . . .* (*The Interview that Dies*, 1989), *Vervalsing zoals ze is, onvervalst* (*Fake the Way She Is, Without Faking*, 1992) and *Een doodnormale vrouw* (*A Very Ordinary Woman*, 1995), all with his muse Els Deceukelier, as well as *De keizer van het verlies* (*The Emperor of Loss*, 1996 with Dirk ROOFTHOOFT). As a visual artist, he is present in museums and exhibitions all over the world. Fabre's universe is the unique product of his own imagination: throughout his work his fascination with border zones becomes apparent, in between order and chaos, light and darkness, often transforming from one to the other through a process of metamorphosis.

Falk, Rossella (1926–) Actor and director, Italy. After a period of training at the National Academy of Dramatic Art in Rome, Rossella Falk made her theatrical debut at the Piccolo Teatro, where she worked from 1949–51. She then worked briefly with the Morelli–Stoppa cooperative and, for a period of almost twenty years, with Giorgio de Lullo, Romolo Valli and Anna Maria GUARNIERI at the Compagnia dei Giovani. Among her most interesting productions are Diego Fabbri's

La bugiarda (*The Liar*, 1955), directed by Giorgio de Lullo, Giuseppe PATRONI GRIF-FI's *Metti, una sera a cena* (*Someone is Coming to Dinner*, 1967) and, more recently, Schiller's *Maria Stuart* (1983), directed by Franco Zeffirelli, and Terence MCNALLY's *Master Class* (1998). Throughout the last forty years Falk has interpreted a large number of both classical and contemporary roles revealing a great spirit of adaptability and an elegant and refined acting style. Falk, who has also made a number of film appearances, most importantly Federico Fellini's *Otto e mezzo* (*Eight and a Half*, 1963), has recently started adapting and directing her own work.

Falls, Robert (1954–) Director, USA. Falls graduated in playwrighting and directing at the University of Illinois. From 1977–85 he was artistic director of the Wisdom Bridge Theatre in Chicago, and since 1986 he has run the Goodman Theatre, Chicago, where he places more emphasis on the classics than did his predecessor Gregory MOSHER. His approach has been called fearless and cinematic. Productions include Brecht's *Leben des Galilei* (*Life of Galileo*), O'Neill's *The Iceman Cometh* and Horton Foote's *The Young Man from Atlanta* (1997). His 1999 Broadway production of MILLER's *Death of a Salesman* received critical acclaim.

Faridi, Humayun (1952–) Actor, Bangladesh. Faridi's major achievements include performances in the role of Takkhak in Salim AL-DEEN's *Shakuntala* (with Shubarna MUSTAFA in the title role, Saisul ASAD as Vishwamitra, directed by Nasiruddin YOUSUFF, 1978), Chhaya-ranjan in Al-Deen's *Kittan Khola* (*The Fair of Kitta Khola*, with Shubarna Mustafa as Banasribala, Shimul YOUSUFF as Dalimon, Asad as Bayati, set designs by Jamil AHMED, directed by Nasiruddin Yousuff, 1981), Keramat in Al-Deen's *Keramat Mangal* (*The Epic of Keramat*, with Shimul Yousuff as Shamala, set designs by Jamil

Ahmed, directed by Nasiruddin Yousuff, 1985) and the title role in an adaptation of Brecht's *Arturo Ui* (directed by Klaus Klusenberg, 1988). Faridi is a charismatic actor whose virtuosity lies in presenting an exploration of the unknown and the unfamiliar with precise timing and striking effect. He is a member of Dhaka Theatre (one of the leading theatre groups in Bangladesh), and is extremely popular in film and on television.

Fatunde, Tunde (1951–) Dramatist, Nigeria. Among Nigerian dramatists, Fatunde is distinguished by his highly agit-prop style of drama and theatre structure and also for his radical advocacy of pidgin as a viable language for serious socio-political theatre since it is the language that most Nigerians, irrespective of class and education, can speak and understand. Because of his view of theatre as a weapon for exposing and challenging the status quo, the recurring theme of his plays is the unending economic and political exploitation of the masses in the context of an authoritarian state divided strictly along class lines. Plays include *Blood and Sweat* (1985), *No More Oil Boom* (1985), his first pidgin play, *No Food, No Country* (1985), *Oga, Na Thief Man* (1986) and *Water No Get Enemy* (1989). Fatunde's theatre is part of the new radical and revolutionary theatre aesthetic in Nigeria which includes playwrights such as Femi OSOFISAN, Bode SOWANDE, Olu OBAFEMI, Tess ONWUEME and the later plays of Ola ROTIMI.

Fedoryshyn, Iaroslav (1955–) Director and actor, Ukraine. In 1976 Fedoryshyn received his degree from the Ivan Kotliarevs'ky Institute for Arts, Kharkiv, Ukraine, and worked as an actor at different Ukrainian theatres. In 1989 he graduated from the Russian State Academy for Theatre Arts (GITIS), in Moscow, where he was trained as a director under the master Anatoly Efros. In 1990 Fedoryshyn founded the Theatre Voskresinnia

(Revival), L'viv, serving as its artistic director and producer. Since then he has staged nine productions including Nina Sadur's *Who are We...* (1992), Valerii Shevchuk's *Pochatok zhakhu* (*The Beginning of Horror*, 1993), Byron's *Cain* (1994), Chekhov's *Tri sestry* (*Three Sisters*, 1995) and Strindberg's *Till Damaskus* (*To Damascus*, 1997). The production of Claudel's *L'annonce faite à Marie* (*Annunciation of the Blessed Virgin Mary*, 1991) was a success at Edinburgh Festival in 1994, also winning a first prize at the International Theatre Festival Golden Lion, Ukraine (which he founded in 1992) as well as at the Gozhuw Festival, Poland. His productions embrace a psychological–plastic methodology which joins the school of Stanislavski, Kurbas and the plastics of Eastern Art.

Feit, Luc (1962–) Actor, Luxembourg. After graduating from the Staatliche Schauspielschule in Stuttgart in 1986, Feit joined the Stadttheater in Ingolstadt where he was a resident actor from 1988–90, playing Riccault in Lessing's *Minna von Barnhelm*, Merkur in Kleist's *Amphitryon* and Erich in Fassbinder's *Katzelmacher*. Thereafter, he could be seen as Wurm in Schiller's *Kabale und Liebe* (*Intrigue and Love*, 1990–1, Saarländisches Staatstheater), Cal in Koltès's *Combat de nègre et des chiens* (*Black Battles with Dogs*, 1991, Stadttheater Erlangen), Herr in Kandinsky's *Violett* (1994, Sprengelmuseum Hannover) and Doktor in Büchner's *Woyzeck* (1995, Volksbühne Berlin). He has also frequently featured in Frank HOFFMANN's productions, among others in Goethe's *Faust I* (designed by Jean FLAMMANG, with Pol GREISCH), in Schiller's *Die Räuber* (*The Robbers*), portraying the role of Karl Moor with great enthusiasm and dexterity, in *Macbeth* as Macduff (1992–6, Théâtre des Capucins, Luxembourg) and in Ondaatje's *The Complete Works of Billy the Kid* as Tom (1996, Théâtre National de la Colline, Paris). He also

appeared in a number of films, both national and international.

Fennario, David (1947–) Dramatist, Canada. Childhood poverty in a working-class district of Montréal influenced Fennario's Marxist approach. *On the Job* (1973) and *Nothing to Lose* (1977) deal with workers rebelling, under the influence of alcohol, against unacceptable working conditions. Fennario's plays continue to be successful due to his gift for dialogue and his ability to create convincing characters. *Balconville*, sometimes billed as Canada's first bilingual play, received the Chalmers Award in 1979. His 1990 play *The Death of René Lévesque* received mixed reviews. Fennario later left mainstream theatre to focus on community theatre work.

Fierstein, Harvey (1954–) Dramatist and actor, USA. Fierstien studied at the Pratt Institute, and first appeared as an actor in Andy Warhol's *Park* at La MaMa theatre (1971). In 1981 his autobiographical play *Torch Song Trilogy*, in which he also performed, proved a major success, winning several awards. The play deals with various views on male homosexuality, and is regarded as the first indication that a previously marginalized subject had entered the mainstream. Later, Fierstein wrote the book for the commercially successful musical *La Cage Aux Folles*. In another trilogy, *Safe Sex* (1988), Fierstein tackles the AIDS issue in his own particular way. A strong advocate for gay rights, he now works regularly as a film actor in supporting roles.

Filatov, Leonid (1946–) Actor, director and reciter, Russia. Following his graduation from Schukin Theatre College in 1969, Filatov worked as an actor with the Moscow Drama (Taganka) Theatre headed by Yuri LIUBIMOV, where he returned (after director Liubimov returned to Russia from exile) after two seasons with the Sovremennik Theatre.

Later he made a film based on the story of misfortunes of the Taganka theatre and its struggle with Soviet censorship (*Suns of a Bitch*). Main roles as an actor include the Master in Bulgakov's *Master i Margarita* (*The Master and Margarita*, 1977), and Baron and Don Carlos in Pushkin's *Pir vo vremya chumi* (*Feast amidst Plague*, 1989). Leading parts in two films about contemporary Russian life, *Ekipazh* (*The Team*, 1980) and *Zabytaya melodiya dlya fleity* (*A Forgotten Melody for a Flute*, 1987) brought him a country-wide popularity and film awards. Filatov is also a brilliant reciter and storyteller, writing poems and tales full of humour and biting satire. Now seriously ill, he has launched a television project 'Let' s Remember...' devoted to actors and actors who died unexpectedly or committed suicide. The programme was awarded a special prize by the National Television Academy.

Filho, Antunes (1929–) Director, Brazil. Filho received a scholarship from the Italian government for a traineeship with the Piccolo Teatro di Milano under Giorgio Strehler, from where he contacted the Berliner Ensemble, Roger Planchon and others. He was able to visit Japan at the invitation of the Japan Foundation. A member of the International Committee of Theatre Olympics, he is creator and founder of CPT, Centro de Pesquisa Teatral in São Paulo, where he still teaches and trains actors, discovering new techniques for the theatre through workshops and research. Filho is also involved in teaching at various other institutions. Among his many productions are Lorca's *Yerma*, Arthur MILLER's *The Crucible*, Wesker's *The Kitchen*, *Peer Gynt* by Ibsen, *Waiting for Godot* by Beckett, Edward ALBEE's *Who's Afraid of Virginia Woolf?*, and *Bonitinha, mas Ordinaria* and *O Eterno Retorno* by Nelson Rodrigues.

Finney, Albert (1936–) Actor, Great Britain. Finney trained for the stage at the Royal Academy of Dramatic Art. In the title role of Keith Waterhouse's *Billy Liar* (1961), he attracted major public attention. His physical stature and rich voice give him an impressive stage presence, and he excels in tough, earthy characters, including the title role in Osborne's *Luther* (Paris International Festival, 1961), Jean in Strindberg's *Fröken Julie* (*Miss Julie*, National Theatre, 1965) and Hamlet in Peter HALL's first production as artistic director of the National Theatre in 1975. Major parts since then have been in Arden's *Sergeant Musgrave's Dance* (1984), Lyle Kessler's *Orphans* (1986), Ronald Harwood's *Another Time* (1989) and *Reflected Glory* (1992), and *Art* by Yasmina Reza (1996).

Fisher, Rodney (1939–) Director and dramatist, Australia. Fisher started directing at the University of Queensland and then studied at the National Institute of Dramatic Art, Sydney. He has worked with all the major Australian theatre companies and has won numerous awards. For many years he was David WILLIAMSON's first choice as director (often working in collaboration with designer Shaun GURTON), and Fisher directed many Williamson premieres. Fisher's often scholarly directorial imprint is always clear in his productions, as is his political commitment: in 1969, in collaboration with George Ogilvie, Fisher wrote and directed *A Long View*, which attempted to present the white invasion of Australia from an Aboriginal perspective – this at a time when Aboriginal citizenship had only just been conceded (1967). While working as associate director at the State Theatre Company of South Australia in the 1970s, Fisher directed several explicitly socialist productions; Fisher also collaborated with Robyn ARCHER in writing and devising *A Star is Torn*. In 1992 Fisher directed Karin Mainwaring's bleak outback tragedy *The Rain Dancers*, a production which included film actor Bryan Brown's return to the stage after an absence of ten years. In 1994 Fisher directed *King Lear* for the Sydney Theatre Company.

Fissoun, Petros (1935–) Actor and director, Greece. Fissoun trained at the Karolos Koun Drama School and has worked as a leading actor at both the National Theatre of Greece and the National Theatre of Northern Greece, in plays by Chekhov, Pirandello, Shakespeare and Strindberg, as well as in all the major Greek tragedies by Sophocles, Euripides and Aeschylus. Besides stage work, which led him on tour to the USA, Canada, Romania and Spain, he has a distinguished career in radio, television and film. In 1983 he became a City Counsellor for Athens.

Flammang, Jean (1954–) Designer and director, Luxembourg. Originally trained as an architect and a town planner, Flammang began his career in theatre as an assistant to Johannes Schütz at La Monnaie in Brussels and at the Schauspielhaus in Bochum (Germany). Since 1990, he has worked as a freelance stage and lighting designer for the theatre and opera in Germany, Belgium, France and Luxembourg. His collaboration on Frank HOFFMANN's production of Goethe's *Faust* (1993, Théâtre des Capucins, with Luc FEIT) was particularly lauded. His debut as a director, Werner Schwab's *Die Präsidentinnen* (*The Presidents*, 1997, Théâtre du Centaure, with Michèle CLEES), was similarly warmly received. Flammang's formation as an architect is instrumental to his creation of theatrical spaces which, with the play of the actors, develop a life of their own.

Flimm, Jürgen (1941–) Director, Germany. Flimm was an assistant director at the Münchner Kammerspiele. After seasons as director in Mannheim and Hamburg, he worked freelance between 1974–9, was artistic director of the Schauspielhaus Köln, and between 1985–98 was artistic director of the Thalia Theater in

Hamburg. Among his productions are Büchner's *Leonce und Lena* (1973), Ibsen's *Peer Gynt* (1985), Chekhov's *Platonov* (1989), *King Lear* (1992), *Richard III* (1993), David MAMET's *Oleanna* (1994), *Tartuffe* by Molière (1996) and *As You Like It* (1998). His 'directorial focus centers on the examination of the individual caught within political, social, or psychic conflicts. Flimm views the nature of the actor's performance as critical in his productions, as is the scenographic space in which the actor is placed. He prefers concentrated psychological spaces which will frame the character and the action in an evocative, associational manner.'

Florentiny, Jeff (1951–) Author, director and actor, France and Martinique. An experienced secondary school teacher of English with a degree from the Université Antilles-Guyane, who has participated in several short courses in drama, Florentiny has moved from acting into translating and adapting plays from the West Indian repertoire into French and French Creole. He directed his highly successful version of Trevor Rhone's wry comedy of tourism, *Smile Orange* (*L'Orange*, 1991), for Bérard Bourdon's Poutyi pa Teyat group, and has translated Rhone's *Two Can Play*, WALCOTT's *Dream on Monkey Mountain* and some Trinidadian one-act plays. *Dodin* (*Dodin's Defeat*, 1996), based on a rueful short story by Samuel Selvon, was awarded the Sony Rupaire Prize for a Creole play, and has proved extremely popular with audiences in the Caribbean and in France. A personable actor on stage and screen, Florentiny enjoys the challenge of using the language varieties of the Caribbean to create meaningful comedy.

Flotats, Josep Maria (1939–) Actor and director, Spain. Having trained as an actor in Strasbourg, Flotats worked in Paris, for a year with Joan Littlewood and for an extended period at the Comédie Française.

He was invited back to Catalonia and ran his own subsidized company at the Poliorama Theatre in Barcelona from 1985–94. There he took up directing and recreated in Catalan some of the main roles he had performed in Paris, such as Rostand's *Cyrano de Bergerac* (1985) and the patient in Brian Clark's *Whose Life is it Anyway* (1987). His original French performance in Clark's play had won him a Best Actor of the Year award in 1980. Flotats demands long rehearsal periods, stresses the tempo of his productions and is proud of his attention to detail, often helping with the stage design and adapting texts himself. Other important plays performed at the Poliorama were Wedekind's *Frühlings Erwachen* (*Spring Awakening*, 1986), Musset's *Lorenzaccio* (1988), Molière's *Le misanthrope* (*The Misanthropist*, 1989) and SHEPARD's *True West* (1990). Following criticisms that he had directed no Catalan plays, he starred in his own monologue version of the writings of Josep Pla (1990) and adapted *Cavalls de mar* (*Sea Horses*, 1992) by Josep Lluís and Rodolf Sirera. Flotats lasted one year (1997–8) as the first director of the new Catalan National Theatre in Barcelona, where he directed Tony Kushner's *Angels in America*. He now works in Spanish as well as Catalan.

Fo, Dario (1926–) Director, dramatist and performer, Italy. Fo began his theatrical career as a set designer and performer of comic sketches and political cabaret. Together with his wife and long-term collaborator Franca RAME, he founded the theatre cooperative Nuova Scena (1968) which, under the auspices of the Communist Party, performed dialectical political pieces in unconventional theatrical spaces, including factories, universities, mental hospitals and prisons. In 1970 he and Rame discontinued collaboration with the Party and founded the theatre collective La Comune, which sought to expose the corruption and oppression of the capitalist system. Fo has written, acted and directed pieces for radio, television and the theatre, and some of his more theoretical writings are collected in *The Tricks of the Trade* (1991). Amongst his most notable plays are *Mistero Buffo* (1969), *Morte accidentale di un anarchico* (*Accidental Death of an Anarchist*, 1970) and *Non si paga, non si paga* (*Can't Pay, Won't Pay*, 1974). A versatile mime, improviser, opinion maker and political satirist, Fo has been one of the most authoritative voices of the Italian theatre scene, offering a commentary on the changes and transformations affecting Italian society over a period spanning from the late 1940s to the present day. In 1997 the significance of this contribution was recognized by the award of the Nobel Prize.

Fomenko, Peter (1932–) Director and actor, Russia. He graduated from the State Institute of Theatre Art. In the 1960s he performed several parts on television, and later joined the Taganka Theatre in Moscow. From 1972–5, Fomenko was a director at Leningrad Comedy Theatre, and from 1977–82 was its artistic director. In 1982 he left Leningrad for Moscow. His production of Tolstoy's *Plody Prosveschenniya* (*Fruits of Enlightenment*, 1985) won him popularity in the Moscow theatre scene, and *Caligula* by Camus at the Mossovet Theatre (1990) brought him his first theatre prize. In the late 1980s he started training actors at the Russian Academy of Theatre Art (RATI), and in 1993 he founded his own theatre based on a student group of RATI. Fomenko combines and promotes different traditions of twentieth-century Russian theatre: his passion for paradox and fantasy shows an impact of Meyerhold's ideas. At the same time, he is a thorough psychologist: his students successfully performed Turgenev's *Mesjac v derevne* (*A Month in a Country*) and Ostrovsky's *Volki I Ovcy* (*Wolves and Sheep*). He also presented quite an unusual interpretation of Pushkin's *Pikovaja Dama* (*Pique*

Dame, 1995). His most recent production was Chekhov's *Vaudevilles* (1997).

Font, Joan (1949–) Director and actor, Spain. Font did some training under Jacques Lecoq in Paris and has headed the Catalan performance group Comediants from its inception in 1971. Influenced by groups such as Bread and Puppet Theatre (with whom they have worked), Comediants have developed their own brand of open air carnival performance by reviving and adapting the traditions of Catalan fiestas with the use of acrobatics, music, huge masks and sophisticated fireworks. (Audiences frequently complain of burnt clothing after a show.) Venues used range from the aqueduct in Segovia to the Sydney Opera House. Their important productions include: *Moros i cristians* (*Moors and Christians*, 1975), *Sol, solet* (*Sun, Little Sun*, 1979), *Dimonis* (*Devils*, premiered in Venice in 1981), *La nit* (*Night*, 1987) and *Llibre de les bèsties* (*Book of Beasts*, 1995). In 1992 they organized the spectacular closing ceremony to the Barcelona Olympic Games, involving 850 participants. Since 1975, Comediants have mostly been resident in Canet de Mar, a Catalan coastal village. In 1981 they started the Festival of Street Theatre in T'àrrega. Despite a disastrous fire in 1990, Comediants continue to use their home base for teaching, making costumes and masks, and as a film set. The group tours all over the world. It also makes television programmes and produces books and recordings.

Forbes, Leonie Evadne (1937–) Actor, Jamaica. Trained at the Royal Academy of Dramatic Art in London, Forbes has performed in Jamaica, England, Ireland, Germany, Australia, the Caribbean, USA, Canada and India. She has appeared on stage, radio, film and television. Among her major stage roles are Cleopatra in *Anthony and Cleopatra*, Kattrin in Brecht's *Mutter Courage und ihre Kinder* (*Mother Courage and her Children*), Miss Aggie in Trevor Rhone's *Old Story Time*, Queen Ojuola in Ola ROTIMI's *The Gods are not to Blame* and Desiree in *A Little Night Music*. She is a lecturer in voice and speech at the Jamaica School of Drama. For her work, she has received several major awards.

Foreman, Richard (1937–) Director, designer and dramatist, USA. After receiving a BA from Brown University and an MFA in playwrighting from Yale, Foreman worked with the playwrighting unit of the Actors' Studio, writing in the style of Clifford Odets and Arthur MILLER. In 1968 he created the Ontological-Hysteric Theatre, 'which playfully altered perceptions of space and language. Influenced by the poet Gertrude Stein, his early plays, such as *Total Recall (Sophia=Wisdom): Part 2* (1970) and *Hotel China* (1971) introduced his highly formalistic uses of displacement, ritual, fragmentation and repetition, all of which have joined the currency of postmodernism. His scenography is rough, intentionally ugly at times, multi-referential and disjunctive. His early designs for his own plays, such as *Pain(t)* (1974) and *Rhoda in Potatoland* (1974) were typified by Victorian décor, strings criss-crossing the space, Renaissance framing devices, and a constant shifting of space and perspective.'

Fornés, Mara Irene (1930–) Dramatist, director and designer, USA. Born in Cuba, Fornés emigrated to the USA in 1945. She has worked as designer and teacher of creative writing and has directed her own and other plays. Among her plays and musicals are *Tango Palace* (1964), *Promenade* (1965), *Dr Kheal* (1968), *Molly's Dream* (1968), *Fefu and her Friends* (1977), *The Danube* (1982), *The Mothers* (1986) and *Oscar and Bertha* (1991). Although these deal with 'serious individual, national and global problems...they are most acclaimed for their zany, whimsical humour and the use of innovative cinematic techniques'.

Forsström, Ralf Åke (1943–) Designer, Finland. Trained at the Academy of Industrial Arts in Helsinki, he travelled to Japan, Indonesia, Egypt and the USA for further studies. He worked as artistic director of Pistolteatern (Sweden), as scenographer at the Swedish Theatre in Helsinki, Stockholm City Theatre and Helsinki City Theatre. In addition to theatre, he designed many productions for the Savolinna Opera Festival and Finnish National Opera. Recipient of several major awards, Forsström has also designed in other Nordic countries as well as the USA, France, Germany, Japan and China. Major credits include *The Tempest* (1982, awarded at Prague Quadriennale 1983), *Katariina Suuri* (*Cathrine the Great*) by Laila Hietamies (1996) and the musical *Pojken Blå* (1999). Through Ralf Forsström's work, scenography in Finland underwent a renewal, coming to be recognized as an independent art form. Modern visual arts have influenced his work, which he himself relates to kinetic lightworks and installations.

Foster, Gloria (1936–) Actor, USA. Foster trained for the theatre at the University of Chicago Court Theatre and with Bella Itkin at the Goodman Theatre. She is an African-American actor, who scored her major successes playing non-black characters: her many parts include Andromache in Euripides's *Troades* (*The Trojan Women*), Ranevskaya in Chekhov's *Visnevyi sad* (*The Cherry Orchard*, 1973), the title role in Brecht's *Mutter Courage und ihre Kinder* (*Mother Courage and her Children*, 1980), the mother in Lorca's *Bodas de sangre* (*Blood Wedding*, 1992) and one of the two characters in Emily MANN's *Having Your Say* (1999). Her work is embued with extraordinary grace and intelligence. She is one of the few great American actors in classic plays.

Foster, Norm (1949–) Dramatist, Canada. Foster is one of Canada's most produced and prolific playwrights. His best-known

play is *The Melville Boys*, which won the Los Angeles Drama League Critics Award in 1988. It is the story of two brothers, one of whom is terminally ill, spending a weekend together at a lakeside cabin, where they meet and have relationships with two sisters. Like much of Foster's work, it is romantic comedy heavily tinged with serious themes: the irrevocability of death or the repressiveness of religion. He has also written *The Affections of May* and *Wrong For Each Other* (1992), *A Foggy Day* (1998) and *Ethan Claymore* (1998).

Fox, Fernand (1934–) Actor, Luxembourg. After attending the Cours de Diction et d'Art Dramatique at the Conservatoire de Luxembourg, he became a comedian with the Compagnons de la Scène before joining the then new Kasemattentheater (founded by Tun Deutsch) as a resident actor in 1970. Besides performing in many plays, both contemporary and classical, on the company's stage in the ancient catacombs of Luxembourg, he hosted the Cabaret littéraire at his own café Theaterstuff. This and his many appearances on television and in film have made his a household name. However, he earned widespread critical recognition for his work as an actor with his portrayal of Willy Loman in MILLER's *Death of a Salesman* (1992, Théâtre des Capucins, with Patrick HASTERT) and of the double bass player in Patrick Süskind's monologue *Der Kontrabaß* (*The Double Bass*, 1993, Théâtre du Centaure) where his dexterity was praised.

François, Juliette (1925–) Actor, Luxembourg. After her training in singing, diction and dramatic art at the Conservatoire de Luxembourg, François co-founded the Compagnons de la Scène. She also acted in numerous musicals in the French language. Her most notable interpretations are The First Woman in Henri Ghéon's *Chemin de la Croix* (*The Way of the Cross*), the title role in J.P. Wenzel's *Loin* d'Hagondange (*Far from Hagondange*) and the Mother in Bernard Kops' *The Dreams of Anne Frank*. She has also featured in many of Pol GREISCH's plays.

François, Guy-Claude (1940–) Designer, France. François studied at the School of the Louvre and at the School of National Arts and Theater Techniques, and has worked with Ariane MNOUCHKINE's Théâtre du Soleil since 1975, appearing in *L'âge d'or* (1975), Mann's *Méphisto, The Novel of a Career* (1979–80), *The Shakespeare Cycle* (1981–4), Hélène CIXOUS's *The Terrible but Unfinished Story of Norodom Sihanouk, King of Cambodia* (1985), *The Indiad or the India of their Dreams* (1987–8) and *La ville parjure ou le réveil des Erinyes* (*The Perjury City or the Awakening of the Furies*, 1994), *Les Atrides* (1990–3) and Molière's *Tartuffe* (1995). He has also collaborated with architects such as Renzo Piano, Andrault and Parat, and Robert Reichen in the conception of performance stages, including the POPB of Bercy (Paris), the Cour d'honneur of the Papal Palace at Avignon, the IRCAM in the Georges Pompidou Centre, the Grande Halle de la Villette and the restoration of the National Opera of Paris. He won a major prize for his setting of the film *Molière* (written and directed by Mnouchkine) in 1979. He has worked with film directors as Bertrand Tavernier (*La Passion de Béatrice, La vie et rien d'autre*), Philip Kauffman (*Henri and June*) and James Ivory (*Jefferson in Paris*).

Fraser, Brad (1959–) Dramatist, Canada. Fraser won his first Alberta Culture Playwriting competition when he was seventeen years old. In 1981–2 his play *Wolfboy* premiered at Saskatoon's 25th Street Theatre. In 1986 Fraser became playwright-in-residence at Edmonton's Workshop West. His most famous play is *Unidentified Human Remains and the True Nature of Love*, which deals with young Edmontonians who search for true love and good sex against a backdrop of urban violence. The exploration of gay and straight sexuality, coupled with a unique voice that is brash and cynical, are hallmarks of his work. Recent plays includes a stage musical version of Craig Russel's *Outrageous, Poor Superman* (1994), and *Martin Yesterday* (1998).

Frayn, Michael (1933–) Dramatist, Great Britain. Frayn's play *Alphabetical Order* (1975) was his major breakthrough. Subsequent plays frequently took an ironic look at different spheres of life: *Make and Break* (1980) is set in the business world, while *Noises Off* (1982), Frayn's most popular success so far, deals with life in the theatre from the backstage perspective. *Benefactors* (1984) shows the problems involved in high-rise architecture. *Look, Look* was criticized for structural problems. *Here* (Donmar Warehouse, 1993) plays with the concept of time. More recently, the Royal National Theatre produced *Copenhagen* (1998), directed, as with many of the first productions of Frayn's plays, by Michael BLAKEMORE. Frayn has also been very successful with translations of Russian drama, mainly Chekhov.

Freibergs, Andris (1938–) Designer, Latvia. Freibergs trained in the Stage Design Department of the Latvian Academy of Art, where he has taught since 1971, currently serving as head of department. Between 1965–73 he was set designer at the Academic Drama (now National) Theatre in Riga (Sophocles's *Electra* and *Henry IV* as notable productions), and he undertook freelance work in Latvia, Russia and Estonia, both in theatre and opera. From 1971–91 he was chief scenographer at the Youth Theatre in Riga. Here he 'skilfully combined metaphoric imagery with functional and maximum use of space. Each production found the key to poetic originality'. More recent productions include Strindberg's

Spöksonaten (*Ghost Sonata*) and Racine's *Phèdre*.

French, David (1939–) Dramatist and actor, Canada. French is regarded as one of Canada's most important dramatists. He studied acting at Al Saxe Studio, Toronto, at Pasadena Playhouse, California, and at Lawlor School of Acting, Toronto. From 1960–5 he worked as an actor in Toronto. His first play, *Leaving Home*, was produced in 1972, directed by Bill GLASSCO. It is the first of four (to date) Mercer plays, which tell the story of a Newfoundland family immigrating to Toronto in the 1940s. In these plays, French's tone is sometimes bitterly realistic, as in *Of The Fields Lately*, and sometimes lyrical, as in the vastly popular *Salt Water Moon*. Apart from the Mercer plays, *Jitters* (1980), a play about the theatre, sometimes compared to Michael FRAYN's *Noises Off*, has been called the best English-Canadian comedy. French's recent play *Silver Dagger*, a mystery-thriller, opened at the Bluma Appel Theatre in Toronto in 1993.

Freyer, Achim (1934–) Designer and director, Germany. Freyer studied graphic design in East Berlin, followed by two years as master-student with Bertolt Brecht at the Akademie der Künste. After Brecht's death in 1956, Freyer initially worked as a freelance painter, returning to the stage only after the GDR authorities had prohibited his work. The early phase of design for the theatre is characterized by artificiality and non-illusionistic effects. In 1972 Freyer emigrated to West Germany, working with, among others, Claus PEYMANN in Stuttgart. For many years, Freyer concentrated on designing for opera, some of which he also directed. In the 1990s he has returned to the theatre, creating the sets for Claus Peymann's productions of Ibsen's *Peer Gynt* and *Zurüstungen für die Unsterblichkeit* (*Preparing for Immortality*) by Peter HANDKE (1997). In 1999 he directed the

first production of Franz Xaver KROETZ's *Die Eingeborene* (*The Native Woman*) in Vienna. As a director, he is influenced by his designs, working in images, and in the spaces he creates.

Friel, Brian (1929–) Dramatist, Ireland. Friel began writing short stories in 1950 under contract to the New Yorker magazine; his first radio plays were produced by BBC Northern Ireland in 1958. Recognition as a playwright of major significance came with *Philadelphia, Here I Come!* (1964), first produced at the Gaiety Theatre, Dublin, which foregrounded themes of exile and emigration indelibly stamped on the collective Irish consciousness. His subsequent prolific output includes *Lovers* (1967), *The Freedom of the City* (1973) and *Faith Healer* (1979). Together with actor Stephen REA, he founded the Field Day Theatre Company in 1980, which combined educational and political as well as theatrical goals, and which produced his celebrated *Translations* (1980), a savage critique of British colonialism and cultural appropriation in Ireland masquerading as a love story, and *Making History* (1988). International awards and acclaim continued with *Dancing at Lughnasa* (1990), directed by Patrick MASON at the Abbey Theatre, Dublin, which won a Tony award for Best Play at the Plymouth Theatre, New York. In 1994 he turned to directing his own plays, *Molly Sweeney* (1994) at the Gate Theatre, Dublin, and *Give Me Your Answer, Do!* (1997) at the Abbey Theatre. His version of Chekhov's *Djadja Vanja* (*Uncle Vanya*) was staged at the Gate Theatre as part of the 1998 Dublin Theatre Festival, directed by Ben BARNES.

Froboess, Cornelia (1943–) Actor, Germany. As a child and teenager, Froboess was popular as a singer and actor in light entertainment films. She took private acting lessons in Berlin and made her professional debut in 1963. After seasons in Braunschweig and freelance work in

Berlin, Hamburg and Munich, she joined the Münchner Kammerspiele in 1972. Her voice, gestures and facial expression make her one of the most intensive actors of her generation, whose many roles show preference for broken, seeking and doubting women: Sonja in Chekhov's *Djadja Vanja* (*Uncle Vanya*), Recha in Lessing's *Nathan der Weise* (*Nathan the Sage*), the title roles in Lessing's *Minna von Barnhelm* (directed by Dieter DORN) and Wedekind's *Lulu*, Ellida Wangel in Ibsen's *Fruen fra havet* (*The Lady from the Sea*), Cäcilie in Goethe's *Stella*, Viola in *Twelfth Night* and Xenia in Edward BOND's *Summer* (directed by Luc BONDY). She has worked extensively with Dieter Dorn and Thomas LANGHOFF.

Fudda, Asaad (1938–) Director and actor, Syria. Fudda trained in Cairo, and then went to Paris for an apprenticeship. He was appointed artistic director of Damascus National Theatre, then general manager of Theatre and Music in Syria. He directed over twenty-three productions during his career, including Dostoyevsky's *Brat'ia Karamazovy* (*The Karamazov Brothers*), Molière's *Dom Juan*, Lorca's *Bodas de sangre* (*Blood Wedding*) and Slawomir MROZEK's *Tango*. He collaborated with several Syrian and Arab playwrights, especially Sa'dallah Wannus from Syria. He directed his *An Evening with Abu Khalil Al-Kabbanni*, *The King is the King* for the Damascus National Theatre and *The Adventure of Slave Jaber's Head* for Weimar's National Theatre in Germany. Fudda attempted playwriting twice: *Hikaya Bila Nihaya* (*A Tale Without an End*) and *Hikayat Rifeya* (*Pastoral Tales*). He directed Syria's top stars, including Muna WASEF, Duraid LAHAM and his own wife Maha Saleh. He is a well-known actor, who played the lead in Arthur MILLER's *Death of a Salesman*, Shaw's *Saint Joan*, Sophocles *Oidipus tyrannos* (*King Oedipus*), Dürrenmatt's *Der Besuch der Alten Dame* (*The Visit*) and Gogol's *Zapiski Sumasshedshego* (*The Diary of a Madman*). He starred in thirty-five television serials and five feature films, winning three prizes in pan-Arab festivals.

G

Gabai, Sasson (1947–) Actor, Israel. After training at the Theatre Department at Tel Aviv University, Gabai became famous for his comic roles (in plays by Goldoni and Molière). For several years he worked at the Jerusalem Khan Theatre in the group directed by Mike Alfreds. Later he played character parts in plays by Hanoch LEVIN and SOBOL and in classics, such as Claudius in *Hamlet*. Gabai has also played extensively in films and television series, like LERNER's *Kastner*, a docudrama about the trial against an Hungarian Jew who negotiated with Adolf Eichman during the Second World War.

Gábor, Miklós (1919–) Actor and director, Hungary. He trained at the Academy of Theatre and Film Art and joined the Madách Theatre in 1941. Between 1945–54 he was a member of the National Theatre in Budapest, and between 1954–75 a member of the Madách Theatre. It was here that he first acted the role of Hamlet in 1962, a performance which brought him international fame. Further stages in his career were the Katona József Theatre of Kecskemét, the Népszinház in Budapest, and the Független Színpad. Since 1995 he has been a member of the Budapest Chamber Theatre. Major roles include Boy (Cocteau's *Les parents terribles* (*The Terrible Parents*)); Romeo, Jaques (*As You Like It*); Fool (*King Lear*); Iago, Richard III, Prospero, Shylock, Dom

Juan (Molière), Alceste (Molière's *L'avare* (*The Miser*)) and George (ALBEE's *Who's Afraid of Virginia Woolf?*). After numerous state and professional awards, at seventy-five he received the Life Achievement Award at the 26th Hungarian Film Festival. Since 1970 he has also worked as a stage director. Major projects have been Shaw's *Man and Superman*, MROZEK's *Portret* (*Portrait*), Goethe's *Torquato Tasso* and and Oscar Wilde's *The Importance of Being Earnest*. In 1988 Gábor exhibited his graphics and paintings. He has published his diaries and theatre theoretical writings in several volumes. He has been described as a theatre personality of enormous intellect who goes deeply into his roles and builds them up with lots of emotion.

Gaden, John (1941–) Actor and director, Australia. An actor of great range, Gaden performed many leading roles with Nimrod Theatre in Sydney during the 1970s. Gaden moved into directing when he became artistic director of the State Theatre of South Australia (1986–9). Here pragmatic programming helped the theatre recover from a period of disappointing box office income; Gaden himself was often both directing and acting. He co-directed several productions with Gale EDWARDS and their success as a collaborative team lasted several years. Gaden has played classical roles – Lear, Prospero,

Menenius, Leontes and Richard II, as well as having success with roles in STOPPARD, WILLIAMSON, SEWELL, HAMPTON and RUDKIN. He has performed in Robyn ARCHER's *Kold Komfort Kaffee* and *Scandals* and has directed big box office successes, such as *The Life and Adventures of Nicholas Nickleby*. Gaden's versatility is striking, but his forte is roles demanding intelligence, control and wit.

Gaitanopoulos, Jenny (1938–) Actor, Cyprus. She trained in the drama section of the Greek Academy of Music and attended the drama school of Karolos Koun. Major parts include many title roles in ancient Greek tragedies, Olga in Chekhov's *Tri sestry* (*Three Sisters*), Ranevskaya in *Visnevyi sad* (*The Cherry Orchard*), Mrs Venable in Tennessee Williams's *Suddenly Last Summer* and Hanna in *Night of the Iguana*, the title role in Schiller's *Maria Stuart*, Elizabeth in Arthur MILLER's *The Crucible* and Mother in Marsha NORMAN's *'night Mother*. She approaches her parts seriously, paying a lot of attention to characterization details, well assisted by her good, clear voice and excellent diction.

Gajos, Janusz (1939–) Actor, Poland. He graduated from the State Theatre and Film Academy in Łódź, where he began his career before moving to Warsaw in 1970. He has been a member of the Teatr Powszechny since 1985. Major roles include Astrov in Chekhov's *Djadja Vanja* (*Uncle Vanya*), He in *The Bench* by Alexander Gelman, Waclaw in *Maz I Zona* (*Husband and Wife*) by Aleksander Fredro, Kotchkaryev in Gogol's *Zenit'ba* (*The Marriage*) and the title role in *Macbeth*. He created many important roles for television, and has a distinguished film career. An actor with supreme technical skills, he specializes in characters hiding their deep inner life, layers of lyricism and sober experience under their rough appearance.

Galán, Eduardo (1957–) Dramatist and critic, Spain. A prominent literary critic throughout the 1980s, Galán turned his attention emphatically to theatre in the 1990s writing intelligently on the country's theatrical climate for a range of newspapers and magazines. His first professionally produced play, *La posada del arenal* (*The Inn on Sandy Ground*, 1990), co-authored with Javier Garcimartín and set in seventeenth-century Madrid, drew on classical antecendents. His most recent work, however, has been firmly located within the landscape of contemporary Madrid. *Anónima sentencia* (*Anonymous Sentence*, 1993) and *Mujeres frente al espejo* (*Women in Front of a Mirror*, 1996, directed by Juan Carlos PÉREZ DE LA FUENTE) have both chronicled issues around professional and private lives juggled in an ambitious and increasingly dehumanised culture. Also prominent in promoting theatre for children (as both an author of plays for children and President of the Spanish association for Children and Young People's Theatre (AETIJ)), Galán's theories on the role of theatre are documented in his 1996 published study *Reflexiones en torno a una política teatral* (*Reflections on a Theatrical Politics*). Since 1996 Galán has been General Subdirector of Theatre at the Ministry of Education and Culture.

Gálffi, László (1952–) Actor, Hungary. Gálffi trained at the Academy of Theatre and Film Art, joined the Vígszínház in 1975 and has been member of the company ever since. He is a frequent guest at other theatres and also a popular film and television actor. He put together recital evenings of poems by Villon and Rimbaud. At the 1996 Sitges Theatre Festival, he led an actors' training workshop based on Chekhov's *Visnevyi sad* (*The Cherry Orchard*). Major roles include Alan Strang (SHAFFER's *Equus*), Richard II, Mozart (Shaffer's *Amadeus*), Arthur (MROZEK's *Tango*), Orin (O'Neill's *Mourning Becomes Electra*), Krapp (Beckett's *Krapp's*

Last Tape), Prince von Berg (MILLER's Incident at Vichy), Edward II (Marlowe) and Iago. He has been described as an intellectual, sensitive, vibrant personality with boyish charm, a modern actor type with a capability for renewal.

Gallacher, Frank (1943–) Actor, Australia. Born in Great Britain, he moved to Australia in 1963 and has been a major actor for the Melbourne Theatre Company during the 1980s and 1990s. Gallacher has a tough, energetic stage presence which has served him well in a variety of dramatic roles, such as a no-nonsense Macbeth for the MTC (playing in tandem with Stephen SEWELL's Dreams in an Empty City), and an earthy, dynamic Caliban in Gale EDWARDS's MTC Tempest. He projected intense anguish as Eric, a man torn between the present and his POW past in Jill SHEARER's Shimada (MTC 1986); his John Proctor in Arthur MILLER's The Crucible (1991) was a raw, passionate man bursting with rage at his impotence and inability to stop the miscarriages of justice.

Gallis, Paul (1943–) Designer, The Netherlands. Paul Gallis is a self-taught designer. After working as an accountant and in a pet shop, he was introduced to the theatre by director Paul Vermeulen Windsant. His first set design was Eva Perón in the 1974 Holland Festival. Gallis is primarily known for his work with director Gerardjan RIJNDERS at both the Globe company (1977–85) and Toneelgroep Amsterdam (from 1987). Possibly his most daring design was for Jane Bowles's In the Summerhouse (1984), with its dark diaphragm-like frame that opened up into 'slots' through which the audience could witness the stage. Gallis's work often has a monumental trait (Ballet, 1990), although he is good at a lurid sort of realism too (De Hoeksteen (The Corner Stone), 1988). In the past years he has started to design for large-scale musicals, like Cats and Phantom of the Opera,

and for opera, such as Le Nozze di Figaro (The Marriage of Figaro) at the Nice Opera House, France. Gallis was awarded the Proscenium Prize in 1991.

Gambon, Michael (1940–) Actor, Great Britain. Although known as a reliable performer throughout his career, Gambon's breakthrough did not come until the 1970s, when he played Jerry in Peter HALL's National Theatre production of PINTER's Betrayal (1978). At the National Theatre, further successes include the title role in Brecht's Leben des Galilei (Life of Galileo, 1980), AYCKBOURN's A Chorus of Disapproval (1985) and A Small Family Business (1987), and David HARE's Skylight and Volpone (1995). For the Royal Shakespeare Company, Gambon played King Lear, Anthony in Anthony and Cleopatra (1982), and, more recently, in Yasmina Reza's L'homme du hasard (The Unexpected Man, 1998). Quiet and unassuming, Gambon develops a depth of feeling that comes across as genuine and thus lingers in the spectators' memory for a long time.

Gao Xing Jian (1940–) Dramatist, China. In the early 1980s, Gao became a dramatist in residence in Beijing People's Art Theatre, where he led Beijing's experimental theatre movement. From 1982–8 a series of his plays including Jue Dui Xin Hao (Absolute Signal), Che Zhan (The Bus Stop) and Ye Ren (Wild Man) were presented at Beijing People's Art Theatre under the direction of LIN Sao Hua. He also had strong influence on Chinese theatre as a theorist: he re-examined the Chinese theatrical heritage from the perspectives of Artaud and Brecht. In 1989 he left China and has since lived in exile in France, where he has published a number of successful novels and plays and exhibited his paintings. The latest production of his work, Bi An (The Other Shore) was presented by MO Sen in 1994 in Beijing.

Garas, Deszõ (1934–) Actor and director Hungary. After training at the Academy of Theatre and Film Arts, he worked for Madách Theatre (1964–76), 25th Theatre of Budapest, MAFILM, a company of screen actors (1977–90), Szigligeti Theatre of Szolnok and Mûvész Theatre (1993–4), and now works freelance. He is a versatile and popular artist with an acrid personality and talent for a grotesque-ironic style. Major parts include Cardinal Barberini (Brecht's *Leben des Galilei* (*Life of Galileo*)); Peachum (Brecht–Weill, *Die Dreigroschenoper* (*The Threepenny Opera*)); Sosias (Kleist's *Amphitryon*); AA (MROZEK's *Emigranci* (*Emigrants*)); Prospero (*The Tempest*); Merlin (DORST's *Merlin oder Das Wüste Land* (*Merlin or The Waste Land*)); and Estragon (Beckett's *Waiting for Godot*). Productions he has directed include Péter Müller's *Final Performance*, Emerich Kálmán's *The Csardas Princess*, Schwajda's *The Miracle*, *The Tempest* (at the Puppet Theatre, winner of Best Director at National Theatre Festival in 1988), and Bronte-Schwajda's *Wuthering Heights*.

Gas, Mario (1947–) Director and actor, Spain. Born in Montevideo, Uruguay, into a family of performers, Gas has worked prolifically since the 1960s, first within the university and independent theatre movement and then with the larger and more established companies including the Centre Dramàtic de la Generalitat de Catalunya, Compañia Núria Espert and the Centro Dramático Gallego. He has directed over thirty-five productions and performed in over forty pieces where his directors have included Lluís PASQUAL, Jorge LAVELLI and John Strasberg. As a director, he is admired for his eclecticism and versatility – he is equally at home with the classics, new writing, musicals and opera – and the clarity and elegant choreography of his productions. He has worked at the most important venues in Barcelona including the Poliorama (*Sweeney Todd*, 1995), the Liceu (*Un ballo in maschera*, 1988), The Romea (Schnitzler's *La Ronde*, 1986), The Condal (*¡Ai, doctor quina neurosi!* (*Oh Doctor! What a neurosis*, 1987)). Although largely associated with the Catalan stage, his productions for Madrid's Centro Dramático Nacional include Dürrenmatt's *Frank V* (1989), Williams's *The Glass Menagerie* (1994) and Valle-Inclán's *Martes de Carnaval* (*Carnival Tuesday*, 1995). Gas's first film as director, *El pianista* (*The Pianist*, 1997), featuring a superb score by Carles Santos, was a stylish study of two musicians marked by the strong visual sense which characterizes his stage work.

Gaskill, William (1930–) Director, Great Britain. Gaskill's early career in the theatre was influenced by his involvement with Joan Littlewood's workshop in 1955. He directed at the Royal Court, including Arden's *The Happy Haven* (1960), at the Royal Shakespeare Company and at the National Theatre. From 1965–73 he was artistic director at the Royal Court, where his productions include Edward BOND's *Saved* (1965) and *Early Morning* (1968). Since then he has been associated with Joint Stock (1974–83), an independent theatre company, and the National Theatre, where he directed Goldsmith's *She Stoops to Conquer* (1984), Bulgakov's *Black Snow* (1991) and Pirandello's *I giganti della montagna* (*The Mountain Giants*, 1993). Gaskill's work is characterized by clarity of argument, and a tendency towards a realistic style.

Gassman, Vittorio (1922–) Actor and director, Italy. After graduating from the National Academy of Dramatic Arts in Rome, Gassman rapidly emerged as one of Italy's leading actors. Best known for his interpretations of classical parts, such as the title roles of Vittorio Alfieri's *Oreste* (1950), directed by Luchino Visconti, *Hamlet* (1952) and Seneca's *Thyestes* (1953), which he co-directed with Luigi SQUARZINA, as well as his more recent interpretation of passages from Dante's *Divina Commedia* (*Divine Comedy*, 1997), Gassman was also a founding member of a number of influential theatre companies, with which he worked on both classical and contemporary plays. Amongst his numerous film appearances are *Riso Amaro* (*Bitter Rice*, 1949) directed by Giuseppe de Santis, *I soliti ignoti* (*Unidentified People*, 1958) directed by Mario Monicelli, *Profumo di donna* (*Scent of a Woman*, 1974) directed by Dino Risi and, more recently, *Sleepers* (1997) directed by Barry Levinson and also starring Dustin Hoffman and Robert De Niro. Whether on stage or on the screen, Gassman has time and again thrilled his audiences in daring interpretations of both classical and contemporary works. A uniquely passionate and eclectic performer, Gassman is not only one of Italy's most popular and respected actors, but also an icon of post-Second World War theatre and film.

Gavran, Miro (1961–) Dramatist and director, Croatia. With more than twenty plays to his credit, translated into many languages, Gavran is one of the most often performed Croatian playwrights of the 1990s. He also writes novels, short stories, radio dramas, poetry, children's plays and screenplays for film and television. He worked as a dramaturg (1986–9) and art manager (1989–92) at the &TD Theatre. From 1990–2 he worked as drama lecturer at the Creative Writing Workshop. In 1993 he founded the literary review *Plima* (*The Tide*) and worked as its editor for three years. Serious plays with a touch of melodrama include *Noće bogova* (*The Night of the Gods*, 1986), *Ljubavi Georgea Washingtona* (*George Washington's Loves*, 1988), *Čehov je Tolstoju rekao zbogom* (*Chekhov Told Tolstoy Goodbye*, 1989), *Shakespeare and Elisabeth* (1994) and *Zaboravi Hollywood* (*Forget about Hollywood*, 1996). He wrote several comedies

such as *Muž moje žene* (*My Wife's Husband*, 1991) and the grotesque *Pacijent doktora Freuda* (*Doctor Freud's Patient*, 1993). The main theme of his comedies is the male/female relationship (marital, love, adulterous) resolved without tragical consequences for the characters. The basic characteristics of his plays are fluent dialogues and unexpected turning points in the plot. His sentences are perfectly suited to the actors. In 1994 he added directing to his credits.

Gbadamosi, Gabriel (1961–) Dramatist, Nigeria. Gbadamosi is based in the United Kingdom (where there are other overseas-based African artists such as Wole SOYINKA, Ngugi WA THIONG'O, Tess ONWUEME, Zakes MOKAE and Esiaba IROBI). His best known works for the theatre are *No Blacks, No Irish*, *Shango*, *Abolition* and *Eshu's Faust*. He has also written a play for BBC television entitled *Friday's Daughter*. For a time he was writer-in-residence at the Manchester Royal Exchange Theatre, and most recently he worked with the European Theatre Convention in Portugal. He also travelled across West Africa as a Winston Churchill Fellow looking at theatre traditions and practices. Despite living in the United Kingdom, Gbadamosi's plays, especially *Eshu's Faust* and *Shango* are still inspired and informed by Yoruba myths and theatre sensibilities.

Geary, David (1963–) Dramatist, New Zealand. He trained as an actor at the New Zealand Drama School, but turned to playwriting, his first success being *Pack of Girls* (Downstage, 1991) which won the Bruce Mason award for most promising playwright. His more notable plays since then are *Lovelock's Dream Run* (Auckland Theatre Company, 1993, directed by Raymond HAWTHORNE) and *The Learner's Stand* (Circa Theatre, 1995, directed by Susan WILSON). His work (these three plays feature a female rugby game, Lovelock's race at the Berlin Olympics and a sheep-shearing shed) excites directors and actors through its imaginatively daring theatricality.

Geddes, Tony (1947–) Designer, New Zealand. He completed an Honours Diploma in Fine Arts at the Ilam School of Art, University of Canterbury, but it was only after some years as a secondary school teacher that his paintings caught the attention of Elric HOOPER and he was invited to design for the Court Theatre, Christchurch. Work like that for Tom STOPPARD's *On the Razzle* (1982) won him appointment there as full-time designer in 1983. He has since designed more than one hundred productions, recently acclaimed examples being Goldsmith's *She Stoops to Conquer* (1995) and Brecht's *Mutter Courage und ihre Kinder* (*Mother Courage and her Children*, 1996). Having to please much the same audience year by year, he enjoys working on plays which challenge through their novelty, or (like Shakespeare) through their familiarity, and like his usual director Elric Hooper, he avoids any conscious personal style, preferring to search out that appropriate to each play.

Geiogamah, Hanay (1945–) Dramatist and director, USA. He is a Kiowa–Delaware Indian from Oklahoma. In 1972 he founded the Native American Theatre Ensemble, and utilized the civil rights energies of the 1970s to create plays by, for and about Indians that are grounded in Indian aesthetics and values, and based in natural Indian idioms and gestures. In the early 1970s the company toured the USA and several European countries. In 1987 Geiogamah became director of the American Indian Dance Theatre. His published plays, *Body Indian* (1972), *Foghorn* (1973) and *49* (1975), mix politics, history, Indian familial and tribal traditions, humour, pathos and spirituality in an integrated style that is typical of Indian aesthetics and thought. 'Geiogamah's plays move fluidly through time, in a more cyclical and multilayered manner than Western linear chronology.'

Gelbart, Larry (1923–) Dramatist, USA. Gelbart is among the most distinguished writers of comedy in contemporary America. An early success was *A Funny Thing Happened on the Way to the Forum*, followed by *Mastergate* (1989), *Feats of Clay* (1991), the television series *M*A*S*H**, the film script for *Tootsie* with Dustin Hoffman, and the book for *City of Angels*, a very successful musical (New York, 1989 and London, 1993). His plays and screenplays reveal as much pain as laughter in his sharp observations of human nature. His 1976 adaptation of Jenson's *Volpone* captures the wit and cruelty of that work. In 1990, Gelbart received the Lee Strasberg Award for Lifetime Achievement.

Gélinas, Gratien (1909–) Dramatist and actor, Canada. An icon of Québecois popular culture, Gélinas created the urban backstreet character Fridolin for CBC radio in 1937. He went on to perform in many popular stage revues called Les Fridolinades, based on that character, which firmly established 'the tone of much of the country's subsequent neo-naturalist drama and comedy' and also 'the amiable Québecois Everyman character that would mark many of Gélinas's later works'. He wrote his most influential play *Tit-Coq*, a love story set against the backdrop of Québec society during the Second World War, in 1948. He founded the Comédie-Canadienne in 1957, a theatre company which produced most of Gélinas's work as well as the work of several other important playwrights, including Marcel DUBÉ. Gélinas's most recent play, in which he also performed, was *Le Passion de Narcisse Mondoux* (*The Passion of Narcisse Mondoux*, 1986).

Gems, Pam (1925–) Dramatist, Great Britain. Gems began writing plays only after her children had grown up. In the 1960s and 1970s she had been interested in the feminist movement, and in socialist politics. Feminism in its broadest sense is at the centre of her plays, such as *Queen Christina* (Royal Shakespeare Company, 1977), *Piaf* (Royal Shakespeare Company, 1978, directed by Howard DAVIES, with Jane LAPOTAIRE as Piaf), and *Camille* (Royal Shakespeare Company, 1982). Some critics consider such adaptations of existing material, or versions of Chekhov's *Djadja Vanja* (*Uncle Vanya*, 1992) and *The Blue Angel* (1992) as more successful than original plays such as *Deborah's Daughter* (1994). At the Royal National Theatre, John CAIRD directed *Stanley* (1996), with Anthony SHER in the title role of painter Stanley Spencer. In 1997 Gems added *Marlene*, a play about Marlene Dietrich, to her canon of bio-plays.

Germain, Greg (1947–) Actor, France and Guadeloupe. Tall, well-built star of LAOU's award-winning *Mélodie de brume à Paris* (*Misty Paris Melody*) and winner of the 1986 Senghor prize for best actor, Germain is equally popular on the stage and the screen. On stage he has played in several Bourseiller productions and took lead roles in Arrabal's *Bella Ciao*, *Othello* and TABORI's *Nigger Lover*. Cinema credits include the leads in *Marmito* and Adam in Aul's musical *L'Ile heureuse* (*The Happy Island*). Among his varied television roles, he has starred in four episodes of the television series *Médecins de nuit* (*Night doctors*) and the American production *Hi Champ*. 1997 saw his adaptation of WALCOTT's *Pantomime* for the Paris stage, which toured widely. In 1998 he spearheaded an ambitious programme of six plays representing the Théâtre d'Outre-Mer en Avginon (TOMA), a showcase of black French theatre, for which he contributed a one-man dramatization of Chamoiseau's runaway slave in *Le Vieux homme et le molosse* (*The Old Man and the Hound-Dog*). He is Presi-

dent of Cinédom+, which aims to forge links among artistes of the Caribbean diaspora.

Gessesse, Tsefaye (1937–) Actor, dramatist and director, Ethiopia. Gessesse, who began as an amateur actor, is second only to Tsegaye Gabre-Medhin as the foremost Ethiopian dramatist and director. He was for a while a resident director at the Haile Selassie 1 Theatre (now the National Theatre) in Addis Abeba when Gabre-Medhin was the general manager, and later took over control of the Ethiopian professional theatre company, The Ager Fikir, in 1974. In 1976 he assumed control of the National Theatre when Gabre-Medhin was removed as a result of problems with the actors. He too was sacked by the government in 1983 because of his efforts to improve the working conditions of actors in the company. Gessesse's plays include *Yeshi* (a play about the problems of urban prostitution), *Iqaw* (1975), *Tehaddiso* (*Renaissance*, 1979) which explores the issue of state repression and coercion, *Theatre Sidada* (*When Theatre Begins to Crawl*, 1989) which thematically and stylistically stretches the frontiers of both realism and supernaturalism. It is mainly as a director that Gessesse is best known, especially for his courageous style in mounting plays that challenged the status quo and for which he was never popular with the authorities.

Gielgud, John (1904–) Actor and director, Great Britain. From a theatrical family, Gielgud studied at Lady Benson's School and at the Royal Academy of Dramatic Art. One of the most important actors in Britain this century, Gielgud became especially renowned for his portrayals of Shakespeare characters; noble bearing and excellent elocution made him an ideal Hamlet (he played that part more than 500 times). Gielgud also appeared in modern and contemporary work, such as Gayev in Chekhov's *Visnevyi sad* (*The*

Cherry Orchard), SHAFFER's *The Battle of Shrivings* and PINTER's *No Man's Land*. His last stage appearance to date was as Sir Sydney Cockerell in Hugh White-more's *The Best of Friends* (1988). Giel-gud has also enjoyed a remarkable film career, and continues to appear in this medium.

Gill, Peter (1939–) Director, dramatist and actor, Great Britain. Gill began as an actor in 1957 and moved into directing by 1965. He directed *Twelfth Night* for the Royal Shakespeare Company in 1974, and *A Patriot for Me* by John Osborne in 1995. He has been associated mainly with the National Theatre since 1980. There he directed Christopher HAMPTON's *Tales from Hollywood* (1983), Sam SHEPARD's *Fool for Love* (1984) and O'Casey's *Juno and the Paycock* (1989). Gill ran the National Theatre Studio, designated to encourage new writing. In 1997, his new play *Cardiff East* was premiered at the Royal National Theatre, designed by Alison CHITTY.

Gillies, Max (1941–) Actor, Australia. Gillies was a drama teacher for many years before becoming involved with the politically committed, left-wing Austra-lian Performing Group at the Pram Fac-tory in Melbourne. There he played in group-devised works and political revues. Gillies is a great impersonator, particu-larly of right-wing politicians, and this talent has been put to extensive use in various satirical theatre shows and on television. Gillies had an early success with the one man show *A Stretch of the Imagination* by Jack Hibberd, which he revived for the Melbourne and Sydney Theatre Companies in 1991. Gillies also created roles in the early Stephen SEWELL plays *Traitors* and *Welcome the Bright World*, and he has played in AYCKBOURN's *A Chorus of Disapproval* for the MTC. His manic head of department in David WILLIAMSON's *The Department* was mem-orable. Gillies has also toured Australia

with *'Allo 'Allo*. In 1996 he performed the satirical revue *Gillies Live at the Club Republic*.

Gimeno, Luis (1927–) Actor and director, Mexico. He attended classes in piano, violin, singing and music theory at the Conservatorio Superior de Musica, Barce-lona, while studying philosophy at the University. In Mexico, he started as an actor with the Dramatic Art School, which belongs to the National Institute of Fine Arts. A character actor, he played the central roles in Gogol's *Revizor* (*The Government Inspector*), Molière's *Le bourgeois gentilhomme* (*The Citizen as Nobleman*), *King Lear* and Falstaff in *The Merry Wives of Windsor*, Ben Jon-son's *Volpone* and many others, covering the whole range of theatrical genres. In addition to his acting career, he served as director of the National Theatre Com-pany for eighteen years, and has directed many operas.

Glass, Joanna (1936–) Dramatist, Ca-nada. Glass made her breakthrough into professional theatre with two one-act companion pieces, *Canadian Gothic* and *American Modern*, at the Manhattan Theatre Club in 1972. Her play *Artichoke* (1979) was a critical success, both in Canada and the United States. In 1984, *Play Memory* was performed on Broad-way and received a Tony nomination. The work is largely autobiographical, dealing with a dysfunctional family – in particu-lar, with the relationship of an abusive, alcoholic father and his young daughter – in Saskatoon. *If We Are Women* (1995) has been produced across Canada. A compelling lyricism and an evocative use of language are hallmarks of Glass's work.

Glassco, Bill (1935–) Director and actor, Canada. He studied acting and directing at New York University. In 1971, Glassco, together with his wife Jane, founded Tarragon Theatre in Toronto, dedicated to new Canadian writing. Productions of plays by David FRENCH (*Leaving Home*, 1972), and David Freeman as well as English-language premieres of plays by Michel TREMBLAY proved very successful. Since 1982, Glassco has been working mainly freelance, apart from four years as artistic director of CentreStage in Toronto (1985–9). Glassco has built a reputation for nurturing new and exciting Canadian dramatists; he has developed long-standing professional relationships with writers like Freeman and French as well as Michel Marc Bouchard and Guy Vanderhaege. 'He has called the impulse behind his work the need for the "celebratory communication" with the audience.'

Glittenberg, Rolf (1945–) Designer, Germany. Glittenberg studied design with Teo Otto and Wilfried MINKS. After freelance designs in Munich, Bochum, Zürich, Hamburg and Köln, Glittenberg, often working with his wife Marianne, became head of design at Jürgen FLIMM's Thalia Theater in Hamburg in 1986. Early designs include Luc BONDY's productions of Edward BOND's *The Sea*, Ibsen's *Gengangere* (*Ghosts*), Beckett's *Happy Days* and *Macbeth*. More recently, he has designed Büchner's *Woyzeck*, *Twelfth Night*, Klaus POHL's *Die Schöne Fremde* (*The Beautiful Stranger*) and *Romeo and Juliet* (Thalia Theater, Hamburg, 1997), Thomas HÜRLIMANN's *Das Lied der Heimat* (*The Song of Homeland*, Zürich, 1998), and Brecht's *Baal* and Ibsen's *Fruen Fra Havet* (*The Lady from the Sea*, Thalia Theater Hamburg, 1998). His scenic spaces and costumes are often characterized by polished elegance, frequently (and at times to excess) taking up whatever is currently fashionable.

Goh, Boon Teck (1971–) Dramatist and director, Singapore. The latest addition to the Singapore theatre scene, Goh is the artistic director of one of the most innovative and dynamic professional theatre companies in Singapore, the Toy Factory Theatre Ensemble. Goh began his career as an actor in 1989 under the tutelage of Kuo Pao Kun and has since graduated to becoming a full-time dramatist and director. Effectively bilingual in both Chinese and English, Goh experiments extensively with style and material both east and west. His works include site-specific performances like *OsEAN* (1993), which was performed at the pool of the Pan Pacific Hotel in Singapore; *Posteterne* (1992), which was a postmodern re-writing of the Chinese folklore of the Butterfly Lovers, and his most acclaimed work to date, *Titoudao* (1994), which he wrote and directed. A collage of memories and events from his mother's life as an Chinese opera performer, the play was muscular in structure and thought-provoking in its issues. Recently returning from his BA degree in drama from Rose Bruford College, London, Goh has since directed a total of five plays in 12 months, ranging from a musical (*Guys And Dolls*) to a Chinese Classic from China (Cao Yu's *Storm*).

Gökçer, Cüneyt (1920–) Director and actor, Turkey. A graduate from the Theatre Department of the Ankara State Conservatory in 1942, Gökçer worked with Carl Ebert as stage assistant and as stage and mime instructor. As a director, he first staged Goethe's *Faust* in 1946. Between 1947–83 he was a director and actor at the Turkish State Theatres, serving as general director of the Turkish State Theatres between 1958–78 and between 1980–3. In addition, he staged and acted in plays in Paris, Athens, Venice and Cyprus. Major credits include Sophocles's *Antigone*, *Julius Caesar*, *Twelfth Night* and Wilder's *Our Town*, as well as musicals such as *Kiss Me Kate*, *Fiddler on the Roof* and *My Fair Lady*. Directing credits include Arthur MILLER's *The Crucible* (1970), Max Frisch's *Andorra* (1972), SHAFFER's *Equus* (1975) and ALBEE's *Who's Afraid of Virginia Woolf?*. He also directed various operas and has acted in film and on television. His most recent production, Terence MCNALLY's *Master Class* (1997, Ankara State Theatre), shows the inexhaustible strength of his artistic skill. His respect for the dramatist will always dominate temptations of dazzling an audience with staging or design effects.

Göncz, Árpád (1922–) Dramatist, Hungary. Göncz studied law and agriculture. Because of his involvement in the 1956 revolution, he was sentenced to life imprisonment in 1958 and was released by amnesty in 1963. He has been writing since his youth, but until 1965 none of his workplaces were connected to his writing or translating activities. Between 1965–90 he worked as a freelance writer and translator, and since 1990 he has been the President of the Hungarian Republic. His play *Magyar Médea (Hungarian Medea)*, dedicated to and first performed by the late actress Mari Szemes, has been translated into several languages and also performed abroad. The world premiere of his play *Bars* was held in Timisoara (Romania) at the Csiky Gergely Theatre in 1992. (The play was translated into Spanish in 1995). His play *Kö a kövön (Stone upon Stone)* was performed at the Budapest National Theatre, and the *Pisszimista komédia (Pessimistic Comedy)* at the Merlin Theatre. Six of his plays were published in 1990 under the title *Mérleg (Balance)*. His plays seek answers to the most important dilemmas of his own generation. As he puts it, he builds up a 'crystal-net' for himself and his contemporaries in the fluidity of the age.

Goldflam, Arnošt (1946–) Dramatist, director and actor, Czech Republic. Goldflam studied directing at the Brno Academy of Performing Arts. Since 1978, he has worked as a resident director (and actor) in the experimental Hanácké theatre in Prostejov (now the HaDiO theatre in Brno), where he presented a number of

his own plays including *Závist (Jealousy, 1981)*, *Návrat ztraceného syna (The Return of the Lost Son, 1983)*, *Písek (Sand, 1988)* and *Nekolik historek zde zivota Bédi Jelínka (Stories from the Life of Béd'a Jelínek, 1995)*. A frequent theme of his plays is the conflict of generations and the 'history of the soul' in a social context. His loose structure relates to the anti-illusionary and associative style of HaDiO theatre. Goldflam also wrote several monodramas (*Biletárka (The Usherette)*, 1983; *Cervená knihovna (Romance Novels)*, 1985), concentrating on character distortion and unmasking the psychic complex. On the domestic stage he has directed Kafka's *Der Prozeß (The Trial, 1989)*, Ladislav Klíma's drama *Lidská tragikomedie (Human Tragicomedy, (1991)* and Dostoyevsky's *Idiot (The Idiot, 1993)*.

Gómez, José Luis (1940–) Actor and director, Spain. He attended the Instituto Dramático of Westfalia and later studied with Lecoq, Grotowski, and Strasberg. After working in Germany as an actor, he went back to Madrid and in the early 1970s directed Kafka's *Bericht an eine Akademie (Report to an Academy)* and Büchner's *Woyzeck*. Between 1979–81 he was co-director (with Nuria ESPERT and José Támayo) of the Centro Dramático Nacional. His inaugural production as artistic director of the Teatro Español of Calderón's *La vida es sueño (Life is a Dream)* was perceived as one of the theatrical highlights of the year. He revived it at the Paris Odéon-Théâtre de l'Europe in 1992. During the 1980s he also enjoyed a conspicuous success with a revisionist much acclaimed Civil War comedy ¡Ay, Carmela! (1986) by José SANCHÍS SINISTERRA, later made into a film by Carlos Saura. During the 1990s he has gone on to found the Teatro de la Abadía in Madrid. Both a theatre and theatre school, its productions have offered audiences imaginative interpretations of key Spanish plays. As an actor, he has worked with a range of film and theatre directors including José Carlos PLAZA, for whom he took the title role in a contentious production of *Hamlet* (1989), Carlos Saura, Ricardo Franco and Pilar Miró.

Gosch, Jürgen (1943–) Director and actor, Germany. Gosch trained at the Schauspielschule in East Berlin (1962–4). Between 1965–79 he worked as an actor and director with various GDR theatres. Jürgen FLIMM invited him to join the Schauspielhaus in Köln as director between 1981–5. He also worked at the Thalia Theater in Hamburg in Flimm's first season as artistic director there. Between 1988–90 Gosch, many of whose productions have been associated with great rituals, was co-artistic director of the Schaubühne am Lehniner Platz in Berlin. He directed Beckett's *Endgame* in Bochum (1991) and Chekhov's *Djadja Vanja* (*Uncle Vanya*) in Frankfurt (1992). Since 1993 he has been a director with the Deutsches Theater in Berlin, where productions include Kleist's *Amphitryon* (1993, with Daniel MORGENROTH), *As You Like It* (1996), Beckett's *Waiting for Godot* (1996), *A Midsummer Night's Dream* (1997), Peter HANDKE's *Zurüstungen für die Unsterblichkeit* (*Preparing for Immortality*, 1997) and Schiller's *Die Jungfrau von Orleans* (*The Virgin of Orleans*, 1998).

Gotanda, Philip Kan (1950–) Dramatist and director, USA. As a third-generation Japanese American, Gotanda is the leading Asian American dramatist. All his plays deal with diaspora experience in the USA. *Song for a Nisei Fisherman* (1980) and *The Wash* (1987) have been characterized as lyrical and naturalistic, whereas *Yankee Dawg You Die* (1987) is more satirical, and *Fish Head Soup* (1991) is surreal. 'His best work conveys the Asian–American milieu with a directness and compassion that render it universal.'

Göthe, Staffan (1944–) Dramatist, actor and director, Sweden. Göthe studied at the University of Uppsala and trained at the Drama School in Gothenburg. In the 1970s he contributed to a revival of Swedish children's theatre. In his plays he uses the imagination, freedom of form and story-telling techniques. Titles include *En Natt in Februari* (*One Night in February*), *Den Gråtande Polisen* (*The Crying Policeman*) and *En Uppstoppad Hund* (*A Stuffed Dog*). Although anchored in reality, Göthe would never write in a purely realistic style, preferring to use all the theatre's devices and instruments at his disposal.

Gotscheff, Dimiter (1943–) Director, Bulgaria and Germany. Born in Bulgaria, Gotscheff worked as a student of and assistant to director Benno Besson. In 1979 he returned to Bulgaria, where he established his reputation as a director in 1983 with a production of Heiner Müller's *Philoktet*. Since 1986 he has worked mainly in Germany, in Köln and Düsseldorf. Gotscheff's productions, which include Strindberg's *Fröken Julie* (*Miss Julie*, 1991), and Klaus POHL's *Die schöne Fremde* (*The Beautiful Stranger*, 1992), 'show the state of our civilization through passions and tell us about the beauty and the pain of the body'. More recent productions include Lorca's *Dona Rosita* and Walser's *Die Zimmerschlacht* (*The Battle in the Room*) in Bochum (1996), *Texte* by Heiner Müller in Düsseldorf (1996), Müller's *Germania 3 Gespenster am toten Mann* (*Germania 3 Ghosts at the Dead Man*) in Hamburg (1997), PINTER's *Ashes to Ashes* (1998, Bochum), and *King Lear* (1999, Hamburg, with Josef Bierbichler in the title role).

Gow, Michael (1955–) Dramatist, actor and director, Australia. Gow's most popular play *Away* has been an international success. Gow has great energy for and dedication to promoting Australian work overseas. *Sweet Phoebe* (1995) about the breakdown of a yuppie couple's relationship, played in London and South Africa as well as Australia. Gow has also worked a great deal with young people. *The Kid* (1986) is a dark comedy that deals with nightmare crises involving young people, and *All Stops Out* was written for young people dealing with pressure over examinations. Gow's plays often deal with families and generational conflict, with crises in sexuality and with cultural colonization; the latter reaches its most explicit statement in *Europe*, a parable of the theatrical relations between old Europe and young Australia. *Furious* centres around a gay playwright trying to come to terms with his family history and with criticism of his work. Gow is an associate director with the Sydney Theatre Company and has described himself as 'the champion of the no-interval play'.

Graber, Yossi (1933–) Actor, Israel. Graber trained at the Royal Academy of Dramatic Art, London. After several years in South Africa and England where he mainly played roles as a foreigner, his career led him to the Haifa municipal theatre and later to the Cameri Tel Aviv municipal theatre, with numerous major roles like the King (in *The King and I*), Harpagon in Molière's *L'avare* (*The Miser*), the Priest in Brecht's *Mutter Courage und ihre Kinder* (*Mother Courage and her Children*) and Shylock in *The Merchant of Venice*. Graber has also created numerous productions for children, played on television as well as in the puppet theatre, together with Arik Smith, and has played in both Israeli and foreign films.

Grant, Tracy (1961–) Designer, New Zealand. Grant began work as a window dresser before becoming stage manager at Centrepoint Theatre, Palmerston North, in 1981–2. She then moved into design, training and establishing herself in her profession at the Mercury Theatre, Auckland, where she became head of design

and, in 1987, associate director. In that year, a travelling fellowship enabled her to study theatre design in America, Britain and Europe. Since 1991 she has been a freelance designer. Amongst admired work, for both design and costumes, are Chekhov's *Wild Honey* (1985) at the Mercury, and Brian FRIEL's *Dancing at Lughnasa* (1995) and Tom STOPPARD's *Arcadia* (1997), both for the Auckland Theatre Company. She has acknowledged the influence in her work of Josef SVOBODA and Frank Lloyd Wright. Her most celebrated success has been in operatic design both in New Zealand and Australia. In 1997 she gained a Bachelor of Spatial Design degree from the Auckland Institute of Technology.

Grashof, Christian (1943–) Actor, Germany. Grashof trained for the stage at the Staatliche Schauspielschule in East Berlin. After three years in Karl-Marx-Stadt (Chemnitz), he joined the Deutsches Theater in Berlin in 1970 where he has remained since, apart from guest appearances at Jürgen FLIMM's Thalia Theater in Hamburg and two seasons (1990–2) at the Schiller Theater in Berlin. His career is closely associated with director Alexander LANG, whose main protagonists he has played, including Danton and Robespierre in Büchner's *Danton's Tod* (*Danton's Death*, 1981). More recent productons include Chekhov's *Djadja Vanja* (*Uncle Vanya*, 1995, where he played the title role), Beckett's *Waiting for Godot* (1996) and Rosmer in Ibsen's *Rosmersholm*. He excels in playing unhappy lovers, or vain, self-centred windbags with a nervous presence which, however, can be threatened on occasion by crude mannerisms.

Gravina, Carla (1941–) Actor, Italy. Carla Gravina's career started in the film industry in the mid-1950s when she appeared in films such as Martin Ritt's *Jovanka e le altre* (*Five Branded Women*, 1960), Nanni Loy's *Un giorno da leone* (*A Day as a Lion*, 1961), Gianni Puccini's *I sette* *fratelli Cervi* (*The Seven Brothers Cervi*, 1968) and, more recently, Ettore Scola's *La terrazza* (*The Terrace*, 1980) and Margarethe von Trotta's *Il lungo silenzio* (*The Long Silence*, 1993). In the theatre, she attained national fame in *Romeo and Juliet* (1960), Peter Weiss's *Marat/Sade* (1967) and Luigi Pirandello's *Come tu mi vuoi* (*As You Desire Me*, 1985). Gravina, who is also very active in politics and was a member of parliament between 1980–3, is one of Italy's most popular actors. Her performance skills are versatile, characterized by a bold and eclectic capacity to reinvent herself both on stage and on screen.

Gray, Simon (1926–) Dramatist, Great Britain. Gray attended Dalhousie University, the University of Halifax in Nova Scotia, Canada, and Trinity College, Cambridge, and for many years was lecturer in English at Queen Mary and Westfield, University of London. Following *Wise Child* (1967), Gray had his first major success with *Butley*, directed by Harold PINTER, who has become closely associated with Gray's work, and with Alan BATES in the title role. Further successful plays were *Otherwise Engaged* (1975), *Close of Play* (1979, National Theatre, with Sir Michael Redgrave), *Quartermain's Terms* (1981), *Melon* (1987) and *Hidden Laughter* (1990). *Cell Mates* (1995) was a critical success on the opening night but had to close quickly following the sudden departure of the main actor. In 1997, *Life Support* was directed by Harold Pinter and starred Alan Bates.

Gray, Spalding (1941–) Actor and dramatist, USA. Gray established himself initially as a traditional actor, and joined Richard Schechner's Performance Group in 1970. Together with Elizabeth LE COMTE and others, he founded Wooster Group in New York in 1975. His series of thirteen highly autobiographical monologues, including *Swimming to Cambodia*

(1984) have been highlighted as without peer. Gray has the mesmerizing ability to transport his audience into his own particular world and allow them to find some part of themselves there.

Greene, Graham (1952–) Actor, Canada. Greene was born on the Six Nations Reserve near Brantford, Ontario. In the 1980s Greene played several roles at Théâtre Passe Muraille, including the Crow in Linda GRIFFITH's *Jessica*. In 1989, he won a Dora Mavor Moore Award for best actor as Pierre St Pierre in Tomson HIGHWAY's *Dry Lips Oughta Move To Kapuskasing*. Major successes in film include an emotionally disturbed Lakota Vietnam veteran in the motion picture *PowWow Highway*, Kicking Bird in Kevin Costner's *Dances With Wolves* (for which he won an Academy Award nomination) and Arthur, a murderous native activist, in the film *Clearcut* (1991). His acting is distinguished by a strong physical presence and a quirky sense of humour.

Greenwood, Jane (1934–) Designer, USA. Born in Britain, Greenwood trained at the Liverpool Art School as well as the Central School of Arts and Crafts in London. She began her career as a costume designer in Britain in 1957, moving to the USA in 1963. She has designed costumes for numerous classical or contemporary plays, such as *Measure for Measure* (1973), Chekhov's *Cajka* (*The Seagull*, 1980), *Othello* (1991), HARE's *The Secret Rapture* (1989), MILLER's *The Last Yankee* (1993), Alfred Uhry's *The Last Night of Ballyhoo* (1997) and Augustus and Ruth Goetz's *The Heiress* (1997, adapted from Henry James). She has also served as professor of design at Yale University. Her costumes are characterized by careful attention to well-researched historical dress that is then subtly influenced by her appreciation of contemporary design and fashion.

Greisch, Pol (1930–) Dramatist and actor, Luxembourg. Greisch attended the Cours de Diction et d'Art Dramatique at the Conservatoire de Luxembourg. As an actor, he appeared in many productions of the country's companies, most notably as Wagner in Goethe's *Faust* (1993, Théâtre des Capucins, directed by Frank HOFFMANN and designed by Jean FLAMMANG, with Luc FEIT). However, since his first play *Äddi Charel* (*Good-bye, Charles*, staged 1966 at the Théâtre Municipal de Luxembourg), his major contribution to the theatre in Luxembourg has been the writing of plays whose recurring theme is the everyday tribulations of so-called normal people, spiked with astute and comical observations on parochial preoccupations. Published widely, he is also a novelist and poet, writing in three languages.

Griem, Helmut (1932–) Actor and director, Germany. Griem has acted with the main theatres in Hamburg, Köln, Munich and Berlin, in addition to an international film career. He is currently a member of Münchner Kammerspiele, where he has added directing to his credits (Orton's *Entertaining Mr Sloane*, Synge's *The Playboy of the Western World* and Klaus POHL's *Die Schöne Fremde* (*The Beautiful Stranger*)). 'When choosing texts to direct, he has a decided preference for well-made plays. He sees no problems as a director working with the actors at the Kammerspiele, because they have known each other from other theatres and all appreciate working together.'

Griffiths, Linda (1953–) Actor and dramatist, Canada. She trained at the National Theatre School, and developed an early association with 25th Street Theatre in Saskatoon, where she co-wrote *OD in Paradise* (1983) and *Jessica* (1984, winner of Dora and Chalmers awards). Her breakthrough came with the one-woman show *Maggie and Pierre*, which she also co-wrote (with Paul Thompson), about

Pierre and Maggie Trudeau. She appeared in many of Thompson's collective creations at Théâtre Passe Muraille, for which she also wrote or co-wrote new plays. In 1996, her play *The Duchess* was produced at Alberta Theatre Projects, directed by Paul Thompson. Although her acting work has been solid, in the 1990s Griffiths devoted most of her attention to playwriting.

Griffiths, Trevor (1935–) Dramatist, Great Britain. Called the most politically literate playwright since Shaw, Griffiths first drew attention to his plays in 1970 with *Occupations*, staged by the Royal Shakespeare Company. *Comedians* (1975) deals with the social and class implications of comedy, and starred Laurence Olivier, as did *The Party* at the National Theatre in 1973. This was a penetrating study of the impotence of the left, providing a critique from the inside. The form of the play strikingly mirrors the contents: rather than ending in a structural climax, the play winds down and tails off, just as the endeavours of the characters portrayed. In 1992 Griffiths took up the Gulf War from the Arab perspective in *The Gulf Between Us*.

Grüber, Klaus Michael (1941–) Director, Germany. After studies at drama school in Stuttgart, Grüber was an assistant stage manager with Giorgio Strehler. From 1969–73 he worked in Bremen, achieving major acclaim for his production of *The Tempest*. Since 1973 he has been associated mainly with the Schaubühne in Berlin, with guest work in Bremen, Stuttgart and Frankfurt. Major achievements include the productions of Kleist's *Penthesilea* (1970), Pirandello's *Sei personaggi in cerca d'autore* (*Six Characters in Search of an Author*, 1981), Büchner's *Danton's Tod* (*Danton's Death*, 1989), *Hamlet* (1981, with Bruno Ganz, Jutta LAMPE and Edith CLEVER), Kleist's *Amphitryon* (1991, starring Otto SANDER, Jutta LAMPE and Imogen Kogge) and Goethe's *Iphi-*

genie (1998). 'Grüber is an expert at working the magic of dreamlike scenarios, or inventing visions of the dark sides of life.'

Gryegorzewski, Jerzy (1939–) Director and designer, Poland. Gryegorzewski trained at the Fine Arts Academy of Lódź and the State Theatre Academy of Warsaw. Until 1973 he worked in Lódź, where he made his debut with Brecht's *Der Kaukasische Kreidekreis* (*The Caucasian Chalk Circle*). From 1973–5 he worked closely with Teatr Ateneum in Warsaw, and between 1975–81 with Teatr Polski in Wroclaw. Since 1973 he has also worked at Stary Teatr in Cracow, and since 1982 he has been the director of Teatr Studio in Warsaw. Main theatre credits include Wyspianski's *Wesele* (*The Wedding*), Chekhov's *Djadja Vanja* (*Uncle Vanya*) and *Cajka* (*The Seagull*), *Ten Portraits with the Seagull in the Background*, based on Chekhov's *Cajka*, *The Death of Ivan Ilyich* after Tolstoi, *Love Unspoken, Face Unbroken* on motifs of the operetta by Léhar and Kálmán, and *La Bohème* after Wyspianski. His productions are often variations or improvisations based on literary text, and the text is usually dominated by the visual aspect. The combination of visual elements, sound and movement create a dream-like atmosphere. Gryegorzewski often designs sets for his productions.

Guare, John (1938–) Dramatist, USA. Guare obtained an MFA from Yale University School of Drama. His work 'is characterized by frank theatricality, lyrical quality, autobiographical base, and satiric vivacity'. Major plays include *The House of Blue Leaves, The Landscape of the Body* and *Six Degrees of Separation*, his most successful play to date, in which a young black man storms into a Fifth Avenue apartment pretending to be a movie star's son and promising his upper-crust hosts bit parts in a movie. The fact that this con artist could learn his new role so quickly and perform it so perfectly that no one suspected his being an upstart dramatizes the artificiality of social distinction.

Guarnieri, Anna Maria (1934–) Actor, Italy. After training at the Teatro Piccolo in Milan, Anna Maria Guarnieri made her theatrical début in 1954. Between 1955–63 she worked at the Compagnia dei Giovani with Rossella FALK and Romolo Valli. After 1964 she was directed mainly by Mario MISSIROLI, for whom she interpreted some memorable female roles in plays such as Luigi Pirandello's *I giganti della montagna* (*The Mountain Giants*, 1980), Carlo Goldoni's *Trilogia della villeggiatura* (*The Holiday Trilogy*, 1981), *Antony and Cleopatra* (1982). She also appeared in Pirandello's *La ragione degli altri* (*The Reason of Others*, 1998) directed by Massimo CASTRI. Guarnieri has time and again enchanted her audiences by offering loyal and evocative interpretations of classical female roles.

Gudzuhn, Jörg (1945–) Actor, Germany. Gudzuhn trained at the Staatliche Schauspielschule in East Berlin. After seasons in Karl-Marx-Stadt (Chemnitz) and Potsdam, he worked with the Maxim Gorky Theater in East Berlin (1976–87). In 1987 he joined the Deutsches Theater in Berlin. Carried by his strong physical presence and charisma, he appears able to bring to life both classical and contemporary characters with effortless indolence. Major parts include Adam in Kleist's *Der Zerbrochene Krug* (*The Broken Jug*, 1990, directed by Thomas LANGHOFF), Leicester in Schiller's *Maria Stuart* (1991), Valmont in Heiner Müller's *Quartett* (1991), the title role in Klaus POHL's *Karate Billy kehrt zurück* (*Karata Billy Returns*, 1992, directed by Alexander LANG), the title role in *Othello* (1998, directed by Lang) and the teacher in Dürrenmatt's *Der Besuch der Alten Dame* (*The Visit*, 1999, directed by Thomas Langhoff).

Gürzap, Arsen (1946–) Actor and director, Turkey. Arsen Gürzap graduated in 1967 from the theatre department of the Anakara State Conservatory with the highest grade. She even started acting at the state theatres while she was a senior student at the theatre department, thus becoming the first student actor ever to appear on the Turkish state theatre stage. In 1978 she joined İstanbul State Theatre and in 1986 İstanbul City Theatre. In addition, she has taught phonetics and acting. Arsen Gürzap is a dignified actor who has excelled in powerfully demanding parts, portraying successfully the internal conflict of characters who strive to maintain their integrity. She has acted in famous plays such as MILLER's *Crucible*, Pirandello's *Sei personaggi in cerca d'autore* (*Six Characters in Search of an Author*), Osborne's *Look Back in Anger*, Ibsen's *Hedda Gabler* and Molière's *Le misanthrope* (*The Misanthropist*). Her directing credits include Harwood's *The Dresser* and MILLER's *Orchestra*. She received the best actor award from Ankara Arts Lovers Association, Arts Institution, and took part in various television theatre programmes.

Gunter, John (1928–) Designer, Great Britain. Gunter trained at the Central School of Art and Design. After initially working in regional theatres and in Europe, he became resident designer at the Royal Shakespeare Company in 1966. He is one of the leading designers in Britain, working in theatre and opera with eminent directors such as Peter HALL (SHAFFER's *The Gift of the Gorgon*, RSC, 1992; *Piaf*, West End, 1993; *Julius Caesar*, RSC, 1995; and in Peter Hall's company at the Old Vic and the Picadilly Theatre) and Richard EYRE (*High Society*, West End, 1987; *Hamlet*, National Theatre, 1989; *Skylight*, by David HARE, Royal National Theare, 1996).

Guo Shi Xing (1952–) Dramatist, China. Following the completion of a distance learning programme at the School of Journalism, People's University, and a career in journalism with *Beijing Evening News*, Guo wrote *Niao Ren* (*The Bird Master*), *Qi Ren* (*The Go Master*) and *Yu Ren* (*The Angling Master*). The three works were presented by Beijing People's Art Theatre and directed by LIN Zhao Hua between 1993–7. They form his 'men of leisure' trilogy, in which he seeks to show the destructive powers of obsessions. The dramatist explains that they embody the spirit of Zen and that they offer 'unexpected readings of human existence'. His most recent work is *Huai Hua Yi Tiao Jie* (*A Street of Obscenities*), which was brought to stage by Jin Hui Meng in The Central Experimental Theatre in 1998.

Guretzki, Miriam (1954–) University, where she later took up a teaching position while at the same time remaining active as a designer. She has worked in most of the Israeli theatres as well as for the Polish stage. Among her more noteworthy productions are *Ochlim* (*Eating*) by Aharon Shabtai at the Jerusalem Khan Theatre in 1979 (directed by RONEN), Chekhov's *Cajka* (*The Seagull*, 1984) at the Be'er Sheva Municipal Theatre (directed by SNIR) and Middleton's *The Changeling* (also Be'er Sheva, 1994, directed by the American director Robert Woodrop). Guretzki has made an interesting contribution to a postmodern, fragmentary stage space, which develops dynamically throughout the performance. She has also applied this approach in productions of realistic plays, as in Ibsen's *Hedda Gabler* produced at the Haifa Municipal Theatre in 1993.

Gurevitz, Miki (1951–) Director, Israel. Gurevitz trained as an actor at the Nissan Nativ Studio in Tel Aviv where he also started to direct his fellow students and has taught in this school for several years. Gurevitz is known for his ability to inspire young actors and his inventive use of the stage, often creating unexpected effects. He has directed many classics

(*Macbeth*, *Much Ado About Nothing*, *A Midsummer Night's Dream*) as well as Israeli plays and satirical productions at most of Israel's major theatres. He has also written a number of plays which he has directed himself.

Gurr, Michael (1961–) Dramatist, Australia. Gurr's early training was via National Theatre Drama School workshops (1972–6). As a young playwright in residence at the Melbourne Theatre Company in 1982, Gurr saw several of his plays produced or presented as rehearsed readings, including *A Pair of Claws* (1983), *Magnetic North* (1983) and *Dead to the World* (1986). Gurr's early plays often contained an absurd element, but his later plays use almost filmic realism and feature very short elliptical scenes. These later plays also contain a strong moral element, the favourite targets being moral corruption in politics, diplomacy, journalism and do-gooding; for example *Sex Diary of an Infidel* (1992) deals in the multi-layered corruption exposed when an award-winning Australian journalist sets out to write about sex tours to the Philippines. *Underwear, Crash Helmet and Perfume* (1994) has an election campaign in its background. *Jerusalem* (1996) questions the impact and motives of characters crusading to make the world a better place.

Gurton, Shaun (1948–) Designer, actor and director Australia. Gurton's work ranges across many areas of theatre but he is best known for his theatre design. Gurton has also worked in multimedia: at the St Martin's Arts Centre, Melbourne he set up a multimedia arts complex specifically aimed at young people, and at the World Expo in Brisbane (1988) Gurton designed the Rainbow Serpent Theatre multimedia performance based on Aboriginal legend. Gurton assisted on the design of *Evita* in London, and then supervised the Australian production. He was Associate Director and designer for the South Australian Theatre Company, Adelaide for many years. He has also designed several premiere productions of plays by David WILLIAMSON, working with director Rodney FISHER. In 1991 he designed a high-tech set for Simon PHILLIPS's modern dress production of *Julius Caesar* in Adelaide, a production which featured a female Mark Antony and Casca; Phillips subsequently revived this production with Robyn NEVIN as Mark Antony in Melbourne and Brisbane.

Gutierrez, Gerald (1952–) Director, dramatist and actor, USA. Gutierrez attended Juillard School of Music and Drama. In 1977 he directed MAMET's *A Life in the Theatre*, and other credits include *Much Ado About Nothing* (1986), *Emily* by Stephen Metcalf and the musical *The Most Happy Fellow* (1991). His 1994 production of Augustus and Ruth Goetz's *The Heiress* drew rave notices and won a Drama Desk Award for Best Direction. His style is traditional, but he is very accomplished in a wide variety of theatrical forms.

Gwon Seong-Deok (1940–) Actor, Korea. Gwon trained at Joong-Ang University. Having spent seven years at Gagyo, Gwangjang, Jayoo Theatre Company, Gwon joined the Korean National Theatre in 1972 and became the President of the company in 1992. He performed as Peter in ALBEE's *Zoo Story* (1965, 1970), the title role in Dürrenmatt's *Romulus der Große* (*Romulus the Great*, 1970 and 1978), OH Tae-Seok's *Hanmanseon* (*Korea-Manchuria-A Ship*, 1982), Leader of the Troops in LEE Kang-Baek's *Biong Saong* (1986, directed by LEE Sung-Gyu), Cheon Sang-Byeong in *Gwicheon* (*Back to Heaven*, 1992) and the Doctor in Ariel Dorfman's *Death and the Maiden* (1998, directed by SOHN Jin-Chaek). Gwon has the talent to perform the role of the ordinary person and to create strong characters by using different minor actions.

H

Haavikko, Paavo Juhani (1931–) Dramatist and poet, Finland. Haavikko has written plays for the theatre, for radio and for television, as well as opera librettos, poems, aphorisms, novels, short stories and historical texts. His plays include *Ylilääkäri* (*The Superintendent*, 1968), *Audun ja jääkärhu* (*Audun and the Polar Bear*, 1967), *Agricola ja kettu* (*Agricola and the Fox*), *Ratsumies* (*The Horseman*, 1974, play and libretto), *Rauta-aika* (*Iron Age*, 1982, a play for television), *Kullervon tarina* (*Kullervo's Story*, 1982), *Englantilainen tarina* (*An English Story*, 1990), *Anastasia ja minä* (*Anastasia and I*, 1995, Winner of the Nordic Drama Award 1996) and *Airo ja Brita* (*Airo and Brita*, 1998). Haavikko examines the human condition, different kinds of people's contacts with others in changing circumstances; the study is extended by means of anachronism from individual events to the general. He further studies the whole of human history from the remote past to events foreshadowing the final entropy. Haavikko analyses old and new gods, religions and ideologies, the roles of man and woman, rules, subjects, rogues both great and small, rich and poor, humanists, psychiatrists, family histories, soldiers and civilians of various ranks; sometimes the dead rise to speak from beyond the grave. As a result of such examining, Haavikko concludes that human cruelty cannot be shed, and that everything repeats itself.

Hacks, Peter (1928–) Dramatist, Germany. Hacks studied philosophy, sociology, German and drama in Munich, obtaining his doctorate in 1951. In 1955 he emigrated to East Berlin, joined Brecht's Berliner Ensemble from 1960–3, and has been a freelance dramatist since. He chose the servility and automatic obedience of the Prussian tradition as primary targets for his historical comedy *Die Schlacht bei Lobositz* (*The Battle of Lobositz*, 1957). In the 1960s, together with the late Heiner Müller, he set new standards for dealing with inherent contradictions of socialist society. History is also dominant for Hacks's later writing. In the 1970s, for example, two of his plays proved particularly popular: *Das Jahrmarktsfest zu Plundersweilen* (*The Market Festival at Plundersweilen*) and *Ein Gespräch im Hause Stein über den abwesenden Herrn von Goethe* (*A Conversation at the Stein Residence about absent Mr von Goethe*). In his plays he tries to combine classicism and the everyday.

Hadjisavvas, Minas (1948–) Actor, Greece. Trained at the National School of Dramatic Arts, Athens, as well as with René Simon, Paris, Hadjisavvas has worked mainly for the National Theatre of Greece, the Art Theatre of Karolus Koun, and the Open Theatre of Yiorgos Michailidis, and played a number of leading roles in plays by Aeschylus (Aga-memnon in the *Oresteia*), Sophocles, Euripides, Aristophanes, Shakespeare (Hamlet, Oberon), Chekhov (Vershinin, Platonov), Wedekind, Beckett (Willy in *Happy Days*) and Brecht (Azdak in *Der Kaukasische Kreidekreis* (*The Caucasian Chalk Circle*)).

Hadlow, Mark (1957–) Actor, New Zealand. Hadlow trained at the Theatre Corporate Drama School, Auckland, and a year later joined the Mercury Theatre Company there. He established his claim to be one of the country's finest comic talents at the Court Theatre in Christchurch, where by 1993 he had already appeared in some twenty-five roles, notably Toad in Kenneth Grahame's *Wind in the Willows* and Babs in Brandon Thomas's *Charley's Aunt*. In 1992, under Colin MCCOLL's direction, he made Tobsha Learner's *Sensitive New Age Guy* his own, appearing to acclaim throughout New Zealand and at the 1996 Edinburgh Festival. His comic roles of Grumio in *The Taming of the Shrew*, Riff Raff in Richard O'Brien's *The Rocky Horror Show* and Herod in the New Zealand tour of Tim Rice and Andrew Lloyd Webber's *Jesus Christ Superstar* have also been critically esteemed. In 1995 he was named Entertainer of the Year.

Halász, Péter (1943–) Actor, director and writer, Hungary. Between 1962–6 Halász was a member of the Universitas Ensemble, and in 1969 he organized the Kassák House Studio, which was later banned and operated from 1972 in a private home. In 1976 he left the country with several members of the ensemble; they settled first in Paris, and then in 1977 founded the Squat Theatre in the United States. Since 1992 Halász has been working again in Hungary. In the 1994/95 season he organized a unique project at the studio of the Katona József Theatre (Kamra): each evening for a month, he and members of the company chose an article of the daily newspapers and created-improvised one-off performances, based on the events of the day. Major works include *Testvérballada* (*Brother Ballad*), *A skanzen gyilkosai* (*Killers of the Skanzen*), *Andy Warhol utolsó szerelme* (*The Last Love of Andy Warhol*), *Mr Dead and Mrs Free*, *A kínai* (*The Chinese*), *Önbizalom* (*Ambitionu*), *Sanyi és Aranka* (*Sanyi and Aranka*) and *Pillanatragasztó* (*Instant Glue*). Altogether, Péter Halász is one of the most unique representatives of Hungarian avant-garde theatre.

Hall, Peter (1930–) Director and actor, Great Britain. Hall began acting and directing while a student at Cambridge University. His position as a first-rate director was established when he directed the first British production of Beckett's *Waiting for Godot* in 1955 (revived with Ben KINGSLEY in the cast, in 1997). In 1960 he was appointed director of the Shakespeare Memorial Theatre, Stratford-upon-Avon, where he founded the Royal Shakespeare Company (RSC) later that year. Hall developed a specific style of playing Shakespeare which he called selective naturalism, characterized by close attention to the text and a balance between intellectual and emotional appeal. Among his productions with the RSC, *The War of the Roses* (1964) was perhaps most memorable. He left the RSC in 1968, and, enjoying power and theatre management, took over from Lord Olivier as director of the National Theatre (1973–88). Major productions include SHAFFER's *Amadeus* (1979, with Paul SCOFIELD, Simon CALLOW and Felicity KENDAL in the cast) and Aeschylus's *Oresteia* (1981), which toured to Greece. Since then he has worked with his own commercial production company, taking residence at the Old Vic in London in 1997 and at the Piccadilly Theatre in 1998. Hall has also directed opera and film. His productions are theatrical, meticulous and inspired.

Hall, Roger (1939–) Dramatist, New Zealand. After immigrating from England, Hall trained as a teacher and studied at Victoria University of Wellington, at the same time beginning to write sketches for student and professional revues. His first full-length play *Glide Time* (Circa Theatre, Wellington, 1976) helped establish a new wave of indigenous playwriting. This, along with his second play, *Middle Age Spread* (Circa, 1977), which also broke New Zealand attendance records and ran for over a year in London, winning the Comedy of the Year award there in 1979, have proved his most successful works. He has continued to write a play a year since, seldom unsuccessfully; examples include *The Share Club* (1987), *Conjugal Rites* (1989) and *Social Climbers* (1995). He often chooses topical issues to satirize, but is at his best when he undercuts his complacent yet dissatisfied middle-class characters with a degree of warmth and sympathy.

Hampton, Christopher (1946–) Dramatist, Great Britain. It is not easy to pigeonhole Hampton's dramatic output, which is characterized by a variety of themes, subjects and styles. His early career is associated with the Royal Court Theatre, where *The Philanthropist* was staged in 1970 and *Savages* in 1973. The National Theatre produced *Tales from Hollywood*, a play about European war exiles in 1940s Hollywood (1982), and *White Chameleon*, a strongly autobiographical play (1991, directed by Richard EYRE). Apart from original plays, Hampton has written several 'new versions' of plays, such as Ibsen's *Hedda Gabler* for the National Theatre (1989, with Juliet STEVENSON, directed by Howard DAVIES) and Ibsen's *En Folkefiende* (*An Enemy of the Poeple*, 1997, Royal National Theatre, directed by Trevor NUNN, designed by John NAPIER and starring Ian MCKELLEN). His stage version of *Les Liaisons Dangereuses* (Royal Shakespeare Company, 1986, with Alan RICKMAN and Juliet

Stevenson, directed by Howard Davies) was a major success and served as the basis of two different film adaptations.

Han Sheng (1960–) Designer, China. Han received an MA in stage design from the Shanghai Academy of Drama (1988), where he is now associate professor of stage design. His main works include designs for Ma Zhong Jun's *Da Qiao* (*The Big Bridge*, 1991), *Twelfth Night* (1986), SHA Ye Xin's *Christ, Confucius and John Lennon* (1988), Cao Lu Sheng's *Bai Niang Niang* (*Lady White Snake*, 1990), Wei Ming Lun's *Zhong Guo Gong Zhu Du Lan Duo* (*Chinese Princess Turandot*, 1995), Yang Bao Chen's *Beijing Wang Bei Shi Bei Da Huang* (*To the North of Beijing Lies the Big Wilderness*, 1995) and Zhao Yao Min's *Ge Xing Yu Xing Xing* (*The Gorilla and the Pop Star*, 1998). He works towards a smooth and unobtrusive integration of set and stage action.

Han Myung-Gu (1960–) Actor, Korea. Han trained at the Seoul Institute of Arts and soon afterwards joined the Mokhwa Repertory Company in 1984 as one of its founder members. In many of his works he was closely involved with OH Tae-Seok, the head of the company. Han played Son in *Choonpoongeui Cheo* (*Choonpoong's Wife*, 1986), Lee-Gae in *Tae* (*The Navel Cord*, 1986), Officer Yoon in *Jajeongeo* (*Bicycle*, 1987), and acted the title role in *Boojayoochin* (*The Struggle between King and the Crown Prince as a Father and Son*, 1987), the Shipowner in *Simcheonginun Wae Indangsooe Doobeon Momul Deonjeotnunga?* (*Why did Shimcheong throw herself into the Indangsoo Sea twice?* 1990), Kitahara in *Doraji* (*Ballon Flower*, 1992) and the Crown Prince of the Baekje Kingdom in *Baekmagang Dalbame* (*Moonlight of the River Baekma*, 1993), which were written and directed by Oh Tae-Seok. He sometimes acted for other companies, playing Lee Gang-Gook in

Jeong Bok-Gun's *Na Kim Soo-Im* (*Me, Kim Soo-Im*, 1997), and Jang Woo-Je's *Mokpoeui Noonmool* (*Tears of Mokpo City*, 1998). Han has the unique talent to express the theatricality of primitive performances using a modern method. He was awarded the Dong-A Theatre Prize for best actor in 1992 and 1997.

Hands, Terry (1941–) Director, Great Britain. Hands founded the Everyman Theatre in Liverpool in 1964. In 1966 he joined the Royal Shakespeare Company as artistic director of the touring section. From 1967–1977 he was associate director, and from 1978–1991 joint artistic director (with Trevor NUNN) of the RSC. Among many productions of Shakespeare, a series of productions of all the history plays, with Alan Howard playing the respective Kings, was striking because of the geometrical formations of the characters on the stage, emphasized by symbolical patterns of spotlights. In addition, Hands directed Peter Nichols's *Poppy* (1982), Peter Barnes's *Red Noses* (1986), Chekhov's *Cajka* (*The Seagull*, 1991) and Marlowe's *Tamburlaine* (1993). Since 1997 he has been director of Theatr Clwyd in Mold, Wales, where productions include AYCKBOURN's *The Norman Conquests* (1998) and *Twelfth Night* (1999). A 1996 mini-profile of Hands in the *Guardian* reads: 'At heart, a European populist in the tradition of Jean Vilar. At his best … a great animator of a text. … His contribution to the RSC – where he was the first really to give women directors their head – has been underrated and his productions have always looked astonishing.'

Hanicka, Barbara Maria (1952–) Designer, Poland. Hanicka graduated from the Academy of Fine Arts in Cracow. Important productions include Brecht's *Die Dreigroschenoper* (*The Threepenny Opera*, Teatr Studio, Warsaw, 1986), Ronald Harwood's *The Dresser* (Teatr Powszechny, Warsaw, 1986), Euripides's

Medeia (Teatr Powszechny, 1988), Ibsen's *Peer Gynt* (Teatr Studio, Warsaw, 1991), *Dom Juan* by Molière (Comédie de St.Etienne, France, 1994, and Teatr Studio, Warsaw, 1996), and *La Bohème* after Wyspianski (Teatr Studio, Warsaw, 1995). Working mostly with Grotowski and devoted to his poetics, she designs costumes operating numerous cultural and historical quotations, non-naturalistic, both conceptual and literary as well as visual.

Hannah, Dorita (1961–) Designer, New Zealand. Hannah has an Honours degree in architecture from Auckland University and lectures in architecture at Victoria University of Wellington, but she also trained in production design as a resident designer at the Mercury Theatre, Auckland, in 1985, and has since 1991 been regularly involved in set and costume design in Auckland and Wellington. She has particularly enjoyed working on new plays, and since 1994 has made a name in bi-cultural productions. Her design for *Nga Tangata Toa* by Hone KOUKA (Taki Rua Theatre, Wellington, 1994) was widely recognized, being chosen for the 1995 Prague Quadrennial, and she won an award for design for Dürrenmatt's *Der Besuch der alten Dame* (*The Visit*, Downstage Theatre, Wellington, 1996). She has also worked on the design or re-development of theatre buildings in England and New Zealand.

Harcourt, Kate (1927–) Actor, New Zealand. Harcourt trained as a singer at the Melbourne University Conservatorium and the Joan Cross Opera School, London, but it was only in her fifties, after extensive work on children's radio programmes, that she developed a name for her roles as an older family mother. Notable examples have been parts in the premières of Roger HALL's *Prisoners of Mother England* (1979) and RENÉE's *Wednesday to Come* (1984), and in Lorca's *La casa de Bernarda Alba* (*The House of*

Bernarda Alba, 1989), all at the Downstage, Wellington. Though generally found in subordinate roles, she has an ambient warmth that endears her to her audiences. She has also appeared in television drama and films.

Harcourt, Miranda (1962–) Actor, New Zealand. After training at the New Zealand Drama School, Harcourt began her career at the Fortune Theatre, Dunedin, where she presented Leah Poulter's solo piece about a prostitute, *Kaz: A Working Girl* (1985), and learnt sign language for the part of Sarah Norman in Mark Medoff's *Children of a Lesser God* (1986). Both productions toured, and established a pattern: she has chosen work of social concern, often presented in prisons or to the emotionally or physically disabled, work sometimes co-written and devised by herself, or more usually a production in which she has been a driving force. In 1990–1 she spent a year at the Central School of Speech and Drama, London, studying drama therapy. With Justice Department sponsorship, she and William Brandt prepared *Verbatim* (1993), another solo piece which toured widely. She is esteemed by directors as an 'excellent craftsperson' who is wholly committed, and she has a striking stage presence.

Hardy, Gérard (1935–) Actor, France. Hardy joined Ariane MNOUCHKINE's Théâtre du Soleil in 1967, where he played in Arnold Wesker's *The Kitchen* (1967), *A Midsummer Night's Dream* (1968), *The Clowns* (1969), *1789* and *1793* (1971–2). He was Chevalier d'Assoucy in the film *Molière*, written and directed by Mnouchkine and played a brilliant Hoefgen, the title role in *Méphisto, The Novel of A Career* by Klaus Mann. At the Théâtre du Soleil he also developed the notion of collective service, which was based on Jean Vilar's conception of public service and theatre. The goal was to attract a broader public to the theatre, and in this he was very successful. He worked with many other theatre directors, appearing as Horgauer in Brecht's *Baal* (1975, directed by André Engel), and Tardiveau in Labiche's *Chapeau de paille d'Italie* (*The Italian Straw Hat*, 1997, directed by Georges Lavaudant). He worked with the Polish movie director Andrej WAJDA on the film *Danton* in 1977.

Hare, David (1947–) Dramatist, Great Britain. Hare was the Royal Court's literary manager from 1969–70, and resident dramatist from 1970–71. Successful plays include *Slag* at the Royal Court (1970), *Brassneck*, written together with Howard BRENTON (1973), and *Fanshen* (1975). The National Theatre has staged many of his plays, including *Plenty* (1978), *The Map of the World* (1983), *Pravda* (again with Brenton) and *The Secret Rapture* (1989). In the early 1990s Hare wrote a trilogy of plays about contemporary Britain which were again produced at the Royal National Theatre, all directed by Richard EYRE. *Racing Demon*, considered the most successful, deals with the Church of England; *Murmuring Judges* scrutinizes the legal system in Britain, and *The Absence of War* takes a very close look at politics, showing the inner mechanisms of a Labour Party election campaign. In writing this play, Hare benefited much from having been allowed to sit in on the Labour Party's meetings during the 1992 election campaign. Hare continued his successes with *Skylight*, starring Michael GAMBON, *Amy's View* (1997, with Judi DENCH), both at the Royal National Theatre directed by Richard Eyre, and *Via Dolorosa* (1998, Royal Court, directed by Stephen DALDRY).

Harifai, Zahirira (1930–) Actor, Israel. Harifai trained at the Cameri Studio, continuing as an actor at the Cameri Tel Aviv municipal theatre. In 1961 Harifai was among the founders of the Haifa municipal theatre, where she played Grusha in Brecht's *Der Kaukasische Kreidekreis* (*The Caucasian Chalk Circle*) and Kattrin in Brecht's *Mutter Courage und ihre Kinder* (*Mother Courage and her Children*), a role she also played later at the Camei theatre. She has played leading roles in many of Hanoch LEVIN's plays as well as in several Israeli films.

Harris, Julie (1925–) Actor, USA. Harris attended Yale University School of Drama and trained at the Perry-Mansfield School of Dance and Theatre as well as at the Actors' Studio. Harris has enjoyed a distinguished career on stage, in film, on television and on radio. Among her major stage credits are Margery Pinchwife in Wycherley's *The Country Wife* (1957), Juliet in *Romeo and Juliet* (1960), Blanche in Williams's *A Streetcar Named Desire* (1967) and Emily Dickinson in a one-woman show, *The Belle of Amherst* (first in 1976). In 1988 she toured the USA as Daisy in Alfred Uhry's *Driving Miss Daisy*; in 1992–3 she toured in SHAFFER's *Lettuce and Lovage*; and in 1997 she played Miss Helen in FUGARD's *The Road to Mecca* and appeared in a rehearsed reading of O'Neill's *A Long Day's Journey into Night*. Critics have admired her 'air of vulnerability and fragility, coupled with remarkable stage techniques'.

Harrison, Wayne (1953–) Director and actor, Australia. Artistic director of the Sydney Theatre Company (STC) from 1990–8, Harrison has steered the company through a difficult period financially, with funding cuts on the increase, and has overseen several extremely successful seasons. Harrison has extensive theatre experience: he was a child actor and a dramaturg (he directed Dramaturgical Services Inc. 1987–90 and was dramaturg at STC 1981–7), and he has also worked alongside Philip Parsons on Elizabethan style productions of Renaissance plays. In 1996 the relationship between director,

playwright and designer became debated in the national press when David WILLIAMSON attacked Harrison and designer John Senczuk for their production of Williamson's play *Heretic*. In box office terms, one of Harrison's most successful productions has been the Mary Morris adaptation of Morris Gleitzman's *Two Weeks with the Queen*.

Haspari, Shmuel (1954–) Dramatist and director, Israel. Haspari studied philosophy and theatre at Tel Aviv University, and began his directing career in fringe theatre productions at the Acco festival for alternative theatre. His trilogy – *Kiddush*, *Chametz* and *Shiva* – deals with contemporary Israeli families living in the shadow of the Holocaust, confronting their religious and national identities. It has been one of the most successful productions on the Israeli stage. Haspari directs his own plays but has also directed other plays such as Tony Kushner's *Angels in America*. He has written and directed a film, *Sh-chur*, about mystical practices among Moroccan Jews in Israel.

Hastert, Patrick (1959–) Actor, Luxembourg. Hastert attended the University of the Saarland, Saarbrücken and the Conservatoire de Luxembourg, where he has taught diction and dramatic arts since 1987. Hastert is an accomplished multilingual actor and has appeared in most major productions of the country, both in classical and contemporary repertory. Most notably, he has portrayed Jean in Ionesco's *Les Rhinocéros*, the Soldier in Stravinsky's *L'Histoire du Soldat* (*The Soldier's History*), the Actor in Woody Allen's *God*, Happy in MILLER's *Death of a Salesman* (1992, Théâtre des Capucins, with Fernand FOX) and, with great aplomb, Leopold in Howard BARKER's *The Europeans* (1995, Théâtre d'Esch, directed by Eric SCHNEIDER). Hastert won acclaim for his playing of Philip in the world premiere of Alexey Shipenko's two-hander *Moskau-Frankfurt* (1994,

Théâtre des Capucins, directed by the author, designed by Jeanny KRATOSCH-WILL, with Jean-Paul MAES). He has also featured in many films.

Haumann, Péter (1941–) Actor and director, Hungary. Haumann trained at the Academy of Theatre and Film Arts and joined the Csokonai Theatre in Debrecen, and between 1966–70 was with the National Theatre of Pécs. From 1970–2 he worked at the 25th Theatre of Budapest. After a season with the József Attila Theatre, he joined the Madách Theatre in 1973. Between 1988–91 he was with the National Theatre of Budapest. In 1991 he joined the Arizona Theatre, then the Radnóti Theatre, and since 1994 he has been member of the Katona József Theatre. Haumann is also a popular screen and television actor, who recently added directing to his credits. Major roles include Woyczeck (Büchner's *Woyzeck*), Arturo Ui (Brecht's *Der Aufhaltsame Aufstieg des Arturo Ui* (*The Resistable Rise of Arturo Ui*)), Benedick (*Much Ado About Nothing*), Eddie Carbone (MILLER's *View from a Bridge*), Norman (Harwood's *The Dresser*), Estragon (Beckett's *Waiting for Godot*), Harpagon (Molière's *L'avare* (*The Miser*)) and Judge Adam (Kleist's *Der Zerbrochene Krug* (*The Broken Jug*)). Haumann is a strong character actor with dramatic strength, special humour and clown characteristics.

Haußmann, Leander (1959–) Director and actor, Germany. Haußmann trained at the Hochschule für Schauspielkunst 'Ernst Busch'. After seasons as an actor and director in Pachim, he joined the Deutsches Nationaltheater in Weimar, where he directed Büchner's *Leonce und Lena* (*Leonce and Lena*) and Ibsen's *Et Dukkehjem* (*A Doll's House*), as well as Schiller's *Kabale und Liebe* (*Intrigue and Love*) in Frankfurt an der Oder. In each case, a classical text was re-interpreted but not destroyed, as in the productions of Frank CASTORF, who is a major influ-

ence on Haußmann's style. 'Where Castorf comes across as intellectual, Haußmann seems rather naive without being simplistic.' Following productions in Frankfurt am Main, Munich, Weimar, Vienna and Berlin, Haußmann has been Intendant at Schauspielhaus Bochum since summer 1995, where recent productions include Sophocles's *Antigone*, *The Taming of the Shrew*, *Much Ado About Nothing* and Brecht's *Die Dreigroschenoper* (*The Threepenny Opera*).

Havel, Václav (1936–) Dramatist, Czech Republic. Havel worked as a theatre technician, and later as an assistant director and dramaturg (in 1966 he completed his studies at the Prague Academy of Performing Arts) at the Prague Theatre on the Balustrade Na zábradlí, where he and Jan Grossman contributed to making that venue one of the most important of the 1960s. It was here that his first plays were performed, including *Zahradni Slavnost* (*The Garden Party*, 1963, directed by Otomar KREJČA), *Vyrozumení* (*The Memorandum*, 1965, directed by Grossman), *Ztizena moznost soustredení* (*Hindered Concentration* 1968). His plays comprised a specifically Czech variation of absurd drama, demonstrating the bureaucratic mechanisms that reduce the individual. After the invasion of the Warsaw Pact forces in August 1968, Havel became a leading dissident, and was imprisoned several times. His plays were banned in Czechoslovakia until the fall of communism in 1989. Beginning with the autobiographical one-act *Audience* (1976, Burgtheater Vienna), the question of human identity gradually comes to the surface in *Largo Desolato* (1985, Burgtheater Vienna), the transposition of the Faust theme in *Pokoušeni* (*Temptation*, 1986, Burgtheater Vienna), and the political allegory *Asanace* (*Slum Clearance*, premiered 1989, Zürich). From 1989–92 he was the president of the Czech and Slovak Federal Republic, and has been president of the Czech Republic since 1993.

Hawthorne, Nigel (1929–) Actor, Great Britain. Born and raised in South Africa, Hawthorne made his London debut in 1951. In 1968 he played Prince Albert in Edward BOND's *Early Morning* at the Royal Court, directed by William GAS-KILL. At the Royal Court he also appeared in *Total Eclipse* (1968) by Christopher HAMPTON. Major parts since then include Brutus in *Julius Caesar* (Young Vic, 1972), the title role in Chekhov's *Djadja Vanja* (*Uncle Vanya*, 1979), Orgon in Molière's *Tartuffe* (1983) and STOPPARD's *Hapgood*, with Felicity KENDAL. In 1991 he played the title part in Alan BENNETT's *The Madness of King George III* (directed by Nicholas HYTNER), a major success for the Royal National Theatre, later made into a film. He appeared on Broadway in the lead of William Nicholson's *Shadowlands* (1992), repeating the role he had created in London in 1989. Hawthorne is also well known from television, especially for the series *Yes Minister*.

Hawthorne, Raymond (1936–) Director and actor, New Zealand. After three years with the New Zealand Players, Hawthorne trained at the Royal Academy of Dramatic Art, London, and was a member of staff there for twelve years. He joined the Mercury Theatre, Auckland, in 1971 as director, actor and tutor, but a passion for training actors led to his founding Theatre Corporate in Auckland, where he achieved outstanding artistic results with mostly younger casts. From 1985–92 he was artistic director at the Mercury Theatre, where he became particularly renowned as a director of musicals and opera. Since then he has been a freelance director and has run popular acting classes. He is known for a theatrical rather than naturalistic style, and for his skill in managing large casts with grace and precision. Notable productions amongst many include Wedekind's *Früh-*

lings Erwachen (*Spring Awakening*, 1979) and Chekhov's *Tri sestry* (*Three Sisters*, 1984) at Theatre Corporate and Arthur MILLER's *A View from the Bridge* (1989) at the Mercury. Not one to spare himself and known as a hard taskmaster, he has the power to win total commitment to his productions.

Hayat, Abul (1944–) Actor, Bangladesh. Hayat's illustrious career in theatre is distinctly remembered for the roles of Sitanath in Badal Sircar's *Baki Itihas* (*The Other Side of History*, with Sarah ZAKER as Kona and Ataur RAHMAN as Saradindu, 1973), the title role in Walliullah's *Bahipeer* (directed by Zia HYDER with Ataur Rahman as Jamidar, Asaduz-zaman NOOR as Jamidar's son and Sarah Zaker as Peer's wife, 1974), Matti in an adaptation of Brecht's *Herr Puntila und sein Knecht Matti* (*Mr Puntila and his Servant Matti*, directed by Noor with Aly ZAKER as Puntila, 1977), Pozzo in a translation of Beckett's *Waiting For Godot* (directed by Ataur RAHMAN, with Noor as Vladimir, 1984), and as the Lawyer in an adaptation of Dorfman's *Death and the Maiden* (directed by Sarah Zaker, with Noor as the Doctor, 1993). These roles have identified him as an actor who is a master of subtle interplay of emotion and nuances. Hayat is also a popular and renowned television, radio and film actor. He is one of the founder members of Nagorik Natya Sampradaya (a leading theatre group in Bangladesh) and has extensively performed abroad.

Helminger, Nico (1953–) Dramatist, Luxembourg. Helminger studied German and Latin language and literature and drama in Luxembourg, Saarbrücken, Vienna and Berlin. His first theatrical experiences were with student amateur theatre and children's theatre. In the 1970s and 1980s, he belonged to a group of authors who revived the Luxembourg language theatre. His breakthrough came in 1982 with the Theatre GMBH's controversial production of *rosch oder déi lescht rees* (rog or the last voyage) at the Escher Schluechthaus arts centre, a play dealing in a radically inventive style with a group of outcasts who struggle to define their condition and the inner ravages caused by the economic crisis of the country's steel industry. Similar themes are recurring in Helminger's later plays *Atlantis, Happy Birthday* (1986) and *Miss Minett* (1993). He found a new direction in the libretto to Camille Kerger's opera *Melusina* which was premiered together with Helminger's two-hander *Vorspiel* in 1995 at the Théâtre d'Esch (both directed by Frank HOFFMANN). He is also a novelist and poet, writing in German and Luxembourgeois, and has written a series of innovative radio plays.

Henare, George (1945–) Actor, New Zealand. Henare broke off training at Ardmore Teachers' College to join the New Zealand Opera Company (1965–71), but at the same time developed theatrical skills in radio and television as well as through New Zealand Maori Theatre Trust productions. He was particularly associated with the Mercury Theatre, Auckland, first appearing there in 1971 and joining as a lead actor in 1972, taking, like other successful New Zealand actors, as many as six leading parts in a year. Notable roles there have been King Lear (1974) and Polonius in *Hamlet* (1990). Only occasionally did he appear elsewhere, for example as Midge in Herb Gardner's *I'm Not Rappaport* (1987) and Othello (1989), both at the Downstage, Wellington. Even before the collapse of the Mercury Theatre in 1992 he was veering back towards musicals and opera, and he has worked in those areas increasingly since, both in New Zealand and Australia.

Henig, Ofira (1961–) Director, Israel. Henig trained at the Kibbutz seminar and received the first price at a student theatre festival in Moscow for her production of

SHAFFER's *Equus*. She began her directing career at the Bet-Zvi theatre school, directing for example, Sherman's *Bent*. Between 1991–93 she was the 'house' director at Habima (Williams's *The Glass Menagerie* and Strindberg's *Fordringsägare (Creditors)* as well as Israeli plays). In 1996 she was appointed as artistic director of the Khan Jerusalem municipal theatre where she is developing a young ensemble and has directed several new Israeli plays.

Henley, Beth (1952–) Dramatist and actor, USA. Henley originally worked as an actor, which shows in the strong female characters in her plays. Important titles include *Crimes of the Heart* (1979), *The Miss Firecracker Contest* (1980), *The Debutante Ball* (1985), *The Lucky Spot* (1987) and *Control Freaks* (1992). The plays often provide a humorous treatment of death, disaster and freakish accidents: Sam SHEPARD has called *Abundance* Henley's 'most ambitious and richly textured play. Dealing with conflicting images of the American frontier and a reversal of character, one might call it a feminist *True West*'.

Henry, Martha (1938–) Actor and director, Canada. Born in Detroit, Martha Henry studied at the Carnegie Institute of Technology (Pittsburgh) and later, after moving to Canada in 1959, at the National Theatre School. In 1961 she made her debut at the Stratford Festival, where she has been performing regularly since, notably as Miranda in *The Tempest* (1961), Isabella in *Measure for Measure* (1976) and Goneril in *King Lear* (1980). She was also associated with the Manitoba Theatre Centre (1961–82) and was artistic director of the Grand Theatre, London, Ontario (1988–95), where she directed numerous productions. For her continued and distinguished success in the theatre, Martha Henry has received several honorary titles from Canadian universities as well as national awards. She is a Companion of the Order of Canada. Henry is justly famous for her attention to detail as an actor and for her intelligent and sensuous portrayal of character.

Henshaw, James Ene (1924–) Dramatist, Nigeria. Henshaw's plays elegantly mix a tragic impulse with an essentially comic mode. Without formal training in the theatre, Henshaw occupies a position between the coarse plays of the Onitsha Market literature tradition and the more dramatically sophisticated plays of Wole SOYINKA, J.P. CLARK-BEKEDEREMO and the other university-trained dramatists. His plays include *This is Our Chance* (first produced in Dublin in 1947 and published in 1957), *A Man of Character* (1957), *Jewels of the Shrine* (1957), *Children of the Goddess* (1964), *Companion for a Chief* (1964), *Magic in the Blood* (1964), *Medicine for Love* (1964), *Dinner for Promotion* (1967), *Enough is Enough* (1976) and *A Song to Mary, Irish Sister of Charity* (1984).

Henwood, Ray (1937–) Actor, New Zealand. Henwood emigrated to New Zealand as a teacher and forensic toxicologist after studying at University College, Swansea, but became one of Wellington's leading actors from 1966, especially at the Downstage Theatre, and from 1976 at the Circa Theatre, which he co-founded. He created the part of Hugh in Roger HALL's *Glide Time* (1976) and played Brack in the Colin MCCOLL production of Ibsen's *Hedda Gabler*, which was invited to the Edinburgh Festival in 1990. His highly successful one-man show *No Good Boyo*, based on the life of Dylan Thomas, toured New Zealand and Australia in the early 1980s and has been revived since. Otherwise seldom seen outside Wellington, his skills have been sometimes unfairly discounted from over-exposure, for he is a reliable actor of considerable presence who builds subtly distinct and consistent characterizations.

Heras, Guillermo (1952–) Actor and director, Spain. Very much associated with the alternative theatre movement of the 1970s, Heras enjoyed a strong association with Tábano and then went on in 1983 to take over the directorship of the CNNTE (Centro Nacional de Nuevas Tendencias Escénicas), at the time perhaps the most innovative and adventurous company in Spain. From 1984–93 he promoted many young emerging dramatists and staged much eclectic dance theatre as well as productions with a strong visual appeal, amongst them *Geografía* (*Geography*) by Alvaro del Amo (1985), *Hilo seco* (*Dried Thread*) by Marisa Ares (1986) and *La soledad del guardaespaldas* (*The Loneliness of the Bodyguard*) by Javier Maqua (1987). As well as promoting the work of contemporary Spanish playwrights, Heras brought a range of international works to a wider Spanish audience. These include the premiere of Bernard-Marie Koltès's *Dans la solitude des champs de coton* (*In the Solitude of Cottonfields*) (1990) and Steven Berkoff's *Greek* (1992). After the closure of the CNNTE, Heras has continued working as a director both in Spain and in Latin America.

Hermanis, Alvis (1965–) Director, actor and designer, Latvia. Hermanis graduated from the Latvian State Conservatory Theatre Department in 1988. In his productions, which include *Madame de Sade* by Mishima and an adaptation of Wilde's *The Picture of Dorian Gray*, he emphasizes small stages, powerful aesthetics, sensuality and atmosphere. He considers himself one of the first directors to attempt to use cyberpunk aesthetics and philosophy in modern theatre. A critic wrote of his production of *Madame de Sade*: 'Hermanis...discovers a world of desire where Time, Place and Truth no longer exist. Theatre here is a ritual that ascends to the heights of poetry and music.'

Herrmann, Edward (1943–) Actor, USA. Herrmann trained at the London Academy of Music and Dramatic Art (1968–9). He played Raymond Brock in David HARE's *Plenty* (1982), T.S. Eliot in Michael Hastings's *Tom and Viv* (New York and London, 1985), Siegfried Sassoon in Stephen MacDonald's *Not About Heroes* (1985), and appeared in Richard Nelson's *The End of a Sentence* and Rattigan's *The Deep Blue Sea* (1998, directed by Mark LAMOS). Critics have commented on his ability to fade into the people he portrays. He is regularly cast in biographical roles also in film and television, having twice played Franklin Roosevelt. He also starred as baseball great Lou Gehrig.

Herrmann, Karl-Ernst (1936–) Designer, Germany. Herrmann studied at the Meisterschule für Kunsthandwerk and the Hochschule für Bildende Künste in Berlin. From 1962–9 he worked for Kurt Hübner in Ulm and Bremen, where he also started designing for Peter STEIN, whose main designer he later became at the Schaubühne am Halleschen Ufer and Lehniner Platz. He has also worked with Claus PEYMANN (Bochum and Vienna), Frank-Patrick STECKEL and Luc BONDY. Since 1982 he has directed opera, often with his wife Ursel. Herrmann's set designs are not obvious at first sight, they develop in the spectator's mind in the course of the performance. They contain a secret. Recent work includes Marlowe's *Edward II* (1998, directed by Peymann in Vienna), and TURRINI's *Die Liebe in Madagaskar* (*Love in Madagaskar*, 1998, Vienna).

Herzberg, Judith (1934–) Dramatist, The Netherlands. The daughter of author Abel Herzberg, who wrote about the horrors of the Nazi camps, Judith remained hidden during the war. She used her experiences as a 'second generation' Jew in her best-known play *Leedvermaak* (*The Wedding Party*, 1982). It is situated at a wedding where the events of many years ago still rear their head in apparently 'normal'

lives. Principally, Herzberg is a poet, writing about small but meaningful events in a deceptively simple style. In 1997 she was awarded the prestigious P.C. Hooft Prize for her poetry. Herzberg took up playwriting in the 1970s, learning from practice. The Baal company, directed by Leonard Frank, with actors Kitty COURBOIS and Trudy DE JONG, put on many productions of her work, including *Leedvermaak, En/of* (*And/Or*, 1983) and her adaptation of *The Dibbuk* (1984). A great champion of her work is Jan Joris LAMERS, who directed a much-praised version of *Kras* (*Scratch*, 1989). Recently Herzberg wrote *Rijgdraad* (*Tacking Thread*, 1996), a sequel to *Leedvermaak*. Herzberg's poignant plays appear straightforward, but they bend reality. Many of them have been translated, and many have been produced in Germany. Herzberg also wrote the script for the film *Charlotte*.

Herzog, Jens Daniel (1964–) Director, Germany. Herzog began as an assistant director with Dieter DORN and Hans Lietzau at the Münchner Kammerspiele, where he has worked since on his own productions, which include *New York, New York* by Marlene Streeruwitz (1993), Beth HENLEY's *The Debutante Ball* (1993), Molière's *Tartuffe* (1995) and *Gleichgewicht* (*Balance*) by Botho STRAUSS. At the Thalia Theater in Hamburg he directed *A Midsummer Night's Dream* (1996) and Peter Handke's *Zurüstungen für die Unsterblichkeit* (*Preparing for Immortality*, 1997), followed by Chekhov's *Cajka* (*The Seagull*) in Munich (1997) and Lessing's *Minna von Barnhelm* in Vienna (1998, with Anne BENNENT in the title role).

Heuer, Marlies (1952–) Actor, The Netherlands. Born into an acting family, Marlies Heuer studied at the mime department of the Amsterdam Theatre School. She graduated in 1976 and was subsequently involved in creating and playing in various fringe productions. Apart from a brief stint at the large, mainstream company Toneelgroep Amsterdam (from 1987–90), she has always remained an independent actor who often makes her own productions. She was involved in *Silicone* by Gerardjan RIJNDERS (with Cas ENKLAAR), and beautifully adapted Nathalia Ginzburg's novel *È stato così* (*The Way of Was*) for the stage, playing the lead role of a grey, tormented housewife. This strongly contrasted with her normal appearance, with its sensual mysteriousness and precise way of moving. In 1991 Heuer joined Matin VAN VELDHUIZEN to lead the Carrousel company. This provides her with a steady base for her productions, and she often plays in van Veldhuizen's productions, for example in Shaw's *Mrs Warren's Profession* (1995) and as an excellent Hedda in Ibsen's *Hedda Gabler* (1998). Heuer teaches at the mime department of the Amsterdam Drama School.

Hewett, Dorothy (1923–) Dramatist, poet and novelist, Australia. In the midst of the blokish renaissance of Australian drama in the early 1970s, while so many new plays were devoted to the rocker and his rituals, Hewett was proclaiming that a woman's life was as heroic as an Arthurian quest in *The Chapel Perilous* (1971). Hewett's plays have inspired and infuriated feminists and anti-feminists alike. Her intensely autobiographical playwriting is often anti illusionistic, non-linear and overtly theatrical, and mixes styles (poetry, melodrama, musical). Her musical play *The Man from Mukinupin*, written for the sesquicentenary of Perth, is a sophisticated piece simultaneously celebrating white culture but also acknowledging the genocide practised against Aboriginal people. Hewett's first play, *This Old Man Comes Rolling Home* (1966), is a predominantly realistic evocation of inner city Sydney life. Hewett has written musicals, rock operas, radio plays, plays for children, poetry, novels and autobiography.

Heyme, Hansgünther (1935–) Director and actor, Germany. Heyme began his career in the theatre as an assistant director and actor in Mannheim (1958–60), and subsequently held positions as director in Wiesbaden (1961–7), as artistic director in Köln (1968–1978), director in Stuttgart (1980–5), and artistic director in Essen (1985–92) and Bremen (1992 – 3). Since 1993 he has worked freelance. Heyme, who regards the theatre as subsidized opposition, is a typical representative of political theatre, often radically modernizing classical plays in order to comment on our contemporary life.

Hickey, Tom (1944–) Actor and director, Ireland. Hickey trained at the Stanislavski Studio, Dublin and was a founder member of Dublin's Focus Theatre in 1967. His roles at the Abbey Theatre, Dublin, include J.P.W. King in *The Gigli Concert* by Tom MURPHY (1983) and Roulston in Frank MCGUINNESS's *Observe the Sons of Ulster Marching towards the Somme* (1985), both directed by Patrick MASON. During the 1980s Hickey collaborated with Patrick Mason and playwright Tom MAC INTYRE at the Peacock Theatre, Dublin, on a series of theatre-of-image plays, including the controversial *The Great Hunger* (1983). Hickey's method training and vibrant physical presence on stage were strong elements of his portrayal of Patrick Maguire and thus of *The Great Hunger's* success. Roles at the Gate Theatre, Dublin, include Vladimir in Beckett's *Waiting For Godot* (1988), Mr Hardcastle in Goldsmith's *She Stoops to Conquer* (1995), directed by Jonathan MILLER, and Dermot in Bernard Farrell's *Stella by Starlight* (1996). His most recent work inludes Judge/Morris in MacIntyre's *Caoineadh Airt uí Laoghaire* (*The Lament for Art O'Leary*, 1998) and Mr Cassidy in Marina Carr's *By the Bog of Cats* (1998). Plays directed by Hickey include *Strawboys* by Michael Harding for the Peacock Theatre (1987).

Highway, Tomson (1951–) Dramatist, Canada. Highway uses total theatre – song, dance, spectacle – to create a powerful and often surreal depiction of the lives of Canadian natives. At the same time, he tries to make non-native audiences familiar with native culture and spiritual mythology. *The Rez Sisters* (1986), about women in an Indian reservation, was followed in 1989 by *Dry Lips Oughta Move to Kapuskasing*, about the men in the same reservation. The central figure in both plays is Nanabush, the trickster, a key character in Ojibway spiritual mythology. Highway has won Dora and Chalmers Awards, and he has served as artistic director of Native Earth Performing Arts (1986–92), where most of his plays have been produced.

Hinds, Ciarán (1953–) Actor, Ireland. After training at the Royal Academy of Dramatic Art, London, Hinds joined the Citizens' Theatre Glasgow, where roles included McLeavy in Orton's *Loot* (1977), Captain Boyle in O'Casey's *Juno and the Paycock* (1983) and the title role in *Richard III* (1988). His striking appearance, stature and charisma contributed greatly to the Citizen's many design-oriented productions. In Ireland he played Giovanni in Ford's *'Tis Pity She's a Whore* and Jack Worthing in Wilde's *The Importance of Being Earnest* (1985), both directed by Garry HYNES of Druid Theatre, Galway. His international profile was raised by joining Peter Brook's multinational company (CIRT) in Paris for *The Mahabharata* (1987, and on tour 1988), in which he played the roles of Nakula (one of the Pandava twins) and Ashwattaman (son of Drona). He has made many appearances in London since, at the Donmar Warehouse, Royal Court and at the Royal National Theatre, where he appeared as Man One in Stephen DALDRY's production of Sophie Treadwell's *Mach-*

inal and recently Larry in Patrick Marber's *Closer* (1997). His extensive television career includes Potter's *Cold Lazarus*, and his many film appearances include *December Bride*, *Circle of Friends* and *Some Mother's Son*.

Hipólito, Carlos (1956–) Actor, Spain. After graduating in Architecture, Hipólito studied acting with William Layton, Miguel Narros and José Carlos PLAZA in Madrid. Associated with the TEI (Teatro Español Independiente), the independent theatre movement, he worked as an actor in productions such as the splendid *El concierto de San Ovidio* (*The Concert of Saint Ovidio*), a masterpiece of the 'realista' generation by Antonio Buero Vallejo, directed by Miguel Narros in 1986, and in O'Neill's *Long Day's Journey Into the Night* in 1989. Since the beginning of the 1990s he has enjoyed extensive residencies with the Compañia de Teatro Clásico (National Classical Company) in plays like Calderón's *El medico de su honra* (*The Doctor of His Honour*) in 1995, a production designed by the company's artistic director Adolfo MARSILLACH, and Molière's *Le misanthrope* (*The Misanthropist*), directed by Ariel García Valdés in 1996. A slight, blond actor, his lithe features, agility and vulnerabilty have made him one of the most respected classical actors in Spain. More recently he has gained a wider popular base with performances in Yasmina Reza's *Art* (1998–9) and his extensive work in film and television.

Hirata Oriza (1962–) Dramatist and director, Japan. Hirata toured the world by bicycle on his own when he was sixteen. This opened his eyes to the world and made him interested in the position of Japan in Asia. In 1982 he founded Seinendan (the Young People's Association Theatre Company) with his fellow students at ICU International Christian University. In 1984 he built Agora Gekijô (the Agora Theatre), Komaba in Tokyo, which has become the office and the theatre of the company. His plays includes *Kaijin* (*The Sea God*) and *Sôru Shimin* (*The Citizen of Seoul*) in 1989, and *Kagaku-suru Seishin* (*A Scientific Mind*) in 1990. *The Citizen of Seoul* was translated into Korean and staged by Hirata in Seoul in 1993. In his direction, Hirata puts the emphasis on the language and tries to establish a new acting method in which actors' prime concerns are the way of phrasing the text and the tone of the voice. Because of this feature, his theatrical style is said to fall into the category of 'the Theatre of the Quiet'.

Hirsch, Judd (1935–) Actor, USA. Hirsch trained at the American Academy of Dramatic Arts, the Herbert Berghof Studios, at Gene Frankel Studio, and with Uta Hagen, Viveca Lindfors and Bill Hickey. Although Hirsch is well-known for his many successful television series, such as *Taxi* (1978–83), he has a considerable record of acting in the theatre. He received an award for his part of Wiseman in Feiffer's *Knock Knock* (1975), played Trigorin in Chekhov's *Cajka* (*The Seagull*, 1983), and won further awards for the part of Nat in Herb Gardner's *I'm Not Rappaport* (1985–6) and the one-man show *Conversations with My Father* (1991 onwards). In 1998 he appeared in the Matthew WARCHUS Broadway transfer of his orignal London production of Reza's *Art*. He is a superb comic actor who brings an enormous urban intelligence to all of his roles.

Hlaváčová, Jana (1938–) Actor, Czech Republic. After studying at the Prague Academy of Performing Arts, Hlaváčová was a member of the Plzeò theatre for five years, before joining the Prague National Theatre in 1965. Here she soon established her name with complex female parts (Madame de Merteuil in HAMPTON's *Les Liaisons Dangereuses*, 1988) and tragic heroines (Clytemnestra in Aeschylus's *Oresteia*,

1981), for which she is suitably equipped physically with a noble figure, an alto voice and a beautiful face. She is also comfortable in comic roles (Beatrice, *Much Ado about Nothing*, 1976), and endows her characters with the attractive and seductive charm of her mature womanhood. In all her actions she emphasizes the features of creativity, energy, and self-assurance. Since 1994, she has been acting at the Vinohrady theatre, where her roles include Christine in O'Neill's *Mourning Becomes Electra* (1995).

Ho, Jeffrey (1956–) Actor and director, China (Hong Kong SAR). Trained at York University and at the National Theatre School of Canada in Montréal, Ho joined the Hong Kong Repertory Theatre (HK Rep) in 1979 as a full-time actor. Ho has played a variety of characters in close to a hundred productions. He was Judge Brack in Ibsen's *Hedda Gabler* (1983), Marquis de Sade in Peter Weiss's *Marat/Sade* (1984), Lear in *King Lear* (1993, directed by Daniel YANG) and Black Elk in Christopher Sergel's *Black Elk Speaks* (1994, also directed by Yang). Ho was the Producing Artistic Director of the Wanchai Theatre Company, a leading amateur theatre group, from 1987–92. Later, Ho rejoined the HK Rep, where he directed AYCKBOURN's *Absurd Person Singular* (1993), Dürrenmatt's *Der Besuch der Alten Dame* (*The Visit*, 1994), Raymond TO's *Miss To Sup-neung* (1996), Carlo Goldoni's *Il servitore di due padroni* (*The Servant of Two Masters*, 1995) and Molière's *Le malade imaginaire* (*The Imaginary Invalid*, 1998). Since 1993, Ho has been the assistant artistic director of the HK Rep.

Hodgman, Roger (1943–) Director, Australia. Married to actor Pamela RABE, Hodgman directed for ABC television in Tasmania (1965–70) before working in theatre in London and Canada (Artistic Director of the Vancouver Playhouse 1978–81). In Canada, the experience of working with Tennessee Williams made a big impact on Hodgman, and his work there seems to have been more experimental than some productions in Melbourne. Hodgman was Dean of Drama at the Victorian College of the Arts, Melbourne, before becoming artistic director of the Melbourne Theatre Company in 1987, taking over from John Sumner who had held the post for thirty-two years. Hodgman has directed a wide range of theatre at the MTC although it has tended to be staple subscriber audience fare, something Hodgman argues is inevitable given that so much of the MTC's funding goes on rent for the company's tenancy of the Victorian Arts Centre.

Höpfner, Ursula (1949–) Actor, Germany. Höpfner trained in dance at the Hochschule für Musik und Theater in Hannover. After a season at the Staatstheater in Hannover, she joined the ballet company of the theatre in Bremen. Here she met George TABORI, whom she married. They have worked together since, in Munich (Kammerspiele, 1978–81), at Tabori's Theater der Kreis in Vienna (1986–90), and freelance, frequently in Bochum. Since 1990 she has been a member of the Burgtheater in Vienna, working again with Tabori (most recently in Beckett's *Endgame*, 1998, with Gert VOSS in the cast), and also appearing in productions directed by Claus PEYMANN and Manfred KARGE.

Hoffmann, Frank (1954–) Director and dramatist, Luxembourg. After studying literature and philosophy in Luxembourg and Heidelberg, Hoffmann was accepted as a research assistant at the university of Heidelberg from 1978–83, where he completed his doctoral thesis on Michel Foucault. Thereafter he turned his attention to theatre, and became assistant to David MOUCHTAR-SAMORAI from 1981–2. Since 1983 he has worked as a freelance director of plays and operas in Germany, Switzerland, France and Luxembourg. He

was named best young director by Theater Heute in 1990, best director for the production of Odön von Horváth's *Geschichten aus dem Wiener Wald* (*Tales from the Vienna Woods*) at the Schauspiel Bonn in 1993, and won the Prix Lyons for his artistic work in 1995. In the same year, he directed the world premiere of Camille Kerger's opera *Melusina* (libretto by Nico HELMINGER) in conjunction with the author's *Vorspiel*. He is also the director of two films: *Die Reise Das Land* (*The Journey the Land*) and *Schacko Klak* (*Top Hat*, winner of Best Director at the Festival of Teheran) and has written three plays: *Der Kitsch bei Max Frisch* (*The Kitsch with Max Frisch*, 1983), *Genet – Der Zerbrochene Diskurs* (*Genet – The Broken Discourse*, 1984) and *Trilogie der Wut* (*Trilogy of Wrath*, 1985).

Hoff Monsen, Helge (1942–) Designer, Norway. Hoff Monsen graduated from Bergen Kunsthandverskole and trained at the Akademia Sztuk Picknych, Krakow, Poland, as student of Professor Stopka. He has worked in residence at most Norwegian theatres. From 1976–82 he was at the Rogaland Theatre, Stavanger, (productions include *Coriolanus*, and Euripides/Sartre's *Women of Troy*). In 1982–6 he was at Den Nationale Scene, Bergen (productions include *As You Like It*, and Lessing's *Nathan der Weise / Nathan the Sage*). Since 1986 he has been resident designer at Det Norske Teatret, Oslo (productions include Ibsen's *Kongs-Emnerne* (*The Pretenders*), *Figaro* by Beaumarchais and Mishima's *Madame de Sade*). Many of his sets are technically very simple but rich in detail. He has been described as basically 'a painter, not an architect, and his colours are wonderfully rich in range and depths'. Hardly a realistic designer, 'his voice is that of a poet, beautiful, passionate and very often grotesque'.

Hoger, Hannelore (1941–) Actor and director, Germany. Hoger trained with

Eduard Marcks at the Staatliche Hochschule für Musik und Darstellende Kunst in Hamburg. In 1961 she joined the company of Kurt Hübner in Ulm, where she first met Peter ZADEK. She later followed him to Bremen, Stuttgart, Bochum and Hamburg. Since 1986 she has worked freelance as an actor and director. She excels in giving convincing and lifelike portrayals of strong-willed, self-confident and independent women. Major parts include Anna in *Richard III* (1968), the Fool in *King Lear* (1974), the title role in ACHTERNBUSCH's *Susan* (1980), Irina in Chekhov's *Cajka* (*The Seagull*, 1984), Irma in Genet's *Le balcon* (*The Balcony*, 1989) and, more recently, TURRINI's *Alpenglühen* (*Glowing Alps*, Berlin, 1993).

Holbrook, Hal (1925–) Actor, USA. Holbrook trained with Uta Hagen at the Herbert Berghof Studios. After his debut with a stock company in 1942, he won major acclaim with his one-man show *Mark Twain Tonight!* (first 1954). Other parts include Quentin in MILLER's *After The Fall* (1964), Odets's *The Country Girl* (1984) and more recently, classical parts such as the title roles in *King Lear* (1990), Chekhov's *Djadja Vanja* (*Uncle Vanya*, 1991), Shylock (1991), and Willy Loman in Miller's *Death of a Salesman* (1994). In 1997 he appeared in Wasserstein's *An American Daughter* opposite Kate NELLIGAN. His work reveals an enormous range and exceptional dramatic imagination. No American actor of his generation has succeeded in so many different forms and styles.

Hollingsworth, Margaret (1940?–) Dramatist, Canada. Born in Britain, Margaret Hollingsworth emigrated to Canada in 1968 where she obtained an MFA in theatre and creative writing from the University of British Columbia, Vancouver (1974). She has held several teaching positions in Canadian universities. Her first full-length play was *Mother Country*

(1980), followed by, among others, *Alma Victoria* (1990) on a topic also dramatized by Terrence Rattigan in *Cause Celèbre* and in Simon GRAY's *Molly*, and *Making Greenpeace* (1992). Her work is wide-ranging in style and subject, with sexuality, the search for a home and war as recurring themes. Her recent play *In Confidence* (1994) was produced at the New Play Centre in Vancouver.

Hollmann, Hans (1933–) Director, Austria. Hollmann trained as an actor and director at the Max Reinhardt Seminar in Vienna. Plays by Kraus, Arthur Schnitzler and Elias Canetti have been at the centre of Hollmann's work, but he has also directed many important plays of the canon. 'He is regarded as a perfectionist, whose curiosity and foolhardiness have added provocative, colourful and witty productions to the German speaking theatre.' Recent work includes HANDKE's *Zurüstungen für die Unsterblichkeit* (*Preparing for Immortality*, Frankfurt, 1997), Sternheim's *Die Hose* (*The Trousers*, 1998, Frankfurt), and Oscar Wilde's *The Importance of Being Earnest* (Berlin, 1998).

Holmberg, Kalle (1939–) Director, Finland. Holmberg trained at the Finnish Theatre School and was a director at the Helsinki Student Theatre, Helsinki City Theatre (1965–70), principal of the Finnish Theatre School (1968–71), film director with the Finnish Broadcasting Company (1977–81) and chief director at Helsinki City Theatre (1984–93). In addition, he has directed in Gothenburg, Budapest, Oslo and Los Angeles. Major productions include *Richard III*, *Macbeth*, Schiller's *Die Räuber* (*The Robbers*), Molière's *Tartuffe* and numerous opera productions. He has been called an *enfant terrible*, critically assessing national values and theatrical conventions.

Holtz, Jürgen (1932–) Actor, Germany. Holtz trained at the Theaterinstitut in

Weimar and the Theaterhochschule in Leipzig. After seasons in Erfurt, Brandenburg/Havel, Greifswald and the Volksbühne in Berlin, he worked with the Deutsches Theater in Berlin (1966–74), the Berliner Ensemble (1974–7), and the Volksbühne (1977–83). He came to West Germany in 1983, working with directors such as B.K. Tragelehn, Einar SCHLEEF, Heiner Müller, Manfred KARGE and Thomas LANGHOFF. After two seasons at the Bayerisches Staatsschauspiel in Munich, he has been with the company of the theatre in Frankfurt since 1985. His artistry with language is remarkable, and he is equally at home playing power-hungry rulers or cunning and thoughtful comedians. Notable roles include Claudius in *Hamlet* (1985), Gloucester in *King Lear* (1990, with Marianne HOPPE in the title role, directed by Robert WILSON), the one-man show *Katarakt* by Rainald Goetz (1992) and, more recently, in Jürgen GOSCH's production of Schiller's *Die Jungfrau von Orleans* (*The Virgin of Orleans*, 1998).

Holtzmann, Thomas (1927–) Actor, Germany. Holtzmann took private acting lessons in Munich. After employment in Schleswig, Nürnberg and Köln, his breakthrough came in 1961 in Berlin when he played the title role in Kleist's *Prinz Friedrich von Homburg*. Following roles in Berlin, Salzburg, Munich and Vienna, he has been a permanent member of the Münchner Kammerspiele since 1977, where important parts include Malvolio (1980), Vladimir in Beckett's *Waiting for Godot* (1984, directed by George TABORI), Gloucester in *King Lear* (1992) and Prospero in *The Tempest* (1994). Very tall, haggard, with a markedly furrowed face, Holtzmann has been for many years one of the most striking performers on the German-speaking stage.

Homar, Lluís (1957–) Actor and director, Spain. After graduating in law from the

University of Barcelona, Homar worked with a number of independent theatre groups within Catalonia, gaining an increasing reputation as a versatile performer. In 1976, together with Fabià Puigserver, Lluís PASQUAL and Anna LIZARÁN, he inaugurated the Teatre Lliure in Barcelona, a theatrical venture which was to see him perform in more than thirty productions. These include Büchner's *Leonce und Lena* (1977), Chekhov's *Tri sestry* (*Three Sisters*), Molière's *Le misanthrope* (*The Misanthropist*) in 1982, a dazzling rendition of Strindberg's *Fröken Julie* (*Miss Julie*) in 1985, and Heiner Müller's *Quartett* in 1994. These productions defined the Lliure as the most consistently innovative venue for Catalan-language theatre. Following the death of Fabià Puigserver in 1992, Homar took over the company's artistic directorship. During the following six years he worked increasingly as a director, collaborating with artist Frederic AMAT on a production of Schiller's *Die Räuber* (*The Robbers*, 1998) as well as fostering the work of young directors. He was replaced as artistic director by Lluís Pasqual and Guillém Jordi Graells in 1998. During the 1980s he has also made a number of cameo appearances in films such as Mario Camus's *Después del sueño* (*After the Dream*, 1992) and Ventura Pons's *El perquè de tot plegat* (*What It's All About*, 1994).

Hooper, Elric (1936–) Director and actor, New Zealand. Following studies at Canterbury University, where he fell under the theatrical spell of Ngaio Marsh, and the London Academy of Music and Dramatic Art, Hooper worked in the Old Vic Company (1960–3) and Joan Littlewood's Theatre Workshop (1964–5), as well as with various other British and European companies. He returned to a career of acting and directing in New Zealand in 1974, becoming in 1979 artistic director of the Court Theatre, Christchurch, a position he has held since: an exceptional tenure in New Zealand. He has made his name as a master of European and twentieth-century classics, and although sometimes said (rather unfairly given his audience's demands) to be cautious in choice of play, he can also point to highly successful productions of newly commissioned plays like Bruce Mason's *Blood of the Lamb* (1980) and of new overseas works like Tony Kushner's *Angels in America* (1993). He has also directed notable productions of opera. Style he believes is to be found within the play, not imposed from without, and his productions are always responsible to the text, highly intelligent and finely finished.

Hopkins, Anthony (1937–) Actor, Great Britain. Hopkins trained for the stage at the Royal Academy of Dramatic Art and Cardiff College of Music and Drama. He has been associated with the National Theatre since 1966, where major roles include Edgar in Strindberg's *Dödsdansen* (*Dance of Death*, 1967), *Coriolanus* (1971) and *Macbeth* (1972). He spent many years in America working on films, but, having overcome his alcoholism, returned to the National Theatre in 1985 to take the lead in *Pravda* by Howard BRENTON and David HARE. Since then he has played King Lear and Anthony there, as well as the lead in David HWANG's *M. Butterfly* for the West End (1989). Following his major successes in Hollywood films, especially Hannibal Lecter in *The Silence of the Lambs*, he has appeared on stage less frequently.

Hoppe, Marianne (1911–) Actor, Germany. Hoppe trained with the Deutsches Theater in Berlin and took private lessons with Lucie Höflich. In her long and distinguished career, she has played at all the major theatres in Germany. Most notably she was with her husband Gustaf Gründgens in Berlin, Düsseldorf and Hamburg. Active well into her old age, she played Madeline in *Savannah Bay* by Marguerite Duras in 1986, and in 1990

she played the title role in *King Lear*, directed by Robert WILSON.

Horowitz, Danny (1941–) Dramatist, Israel. Since his debut with *Brothers* in 1969 Horowitz has written plays about a broad range of Jewish and Israeli subjects. His best-known plays, confronting different aspects of Jewish identity, are *Cherli Ka Cherli* about the archetype of the mythological Israeli hero figure, (which premiered at the Jerusalem Khan Theatre), *Yossele* (which premiered at La Mama in 1982), and *Daf min Ha-Talmud* (*A Page from the Talmud*, 1984) where he goes back to traditional Jewish sources. In *Hadod Artur* (*Uncle Artur*) Horowitz has taken up the painful memories from the Holocaust. He has also published a book about Israeli Arab (Palestinian) actors. He teaches at the Kibbutz seminar.

Howard, John (1952–) Actor and director. Australia. Trained at the National Institute of Dramatic Arts, Sydney, Howard has a very powerful, physically imposing and intelligent stage presence and he has played starring roles for most of the major theatre companies in Australia. Particularly notable were his performances as the leads in David EDGAR's adaptation of *Nicholas Nickleby*, *Coriolanus*, Aphra Behn's *The Rover* and, most acclaimed of all, John Proctor in Arthur MILLER's *The Crucible* for the Sydney Theatre Company. In Australian plays, Howard has starred in David WILLIAMSON's *Dead White Males* and *Top Silk*, Louis NOWRA's *The Incorruptible* and Nick ENRIGHT's *Mongrels*. Howard has also appeared in film and television and has been working as an associate director of the Sydney Theatre Company with the Australian People's Theatre, which is dedicated to combining multiculturalism and popular theatre.

Howe, Tina (1937–) Dramatist, USA. Following several plays indebted to the Theatre of the Absurd, including *The*

Nest (1969), *Birth after Birth* (1973), *Museum* (1976) and *The Art of Dining* (1979), Howe's breakthrough came with *Painting Churches* (1983), an autobiographical play about a painter making peace with her parents. In this and subsequent plays such as *Coastal Disturbances* (1986), *Approaching Zanzibar* (1989) and *One Shoe Off* (1993), she is a 'marvellously perceptive observer of contemporary mores. At her best, Howe's comedies probe beneath the surface to reveal the mixture of humorous and horrific to which modern culture is a barely adequate response'.

Ho-You-Fat, Yasmina (1964–) Actor, France and Guyane. Qualified in arts, theatre and especially social anthropology, she has also studied method acting and singing. Ho-You-Fat began acting as a schoolgirl in Cayenne with parts in Elie STEPHENSON's plays such as *O Mayouri* (*Working Together*, 1979), and then acted with Jules-Rosette's Théâtre Noir, playing and touring in Marie-Line Ampigny's adaptation *Carmen la Matadore* (*That Feisty Carmen*, 1983), and adaptations of novels and folktales. In 1993 she founded the Pitt à Pawol (Cockpit of Words), a regular series of encounters over a theme or new work in Caribbean literature, where dramatic readings, music and discussion allow authors to meet and debate with a keen and informed section of their public. The series continues, increasingly touring the Caribbean after a presentation in Paris and widening the range of authors. Ho-You-Fat has also undertaken some film and television work. In 1997–9 she appeared in the dramatic version of Chamoiseau's *Chemin d'Ecole* (*School Days*).

Hrůza, Luboš (1933–) Designer, Czech Republic and Norway. After studying scenography at the Prague Academy of Performing Arts, Hrůza became the resident designer of the Bezruč theatre in Ostrava, and as of 1965, of the Prague

Činoherní Club. He has demonstrated his sense of relief composition on the shallow stage, assembled with an inventive combination of authentic and mock-up details in productions including O'Casey's *Midnight Adventure* (1965), SMOČEK's *Podivné odpoledne doktora Zvonka Burkeho* (*The Strange Afternoon of Dr Zvonek Burke*, 1966, directed by Smoček), and Gogol's *Revizor* (*The Government Inspector*, 1967, directed by Jan KAČER). After emigrating to Norway in 1969, he became resident scenographer and in 1972 head scenographer of the Nationalteatret in Oslo, where he developed that conception of Czech scenography which forms the stage as a changeable space–time. Sincer the fall of communism in Czechoslovakia he has returned from time to time to Prague stages (for example, the set and costumes for the modern dress production of Molière's *L'avare* (*The Miser*, 1992) at the Činoherní Club).

Hu Zong Wen (1922–) Actor, China. With neither university education nor professional training, Hu joined Beijing People's Art Theatre in 1952. She appeared in many major parts in the Soviet Russian plays which dominated the Chinese stage in the 1950s. She played the eponymous heroine in Jin Jian's *Zhao Xiao Lan* (1952), Sifeng in Cao Yu's *Lei Yu* (*Thunderstorm*, 1954) and Mariane in Moliere's *L'avare* (*The Miser*, 1959), Wu Su Xin in Su Shu Yang's *Dan Xin Pu* (*Devoted Heart*, 1978), Kang Shun Zi in Lao She's *Cha Guan* (*Teahouse*, 1979) and Hu Niu in Mei Qian's dramatization of Lao She's *Luo Tuo Xiang Zi* (*The Camel Son*, 1980). She is known for her understated and natural acting.

Huang Hai Wei (1959–) Designer, China. Huang graduated from the Department of Stage Design at the Hunan Provincial Art School in 1980, and from the Department of Stage Design at the Central Academy of Drama in 1988. From 1992–4 he studied at L'Ecole Supérieure Nationale de L'Art Dramatique de Strasbourg with a scholarship awarded jointly by the French Ministry of Culture and the Ministry of Foreign Affairs. Since 1994 he has been teaching stage design in The Central Academy of Drama. He designed sets for Wu Zu Guang's *Niu Lang Yu Zhi Nu* (*The Cowboy and the Weaver Girl*, 1986), Alexei Arbuzov's *Little Boar* (1988), and Euripides's *Bakchai* (1995, for which he also designed the masks). In 1997 he designed the set for Shanghai People's Art Theatre's production of Yao Yuan's *Shang Yang*, the set and mask for Florence Opera House's triumphant *Turandot* (directed by Zhang Yi Mou), Zheng Tian Wei's *Gu Wan* (*Antiques*) at Beijing People's Art Theatre, and, most recently, the Chinese classic *Mu Dan Ting* (*The Peony Pavilion*) by the Ming playwright Tang Xianzu, a co-production between Lincoln Centre and Shanghai Kunqu Traditional Opera Company (1998). He has expressed his understanding of the aesthetics, ideas and forms of Chinese traditional theatre in the productions of Chinese themes he designed.

Hubay, Miklós (1918–) Dramatist, Hungary. After studies at the Pázmány Péter University, Hubay became editorial secretary of Nouvelle Revue de Hongrie in 1940. In 1942 he went to Geneva on a scholarship, and between 1945–8 served as director of the Geneva Hungarian Library. From 1949–57 he worked as a teacher of drama history at the Academy of Theatre and Film Art, and from 1955 as dramaturg at the National Theatre of Budapest for two years. Between 1974–88 he was teacher of Hungarian literature at the University of Florence. His plays are constantly on repertory at home and abroad. They include *Egy szerelem három éjszakája* (*Three Nights Of a Love Affair*, 1961), *C'est la guerre* (1962), *Késdobálók* (*Knife-Throwers*, 1964), *Zsenik iskolája* (*A School Of Geniuses*, 1966), *Freud vagy az álomfejtö álma* (*Freud, or the*

Dream of the Dream-Reader, 1984) and *Where Has the Rose's Spirit Gone* (1997). A common feature of his plays of different subjects, genres and styles is that they are all based upon the contradiction between social and particular existence. His heroes are people with a mission, who, due to their personalities and ideas, get into conflict with the expectations of their society.

Hübchen, Henry (1947–) Actor and director, Germany. Hübchen trained at the Staatliche Schauspielschule in East Berlin. Following employment in Magdeburg, he joined the Volksbühne in East Berlin in 1974, appearing in several of Heiner Müller's plays. Since 1985 he has become one of the main actors working with director Frank CASTORF, appearing among other roles as Claudius in *Hamlet* (1989), Fernando in Goethe's *Stella* (1990), Franz Moor in Schiller's *Die Räuber* (*The Robbers*) and the title role in Molière's *Le misanthrope* (*The Misanthropist*). Productions he directed include Horvath's *Glaube, Liebe, Hoffnung* (*Belief, Love, Hope*) and Goethe's *Clavigo* (1990).

Hürlimann, Thomas (1950–) Dramatist, Switzerland. Hürlimann studied philosophy in Zürich and Berlin, followed by three years as assistant director and dramaturg at the Schillertheater in Berlin. His first play, *Großvater und Halbbruder* (*Grandfather and Half-brother*), was produced in 1981. It deals with the way an emigrant is treated in a Swiss village. In *Stichtag* (*Key Date*, 1985), Hürlimann wrote about a very personal topic, his brother's long illness and death from cancer. *Das Lied der Heimat* (*The Song of the Homeland*) was premiered in 1998 in Zürich. 'Hürlimann has been called a specialist in melancholy and dark humour.'

Hussein, Ebrahim (1943–) Dramatist, Tanzania. Ebrahim Hussein was the first highly educated Tanzanian writer (BA in theatre arts from the University of Dar es Salaam) to choose to write his plays in Swahili, his mother tongue. Hussein's theatre can be said to have emerged out of the *taarab*, a tradition of extempore poetry compositions/recitations in Swahili, the *baraza*, a form of formal men's talk sessions and the impromptu tradition of short poetry recitations at weddings. His best published Swahili plays are *Kinjiketile* (1970) and *Mashetani* (*Devils*, 1971), two plays that deal with Tanzanian history (past and recent), the politics of both resistance to colonialism and the tensions of the Tanzanian revolution. Other plays include *Wakati Ukata* (*Time is a Wall*, 1970), *Alikaona* (*She was Punished*, 1970), *Jogoo Kijijini* (*A Cock in the Village*, 1976), *Ngao ya Jadi* (*The Ancestral Shield*, 1976) and *Arusi* (1980). A central theme which runs through Hussein's drama is the concern with the unending struggle to create a just society in Tanzania.

Husseini, Haya (1962–) Dramatist, Jordan. Husseini obtained a Diploma in Education from the University of Western Australia and a BA in English and Spanish from the University of Birmingham. After some time as a teacher of English, she now works as a journalist with *Jordan Times* in Amman. Initially her plays, including *Shades of Eve*, *Spirals* and *The Lights of Jericho*, were inspired by the conflict between East and West. She wanted to deconstruct what she knew of both, expose their similarities and differences, and revel in undoing their established literary structures and norms. In due course, her interest shifted to issues grounded in the political and religious roots of Jordan. Her writing is characterized by a sense of opposed elements placed casually together.

Hutt, William (1920–) Actor, Canada. Born in Toronto, Hutt began performing at Hart House Theatre. He joined the Stratford (Canada) Festival's first company in 1953 and has been a regular on the Stratford stage since then. His prodigious range is demonstrated in the variety of roles he has played at Stratford, including Prospero (*The Tempest*), Feste (*Twelfth Night*), the title role in Molière's *Tartuffe*, Trigorin (Chekhov, *Cajka* (*The Seagull*)), Lady Bracknell (Wilde, *The Importance of Being Earnest*), Vanya (Chekhov, *Djadja Vanja* (*Uncle Vanya*)), Falstaff and Titus Andronicus. He has appeared on Broadway in Shaw's *Saint Joan* and as James Tyrone in the Bristol Old Vic production of *A Long Day's Journey into Night* (1959), and in the 1995 motion picture with Martha HENRY. Hutt is well-known for his mellifluous voice and, in his more recent work, for his economy and subtlety onstage.

Hwang, David Henry (1957–) Dramatist, USA. Hwang attended Yale University School of Drama. He scored his major success with *M. Butterfly* (1988, London 1989 with Anthony HOPKINS), a complex play about the relationship between a French diplomat and his Chinese mistress who turns out to be a man. Other plays include *FOB* (1978), *Broken Promises* (1983), *Rich Relations* and *Golden Child* (1997). Hwang is interested, as he himself says, 'in the dust that settles when worlds collide. Sometimes these worlds are cultural, as in my exploration of a Chinese past meeting an American present. Sometimes they are spiritual, as in *Rich Relations*, where the gung-ho materialism of a California family struggles with its Christian mysticism. Most of the time I also try to walk the fine line between tragedy and comedy.'

Hyder, Zia Dramatist and director, Bangladesh. Hyder trained in theatre at the University of Hawaii from 1966–8. Important among his original works as a playwright are *Shubhra, Sundar, Kalyani, Ananda* (*The Four Passengers*, 1970) and *Elebele* (*The Baloney*, 1981). An allegorical-symbolist play, *Shubhra, Sundar, Kalyani,*

Ananda shows that it is impossible for human society to attain perfection in which peace and happiness can exist. Hyder has translated Sartre's *Huis clos* (*No Exit*, 1969) and Gogol's *Zenit'ba* (*The Marriage*, 1970) jointly with Ataur RAHMAN. He has directed translations of Sophocles's *Oidipus tyrannos* (*King Oedipus*, 1969), Camus's *Le Malentendu* (*Cross Purposes*, 1973), Sartre's *Hus clos* (*No Exit*, 1987) and his own *Elebele* (1990). Zia Hyder has also published five collections of essays on theatre, four volumes of history of world theatre and a volume on Stanislavski, all in Bengali. Professor of Theatre at the Chittagong University, Hyder has travelled extensively abroad to attend various seminars and workshops.

Hyland, Frances (1927–) Actor, Canada. Hyland studied acting at the University of Saskatchewan and at the Royal Academy of Dramatic Art, London. She made her London debut as Stella in Tenessee Williams's *A Streetcar Named Desire* (Aldwych, 1950). Returning to Canada, she performed leading roles with the Stratford (Canada) Festival, the Canadian Players, the Manitoba Theatre Centre, the National Arts Centre and the Vancouver Playhouse (where she played Rita Joe in the celebrated premiere of George Ryga's *The Ecstasy of Rita Joe*). In 1997 she played Augusta Caulfield in Raymond Storey's *South of China* at the Citadel Theatre in Edmonton. Hallmarks of Hyland's acting style are her truthfulness, her vulnerability and her attention to psychological detail. She has won the Governor-General's Award for lifeime achievement in the arts.

Hyman, Earle (1926–) Actor, USA. Hyman trained with Eva le Gallienne at the American Theatre Wing, and at the Actors Studio, New York City. His stage debut was in 1943, and he has played major parts in many productions since then, including the title role in *Othello*,

Vladimir in Beckett's *Waiting for Godot* (1957), Cominius in *Coriolanus*, Hoke Coleburn in Alfred Uhry's *Driving Miss Daisy* (1987), Pickering in Shaw's *Pygmalion* (1991) and the title role in Ibsen's *Bygmester Solness* (*The Master Builder*, 1992). Since 1957, Hyman has been a teacher at the Herbert Berghof School of Acting in New York City. His work is filled with grace and intelligence. This was clearly evident in his performance of Gayev in Chekhov's *Visnevyi sad* (*The Cherry Orchard*, 1973), which was one of the finest portrayals of that role in the last twenty-five years.

Hynes, Garry (1953–) Director, Ireland. In 1975, Hynes established Galway's Druid Theatre Company with actors Mick LALLY and Marie MULLEN. In 1983 Tom MURPHY became Druid's playwright-in-association, and in 1985 Hynes directed the first productions of his *Conversations on a Homecoming* and *Bailegangaire*, the spareness of her direction underlining the strength of these plays. From 1990–4 Hynes was artistic director of the Abbey Theatre. Her work during this controversial period in her career included *Famine* by Tom Murphy and O'Casey's *The Plough and the Stars* (1991), whose expressionist interpretation upset traditionalists. Hynes's commitment to the work of young playwrights is evident in her sparse, uncompromising staging of *Portia Coughlan* by Marina CARR for the Peacock Theatre, Dublin (1996), the Druid Theatre/Royal Court co-production of Martin McDonagh's *The Beauty Queen of Leenane* (1996), and the *The Leenane Trilogy* by McDonagh (1997) for Druid Theatre and at the Duke of York's Theatre, London. Hynes has also directed for the Royal Shakespeare Company, the Royal Exchange, Manchester and the Royal Court Theatre, London, where she is an associate director. In 1998 Hynes directed the première of Arthur MILLER's *Mr Peters' Connections* on Broadway and became the first ever female director to win a Tony award, for the Druid production of *The Beauty Queen of Leenane*.

Hytner, Nicholas (1956–) Director, Great Britain. Hytner studied in Cambridge, where he had already begun directing. Via Kent Opera, the Northcott Theatre in Exeter and the Leeds Playhouse, he arrived at the Royal Shakespeare Company in 1988, directing *Measure for Measure* and then the large-scale musical *Miss Saigon* in the West End (1989). At the Almeida he directed Ben Jonson's *Volpone*; at the National Theatre, he directed SOBOL's *Getto*, Alan BENNETT's adaptation of *The Wind and the Willows*, and especially the successful *The Madness of George III* by Alan Bennett (starring Nigel HAWTHORNE in the title role), which was later made into a film, also directed by Hytner. More recently, he directed Martin McDonagh's *The Cripple of Inishmaan* at the Royal National Theatre.

I

Ichikawa Danjûrô XII (1946–) Kabuki
actor, Japan. The first son of Ichikawa
Danjûrô XI, he succeeded to the present
stage name by playing Sukeroku in *Suker-
oku Yukari no Edo-Zakura* (*Sukeroku:
Flower of Edo*) by Jihei Tsuuchi and
Hanemon Tsuuchi, Benkei in *Kanjincho*
(*The Subscription List*) by Gohei Namiki,
Narukami Shonin in *Narukami Fudo
Kitayama Zakura* (*Saint Narukami and
the God Fudo*) by Hanjuro Tsuuchi, Abun
Yasada and Mansuke Nakada, and Ka-
makura Kengoro in *Shibaraku* (*Wait for a
Moment*) by Ichikawa Danjûrô I at the
Kabuki Theatre in Tokyo in 1985. His
acting style is dynamic, bold, loud and
cheerful, which represents the artistic
family tradition of the Danjûrô family
aragoto (rough) style. His *mie*, expressions and postures on stage, is exquisitely
beautiful and authentic. When Danjuro
XII plays a role in *sewamono* (domestic)
plays, he draws his audience into the
drama by his restrained acting. Thus
Danjuro XII is one of the most important
and acomplished Kabuki actors both in
name and reality. He toured the USA in
1985, Australia in 1988 and Europe in
1989.

Ichikawa Ennosuke III (1939–) Kabuki
actor and director, Japan. The first son of
Ichikawa Danshirô III, he succeeded to
this stage name in 1963. In 1968 Ennosuke revived some of the traditional techniques of Kabuki in *Yoshitsune Senbon
Zakura* (*Yoshitsune Thousand Cherry
Trees*) by Izumo Takeda, Shoraku
Miyoshi and Senryu Namiki, at the National Theatre. He revived the traditional
elements of Kabuki acting such as *keren*
(playing to the audience) with acrobatic
movements, *hayagawari* (instant costume
change) and *chunori* (the mid-air stunts)
in his productions, and has restored the
spectacle and the liveliness in Kabuki in
his productions. Ennosuke acts and
dances both male and female parts. His
acting style is energetic and athletic. He
also produces 'Super Kabuki' in a more
elaborate, grand, visual and modern style
of Kabuki, for example *Oguri* (1982) and
Yamato Takeru (*Takeru Yamato*, 1986).
He also directed an opera, *Coq D'or*
(1984) at Théâtre Chatèle in Paris. A
Chinese opera, *Ryuo* (*King Ryu*, 1989)
was a joint production with the Peking
Opera Academy. Ennosuke has played an
important role in restoring the spirit of
Kabuki as the people's theatre while at the
same time exploring the possibilities of
Kabuki.

Idlbi, Hussein (1939–) Director, Syria. He
trained in Austria. In Syria, he directed
for several years in Aleppo, the second-
largest city in the country, becoming
Artistic Director of its People's Theatre.

He worked closely with playwright Walid IKHLASSI and produced his first play *Al-Ayamu'lati Nansaha* (*The Days We Forget*), which was among several plays he directed there. He then joined Damascus National Theatre, where he directed several productions including Kleist's *Der Zerbrochene Krug* (*The Broken Jug*), Molière's *L'avare* (*The Miser*), Riad Ismat's *Lubato 'l-Hub Wa'l-Thawra* (*The Game of Love and Revolution*) and Sean O'Casey's *Juno and the Paycock*. He is considered a traditional director, whose work started out quite promising but became disappointing later in his career.

Igawa Tôgo (1946–) Actor, Japan. Igawa trained at Haiyû-za (the Actors' Theatre) and Tôhô Gakuen Drama Schools and became a founder member of Engeki Centre (the Black Tent Theatre) in 1969. After moving to the UK, from 1986–8 he acted in productions of the Royal Shakespeare Company and played the parts of El Jefe in Howard Sackler's *The Great White Hope*, Alcade in Trevor NUNN's production of Thomas Haywood's *The Fair Maid of the West* and Sebastian in Aphra Behn's *The Rover*. As a member of the Total Theatre group, he played the role of Japanese Man in Strindberg's *Stora landsvägen* (*The Great Highway*) at the Gate Theatre in 1993 and 1994. He also played Takano in the translation of *Epitaph for the Whales* by SAKATE Yoji at the Gate Theatre in 1998.

Ikhlassi, Walid (1935–) Dramatist, novelist and short story writer, Syria. Although he studied agricultural engineering, he became one of the top literary figures. He lives in Aleppo, the second largest city to the north of Syria. His prose and dramatic writing developed together. His first produced play, *Al-Ayamu'lati Nansaha* (*The Days We Forget*, 1969), produced by The People's Theatre in Aleppo, dealt with a national theme during the French mandate. His other contributions include, *Kayfa Tas'ado Duna An Taka*

(*How to Climb up without Falling*, 1973); *Sahra Dimocratya Ala'l'Khashaba* (*A Democratic Evening on the Stage*, 1979); *Itlaku l-Nari Mina'l-Khalf* (*Firing from the Back*, 1981); *Ors Sharqi* (*An Eastern Wedding*, 1981); and *Oedipus* (1981). His *Maqam Ibrahim Wa Saffia* (*The Shrine of Ibrahim and Saffia*, 1981), was his last major play, considered by critics his best because it dealt with the confrontation between love and traditions in a tragic story with a credibility that resulted in a catharsis. Its success carried it to Damascus as a play for television. In general, Ikhlassi is heralded more as a novelist and short story writer than a dramatist, because he experimented on the basis of literary rather than theatrical experience.

Ikranagara (1943–) Dramatist, performer, director and designer, Indonesia. Ikranagara studied medicine in Yogyakarta and psychology in Jakarta. Having left Bali to attend university in Yogyakarta, he performed with several theatre companies including W.S. RENDRA's Bengkel Theatre. He moved to Jakarta where he continued to perform, translate and adapt plays for a number of companies. In 1975 he formed his own group, Teater (Siapa) Saja which has performed twenty-four of his own plays. He has given lectures, workshops and performances throughout the United States and Southeast Asia, and in 1990–1 was a Fulbright visiting artist in the theatre department of Ohio State University. Plays include *Era of the Bat* (a one-man mask theatre based on Balinse Topeng Pajegan), *Rites of the Mask*, *Zaman Kalong*, *Tok Tok Tok*, *Ssst!*, *Gusti* and *Byurrr...!* He describes his approach as total theatre, born of his interest in ritual and his Balinese heritage. He is also a poet, editor of the literary magazine *Horison* and a regular contributor to the Malaysian journal *Tenggara*. Two volumes of his plays and two of his poetry are published in Indonesian, and he is currently writing a history of Indonesian theatre in English. As a performer and director, he is energetic and innovative; as a writer he balances the boldly satirical with the surreal to create a strange and vivid theatrical world.

Ilie, Gheorghe (1940–) Actor, Romania. After graduating from the Bucharest Institute of Theatre and Film (1967), Ilie joined the National Theatre of Craiova where he became one of the most important members of the company. To date he has performed about eighty-six parts, most of them major roles in Romanian and world repertory by authors such as I.L. Caragiale (in all his comedies), D.R. POPESCU (*Paznicul de la depozitul de nisip* (*The Guardian at the Sand Storehouse*) and *Piticul din grădina de vară* (*Dwarf in the Summer Garden*)), A. Baranga, Tudor POPESCU, Marin Soreseu and also Calderón, Gogol, Gorky and Shaw (Alfred Doolittle in *Pygmalion*). The roles which brought him national and international acclaim were Aaron in *Titus Andronicus* and Theseus in *Phèdre* (after Seneca and Euripides), directed by Silviu PURCĂRETE. In 1995–6 he played Caliban in *The Tempest* at the Nottingham Playhouse and Theatre Clwyd Company, under Purcărete's direction. Critics praised his energy and technical ability.

Iliev, Konstantin (1937–) Dramatist, Bulgaria. Iliev studied German at Sofia University, graduating in 1961, and obtaining his Ph.D. with a thesis on Swiss dramatist Friedrich Dürrenmatt. The productions of his first plays, *Longing for Colours* (1961) and *Without You in October* (1968), were prohibited for ideological reasons. His first work to be staged was *Music from Shatrovets* (1973), followed by *The Window* (1978), *Basils for Draginko*, (1979), *Easter Wine* (1981), *Nirvana* (1983), *Odysseus Travels to Ithaca* (1984), *Red Wine for Good Bye* (1990) and *Canine Holy Mother* (1995). Since 1995 Iliev has been head dramaturg at the National Theatre. Major topics in his plays are the collision between political power and the

ethos of individuals, and the tragic discrepancy between ideal and reality.

Inoue Hisashi (1934–) Dramatist and novelist, Japan. Inoue first became known as a television scriptwriter for the NHK TV's children's puppet play series, *Hyokkori Hyôtan Island*, in the 1960s. With his play *Nihon no Heso* (*Japan's Navel*, 1969), he gained attention as the author of a new comedy. Further plays include *Yabuhara Kengyô* (*Yabuhara the Blind Monk*, 1973), *Keshô* (*Greasepaint*, 1982) and *Zutsû Katakori Higuchi Ichiyô* (*Headache, Stiff-Shoulders and Higuchi Ichiyô*, 1984). He became the head of the Komatsu-za Theatre Company in 1983, where he writes plays as a resident writer. *Keshô* (*Greasepaint*, 1982), in the collection of one-woman plays, *Haha* (*Mothers*), directed by KIMURA Kôichi, was toured in Europe and the USA in 1986 and 1989. British actor Frances DE LA TOUR went to Japan to study the movements of the play and acted *Greasepaint* in English translation at the Lyric Hammersmith, London in 1993.

Iordache, Stefan (1941–) Actor, Romania. Iordache graduated from the Institute of Theatre and Film in Bucharest in 1963. As an actor of the Nottara Theatre in Bucharest, he played major parts in a large variety in plays by I.L. Caragiale (Rica Venturiano in *O noapte furtunoasă* (*A Stormy Night*)), Dostoyevski (Raskolnikov in an adaptation of *Prestuplenie I nakazanie* (*Crime and Punishment*)), Jean Anouilh (*Antigone*), and Shakespeare (*Hamlet*, an especially notable achievement under the direction of Dinu Cernescu in 1974). In 1978 he joined the Teatrul Mic (Little Theatre), where he played a wide range of main roles in Pirandello's *Vestire gli ignudi* (*Let's Dress the Naked*) and Bulgakov's *Master i Margarita* (*The Master and Margarita*), both directed by Cătălina BUZOIANU, and also in MROZEK's *Emigranci* (*Emigrants*) and the title role in *Richard III*, directed by Silviu PURCĂRETE. At the National Theatre in Craiova, he played the title role in *Titus Andronicus*, again directed by Purcarete. Back at the Nottara Theatre, he played *The Prince of Darkness* by Iris Murdoch (1994) and at the Comedy Theatre, and in 1995, General Tcharnota in *Beg* by Bulgakov, directed by Cătălina Buzoianu. A special voice timbre, elegant movement and a capacity for refined emotionality are marks of his acting.

Irobi, Esiaba (1960–) Actor, dramatist and director, Nigeria. Irobi is a sensitive artist whose playwriting and acting show committed and constant experimentation with both dramatic form and staging techniques. His plays include *Nwokedi, What Song Do Mosquitoes Sing?*, *Hangmen Also Die*, *Gold, Frankinsence and Myrrh*, *Why the Vulture's Head is Naked*, *The Other Side of the Mask*, *Am I Too Loud?*, *A Tent to Pass the Night* and *The Fronded Circle*. Among his acting credits are Styles/Buntu in John KANI, Athol FUGARD and Winston NTSHONA's *Sizwe Bansi is Dead* (1982 and 1986), Elesin Oba in Wole SOYINKA's *Death and the King's Horseman* (1982), and Duncan and later Macbeth in *Macbeth* (directed by Ossie ENEKWE and co-starring Toni DURUAKU as Macbeth). His directing credits include co-directing *Sizwe Bansi is Dead* (1986), *Romeo and Juliet* and *Death and the King's Horseman* (Plymouth, 1992).

Isidori, Marco (1948–) Directror, dramatist and actor, Italy. In 1984, Marco Isidori founded, together with the painter and set designer Daniela Dal Cin and the performer Maria Luisa Abate, the theatre company Marcido Marcidorjs e Famosa Mimosa. Since then, Isidori has been exploring the boundaries of dramatic form by abolishing the notional separation between the world of the stage and the auditorium. Considered to be one of Italy's most interesting directors, Isidori has so far focused his work on classical texts. Among his most notable productions are

Studio (*Study*, 1986), *Palcoscenico ed Inno* (*Stage and Hymn*, 1991), *Spettacolo* (*Spectacle*, 1993) and *Happy Days in Marcido's Field* (1997).

Ismat, Riad (1947–) Dramatist, critic and director, Syria. Ismat trained in the UK at the Drama Centre, the Mime Centre, the BBC and University College, Cardiff. In the USA, he trained in San Francisco with Jean Shelton and Mark Epstein, and worked as an assistant to Joseph CHAIKIN. His plays include *Lubato 'l-Hub Wa'l-Thawra* (*The Game of Love and Revolution*, 1975), *Al-Hidad Yaleek Bi-Antigone* (*Mourning becomes Antigone*, 1978) and *Columbus* (1989). *Sinbad* (1981), and *Layali Shahryar* (*Shahryar's Nights*, 1982) are adaptations from *The Arabian Nights*. *Shahryar's Nights* premiered in English at the Sherman Arena, Cardiff, directed by Ismat, who also revived it in 1995 at the Damascus National Theatre. Television credits include the mini-series *Al-Fannan Wa'l-Hub* (*The Artist and Love*, 1985), and the twenty-three-episode serial *Taj Min Showk* (*A Crown of Thorns*), a saga set in the pre-Islamic Arabian desert. Ismat aims to bridge the gap between Arabian and Western cultures by tackling such immortal themes as freedom and democracy, inspired mostly by his own heritage and international classics. More recently, he wrote and directed the first Syrian musical comedy, *Safar El-Narjes* (1997), set his production of Tennessee Williams's *A Streetcar Named Desire* in Damascus in the 1950s, and commemmorated Brecht's anniversary with a production of *The Visions of Simone Machard* (1998).

Ispirescu, Mihai (1941–) Dramatist, Romania. Ipirescu emerged as a playwright in 1977 with *Concediu Nelimitat* (*Unlimited Holidays*), produced at the Toma Caragiu Theatre in Ploiesti. The satirical comedy *Trăsura fa scară* (*The Coach at the Porch*, 1983) won recognition from critics and audiences, as did *Tehnica* *raiului* (*Heaven's Technique*, 1997). Ispirescu's plays follow the style of a parable containing humour and tragical warnings alike. Awarded many prizes, he is a founder of the Romanian Humorists' Association and editor in chief of the humoristic publication *Moftul Român* (Romanian Trifle).

Iwamatsu Ryô (1952–) Dramatist, director and actor, Japan. Iwamatsu attended the Jiyû Gekijô Drama school before becoming a member of Gekidan Tokyo Kandenchi (the Tokyo Electric Battery Theatre Company) (1976–91). Initially Iwamatsu helped the actors' improvisations, then became the company's resident playwright and director. His plays include *O-cha to Sekkyô* (*Tea and Lecture*, 1986), *Futon to Daruma* (*Futon and Daruma*, 1988) *Tonari no Otoko* (*The Man Next Door*, 1990) and *TV Days* (1996). Iwamatsu is one of the leading playwrights in the trend of 'the Theatre of the Quiet' which appeared in the late 1980s. The power of dialogues and drama created by words and pauses are closely examined in this sort of theatre. His drama shows close resemblance to that of PINTER.

J

Jacobi, Derek (1938–) Actor, Great Britain. Jacobi first appeared on the stage in 1960 at the Birmingham Repertory Theatre. He is well-known for his portrayal of the title character in the television series *I Claudius*, and, more recently, *Cadfael*. A beautiful voice is helpful in rendering his classical characters highly poetic. An air of innocence makes him vulnerable. He has a distinguished career both in Shakespeare, such as *Hamlet* (1977, also television), *Richard II* (1988), *Richard III* (1988) and *Macbeth* (1993, Royal Shakespeare Company, directed by Adrian NOBLE, with Cheryl CAMPBELL as Lady Macbeth), and in modern and contemporary plays (Whitemore's *Breaking the Code*, 1986, Anouilh's *Beckett*, 1991 and the title role in Chekhov's *Djadja Vanja* (*Uncle Vanya*), 1996).

Jalan, Shyamanand (1934–) Director, India. Jalan brought post-independence Hindi theatre into Bengal with the first production of Mohan Rakesh's *Ashad ka ek Din* (1960). He is one of the founder members of the Anamika theatre group, which committed itself to the ancient *rasa* theory. Some of his notable productions include his *Janata Ka Shatru*, (an adaptation of Ibsen's *En Folkefiende* (*An Enemy of the People*)), Badal SIRCAR's *Evam Indrajit*, Mohan Rakesh's *Adhe Adhure*, Vijay TENDULKAR's *Sakharam Binder*, Girish KARNAD's *Tughlaq*, Kalidasa's *Shakuntala* and G.P. DESHPANDE's *Uddhwasta Dharmashala* (*A Man in Dark Times*). He has explored the relevance of the ancient *rasa* theory in his productions and sometimes uses pop or jazz, as for instance in his recent production of his play *Ram Kalha, Ram Kahani*.

Jančar, Drago (1948–) Dramatist, Slovenia. He studied law and worked as a journalist, editor and freelance writer. In 1975 he was sentenced for 'enemy propaganda'. In 1985 he went to the USA as a Fulbright fellow, in 1988 he was in Germany with a Bavarian scholarship for writers. From 1987–91, he was president of the Slovenian PEN Centre. His novels and short stories have been translated into many languages and have won several prizes. Major plays include *Profesor Arnož in njegovi* (*Professor Arnož and His Followers*, 1982), *Veliki briljantni valcek* (*The Brilliant Grand Waltz*, 1985), *Nocni prizori* (*Night Scenes*, 1986), *Zalezujoc Godota* (*Stakeout on Godot*, 1987), *Klementov padec* (*Klement's Fall*, 1987), *Dedalus* (1988), *Dvoboj* (*Duel*, 1992) and *Halstst* (*Hallstatt*, 1994). The surrealist *Brilliant Grand Waltz* was considered by Jan Kott as 'one of the best works to come out of the Communist countries, as good as anything being written in the eighties'.

Jang Min-Ho (1924–) Actor, Korea. Jang trained at the Joseon Actors' School. Since his first appearance in 1947, Jang has been recognized as a follower of the realistic trend in modern Korean theatre. He has performed the largest number of title roles on the modern Korean stage, including Guss in Anderson's *Both Your Houses* (1954), the title role in Goethe's *Faust* (1965, 1979, and 1984), Lee Soon-Sin in *Seongwoong Yi Soon-Sin* (*Admiral Soon-Sin Lee*, 1973, in the opening programme of the New National Theatre of Korea), Father in OH Tae-Seok's *Sachoogi* (*Adult at Puberty*, 1979) and Sin Che-Ho in *Kumhanul* (*Heaven in a Dream*, 1987, directed by KIM Suk-Man). Jang received the honourable title of 'actor of no failure' from Korean drama critics. He was the president of the Korean National theatre from 1967–71 and 1979–87.

Janžurová, Iva (1941–) Actor, Czech Republic. A graduate of the Prague Academy of Performing Arts, Janzurová worked for a year in the Liberec theatre, whence she moved to the leading Prague Vinohrady theatre. It was here she developed her extraordinary range in dozens of characters such as Jana in Anouilh's *L'Alouette* (*The Lark*, 1965), Josie in O'Neill's *A Moon for the Misbegotten*, 1969 and Madame von Stein in Peter Hacks's *Ein Gespräch im Hause Stein über den abwesenden Herrn von Goethe* (*A Conversation in the Stein Residence About the Absent Mr von Goethe*, 1977). She has been a member of the Prague National Theatre since 1987, where she played Dorina (Molière's *Tartuffe*, 1988), the Old Woman (Ionesco's *Les chaises* (*The Chairs*), 1992, directed by Jan KAČER) and Gina Ekdal (Ibsen's *Vildanden* (*The Wild Duck*), 1993). The trademark of her acting is the contrast between the exterior mad, confused expression and the interior world of the characters. This contrast

allows her a tragicomic effect as well as capturing one of the key themes of modern times: the disoriented relationship of human beings to the external world.

Jelinek, Elfriede (1946–) Dramatist, Austria. Jelinek studied piano and composition at Wiener Konservatorium, as well as theatre and art history. Besides plays for the stage, including *Clara S*, *Krankheit oder Moderne Frauen* (*Illness or Modern Women*, 1987), *Totenauberg* (1990) and *Raststätte oder Sie machens alle* (*Inn, or They All Do It*, 1994), and radio, she has written poems and novels. 'Any attempts by critics to stir up a scandal around her radical texts have failed, because of their artificiality, brokenness and hermetically closed language.'

Jernidier, Joël (1965–) Actor, France and Guadeloupe. An ambitious and very personable member of a keen theatrical family, Jernidier initially took part in workshops and plays with brother José, then graduated with much success in 1990 from the Cours Florent, Paris. He took part in the celebration of black poetry *Cent vers sans chaînes* (*A Hundred Unchained Verses*, 1991) in festivals in Morocco and Senegal, and in a production of Koltès *Dans la solitude des champs de coton* (*In the Solitude of the Cotton Fields*) by the TNP Villeurbanne. Back in Guadeloupe, he joined, as 'Madame le Président', in the virtuoso masking of Michèle Montantin's *Vie et mort de Vaval* (*Life and Death of Carnival*, 1991), played in the popular work for children's theatre, *Les Deux Bossus et la Lune* (*The Two Hunchbacks and the Moon*), in Gerty DAMBURY's *Madjaka ou la fin du Bal* (*The Party's Over*), and in *Carêmes* (*Dry Seasons*, 1998). Film roles include Codou in Christian Lara's *Sucre amer* (*Bitter Sugar*, 1997).

Jernidier, José (1959–) Actor, author and director, France and Guadeloupe. On returning from France, where he studied photography, Jernidier joined a drama workshop in Petit-Bourg and launched into satirical comedy in Creole with his group TTC (Théâtre Tradition et Culture) + Bakanal. After a collective creation *Plus Bakanal* (*More Bacchanal*, 1985) and other plays mocking the media and consumer society, his nostalgic comedy *Moun Koubari* (*The Folk of Locust Tree Village*, 1990) was a popular hit and toured the French Caribbean and France, to be followed in 1996 by *Mal Maké* (*Branded Bad*). Though farcical in method, Jernidier's comedy springs from observation of the clash of values as a distinctive rural society is exposed to assimilation by French urban pressures. His work attracted the attention of Maryse CONDÉ, and after a folk play on slavery, *Les Sept voyages de Ti Noel* (*The Seven Journeys of Little Noel*), he took the role of Toussaint-L'Ouverture in Condé's *An Tan Revolisyon* (*Revolution Time*, 1989), as well as assisting director Sonia Emmanuel. He subsequently directed and played in Condé's *Comédie d'Amour* (*The Comedy of Love*, 1993). Inspiring much loyalty from his small semi-professional group, Jernidier has made his mark especially in Guadeloupean comedy in Creole.

Jivanov, Emilia (1938–) Designer, Romania. Soon after graduating from the Fine Arts Institute N. Grigorescu in Bucharest in 1963, Jivanov joined The National Theatre in Timişoara and has been working there since, creating set and costume designs for more than ninety productions. She has collaborated also with the National Theatre in Târgu Mures, the National Theatre in Bucharest, the State Theatre in Oradea and others. Among her most acclaimed designs are many plays by Romanian authors, such as Dumitru Radu POPESCU (*Mormântul călăretului avar* (*The Grave of an Avar Horseman*), *Dalbul pribeag* (*The Wanderer*)) and Matei VISNIEC (*Arthur osânditul* (*Arthur the Convict*)), and by world classics and contemporary authors such as

Shakespeare, Chekhov (*Tri sestry* (*Three Sisters*), *Djadja Vanja* (*Uncle Vanya*)), Goldoni, Gorki, Peter Weiss and Ibsen. Recipient of many awards, she participated in national and international exhibitions in Bucharest, Novi Sad and Prague (Ouadriennale). Emilia Jivanov is acclaimed for her capacity of creating settings with a poetical touch, where light and colour radiate emotional power.

Johnson, Terry (1955–) Dramatist and director, Great Britain. Johnson shot to fame with *Insignificance* (1982), which had the curious combination of Marilyn Monroe, Einstein, McCarthy and Joe diMaggio as characters. Some subsequent plays did not live up to the quality of this first success, until *Hysteria*, about a meeting between Freud and Dali, and *Dead Funny*. More recently, he has directed a few productions at the Royal National Theatre, including his own *Cleo, Camping, Emanuelle and Dick* (designed by William DUDLEY).

Jones, Gillian (1947–) Actor, Australia. Trained initially as a ballet dancer before graduating from the National Institute of Dramatic Art, Sydney in 1968, Jones has played a wide variety of roles, classical and modern, including Viola in *Twelfth Night*, Gertrude in *Hamlet* and Barbara in Michael GOW's *Europe*. Jones is particularly known for her work with directors Neil ARMFIELD at Company B, Belvoir St, Sydney, Rex Cramphorn at his Performance Syndicate, and Jim SHARMAN. Jones was in the original Australian *Hair*, and went on to work with Sharman at the Lighthouse ensemble in Adelaide. She brings intensity and intelligent clarity to her roles along with a sense of discipline and a powerful sensuality, and has rarely played comic roles. Jones also wrote and performed the monodramas *Passengers in Overcoats* and *Anorexia Sometimes*.

Jones, Marie (1951–) Dramatist and actor, Ireland. Marie Jones was writer-in-residence with Charabanc Theatre Company, Belfast from its foundation in 1983 until 1990. Plays for the company included *Lay up your Ends* co-written with Martin Lynch (1983), *Gold in the Streets* (1986) and *Weddin's, Wee'ins and Wakes* (1990). Jones's work has taken an unerring look at Irish society, having addressed such issues as life in a block of high-rise flats in 1980s Belfast in *Somewhere Over The Balcony* (1988). By cofounding and writing for Charabanc, Jones not only staged the condition of Irish women but actively placed women on the Irish stage. She has consolidated her position as a leading Irish playwright as a founder member of Dubbeljoint Theatre Company, Belfast, where she is writer-in-residence and associate director. Her work for the company includes *A Night in November* (1994), *Women on the Verge of HRT* (1996) and *Stones in his Pockets* (1996). Jones has also written for Replay Theatre in Education Company, for radio and television. As an actor, Jones has worked extensively with Charabanc, Dubbeljoint, and on radio and film.

Jude, Nouman (1945–) Designer, Syria. Jude studied in St Petersburg, Russia. After his return to Syria, he designed sets, costumes and lighting for over ninety productions for theatre, television and film. For the Damascus National Theatre, he designed Sean O'Casey's *Juno and the Paycock*, and Sa'dallah Wannus's *The King is the King*. For the Experimental Theatre he designed the sets of all Fawaz Sajer's productions. He participated in international exhibitions in Egypt, Tunisia and Germany and won prizes. He is the only Arabic member of OISTAD, an international organization of theatre designers, and participated in its two conferences in Prague in 1991 and 1995, winning in the later the third prize among artists from forty-three countries. He designed the set for the first Syrian opera coproduction with the support of the British

Council, Henry Purcell's *Dido and Aeneas*. He taught design at the Syrian Academy of Dramatic Arts for sixteen years, before moving to teach in Kuwait.

Juliani, John (1940–) Director, Canada. Juliani trained as an actor at the National Theatre School. After two seasons at the Stratford Festival, he joined Simon Fraser University, British Columbia, to teach theatre. Here he developed experiments in theatre called Savage God, with an emphasis on 'economy, flexibility and mobility'. He continued his work while at York University, Toronto (1974–6) and Edmonton (1976–81). Since 1981 he has worked as CBC radio drama producer in Vancouver as well as a freelance director for theatre, film and television.

Junker, Marja-Leena (1945–) Actor and director, Luxembourg. After graduating from the Conservatoire de Luxembourg, the Finnish-born Junker joined the Théâtre du Centaure and played a great number of roles in both classical and contemporary repertory, mostly in French. She was particularly lauded for her performance of Cocteau's monologue *La Voix Humaine* (1985–9, Luxembourg, Paris and Athens). She also won great acclaim for the parts of Ysé in Claudel's *Partage de Midi* (*Noontide*, 1989, Théâtre des Capucins), Martha in ALBEE's *Who's Afraid of Virginia Woolf?* (1992, Théâtre d'Esch, with Philippe NOESEN and Myriam MULLER, designed by Jeanny KRATOSCHWILL) and Mama in Coline Serreau's *Lapin Lapin* (1996). In 1992 she assumed the artistic directorship of the Théâtre du Centaure and has since directed the company's productions of Molière's *Les fourberies de Scapin* (1993), Lyie Kessier's *Orphans* (1996) and Camus's *Les Justes* (*The Just*, 1997). Junker is an actor of immense stage presence and emotional depth and, through her teaching, has inspired many younger theatre artists.

Jurisic, Melita Actor, Australia. Born in Croatia, Jurisic is now based in Melbourne and began her career there with the Actors Company. Jurisic has played a variety of extraordinary roles with astonishing, sometimes blazing intensity. Jurisic created the role of Betsheb in Louis NOWRA's *The Golden Age* with a sense of animal vitality, otherness, weirdness and passion which was extremely powerful. She appeared in several of Nowra's early works, first working with him at the Lighthouse Company in Adelaide, which she joined in 1982 and where she also played in *A Midsummer Night's Dream*, Brecht's *Mutter Courage und ihre Kinder* (*Mother Courage and her Children*) and Kleist's *Prinz Friedrich von Homburg*. More recently she played Gretchen in the Melbourne Theatre Company's production of Goethe's *Faust*, six different roles in CHURCHILL's *Mad Forest*, a hundred year old Balinese woman in Graeme Shiel *Bali Adat* and Cordelia in a SUZUKI-influenced *Lear* at Playbox, Melbourne. Jurisic's acting is visceral; her stage presence is compelling and she is unafraid to seek out extremes within the characters she plays.

Justin-Joseph, Annick (1949–) Director and writer France and Martinique. With diplomas in movement, mime and drama, her gentle determination and commitment to the development of Martinican theatre have informed her roles as head of the SERMAC theatre workshop (1977–81), founding director of the Théâtre de la Soif Nouvelle (1982–7), head of the Centre Dramatique Régional (1987–9) and municipal cultural administrator (1995–). After an interlude of study she returned to Martinique in 1992 to work with a group of disadvantaged children, with whom she created the bilingual musical *Rosia Siguine O* (1996). She is fascinated with local history and motivated by 'the aesthetic of our traditions'. Her directing credits include montages poétiques, Placoly's *Massacre au bord de mer* (*Massacre on the Seashore*, 1989), a television adaptation of Ina Césaire's *Dame Kéléman* for RFO, and a commissioned piece for the Museum of Pre-Columbian Art. Among those with whom she has worked, she particularly credits SOYINKA, whom she assisted on *Trials of Brother Jéro* for the 1984 Festival of Fort-de-France, with inspiring the direction of her company Carib Studio.

K

Kačer, Jan (1936–) Director and actor, Czech Republic. Kačer studied direction at the Prague Academy of Performing Arts and began work for the Youth Theatre in Ostrava (1959–64), where he directed Brecht's *Mutter Courage und ihre Kinder* (*Mother Courage and her Children*, 1961) and *Romeo and Juliet* (1962). In 1965 he co-founded the experimental Činoherní Club in Prague, whose profile was further shaped by Kačer's productions of Gogol's *Revizor* (*The Government Inspector*, 1967) and Chekhov's *Visnevyi sad* (*The Cherry Orchard*, 1969), *Djadja Vanja* (*Uncle Vanya*, 1973) and *Cajka* (*The Seagull*, 1975), in which he always tried to bring the dramatic and comic qualities of the text to a head. He also played the part of Raskolnikov in Dostoyevsky's *Prestuplenie I nakazanie* (*Crime and Punishment*, 1966). Politically persecuted, he was forced to leave Prague and worked in Ostrava until returning again in 1986. His direction is marked by a large range of styles, both in terms of means as well as repertoire, from the absurd (Ionesco's *Les chaises* (*The Iva* JANŽUROVÁ and Miroslav DONUTIL) to poetic drama (Ibsen's *Peer Gynt*, National Theatre, 1995). He works in small and large venues, with puppet theatre and in the opera.

Kadyrova, Larysa (1943–) Actor, Ukraine. Kadyrova trained at the Drama Studio at the Maria Zan'kovets'ka Ukrainian Drama Theatre (L'viv), graduating in 1963. In 1981 she received a degree from the Karpenko-Kary Institute for the Art of the Theatre, Kiev. Her major roles at the Maria Zan'kovets'ka Ukrainian Drama Theatre, L'viv (1963–93) in productions directed by Serhii DANCHENKO and Alla Babenko include Donna Anna in Lesia Ukrainka's *Kam'ianyi hospodar* (*The Stone Host*, 1971), Mavka in Ukraina's *Lisova pisnia* (*The Forest Song*, 1983), Larisa in Ostrovsky's *Bespridanittsa* (*The Dowerless Girl*, 1985), the title role in Racine's *Phèdre* (1988) and Natalia Petrivna in Volodymyr Vynnychenko's *Brekhnia* (*The Lie*, 1991). Kadyrova is an actor of an intellectual plane; exalted refinement and nervousness are characteriztic of her heroines. Since 1993 she has been an actor of the Ivan Franko Ukrainian Drama Theatre, Kiev where she played Rebecca in *Rosmersholm* by Ibsen (1994). Kadyrova has also appeared in the role of Ranievskaia in Chekhov's *Visnevyi sad* (*The Cherry Orchard*, 1996), at the Les' Kurbas Molodizhny Theatre, L'viv, directed by Volodymyr KUCHYNS'KY.

Kahn, Michael (1940–) Director, USA. Kahn graduated from New York's High School of Performing Arts, and trained with Michael Howard and the Actors Studio. In a prolific career, he has directed numerous productions in all genres and styles. He was artistic director of the American Shakespeare Theatre (1969–74), McCarter Theatre (1974–9) and the Acting Company (1978–88). Since 1986 he has been very successful as artistic director of the Shakespeare Theatre at the Folger in Washington. Kahn is mainly known for his Shakespeare productions. His work places great emphasis on clear story telling and fine speaking with little regard to directorial concepts.

Kainy, Miriam (1942–) Dramatist, Israel. Kainy studied history at Tel Aviv University. Her first play *Hashiva* (*The Homecoming*, produced 1973 and 1975) and *Hem* (*They*, produced together with Joseph CHAIKIN in 1980) dealt with the Arab–Israeli conflict as an expression of the experience of the outsider/other. In her later plays like *Bavta* (1986), *Sof Onat Hachlomot* (*The End of the Dream Season*, 1991) and *Bianca* (1995), she has focused on female issues. Kainy has also written screenplays for television and radio plays and is active as a translator and has adapted several plays.

Kállai, Ferenc (1925–) Actor, Hungary. After training at the Academy of Theatre and Film Art he joined the Belvárosi Theatre in 1945, and from 1948 until his retirement in 1986 he was a member of the National Theatre. Since 1977 he has been a teacher at the Academy of Theatre and Film Art, and since 1981 the president of the Hungarian Theatre Art Association. Between 1985–9 he served as an MP. A significant screen actor, he became the symbol of an era in the leading role of Péter Bacsó's political satire *A tanú* (*The Witness*). Major roles include Romeo (*Romeo and Juliet*), Edmund (*King Lear*), Jourdain (Molière's *Le bourgeois gentilhomme* (*The Citizen as Nobleman*)), Orgon (Molière's *Tartuffe*)), Stockmann (Ibsen's *En Folkefiende* (*An Enemy of the People*)), Volpone (Ben Jonson's *Volpone*), Mayor (Gogol's *Revizor* (*The Government Inspector*))

and Polonius (*Hamlet*). Kallai is convincing as dramatic hero, petty tyrant or suppressed ordinary man. In some plays (like the Hungarian national tragedy, József Katona's *Bánk Bán* (*Banus Bánk*)) he played several roles during his career.

Kaloč, Zdeněk (1938–) Director and dramatist, Czech Republic. Kaloč studied direction at the Prague Academy of Performing Arts. In all his productions, he joins psychologicalism with the stage metaphor. From 1962–6 he worked at the Mrštík Brothers theatre, where he directed, amongst others, Dürrenmatt's *Die Physiker* (*The Physicists*, 1964). His productions of Euripides's *Troades* (*The Trojan Women*) and Shudraka's *Mrcchakatika* (*The Little Clay Cart*), both in 1968 at the National Theatre, were characterized by a poetically and musically stylized stage form. He has often reworked the dramatic text quite fundamentally, such as Pushkin's *Boris Godunov* (1970), and has directed his own prose adaptations (Tolstoy's *Vojna I mir* (*War and Peace*), 1970; Dostoyevsky's *Brat'ia Karamazovy* (*The Karamazov Brothers*), 1995), which are informed by his interest in Russian authors and their fascinating portrait of the human soul. He is also inclined to Paul Claudel, with productions of *Annonce faite à Marie* (*Annunciation to Mary*, 1991), and *Le Soulier de Satin* (The Satin Slipper, 1993). Among his own plays are *Mejdan na písku* (*Party on the Sand*, 1977), *Holátka* (*The Nestlings*, 1982) and *V zajetí nezne chiméry* (*In the Clutches of the Gentle Chimera*, 1985).

Kalyagin, Alexander (1942–) Actor and director, Russia. Kalyagin started his career in the theatre as an amateur actor. Later he trained at the Schukin Theatre College in Moscow. He joined the Taganka Theatre Company, where he successfully played Galileo in Bertolt Brecht's *Leben des Galilei* (*Life of Galileo*). After that he joined the Moscow Yermolova Theatre. Since 1976 he has worked with the Moscow Art Theatre. His most important parts with the Moscow Art Theatre include Popryschin in Gogol's *Zapiski Sumasshedshego* (*Diary of a Madman*), Orgon in Molière's *Tartuffe* and Protassov in Tolstoy's *Zivoj Trup* (*Living Corpse*). Kalyagin is a brilliant comic actor, assisted by his round face and rather stout figure. Nevertheless, he is also an accomplished performer of serious drama, mainly Gorky and Chekhov. He toured for some seasons in France with his partner Anastasya Vertynskaya, giving lessons in dramatic art to foreign colleagues. In 1993 he founded his own theatre, Et Cetera, playing Chekhov and other Russian classics. Kalyagin has a profound interest in actor training and is a professor at the Moscow Art Theatre Studio.

Kambar, Chandrasekar (1937–) Dramatist and actor, India. Kambar has written more than twenty plays in Kannada, some socio-political, such as *Jokumaraswamy* and *Rishyasirunga*, and more recently comedy, such as *Siri Sampige*. His most significant contribution to Indian theatre is the use of Bayalata, the folk form of North Karnataka, and the Sangya-Bayalata, a folk play of Karnataka. In his plays, he is concerned with human relation with the beyond. Winner of many awards, he is the chairman of Karnataka State Nataka Academy, and has also acted in some of his plays.

Kambarev, Stoyan (1953–) Director, Bulgaria. He trained at the National Academy of Theatre and Film Arts, Sofia (1979–83). In addition, he studied at the Silvio D'Amico Theatre Academy and La Sapienza University in Rome and at the Vispyanski Theatre, Katowice, Stary Theatre and Bagatela Theatre, Cracow, Poland. His major productions include Sam SHEPARD's *Fool for Love* (1986), Beckett's *Happy Days* (1988), Gogol's *Revizor* (*The Government Inspector*, 1992), *Die Zeit und der Raum* (*The Time and the Room* by Botho STRAUSS, 1992),

and *January* by Bulgarian dramatist Yordan RADICHKOV (1995). His strength lies in his ability to recognize the qualities of space as the basis for the structure of performance, especially in terms of his choice of unconventional spaces. Mutual relationship with the actors, in the process of which both sides are challenged to improvisations, characterizes his work as a director.

Kancel, Harry (1948–) Actor and director, France and Guadeloupe. A trained teacher, Kancel began by organizing short plays as leisure activity for young people on free afternoons. He took part in the 1970 workshop run by Jean-Marie Serreau, out of which Arthur LÉRUS and others constituted the Théâtre du Cyclone. Until 1978 he was closely involved in Cyclone's annual collective productions, then worked independently. Since 1982 he has mainly directed works by Jean-Michel Palin, with whom he created a small group Pawol a Nèg Soubarou' (Words of a Roots Man), named after their play, also called *L'arbre aux masques* (*The Tree of Masks*, 1984) in which Kancel played an ancient black man interrogated by a little girl. As well as a number of poetic 'montages' on Caribbean texts, Kancel has directed Henri Corbin's *Baron samedi* (1989), Lucie Julia's *Jean-Louis: un nègre pièce d'Inde* (*Jean-Louis: A Negro, Piece of India*, 1991), Jean Metellus' *Anacoana* (1993) and Raymond Boutin's *Cris et silence* (*Cries and Silence*, 1995). He has become a leading exponent of serious Guadeloupean theatre with a special interest in demonstrating the poetic possibilities of dialogue in Creole as well as French.

Kang, Waldo (1936–) Dramatist, Korea (also known as Pagoon or Pagune). He attended Seoul National University, studied at the University of Indiana, Bloomington, USA and received a Ph.D. degree in philosophy from Columbia University, New York. From the early 1960s, he wrote one-act plays for fringe theatres in New York, including *Among Dummies* (1962, Cafe Cino Theatre), *Head Hunting* (1962, at Cafe La MaMa) and *Between Yesterday and Tomorrow* (1964). Since the mid-1980s, Kang has been involved in Korean theatre, writing some plays in Korean including *Eocheonji Dolyeonbyeoni* (*Mutating for No Reason*, 1988), *Beondaegijeon* (*Tales of Pupae*, 1990) and *Bakdeongi Romance* (*Romance of a Ground*, 1995). All these works deal with the typical pattern of human behaviour in hazardous situations.

Kani, John Bonisile (1943–) Actor, South Africa. Kani acquired his performing skills through workshops with the Serpent Players. *Sizwe Bansi is Dead* (1976), which had evolved out of workshops and improvisations, is the play that launched the international acting careers of John Kani and his co-actor and devisor, Winston NTSHONA. However, the play did more than that, for more than any other play before or even after it, except possibly *Woza Albert!*, it brought the evil of apartheid onto the international stage. Kani was remarkable in his twin roles of Styles and Buntu. Kani has subsequently featured in many of Fugard's other plays, including Sam in *Master Harold and the Boys*, and leading characters in *Playland*, *Marigolds in August*, *The Island* and most recently *My Children! My Africa!* in which he plays Mr M (the school teacher stoned to death at the end for betrayal). Kani's performance in all these and other plays in which he has appeared has been acclaimed locally and internationally. He is the complete performer, who brings to his roles an inner life, fire and joy that are peculiarly his own. Other credits include Jean in Strindberg's *Fröken Julie* (*Miss Julie*), and the title role in *Othello*.

Kanze Hideo (1927–) Nôgaku shite actor, actor and director, Japan. The second son of Kanze Tetsunojôgasetsu VII and a member of Kanze School of nô, he was initially taught by his father and Kanze Kasetsu. After the Second World War he changed to Kita School and studied under Kita Roppeita VI and Kita Minoru. He once left nô in 1958 but in 1979 returned to the Kanze School. He formed Seinen Geijutsu Gekijô (The Youth Art Theatre Company) with the playwrights Yoshiyuki Fukuda and Ken Miyamoto, and also formed Jiyû Gekijô (the Freedom Theatre Company) with SATÔ Makoto in 1966. He acted in *Shigosen no Matsuri* (*Requiem on the Meridian*, 1979) by KINOSHITA. He appeared in the film of *Suna no Onna* (*The Woman in Dune*) by Abe Kôbô, which won an award at the Cannes International Film Festival. He was also involved in the productions of Greek tragedies by Mei no Kai (The Group Mei Theatre Company). Since returning to nô, he has revived old nô plays such as *Ikenie* (*The Sacrifice*), *Sanekata* and *Take* (*The Banboo*). He has attended many international theatre festivals to introduce nô widely to the world. Kanze Hideo was one of the forerunners of the new theatre movement of the 1960s. His open-minded and courageous attitude and an attempt to bridge traditional and modern theatre by recognizing Japanese theatre as a whole have contributed tremendously to theatre in Japan. Apart from acting, he directs plays, operas and choreographs dance.

Kara Jûrô (1940–) Dramatist, director, artist and novelist, Japan. Kara attended Seihai Drama School. He felt that socialist realism did not satisfy his appetite for theatre, and went back to his student theatre group and renamed it Jôkyô Gekijô (the Situation Theatre Company, inspired by Sartre). Kara's concept of drama, and of theatricality was completely different from the *shingeki* paradigm. Soon he became one of the leading figures of *angura* (the underground or alternative) theatre movement of the 1960s. The company was widely known as Aka Tento (Red Tent) because of their mobile big red tent theatre, and the performances were given in a shrine precinct, on the street or by a pond in the park. His plays include *Shôjo Kamen* (*Virgin's Mask*, 1969, directed by SUZUKI), *Nito Monogatari* (*The Tale of Two Cities*, Seoul, 1972), *Bengaru no Tora* (*The Bengalese Tiger*, Bangladesh, 1973) and *Binro no Fuin* (*The Seal of Binro*, Taiwan, 1992). His concept of internationalism focuses on Japan's neighbouring countries in Asia. His plays attract other theatre directors. For example, *Shitaya Mannen-cho Monogatari* (*The Story of Shitaya Mannen Street*, 1981), and *Taki no Shiraito* (*The Water Jugglar*, 1989) were both directed by NINAGAWA.

Karanth, B.V. (1929–) Director, India. One of the controversial directors of the Indian scene, Karanth received early education at the Gubbi Theatre Company. He was the director of the National School of Drama, director of the Bharatiya Bhavan, Bhopal and director of the drama institute Rangayana in Mysore. Some of Karanth's best-known productions are Girish KARNAD's *Tughlag* and *Hayavadana*, Badal SIRCAR's *Evam Indrajit*, KAMBAR's *Jokumaraswamy*, TENDULKAR's *Ghashiram Kotwal* and *Birnam Vana*, an adaptation of *Macbeth*. He has composed music for many theatre productions including his own, and has directed some avant-garde films like *Chomana Dudi* and *Vamsa Viruksha*. Karanth pursues a restless quest for the meaning of the arts in the modern world.

Karashevs'ky, Volodymyr (1955–) Designer, Ukraine. In 1981 Karashevs'ky received his degree from the Taras Shevchenko Kiev State Institute for Arts, the Faculty of Painting, Theatrical Department (the workshop of Daniil LIDER). He is one of the most original modern Ukrainian scenographers. He designed many successful experimental projects including Shal'tianis's *'Skazka o Monike* (*The Fairy Tale about Monika*, Kiev, 1978), *Pam'iat'*

(*The Memory*, after Borys Oliinyk, Kiev, starring Bohdan STUPKA, 1987), Valerii Shevchuk's *Sad bozhestvenukh pisen'* (*The Garden of Divine Song*, Kiev, directed by Oleksii KUZHEL'NYI and starring Bohdan Stupka, 1989), Peter SHAFFER's *Lettuce and Lovage* (Sevastopol', 1989 and St. Petersburg, 1996), *Iago*, after *Othello* (Kiev and Edinburgh, 1994), Lesia Ukrainka's *Oderzhyma* (*One Possessed*, Kiev and Augsburg, Germany, directed by Serhii PROSKURNIA, 1995) and *Brat'ia Karamazovy* (*The Karamazov Brothers*, after Fedor Dostoevsky, Moscow and Kiev, directed by Iuri LIUBIMOV, 1997). Karashevsky avoids stage properties in his scenic designs, and is drawn to the synthesis of functional subjective structures and philosophical generalization.

Karge, Manfred (1938–) Director, actor and dramatist, Germany. Karge studied at the Staatliche Schauspielschule in East Berlin. From 1961–8 he worked at the Berliner Ensemble, where he directed many Brecht productions together with Thomas LANGHOFF. Karge and Langhoff continued their co-directions when Karge joined the Berliner Volksbühne (1969–78). From 1986–93 Karge regularly directed at the Burgtheater in Vienna under Claus PEYMANN's artistic directorship. In many of his productions, Karge also played leading parts. More recent work includes Hassenreuther in Hauptmann's *Die Ratten* (*The Rats*) at the Maxim Gorky Theatre in Berlin (1997). His productions are often shrill in making their point; as a result, critical and audience response is split between enthusiatic support and harsh rejection.

Karlík, Josef (1928–) Actor, Czech Republik. Karlík studied at the Brno Conservatory joined the State (today the National) Theatre in Brno in 1956, where he has remained to this day, taking lead roles from the early 1960s. He literally acts with his entire body, and can be nimble despite his heaviness, as could best be seen in his acrobatic rendition of Puck (*A Midsummer Night's Dream*, 1977). His non-illusionary style, which is heavily theatrical, and his exaggerated expression and demonstrative figure find their best application in the plays of Brecht, as in Azdak in *Der Kaukasische Kreidekreis* (*The Caucasian Chalk Circle*, 1959), the title role in *Leben des Galilei* (*Life of Galileo*, 1978), and as Dürrenmatt's *Romulus der Große* (*Romulus the Great*, 1965), Edgar in Dürrenmatt's *Play Strindberg* (1969) and Ill in *Der Besuch der Alten Dame* (*The Visit*, 1991). At the same time he presents brilliant portraits of psychologically complicated characters, such as Stepan Verkhovensky (Dostoyevsky/Camus: *Besy* (*The Possessed*, 1992) and Serebryakov (Chekhov's *Djadja Vanja* (*Uncle Vanya*, 1996).

Karnad, Girish Ragunath (1938–) Dramatist and actor, India. Karnad is influenced by his native tradition as well as impressions gained during his training and education in the West (Rhodes Scholar, Oxford, Fulbright scholarship, visiting professorship in Chicago and writer-in-residence at the Tyrone Guthrie Theatre), especially Shakespeare and Anouilh. His first play, *Yayati*, and many other plays in Kannada including *Hayavadana*, *Bali*, *Naga-Mandala*, *Tale Dhanda* and his recent *Agni Mattu Male*, re-interpret Indian myths and folk stories in a contemporary sensibility, mixing Indian and Western theatre techniques; he also translates many of his own plays into English. His *Tughlag*, a political play, was directed by Ebrahim ALKAZI. He served as chairman of the Sangeeth Natak Academy, has directed many films and is also an actor of repute.

Karya, Teguh (1937–) Director, Indonesia. Karya trained at ATNI (Academi Teater Nasional Indonesia) and ASDRAFI (Academi Seni Drama dan Film), Yogyakarta. A seminal figure in the development of modern Indonesian theatre, Teguh Karya founded his Teater Popular in the early 1960s in Jakarta. The company performed translations and adaptations of classics by Molière, Ibsen, Gogol, Büchner and Strindberg, as well as plays by Coward, KOPIT, Hartog, Lorca, Čapek, PINTER, Brecht and Tennessee Williams. Karya also directed productions of original plays by contemporary Indonesian playwrights Putu WIJAYA and W.S. RENDRA. Karya provided a training ground for many young theatre artists who have since established their own companies or found success in film and television. Karya himself is now a distinguished film director.

Kasapoğlu, Işil (1955–) Director, Turkey. After graduating from the Theatre Department of the Sorbonne in 1981, Kasapoglu worked at the Pierre Vial Theatre Workshop of the Paris State Conservatory. Productions he directed between 1978–83 in Paris include Gogol's *Mertvye dusi* (*Dead Souls*). In 1983, he founded his own theatre group, Théâtre â Venir. In 1987, he joined İstanbul Municipality City Theatres to direct Goldoni's *Il servitore di due padroni* (*The Servant of Two Masters*), *King Lear* and Gogol's *Revizor* (*The Government Inspector*). Between 1991–6 he directed various plays in Turkey for different theatre companies: *Macbeth*, *Twelfth Night* and *Measure for Measure* for Diyarbakir State Theatre, and *The Merchant of Venice* for Trabzon State Theatre. In 1997, he established İzmir City Theatre and directed a controversial *Hamlet*. In general, Kasapoglu is interested in revealing new dimensions of well-known plays. Highly aware of the give-and-take relationship between text/director and director/actors, his productions manage to ignite and sustain audience interest.

Kasoma, Kabwe (1933–) Dramatist, Zambia. Kasoma came to the University of Zambia as a mature student after his active involvement in the local politics of the Copper Belt during the independence struggle. His university education was to improve his prospects for a career in politics. Kasoma started his playwriting career as a hobby, but his stay at university helped him to develop his perception of his role as a politically aware playwright. Like Steve CHIFUNYISE, he is a product of the Chikwakwa Theatre experience, learning and honing his dramatic skills and technique through participation in the projects and tours of Chikwakwa. His plays are in the main concerned with exploring the social problems of Zambia. Following in the style of Chikwakwa, Kasoma's plays make extensive use of traditional Zambian folk forms of dance, music, ritual, movement, mime and storytelling techniques to ensure mass/popular appeal. His major works are *The Poisoned Cultural Meat*, *The Fools Marry*, *The Black Mamba Plays* (a trilogy on Kenneth Kaunda and the Zambian struggle for independence) and *Distinction*.

Kaul, Bansi (1949–) Director, India. Kaul graduated from the National School of Drama, New Delhi, specialized in stagecraft and later joined the School as a professor. He has directed more than a hundred plays and a number of workshops. In 1986 he founded the Rang Vidushak, a repertory in Bhopal, where he has been working with actors, clowns and acrobats in an attempt to evolve a new theatre idiom rooted in the physical culture of the country. Recently Kaul directed *Sooch ka Doosara Naam*, a collage of wisdom tales. It set a trend of using folk tales as narrative in theatre. He has also directed Western plays like Beckett's *Waiting for Godot*, Gogol's *Revizor* (*The Government Inspector*), Ben Jonson's *Volpone* and many Indian plays.

Kauzlarić Atač, Zlatko (1945–) Designer and director, Croatia. Kauzlaric Atae trained at the Academy of Fine Arts in Zagreb, where he now works as a professor. From the mid-1960s he had many individual and group exhibitions at home and abroad. From 1970–8 he was a member of the Biafra Group. He worked for almost all Croatian theatres. His own poetics of design developed gradually, passing several phases, from shock design through structural design to design of symbols or signs. He makes no attempt at naturalistic presentation but, whenever possible, gives up illustrative scenery. He always tries to find a balance between the dynamics of dramatic action and its visual expression, often using comic book elements in his designs. His recent aim has been a highly functional setting included in the dramatic action and placed on equal footing with other elements of the performance. He designed his first set in 1974 for Brecht's *Im Dickicht der Städte* (*Jungle of Cities*). His major designs include Krleža's *Banquet in Blitva* (directed by PARO, 1981), Lisinsky's opera *Porin* (1993) and Chekhov's *Ivanov* (directed by KUNČEVIČ, 1978). He also worked abroad, in Slovenia, Bosnia-Herzegovina, Malta and Germany. In 1996 he directed Verdi's *Rigoletto*, making the spatial outlook of the stage the basis of his direction.

Keane, John B. (1928–) Dramatist, Ireland. Keane's first play *Sive* was produced by the Listowel Drama Group. Among his later plays, *The Field* was produced by Gemini Productions at the Olympia Theatre, Dublin (1965) and *Big Maggie* was produced by Gemini Productions at the Opera House, Cork (1969). Joe DOWLING, as artistic director of the Abbey Theatre in the 1980s, instigated a reappraisal of Keane's work as directed by Ben BARNES. *Sive* was produced at the Abbey Theatre in 1985, followed *The Field* with Niall TÓIBÍN as the Bull McCabe in 1987 and *Big Maggie* with Brenda Fricker in the title role in 1988. *Sharon's Grave* was directed by Ben Barnes for the Gate Theatre, Dublin in 1995. In August 1998

Keane was awarded the prestigious Gradam Award by the National Theatre Society (Abbey and Peacock Theatres) in recognition of his contribution to Irish theatre, a remarkable yet fitting gesture given his lack of recognition by the National Theatre earlier in his career. A native of Listowel in County Kerry, where he still lives, Keane's background has enriched his drama, which remains extremely popular with amateur drama groups. Keane's profile was raised considerably by the film version of *The Field*, directed by Jim Sheridan in 1991, with Richard Harris as the Bull McCabe.

Kelly, David (1929–) Actor, Ireland. Kelly's international fame in television sitcoms belies his extensive fifty-year career as a critically acclaimed theatre actor, having trained at the Abbey Theatre, Dublin. A former member of Joan Littlewood's Theatre Workshop in London (playing in Beckett's *Waiting for Godot*) and of John Neville's Nottingham Playhouse, he gave the first solo performance in Ireland of Beckett's *Krapp's Last Tape*, produced professionally at Trinity College, Dublin, in 1959. He played this role again in the 1992 Beckett Festival at the Gate Theatre, Dublin, which subsequently toured to Chicago, Seville and New York. His career includes work with major directors such as Polanski, Olivier and MacLiammóir. Recent roles at Dublin's Abbey Theatre include Giles Corey in Arthur MILLER's *The Crucible* (1995), and the kleptomaniac Jack in Brian FRIEL's *Give Me Your Answer, Do!* (1997). In his many roles he has been noted for his comic sensitivity and sense of pathos.

Kemp, Jenny (1949–) Director and dramatist, Australia. Kemp's style is very distinctive and she creates extremely visual texts (often inspired by the art of Paul Delvaux) which are non-linear, cyclical and associative. Although Kemp has worked in the mainstream (Melbourne

Theatre Company, the State Theatre of South Australia), she started working in theatre with the alternative Stasis Group at The Pram Factory, Melbourne, and her self-authored work is often slightly esoteric, although breathtakingly beautiful. Using music, fragmented language and language as music, Kemp's play texts often work as soundscapes with unstable and infinitely varying meanings. Of the productions Kemp has authored and directed, *The Call of the Wild* (1989) played with the notion of the gaze as well as offering sumptuously beautiful visions to the audience; *The Black Sequin Dress* (1996) used repetition and dream to explore experience and psyche; and *Remember* (1992) explored interiority, memory and the survival of trauma.

Kendal, Felicity (1946–) Actor, Great Britain. Kendal was born in India where she toured with her parents' theatre company, making her debut at the age of nine as Puck in *A Midsummer Night's Dream*. Since 1965 she has been in Britain, where she scored successes in AYCKBOURN's *The Norman Conquest* (1974) and seasons at the National Theatre including Constanze in SHAFFER's *Amadeus* (1979, with Paul SCOFIELD, and Simon CALLOW, directed by Peter HALL) and Desdemona (with Scofield as Othello, again directed by Hall). Recently she has become associated mostly with revivals and new plays by Tom STOPPARD, ranging from *The Real Thing* (1982) to *Indian Ink* (1994). In 1997 she joined Peter Hall's company at the Old Vic in London, appearing opposite Michael PENNINGTON in Granville-Barker's *Waste* and as Arkadina in Chekhov's *Cajka* (*The Seagull*), both directed by Hall.

Kente, Gibson (1932–) Director and theatre manager, South Africa. Kente's early cultural influences were Christian hymns and Xhosa traditional music. He joined the Union of South African Artists (USAA) and set up his own theatre company, which was to produce mostly vaudeville/musical dramas for black township audiences. His musical *Sikalo* set the basic pattern for the township musical with its successful and later widely adopted formula and format of situations and popular/stock characters that the township audiences find endearing. Inspired by the commercial success of the politically committed *Sizwe Bansi is Dead* (by Athol FUGARD, John KANI and Winston NTSHONA), Kente wrote *How Long* (1974). In 1976, Kente was arrested while working on a film version of *How Long*. On his release in 1977 he returned directly to theatre work, but it was evident that the brush with the law had changed his new style and subject; his next musical, *Can You Take I* completely avoided politics, as did his subsequent productions, including *Mama and the Load*.

Kenter, Müşfik (1932–) Actor and director, Turkey. Following two years with the Children's Theatre of the Ankara State Theatre, Kenter trained at the Theatre Department of the Ankara State Conservatory. He worked for the Ankara State Theatre between 1955–9. Going to Istanbul, with his sister Yıldız KENTER, he joined Karaca Theatre under the directorship of Muhsin Ertugrul in 1959. During the 1960–1 season he co-founded Site Players Group with his sister and friends. After the 1961–2 season the same group became Kent Players, which has been active until the present day. Since 1959, he has been directing and acting in numerous plays of internationally known playwrights such as PINTER, Osborne, Ionesco, Brecht, Shakespeare, MILLER, Chekhov, AYCKBOURN, Gorky, O'Neill and Tennessee Williams, and Turkish dramatists such as Mehmet BAYDUR, Turgut Özakman and Adalet Ağaoğlu. In acting, he approaches his roles with incomparable sensitivity and portrays his characters with admirable credibility and consistency. Scholarships from the British Council and from the Rockefeller Foundation enabled him to study theatre in Britain, Europe and the USA. He travelled widely, acting in former Yugoslavia, the USA, Russia, Germany and the Turkish Republic of Cyprus. He has also contributed to the Turkish theatre world by his publications on theatre. As well as being a renowned actor and a director, he has gained fame in film.

Kenter, Yıldız (1928–) Actor, director and artistic director, Turkey. Following her graduation from the Ankara State Conservatory's Theatre Department in 1948, Kenter spent eleven years as an actor and a director at the Turkish State Theatres. After receiving a Rockefeller Scholarship, she studied acting and new techniques of teaching drama at the American Theatre Wing, Neighbourhood Playhouse and at Actors Studio. On her return to Turkey, she founded her own company, The Kent Players, with her actor brother, Müşfik KENTER and her actor husband Şükran Güngör, in 1962. In 1968, she moved into her own theatre in İstanbul, Kenter Theatre, of which she is the artistic director. She has performed and directed over 100 plays in Turkey and abroad, including works by Shakespeare, Chekhov, Gorky, Brecht, Ionesco, PINTER, AYCKBOURN, Arthur MILLER, ALBEE and Tennessee Williams as well as many Turkish dramatists. As an actor, her performances are based on a persistent 'action–reaction' principle: she immediately establishes an interaction with her audience. While in character as Maria Callas in Terence MCNALLY's *Master Class* (1998), she gave a master class to opera singers. At the same time, she also gave a master class in acting to her audience.

Kertonegoro, Madi (1955–) Performer and director, Indonesia. Kertonegoro is a self-taught painter, writer, actor, dancer, choreographer and director from Central Java who now lives and works in Bali. Basing his work on traditional models,

Kertonegoro strives to create a total theatre of drama, dance and music. Major pieces include *Resi Jaran Goyang* (*Crazy Horse Bishop*, 1981) and *Bunga Bangkai* (*Corpse Flower*, 1982) with Teater Mentah, Denpasar and *Release from World Disaster* created with the villagers of Petulu Gunung (1988) Since 1991 he has concentrated his efforts upon establishing the Dayu Putih Foundation. He sees 'the theatrical process as spiritual process' and the foundation combines aspects of esoteric philosophy and performance for spiritual development. In 1997 he was collaborating on a stage adaptation of his 1987 novel *The Guard of Ubud Corner*.

Khadour, Mahmoud (1943–) Director, Syria. After training in Moscow he worked briefly in Aleppo, where he directed three productions, including Walid IKHLASSI's *Yawma Askatna Taera'l-Wahm* (*The Day When We Shot down the Bird of Illusion*, 1974). Then he moved to Damascus, where he worked with its National Theatre. His collaboration with Mamdoub Adwan was notable, he directed his liberal adaptations: *Hamlet Wakes up Late* (1978) and *Don Quixote* (1979), as well as his original scripts, *Zeyaratul-Malika* (*The Queen's Visit*, 1981) and *Al-Khaddameh* (*The Maid*, 1984). He also directed Aleksei Arbuzov's *The Promise* (1980) and Peter SHAFFER's *Black Comedy* (1981). His latest contribution is *Nabukhaz Nasser* (1998), based on a play by a new playwright, Talal Naser'l Deen.

Khan, Tariq Anam (1953–) Actor and director, Bangladesh. Tariq Khan trained at the National School of Drama, India, from 1976–9. His commendable acting career includes title roles in the translations of *Othello* (with Ferdausi MAJUMDAR as Desdemona and AL-MAMUN as Iago, 1981), Girish KARNAD's *Tughlaq* (also directed by him, 1992), adaptations of Molière's *L'avare* (*The Miser*, directed by Kamaluddin NILU, 1983) and Balraj Pundit's *Panchwan Sawar* (*The Paper*

Tiger, directed and designed by Jamil AHMED, 1982). Possibly his most striking directorial venture is Syed HUQ's *Juddha Ebang Juddha* (with Ferdausi Majumdar as Rabeya, Al-Mamun as Barkatullah and Ramendu MAJUMDAR as Kalimullah, 1986). His production of *That Scoundrel Scapin* has been particularly praised for his 'ability to improvise without distorting Molière's text'. His unique quality as an actor and director lies in his capability for combining a sense of stability with explosive energy. He has adapted a number of plays and is the founder director of Natya Kendra (an important theatre group in Bangladesh). He has also extensively toured abroad as a designer for performance troupes from Bangladesh and is a well-reputed television and film actor.

Khostikoiev, Anatolii (1953–) Actor, Ukraine. Khostikoiev graduated from the Karpenko-Kary Institute for the Art of the Theatre, Kiev (1974) and gave his debut at the Maria Zan'kovets'ka Ukrainian Drama Theatre, Lviv in the role of Chernysh in *Praporonostsy* (*Standard-Bearers*) after the novel by Ukrainian writer Oles' Honchar (directed by Serhii DANCHENKO, 1975). In 1978 he joined the Lesia Ukrainka Russian Drama Theatre, Kiev. Since 1980 he has been an actor at the Ivan Franko Ukrainian Drama Theatre, Kiev. Khostikoiev is an actor of brilliant appearance and deep dramatic temperament, a wonderful character actor. Major roles include Astrov in Chekhov's *Djadja Vanja* (*Uncle Vanya*, 1985), Aenei in *Eneida* (*Aeneid*) by Ivan Kotliarevsky (1986) and Komandor in Lesia Ukrainka's *Kam'ianyi hospodar* (*The Stone Host*, 1988). He has recently appeared with a very successful work in Hrynyshyn's and Zholdak's adaptation of *Shveik* after Hashek, playing four extremely different roles (1996). He has also appeared in many films.

Khuri, Makram (1945–) Actor, Israel/-Palestine. Khuri trained at Mountview

Theatre School in London and has played both in Hebrew and Arabic in bilingual productions of Joseph CHAIKIN's and Miriam KAINY's *They* (1980) and appeared as an Arabic-speaking Didi in an Israeli production of Beckett's *Waiting for Godot* (directed by Ilan RONEN at the Haifa Municipal Theatre), and in many Hebrew productions. Among the roles where his Palestinian background was interestingly used, Lopachin in Chekhov's *Visnevyi sad* (*The Cherry Orchard*) at the Habima theatre is worth noting. Khuri is co-founder of the Arab-speaking theatre, Beit-Hagefen, in Haifa. In 1987 he received the Israel prize, an unusual distinction for a non-Jewish artist. Has also played on film and television.

Kilroy, Thomas (1934–) Dramatist, Ireland. Kilroy held a professorship in Modern English at University College Galway. As a dramatist, he is drawn to what he describes as 'the moral see-saw on which the character is placed' and 'how this moral see-saw tips'. This fascination can be seen particularly in *Double Cross*, first produced by Field Day Theatre Company, Derry, in 1986. *Double Cross* juxtaposes the lives of two men, Brendan Bracken and William Joyce (Lord Haw-Haw) and their involvement in the Second World War. The play, a theatrical study of the shaping of identity, used various staging techniques to allow the characters to acknowledge each other while being played by the one actor; in Field Day's acclaimed production, Stephen REA played both Bracken and Joyce. Other plays by Kilroy include *The O'Neill* (1969), *Talbot's Box* (1977), and versions of Chekhov's *Cajka* (*The Seagull*, 1981) and Pirandello's *Sei personaggi in cerca d'autore* (*Six Characters in Search of an Author*, 1996). In 1997 Kilroy's *The Secret Fall of Constance Wilde* (about the love triangle of Constance, Oscar and Lord Alfred Douglas) was directed by Patrick MASON at the Abbey Theatre and toured to the Melbourne Festival in 1998.

Kim Ara (1956–) Director, Korea. Kim trained at Hunter College Graduate School in New York, and is renowned for being able to combine logical and emotional elements in one production. Since 1986, she has directed Williams's *The Rose Tattoo* (1986), Chung Bok-Gun's *Dokbae* (*The Poison Glass*, 1988), Peter SHAFFER's *Equus* (1990) and *Captured Soul* (1991, produced by the Korean National Theatre). After establishing the Muchon Theatre Group in 1992, she directed Chung's *Soomun Mool* (*Hidden Water*, 1992), Jang Jeong-Il's *Oedipuswaeui Yeohaeng* (*A Journey with Oedipus*, 1995), Jang's *Isesang Gut* (*The End of the World*, 1996) and LEE Kang-Baek's *Naema* (1998). These productions share the theme of exploring the internal human being. In 1996, she moved to the countryside where she built 'Theatre in the Mountain', in order to establish a unique acting style through the collective life of the company, and produced Sophocles's *Oidipus tyrannos* (*King Oedipus*, 1997).

Kim Hyun-Sook (1954–) Designer, Korea. Kim trained at the University of Illinois, Chicago (MA in costume design) and the University of Illinois, Urbana (MFA in costume design). She has tried to modernize and reconstruct Korean traditions by using a variety of materials in sets and costumes. She worked as a costume and set designer for Jeong Bok-Gun's *Dokbae* (*Poison Glass*, 1988, directed by KIM Ara), KIM Kwang-Lim's *Jip* (*House*, 1994), Woo Bong-Gyu's *Noongot* (*Snowflakes*, 1995, directed by KIM Suk-Man), the musical *MyeongSeong Hwanghoo* (*Empress Myeong-Seong*, 1995, starring YOON Suk-Hwa), Kim Ji-Won's *Gooreongi Sinranggwa Gueui Sinboo* (*Serpent Bridegroom and His Wife* (1996, directed by CHOI Hyung-In), LEE Gun-Sam's *Choonhyanga Choonhyanga!* (*Choon-Hyang!*, 1996, directed by Kim Kwang-Lim), *Saeduldo Sesangul Tunungoona* (*Even The Birds are Leaving*, 1997, directed by Kim Suk-Man) and *Yoorangeui*

Norae (*Song of Wandering*, 1998, written and directed by KIM Myeong-Gon).

Kim Jae-Kun (1947–) Actor, Korea. Kim trained at the Seoul Institute of Arts and soon afterward joined the Korean National Theatre, performing in *Seongwoong Yi Soon-Sin* (*Admiral Soon-Sin Lee*, 1973, by Lee Jae-Hyeon), *Namhansanseong* (*Mountain Castle of Namhansan*, 1974, by Kim Eui-Kyung), *Moolbora* (*Spray*, 1978, by OH Tae-Seok), *Sachoogi* (*Adult at Puberty*, 1979, by Oh Tae-Seok), *Yennal Yetjeoge Hwei Hwei* (*Shoo Shoo Once upon a Time*, 1985, by CHOI In-Hoon), *Biong Saong* (1986, by Lee Gang-Baek, directed by LEE Sung-Gyu), *Yennal Yetjeoge Hwei Hwei* (*The Heaven in a Dream*, 1987, by Cha Beom-Seok, adapted and directed by KIM Suk-Man), Ibsen's *Vildanden* (*The Wild Duck*, 1987), Sophocles's *Oidipus tyrannos* (*King Oedipus*, 1990), *So* (*Cow*, 1991, by Yoo Chi-Jin), *Maengjinsadak Gyeongsa* (*The Maeng Family's Happy Day*, 1992, by Oh Young-Jin), *Pigojigo Pigojigo* (*Blooming Falling Blooming Falling*, 1993, by LEE Man-Hee), *Choonhyanga Choonghyanga!* (*Choon-Hyang!*, 1996, by LEE Gun-Sam, directed by Kim Kwang-Lim), and *Faust 1997* (adapted and directed by LEE Youn-Taek). As an actor with a friendly traditional appearance, Kim has specialized in parts which portray the contemporary Korean, living between the traditional and industrialized eras.

Kim Kwang-Lim (1952–) Director and dramatist, Korea. Kim trained at UCLA (MA, theatre arts), and has directed his own plays, including *Dallajin Jeosung* (*The Other World is Changed*, 1987, with CHOI Hyung-In), *Sarangul Chajaseo* (*In Search of Love*, 1990), *Jip* (*House*, 1994) and *Nalboreowayo* (*Come to See Me*, 1996). He has also directed *Apa Eolgool Yepooneyo* (*Your Face is Beautiful, Dad!*, 1987, by Kim Min-Gi), Franz Xaver KROETZ's *Nicht Fisch Nicht Fleisch* (*Neither Fish Nor Meat*, 1988, with Choi

Hyung-In in the cast), *Bookeo Daegari* (*Head of a Dried Pollack*, 1993, by LEE Kang-Baek) and *Choonhyanga Choonghyanga!* (*Choon-Hyang!*, 1996, by LEE Gun-Sam). Kim's main theme in both written work and directing expresses the difference between practical reality and ideal social justice.

Kim Seong-Nyu (1950–) Actor, Korea. Kim graduated from Dan-Gook University (BA, classical Korean music). Born into a theatre family with dramatist-actor parents, she first appeared on stage at the age of five. Soon after her professional debut as an actor, performing the title role in Oh Young-Jin's *Hanneui Sungcheon* (*Ascension of Hanne*, 1975), Kim crossed genres from realistic theatre to musicals and Korean traditional performances. She performed the title role in *Porgy and Bess* (1975), Soondan in OH Tae-Seok's *Baekmagang Dalbame* (*In a Moonlight on the River Bakma*, 1991) and Man-Hee LEE's *Doejiwa Otobai* (*The Pig and the Motorcycle*, 1993). In 1986, she founded the Michoo Theatre Company with her husband, director SOHN Jin-Chaek and played The Chief Mourner in *Jikimi* (*The Keeper*, 1987), Paulina in Dorfman's *Death and the Maiden* (1992), the Head Mistress in YOUN Dai-Sung's *Namsadangeui Hanul* (*Sky of Namsadang the Wandering Troupe*, 1993) and performed title roles in many Madang-Guk performances, such as *Sim-Cheongjeon* (*The Story of Sim-Cheong*, 1988) and *Choon-Hyangjeon* (*The Story of Choon-Hyang*, 1995), both produced and directed by Sohn Jin-Chek.

Kim Suk-Man (1951–) Director, Korea. Kim trained at the University of California, Berkeley (BA in dramatic arts) and New York University Graduate School (MA in performance studies). Returning to Korea after eleven years in the USA, Kim started a new era of political drama for Korean intellectuals, adapting elements of epic theatre, cinema and documentary production. As a member and president of the Yeonwoo Stage Company, he directed *Hansi Yeondaegi* (*Mr Han's Chronicle*, 1985), Hyun Ki-Young's *Byeonbange Woojitnun Sae* (*The Crying Bird in the Periphery*, 1987, with CHOI Hyung-In in the cast), *Saeduldo Sesangul Tunungoona* (*Even the Birds are Leaving*, 1988), his own *Choi Seonsaeng* (*Miss Choi, Our Teacher*, 1990) and Yoo Jin-Oh's *Parkcheomji* (*Park, Esquire*, 1991). For the Korean National Theatre, he adapted and directed *Goomhanul* (*Heaven in a Dream*, 1987, by Cha Beom-Seok) and Woo Bong-Gyoo's *Noongot* (*Snowflakes*, 1995). His main theme is the unintentional ruin of personal life resulting from political circumstances.

Kimele, Mara (1943–) Director, Latvia. In 1963 Kimele graduated from the Theatre Arts Department of the Latvian State Conservatory, and continued her training as a director at the Anatoly Efros Master Class in Directing at the Moscow Theatre Institute, graduating in 1969. She has led several major companies in Latvia, and has become one of the most interesting and challenging directors in Latvia. An experience ranging over twenty-five years gives her the possibility to develop clear expression and precise form. This has, however, not hampered her readiness to experiment. Adapting performance styles to the psycho-physical peculiarities of the individual actor, Kimele creates an inner world full of intellectual and spiritual tension. She utilizes theatrical models of past and present, and searches for inspiration from other art forms. Major productions include *Othello*, *King Lear*, Anouilh's *Medea* and Peter Nichols's *Passion Play*.

Kimoulis, George (1956–) Actor and director, Greece. Kimoulis trained in popular experimental theatre and at Veaki's Drama School. In 1986 he founded the Contemporary Theatre of Athens, whose drama school he now leads. His roles include the classical repertory, Shakespeare (Hamlet, Macbeth, Petrucchio), Chekhov (Treplev, Platonov, Ivanov), and contemporary parts such as Clive in SHAFFER's *Five Finger Exercise*. He has directed Chekhov's *Cajka* (*The Seagull*), Gogol's *Revizor* (*The Government Inspector*), *The Taming of the Shrew* and many other productions. In addition, he has translated many plays into Greek, such as *Rumours* by Neil SIMON and Strindberg's *Fröken Julie* (*Miss Julie*).

Kimura Kôichi (1931–) Director and translator, Japan. Kimura joined Bungaku-za (The Literature Theatre Company) in 1955 and translated and directed Arnold Wesker's *The Kitchen* in 1963. He continued to stage Wesker's trilogy, *Chicken Soup with Barley, Roots* and *I'm Talking about Jerusalem*. His production of *A Streetcar Named Desire* by Tennessee Williams in 1964 was a success, and productions by British contemporaries such as Osborne, Arden and Robert Bolt followed. He also staged plays by Miyamoto Ken, Mizukami Tsutomu and INOUE Hisashi. He co-founded Gogatsu-sha (Theatre Group May) in 1973, and the company's first production was *Yabuhara Kengyô* (*Yabuhara the Blind Monk*) by Inoue. Kimura left Bungaku-za and formed the Chijin-kai Theatre Company in 1982. There he directed *Keshô* (*Greasepaint*, by Inoue) which was one of six plays collected for one-woman plays *Haha* (*Mothers*). *Keshô* was performed in Europe and the USA in 1986 and 1989. Watanabe Misako played the part of the leader of the touring company and won critical acclaim for her one-woman performance.

Kingsley, Ben (1943–) Actor, Great Britain. Kingsley made his debut as an actor on a schools tour with Theatre Centre. He was for many years associated with the Royal Shakespeare Company, where major parts include Demetrius in Peter BROOK's production of *A Midsummer*

Night's Dream (1970), Squeers in Trevor NUNN's production of *Nicholas Nickleby* (1980) and title roles in *Hamlet* (1975) and *Othello* (1986). His outstanding portrayal of Gandhi in Attenborough's film (1982) won him an Academy Award, brought international fame and led to many further leading roles in major films, from PINTER's *Betrayal* (1983) to Spielberg's *Schindler's List* (1994). After a long break, Kingsley returned to the theatre in Peter HALL's production of Beckett's *Waiting for Godot* at the Old Vic, London (1997). He brings a remarkably felt depth of emotion to all his roles, greatly supported by a rich vocal range.

Kinoshita Junji (1914–) Dramatist, Japan. Kinoshita wrote plays based on traditional Japanese stories. Most important, *Tsuru Nyôbô* (*A Crane Wife*), which was revised as *Yûzuru* (*Twilight Crane*) in 1949 and had been performed more than 1,000 times by 1984, has made its way into school textbooks and is considered one of the classics of modern Japanese drama. The play has been adapted to the other forms of theatre such as nô, Kabuki and opera. His other plays are *Kaeru Shôten* (*The Ascension of a Frog*, 1951), *Ottô to Yobareru Nihon-jin* (*A Japanese called Ottô*, 1962), *Kami to Hito no Aida* (*Between the God and Man*, 1972) and *Shigosen no Matsuri* (*Requiem on the Meridian*, 1979). In these plays, Kinoshita discusses issues such as socialist political movements in Japan and the Japanese nation's responsibility for the Second World War. He adopts the syle of socialist realism, *shingeki* orthodoxy. Kinoshita also examines the nature of the Japanese language in his plays.

Kirchhoff, Corinna (1958–) Actor, Germany. Kirchoff trained at the Schauspielschule Berlin, and since 1983 she has been a member of the Schaubühne am Lehniner Platz. She has developed a way of using language that is rich in nuances, giving way at times to mannerisms. She is frequently cast in the parts of unhappy, bored women spoilt by luxury. In 1984 she played Irina in Peter STEIN's production of Chekhov's *Tri sestry* (*Three Sisters*, with Jutta LAMPE and Edith CLEVER as her sisters). Further parts include the title role in *Die Fremdenführerin* (*The Tourist Guide*) by Botho STRAUSS (1986, directed by Luc BONDY), Herminone in Bondy's production of *The Winter's Tale* (1990) and the title role in Ibsen's *Hedda Gabler* (1994, directed by Andrea BRETH). She also appeared in Mishima's *Madame de Sade* (1996), and played Elena in Chekhov's *Djadja Vanja* (*Uncle Vanya*), 1998) and the title role in Goethe's *Stella* (1999), both directed by Breth.

Kirchner, Ignaz (1948–) Actor, Germany. Kirchner trained at the Schauspielschule Bochum. Following freelance work in productions by Wilfried MINKS at the Freie Volksbühne Berlin, and seasons in Stuttgart (1974–8), Bremen (1978–81) and the Münchner Kammerspiele (1982–6), he was a member of the Burgtheater in Vienna from 1987–92, where major parts include Iago in George TABORI's production of *Othello* (with Gert VOSS in the title role). Since 1992, Kirchner has worked at the Deutsches Theater in Berlin, playing among other roles Sosias in Kleist's *Amphitryon* (1993, directed by Jürgen GOSCH), but also appearing elsewhere, for example in Beckett's *Endgame* (1998, Vienna, directed by Tabori, with Voss and Ursula HOEPFNER in the cast).

Kishida Kyôko (1930–) Actor and writer, Japan. Kishida is the second daughter of Kishida Kunio (1890–1954), who was one of the leading dramatists of modern Japanese theatre. She is a founder member of Engeki Syûdan En (The Circle Theatre Company). The roles she has acted in Japanese translations include Salome in Wilde's *Salome* (1959), Lady Macbeth (1975) and Blanche in Williams's *A Streetcar Named Desire* (1990). Kishida also acts in contemporary plays by Japanese dramatists such as BETUYAKU Minoru, SHIMIZU Kunio and ÔTA Shôgo. She acted the Woman's part in Ôta's two-hander *Sarachi* (*Vacant Lot*), which toured in the USA in 1996 and in Poland in 1997. Kishida understands the styles of the dramatists' works and their theatrical languages and materializes those elements in her acting. She played the role of the woman in the film of *The Woman in Dune* by Kôbô Abe, which won an award in the Cannes International Film Festival.

Kiyingi-Kagwe, Wycliffe (1934–) Dramatist, Uganda. Kiyingi-Kagwe is seen by many as the moving spirit behind modern Ugandan theatre. In 1954 he founded African Artists' Association, the first all-Ugandan theatre company. Kiyingi-Kagwe's theatrical style is essentially farcical, with topical satire which he employs for social commentary in the style of George Bernard Shaw and Sean O'Casey, whose influence he readily acknowledges. His plays have remained popular, especially his television plays, which are seen by a wider Ugandan audience. His major plays and productions include the radio series *Wokulira* (*By the Time You Grow Up*, begun in 1961), the television series *Buli Enkya, Buli Ekiro* (*Day In, Day Out*, begun in 1962), *Gwosussa Emwanyi* (*The Ignored Guest becomes the Saviour*, 1962), his first full-length play *Lozio ba Cecilia* (*Lozio, Cecilia's Husband*, 1972, performed in the Luandan language) and *Muduuma kwe Kwaffe* (*Muduuma Our Home*, 1977).

Kline, Kevin (1947–) Actor, USA. Kline obtained a BA in speech and theatre from Indiana University in 1970 and graduated with a diploma from the Juillard Drama Centre in 1972. He began his professional career in 1970, and from 1972–6 he appeared mainly with the Acting Company in New York City, of which he was a founder member. His roles include Vershinin (Chekhov, *Tri sestry* (*Three Sisters*)) and Friar Peter in *Measure for*

Measure. In 1980 he won awards for playing the pirate king in Gilbert and Sullivan's *The Pirates of Penzance*. Following the beginning of his film career in 1983, he continued performing in the theatre with title roles in *Richard III* (1983), *Henry V* (1984) and *Hamlet* (1986 and 1990). In 1993 he was appointed artistic associate of the New York Shakespeare Festival, and played the Duke in *Measure for Measure*. Now frequently seen in starring roles in film, he is particularly adept at physical humor.

Ko Tin-lung (1954–) Director, actor and dramatist, China (Hong Kong SAR). In 1983, Ko began his acting career at the Hong Kong Repertory Theatre. In 1987, he received the Lee Hysan Foundation Grant from the Asian Cultural Council and visited various theatre companies in New York. Returning to Hong Kong in 1989, he became the assistant artistic director of the Hong Kong Repertory Theatre, where he wrote and directed *One of the Lucky Ones* (1990, revived in 1991) and directed Raymond TO's *Tokyo Blues* (1991), *I Have a Date with Spring* (1992, revived in 1993) and *The Legend of the Mad Phoenix* (starring TSE Kwan-ho, 1993 and 1995). Ko became the artistic director of the Chung Ying Theatre Company in 1993. For Chung Ying (literally, 'Chinese–English'), his major success came with *The School and I* (1993), winning the fourth Hong Kong Drama Awards for best director. Ko's recent directions also include *The First Emperor's Last Days* (1998, by Tan Tarn How) and his own play *The Merchant of China* (1999), dramatizing the life of a Chinese businessman, Hu Xu-yin, for the opening programme of the twentieth anniversary celebration series of the Chung Ying.

Koenig, Leah (1933–) Actor, Israel/Palestine. Daughter of two famous Yiddish actors, Koenig started her stage career in Romania at the age of sixteen. She emigrated to Israel in 1961, where she has played numerous roles, mainly at the Habima theatre. Most remembered roles are her Mother Courage (Brecht), the mother in Lorca's *Bodas de sangre* (*Blood Wedding*) and Laura in Strindberg's *Fadren* (*The Father*). In 1987 she received the Israel Prize. She has also appeared in many films.

Koltai, Ralph (1924–) Designer, Great Britain. Born in Germany, Koltai trained at the Central School of Arts and Crafts, Holborn, London, and has designed for theatre and opera worldwide. For many years he was an associate of the Royal Shakespeare Company. Major theatre credits include Brecht's *Der Kaukasische Kreidekreis* (*The Caucasian Chalk Circle*), Sophocles's *Oidipus tyrannos* (*King Oedipus*, 1974), *Hamlet* (RSC, 1981), *Troilus and Cressida* (RSC, 1985), *Othello* (RSC, 1986, with Ben KINGSLEY in the title role) and the musical *My Fair Lady* (1993). He is known for his 'contemporary and sometimes experimental approach to scenic design, and employs modern-day materials and techniques'.

Koman, Jacek Actor, Australia. Koman obtained an MA from the State Academy of Film, Television and Theatrical Studies, Łódź, Poland in 1978. After moving to Australia in 1981, Koman first worked in Perth and was acclaimed for his performance in Slawomir MROZEK's *Emigranci* (*Emigrants*, 1987), a play he returned to in Melbourne in 1990. Koman was associated for several years with Jean-Pierre Mignon's Anthill theatre in Melbourne, where he appeared in a wide variety of plays ranging from Molière's *Le malade imaginaire* (*The Imaginary Invalid*) to Beckett's *Endgame*. Koman was particularly praised for his comically lugubrious, Chaplinesque Estragon to Alex Menglet's Vladimir in Mignon's production of Beckett's *Waiting for Godot* for the Melbourne Theatre Company. Koman has a great stillness onstage, which can be extremely

powerful and was put to good use in Neil ARMFIELD's production of *Hamlet*, in which he played a Claudius who had a focused coldness in his drive for power and whose relationship with Gertrude was devoid of sensuality. Koman then played Roy Kohn in Armfield's 1994 production of Kushner's *Angels in America*, a performance which was highly praised for its chilling portrayal of a power-hungry evil.

Komine Lili (1947–) Designer, Japan. Komine first worked for the production department of the Shiki Theatre Company, and joined the Royal Shakespeare Company in the UK from 1970–2. Her designs in Japan include *Romeo and Juliet* (1974), Sophocles's *Oidipus tyrannos* (*King Oedipus*, 1976), Brecht's *Die Dreigroschenoper* (The Threepenny Opera, 1977) and *The Tempest* (1987), directed by NINAGAWA and produced by the Tôhô Company. She designed the costumes for Ninagawa's production of Mishima's *Kantan and Sotoba Komachi* in Edinburgh, New York and Canada (1991) and also his *Tango Fuyu no Owari ni* (*Tango at the End of Winter*), an English adaptation of a play by SHIMIZU Kunio at the Royal National Theatre in London in 1991. She sometimes uses the elements of the costumes found in traditional Japanese theatre, nô and kyogen.

Komorowska, Maja (1937–) Actor, Poland. Trained at the State Theatre Academy in Cracow, Komorowska started her career with Jerzy Grotowski at his Theatre of 13 Rows in Opole, then the Theatre Laboratory in Wroclaw. Later she worked at Teatr Wspolczesny and Teatr Polski in Wroclaw, and since 1992 she has been a member of the Teatr Wspolczesny in Warsaw. Her main stage credits include the title roles in Sophocles's *Antigone*, Strindberg's *Fröken Julie* (*Miss Julie*), Hamm in Beckett's *Endgame* and Winni in *Happy Days*, Lettuce in Peter SHAFFER's *Lettuce and Lovage*, Claire Zacanassian in

Dürrenmatt's *Der Besuch der Alten Dame* (*The Visit*) and Ambassador's Wife in MROZEK's *Ambassador*. Komarowska is also a distinguished film actor, working with Zanussi, Wajda and Kieslowski. An actor of deep and potent emotions, she is particularly good in tragedy, pathos and lyricism, creating heroines of spiritual power and nobility, or sensitive and educated unmarried women, full of sympathy and warmth towards other people.

Kon, Stella Dramatist, Singapore. Stella Kon has been credited with putting Singapore on the International theatre map. Her best-known play, *Emily of Emerald Hill* (1983), was the first Singapore play to be performed at the Edinburgh Fringe Festival in 1986 and has enjoyed much revival. In total, it has been revived some thirty-seven times in Singapore and Malaysia. The play is a monodrama that tracks the life of a Peranakan (Straits-born Chinese) matriarch and showed great fondness towards a vanishing culture in Singapore. A Peranakan herself, Kon's depiction of Emily Gan in the play has been widely acclaimed as one of the most sensitive portraits of women in Singapore. Since then, Kon has written *Dragon Teeth's Gate* (1986) and *Butterflies Don't Cry* (1989). She is divorced and has two sons, who live in London and Sydney respectively. With six grandchildren, Stella herself is becoming the matriarch of an extended family.

Konečný, Jan (1951–) Designer, Czech Republic. After studying at the Technical College in Brno, Konečný attended Josef SVOBODA's architecture atelier in Prague. Since the end of the 1970s he has been working regularly with Moravian experimental studios (Ha theatre, the Goose on a String (Husa na provázku) theatre), playing in non-typical spaces. He often uses simple geometric constructions and relies on the proximity of the spectators surrounding the playing space. Among larger venues, he has worked repeatedly with the Municipal Theatre in Zlín, for which he designed the set for HAVEL's *Zahradní Slavnost* (*Garden Party*, 1990). He teaches at the Brno Academy of Performing Arts.

Kopit, Arthur (1937–) Dramatist, USA. Kopit studied at Harvard University. His first play, *Oh Dad, Poor Dad, Mamma's Hung You in the Closet and I'm Feelin' So Sad*, a parody of the Oedipus complex, launched Kopit's success as a playwright. It also gained him the label of absurdist, an inaccurate assessment of Kopit's later work, including *The Road to Nirvana* (1991). The early play does, however, show some of Kopit's most striking characteristics: 'a faculty with language, an ear for the cliches of art and life, an eye for the effective stage image, a strategic use of caricature, and the talent for being funny about a subject that is not at all comic'.

Kosky, Barrie (1967–) Director, Australia. Known for his shock tactics and the boldness of his theatrical vision, Kosky initially directed mostly opera; he claims his passion for opera began when he saw his first opera at the age of seven. Kosky founded his own theatre company, Treason of Images, when he was eighteen. His Jewish theatre company Gilgul won awards for its 1991 production of Solomon Ansk's *The Dybbuk*, which was performed in a disused factory in St Kilda, Melbourne. Kosky's strident confidence has led to accusations of arrogance; when he directed Therese Radic's *The Emperor Regrets*, Radic claimed Kosky completely ignored her wishes. Kosky has been quoted as saying 'writers' theatre is dead' and his Gilgul production *The Wilderness Room*, about five Jews travelling to Australia on the First Fleet, was devoid of dialogue, relying on song, images and props to communicate. Kosky was artistic director of the 1996 Adelaide Festival of Arts.

Kotler, Oded (1937–) Actor and director, Israel. Kotler started as a youth actor and completed his training with the Actors Studio and the Neighbourhood Playhouse in New York. After a number of leading roles at the Cameri Tel Aviv municipal theatre, he founded a small theatre called The Actors' Stage which was later incorporated into the Haifa municipal theatre. For a decade from 1970, Kotler was the artistic director of this theatre introducing new playwrights like Hanoch LEVIN, Yehoshua SOBOL and Hillel MITTELPUNKT. In 1980 Kotler founded the Acco festival for alternative theatre, and in 1981 was co-founder of the Neve Zedek theatre centre, a provocative political theatre. After directing the Israel Festival for a few years, he returned to the Haifa municipal theatre in 1990. As well as his stage roles and the plays he has directed, Kotler is also known for his many film roles, and in 1967 he received the Golden Palm at the Cannes Film Festival for best actor in the Israeli film *Three Days and a Child*.

Kouka, Hone (1968–) Dramatist, New Zealand. An Honours degree at Otago University led to training as an actor at the New Zealand Drama School, but Kouka quickly turned to playwriting, appearing in his own solo piece *Mauri Tu* in 1991. With Hori Ahipene, he wrote *Hide 'n' Seek* (1992), winning the Bruce Mason award for most promising playwright in that year. He joined Colin MCCOLL as co-artistic manager of the Taki Rua Theatre, Wellington, in 1993, where *Nga Tangata Toa*, directed by McColl, won an award for best new play in 1994. This production and that of *Waiora* (1996) have both travelled by invitation to Europe. Although his plays feature Maori characters and family relationships, he can be seen to be achieving his aim to transcend the limiting label of 'Maori' playwright.

Kozak, Bohdan (1940–) Actor and director, Ukraine. Kozak graduated the from L'viv State Ivan Franko University, Faculty of Philology (1972) and trained at the Drama Studio at the Maria Zan'kovets'ka Ukrainian Drama Theatre (L'viv, 1963). Later he joined this theatre, where he played over 100 roles in productions directed by Serhii DANCHENKO, Alla Babenko and Fedir STRYHUN, including Clarence in *Richard III* (1976), Iago in *Othello* (1985), the title role in *Macbeth* (1992), Polonius in *Hamlet* (1997), Arbenin in Lermontov's *Maskarad* (*Masquerade*, 1982), the title role in Molière's *Tartuffe* (1986), Vozny in Ivan Kotliarevs'ky's *Natalka Poltavka* (1991) and Tesman in Ibsen's *Hedda Gabler* (1993). Directing credits include Chekhov's *Tri sestry* (*Three Sisters*, 1982), Zapolska's *Zhabusya* (1994) and *French Vaudevilles* by Labiche (1997). He worked as a teacher (1978–86) at the Drama Studio at the Maria Zan'kovets'ka Ukrainian Drama Theatre. Since 1990 he has been teaching at the Drama Faculty of Mykola Lysenko Conservatory, L'viv. The artistic method of Bohdan Kozak takes its inspiration from the theatre of Europe. In addition, he experiments with non-linear forms of theatre.

Krasinski, Janusz (1928–) Dramatist, Poland. Krasinski worked as one of the editors of the radio drama department, and was co-editor of the weekly *Kultura* and of the monthly theatre magazine *Dialog*. A member of PEN and the Polish Writer's Association, his main plays include *Czapa Czyli Smierc na Raty* (*Death in Instalments or The Black Cap*), *Wkrótce Nadejda Bracia* (*The Brothers Will Come Soon*), *Kochankowie z Klasztoru Valldemosa* (*The Lovers from Valldemosa*), *Obled* (*Madness*, an adaptation of a novel by Jerzy Krzysztón) and *Krzak Gorejacy* (*The Burning Bush*). His themes are the individual versus the destructive power of ruling authorities, the price of truth, the importance of self-identity, protest against capital punishment and insensibility.

Kratoschwill, Jeanny (1960–) Designer, Luxembourg. Kratoschwill graduated in costume and stage design at the Hochschule für Musik und Darstellende Kunst, Mozarteum in Salzburg. She gained practical experience at the Stadt-theater in Trier, the Ruhrfestspiele in Recklinghausen and the Salzburger Fest-spiele. Since 1986, she has worked as a freelance costume and stage designer in Luxembourg, Belgium, France and Ger-many and has collaborated on most of the Luxembourg's major productions, such as ALBEE's *Who's Afraid of Virginia Woolf?* (1992, Théâtre d'Esch, with Philippe NOE-SEN, Marja-Leena JUNKER and Myriam MULLER), MILLER's *Death of a Salesman* (1992, with Fernand FOX and Patrick HASTERT), Schiller's *Die Räuber* (*The Robbers*, 1995, directed by Frank HOFF-MANN, with Luc FEIT) and Jean-Paul MAES's *Good Night Sweet Heart* (1996, Théâtre des Capucins). For the world premiere of Alexey Shipenko's *Moskau Frankfurt* (1995, Théâtre des Capucins, with Jean-Paul Maes and Patrick Hastert), she designed the remarkable stage artefact of an aeroplane's wing on which the play's protagonists travel across Europe. Kra-toschwill has also worked as a costume designer on several films.

Krejča, Otomar (1921–) Director and actor, Czech Republic. Krejča played Othello (1951), Molière's Dom Juan (1957) and Malvolio (1963) at the Prague National Theatre. As the head of its theatre department (1956–61), he selected new plays by Czech authors and directed the first production of HAVEL's *Zahradní Slavnost* (*Garden Party*, 1963 in the Theatre on the Balustrade (Na zábradlí)). In 1965, he founded the Theatre Beyond the Gate (Za branou), where productions include Chekhov's *Tri sestry* (*Three Sis-ters*, 1966), Musset's *Lorenzaccio* (1969) and Chekhov's *Cajka* (*The Seagull*, 1972). After his theatre was closed by the autho-rities, he directed abroad until 1989, including Goethe's *Faust* (1976, Burg-

theater Vienna), and Beckett's *Waiting for Godot* (1978, Festival d'Avignon). In 1991, he launched the Theatre Beyond the Gate II (Za branou II) with Chekhov's *Visnevyi sad* (*The Cherry Orchard*). After closing of this theatre 1994, he directed as a guest at Comédie Française and at Prague National Theatre (Goethe's *Faust*, 1997). Krejča is particularly sensitive to the strong internal drama of Chekhov's characters. His productions are distin-guished by the complex combination of the stage components, frequent reworking of the text, and the psychological base of the acting developed from the principles of Stanislavski.

Krisanc, John (1956–) Dramatist, Canada. Krisanc's plays include *Crimes of Inno-cence* (1976), *Uterine Knights* (1979), *Tamara* (1981, Los Angeles Drama Critics' Circle Award) and *Prague* (1984, Governor General's Award), all directed by Richard Rose. The plays are character-ized by a melodramatic exploration of the role of the artist, by experiments with simultaneous staging and by innovative use of space. Krisanc is a founding mem-ber of the Necessary Angel Theatre Com-pany in Toronto. His latest play is *The Half of It* (1989).

Krishnamoorthy, N. (1951–) Designer, In-dia. Krishanmoorthy founded the Soorya Stage and Film Society in Thiruvanantha-puram. Music, dance and film festivals organized by the society have become major cultural events in the country. He has also designed and presented a number of sound and light shows, including *Ta-maso ma Jyothirgamaya*, *Veluthampi Da-lava*, *Sthree Parvam*, *Deep Shika Anjali* and *Soorya Kanti*. He has led troupes of Indian performing artists to Sweden, Ja-pan, Britain and Germany and has de-signed the sets for performances. A concern with geometrical forms charac-terizes his work.

Kroetz, Franz Xaver (1946–) Dramatist, director and actor, Germany. Kroetz trained at the Max Reinhardt Seminar in Vienna. Between 1966–70 he worked as an actor, mainly in small parts. He began writing plays in 1968, specializing in realistic folk plays in Bavarian dialect. A phase of agitprop writing was followed by renewed emphasis on critically realistic folk theatre, combining precise observation with communist optimism. Following major plays in the 1980s, including *Nicht Fisch, nicht Fleisch* (*Neither Fish nor Meat*, 1981), *Furcht und Hoffnung der BRD* (*Fear and Hope of the FRG*, 1983), *Bauern sterben* (*Farmers Dying*, 1985) and *Heimat* (Home, 1987), as well as major success as an actor on television, he withdrew from the theatre for several years, facing a major writing block. Since 1994 he has returned to writing for the stage, most recently with *Die Eingeborene* (*The Native Woman*, 1999, Vienna, directed by Achim FREYER). He has also added directing to his credits (including, in 1998, Brecht's *Herr Puntila und sein Knecht Matti* (*Mr Puntila and his Servant Matti*) in Munich).

Kuchyns'ky, Volodymyr (1958–) Director, Ukraine. Kuchyns'ky trained at the Russian State Academy for Theatre Art (GITIS), Moscow (with Mark ZAKHAROV and Anatoly VASSILYEV, 1984–8). As a resident director at the Maria Zan'kovets'ka Ukrainian Drama Theatre, L'viv, he staged *Marusia Churai*, after Lina Kostenko (1987). Kuchyns'ky is a founder and artistic director of Les Kurbas Theatre, L'viv (1988). He created about twenty theatre productions, including *The Court of Henry III*, after Dumas (1988), Hryhorii Skovoroda's *Blahodarnyi Erodii* (*Grateful Erodii*, 1993), *Zabavy dlia Fausta* (*Games for Faust*) after Dostoevsky's *Prestuplenie i nakazanie* (*Crime and Punishment*, 1994), *Apokryfy* (*Apocrypha*) after the works of Lesia Ukrainka (1995) and Chekhov's *Visnevyi sad* (*The Cherry Orchard*, 1996). International

theatrical collaborations include the International Laboratory of Anatoly Vassilyev (directing participant, Moscow, 1988–94), the Theatrical Laboratory conducted by Peter BROOK (Moscow, 1990), Les Kurbas Theatre with Yara Arts Group at La MaMa (New York, 1994), Les Kurbas Theatre at the Saratoga International Theatre Institute (New York, 1996) and Les Kurbas Theatre at the Work Centre of Jerzy Grotowski (Pontedera, Italy, 1996). Kuchyns'ky has conducted theatre training workshops since in Kiev, Kharkiv, L'viv and Sevastopol' (Ukraine), Moscow and St Petersburg (Russia), Krakow and Warsaw (Poland), New York City, Boston and Philadelphia (USA), and Pontedera (Italy).

Kugrèna, Làsma (1952–) Actor, Latvia. Since her graduation from the Latvian State Conservatory in 1975, Kugrèna has been working with the Latvian National Theatre. Among her roles are Juliet (1984), Queen Elizabeth in Schiller's *Maria Stuart* (1989) and the title role in Ibsen's *Hedda Gabler* (1991), about which a critic wrote: 'Kugrèna's star was born as Juliet, grew brighter and solidified with her Queen Elizabeth. Kugrèna has intricately etched Hedda Gabler's destructiveness. Enveloped in a fog of mystery, she enters and exits and lives her true life like one of Renoir's enigmatic women.'

Kunčevič, Ivica (1945–) Director, actor, Croatia. Kunčevič trained at the Academy of Dramatic Art, Zagreb. From 1969–77 he worked at the Theatre Marin Držić in Dubrovnik and from 1977–82 at the Zagreb Theatre Gavella. In 1992 he became a resident director of the Croatian National Theatre in Zagreb. He has directed more than seventy productions from a worldwide repertory, including Sophocles, Jonson Ibsen, Checkov, Ionesco, Genet and, in particular, Shakespeare (*Julius Caesar* (1974), *Macbeth* (1977), *Romeo and Juliet* (1986), *Troilus and Cressida* (1990), *Measure for Measure*

(1991), *The Merchant of Venice* (1995) and *King Lear* (1998)). He is equally known for his productions of Croation authors, especially the Dubrovnik writers Držić, Gundulić and Vojnović. He prefers working with the same circle of people (including set and costume designers, composers, dramaturgs and actors). Many productions are characterized by his radical changes in text, believing that a text comes to life only as a performance. The starting point of his direction is the spatial outlook of the stage. In addition to directing, Kunčević tried his skill as an actor both in theatre and on film. In Ante Babaja's film *Kamenita vrata* (*The Stone Gates*) he played the part of doctor Boras. In his own adaptation of Dostoyevsky's *Brat'ia Karamazovy* (*The Karamazov Brothers*) he played Alyosha.

Kuo Pao Kun (1939–) Dramatist and director, Singapore. Kuo is revered as the leading playwright and director in Singapore. With a career spanning close to forty years, Kuo has been active predominantly in the Mandarin-speaking drama community, but in recent years has crossed over to the English medium. He began in radio drama in 1956, and in 1963 graduated from the National Institute of Dramatic Art in Sydney. In 1965, he founded the Practice Performing Arts School with his wife, Goh Lay Kuan. His career in the late 1960s to 1970s was inextricably linked to political activism which resulted in his arrest and incarceration from 1976–80 under the Internal Security Act of Singapore. Upon his release, Kuo returned to the stage as dramatist/director and in 1985 wrote his first English play, *The Coffin is Too Big For The Hole*. The 1980s saw Kuo experimenting with different styles and techniques: *Silly Little Girl and The Funny Old Tree* (1987) was heavily influenced by Grotowskian methodology. *Mama Looking For Her Cat* (1988) was the first polyglottal and multi-cultural play featuring an mixed ethnic ensemble cast. Kuo's

later plays, namely *Lao Jiu* (1993), and *Descendants of the Eunuch Admiral* (1996), are lyrical and allegorical pieces that make allusions to the Singapore condition. His latest offering, *Spirits Play*, is heavily influenced by nô theatre's narrative and expositional style.

Kusumo, Sardono W. Director, choreographer and performer, Indonesia. Although born in Java, Kusumo spent a period of time in Bali in the 1970s studying with masters Nyoman Kakul and Ketut Rinda, among others. It was there that he created a new Kecak in modern style which, unique among Kecak productions, features the Subali-Sugriwa episode of the *Ramayana*. This spectacular version of the battle of the monkey armies is still performed regularly by the people of Teges Kangin, Peliatan village. As part of the burgeoning Jakarta arts scene, he was also influenced by W.S. RENDRA's Mini-Word Theatre and created the theatre piece *Dongeng dari Dirah*. He is now known primarily as a dancer and choreographer.

Kuzhel'ny, Oleksii (1953–) Director, Ukraine. Kuzhel'ny graduated from the Karpenko-Kary Institute for the Art of the Theatre, Kiev in 1983 (the course of Volodymyr Nelli and Mikhail Rudin). In 1987 he founded the Studio for the Art of Theatre Suzir'ia (Galaxy). At his theatre he has directed *Sad bozhestvennykh pisen'* (*The Garden of the Divine Songs*, 1989) by contemporary Ukrainian author Valerii Shevchuk, *The Eradiation of Parenthood* by Karol Voityla (Pope John Paul II) (1993) and *The Letter of the Stranger* after Zweig (1994). Since 1993 he has been the organizer and director of the Annual International Festival of Chamber Theatres (Kiev). According to critical opinion, Kuzhel'ny's dramaturgy is marked by moments of spirituality and scenic exposure of the soul.

Kylätasku, Jussi Juhani Ilmari (1943–)
Dramatist, Finland. In addition to plays
for the theatre, including *Runar ja Kyllikki* (*Runar and Kyllikki*, 1974), *Maaria
Blomma* (*Mary Bloom*, 1980), *Haapoja*
(1989), *Hetki Lähtöni Lyö* (1992) and
Caligula (1996), he has written for television, film and radio, as well as poems and
novels. The myth of crime attracts Kylätasku as a playwright. Many of his main
characters are murderers who are seen in
their own social surroundings which provide the reasons for their actions. Kylätasku also turns regularly to historical
events to comment on the politics of
today.

L

Laberge, Marie (1947–) Dramatist, actor and director, Canada. Laberge attended the Conservatoire de l'Art Dramatique. Following several earlier plays, she achieved national acclaim in 1981 with *C'était avant la guerre à l'Anse à Gilles* (*Before the War, Down at l'Anse à Gilles*). Other notable plays include *L'Homme Gris* (translated by Rina Fraticelli as *Night*, 1984), *Aurélie ma soeur* (*Aurelie, My Sister*, 1988) and *Le Faucon* (*The Falcon*, 1991). Her plays feature some recurring themes, including 'the emptiness of personal relationships, the ludic allusions of love, the inbred subservience of women in a patriarchal society founded on religious and political conservatism'.

Labou Tansi, Sony (1947–) Dramatist, Congo. In 1979, Labou Tansi founded the Rocalo Zulu Theatre, the leading theatre company in the Congo that makes use of collectively devised productions which it tours and presents at international festivals and venues, especially in France. Labou Tansi's published plays deal with political and moral issues arising from the numerous dictatorships that have characterized post-independence African states. The plays are *Conscience de tracteur* (*The Conscience of a Tractor*, 1979), *La Parenthèse de sang* (*Blood Parenthesis*, 1981), *Je sous-signé* (*I, the Undersigned*, 1981), *Qui a mangé Madame D'Avoine Bergotha?* (*Who Has Eaten Madam D'Avoine Bergotha?*, 1984), *Antoine m'a vendu son destin* (*Antoine Sold Me His Destiny*, 1986) and *Moi veuve de l'empire* (*I, Widow of the Empire*, 1987). His performed but as yet unpublished plays are *La Rue des mouches* (*The Street of Flies*, 1985) and an adaptation of *Romeo and Juliet*, which was produced in Bordeaux in 1990.

Lagoo, Shreeram (1927–) Actor and director, India. Lagoo established the Progressive Dramatic Association in Pune in 1951. He gave up his practice of medicine to become an actor; much influenced by John GIELGUD and Laurence Olivier, he has become a celebrated actor on the Bombay stage. His first landmark role was in Vasant Rao Kanekar's *Vedyache Char Unhat*. Lagoo adopted Stanislavski's techniques, which he popularized in India. His pioneering of the naturalistic style of acting has been noted, for example in V.V. Shirwadkar's *Natasmrat*. During emergency legislation in India in the 1970s, Lagoo directed Anouilh's *Antigone* to highlight the problem of the state versus the individual.

Laham, David (1934–) Actor and director, Syria. After early success in television, Laham's contribution to theatre began when he co-founded the Thorn theatre in 1969. There he gathered well-known actors, who used their stock characters to pass strong political messages. Their criticism was daring in *Jerk*, *Maraya* (*Mirrors*) and *Baraweez* (*Frames*). Such political theatre soon became fashionable commercially, and Laham abandoned this style for something else: he produced, performed in and co-directed four plays by Mohamed MAGOUT – *Day'at Tishreen* (*The October Village*, 1974), *Ghurba* (1976), *Kasak Ya Wattan* (*Cheers, My Country* (1979) and *Shaqaeq 'l-Nouman* (*Red Anemones*, 1986) – integrating songs and dances with political farce, which made these plays very popular. In 1992 he directed Richard Nash's *The Rainmaker* and a children's play, *Al-Usfoura-l-Sa'ieda* (*The Happy Bird*). Today, Laham confines his work to film and television.

Lally, Michael (Mick) (1945–) Actor, Ireland. Lally worked as an actor with Taibhdhearc na Gaillimhe before becoming a founder member of Galway-based Druid Theatre Company in 1975. His roles with Druid included Uncle Larry in *Wild Harvest* by Ken Bourke (1989). Other roles include Manus in Brian FRIEL's *Translations* (1980), Canon Pratt in *The Field* by John B. KEANE at the Abbey Theatre (1987) and Peter in *The Power of Darkness* by John McGahern, directed by Garry HYNES for the Abbey Theatre (1991). Although Lally has become familiar to Irish television audiences as Miley in RTE's weekly rural soap *Glenroe*, he remains committed to the stage. In 1997 Lally appeared as Mick Dowd in *A Skull in Connemara* by Martin McDonagh (part of *The Leenane Trilogy*), produced by Druid Theatre Company and directed by Garry Hynes. Lally played Raphael Bell in Pat McCabe's *The Dead School*, adapted for the stage by McCabe and produced by Macnas Theatre Company Galway in 1998. His rugged but gentle features and his masterly sense of the comic make him one of the most popular actors in Irish theatre.

Lamers, Jan Joris (1942–) Actor, director and designer, The Netherlands. Jan Joris Lamers is a modern *homo universalis*, who trained as an actor (1960–1), director (1966–9) and sculptor (1968–70). The importance of Lamers in the development of Dutch theatre after 1968 cannot be overestimated. A brilliant didactic, he blazed the trail with anti-illusionary, aesthetic, montage-oriented, highly ironic, rhetorical performances with his Onafhankelijk Toneel and, from 1983, with Discordia. Both are true actors' companies: the actors do everything, from making their own sets and translations to the lighting. Some high points were *The Favourites* (ready-made world classics), *Stijl* (an enquiry into style, 1980), *What happened to Majakovski* (1981), Wilde's *An Ideal Husband* (1982), HANDKE's *Über die Dörfer* (*Across the Villages*, 1983) and many Shakespeare, Bernhard and Schnitzler plays. Lamers championed the work of Judith HERZBERG, directing an award-winning production of her play *Kras* (*Scratch*, 1991). He is also a first-class designer. Recently, his lateral approach to the theatre and his inability to memorize his lines have met with disapproval. However, through working with young actors, he continues to influence the Dutch theatre outside the proscenium arch stages.

Lamos, Mark (1946–) Director and actor, USA. Lamos trained as an actor at the Guthrie Theatre. In 1976 he began directing, first at the Guthrie II (Fugard's *Hello and Goodbye* and Jerome Kilty's *Dear Liar*), then at the California Shakespeare Festival (*Taming of the Shrew*, *Hamlet*, *A Midsummer Night's Dream*). He also served as artistic director of the Arizona Theatre Company (directing Chekhov's *Cajka* (*The Seagull*) and *Twelfth Night*). In 1980 he became artistic director of the Hartford Stage Company, where he has since presented his radical, spectacular and fantastic interpretations of classical plays. Working with scenographer Michael Yeargan, his production of *Twelfth*

Night was staged as a late-night party with Cole Porter piano background. John CONKLIN designed his two-part production of Ibsen's *Peer Gynt*, and he presented *The Greeks* as a nine-play seven-hour marathon. More recently, he directed Rattigan's *The Deep Blue Sea* (1998, with Edward HERRMAN in the cast).

Lampe, Jutta (1943–) Actor, Germany. Lampe took private acting lessons with Eduard Marcks. After first working at theatres in Wiesbaden and Mannheim, she joined the theatre in Bremen where she played Elisabeth in Schiller's *Don Carlos* and, directed by Peter STEIN, Lady Milford in Schiller's *Kabale und Liebe* (*Intrigue and Love*) as well as Leonore in Goethe's *Torquato Tasso*. Since 1971 she has been a member of the Schaubühne am Halleschen Ufer, later Lehniner Platz. There her roles include Solveig in Ibsen's *Peer Gynt*, Rosalind in *As You Like It*, Ophelia in *Hamlet* directed by Klaus Michael GRÜBER, and Alkmene in Kleist's *Amphitryon*. Theatre critic Benjamin Henrichs wrote about her: 'She can look with such large, surprised eyes. She can create the most beautiful, calm songs of voice. She can. She can. She can do anything, masters her abilities as no one else with the Schaubühne. And she does not apply all those means like a primadonna, but with all cleverness'. Recent work includes RONCONI's production of Pirandello's *I giganti della montagna* (*The Mountain Giants*, 1994, Salzburg), and with the Schaubühne she appeared in Mishima's *Madame de Sade*, Borchardt's *Hausbesuch* (*Visit at Home*, 1996, directed by Edith CLEVER), and as Cäcilie in Andrea BRETH's production of Goethe's *Stella* (1999, with Corinna KIRCHHOFF in the title role).

Lan Tian Ye (1927–) Actor, China. Lan studied Western-style painting at the Peking National Academy of Fine Arts in 1944 and acting at the Central Academy of Drama from 1954–6. Upon graduation he joined Beijing People's Art Theatre, where he played the Political Commissar in Cao Yu's *Qing Lang De Tian* (*Clear Sky*, 1954), Zeng Wen Qing in Cao Yu's *Peking Characters* (1957), Sun San in Mei Qian's dramatization of Lao She's novel *Luo Tuo Xiang Zi* (*The Camel Son*, 1957), Butler He and Yu Shi Pu in Tian Han's *Guan Han Qing* (1958), Feng Di Ping in Cao Ming's *Cheng Feng Puo Lang* (*Riding Waves and Winds*, 1961) and Qi Xiao Xuan in Zhao Qi Yang's *Hong Yan* (*Red Cliff*, 1961). He puts an emphasis on carriage and delivery, and seems to specialize in roles as handsome young men.

Lang, Alexander (1941–) Director and actor, Germany. After training as a poster designer and working as a stagehand, Lang studied acting at the Staatliche Schauspielschule Berlin (East). In the GDR, he acted at the Maxim-Gorky-Theater, the Berliner Ensemble, and the Deutsches Theater. In 1985 he made his debut as a director in West Germany, at the Münchner Kammerspiele. After some seasons at the Thalia Theater in Hamburg and the Staatliche Schauspielbühnen Berlin, he now works freelance. His style has been described as radical. In a production of Büchner's *Danton's Tod* (*Danton's Death*), for example, he cast the same actor, Christian GRASHOF, as Danton and Robespierre. Recent productions include Goethe's *Iphigenie in Tauris*, Corneille's *Le Cid*, Goethe's *Tasso*, Sophocles's *Oidipus Tyrannos* (*King Oedipus*), Toller's *Hinkemann* (*Limping Man*, 1998, Munich), DORST's *Wegen Reichtum Geschlossen* (*Closed due to Wealth*, 1998, Munich) and *Othello* (1998, Berlin, with Jörg GUDZUHN in the title role).

Långbacka, Ralf Runar (1932–) Director and writer, Finland. Långbacka was a director at the Little Swedish Theatre and the Swedish Theatre in Helsinki, artistic director of the Åbo Swedish Theatre, director at the Finnish National Theatre, assistant artistic director of the Swedish

Theatre in Helsinki, director at the Gothenburg City Theatre, Sweden, artistic director of Turku City Theatre and artistic director of the Helsinki City Theatre. Långbacka combines precise intellectual analysis with a socially oriented approach in his productions. He has fought to create ensembles of thinking, creative artists. In the 1990s, his influence on theatre in Finland extended into the areas of teaching and theory as he became a noted analyst of theatre and dramatic art. Major theatre credits include Brecht's *Leben des Galilei* (*Life of Galilei*, 1973), Chekhov's *Visnevyi sad* (*The Cherry Orchard*, 1974), Ibsen's *Peer Gynt* (1991), *As You Like It* (1992) and Chekhov's *Tri sestry* (*Three Sisters*, 1998, Copenhagen).

Langhoff, Thomas (1938–) Director and actor, Germany. Born in Zürich, Langhoff attended the Theaterhochschule Leipzig, and between 1963–71 he was an actor in Potsdam. From 1971 onwards he worked as a director in several GDR theatres. Productions include Chekhov's *Tri sestry* (*Three Sisters*, 1979), *A Midsummer Night's Dream* (1980) and Ibsen's *Fruen fra havet* (*The Lady from the Sea*, 1989). Since August 1991 he has been artistic director of the Deutsches Theater, Berlin, where productions include Hofmannsthal's *Der Turm* (*The Tower*), Ostrowski's *Les* (*The Forrest*), Hauptmann's *Der Biberpelz* (*The Beaver Fur* with Dieter MANN), *Das Gleichgewicht* (*Balance*) and *Ithaca* by Botho STRAUSS, Chekhov's *Djadja Vanja* (*Uncle Vanya*), Brecht's *Der Kaukasische Kreidekreis* (*The Caucasian Chalk Circle*, 1998) and Dürrenmatt's *Der Besuch der Alten Dame* (*The Visit*, 1999). He considers theatre 'as a space for various forms of resistance, including an unspectacular reflection of human values'.

Lanoye, Tom (1958–) Dramatist, novelist, poet and performer, Belgium. Lanoye is currently one of the most versatile contemporary Flemish writers. His first poetry collection appeared in 1984. Since then he has published several novels. His work has been translated into German, French, English, Frisian and Afrikaans. He made his debut as a dramatist in 1989 with *De Canadese muur* (*The Canadian Wall*), written in collaboration with his contemporary Herman Brusselmans. After that followed *Blankenberge* (1991), *Bij Jules en Alice* (*At Jules and Alice's*, 1991) and *Celibaat* (*Celibacy*, 1993). More recently he worked on *Ten Oorlog* (*To War!*), an adaptation of Shakespeare's history plays, for the Blauwe Maandag Compagnie in collaboration with Luk PERCEVAL. The eight plays were performed together as part of a grand project during the 1997–8 season. Tom Lanoye's stage writing can be seen as a reaction to today's intellectualist theatre. He searches for the typically Flemish aspects of his roots.

Laou, Julius Amédée (1950–) Dramatist and cinematographer, France and Martinique. Founding director of the Paris-based company La Comédie du 21ème Siècle, the titles of his work reflect themes of alienation and issues of colour. *Ne m'appelez jamais nègre* (*Don't Ever Call Me Nigger*, 1982), is set amidst the European black diaspora, while *Sonate en Solitude Majeure* (*Sonata in Solitude Major*, 1986) explores the jealousy of a white servant towards his famous black employer. His highly successful *Folie ordinaire d'une fille de Cham* (*Ordinary Madness of a Daughter of Ham*) starred Jenny ALPHA in its inaugural 1984 production. New York's Ubu Repertory Theatre produced *Une Autre Histoire ou le malentendu* (*Another Story or The Misunderstanding*). His 1984 prize-winning short fiction film, *Solitaire à micro ouvert* (*Microphone Solo*), was followed by *Melodie de brumes à Paris* (*Misty Paris Melody*), starring Greg GERMAIN. With the full-length *La vieille quimboiseuse et le majordome* (*The Old Sorceress and the*

Valet), Laou revisits his moody exploration of multi-cultural relationships to great critical acclaim. For Avignon in 1998, he wrote and directed a sarcastic anti-racist farce, *Madam Huguette et les français souche de souche* (*Madame Huguette and the True French Stock*).

Lapotaire, Jane (1944–) Actor, Great Britain. Lapotaire trained for the stage at the Bristol Old Vic. Apart from freelance work, she has been associated with the National Theatre, where she has appeared in Strindberg's *Dödsdansen* (*Dance of Death*, 1967) and Sophocles's *Antigone* (1984), and with the Royal Shakespeare Company, where she played the title role in *Piaf* by Pam GEMS (directed by Howard DAVIES), Gertrude opposite Kenneth BRANAGH's *Hamlet* (1992, directed by Adrian NOBLE), and Mrs Alving in Ibsen's *Gengangere* (*Ghosts*, directed by Katie MITCHELL, with Simon Russell BEALE as Osvald). Lapotaire's performances are convincing and impressive because of their emotional intensity, facilitated by her method acting approach.

Lause, Hermann (1939–) Actor, Germany. After training with Ellen Mahlke in Munich, Lause performed in the theatres in Berlin, Essen and Oberhausen, and joined Peter ZADEK in Bochum (1972–7) and Hamburg (1977–9). Since then he has worked freelance, playing major parts (Shylock, Jack Worthing in Wilde's *The Importance of Being Earnest*, Karl Moor in Schiller's *Die Räuber* (*The Robbers*), the title role in *King Lear*) in productions by Werner SCHROETER, Zadek, Luc BONDY and Michael BOGDANOV. More recent work includes Lopakhin in Chekhov's *Visnevyi sad* (*The Cherry Orchard*, Burgtheater Vienna, 1996) and Licht in Kleist's *Der Zerbrochene Krug* (*The Broken Jug*, Bayerisches Staatsschauspiel, Munich, 1997). His strength is in playing sad, funny or grotesque everyday characters.

Lauwers, Jan (1957–) Director, designer and author, Belgium. After studying painting at the Arts Academy in Ghent, he made his theatre debut when he founded the Epigonenensemble (1979). In 1981 this company became a collective (Epigonentheater zlv), which surprised with concrete, direct, strongly visual productions using music and language as their structuring elements. In 1985 the collective was dissolved and Lauwers founded Needcompany. Lauwers's casts are always international. Each production is performed in different languages. Lauwers's training as a visual artist is important for his way of dealing with theatre as a medium: he created a highly individual and revealing theatrical language, which characterizes not only his early, strongly visual productions such as *Need to Know* (1987) and *ça va* (1989), but also his direction of *Julius Caesar* (1990, with actor Dirk ROOFTHOOFT), *Anthony and Cleopatra* (1992), Needcompany's *Macbeth* (1996) and his latest project, *The Snakesong Trilogy* (1994–6, with actor Viviane DE MUYNCK).

Lavelli, Jorge (1931–) Director, France. Born in Argentina, Lavelli studied at the University of Buenos Aires before becoming involved with the Independent Theatre Organization. He directed a number of contemporary Argentinian plays before coming to Paris in 1960 to study in Paris remaining at L'Université du Théâtre des Nations where his contemporaries included Jerôme SAVARY, Copi and Víctor García. His first significant production, a bold and violent staging of Witold Gombrowicz's *Slub* (*The Wedding*) won him the Concours des Jeunes Compagnies in 1963 and with it instant recognition. During the 1960s he gained much acclaim with a series of striking and resolutely non-naturalistic productions of pieces by Eugene O'Neill, Claudel, HANDKE and Arrabal. Throughout the 1970s and 1980s he worked regularly at the most prestigious theatre and opera houses in

Europe including La Comédie Française, La Scala and Bonn's Theater der Stadt. Between 1987–96 he was artistic director of France's newest national theatre, La Colline, where he juggled an impressive repertoire of modern classics and contemporary works. He continues to work freelance, largely in Paris.

Lavia, Gabriele (1942–) Actor and director, Italy. After training at the Academy of Dramatic Art in Rome, Gabriele Lavia rose to national fame by performing in *Titus Andronicus* (1967), directed by Luca RONCONI, and *King Lear* (1973), directed by Giorgio Strehler. In 1975 he founded his own theatre company, which is devoted to neo-naturalistic forms of dramaturgical research and for which he acts and directs mainly classical texts. Lavia, who has also made a number of television and film appearances such as Dario Argento's *Profondo Rosso* (*Deep Red*, 1974), has a compelling stage presence and is a good interpreter of leading male roles. Among his most notable productions are *Othello* (1975), Schiller's *Die Räuber* (*The Robbers*, 1981), Kleist's *Prinz Friedrich von Homburg* (1985) and, more recently, Luigi Pirandello's *Il gioco delle parti* (*The Game of Roles*, 1996) and Ingmar Bergman's *Scenes from a Marriage* (1998). Since 1997 Lavia has been artistic director of the Teatro Stabile Torino.

Lawler, Ray (1921–) Dramatist and director, Australia. Lawler left school at thirteen. He started writing plays as well as acting and directing with the Melbourne Union Theatre Repertory Company. Lawler is best known for his landmark play, *The Summer of the Seventeenth Doll*. This play, which won joint first prize along with Oriel Gray's *The Torrents* in a playwriting competition in 1955, was produced by the Union Theatre Repertory Company and was an enormous success in Australia before transferring to London's West End. *The Doll* was less suc-

cessful in New York, and a very dull film version (*The Canecutters*) does not do the play justice. *The Doll* is a realistic, well-made play set in Melbourne, seventeen years into a relationship between Olive, a barmaid, and Roo, a canecutter who comes south for the lay-off period. In the mid-1950s it very much appealed to Australian audiences tired of watching British and American lifestyles enacted onstage. *The Doll* is frequently studied and revived in Australia, and Lawler eventually wrote two prequels to *The Doll*, *Kid Stakes* and *Other Times*. The phenomenal success of *The Doll* tends to overshadow Lawler's achievements, for example, as a director and dramaturg for the Melbourne Theatre company.

Lébl, Petr (1965–) Director and scenographer, Czech Republic. Lébl studied directing and scenography at the Prague Academy of Performing Arts, and drew attention to himself through the inventive and fantastically graphic amateur productions of *Grotesques* (1985, based on Kurt Vonnegut, Jr), *The Serpent* (1987, based on Mircea Eliade), and *Metamorphosis* (1988, an adaptation of Kafka). In 1988 he began to work in professional theatres, and in 1993 he became artistic director of the Prague Theatre on the Balustrade (Na zábradlí), where he directed Genet's *Les bonnes* (*The Maids*, 1993), Chekhov's *Cajka* (*The Seagull*, 1994), Gogol's *Revizor* (*The Government Inspector*, 1995), Synge's *The Playboy of the Western World* (1995), the musical *Cabaret* (1995) and the new Czech play by J.A. PITÍNSKÝ, *Pokojíček* (*The Little Room*, 1993). With his typical stylistic heterogeneity and radical reinterpretation of the text, he is considered as the most significant representative of the postmodern Czech theatre.

LeCompte, Elizabeth (1944–) Director, USA. A graduate in applied art and art history at Skidmore College, Lecompte joined Richard Schechner's Performance

Group in 1970 as an actor and assistant director. When Schechner left the Performance Group in 1980, LeCompte became artistic director of the Wooster Group, formed at the same venue by LeCompte and other former Performance Group members including Spalding GRAY. Schechner, Richard FOREMAN's use of non-representational gesture and Robert WILSON's 'minimal rather than logical structure' have been influential for LeCompte's work. She has led the Wooster Group to become 'arguably America's most important experimental group'. Her theatre works emerge from process: they are not predetermined.

Lee Byung-Boc (1927–) Designer, Korea. Lee graduated from Ewha Women's University and trained at the Académie de Coupe de Paris. As a costume and set designer, Lee introduced semiotics onto the Korean stage. Her career began in 1966, and she has worked on more than one hundred productions including CHOI In-Hoon's *Eodiseo Mooeosi Doieo Dasi Mannarya* (*When, Where to Meet Again as What*, 1970, with PARK Jung-Ja in the cast) for the Korean National Theatre, Tennessee Williams's *Cat on a Hot Tin Roof* (1974), *Baram Boonun Naledo Gotun Pigo* (*Flowers are Blooming on Windy Days*, 1984), Lorca's *Bodas de sangre* (*Blood Wedding*, 1985, 1988), *Hamlet* (1993), Brecht's *Mutter Courage und ihre Kinder* (*Mother Courage and her Children*, 1997) and *Comedy of Errors*. Her sets and costumes signify the unity of images, patterns and signs.

Lee Chun-Chow (1958–) Director and actor, China (Hong Kong SAR). Lee's professional debut was with the Chung Ying Theatre Company in 1981 as an actor. He appeared in many productions including Carlo Goldoni's *Il servitore di due padroni* (*The Servant of Two Masters*, 1982, directed by Colin George), SHAFFER's *The Royal Hunt of the Sun* (1984,

also directed by George) and Cheung Tat-ming's *The Legend of a Storyteller* (1993, directed by Fredric MAO). Lee also played in his one-man shows, including Kuo Pao-kun's *No Parking on Odd Days* (1987) and James Cheung's *Taxi Driver* (1993). He is chiefly remembered for his leading role in Cheung Tat-ming's musical *Old Master Q* (1994), claiming the Hong Kong Drama Awards for best actor. In 1995, Lee was invited to Singapore for the Festival of Asian Performing Arts with *Old Master Q*. Lee has also adapted and directed numerous popular productions for the Chung Ying. His direction of Leung Ka-kit's *The Professional* (revived in 1998) won him the Best Director in the 1998 Hong Kong Drama Awards.

Lee Gun-Sam (1929–) Dramatist, Korea. Lee trained at the Department of Dramatic Arts, University of North Carolina and at New York University. He was the director of the Min-Joong Theatrical Company during the 1970s and 1980s. Since 1957, Lee has written fifty-two plays, including three plays in English. He is mainly known for his comedies *Wongoji* (*The Manuscript Papers*, 1960), *Daewangun Jooggirul Geoboohatda* (*The Great King Refuses to Die*, 1961), *Je Sipal Gonghwagook* (*The 18th Republic*, 1965), *Gookmool Itsaomnida* (*Taking the Lion's Share*, 1966), *Yooranggukdan* (*Travelling Troupe*, 1971, directed by LEE Sung-Gyu), *Samsipilganeui Yayoohoi* (*A Thirty-day Picnic*, 1974), *Goommeogo Moolmasigo* (*Dreaming and Drinking*, 1981), *Makchatan Donggi Dongchang* (*The Enemies Meet on the Last Train*, 1991), *Yi Seong-Gyeeui Boodongsan* (*The King Yi's Property*, 1994) and *Acasia Gotipun Barame Naligo* (*Wind Spread Acasia Flowers* (1998, with YOON Ju-Sang in the title role). Lee's contribution to Korean theatre is in tackling cultural gravity and introducing modern comedies into the Korean theatre which had been dominated by realistic drama.

Lee Kang-Baek (1947–) Dramatist, Korea. Trained with the Gagyo Theatre Company and at the Korea Playwrighting Workshop. Lee was mainly known for his short plays for the fringe theatre, such as *Daseot* (*Five*, 1971, directed by LEE Sung-Gyu) and *Gyeolhon* (*Marriage*, 1974). From the 1980s, Lee converted his dramaturgy onto a large scale. He wrote *Jokbo* (*Family Tree*, 1981), *Juragieui Saramdul* (*People in the Jurassic Period*, 1982), *Homo Separatus* (1983), *Bomnal* (*One Spring Day*), *Biong Saong* (1986, directed by Lee Sung-Gyu), *Chilsanli* (*The Town of Chilsanli*, 1989), *Bookeo Daegari* (*Head of a Dried Pollack*, 1993, directed by KIM Kwang-Lim) and *Nukim Gukrakgatun Feeling Like Heaven* (1998, directed by LEE Youn-Taek). Lee's greatest talent is his ability to dramatize his main concern, political matters, in the form of allegory.

Lee Man-Hee (1954–) Dramatist, Korea. Lee graduated from Dong-Gook University, Seoul (BA, philosophy of India) and trained as a monk at the Gumsan Buddhist Temple. His first play, *Moondi* (*Lepers*), published in 1983 but staged six years later, received a huge response. Each of his plays, *Gugeotsun Moktak Goomeongsokeui Jakun Eodoomieotsumnida* (*That was a Small Patch of Darkness in the Wood Block*, 1990), *Booljom Geojooseyo* (*Turn Off the Switch, Please*, 1992), *Doejiwa Otobai* (*The Pig and the Motorcycle*, 1993), *Pigojigo Pigojigo* (*Blooming Falling Blooming Falling*, 1993, with GWON Seong-Deok in the cast), *Gurae Woori Amsterdame gaja* (*Let's go to Amsterdam*, 1995), *Dolaseoseo Deonara* (*Don't Look Back When You Leave*, 1996, with CHUNG Kyung-Soon, and HAN Myung-Gu in the cast), *Arumdawoon Geori* (*Beautiful Street*, 1997), *Yongdi Wuie Gaedi* (*Marridge Stories*, 1998) and *Ni Deok Nae Tat* (*Your Virtue My Fault*, 1998), were long-running box office hits. Lee is recognized as the most influential Korean dramatist of the 1990s, described by Korean drama critics as a dramatist dealing with a philosophical theme in a practical way. He is known as 'the alchemist of the Korean language'.

Lee Ming Cho (1930–) Designer, USA. Born in China, Lee studied Chinese watercolour before emigrating to the USA in 1949. In the mid-1950s he became an assistant to Jo Mielziner for five years, and also worked with George Jenkins, Rouben Ter-Arutunian and Boris Aronson. 'Lee virtually changed the US approach to design overnight with his 1964 production of *Electra* for the New York Shakespeare Festival's outdoor theatre in Central Park. The set was a multilevelled thrust stage backed by three highly textured emblematic scenic pieces hanging from a pipe-batten gridwork. The set appeared to be carved out of stone. Lee considers the style he forged in the 1960s an American Brechtianism, although his approach owes more to the visual aesthetics of Brecht's chief designer Caspar Neher than to any reflection of Brechtian theories. In place of poetic realism Lee created sculptural settings of natural materials such as wood and metal; painterly fantasy was replaced by texture; colour and ornament were replaced by formality and spatial relationships.' His work is also well represented in the worlds of opera and dance.

Lee Seung-Chul (1950–) Actor, Korea. Lee was a trainee at the Maekto Theatre Company and with the Seongjowa Theatre Group. He usually took the role of cool, measured, self-controlled characters in urban life. The majority of his performances are in European and American contemporary plays, such as Anthony Shaffer's *Sleuth* (1981), Neil SIMON's *Barefoot in the Park* (1983), Williams's *A Streetcar Named Desire* (1986) and *The Rose Tatoo* (1986, directed by KIM Ara), Willy Russell's *Educating Rita* (1991) and Harold PINTER's *Betrayal* (1991). In

Korean originals, he performed in the musicals *Majimak Choomun Nawa Hamge* (*Why not Have the Last Dance with Me*, 1993, by Joo Chan-Ok) and *Soo-Il Lee & Soon-Ae Shim* (1997, by Kim Sang-Yeol).

Lee Sung-Gyu (1939–) Director, Korea. Lee graduated from the Drama and Cinema Department of Joongang University in 1966. In the same year he established the Gagyo theatre company, and continued with this group until 1979. In 1983 Lee gained an MA from the Department of Performance Studies, New York University. He was the artistic director of the Korean National Theatre from 1985–6, and held the same position in the Noori Korean Theatre Company in New York from 1991–3. During the first fifteen years of his career, Lee directed many European classical plays and Korean originals including LEE Gun-Sam's *Gwanginduleui Chookje* (*The Madmen's Festival*, 1968), *Yoorang Gukdan* (*Travelling Troupe*, 1971) and LEE Kang-Baek's *Naema* (1974). After settling down in Korea in 1993 as the artistic director of the Incheon City Theatre Company, his interests changed to a more fundamental issue, harmony between different cultures. In his recent productions of Dürrenmatt's *Der Besuch der Alten Dame* (*The Visit*, 1994), *The Comedy of Errors* (1994), and *Gooweoldong Scrooge* (*The Scrooge in Town of Gooweoldong*, 1995), he has tried to combine Korean theatrical elements with the European originals.

Lee Tae-Sup (1954–) Designer, Korea. Lee trained at Hong-Ik University (BFA in fine art), Joong-Ang University (MA in theatre art) and Brooklyn College of the City University of New York (MFA in scene design). Lee has been involved in theatre, opera and dance performances. For the theatre, he designed the set of Waldo KANG's *Beondaegijeon* (*Tales of Pupae*, 1990), *Oirowoon Byeoldul* (*Solitary Stars*, 1991), and LEE Kang-Baek's *Mool-geopoom* (*Water Bubble*, 1991), the musical *Goomgoonun Gicha* (*The Dreaming Locomotive*, 1992), *Lost Angels* (1993, directed by KIM Suk-Man, performed at LA City Theatre, USA), *Gwicheon* (*Back to the Haven*, 1993, with GWON Seong-Deok in the cast), OH Tae-Seok's *Jajeongeo* (*Bicycle*, 1994), *The Comedy of Errors* (1997, directed by LEE Sung-Gyu) and Mi-ri Yoo's *Moolgogieui Chookje* (*Fishes' Festival*, 1997), each of them functionally symbolized and minimalized.

Lee Youn-Taek (1952–) Director and dramatist, Korea. Lee studied at the Seoul Institute of Arts. After directing *Citizen K* (1989), and *Ogoo-A Funeral Ceremony* (1990), a mixture of an obsessive attitude with bodies, movements and literary language, he became known as 'a cultural guerrilla' by Korean critics. His main aim is to demolish conventions for reviving primitive theatricality. He continues his experiment with the Yeonhee Street Gang Theatre Group in Pusan (1986–) and the Theatre Laboratory for Our Theatre (1994–). Lee is interested in merging language and body together by staging both classical plays and his own adaptations. His recent works include KIM Eui-Kyung's *Gil Deonanun Gajok* (*A Family on the Road*, 1991), Kim Kwang-Lim's *Hongdongjinun Salaitda* (*Hongdongji is still E[A]live*, 1993, for the Korean National Theatre), OH Tae-Seok's *Viniy Hothouse* (1994), *Cheongbajirul Ipun Faust* (*Faust in Jeans*, 1995), *Moonjejeok Ingan Yeonsan* (*King Yeonsan – A Controversial Figure*, 1995 with YU In-Chon in the cast), *Hamlet* (1996), *Faust 1997* (for the Korean National Theatre) and LEE Kang-Baek's *Nukim Gukrakgatun* (*Feeling Like Heaven*, 1998).

Lei Que Sheng (1936–) Actor, China. After graduation from the acting department of the Central Academy of Drama in 1960, Lei became a member of the Central Experimental Theatre. A versatile actor, in thirty years he played more than two hundred roles in both Chinese and foreign plays. Between the 1970s and 1990s, major parts include Jian Zhen, the Chinese monk who brought Buddhism to Japan in Qi Zhi Xiang's *Jian Zhen Dong Du* (*Jian Zhen's Eastward Voyage*), the eponymous hero in Chen Bai Cheng's *A Q Zheng Zhuan* (*An Anecdotal History of Ah Q*) and Zen Hao in Cao Yu's *Peking Characters*, as well as Falstaff and Ford in *The Merry Wives of Windsor*.

Lepage, Robert (1957–) Director and actor, Canada. Lepage studied at the Conservatoires d'Art Dramatique in Québec and trained in Paris with Alain Knapp. His theatrical work has been vitally influenced by the concepts developed by Théâtre Repère, which recommends 'approaching creation through the slant of resources (objects, sounds, texts, music, etc.) explored through scores...The results of these free explorations are summarised in an Evaluation before being brought out in Representation'. In his own creations (such as *The Seven Streams of the River Ota*, 1996), as well as productions of classics (*A Midsummer Night's Dream*, *The Tempest*, 1992), he has created a theatrical magic often tied to his presence on stage as an actor, but also resulting from mastery of stage space and time. His productions are characterized by a non-linear dreamlike surrealism. Recently, he directed *The Confessional* (1995), which won a Genie Award for Best Canadian Film, and *La Géométrie des miracles* (The Geometry of Miracles, 1997), a theatrical inquiry into the works of Frank Lloyd Wright.

Lepage, Sue (1951–) Designer, Canada. Lepage joined the Stratford Festival as an assistant in the paint shop. In 1975, she designed the national tour of REANEY's *The Connellys*. Other major productions include David FRENCH's *Salt-Water Moon* (1984), STOPPARD's *Rosencrantz and Guildenstern are Dead* (1985) and Brecht's *Mutter Courage und ihre Kinder*

(*Mother Courage and her Children*). Rather than reflecting a personal style, her designs emphasize the meaning of the play: 'texture is a vital element in her work, whether conveyed through a wealth of detail or with extreme simplicity'.

Lerner, Motti (1949–) Dramatist and director, Israel. Lerner studied Literature at the Hebrew University in Jerusalem and began his theatre career as dramaturg and director at the Khan Jerusalem municipal theatre. His play *Kastner*, about a historical figure with that name who negotiated with Eichmann for releasing Jews and was later accused of collaboration with the Nazis, was performed at the Cameri Tel Aviv municipal theatre. It was later followed by a television series about the trial itself. His play *The Pangs of Messias* presents an apocalyptic vision of the settlers in the occupied territories, and *Else* deals with the life of poetess Else Lasker-Schueler in Jerusalem.

Lérus, Arthur (1948–) Actor, director and author, France and Guadeloupe. Trained as a teacher in special education, Lérus was inspired by Jean-Marie Serreau's 1970's drama workshops to found the group Théâtre du Cyclone, which has proved an enduring focus for independent dramatic creation. With Lérus and his wife as anchor, Cyclone has aimed to transpose in dramatic form core issues of Guadeloupean resistance – against the pressures of urbanization and migration, and corrupt political mores – using dynamic symbolism, music and dialogue in Creole. Well received in Fort-de-France at the annual summer festivals, noteworthy productions include the collective creations, *Nuit blanche* (*White Night*, 1975), the biography of a militant youth; *Ma Man Nasis sek* (*Mrs Nassis's Pond is Dry*, 1978) exposing injustice over rural water shortages, written by Lérus; *Atoufanm* (*Lassie*, 1986), about a mother and her dog faced with relocation in a tower block while her son lives in France; and

Oti Tannis? (*What's become of Tannis?*, 1988), a search for treasure (values) by three characters on a derelict beach. In 1998, *Karata*, a fable using Egyptian and Inca mythology to reflect on terrorist violence and the choice of values, was put on at the Artchipel. Nicknamed 'Mandingo', Lérus radiates a quiet moral and theatrical authority, rooted in his tenacious independence.

Lev Ari, Shimon (1942–) Actor, Israel. Lev Ari studied acting at Tel Aviv University. His first main role was Happy in Arthur MILLER's *Death of a Salesman*. He has also played Vladimir in Yossi YZRAE-LI's production of Beckett's *Waiting for Godot*, as well as in three additional productions of this play, Edgar in Strindberg's *Dödsdansen* (*Dance of Death*) as well as Sender in Hanan SNIR's production of *The Dybbuk* at the Habima theatre in 1998. His one-man show *Vincent* by W.G. Smith was a long-running success (1975–81). He has also played in several television series. Lev Ari is founder and director of the Tel Aviv University theatre archives.

Levi, Rakefet (1968–) Designer, Israel. Levi studied at the Ramat Hasharon Arts College and began her career as a designer for children's television programs. She has designed several performances for the Bat-Sheva dance company. In the theatre she has designed both sets and costumes for *Romeo and Juliet* (directed by Rina YER-USHALMI), *Kritat Rosh* (*Beheading*) and *Ashkava* (*Requiem*) (both written and directed by Hanoch LEVIN) and Gilead Evron's *Har lo zaz* (*A Mountain Doesn't Move*, directed by Hanan SNIR). Levi has developed an eclectic postmodern style with highly stylized aesthetic qualities.

Levin, Hanoch (1943–) Dramatist and director, Israel. Levin studied philosophy and literature at Tel Aviv University, where he wrote articles for the students' newspaper and mounted two satirical programmes at the students' club during the late 1960s. Levin is the most prolific and probably the most controversial playwright in Israel. He has published fifty plays, of which about half have been performed on the stage, mostly directed by Levin himself. His third satirical programme *Malkat Ambatia* (*The Queen of the Tub*, 1969) was performed at the Cameri Tel Aviv municipal theatre and caused a major scandal. His satirical revue *Hapatriot* (*The Patriot*), written during the war in Lebanon, was partly censored. His earlier full-length plays from the 70's like *Yaakobi and Leidenthal*, *Chefetz* and *Shitz* are strongly influenced by absurd theatre and depict the everyday life of the characters from a grotesque perspective. In plays like *Hotsaa Lehoreg* (*Execution*), *Yesorei Iov* (*Job's Sorrows*) and *Hazona Hagedola Mibavel* (*The Great Whore of Babylon*) from the early 1980s, Levin developed a more poetic allegorical style, basing his plots on different mythical narratives on the basis of which he made his personal statement. These plays have a strong nihilistic subtext. In plays like *Halvaia Chorpit* (*Winter Funeral*) and *Orzei Hamizvadot* (*Suitcase Packers*) the poetical and the absurd are mixed. His more recent plays like *Hayeled Cholem* (*Dreaming Child*), *Peorei Pe* (*Mouth Open*) and *Kritat Rosh* (*Beheading*) and *Haholchim Bachoshech* (*The People that walked in Darkness*) could be termed horror fantasies, mixing the poetic and the allegorical with strong ideological statements. Among his later plays, *Retsach* (*Murder*) deals with the repeated circles of violence in the Israeli–Palestinian conflict, while *Ashkava* (*Requiem*) like most of his plays dealing with the confrontation with death, is based on three short stories by Chekhov. He has also published short stories and poetry and has written and directed two films.

Levine, Michael (1961–) Designer, Canada. Levine studied at the Ontario College of Art and at the Central School of Art and Design in London, England. He has designed for the Glasgow Citizens' Theatre, the Royal Shakespeare Company, the Old Vic and the English National Opera. His first major success was as co-designer for O'Neill's *Strange Interlude* in London and New York. His surrealistic and imaginative designs for the Shaw Festival have been widely acclaimed.

Levyts'ka, Maria (1955–) Designer, Ukraine. Levyts'ka graduated from the workshop of Daniil LIDER at the Taras Shevchenko Kiev State Institute for Arts. Her first independent work was seen in the experimental production of Calderón's *El principe constante* (*The Constant Prince*) at the Molodizhny Teatr, Kiev, which was banned by the Soviet authorities (1981). At the beginning of the 1980s she worked at the Crimea Maksim Gorky Russian Drama Theatre, Sevastopol', Ukraine, designing set and costumes for Bulgakov's *Master i Margarita* (*The Master and Margarita*, 1981), and Chekhov's *Tri sestry* (*Three Sisters*, 1981). Lately she has been working fruitfully at the Taras Shevchenko Opera and Ballet House (chief designer since 1989), and at the Lesia Ukrainka Russian Drama Theatre, Kiev, including Sheridan's *The School for Scandal* (1995) and *Toibele and her Demon* by Bashevis Zinger and Fridman (1996, Kiev; 1997, Haifa, Israel). She has also made set and costume designs for numerous films, and worked in icon painting and paintings on silk and other fabrics.

Leysen, Johan (1950–) Actor, Belgium. Following studies at the Studio Herman Teirlinck in Antwerp, Leysen worked with several Dutch companies such as De Appel, RO Theatre, Globe and Baal. Since the late 1980s, Leysen has been freelancing all over Europe. Major parts include Jason in Heiner Müller's *Verkommenes*

Ufer Medeamaterial Landschaft mit Argonauten (*Run-down Shore Medeamaterial Landscape with Argonauts*, 1987), directed by Anne Teresa de Keersmaeker, Wittgenstein in the monologue *Wittgenstein Incorporated* (1989), directed by Jan Ritsema (Kaaitheater), and Brutus in *Julius Caesar* (1990), directed by Jan LAUWERS (Needcompany). In 1996 he starred in Heiner Goebbels's *Die Wiederholung/La Reprise/The Repetition*. Leysen also made a reputation in films by directors such as André Delvaux and Jean-Luc Godard.

Li Liu Yi (1961–) Director, China. Following graduation from the directing department of the Central Academy of Drama, Li's major productions include a Sichuan opera version of Brecht's *Der Gute Mensch von Sezuan* (*The Good Person of Sezuan*, 1987) and Su Li Qun's *Zhunag Zhou Shi Qi* (*Zhuang Zhou Tests his Wife*, 1995, designed by YAN Long). He draws on his good understanding of Chinese operatic traditions, and seeks new forms from his own feelings and experiences, refusing to be avant-garde for its own sake. He aims to embrace the audience in the whole theatrical process. His productions reveal an experimental attitude towards stage space and time.

Lider, Daniil (1917–) Designer, Ukraine. Lider trained at the Institute for Painting, Sculpture and Architecture, Leningrad, and has been teaching at the Taras Shevchenko Kiev State Institute for Arts, the Faculty of Painting, Theatrical Department, since 1975. Andrii ALEKSANDROVYCH-DOCHEVS'KY, Volodymyr KARASHERVS'KY and Maria LEVYTS'KA are among his pupils. Lider's designs, for more than 100 productions, were seen in numerous Ukrainian and Russian theatres. Active and metaphoric imagery and deep philosophical interpretation of the subject are characteristic of his work, as well as the polyphony of textures and volumes and the functioning of space. Selected productions include Ivan Kocherha's *Iaroslav Mudry* (Kiev, 1970), Ostrovsky's *Goriachee serdtse* (*The Warm Heart*, Kiev, 1973), *Macbeth* (Khmel'nyts'k, Ukraine, 1977), *King Lear* (The Maly Theatre, Moscow, 1979), Chekhov's *Visnevyi sad* (*The Cherry Orchard*, Kiev, 1980) and Shalom-Aleichem's *Tevie-Tevel'* (*Tevie the Milkman*, Kiev, 1989).

Liensol, Robert (*c*.1930–) Actor, France and Guadeloupe. While studying for an arts degree at the Sorbonne, Liensol developed a passion for the theatre, obtaining walk-on parts in films and at the Comédie Française and TNP. At the Cours Charles Dullin he met other pioneering drama students from the Caribbean and Africa, teaming up with them to found the first professional black theatre company, Les Griots. After several productions directed by Roger Blin, they triumphed in Genet's *Les nègres* (*The Blacks*, 1959) with Liensol as Ville de Saint-Nazaire. Roles followed in productions by several major Paris directors, though Liensol was especially concerned to lend his support to worthwhile black and Third World theatre, including FUGARD's *Boesman and Lena* (1976) and plays by Julius Amédée LAOU. A mainstream success was in the 1991 French version of Alfred Uhry's *Driving Miss Daisy*. His role as the jailer in *L'Exil de Béhanzin* (*King Béhanzin's Exile*) by Guy Deslauriers exemplified the dignity and strength of conviction of this doyen of French Caribbean actors, and gained him an award as Best Francophone actor at Namur (1994).

Lill, Wendy (1950–) Dramatist, Canada. Lill has had a long-standing association with the Prairie Theatre Exchange (in Manitoba), which produced *The Fighting Days* (1982), *The Occupation of Heather Rose* (1985) and *Memories of You* (1988). More recent work includes *Sisters* (1989,

produced at Ships Company in Nova Scotia), *All Fall Down* (1993, Alberta Theatre Projects) and a stage adaptation of *The Glace Bay Miners' Museum*. Her work is characterized by a strong commitment to social and political causes. *The Fighting Days*, for example, chronicles Nellie McClung's rise to prominence as a suffragette. Lill was elected Member of Parliament in 1997.

Lin Zhao Hua (1936–) Director, China. Lin studied acting at the Central Academy of Drama and later became an actor with the Beijing People's Art Theatre. In 1982 he made his directorial debut with GAO Xing Jian's *Jue Dui Xin Hao* (*Absolute Signal*), creating a great stir in the capital. After the initial success he collaborated closely with Gao, staging his *Che Zhan* (*The Bus Stop*) and *Ye Ren* (*Wild Man*). In 1986 he directed Liu Jin Yun's *Uncle Doggie's Nirvana*. He collaborated with designer Xue Dian Jie in staging *Peking Characters* and *Faust*. In 1990 he directed a critically acclaimed studio production of *Hamlet*. In recent years he has produced dramatist GUO Shi Xing's 'men of leisure' trilogy, *Niao Ren* (*The Bird Master*), *Qi Ren* (*The Go Master*) and *Yu Ren* (*The Angling Master*). Lin's name has been closely connected with the experimental theatre in China, which since the end of the Cultural Revolution has seen an increasing emphasis on an 'expressive' approach towards acting and stage presentation.

Linehan, Rosaleen (1937–) Actor, Ireland. After beginning in musicals, by 1962 she was a household name, appearing in satirical revues and her own RTE (Radio Telefis Eireann) television series *Me And My Friend*. Her varied talents include writing music for the smash hit mini-musical *Mary Makebelieve* in 1981 at the Abbey Theatre, Dublin. This was revived at the Gate Theatre, Dublin, in 1993. Since 1985 she has embarked on a 'legitimate' acting career which brought her to work with most major Irish directors. In 1994 her one-woman show, *Mother of All The Behans*, which she co-wrote with Peter Sheridan and which had won an Edinburgh Festival Fringe First in 1989, was revived for the Irish Repertory Theatre, New York. Recent critically acclaimed roles include Mrs Hardcastle in Goldsmith's *She Stoops to Conquer*, directed by Jonathan MILLER at the Gate Theatre, Dublin; Winnie in Beckett's *Happy Days* at the Gate, and on tour to London and New York (1996), directed by Karel Reisz; and Lady Bracknell in Wilde's *The Importance of Being Earnest* (1997) at the Abbey Theatre. In 1990 she won the Radio Telefís Eireann Hall of Fame Award for her contribution to Irish Theatre, and is now widely regarded as a leading actor of the classical repertoire in Ireland.

Liptsyn, Oleg (1960–) Director and actor, Ukraine. Lipstyn studied in the Russian State Academy for Theatre Art (GITIS), Moscow (with Mikhail Butkevich and Anatoly VASSILYEV, 1983–8), and was in residence at the Moscow State Theatre School of Dramatic Art under Vassilyev (1988–90) and at the Schaubühne, Berlin (1991). Liptsyn is founder and artistic director of Theatre Club, Kiev (1989), an international avant-garde theatre company from the Theatre Union of the Ukraine. He directed eighteen theatre productions, among them Sophocles's *Antigone* (1991), an adaptation of *Ulysses* by Joyce (1993) and *Starukha* (*The Old Woman*) by Gogol and Kharms (1995). Liptsyn participated in several international projects. He also conducted several educational projects, such as a practical course in acting at the Konrad Wolf High School of Film and TV (Potsdam-Babelsberg, Germany, 1994), and a practical seminar for acting and directing students at the National School of Drama (Delhi, 1995). As actor and director, he participated in theatre festivals in Austria, Germany, Italy, Canada, France, Hungary, Mexico, Croatia, Spain, the UK, the USA, Poland and Russia.

Liu Shu Gang (1940–) Dramatist, China. Liu graduated from the Acting Department, of the Central Academy of Drama (1958–62). He has published *Shi Wu Zhuang Li Huen An De Diao Cha Fen Xi* (*Fifteen Divorce Cases Analysed*, 1983) and *Yi Ge Si Zhe Dui Sheng Zhe De Fang Wen* (*A Dead Man's Visit to the Living*, 1985), both performed by The Central Experimental Theatre, where he is a dramatist in residence. Although he was trained in the Stanislavski method, he has tried to free himself from its influence. Seen as a modernist by the old generation but as a traditionalist by the young, he seeks to combine stage effect and conceptual depth.

Liu Yuan Sheng (1942–) Designer, China. Liu obtained an MA from the Central Academy of Drama in 1981, where he is professor and dean of the stage design department. His representative designs are Huanh Zhi Long's *Songzanganbu* (1982), Ibsen's *Peer Gynt* (1983), Sophocles's *Oidipus tyrannos* (*King Oedipus*, 1986) and *Antigone* (1988), *Sang Ping Ji Shi* (*Story of Songshuping Village* (1988, by Zhu Xiaoping and Yang Jian), Ibsen's *Brand* (1990), Long Yun Li's *Sa Man Yue Guang De Huang Yuan* (*Moonlit Wasteland*, 1993, directed by XIAO Zhong Xu), Yang Xiao's *Sha Zhao Ping* (*Shazhou Village*, 1994), Chen Jian Qiu's *Ou Ren Ji* (*Adventures of the Marionettes*, 1996) and SHI Xing Guo's *Yu Ren* (*The Angling Master*, 1998). He strives for visual appeal of material and free association of the mind.

Liubimov, Yuri (1917–) Director and actor, Russia. He trained at the Schukin Theatre College in Moscow, and soon became a leading actor of the Vakhtangov Theatre Company. Next he turned to actor training, and a group of his students soon formed the Moscow Drama Theatre, now known all over the theatre world as the Taganka Theatre. In conflict with the authorities because of his non-conformism, he was expelled from the USSR. Between 1983–9 he lived in Israel and worked in different theatres throughout Europe. In Gorbachov's era, Liubimov was reappointed as director of the Taganka and his Russian citizenship was restored. Liubimov combines the lines of Vakhtangov, Meyerhold and Brecht. His trademarks were not only a new artistic style and language, but also his political outlook which he firmly expresses in modern plays and well-known classics alike. One of his most rebellious productions was *Hamlet* (1970), showing Russia rather than Denmark as a prison. Other classic productions include Bulgakov's *Master i Margarita* (*Master and Margarita*), Pushkin's *Boris Godunov*, Pasternak's *Zhivago* and Mozhayev's *Zhivoi* (*Alive*), about the destruction of Russian peasantry by Bolsheviks.

Lizaran, Anna (1944–) Actor and director, Spain. Lizaran attended a course at the Jacques Lecoq School in Paris. Back in Barcelona in 1976, she co-founded the now legendary Teatre Lliure which was to provide Barcelona with a Catalan-language theatre specializing in contemporary and classical works. With Carlota Soldevila and Lluís HOMAR, she was amongst the company's most prestigious performers. Her central performances in the company's most acclaimed works include Ibsen's *Hedda Gabler* (1977), a sensual Julie in Strindberg's *Fröken Julie* (Miss Julie, 1986), Natasha in Chekhov's *Tri sestry* (*Three Sisters*, 1979) and an outstanding performance as the Comtessa Saint-Fond in Mishima Yukio's *Madame de Sade* in 1986. More recently she has appeared in Pasqual's production of Beckett's *Waiting for Godot* (1999) and in a number of well-received films, including Ventura Pons's *Actrius* (1996) and Miguel Albaladejo's *La primera noche de mi vida* (*The First Night of My Life*, 1998). Since

1995 she has also worked increasingly as a director, but it is as an actor of chameleon-like versatility, surprising sensuality and deep intensity for which she is best-known. Increasingly, she has played a key role in the educational programmes for young performers at the Lliure.

Lo Koon-lan (1954–) Actor, China (Hong Kong SAR). Lo's recent appearances were in Richard Sheridan's *The School for Scandal* (Hong Kong Cultural Centre, directed by Henry Woronicz, 1996) and Raymond TO's *The Magic is the Moonlight* (with TSE Kwan-ho, 1997). A former principal actor of the Hong Kong Repertory Theatre (HK Rep), she appeared in over sixty productions, including Antigone in Jean Anouilh's *Antigone* (1991), Regan in *King Lear* (1993, directed by Daniel YANG) and Maggie in Tennessee Williams's *Cat on a Hot Tin Roof* (1995, also directed by Yang). She played Mei Ling in *Those Inconvenient Sisters* (1989, directed by William Hurt) for the Circle Repertory Theatre in New York. For the HK Rep, she also played Kam Lu-lu in Raymond To's *I Have a Date with Spring* (1992), a role she repeated on film in 1993. Lo's portrayal of the leading role in Dürrenmatt's *Der Besuch der Alten Dame* (*The Visit*, 1994) won the Fourth Hong Kong Drama Awards for best actor. Since the early 1990s, Lo has been a familiar face on film and television.

Lobel, Adrienne (1955–) Designer, USA. Trained at Yale University School of Drama and by LEE Ming Cho, Lobel has become 'one of the most daring of postmodern designers', whose sets are 'typified by bold uses of line and colour to create dominant images with a humorous or ironic sensibility'. Lobel has worked with director Peter SELLARS on the Mozart operas *Cosi fan tutte*, *The Marriage of Figaro* and the Glyndebourne production of *The Magic Flute*. Theatre credits both for repertory and in New York include sets and costume for Wedekind's *Lulu*

(1980), Gogol's *Revizor* (*The Inspector General*, 1980), *The Taming of the Shrew* (1986), Harry Kondoleon's *Zero Positive* (1988) and Frances Goodrich and Wendy Kesselman's *Diary of Anne Frank* (1997).

Löscher, Peter (1938–) Director and actor, Germany. Trained as an actor and director in Frankfurt an der Oder, after three years as dramaturg in Wuppertal and some time observing the work of the Royal Shakespeare Company, Löscher has worked mainly in Frankfurt am Main, Theater am Turm, at the Schauspielhaus in Düsseldorf and in Hamburg, as well as in Munich. One of his most remarkable productions was *Die Räuber* (*The Robbers*) by Schiller, which he directed in Düsseldorf, not in the traditional theatre space but in a huge old trade exhibition hall. Recent productions include Pirandello's *Sei personaggi in cerca d'autore* (*Six Characters in Search of an Author*, Bonn, 1994).

Lonza, Tonko (1930–) Actor, Croatia. Lonza trained at the Academy of Dramatic Art in Zagreb. Since his debut at the Dubrovnik Summer Festival in 1953, he has become one of the most renowned actors in Croatia. From 1953–68 he was a member of the Zagreb Theatre Gavella; since then he has been with the Croatian National Theatre in Zagreb. He played Orestes in Aeschylus's *Choephoroi* (*Libation Bearers*, 1956), Oronte in Molière's *Le misanthrope* (*The Misanthropist*, 1960) and Kowalski in Williams's *A Streetcar Named Desire* (1960). In 1963 he gave a deeply tragic portrait of Oedipus in Sophocles's *Oidipus tyrannos* (*King Oedipus*). It was a turning point in his career: he fascinated the audience with his vocal potential and elegance in speaking verse. In 1986 he scored another major success with Pedro Crespo in Calderón's *El alcade de Zalamea* (*The Mayor of Zalamea*). He is one of the most important interpreters of Krleza's characters. He also tried his hand as a director and film

actor. Since 1962 he has been working as a professor of stage speech and acting at the Academy of Dramatic Art in Zagreb.

Loquasto, Santo (1944–) Designer, USA. Loquasto began his career designing for repertory companies (Hartford Stage and Long Wharf Theatre). His New York debut was in 1970. Loquasto also works with modern dance companies (mainly costumes only). 'His actual settings can be monumental structures, immense cubes, heavily textural, or they can be constructed out of interesting components such as pipe, wood, or other found materials. At the other extreme, they can be highly realistic, filled with the clutter of everyday life.' Recent productions include William Luce's *Barrymore* (1997), the musical *Ragtime* (1997) and Leslie Ayvazian's *Nine Armenians* (1999, directed by Lynne MEADOW). He has also been the production designer for motion pictures, including several by Woody Allen.

Lubienski, Tomasz (1938–) Dramatist, Poland. A member of PEN and the Polish Writer's Association, Lubienski graduated in Polish philology from the University of Warsaw in 1960. His most important plays include *Gra* (*A Game*, 1959), *Zegarty* (*The Clocks*, 1970), *Cwiczenia z Aniolem* (*Exercises with an Angel*, 1977), *Smierc Komandora* (*Death of the Commander*, 1984), *Historia z Psem* (*History with a Dog*, 1988) and *Sniadanie do Lozka* (*Breakfast in Bed*, 1994). His plays, produced by theatre, radio and television and frequently published in the theatre monthly *Dialog*, are influenced by an open form of romantic drama. Stage directions, often extended, are of great autonomic importance. His themes are both historic and contemporary.

Lukavský, Radovan (1919–) Actor, Czech Republic. A graduate from the Prague Conservatory, Lukavský first made use of his comic talent and then succeeded in roles as a modest romantic hero, such as

Bill Starbuck in Nash's *The Rainmaker* (Prague Municipal Theatre, 1957). He soon joined the National Theatre, where he performed an up-to-date, rational *Hamlet* (1959) and where he first made thorough use of his expressive understatement, thereby influencing subsequent Czech acting. His characters combine the search for truth, the defence of moral values and a firm ethical base, informed by the actor's masculine, emotionally restrained expression. He is known for the precision of his technique, including the control of his body, and for a quality of stage diction that is without rival in his country. His most accomplished roles include Lysander in Calderón's *El Mágico Prodigioso* (*The Wonderful Wizard*, 1995) and Theatre Director in Otomar KREJČA's production of Goethe's *Faust* (1997). Both his teaching and his acting are informed by Stanislavski's principles.

Luo Jin Ling (1937–) Director, China. Upon graduation in 1961 from the directing department of the Central Academy of Drama, Luo stayed on to teach directing in the same institution, where he is now the deputy director and professor of directing. His directing debut was Shen Xi Meng's *Ni Hong Deng Xia De Shao Bing* (*Guards Under Neon Lights*, 1977). He established his position in Chinese theatre as the first to stage full-scale productions of Greek tragedies in China, directing, among ohers, Sophocles's *Oidipus tyrannos* (*King Oedipus*, 1986), *Antigone* (1988), and Euripides's *Medeia* (1989) and *Troades* (*The Trojan Women*, 1992). At times he introduced elements of Chinese traditional theatre in some of his productions of Greek tragedy, which were well received in the European countries they visited.

Lupa, Krystian (1943–) Director, designer, painter and graphic artist, Poland. Lupa trained at the Academy of Fine Arts in Cracow and studied directing at the State Theatre Academy, where he joined the staff in 1984. Between 1977–86 he worked at Teatr im. Cypriana Kamila Norwida in Jelenia Gora and Stary Teatr of Cracow, and since 1987 exclusively with Stary and abroad. His most important productions include Witkiewicz's *Pragmatysci* (*Pragmatists*, 1981), *Bezimienne Dzielo* (*The Anonymous Work*, 1982), *Maciej Korbowa I Bellatrix* (*Maciej Korbowa and Bellatrix*, 1986), *Miasto Snu* (*The City of Dreams*, Lupa's scenario after *Po Tamtej Stronie* (*On the Other Side*) by Kubin, 1985), *The Dreamers* (Robert Musil, 1988), *The Brothers Karamasov* (Dostoyevsky, 1990), *Malte* (after Rilke, 1991), *Kalkwerk* (after Thomas Bernhard, 1993), *Lunatics* (after Herman Broch, 1995) and *Immanuel Kant* (Thomas Bernhard, 1996). Lupa treats his theatre as an existential and epistemological experience. His first productions (the Witkiewicz ones) were directly devoted to the problem of cognition. Later the ethical issues dominated (showing the influence of Jung), and his work became concerned with man's spiritual situation in times of great cultural change (the age of Aquarius). Lupa has also designed the set for all his productions.

Luzzati, Emanuele (1921–) Scenographer, Italy. After a period of training at the Institute of Fine Arts in Lausanne, Emanuele Luzzati made his theatre debut in 1947 in a production of *Lea Lebowitz*, written and directed by Alessandro Fersen. Luzzati's long career as a painter, set designer, costume designer and cartoonist in various theatres and opera houses all over the world has made him one of Italy's most original and innovative theatre designers. His films *La gazza ladra* (*The Thieving Magpie*, 1965) and *Pulcinella* (1973) have received Academy Awards, and the former has been nominated as one of the most successful animations of all times. Luzzati understands design as an extension of text and often elaborates his materials pictorially.

M

Maan, Trudi (1954–) Designer, The Netherlands. Trudi Maan trained as a handicraft teacher and later as a sculptor at the Van Eyck Academy (1981–3). She got involved in the theatre through Bonheur, a loosely knit circle of actors and artists originating from the Drama School in Arnhem in the mid-1980s. With them, she has shaped many productions. Maan is not a classical 'give me a story and I'll make a picture' kind of designer; in her hands the set, or rather the environment, becomes an additional actor. She turns spaces (like Bonheur's old gym hall in Rotterdam) into theatrical environments, unrecognizable from earlier visits. She also likes to give work by other artists a place in the show. Some titles (all adapted from books and directed by Anneke van Blokland) include *Hotel Bonheur* (1988), *Comptons and Burnetts* (after Ivy Compton Burnett, 1989), *Orlando* (after Virginia Woolf, 1992), *Krazy Kat* (after George Herriman, 1994) and *The Hearing Trumpet* (after Leonora Carrington, 1997). Maan's spunky, irreverent taste shines through, too, in work she does for others. She teaches scenography at the Performing Arts Academy in Utrecht.

Ma'ayan, Dudu (1954–) Director, Israel. Ma'ayan trained at the Tel Aviv University. His first production, *The Inn of Spirits* by Israeli poet-playwright Nathan Alterman, won the first prize at the first Acco festival for alternative theatre. Ma'ayan founded the Acco Centre for theatre, where his five-hour kaleidoscopic performance *Arbeit macht frei von Toitland Europa*, confronting the Holocaust in the contemporary Israeli context, creating interesting analogies between the Holocaust and the Israeli–Palestinian conflict, premiered in 1991. This extraordinary performance has also toured different countries and it has made Israeli alternative theatre internationally known.

Mac Intyre, Tom (1931–) Dramatist, Ireland. Mac Intyre has brought a liberating sense of play to Irish theatre by combining a creative grasp of language with a commitment to theatre of image. Early work includes *Eye Winker Tom Tinker* (1972) and *Jack Be Nimble* (1976), directed by Patrick MASON. During the 1970s in New York, Mac Intyre was influenced by the work of Martha Graham and Pina Bausch, and his work with the American Calck Hook Dance Theatre in Paris resulted in *Doobally – Back Way* (1979). This involvement with dance has strongly influenced Mac Intyre's physical vision of theatre, as evidenced by *The Great Hunger* (1983), an interpretation of Patrick Kavanagh's poem *The Great Hunger* for the stage. Developed in collaboration with Patrick Mason and actor Tom HICKEY, this was a stark compelling work. Their collaboration also included *The Bearded*

Lady (1984) and *Snow White* (1988). Recent work includes the irreverent and highly successful *Good Evening Mr Collins* (1995) and *You Must Tell the Bees* produced in collaboration with Irish Modern Dance Theatre (1996), *The Chirpaun* (1997) and *Caoineadh Airt uí Laoghaire*, a bilingual play taken from the traditional poem *The Lament for Art O'Leary* (1998).

McAnuff, Des (1952–) Director and dramatist, USA. McAnuff founded Dodger Productions in the 1970s. Later he directed some of his own plays at Joseph Papp's Public Theatre. In 1982, he became artistic director of La Jolla Playhouse in San Diego, where he directed both classics (Chekhov's *Cajka* (*The Seagull*, 1985)) and new plays. As in Keefe's *Gimme Shelter* at the Brooklyn Academy of Music (1978), McAnuff frequently combines pop music and culture and more traditional forms of theatre. This, together with his willingness to explore contemporary political and ethical questions distinguish his direction.

McCalla, Barbara Stanwyck (1947–) Actor, Jamaica. McCalla is a qualified attorney at law (she holds BA and law degrees from the University of the West Indies). She trained at the Jamaica School of Drama. In her distinguished career, she has played in traditional theatre (Makak in Derek WALCOTT's *Dream on Monkey Mountain*, Gloria in Trevor Rhone's *Two Can Play*, and Miss Aggie in Rhone's *Old Story Time*, as well as Bloody Mary in *South Pacific*). In addition, she has appeared in film, on radio and on television. She seeks continually to find more and more challenging roles which will help her to refine her craft. Her general sensitivity to the needs of fellow actors make her a reliable working companion.

McCarten, Anthony (1961–) Dramatist, New Zealand. After completing a BA at Victoria University of Wellington in which he abandoned political science for drama and creative writing, and with only a brief apprenticeship at a small Wellington theatre, McCarten wrote in collaboration with Stephen Sinclair the farcical comedy *Ladies' Night* (1987), which was an immediate hit in New Zealand and Australia, has been performed in the United States and in Europe, and enjoyed extensive British tours during the early 1990s. His early work may be 'brazenly populist', but later plays such as *Via Satellite* (1991) and *F.I.L.T.H.* (1995), though achieving more moderate success, have been at the same time wittier and more thought-provoking. Overall, his popularity leapfrogs any critical hesitation and his success is already second only to Roger HALL's.

McColl, Colin (1948–) Director and actor, New Zealand. After professional training limited to a drama school in Christchurch, McColl first appeared in Wellington as an actor at the Downstage Theatre in 1968. Several years of theatrical experience in England followed. He returned to the Downstage as associate artistic director (1974–7), and after three years in Australia became artistic director (1984–92). Though unavoidably restricted by his audience to a middle-class choice of play, he aimed for a theatricality and fresh interpretation which resulted in startlingly unconventional productions of plays like Oscar Wilde's *The Importance of Being Earnest* (1991). He was the first New Zealand director invited to the Edinburgh Festival with his (equally unconventional) production of Ibsen's *Hedda Gabler* (Downstage, 1990). This went on to the inaugural Ibsen Festival in Oslo, where McColl returned in 1991 to direct a Norwegian cast in Ibsen's *The Vikings at Helgeland*. In New Zealand, he has consciously presented twentieth-century European classics from a contemporary New Zealand perspective, for example Dürrenmatt's *Der Besuch der alten Dame* (*The Visit*, 1996). He has also directed several premières of New Zealand plays, including John Broughton's *Michael James Manaia* (1991) and Hone KOUKA's *Nga Tangata Toa* (1994).

McCowen, Alec (1925–) Actor, Great Britain. McCowen trained for the theatre at the Royal Academy of Dramatic Art. Milestones in his long and acclaimed career have been the Fool in Peter BROOK's production of *King Lear* (1962, with Paul SCOFIELD as Lear), Martin Dysart in Peter SHAFFER's *Equus* (1973) and his solo performance of St Mark's Gospel (first 1978). As Alceste in Molière's *Le misanthrope* (*The Misanthropist*) opposite Diana RIGG's Célimène, he movingly cut through intellectual insincerity and hypocrisy of society. More recently he appeared in Stephen Churchett's *Tom and Clem* opposite Michael GAMBON in the West End (1997) and at the Royal National Theatre as Storyteller in John CAIRD's production of *Peter Pan* (adapted by Caird and Trevor NUNN).

McCusker, Stella (1942–) Actor, Ireland. Stella McCusker has worked extensively in Ireland both north and south, and has worked with Northern Irish playwrights Stewart Parker, Graham REID, Ron Hutchinson and Robin Glendinning. Her roles include Mrs Tancred in Joe DOWLING's production of O'Casey's *Juno and the Paycock* (1986) and Vi in the first production of Christina REID's *The Belle of the Belfast City* at the Lyric Theatre (1989). In 1992 McCusker appeared as Lizzie Boles in the acclaimed Druid Theatre production of Vincent Woods's *At The Black Pig's Dyke*, directed by Maeliosa Stafford and revived in 1994 for a national and international tour. McCusker played Julie in the first production of *The Mai* by Marina CARR (1994) and Marianne Scully in the first production of Carr's *Portia Coughlan* (1996). Recent roles with the RSC Stratford include the Mother in *Roberto Zucco* by Koltès (1997) and Maurya in Synge's *Riders to the Sea* as part of *Shadows*, a presentation

of the work of Synge and Yeats as directed by John CROWLEY (1998). As a trained singer, McCusker has brought a musical dimension to her many roles. She has also worked on radio, television and film, with credits including *Ballykissangel* for BBC television.

McGovern, Barry (1948–) Actor, Ireland. After training at the Abbey School of Acting, McGovern spent two years with the RTE (Radio Telefis Eireann) Players working as a radio actor. Throughout his stage career he has played many roles on the Abbey Theatre stage in plays ranging from Molière and Shakespeare to O'Casey. Perhaps his most significant role at the Abbey was his performance of Father Jack in the world première of Brian FRIEL's *Dancing at Lughnasa* (1990). He is, however, more closely associated with the work of Samuel Beckett. In 1985 he won a Harveys Theatre Award for *I'll Go On*, a one-man Beckett show (made up of texts from the novels *Molloy*, *Malone Dies* and *The Unnamable*) selected by McGovern and Gerry Dukes. His version of Krapp in *Krapp's Last Tape* (1996) was a towering display of meticulousness and sensitivity. He has written music for many shows and collaborated on the lyrics for two musicals, *The Happy-Go-Likeable Man* and *Thieves' Carnival* with actor Bryan Murray. He also has directed plays and operas.

McGrath, Tom (1935–) Dramatist and director, Great Britain. McGrath began his career as a BBC television director and writer. In his plays, he initially pursued a clearly socialist agenda (*Events While Guarding the Bofors Gun*). After 1968 his style became more popular, including songs in a loose structure. For the Everyman Theatre, Liverpool, he wrote *Soft, or a Girl* (1971). He founded the company 7:84 (7 per cent of the population control 84 per cent of national wealth), which had a decidedly socialist political agenda. Plays written for 7:84

include *Black Oil* (1973) and *Blood Red Roses* (1980). McGrath resigned as artistic director in 1988. Recent work includes *Border Warfare* (1989), *John Brown's Body* (1990) and *Watching for Dolphins* (1991).

McGuinness, Frank (1953–) Dramatist, Ireland. McGuinness is the most innovative Irish playwright of international renown, whose prolific output is marked by an extraordinary sensitivity to opposing traditions and sensibilities in contemporary Ireland. *Observe the Sons of Ulster Marching Towards the Somme* (Peacock Theatre, Dublin, 1985) questions the myths and loyalties of eight Ulster Protestants fighting for the British at the Battle of the Somme in 1916, to reveal an emotional and moral battle raging beneath an expressionistic dance of death representing the First World War. McGuinness's most commercially successful play to date, *Someone Who'll Watch Over Me* (Hampstead and Vaudeville Theatres, London, 1992 and Booth Theatre, New York), featured the plight of three western hostages in an unnamed Middle Eastern country. Other plays include *The Factory Girls* (1982) and *The Bird Sanctuary* (1992), an allegory for Ireland's endangered species, the Protestant family in the crumbling big house in South Dublin. In 1997 *Mutabilitie* (Royal National Theatre, London, directed by Trevor NUNN) brought Shakespeare and Spenser to Ireland. He is also renowned for his translations/versions of European classics and the plays of Ibsen in particular, including NINAGAWA's production of Ibsen's *Peer Gynt* (1992) and *Et Dukkehjem* (*A Doll's House*, London and New York, 1997).

McKellen, Ian (1939–) Actor, Great Britain. Towards the beginning of his prestigious career McKellen was romantic, emphasizing verbal music. In maturity, he has became capable of extraordinary realism: he played Iago in Trevor NUNN's

production of *Othello*, as an ageing army officer reduced to vocal mannerisms. He appeared with the National Theatre (title parts in *Coriolanus*, Chekhov's *Djadja Vanja* (*Uncle Vanya*) and *Richard III*), the Royal Shakespeare Company (most notably *Macbeth* with Judi DENCH, 1975), as Salieri in SHAFFER's *Amadeus* for its transfer to Broadway (1991), and in AYCKBOURN's *Henceforward* (1988). In 1997 he played Dr Stockman in Christopher HAMPTON's version of Ibsen's *En Folkefiende* (*An Enemy of the People*) at the Royal National Theatre, directed by Trevor NUNN and designed by John NAPIER.

McNally, Terence (1939–) Dramatist, USA. McNally began his career with one-act plays which already show his main concerns: 'the theatre, the outsider, long monologues, the hero addressing the audience as a character in the play', which are more fully developed in his full-length plays. *It's only a Play* (1982) deals with theatre on Broadway and has been compared to Michael FRAYN's *Noises Off*. *Frankie and Johnny in the Claire de Lune* (1987) is a romantic love story, later made into a film. *Lips Together, Teeth Apart* (1991) deals with AIDS, and *Master Class* (1995) has Maria Callas as its main character.

McPherson, Conor (1971–) Dramatist, Ireland. On leaving college McPherson co-founded Fly by Night Theatre Company, which produced his early work including *Rum and Vodka* (1992) and *The Good Thief* (1994), winner of a Stewart Parker award. In 1995 *This Lime Tree Bower* transferred to the Bush Theatre London where McPherson became the 1996 writer in residence. *St Nicholas* was subsequently produced at the Bush Theatre in 1997 before touring to New York. The Royal Court Theatre London commissioned a new play from McPherson and produced *The Weir* at the Theatre Upstairs in 1997; the play was then restaged at the Royal Court Theatre Downstairs in 1998, before touring to Brussels, Toronto and Dublin. McPherson's work is notable for a strong element of storytelling, which relies heavily on evocative language, monologue and reportage. However, in recent plays a balance has been struck with an increased use of theatricality. McPherson won Best Screenplay at the San Sebastian film festival for *I Went Down*, directed by Paddy Breathnach and premiered at the 1997 Cannes Film Festival. Other awards include Playwright of the Year at the Ka/Sunday Independent 'Spirit of Life' awards, and an Evening Standard Award, a Critics' Circle Award and a George Devine Award for *The Weir*.

Maddy, Yulisa Amadu Pat (1936–) Actor, dancer, dramatist and director, Sierra Leone. Maddy trained in theatre and acting at the Rose Bruford College of Speech and Drama in Britain. He is the best example of the migrant or roving theatre artist, and he has had an immense impact on theatre, not only in his native Sierra Leone but in many other countries including Nigeria and Zambia. He is the founder-director of Gbakanda Afrikan Tiata, a theatre company which he founded in Freetown in 1969 and which has followed him everywhere he has travelled. His plays include *Alla Gbah* (*The Big Man*, 1967), *Yon Kon* (*Clever Thief*, 1968) and *Obasai* (*Over Yonder*, 1971), *Gbana Bendu* (*Tough Guy*, 1971), *Life Everlasting* (1972), *Big Breeze* (1974), *Big Berin* (1976) and *Drums, Voices and Words* (1985). His productions or plays are always striving for a 'total theatre' in which song, dance, movement and dialogue are completely integrated. A radical and outspoken critic of government, he has been imprisoned a number of times.

Mădescu, Mihai (1936–) Designer, Romania. Madescu graduated from the Fine Arts Institute 'N. Grigorescu', Bucharest,

in 1963 and began his career as scenographer (set and costume design) at Teatrul Tineretului (Youth Theatre) in Piatra Neamtz. After ten years he joined Teatrul Mic – Little Theatre, and in 1978 he joined the Bulandra Theatre, Bucharest, working with major directors, such as Andrei SERBAN (Brecht's *Der Gute Mensch von Sezuan* (*The Good Person of Sezuan*), Goldsmith's *She Stoops to Conquer* and Chekhov's *Visnevyi sad* (*The Cherry Orchard*)), Cătălina BUZOIANU (Ibsen's *Peer Gynt*, Dumitru Radu POPESCU's *Ca frunza dudului din rai* (*Like the Mulberrytree Leaf*) and Sam SHEPARD's *Buried Child*), Silviu PURCĂRETE (*Il Teatro Comico* by Goldoni at Bulandra Theatre) and many others, distinguishing himself as a poet and an architect of the scenic space, a builder of suggestive spatial structures. He was awarded many prizes, and his works gained critical acclaim during international tours to Nancy, Madrid, Copenhagen, Mexico City, Milan and Bogota.

Madzik, Leszek (1945–) Designer, director and dramatist, Poland. Madzik studied art history at the Catholic University of Lublin, where he founded and serves as artistic director of the Visual Stage. His productions and exhibitions were shown at many international festivals. Abroad, he worked with students at the Theatre Academy in Helsinki, the Academy of Arts in Berlin and the Academy of Arts in Amsterdam. Winner of many prizes, he says that he creates the same performance over and over again, a profoundly human reality consisting of emotions and essential states: love, faith, holiness, awe, the sense of mortality and death. His work is often called a theatre of Christian existentialism, religious or cosmic theatre. Among his plays are *Ecce Homo* (1970), *Wieczerza* (*Supper*, 1972), *Wilcoc* (*Moisture*, 1978), *Brzeg* (*The Shore*, 1983), *Wrota* (*The Gateway*, 1989) and *Szczelina* (*The Crevice*, 1994).

Maes, Jean-Paul (1955–) Dramatist, actor and director, Luxembourg. After his graduation from the Hochschule für Musik und Darstellende Kunst in Graz (Austria), he worked as an actor in Germany and Austria before returning to Luxembourg in 1988. Initially directing a number of classical Luxembourg tragicomedies by such authors as Dicks, André Duschcher and Batty Weber (mostly staged at the festival of Steinfort), he soon turned to playwriting. His plays combine parochial peculiarities with themes of life and death and concern themselves with the characters' yearning for escape from the suffocating reality surrounding them. *Manila du mäin hiirzegt Kand* (*Manila My Dearest Child*, 1990, Théâtre des Capucins) was warmly received, and his latest play *Péiténg* (*Pétange*, 1995, Théâtre d'Esch, directed by Eva PAULIN) was particularly lauded for its qualities of language. Besides playing in most of the country's major productions, Maes also portrayed to great acclaim Alexander to Patrick HASTERT's Philip in the world premiere of Alexey Shipenko's two-hander *Moskau-Frankfurt* (1995, Théâtre des Capucins, directed by Shipenko, designed by Jeanny KRATOSCHWILL).

Magout, Mohamed (1943–) Dramatist and poet, Syria. Magout worked in journalism and gained a reputation for his innovative poetry. His first play, *Al-Usfour 'l'Ahdab* (*The Hunchback Bird*, 1967), was written in verse. Its surrealistic style contrasted with the daring political subject of his next play, in prose, *The Clown* (1974): a great historical figure from the past was placed in a paradoxical current age, where he suffers a decline of pride at the hands of the secret police. Magout's sharp satire led him to write soap operas for television, and brought him commercial success, especially since his collaboration with Syria's pan-Arab comedian Duraid LAHAM in *Day'at Tishreen* (*The October Village*), *Ghurba*, *Kasak Ya Wattan* (*Cheers, my Country*) and

Shaqaeq'l-Nouman (*Red Anemones*). After a decade of silence, Magout returned to the theatre in 1998 with *Kharej'l-Serb* (*Astray from the Flock*), directed by Jihad SA'ED. In this he tried to follow his own footsteps with a witty dialogue and many political allusions. The play centres on a theatre troupe trying to revive *Romeo and Juliet* under censorship pressures.

Maharishi, Mohan (1940–) Director and dramatist, India. Maharishi graduated from the National School of Drama, Delhi and later became its director. Currently he serves as head of the theatre department at Punjab University, Chandigarh. An ardent admirer of Brecht and his epic theatre, Mohan Maharishi created an impact on the national stage with his productions of *Mutter Courage und ihre Kinder* (*Mother Courage and her Children*), Shaw's *Pygmalion*, Anouilh's *Antigone* and Kafka's *Der Prozeß* (*The Trial*), as well as plays by Badal SIRCAR, Girish KARNAD and Dharamvir BHARATI, and an experimental film *Ek Tha Raja* (*There was a King*). His latest work, *Einsteen*, is an 'unconventional, innovative experiment in interdisciplinary theatre'.

Majumdar, Ferdausi (1943–) Actor, Bangladesh. With about thirty plays (900 performances) to her credit, Ferdausi Majumdar is possibly the most renowned and respected stage performer in Bangladesh. Important roles in her illustrious career include Ranu in AL-MAMUN's *Subochan Nirbasane* (*Virtue in Exile*, 1974), the daughter of Matabbar in Syed HUQ's *Payer Awaj Pawa Jay* (*At the Sound of Marching Feet*, co-starring and directed by Al-Mamun, 1976), Marjina in Al-Mamun's *Ekhon Duhshomoy* (*Its Bad Times Now*, co-starring and directed by Al-Mamun, 1976), Sharmila in an adaptation of Tagore's *Dui Bon* (*The Two Sisters*, with Ramendu MAJUMDAR as Shashanka and Al-Mamun as Mathur, 1978) and a solo performance in Al-Mamun's

Kokilara (*The Kokilas*, directed by the author, 1989). She is at her best when handling female characters from the Bengali middle classes: these she portrays with delicate detail and probes the emotion with uncanny perception. A schoolteacher by profession and winner of numerous national awards, Ferdausi Majumdar is also popular on radio and television and has toured abroad with her performances.

Majumdar, Ramendu (1941–) Producer and actor, Bangladesh. Majumdar's contribution to theatre in Bangladesh is valuable primarily because of the organizational role he plays. He is the founder general secretary of Theatre (a leading theatre group in Bangladesh), founder chairman and currently presidium member of the Bangladesh Group Theatre Federation, as well as holding several posts within the ITI Bangladesh and worldwide. He is founder editor of *Quarterly Theatre*, the leading journal on theatre in Bangladesh. Also a notable stage actor (Talebali in AL-MAMUN's *Ekhono Kritadas* (*Still a Slave*, 1980), Shashanka in Tagore's *Dui Bon* (*The Two Sisters*, 1978) and Kazi Tobarak in Al Mamun's *Meraj Fakirer Ma* (*The Mother of Meraj Fakir*), 1996), Ramendu Majumdar has extensively travelled abroad attending various seminars and conferences.

Makkonen, Tiina Anitra (1952–) Designer, Finland. Trained at the Academy of Industrial Arts, Helsinki, Makkonen worked at Hämeenlinna City Theatre, Vaasa City Theatre, Turku City Theatre and Helsinki City Theatre. Major productions include Howard BARKER's *Scenes from an Execution* and *The Love of a Good Man*, *A Midsummer Night's Dream* and Brien FRIEL's *Dancing at Lughnasa*. Tiina Makkonen is one of the most individual stage designers in Finland. Of her works, most attention has been aroused by those where instead of an ordinary stage quite different theatre venues have been used, such as old houses, warehouses or cellars. Makkonen loves all that is old and decayed. She thinks that the working of time is very beautiful.

Malina, Jaroslav (1937–) Designer, Czech Republic. After studying at the Academy of Performing Arts in Prague, Malina worked at various regional theatres. During the 1970s, he made his name as a leading representative of 'action scenography'. He most often made use of textiles with a combination of contrasting materials (drapery, wood, plastic wrap, metal), such that the actors would use their characteristic properties as part of the action. Although he mixes non-homogeneous stylistic elements, his set designs work as a whole, such as Büchner's *Leonce und Lena* (1976, at the Činoherní studio Ústí n.L., directed by Ivan RAJMONT) and Euripides's *Medeia* (1981 at Studio Forum, Olomouc). He works with many Czech theatres, from small studios to large venues, including the Prague National Theatre. Since the mid-1980s, elements of painting have increased in his designs (Janáček's *Príhody lišky Bystroušky* (*The Cunning Little Vixen*) at the State Theatre in Ostrava, directed by David Sulkin). He teaches at the Academy of Performing Arts in Prague, and has been its rector since 1995.

Malkovich, John (1953–) Actor, director and sound designer, USA. Malkovich's off-Broadway debut was in 1982 as Lee in SHEPHERD's *True West*, which won him a Theatre World Award. Malkovich is co-founder and member of the Steppenwolf Theatre Ensemble in Chicago, for which he has directed many productions including PINTER's *The Caretaker* (1985). His emotional spectrum is wide: often praised because of his 'extraordinary ability to generate a menacing physical presence on stage', as Biff in a flashback scene in Arthur MILLER's *Death of a Salesman* he showed 'tearful vulnerability'. Other parts include Captain Bluntschli in Shaw's *Arms and the Man* (1985). In 1984, Malkovich began his equally distinguished film career, from which he returned to the theatre in 1991 for Lanford WILSON's *Burn This* (in London, with Juliet STEVENSON), and a portrayal of Lee Harvey Oswald (1994).

Mamet, David (1947–) Dramatist and director, USA. Mamet is today considered as one of the most original American playwrights. Critical studies have frequently picked up on Mamet's 'rhythmic, hypnotic language', which is evident in early one-act plays such as *Duck Variations* (1972) and *Sexual Perversity in Chicago* (1974), as well as full-length plays including *American Buffalo* (1977), *A Life in the Theatre* (1977) and *Glengarry Glenn Ross* (1983). More recently, the controversial *Oleanna* dealt with sexual harassment in the context of political correctness. In general, Mamet's characters 'suffer from, or rather exist in, a subconscious anxiety which both draws them towards the trap and makes them fearful of it'.

Manahan, Anna Actor, Ireland. Manahan trained under Ria Mooney at the Gaiety School of Acting. She has played many roles in the course of her long and successful career, appearing with all the major companies including the renowned Edwards/MacLiammóir Company at the Gate Theatre, Dublin, and Phyllis Ryan and Gemini Productions. She played Mother in Druid Theatre Company's production of FRIEL's *The Loves of Cass Maguire* (1996) and Mag Folan in their production of McDonagh's *The Beauty Queen of Leenane* (1996). Other work includes *Live Like Pigs* by John Arden at London's Royal Court Theatre, Friel's *Lovers* at the Music Box Theatre New York and Boucicault's *The Shaughraun* at the Abbey Theatre, Dublin. Manahan played Mag Folan in *The Beauty Queen of Leenane* and Mary Johnny Rafferty in

A Skull In Connemara, produced as part of McDonagh's *The Leenane Trilogy* by Druid Theatre Company, Galway, in 1997. Manahan is a strong and highly regarded actor, and it is said that John B. KEANE wrote *Big Maggie* for her. Her many film and television appearances include *The Butcher Boy*, *A Man of No Importance*, *The Bill* and *The Irish RM*.

Manaka, Matsemela (1956–) Dramatist and director, South Africa. Manaka is one of the young black South African theatre artists who learned their trade in and around the Market Theatre, founded by Barney SIMON and Mannie Manim. Since 1976, he has been a founder member of the Soyikwa Theatre Group based in Soweto. His most performed and anthologized play is *Children of Asazi*, which explores the themes of homelessness and incest while exposing the negative influence of the apartheid regime in South Africa on the black family and its values. His other plays include *The Horn*, *Egoli, the City of Gold*, *Pula! (Rain!)*, *Imbuba (Unity)*, *Vuka* and *Goree*. Apart from indigenous South African traditions of performance such as Xhosa storytelling, Manaka is influenced by West African theatre, especially that of Wole SOYINKA, and the poor theatre techniques of Jerzy Grotowski. *Egoli*, which evolved out of the workshop influence of Simon and Athol Fugard, was so provocative that the South African government had to ban it in 1979, but not before it had been performed to rave audiences in South Africa and West Germany.

Maniotis, George (1951–) Dramatist, Greece. Maniotis has established himself as a major playwright in Greece. His plays are metaphysical farces, whose dark humour reveals the struggle of the individual to maintain their integrity and identity in a world defined by empty social rituals, technology, the lure of profit and the search for prestige. In plays like *The Match* (1978), *The Hustler or The Art of*

Dreaming (1981) or *Vacation in Heaventown* (1987), Maniotis depicts the isolation of the individual who, regardless of his efforts to resist, is crushed by the social mechanism. Despite their direct language and the dreary realism of their settings, the plays of Maniotis are imbued with poetry.

Mann, Dieter (1941–) Actor, Germany. Mann trained as an actor at the Staatliche Schauspielschule in East Berlin, and since 1964 he has been employed with the Deutsches Theatre, Berlin, where he served as artistic director between 1984–91. On handing over to Thomas LANGHOFF, he expressed his concern that 'the Deutsches Theater should keep a strong ensemble not tempted by better salaries at lower quality West German theatres'. Recent parts include Wehrhahn in Hauptmann's *Der Biberpelz* (*The Beaver Fur*, 1992, directed by Thomas Langhoff), John in David MAMET's *Oleanna* (1994), Kurfürst Friedrich Wilhelm in Kleist's *Prinz Friedrich von Homburg* (1995, directed by Jürgen GOSCH) and *Ithaka* by Botho STRAUSS (Deutsches Theater Berlin, 1997, directed by Thomas Langhoff).

Mann, Emily (1952–) Director and dramatist, USA. Mann studied at the University of Chicago Lab School and trained with Tony Richardson in London and at the Guthrie Theatre, where she began her career as an assistant director. From 1977–9 she was artistic director of Guthrie II, then resident director at the Brooklyn Academy of Music (1981–2). In 1990 she became artistic director of McCarter Theatre, Princeton. Her own plays include *Still Life*, about the aftermath of the Vietnam war, and *Execution of Justice*, about a notorious US trial. Her 'theatre of testimony', using documentary material, is a subjective form of docudrama which allows the writer the freedom to create both the strongest moral statement and the deepest catharsis. More recently she devised and directed *Having*

our Say, based on the book by and about two sisters who lived together happily for more than 100 years. Her directing is Stanislavski-based, and she works from moment to moment exploring how the characters relate to the main idea.

Manzel, Dagmar (1958–) Actor, Germany. Manzel trained at the Staatliche Schauspielschule in East Berlin. She has an enormous stage presence, and her repertory emcompasses all types of roles in most genres. From 1980–3 she worked with Staatstheater Dresden, playing the title role in Schiller's *Maria Stuart*, Eboli in Schiller's *Don Carlos* and Rosalind in *As You Like It*. Since 1983 she has been a member of the Deutsches Theater in Berlin. Major roles there include Portia in *The Merchant of Venice*, the title role in Lessing's *Emilia Galotti*, Merteuil in Heiner Müller's *Quartett*, Lilli Groth in *Das Gleichgewicht* (*Balance*) by Botho STRAUSS (1994, directed by Thomas LANGHOFF) and Kriemhild in Hebbel's *Kriemhild's Rache* (*Kriemhild's Revenge*, 1999, directed by Langhoff). In 1997 she appeared in Langhoff's production of *Ithaka* by Botho Strauß.

Mao, Fredric (1947–) Director and actor, China (Hong Kong SAR). Mao made his Broadway debut in 1976 with the Kabuki-style musical *Pacific Overtures* by Harold Prince and Stephen Sondheim. For thirteen years (1972–85), he acted and directed professionally in the United States with various theatre companies. Mao was the artistic director of the Napa Valley Theatre Company in California before becoming head of acting at the inception of the Hong Kong Academy for Performing Arts in 1985. In recent years, Mao won popular as well as critical acclaim for his directing in Cheung Tatming's *The Legend of a Storyteller* (1993) and Eric Pun's musical *The Kids, the Wind and the City* (1994). His adaptation and direction of Shaw's *Saint Joan* (1997) was regarded as one of the best productions of the 1990s and claimed six awards at the 1998 Hong Kong Drama Awards. For the Hong Kong Repertory Theatre, Mao recently directed Raymond TO's *Forever and Ever* (1999, City Hall Theatre), an original play which depicts the relationship between an AIDS-infected adolescent and his mother. Mao also values the Chinese Opera highly and is an ardent supporter of traditional Chinese theatre in Hong Kong. His direction of Karley NG's *Timeless Love* (1998) was a new attempt at combining traditional Chinese opera with Western acting styles.

Maponya, Maishe (1951–) Dramatist, director and actor, South Africa. Maishe Maponya is one of the angry dramatists of South Africa in the 1970s and 1980s who sought to use their art to engage with and confront apartheid politics. His major plays are *The Hungry Earth* (1981), *Umongikazi* (*The Nurse*, 1983), *Dirty Work* (1985), *Gangsters* (1985), *The Valley of the Blind* (with V. Amani Waphtali, 1987), *Jika* (1988) and *Busang Merop* (*Bring Back the Drums*, 1989). Apart from directing all his plays, Maponya has also directed Don Kinch's *Changing the Silence* (1985), Athol Fugard's *The Coat* (1990), Trevor Rhone's *Two Can Play* (1992) and Lorraine Hansberry's *A Raisin in the Sun* (1992). His theatre shuns the accommodating and survivalist ethos of plays such as Fugard's *Sizwe Bansi is Dead* and Gibson KENTE's *Sikalo*; his plays seek rather to overwhelm the audience with their urgency and demand for action to pull apartheid down. Maponya is also a fine actor and has taken many roles in his own plays.

Maraini, Dacia (1936–) Dramatist, Italy. Dacia Maraini is one of Italy's best-known authors. Apart from writing for the theatre, she also writes fiction and poetry and offers regular contributions to Italian newspapers and magazines. Throughout her long career, Maraini has been exploring social and political issues related to the female condition. In 1969 she founded the Teatro di Centocelle, with which she produced *Manifesto dal carcere* (*Manifesto from Prison*), one of the first feminist plays to be performed in Italy, and in 1973 she founded one of the most interesting Italian feminist theatre companies, the Teatro della Maddalena. Among her most notable plays are *La famiglia normale* (*The Ordinary Family*, 1966), *Il ricatto a teatro* (*Blackmail in the Theatre*, 1968), *La donna perfetta* (*The Perfect Woman*, 1975), *Dialogo di una prostituta con un suo cliente* (*Dialogue Between a Prostitute and One of her Clients*, 1976), *I sogni di Clitennestra* (*The Dreams of Clitennestra*, 1979) and *Lunga vita di Marianna Ucria* (*The Long Life of Marianna Ucria*, 1991).

Marchioro, Marcello (1952–) Director and dramatist, Brazil. Marchioro trained with Carlos Kraide and worked as assistant director with Antonio ABUJAMRA and Emilio di Biasi in Sao Paulo. Later he underwent a training period with the German–Brasilian Theatre Colloquium, a theatre course in Berlin ran by theatre professors and directors including Dieter DORN, Andreas Sippel, Henri Thorau, Celso NUNES, Marcio Aurelio Pires de Almeida and Barbara Heliodora. He considers his productions a continuous research of different kinds of language which link stage work to theatre investigation. Committed to the social and the contemporary, his main theatre productions include Wedekind's *Lulu*, Brecht's *Die Dreigroschenoper* (*The Threepenny Opera*), *Mahagonny*, and *Die Sieben Todsünden* (*The Seven Cardinal Sins*), Thomas Bernhard's *Der Theatermacher* (*The Theatremaker*), *Quai West* by Koltès, Tankred DORST's *Ich, Feuerbach* (*I, Feuerbach*), Arthur MILLER's *The Crucible*, *Hamlet* and *A Midsummer Night's Dream*.

Maréchal, Marcel (1937–) Actor and director, France. Maréchal began his career in Lyon, where he founded the Théâtre du Cothurne and in 1968 the Théâtre du Huitième. In 1975 he founded Le Théâtre de la Criée in Marseilles. He has directed major new work by French dramatists as well as the classical repertory, especially Molière.

Marijnen, Franz (1943–) Director, Belgium. Marijnen went to Poland to work with Jerzy Grotowski. In 1970 he left for the United States, where he directed at La MaMa and founded his own company, Camera Obscura. In 1977, he directed Oskar Panizza's controversial *Das Liebeskonzil* (*The Council of Love*) in Rotterdam, where he became artistic leader of the RO Theatre until 1983. After a period during which he staged several operas, he joined the Schillertheater in Berlin. Since 1993, Marijnen has been manager of the Koninklijke Vlaamse Schouwburg (Royal Flemish Theatre) in Brussels. Marijnen's early productions were rebellious, visually impressive and built on the actor, the result no doubt of his work with Grotowski. In later years the text has gained importance in his work, as shown by his Shakespeare productions at the Koninklijke Vlaamse Schouwburg.

Marinho, Sunmbo Director and designer, Nigeria. Marinho is one of the few designer-directors of the Nigerian stage (together with Demas NWOKO and Domba Asomba). Major works include courageously directing Femi OSOFISAN's *Yungba-Yungba and the Dance Contest* at a time when the government was seriously repressing artists producing work that was critical of politics and politicians. He was also technical director for the premiere of Osofisan's *Midnight Hotel* in 1982 as well as artistic director for the National Theatre production of Kalu UKA's *A Harvest for Ants* (1977) and technical director for Wale OGUNYEMI's *Partners in Business* (directed by the playwright himself as part of Ogunyemi's

fiftieth birthday celebrations at the Arts Theatre, Ibadan in 1989).

Maro Akaji (1943–) Butoh dancer, Japan. Maro first became a member of Jôkyô Gekijô Theatre Company led by KARA Jûro, then studied dance under Tatsumi Hijikata in 1965. He founded the Dai-Rakuda-kan Dance Company with other butoh dancers in 1972. The company's early productions were *Dansu Toko Mashin* (*Dance and Machine*, 1972), *Yobutsushintan* (1973) and *Rancushingi* (1975). Their productions use large and spectacular stage devices and are visual. For example, *Kazesakashima* (*The Wind and Sakashima Island*, 1979) was performed at Shiretoko Peninsula in Hokkaido, the north part of Japan. The contrast of the human bodies with colourful costumes and white make-up against the rock and the vast green sea created extraordinary dynamism in this production. Maro often employs ghosts or supernatural elements as the central topics of his work. *Kaidan Umijirushi no Uma* (*A Ghost Story: A Horse with a Mark of the Sea*) was performed at an open air theatre in Avignon in 1982; during the performance strong winds swept across the stage and contributed to the show. The company was also invited to the American Dance Festival in the same year, and toured the USA and Australia in 1987. They used a large warehouse for their recent work *Ugetsu* (*Ugetsu the Ghost Story*, 1992).

Maron, Channa (1925–) Actor, Israel. Born in Germany where she was a well-known child actress, Maron immigrated to Israel in 1933 and trained at Habima. She was among the founders of the Cameri Tel Aviv municipal theatre. Among her most memorable roles is Mika, a Jewish refugee, in *Ho halach basadot* (*He Went Through the Fields*, 1948) about the Jewish struggle for independence in Israel. She has played a large number of leading roles like Liza Doolittle (in Shaw's *Pygmalion*), Rosalind (in *As You Like It*), Nora in Ibsen's *Et Dukkehjem* (*A Doll's House*), and the title roles in Ibsen's *Hedda Gabler*, Seneca's *Medea* and Schiller's *Maria Stuart*. Maron has also played in films and in television series.

Marrero, José Luis (Chavito) (1926–) Actor, Puerto Rico. Marrero is the husband of actor Mercedes SICARDO. After some postgraduate work at Yale University, he returned to Puerto Rico and worked as an actor and director for the Department of Public Instruction beginning in 1953. One of his early roles was Clarín in Calderón's *La vida es sueño* (*Life is a Dream*), which he toured to Cadiz, Spain and throughout the Americas with the Spanish troupe Lope de Vega. Marrero is a versatile actor, and is known for playing both comic and dramatic roles with some of Puerto Rico's most prominent theatre companies and actors. These include Orgon in Moliere's *La Malade Imaginaire* (*The Imaginary Invalid*, Teatro La Máscara, 1977, directed by Axel ANDERSON), Luis Torres Nadal's *La Santa Noche del Sábado* (*Holy Saturday Night*, Teatro Bohio Puertorriqueño, 1986, with Ernesto CONCEPCIÓN), Ibsen's *En Folkefiende* (*An Enemy of the People*, El Otro Grupo, 1978, with Miguel Ángel SUÁREZ) and Ignacio in Manuel Méndez Ballester's *Tiempo Muerto* (*Dead Times*, Candilejas, 1974, with Lucy BOSCANA and Idalia Pérez Garay).

Marsillach, Adolfo (1928–) Actor, director and dramatist, Spain. Together with Luis Alonso, Marsillach contributed to the creation of the role of scenic director in Spain. Marsillach started performing with the Catalan university theatre and he went to Madrid to direct Antonio Buero Vallejo's play *En la Ardiente Oscuridad* (1950) and Alfonso Sastre's *La Cornada* (1960). In 1968, he put on the revolutionary performance *Marat-Sade* by Peter Weiss, designed by Francisco NIEVA. In 1978, he took on the direction of the

Centro Dramático Nacional, but resigned the following year. In 1985, Marsillach created the Compañía the Teatro Clasico, where he staged non-familiar classic dramatic texts by Lope de Vega, Calderón and Tirso de Molina. From 1989–92 he was the general manager of INAEM (Instituto Nacional de las Artes Escénicas). In 1993, he went back to the Compañía de Teatro Clasico, but in 1996 he was dismissed due to his incompatibility with the Partido Popular. Marsillach has also written successful plays.

Marthaler, Christoph (1951–) Director and composer, Germany. Marthaler studied music and trained at the theatre school of Jacques Lecoq in Paris. For various theatres (Deutsches Schauspielhaus Hamburg, Düsseldorfer Schauspielhaus, Staatstheater Stuttgart, Bayerisches Staatsschauspiel Munich, as well as theatres in Bonn and Zürich) he has composed music. From 1988–93 he worked with the theatre in Basel, and since 1993 he has been a director with the Deutsches Schauspielhaus in Hamburg. Recent productions there include Horvath's *Kasimir und Karoline* (1996). His productions are characterized by slow motion, extended time and repetitions, during which he relentlessly and profoundly dissects the mental basis of the petit bourgeois.

Martial, Jacques (c. 1950?–) Actor, France and Guadeloupe. Martial trained at the Cours Sarah Sanders in Paris and had some early experience with Jules-Rosette's Afro-Caribbean Théâtre noir (1978–9). He co-starred with Sonia Emmanuel in Maryse CONDÉ's *Pension Les Alizés* (1987) as the troubled Haitian doctor in exile, also playing in Condé's version of Trevor Rhone's *Two Can Play* (1985), in the French version of *Little Shop of Horrors* (1986), in *Nuit blanche* (*White Night*, 1997) and in a range of other productions. Screen work includes parts in the prize-winning *Noir et blanc* (*Black and White*, 1986) directed by Claire Devers, in

Wonder Boy (1993) and *Walk the Walk* (1995), and for television a major role as Bain-Marie in the long-running popular police drama *Navarro* (1989–).

Martial, Jean-Michel (1952–) Actor and director, France and Guadeloupe. Martial trained at the Cours Sarah Sanders and with Andréas Voutsinas in Paris, and began a busy career in the 1980s. He has taken part in a wide range of contemporary and classical plays, notably as Jean in Strindberg's *Fröken Julie* (*Miss Julie*, 1988), in the title role as *Ange noir* (*Black Angel*) by Nelson Rodriguez (1996), in Fugard's *A Lesson of Aloes*, in plays by Genet and Shakespeare at the Odéon, and several plays by Julius Amédée LAOU. In 1994 he took a main role in Michèle CÉSAIRE's allegory of Caribbean identity, *La nef* (*The Ship*). His commanding height and a resonantly deep voice have also been in demand for screen work, both in France and with Caribbean directors such as Haitian Raoul Peck (as the male lead in *L'Homme sur les quais* (*Man by the Shore*), 1993). Increasingly, Martial is writing and directing for stage and screen, and he tutors regularly in the professional drama courses at the Artchipel, the Scène Nationale de la Guadeloupe.

Martinez, Mario Ivan Actor, Mexico. Martinez trained at the Emma Pulido Institute of Culture, Mexico City, and at the London Academy of Music and Dramatic Art. In addition, he took singing lessons with Jennifer Tatum in London, Carlos Hinojosa in Mexico and Carol Tingle in Los Angeles. He has appeared on film, and starred in several Mexican prime-time soap operas on television. In the theatre, his roles include Oberon and Malvolio, the psychiatrist in Brian Clark's *Whose Life is it Anyway?*, Andrej in Chekhov's *Tri sestry* (*Three Sisters*), and a one-man show on Shakespeare, *Perchance to Dream*, which won two National Theatre Critics awards and is performed in English and Spanish.

Martínez Lopez, Berta (1931–) Actor and director, Cuba. Martínez attended the Academia Municipal de Arte Dramatico in La Habana. She also studied acting and lighting design in the United States. In 1957 she directed her first production, *El Difunto Senor Pic* (*The Deceased Mr Pic*). In 1961 she joined the theatre group Teatro Estudio, and in 1964 she started experimenting with stage direction becoming one of the most outstanding theatre directors in Cuba. Her work as an actor and director is complemented by her work in education, as well as the design aspects of the theatre. In 1980 and 1983 her production of Garcia Lorca's play *Bodas de sangre* (*Blood Wedding*) travelled to different international festivals, and in 1990 her productions of the plays *El Boticario* (*The Apothecary*), *Las Chulapas* (*The Little Canoes*) and *Celos Mal Reprimidos* (*Badly Repressed Jealousy*) participated in the festival of Moscow. Currently she works with the Hubert De Blanck theatre company.

Martini, Jandira (1945–) Actor and dramatist, Brazil. Martini attended the School of Dramatic Art at the University of São Paulo and studied literature at the Catholic University of Santos. In her own words: 'my years as an actor took me to writing. The daily contact with the audience and the study of their reactions and preferences led me to the path of comedy which is most profoundly rooted in our culture: farce. Though the reviewers look with disdain at this kind of theatre, the audience give us the answer that we need to go on doing what is the most typically Brazilian kind of theatre.'

Martone, Mario (1959–) Director, Italy. Martone founded the alternative theatre company Falso Movimento in 1979. In 1987 he co-ordinated the foundation of the theatre conglomerate Teatri Uniti, whose aim is to facilitate the collaboration of a number of Neapolitan practitioners. Martone's work with Falso Movimento and Teatri Uniti has represented a milestone in Italian alternative theatre. His challenging and subversive use of a variety of media within striking visual performances characterized by fragmentation of dialogue, repetitive movement and the evocative use of figurative elements has influenced a number of alternative theatre companies and represented a model for those interested in innovative multimedia practice. Among Martone's most notable productions are *Musica da camera* (*Chamber Music*, 1978), *Tango glaciale* (*Glacial Tango*, 1982) and *Ritorno ad Alphaville* (*Returning to Alphaville*, 1986). More recently, Martone has also started directing films; among these are the acclaimed *Morte di un matematico napoletano* (*Death of a Neapolitan Mathematician*, 1991) and *L'amore molesto* (*Troublesome Love*, 1995).

Mas, Ida Bagus Nyoman (1951–) Performer and director, Indonesia. Mas trained at STSI (the Academy of Performing Arts), Denpasar. A performer in traditional Balinese dance/drama genres, in 1990 he founded a Kecak ensemble in his own village of Blahkiuh which, in 1993, was selected as the best Kecak group in Bali. As well as performing throughout south Bali, he taught Kecak at the University of Hawaii at Manoa (UHM) in 1995 and was co-director (with I Wayan DIBIA) of the Kecak *Hanoman as Messanger* produced by UHM in that year. In collaboration with Abu BAKAR, he has directed a new Kecak production for Puspita Jaya which premiered at the 1997 Singapore Arts Festival.

Mason, Marshall W. (1940–) Director and actor, USA. Mason trained at the Actors Studio in New York with Lee Strasberg and Harold Clurman. Mason's style of directing is strongly influenced by the method acting approach. Early productions include Ibsen's *Little Eyolf* and Shaw's *Arms and the Man*. In 1965 Mason directed Lanford WILSON's *Balm in Gilead*, and has since directed many of Wilson's plays. In 1969 he co-founded the Circle Repertory Company and was its artistic director until 1986. More recently, he directed Lyle Kessler's *Robben* (1997). His method-based approach revealed itself in productions that were filled with detailed character observations.

Mason, Patrick (1951–) Director, Ireland. Born in Great Britain, Mason studied drama at the Central School London and taught at Manchester University before embarking on a professional career as a director. Currently artistic director of the National Theatre Society, which incorporates the Abbey and Peacock stages, Mason has enjoyed a successful involvement with Irish theatre for over twenty years. He directed the first productions of numerous plays by emerging Irish playwrights, with clarity and a strong sense of symbolism. However, Mason has also stressed the importance of Irish theatre's literary history. He found a careful balance between word and image in such plays as *Observe the Sons of Ulster Marching towards the Somme* (1985) by Frank MCGUINNESS, and *The Gigli Concert* (1983) by Tom MURPHY at the Abbey Theatre. During the 1980s Mason collaborated with Tom MAC INTYRE and Tom HICKEY on a series of plays, including *The Great Hunger* (1983). In 1990 Mason directed Brian FRIEL's acclaimed *Dancing at Lughnasa* for the Abbey. Plays directed while Artistic Director of the Abbey include Sebastian BARRY's *The Only True History of Lizzie Finn* (1995), the Irish premiere of Tony Kushner's *Angels in America Part 1* (1995), the first productions of KILROY's *The Secret Fall of Constance Wilde* (1997) and CARR's *By the Bog of Cats* (1998).

Máté, Gábor (1955–) Actor and director, Hungary. After training at the Academy of Theatre and Film Art, Máté joined the Csiky Gergely Theatre of Kaposvár in 1980 and the Katona József Theatre in Budapest in 1987. Since 1993 he has been a teacher at the Academy of Theatre and Film Art, and since 1994 a board member of the Hungarian Theatre Art Association. Máté is also a significant screen actor and an acknowledged director. Major roles include Hamlet, Claudius (*Hamlet*), Beliayev (Turgenyev's *Mesjac v derevne* (*A Month In The Country*)), Towncrier (Weiss's *Marat/Sade*), Tibor Pálffy (Szomory's *Hermelin*), Mr Martin (Ionesco's *La cantatrice chauve* (*The Bald Soprano*)), Afranius (Bulgakov's *Master Margarita* (*The Master and Margarita*)), Trofimov (Chekhov's *Visnevyi sad* (*The Cherry Orchard*)), Philinte (Molière's *Le misanthrope* (*The Misanthropist*)) and Oberon (*A Midsummer Night's Dream*). Major directorial achievements include Strindberg's *Den starkare* (*The Stronger*), Brien FRIEL's *Dancing at Lughnasa*, STOPPARD's *Rosencrantz and Guildenstern Are Dead* and *Measure For Measure*. Máté is considered a sensitive, thorough, intellectual actor, and an inspired director.

Matheus, Mariann (*c.*1955–) Actor and dramatist, France and Guadeloupe. First attracting attention as a prize-winning young singer, Mariann Matheus appeared from 1974 with the Lonsdale-Puig company, and in 1980 joined Toto Bissainthe to perform and record Caribbean, particularly Haitian, traditional songs. She helped research life histories for Ina CÉSAIRE's two-hander *Mémoires d'Isles* (*Island Memories*, 1983) and created the role of Hermance. After playing the lead in a Creole version of Brecht's *Der Gute Mensch von Sezuan* (*The Good Person of Sezuan*), her poignant songs and grace of movement contributed to the international success of Simone Schwarz-Bart's short play *Ton beau capitaine* (*Your Handsome Captain*, 1987). She alternated the role of the Singer-Storyteller in the Comédie Française 1991 production of Césaire's *Tragédie du roi Christophe* (*The Tragedy of King Christophe*), and took the main part in Placoly's 1992 play *Grand Hotel*. Matheus has always been active in children's theatre. The group Moun San Mélé, devoted to developing musical theatre with and for very young audiences, produced her latest musical folktale, *Ti-Sonson*, which has been followed by *Pawol ti moun* (*Childhood Words*, 1997). A radiant stage presence, Matheus works without affectation to transmit the cultural heritage of the Caribbean to new and often uprooted generations.

Matsumoto Kôshirô IX (1942–) Kabuki actor, Japan. The first son of Matsumoto Kôshirô VIII, later Matsumoto Hakuô I, he succeeded to this stage name by playing Sukeroku in *Sukeroku Yukari no Edo-Zakura* (*Sukeroku: Flower of Edo*) by Jihei Tsuuchi and Hanemon Tsuuchi, and Benkei in *Kanjincho* (*The Subscription List*) by Gohei Namiki, at the Kabuki Theatre, Tokyo in 1981. He played the leading role in a Broadway musical, *The Man of La Mancha* (1970). When his father and his family changed their residential theatre companies from the Shô-chiku Company to the Tohô Company between 1961–79, he played many leading parts in straight plays and musicals. He acted the major roles *Sabu* by Yamamoto Shûgorô, *The King and I* and *The Moon and Six Pence*. He also played Zeami in *Zeami* by YAMAZAKI Masakazu at the Sunshine Theatre in 1987 and in the USA in 1988. He played the king in the London production of *The King and I* in 1990. His latest success is Salieri in Peter SHAFFER's *Amadeus* in translation. Kôshirô is an all-rounder and acts in the styles of kabuki, modern theatre and musical. He is renowned for an intellectual approach to drama and for his characterization.

Mattes, Eva (1954–) Actor, Germany. Mattes already appeared on the stage as a teenager, and worked in dubbing. She is a strong, lively actor, who is convincing in playing women characterized by a strong sense of reality and direct action. From 1972–9 she was a member of the Schauspielhaus in Hamburg, where her parts include the title role in Schiller's *Die Jungfrau von Orleans* (*The Virgin of Orleans*) and Desdemona. She worked much with the late Rainer Werner Fassbinder, both in film and theatre, and with Peter ZADEK (Rosalind in *As You Like It*, Portia in *The Merchant of Venice*, and Tankred DORST's version of *Der Blaue Engel* (*The Blue Angel*)). Heiner Müller's directed her in his *Fatzerl/Germania 2* (1993), and in 1996 she appeared in Chekhov's *Visnevyi sad* (*The Cherry Orchard*) at the Burgtheater in Vienna.

Matthes, Ulrich (1959–) Actor, Germany. Matthes took acting classes with Else Bongers in Berlin. He is a sensitive, nervous actor, who plays mainly characters who are doubting, passive and split. After seasons in Krefeld/ Mönchengladbach, he joined the Düsseldorfer Schauspielhaus in 1985 where he played the title role in *Heinrich oder Die Schmerzen der Phantasie* (*Henry or the Pains of Imagination*) by Tankred DORST, and Otto Weininger in Joshua SOBOL's *Weininger's Nacht* (*Weininger's Night*). In 1986 Matthes moved to the Bayerisches Staatsschauspiel in Munich, and between 1988–92 he worked for the Münchner Kammerspiele. Since 1992 he has been a member of the Schaubühne am Lehniner Platz, Berlin. Over the years, Matthes has worked with directors such as Wolfgang ENGEL, Thomas LANGHOFF, Dieter DORN and Andrea BRETH.

Mauri, Glauco (1930–) Actor, director and dramatist, Italy. After gaining popularity by appearing in a television series based on Fedor Dostoyevsky's *Brat'ia Karamazovy* (*The Karamazov Brothers*) in the 1950s, Glauco Mauri started working in the theatre with Renzo Ricci and, shortly afterwards, with Giorgio ALBERTAZZI and Anna Proclemer. In 1960, he co-founded the Compagnia dei Quattro with Franco Enriquez, Valeria MORICONI and Gabriele LUZZATI. A classical actor with a strong and charismatic stage presence, Mauri has spent his long dramatic career exploring some of the greatest leading roles of Western theatre. Among his most notable performances are Aeschylus's *Oresteia* (1972) directed by Luca RONCONI, Sophocles's *Philoctetes* (1976), *King Lear* (1984), *Twelfth Night* (1986), Luigi Pirandello's *Enrico IV* (*Henry IV*, 1998) and *The Tempest* (1998), which he also directed. Mauri has also made a number of film appearances such as, most notably, Marco Bellocchio's *La Cina è vicina* (*China is Near*, 1967) and Dario Argento's *Profondo Rosso* (*Deep Red*, 1975).

Mauvois, Georges (1922–) Author, France and Martinique. Mauvois left school and worked for some years in the post office, playing an active role in trade unionism and left-wing politics. After clashing with his employers, he left, took a law degree and was called to the bar in Fort-de-France. This first-hand observation of colonial politics and the civil service provides the material for his satirical plays, notably *Agénor Cacoul* (1966), which exposes the corruption at the town hall during a strike of sugar estate workers, and *Man Chomil* (1989), a hilarious exposé of the petty tyranny of a rural postmistress. A pioneer in deploying the resources of both Creole and French for dramatic effect, Mauvois was largely unperformed until the pressure group GEREC (Groupe d'Etudes et Recherches en Espace Créolophone) promoted his work for its linguistic authenticity. Much encouraged by publication of two volumes of his plays and frequent revivals of the less politically controversial works, such as *Misyé Molina* (*Mr Molina*), he is busily writing: recent works include *Arrivé de Paris* (*Newly Come from Paris*, 1995) and a Creole translation of Molière's *Dom Juan* (1996).

Max, Nicole (1961–) Actor, Luxembourg. A graduate of theatre studies at the Sorbonne-Nouvelle in Paris, Max has worked extensively in France and Luxembourg, most notably in Inoué Yashushi's *Le Fusil de Chasse* (*The Hunting Rifle*, Théâtre de Lenche, Marseille) as Shoko, in *A Midsummer Night's Dream* (Théâtre des Capucins, directed by Claudine PEL-LETIER) as Hermia, in *Macbeth* (1996, open air theatre, Berdorf) as Lady Macbeth, and in Büchner's *Leonce und Lena* (1997, Théâtre de la Commune Pandora, Aubervilliers) as Lena. She gained acclaim for her solo performance of Philippe Faure's *Moi j'étas femme dans les tableaux de Modigliani* (*I was a Woman in Modigliani's Paintings*, 1995, Théâtre du Centaure and Théâtre AKTEON, Paris). A versatile actor, she also appeared in many television and cinema films playing leading roles, particularly in Andy Bausch's award winning *Troublemaker* (1987) and its sequel *Back in Trouble* (1997).

Mazia, Edna (1949–) Dramatist, Israel. After writing filmscripts for Israeli director Amos Gutman, Mazia turned more actively to writing for the stage and has become one of Israel's most popular playwrights. Her play *Mischakim Bechatzer Ha-achorit* (*Games in the Backyard*, 1993) a docudrama about a collective rape which shook the Israeli public opinion, earned her fame as a socially engaged playwright. *Sipur Mishpachti* (*A Family Story*) and *Hamordim* (*The Revolters*), both performed at the Kameri Tel Aviv Municipal Theatre, have established her popularity among the audience. She has also published prose and written for television.

Mbowa, Rose (1943–) Actor and dramatist, Uganda. Mbowa's major play is *Mother Uganda* (1987), which she produced in collaboration with the well-known Ugandan musician Jimmy Katumba. This production managed to link music and dances of the many ethnic groups and cultures in Uganda into a very powerful performance piece. Mbowa's other theatrical activities are mainly concerned with community-based theatre projects in the style of the Kamiriithu cultural project in Kenya headed by Ngugi WA THIONG'O and Ngugi WA MIRII. She writes the scripts for these community plays and performances, which are most often issue-based and provide vehicles for all the arts of the theatre, especially the oral/traditional art of the villages to be employed. She was a member of the very talented and highly influential performing group Theatre Ltd, which was founded in Kampala in 1970 and which included famous artists such as Wycliffe KIYINGI-KAGWE.

Mda, Zanemvula Kizito Gatyeni (1948–) Dramatist and director, South Africa. Zakes Mda's academic training let to his current position as Fellow at Yale University. His plays include *We Shall Sing for the Motherland* (1978), *Dead End* (1979), *The Hill* (1979), *Dark Voices Ring* (1979) and *The Road* (1982). They deal with the effects of apartheid on a variety of people. Mda avoids the usual trap of too much polemic at the expense of his art. Of late he has concentrated his efforts on theatre-for-development activities, and in 1993 wrote a book on this genre of theatre. His plays have been widely performed in southern Africa, and some have been performed in the USA, Britain, the former USSR (in a Russian translation) and in France (in French).

Meadow, Lynne (1946–) Director, USA. After training in the directing programme at the Yale University Drama School, Meadow became artistic director of the

Manhattan Theatre Club. She taught at Yale University, the Circle in the Square Theatre School, New York University and SUNY Stony Brook. Meadows prefers to direct plays by living playwrights. Her productions include *Ashes* by David RUD-KIN, David EDGAR's *The Jail Diary of Albie Sachs*, AYCKBOURN's *Woman in Mind* (with Stockard CHANNING) and *Absent Friends*, Lee BLESSING's *Eleemosynary*, Chekhov's *Tri sestry* (*Three Sisters*) with Dianne WIEST, Leslie Ayvazian's *Nine Armenians* (1999, with set design by Santo LOQUASTO), and the musical *Captains Courageous* (1999). 'Her rehearsal method is straightforward: she makes suggestions and asks actors guiding questions about their characters. Her directorial hand seems very subtle, although her productions are careful and highly orchestrated pieces of work.'

Medvešek, Rene (1963–) Actor, director and dramatist, Croatia. Medvešek trained at the Academy of Dramatic Art in Zagreb and then joined the ZKM Theatre (Zagreb Youth Theatre) where parts include Kamilo in Krleža's *Zastave* (*The Flags*, adapted and directed by Paro in 1991). He scored a major success with his portrayal of Leone (sometimes referred to as Croatian Hamlet) in Krleža's *Gospoda Glembajevi* (*The Glembays*), a part usually reserved for the most prominent actors. He was praised for his performance in *A Midsummer Night's Dream* and for several roles he played on film. In the last few years he has rarely acted, but works mostly as an independent author and director of plays for children. His directions are always highly individual creations, emerging from his own original concepts, such as *Zimska bajka* (*The Winter's Fairytale*, 1993), *Hamper* (*Bucket*, 1996) and *Nadpostolar Martin* (*The Shoe of All Shoes*, 1998), for which he received many awards.

Melato, Mariangela (1943–) Actor, Italy. After a period of training at the Accade-

mia dei Filodrammatici, Mariangela Melato started working in the theatre with Luchino Visconti, Dario FO and Luca RONCONI, most famously on Ludovico Ariosto's *Orlando Furioso* (1969) and Aeschylus's *Oresteia* (1972), Karel Čapek's *The Makropulos Affair* (1993) and Eugene O'Neill's *Mourning Becomes Electra* (1997) all directed by Ronconi, as well as Copi's *Tango barbaro* (*Barbaric Tango*, 1997) directed by Elio DE CAPI-TANI. Melato, who throughout the last twenty years has been one of Italy's most popular actors, is a versatile performer who has interpreted a large number of lead roles both in the cinema and in the theatre. Known both for her comic skills and for the interpretation of more challenging politicised roles, Melato has a strong and charismatic presence which she displays both on stage and on the screen. Among her most memorable film appearances are Elio Petri's *La classe operaia va in Paradiso* (*The Working Class Goes to Paradise*, 1971), Fernando Arrabal's *L'albero di guernica* (*The Guernica Tree*, 1975), Giuseppe Bartolucci's *Oggetti smarriti* (*Lost and Found*, 1980) and Cristina Comencini's *La fine è nota* (*The End is Known*, 1992).

Melles, Sunnyi (1958–) Actor, Germany. Melles attended the Otto Falckenberg Schule in Munich, and has been a member of the company of Münchner Kammerspiele since 1980, where her roles include Elisabeth in Schiller's *Don Carlos*, Cressida in *Troilus and Cressida*, Gretchen in Goethe's *Faust*, Maja in Ibsen's *Nå Vi Døde Vågner* (*When We Dead Awaken*) and Delio in *Schlußchor* (*Final Chorus*) by Botho STRAUSS. In Arthur KOPIT's *Nirvana* she portrayed pop star Madonna; critics praised her ability to express the face and the life behind the mask of a mega-star with the enchanted sadness and the wide-eyed freshness of a usurping child.

Mellor, Aubrey (1947–) Director, Australia. Graduated from the National Institute of Dramatic Art, Sydney in 1969. Since 1993, Mellor has been artistic director of Playbox, the Melbourne theatre dedicated to producing new Australian plays. There Mellor has directed many important premieres, including Hannie RAYSON's *Falling from Grace* and *Hotel Sorrento* and Louis NOWRA's *The Incorruptible*. Outside of Playbox, Mellor has directed for all the major Australian companies and has directed both classics and modern European drama (Chekhov, Brecht, Ibsen, HAVEL, FO, CHURCHILL). Mellor has a particular interest in Eastern theatrical styles. He has co-written translations, mostly of Chekhov, aimed specifically at Australian audiences. He taught acting at the National Institute of Dramatic Art for ten years and was artistic director at the Queensland Theatre company 1988–93.

Meng Jin Hui (1965–) Director and dramatist, China. Meng directed PINTER's *The Dumb Waiter*, Cai Jun's *Shen Ye Dong Wu Yuan* (*Midnight Zoo*), Ionesco's *La cantatrice chauve* (*The Bald Soprano*), Beckett's *Waiting for Godot* and *Stirrings of Earthly Thought and Elopement from the Monastery*, a collage piece he composed by conflating a Ming story and a tale from *The Decameron*. Upon graduation from the Central Academy of Drama, he became a director in the Central Experimental Theatre and directed *Stirrings of Earthly Thought*, which he had composed himself, Genet's *Le balcon* (*The Balcony*), *Wo Ai XXX* (*I Love XXX*), which he co-wrote with Shi Hang, Wang Xiao Li and Huang Jin Gang, Büchner's *Woyzeck*, *Twelfth Night*, Hanoch LEWIN's *Jacobi and Leidental* (1997), Shi Xing Guo's *Huai Hua Yi Tiao Jie* (*A Street of Obscenities*, 1998, designed by YAN Long) and Dario FO's *Morte accidentale di un anarchico* (*Accidental Death of an Anarchist*, 1998). Meng's works have been seen in Germany, Japan and Hong Kong. He emphasizes improvisation in rehearsal.

His productions are humorous, irreverent and exaggerated.

Mesguich, Daniel (1952–) Director and actor, France. Mesguich studied at the Conservatoire National Supérieure d'Art Dramatique in Paris and founded the Théâtre du Miroir in 1974. From 1986–8 he was artistic director of the Théâtre Gérard Philipe in Saint-Denis and since 1991 he has held that position at the Théâtre National Lille. Major stage acting credits include the title roles in *Hamlet* and Chekhov's *Platonov*, which he also directed. Further productions directed for the theatre include Marivaux's *La seconde surprise de l'amour* (*The Second Surprise of Love*), Racine's *Bérénice* and Victor Hugo's *Marie Tudor*. He has also directed opera and films, and acted in films.

Micha, Maria (1949–) Actor, Cyprus. A graduate in philosophy from the University of Athens, Micha trained at the Drama School of Karolos Koun. Major stage credits include Abigail in Arthur MILLER's *The Crucible*, Desdemona in *Othello*, Gertrude in *Hamlet*, Beatrice in *Much Ado About Nothing*, Adella in Lorca's *La casa de Bernarda Alba* (*The House of Bernarda Alba*), Yelena in Chekhov's *Djadja Vanja* (*Uncle Vanya*), Natasha in Chekhov's *Tri sestry* (*Three Sisters*), Alison in Osborne's *Look Back in Anger*, Clea in Peter SHAFFER's *Black Comedy*, Helen in Euripides's *Troades* (*The Trojan Women*), Hermione in *Andromache* and Evadne in Aeschylus's *Hiketides* (*Suppliant Women*). Her deep voice supports her strong stage presence.

Miller, Arthur (1915–) Dramatist, USA. Miller is probably the best-known American dramatist. In his own words, he is 'constantly awed by what an individual is, by the endless possibilities in him for good and evil, by his unpredictability, by the possibilities he has for any betrayal, any cruelty, as well as any altruism, any sacrifice'. Miller writes in realistic style about human relationships. The main character of *Death of a Salesman*, Willy Loman, is perhaps the best known character in US drama. This lower middle-class salesman believes fervently in the American dream. This belief destroys him. By creating Willy, Miller taps deep into the American soul. Problems of identity recur often in Miller, especially in *After the Fall* and *Broken Glass* (1994), which deals with Jewish identity. He also addressed issues of responsibility in *The Crucible*, *Incident at Vichy* and his adaptation of Ibsen's *En Folkefiende* (*An Enemy of the People*). Many regard him as the world's most eminent living playwright.

Miller, Jonathan (1934–) Director, Great Britain. Miller has achieved remarkable success as a director both in the theatre and in opera, offering strikingly new interpretations which tend to convince because of their psychological depth (Miller's medical training shows here). Major theatre productions include Chekhov's *Cajka* (*The Seagull*), *Hamlet*, *The Merchant of Venice* and seasons at the Old Vic with *The Tempest* and *King Lear*. His production of *The Taming of the Shrew* for the Royal Shakespeare Company (1987, with Brian COX and Fiona SHAW), was particularly successful.

Minks, Wilfried (1931–) Designer and director, Germany. Minks trained in art and stage design at the Hochschule der Künste in Berlin. He began his career in the theatre in Ulm in 1959 and moved to Bremen in 1962, where he worked with Peter STEIN, Peter ZADEK and Kurt Hübner. Important set designs include Behan's *The Hostage*, *Hamlet* and Schiller's *Die Räuber* (*The Robbers*). Since 1971 Minks has also directed on a freelance basis at all major theatres in Germany. He is currently professor of stage design at the School of Fine Arts in Hamburg, as well as a freelance director and stage designer in Berlin, Hamburg, Munich and Vienna.

Recent productions include *Drang* (*Urge*) by Franz Xaver KROETZ (1996) and *St Pauli Saga* (1997), both at Deutsches Schauspielhaus Hamburg. On the occasion of his sixtieth birthday, the Frankfurter Allgemeine Zeitung wrote: 'Until then, most stages of post-war Germany had been empty. With the *Hostages* in Ulm [1961], they were opened: spaces for projection of images.'

Missiroli, Mario (1934–) Director, Italy. After graduating from the National Academy of Art, Mario Missiroli worked as Giorgio Strehler's assistant between 1959–62. He then started directing his own productions at the Piccolo Teatro, such as Giovanni Testori's *La Maria Brasca* (1960) and T.S. Eliot's *Murder in the Cathedral* (1961). Missiroli, who also directed for film and television, has worked in a number of theatres and opera houses on both classical and contemporary plays. He is best known for his controversial interpretations of classical texts which constitute an intriguing mixture of claustrophobic vaudeville and Freudian and Marxist theory. Among his most notable productions are *Anthony and Cleopatra* (1982–3), Niccolò Machiavelli's *La Mandragola* (1983), Bernard-Marie Koltès's *Combat de Nègre et de Chiens* (*Black Battles with Dogs*, 1984), Euripides's *Medeia* (1996) and August Strindberg's *Pelikanen* (*The Pelican*, 1998).

Mitchell, Katie (1964–) Director, Great Britain. Mitchell began her career as an assistant director with Plaines Plough. In 1989 she joined the Royal Shakespeare Company as an assistant director, from 1990 onwards directing her own productions. In addition she has directed for the Gate Theatre and the Royal National Theatre. Her production of Ibsen's *Gengangere* (*Ghosts*, Royal Shakespeare Company, 1993) with Jane LAPOTAIRE and Simon Russell BEALE was acclaimed for not only exploiting the intimacy of the small stage, but for also exporting the characters' complexity. 'Mitchell has the ability to make pain manifest', Michael Billington wrote, 'You come out both shaken and stirred.' More recent work includes *Beckett Shorts* with Juliet STE-VENSON, *The Mysteries* and Chekhov's *Djadja Vanja* (*Uncle Vanya*, 1998).

Mittelpunkt, Hillel (1949–) Dramatist and director, Israel. Mittelpunkt studied theatre at Tel Aviv University, where he produced his first play. Most of his plays, like *Mei Tehom* (*The Swamp*), *Makolet* (*Grocery Store*), *Buba* and *Parod Zmani* (*Abandoned*) and *Hagag* (*The Roof*) de-pict stereotypes of marginal characters in the Israeli society with great empathy and social involvement. The play, *Gorodish*, about a legendary Israeli general from the Six Days War who lost his reputation in the 1973 war was a great success, show-ing the meaninglessness of military tri-umph. Mittelpunkt has also written two rock operas, *Mami* and *Samara*, satirical programmes and scripts for films.

Mlama, Penina (1942–) Dramatist and theatre director, Tanzania. Mlama writes and devises mostly in Swahili. Her pub-lished plays include *Hatia* (*Guilt*, 1972), *Heshima Yangu* (*My Honour*, 1974), *Pambo* (*Ornament*, 1975), *Talaka si Mke Wangu* (*I Divorce You*, 1976), *Nguzo Mama* (*Mother Pillar*, 1982), *Lina Ubani* (*There is an Antidote for Rot*, which was a collaboration with other Tanzanian playwrights), *Matanga* (1993) and *Dude Dude* (1994). Strongly believing in the potential of theatre as a weapon for social learning and mobilization, Mlama is ac-tively involved in the theatre-for-develop-ment movement which is well-established in Tanzania and other African countries. The key themes of her plays are issues of the struggle for liberation and the estab-lishment of an egalitarian society and personal themes such as the problems arising from divorce, especially as it affects the children caught in the middle.

Mnouchkine, Ariane (1939–) Director, France. Mnouchkine studied at the Sor-bonne, Paris, 1959–62 and at the Univer-sity of Oxford. She participated in amateur theatre at Oxford and subse-quently founded the Association Théâ-trale des Etudiants de Paris, with whom she created her first production, Henry Bauchau's *Gengis Khan* (1961). She toured the Far East (1962–3) and studied improvisation under Jacques Lecoq. The foundation of the Théâtre du Soleil in 1964, with former fellow students, marked the true beginning of her career and her name is now synonymous with that of her company. Her research has been influenced by the principles of Jean Vilar and a belief in a popular theatre. Her dramatic style and art are also marked by traditional Oriental theatre such as kabuki or kathakali. Mnouchkine adapts classical texts, such as Shakespeare or Molière, as well as contemporary ones, such as those by Hélène CIXOUS, but her choice is always inspired by great events of world history.

Mo Sen (1963–) Director and dramatist, China. After graduation from the Chinese department of Beijing Normal University, Mo founded Frog Experimental Theatre in 1987 in Beijing, where he directed Ionesco's *Rhinocéros* and O'Neill's *The Great God Brown*. In 1993 he founded The Workshop, where he directed Gao Xing Jian's *Bi An* (*The Other Shore*), his own *Ling Dang An* (*File Zero*), *Gu Xiang Tian Xia Huang Hua* (*Chrysanthemums of My Home Town*), *Hong Zun Yu* (*Red Herrings*), *Yi Ge Ye Wan Hui Yi De Bao Gao* (*Report on One Night's Memories*), *Yi Yuan* (*The Hospital*) and *Guan Yu Ya Zhou De Kuang Xiang Qu Song Ge Huo Lian Xi Qu* (*Fantasies, Odes, or Etudes about Asia*). He has introduced new European concepts of the theatre to China and presented off-stage reality on stage, thus challenging the traditional idea of the dramatic and the real.

Modisane, Bloke Actor, South Africa. Modisane was a member of the African Music and Drama Association at Dorkay House in Johannesburg, which included notable actors such as Zakes MOKAE, Stephen Moloi and Gladys Sibisi. The group collaborated with Athol Fugard in the writng/creation and performance of *No-Good Friday*, the latter's first township play (performed in 1958) in which Modisane played the part of Shark; Mokae was First Thug while Fugard played Father Higgins, a role later played by Lewis NKOSI because apartheid segregation laws forebade Fugard acting with black actors. Modisane has also featured in other Fugard plays, including playing Outa in *Boesman and Lena* at the London Theatre Upstairs, with Yvonne Bryceland as Lena and Mokae as Boesman, directed by Fugard himself. Modisane's acting has been described as being influenced by the 'method' of Lee Strasberg's Actors Studio, with Marlon Brando as his ideal model.

Mokae, Zakes Actor, South Africa. Most of Mokae's early acting roles were in plays by Athol FUGARD, including First Thug in the Johannesburg premiere of *No-Good Friday* (1958). This performance also featured Fugard and later Lewis NKOSI as Father Higgins, Bloke MODISANE as Shark, directed by Fugard himself. He also played Blackie in *Nongogo* (1959), Zach in *The Blood Knot* (Johannesburg, 1961; London, 1963; Broadway revival, 1985). He also played Outa in the 1970 New York production of Fugard's *Boesman and Lena* with Ruby Dee as Lena and James Earl Jones as Boesman directed by John Berry. In 1982 he played Sam alongside Danny Glover's Willie in Fugard's *Master Harold ... and the Boys* at the Yale Repertory Theatre, a stunning performance that won him a Tony Award. He has also been active in films. His greatest strengths as an actor are his stage presence and his ability to look calm and in control even when his character is near breaking point.

Molina Foix, Vicente (1946–) Dramatist, Spain. After studies in Madrid and London, he taught at Oxford University and the University of the Basque Country. In 1990 he was appointed literary director of the Centro Dramático Nacional at Madrid's Teatro María Guerrero. His first play, *Los abrazos del pulpo* (*The Octopus's Embrace*) was presented at Madrid's premier new writing venue, El Centro National de Nuevas Tendencias Escénicas in 1985. Later, he worked on adaptations of *Hamlet* (1989) and *The Merchant of Venice* (1992), both directed by José Carlos PLAZA as well as an original work, *Don Juan Último* (*The Last Don Juan*) directed by Robert WILSON (1992). He has gone on to work on translations of ALBEE's *Three Tall Women* (1995), Shaw's *Mrs Warren's Profession* (1996) and Williams's *The Rose Tattoo* (1997). His third play, *Seis armas cortas* (*Six Short Arms*) was directed by Adrián Daumas in 1997, and he has recently completed his fourth play, *Lenguas de plata* (*Silver Tongues*). As well as an admired dramatist and translator, Molina Foix is the author of seven published novels, two influential volumes of poetry and two opera librettos. He continues to work as a film and television critic, and has a weekly column in the newspaper *El País*.

Monette, Richard (1944–) Director and actor, Canada. Born in Montreal, Monette left Canada for England in 1969 and landed a role in the West End production of *Oh! Calcutta!*. He returned to Canada in 1972 and played several important roles at the Stratford Festival, including Hamlet, Caliban, Romeo and Berowne. At Toronto's Tarragon Theatre, he delivered a stunning performance as a transvestite in Michel TREMBLAY's *Hosanna*. A passionate and political man of the theatre, Monette is currently artistic director of the Stratford Festival. His direction has been bold and assured, even in his earliest directorial assignment at Stratford, a lively

1988 production of *The Taming of the Shrew*.

Montenegro, Fernanda (1929–) Actor, Brazil. Self-taught, Montenego worked for radio for ten years, for television for twenty years, and she has been on the stage for forty-six years. In her long and distinguished career, she has worked with directors from Italy, France, Poland, Russia and Brazil. Important stage credits include Vivie in Shaw's *Mrs Warren's Profession*, Laudelina in Arthur de Azevedo's *O Mambembe*, and the main female characters in Goldoni's *Mirandolina*, PINTER's *Homecoming*, *Phèdre* by Racine, Noel Coward's *Design for Living* and Beckett's *Happy Days*. She writes: 'All of them are important to me: plays, characters, directors and colleagues. I regard those 46 years as a mosaic where each little stone is essential. With a few exceptions, all of them are great writers, gifted directors and talented actors. I do my work with emotion and workmanship. This is a non-ending job.'

Moore, Claudia (1923–) Actor, Puerto Rico. Born in Green Bay, Wisconsin, Claudia Moore is widely considered to be the First Lady of the English-language theatre in Puerto Rico. She studied informally in New York from 1943–7 at the American Academy of Dramatic Arts, the Fagan School of Dramatic Art and the Henry Davenport Shakespearean Theatre. In 1954, she joined the Little Theatre in San Juan (later known as the Civic Theatre), where she worked with such actors as Raúl Julia, Sally Jessy Raphael and Henry Darrow. Primarily a comic actor, Moore has appeared in numerous professional productions, including the audience participation off-Broadway hit *Tony 'n' Tina's Wedding* (Hotel San Juan, 1994), in which she portrayed the grandmother of the groom. Moore has also performed serious leading roles in the musical *Cabaret*, Frank Marcus's *The Killing of Sister George* and Ira Levin's *Deathtrap*.

Moore, Mary (1945–) Designer, Australia and Great Britain. Moore trained at the Central School of Art, London and worked extensively in the UK (Royal Shakespeare Company, Bristol Old Vic, Royal Court, Monstrous Regiment, Gay Sweatshop and the Women's Project). She moved to Australia in 1981 and now combines lecturing at Flinders University, Adelaide with designing. She designs frequently for Adelaide's Troupe Theatre and the State Theatre Company of South Australia. She has designed classical productions (*King Lear* and *The Winter's Tale*) and for opera (*Abduction from the Seraglio*, *Joan of Arc at the Stake* for the Victorian State Opera), for fringe (Anthill, Melbourne; Red Shed, Adelaide) and for dance. Moore has designed for two of STCSA's productions of neglected plays by early Australian women playwrights: she designed a towering metallic newspaper office set for the 1996 production of *The Torrents* by Oriel Gray, and a claustrophobic 1930s filmic, black, white and grey set for *Morning Sacrifice* by Dymphna Cusack (1994). Moore is particularly interested in unconventional theatre spaces and audience performer relationships.

Morgenroth, Daniel (1964–) Actor, Germany. After attending the Hochschule für Schauspielkunst 'Ernst Busch', East Berlin, Morgenroth soon joined the Deutsches Theater, Berlin, where he played Leslie (Brendan Behan, *The Hostage*), and Tempelherr (Lessing, *Nathan der Weise* (*Nathan the Sage*)). Critical appreciation for his Peer Gynt was especially favourable: 'The change from one extreme to the other is beyond the spectator's comprehension.' Since then, he has established himself as one of the leading young performers with this theatre, appearing as Graf Wetter vom Strahl (Kleist, *Das Käthchen von Heilbronn*), in Kleist's *Amphitryon* (directed by Jürgen GOSCH, 1993), as Siegfried in Hebbel's *Kriemhild's Rache* (*Kriemhild's Revenge*, 1994, directed by Thomas LANGHOFF) and in Marlowe's

Edward II (1999, directed by Wolfgang ENGEL).

Morgenstern, Maia (1962–) Actor, Romania. Morgenstern is a graduate of the Bucharest Theatre and Film Academy (1985). After three years at the Teatrul Tineretului – Youth Theatre in Piatra Neamtz, where she asserted herself as a very promising young actor, she joined the State Jewish Theatre in Bucharest where she played major roles in the Yiddish language, including Sally in the musical *Cabaret*. In 1990 she became an actor of the National Theatre in Bucharest, working with Andrei SERBAN on major roles such as Medea in *The Ancient Trilogy*, Viola in *Twelfth Night*, Varia in Chekhov's *Visnevyi sad* (*The Cherry Orchard*) and Liz Morden in Timberlake WERTENBAKER's *Our Country's Good*, as well as other major roles with other directors such as Strindberg's *Fröken Julie* (*Miss Julie*) and Haya in Jehoshua SOBOL's *Ghetto*. At the Bulandra Theatre in Bucharest she worked with Cătălina BUZOIANU. One of her most notable achievements was Lola Blau in *Heute Abend Lola Blau* (*This Evening, Lola Blau*), a musical by Georg Kreisler, where she demonstrated her multi-faceted talent in singing, dancing and acting both the tragedy and the comedy with a deep insight. Morgenstern, recipient of many awards and prizes, is also a well-known film actor.

Moriarty, Jim (1953–) Actor and director, New Zealand. Moriarty's work for the stage has been much influenced by his experience as a psychiatric nurse and as a recovering alcoholic, as well as by very varied theatrical work from a young age. He played Stanley in *A Streetcar Named Desire* by Tennessee Williams at the Downstage Theatre, Wellington, in 1986, but his most notable role has been the solo character in John Broughton's *Michael James Manaia*, which toured widely and was invited to the 1991 Edinburgh Festival. He has inclined towards roles featuring marginalized men, but recent performances since his recovery from alcoholism have benefited from more objective portrayals. He helped to establish the concept of theatre marae, which combines elements of Maori and Western performance, and established the theatre group Te Rakau Hua o te Wao Tapu, which works in schools, maraes, prisons and alcohol and drug centres.

Moriconi, Valeria (1931–) Actor, Italy. Valeria Moriconi made her debut in the cinema in 1953 with Alberto Lattuada's *La spiaggia* (*The Beach*) and started working in the theatre with Eduardo de Filippo in 1957 in *De Pretore Vincenzo*. In 1960 she founded the influential Compagnia dei Quattro with Franco Enriquez, Glauco MAURI and Gabriele LUZZATI. Subsequently Moriconi appeared in over twenty-five films and two hundred theatre productions, touring theatres all over the world. Among her most notable performances are *Taming of the Shrew* (1962), Carlo Goldoni's *La Locandiera* (*The Mistress of the Inn*, 1964) and *Macbeth* (1972), all directed by Enriquez, Alberto Savinio's *Emma B. vedova Giocasta* (1980–94) directed by Egisto Marcucci, Giovan Battista Andreini's *Due commedie in commedia* (1985) directed by Luca RONCONI, the anonymous fifteenth-century comedy *La Venexiana* (1986) directed by Maurizio Scaparro and Euripides's *Medeia* (1996) directed by Mario MISSIROLI.

Morrison, Conall (1966–) Director and dramatist, Ireland. Morrison is an associate director of the Abbey Theatre, Dublin, and associate artist with Bickerstaffe Theatre Company, Kilkenny. His most successful play, *Hard to Believe*, was performed by Bickerstaffe in Dublin in 1995. Arguably the most talented and versatile of the new breed of Irish directors, he has had critical and popular successes with his productions of the gritty urban dramas of Belfast playwright Gary Mitchell, *In a Little World of Our Own* (1997) and *As the Beast Sleeps* (1998), at the Peacock Theatre, Dublin. To date, the production which has projected Morrison onto the international stage is his own adaptation of Patrick Kavanagh's novel, *Tarry Flynn* at the Abbey Theatre (1997) which toured to the Royal National Theatre, London in 1998. A highly visual and exuberant satire of rural Irish life, this production was aided by the muscular choreography of David Bolger, and entertained a new and young Dublin audience with a picaresque, scathing swipe at rural Catholic values. His sense of the theatrical is a challenge to decades of subservience to text in Irish theatre and earned him the task of directing the revival of the musical *Martin Guerre* for Cameron Mackintosh at the West Yorkshire Playhouse (1998).

Morse, Helen (1946–) Actor, Australia. Graduated from the National Institute of Dramatic Art, Sydney. After several successful film and television appearances (*Caddie, Picnic at Hanging Rock, A Town Like Alice*) Morse has chosen to concentrate on her stage career in Melbourne. Morse has brought elegance, dignity and an extraordinary, paradoxical combination of fragility and strength to many roles, including Katherine Mansfield in Alma DE GROEN's *The Rivers of China*, Barbara in Michael GOW's *Europe* and Paulina in Ariel Dorfman's *Death and the Maiden*. Morse was also able to bring earthy realism to her performance of Rita in Nick ENRIGHT's *Good Works* (national tour, directed by Kim Durban 1995 & 6). Morse likes to go deeply into a character, to seek out an inner life and this seriousness of purpose shows in her considered and intelligent acting. Highlights of her career include Blanche Dubois, Viola and Hedda, but Morse often plays small parts as well as star roles.

Moscato, Enzo (1948–) Director, performer and dramatist, Italy. After graduating in philosophy in 1974, Enzo Moscato worked as a researcher at the University of Salerno. He then founded his own theatre company, the Compagnia di Enzo Moscato, in 1980 and has recently started collaborating with the Neapolitan-based conglomerate Teatri Uniti. Focused around the exploration of life and art in Naples, his pieces are witty and elegant experimental linguistic pastiches with strong political subtexts. Moscato, who has also appeared in a number of films, including Mario MARTONE's *Morte di un matematico napoletano* (*Death of a Neapolitan Mathematician*, 1991), is one of Italy's most adventurous and eclectic theatre practitioners. Among his most notable performances are *Pièce noire* (1985), *Rasoi* (*Razors*, 1991), *Mal-d'Hamlé* (*Hamletache*, 1994) and *Embargos* (1994).

Mosher, Gregory (1949–) Director, USA. Mosher studied theatre at Oberlin and Ithaca colleges as well as at Juillard School. In 1974 he took over the Stage 2 programme at the Goodman Theatre in Chicago. Between 1978–85 he was artistic director of the Goodman, while between 1985–91 he held that position at the Lincoln Centre in New York, where he was criticized for being too successful, running a non-profit company too commercially. Mosher directed many productions, notably first work of dramatists such as Edward ALBEE, Spalding GRAY, John GUARE, Wole SOYINKA, David RABE, Emily MANN, Tennessee Williams and David MAMET. Mosher's work has been described as 'specific, simple, straightforward, and dedicated to the sanctity of the playwright's words'. Since 1997 he has been artistic director of the Circle in the Square theatre. He has argued that one should focus on a play, not an institution. There is something invigorating about devoting oneself to one project at a time.

Mouchtar-Samorai, David (1942–) Director, Germany. Born in Baghdad, raised in Israel and Britain, Mouchtar-Samorai has worked in Germany since 1975, with Heidelberg, Frankfurt, Düsseldorf and, most recently, Bonn, as major stages of his career. Productions include *A Midsummer Night's Dream, Troilus and Cressida*, Kleist's *Amphitryon*, Pirandello's *I giganti della montagna* (*Mountain Giants*), Lorca's *Dona Rosita*, Williams's *Sweet Bird of Youth* (1998, Zürich), Strindberg's *Till Damaskus* (*To Damascus*, 1998), and Schnitzler's *Das Weite Land* (*Undiscovered Country*, 1998). 'Not a director of theories or concepts, his theatre is devoid of illusions, but nevertheless full of sensuality and magic.'

Mrozek, Slawomir (1930–) Dramatist, Poland. Mrozek studied at the Academy of Fine Arts in Cracow, followed by several years as a journalist and then theatre critic. In 1953 he began his literary career by publishing short stories. His first play was *Policja* (*Police*, 1958). From 1963–6 Mrozek lived in Italy, France and Mexico. Landmarks in his career are *Tango* (1965) and *Emigranci* (*Emigrants*, 1974). Mrozek's first plays concentrated on two subjects: lack of identity of an individual subordinated to social role, and the feeling of freedom in relation to terror. These plays were like philosophical parables or allegories. *Tango* introduces the problem of principles, norms and values rejected by contemporary Europe. The way from *Tango* to *Emigranci* was the way to reality in a formal and metaphorical sense. Parable was substituted by concrete observation. More recent work, including *Kontrakt* (*The Contract*, 1986), *Portret* (*Portrait*, 1987) and *Milosc na Krymie* (*Love in the Crimea*, 1994), mirrors this development.

Mtwa, Percy Actor, South Africa. While working as a stores clerk he began dancing and playing music in night clubs. He later formed his own group. His break into professional theatre came in 1979 when Gibson KENTE offered him a part as a singer/dancer in his *Mama and the Load*. With Mbongeni NGEMA, he successfully collaborated on *Woza Albert!*. He is one of the exponents of a black political theatre which began to supplant the apolitical township musicals of Kente. Although known internationally for just two plays, Mtwa has a substantial performing career in South Africa, North America and the United Kingdom. His work has been observed to have close affinities with the poor theatre theories of Jerzy Grotowski. For Mtwa, all the actor has is his body as a means of communicating with the audience, and in the context of apartheid which banned black political plays, the intense physicality and minimal props of the poor theatre provided the appropriate milieu for Mtwa to communicate the anguish and oppression of the black situation to an audience.

Mühe, Ulrich (1953–) Actor, Germany. Mühe trained at the Theaterhochschule Hans Otto in Leipzig. After employment in Chemnitz, Heiner Müller cast him in his *Macbeth* production at the Volksbühne in East Berlin (1982). Since 1983 he has been a member of Deutsches Theater, Berlin, where his roles include Osvald in Ibsen's *Gengangere* (*Ghosts*, 1983, directed by Thomas LANGHOFF), the title role in Goethe's *Egmont* (1986) and the Shakespeare/Müller *Hamlet/Hamletmaschine* (1990). In the early 1990s he repeatedly played with the Burgtheater in Vienna, including the title role in Goethe's *Clavigo*, (1991, directed by PEYMANN) and the professor in David MAMET's *Oleanna* (1993, set design by Wilfried MINKS). He played the title role of Ibsen's *Peer Gynt* (Vienna, 1994, directed by Claus PEYMANN) as a big, dreamy child, and critics praised his virtuosity and commented on the richness of expressions the actor can produce.

Müller, Elfriede (1956–) Dramatist, Germany. Raised on a farm (an experience which influenced at least her first play, *Bergarbeiterinnen (Female Miners)*), she took ballet classes and trained at the Schauspielschule of the Hochschule für Darstellende Künste in Berlin. In *Damenbrise (A Fresh Breeze of Ladies)*, her second play, she wittily deals with the theatre. *Glas* (1990) takes its origin in dance and project work, *Goldener Oktober (Golden October*, 1991) deals with the euphoria and reality of the new relationship between East and West Germany after reunification. In her plays, 'she searches for an openness which allows a poetic treatment of contemporary issues'. Her most recent play, *Die Touristen (The Tourists)*, was premiered in Saarbrücken (1996).

Mugo, Micere Githae (1942–) Dramatist, Kenya. Mugo's theatrical writings include *Daughter of My People, Sing!* (1976), *The Long Illness of Ex-Chief Kiti* (1976) and a radio play, *Disillusioned* (1976). The play for which she is best known internationally is her collaborative effort with Ngugi WA THIONG'O, *The Trial of Dedan Kimathi* (1976). Apart from its radical politics, *Dedan Kimathi* was also remarkable for its integration of songs, dances, mime, flashbacks and storytelling techniques borrowed evidently from traditional folklore into a compelling theatre of visual power and linguistic sophistication. Unfortnately, like many other Kenyan artists who have and are still being persecuted by the government for their outspoken criticism, Mugo now lives in exile.

Mukulu, Alex (1954–) Actor, dramatist and director, Uganda. Alex Mukulu founded a theatre company which was prominent in the early 1980s and was noted for its very professional and accomplished productions. Notable among these were *Wounds of Africa* (1990) and *Thirty Years of Banana* (1991), written and directed by Mukulu himself; he also

played the leading roles in them and in most of the group's other productions. The productions incorporate much dance, music, mime and movement in the manner of other popular Ugandan theatre groups such as Robert Serumaga's Abafumi Players, the Kampala City Players of Byron Kawadwa and the influential Luandan theatre of Wycliffe KIYINGI-KAGWE. Mukulu also wrote his plays in Luandan, but through the staging technique of mime, movement, dance, music and songs that are both topical and satirical, he and his group aim to transcend the language barrier and appeal to all Ugandans as well as to non-Ugandan audiences.

Mullen, Marie (1953–) Actor, Ireland. In 1975 Mullen became a founder member of Druid Theatre Company with director Garry HYNES and actor Mick LALLY. Druid productions were marked by the company's strength as part of the community, a commitment to Irish writing and an extensive rural touring schedule. Mullen added a freshness to The Widow Quinn in Hynes's production of Synge's *The Playboy of the Western World* (1975), and played Peggy in the first production of Tom MURPHY's *Conversations on a Homecoming* (April 1985) and Mary in the first production of Murphy's *Bailegangaire* (December 1985), both directed by Hynes. Mullen has also worked in Britain with the Royal Shakespeare Company in Stratford in the late 1980s, appearing in Congreve's *The Man of Mode* and Timberlake WERTENBAKER's *The Love of The Nightingale*. Since then Mullen played Baby in *The Power of Darkness* by John McGahern, directed by Hynes at the Abbey Theatre, and appeared as Maureen in Martin McDonagh's *The Beauty Queen of Leenane* (1996).

Muller, Myriam (1971–) Actor, Luxembourg. Muller attended the Conservatoire de Luxembourg and the Cours Périmony in Paris (1990–2) and trained at the

Studio Pygmalion under Pascal Luneau in 1996. Her professional breakthrough came with her portrayal of Catherine Holly in Williams's *Suddenly Last Summer* (1989, Théâtre des Capucins, directed by Marja-Leena JUNKER) and of Honey in ALBEE's *Who's Afraid of Virginia Woolf?* (1992, Théâtre d'Esch, with Maria-Leena Junker and Philippe NOESEN, designed by Jeanny KRATOSCHWILL). She received major recognition for her performance in Marie-Claire Junker's monologue *L'enfant des nuages* (1995, Théâtre du Centaure and Théâtre du Tourtour, Paris, designed by Jean FLAMMANG), confirming that she is one of the most promising young Luxembourg actors.

Munitz, Ben-Zion (1943–) Designer, Israel. Munitz is one of the first professional lighting designers in Israel, giving this art form a respected professional status in the country. Munitz has designed for a large number of theatre and opera productions, among the more recent ones Gilead EVRON's *Yehu* and Hanoch LEVIN's *Hayeled Cholem* (*Dreaming Child*). He teaches at Tel Aviv University and many of the lighting designers today in Israel are his former students.

Munte, Jeta (1947–) Actor, Israel. Munte trained at the Romanian National Academy of Dramatic Art and began her professional career on the Romanian stage before immigrating to Israel in 1970. Munte joined the Haifa municipal theatre where she played leading roles like Juliet, Puck and Ariel. Moving to the Cameri Tel Aviv municipal theatre she played roles like Sonia in Chekhov's *Djadja Vanja* (*Uncle Vanya*), Grusha in Brecht's *Der Kaukasische Kreidekreis* (*The Caucasian Chalk Circle*) and Lady Macbeth. She has also appeared in many of Hanoch LEVIN's plays like *Kolam rotsim lichiot* (*Everybody wants to live*), as the mother in *Hayeled Cholem* (*Dreaming Child*) and *Hazona MiOhio* (*The Whore from Ohio*).

Murai Shimako (1929–) Dramatist and director, Japan. Murai studied drama at Butai Geijutsu Gakuin (the Stage Arts School). She then went to Czechoslovakia to do her research in theatre studies at Karel University, and was awarded a Ph.D. in 1967. Murai is a founder member of Katatsumuri no Kai (the Snail Theatre Company). The plays she has directed for the company include Betsuyaku Minoru's *Mae Mae Katatsumuri* (*Dance Dance Sanils*, 1979), *Uketsuke* (*The Information Desk*, 1980), *Ashi no Aru Shitai* (*A Corpse with Feet*, 1982), and *Rokugatsu no Denwa* (*A Phone Call in June*, 1995). Murai has written the plays about the victims of atomic bombs, supported by the active group, Women of Hiroshima Staging Committee. *Ano Hi Ano Ame* (*That Day That Rain*, 1990) deals with the daughter of an A-bomb victim in Hiroshima and the children who are the victims of the Chernobyl. Thus the issue is never described as an unfortunate experience in the past. Other plays include *Hiroshima no onna Hachigatsu Muika* (*Women of Hiroshima*) in the series of *Women of Hiroshima August* (1983), *Bira wa Furu* (*A Shower of Leaflets*, 1984) and *Himawari Le Soleil* (*The Sunflower*, 1990). The plays have been translated into English, French, German, Czech and Spanish, and have been staged in Edinburgh (1988) and Avignon (1989).

Murfi, Mikel (1965–) Actor, director and dramatist, Ireland. Trained at the Ecole Jacques Lecoq, Paris, Murfi was co-founder in 1993 of Barabbas...The Company, which is dedicated to the exploration of clowning, buffoonery and other popular performing traditions such as the commedia dell'arte, and is thus at the forefront of a new wave of 'physical theatre' in Ireland. Murfi and his co-founders devised three critically acclaimed pieces in their first year: *Come Down From The Mountain John Clown, John Clown* (a savage and grim critique of Ireland's urban reality played in red nose), *MacBeth* (a physical realization of Shakespeare's play by a five-man buffoon team) and *Half Eight Mass of a Tuesday* (an observation of the particularly rural Irish tradition of early morning mass with the aid of puppets, miniatures and shadow). Further challenging observations on Irish life were seen in his physically demanding solo performance of a rural tailor in *Strokehauling* (1996). Murfi has also worked for many other companies in the independent sector and also at the Abbey Theatre. More recently gave a towering performance of multiple characters in Lennox Robinson's *The Whiteheaded Boy* directed by Gerard STEMBRIDGE (1997) for Barrabas...The Company. In 1998 Murfi directed *Diamonds in the Soil*, devised by artist Patrick O'Reilly for Macnas Theatre Galway.

Murphy, Tom (1935–) Dramatist, Ireland. Early work includes *On The Outside* (1959, written with Noel O'Donohue), *A Whistle in The Dark* (1961, produced by Joan Littlewood's Theatre Royal at Stratford East), *Famine* (1968), *A Crucial Week in the Life of a Grocer's Assistant* (1969 with Donal McCann), *The Morning After Optimism* (1974) and the acclaimed *The Gigli Concert* directed by Patrick MASON for the Abbey (1983). Also in 1983, Murphy became writer-in-association with Druid Theatre Company, Galway, and in 1985 Garry HYNES directed *Conversations on a Homecoming* and *Bailegangaire* with the company. Murphy's County Galway background gave a local resonance to *Bailgangaire*, which used the Irish tradition of storytelling to take an eloquent look at the lives of three women as they each come to terms with life in the anachronistic modern rural Ireland. Recent work includes *The Patriot Game* (1991), *She Stoops To Folly* (after *The Vicar of Wakefield*, 1996) and *The Wake* (1998) at the Abbey Theatre directed by Patrick Mason.

Murray-Smith, Joanna (1962–) Dramatist, Australia. Murray-Smith's first play *Angry Young Penguins* (1987) was directed by Ewa Czajor. Czajor was murdered soon afterwards and Murray-Smith's play *Atlanta* (1990), dedicated to Czajor, is a fantastic, dream-like play meditating on the impact that the untimely death of a talented young woman has on a group of friends. Murray-Smith's best known play *Love Child* is a hard-hitting, entertaining exploration of the mother/daughter relationship with an unexpected twist. *Honour* (1995) focuses on the break-up of a thirty-two-year marriage, looking particularly at the reactions of the women involved. Murray-Smith has also written novels, a children's book and for television. Her recent plays are remarkable for their spare, fast-paced dialogue, something which contrasts starkly with the drifting, fantastic, hallucinogenic qualities of *Atlanta*.

Murrell, John (1945–) Dramatist and director, Canada. Born in the USA, Murrell was brought up in Canada. After five years as a schoolteacher, he has worked as a playwright and director since. His two major successes are *Waiting for the Parade* (1977), interweaving the stories of five women in Calgary during the Second World War, and *Memoir* (1977), which shows a day towards the end of the life of Sarah Bernhardt. *Memoir* has been translated into more than twenty languages and performed in thirty countries. Later plays include *October* (1988), depicting a fictional meeting of Isadora Duncan and Eleonora Duse, *Democracy* (1991) and *The Faraway Nearby* (1995). Murrell's work is lyrical without being overly melodramatic, and he has a remarkable gift for adapting play structure to pre-existing theatrical forms. In *Waiting for the Parade*, for example, the interweaving stories of five Calgary women in wartime are told using the conventions of music hall.

Musinga, Victor Eleame (1944–) Dramatist and actor, Cameroon. Musinga draws inspiration and material for his writing from the urban experience of his native Cameroon. His plays deal with the common people lost in the conflicting mix of urban and traditional values which characterize city life. Musinga's theatre has very much in common with that of other African popular artists, but especially the plays of the Zambian Kabwe KASOMA. Apart from a similarity in theme, their theatrical style reflects the syncretism of urban life and experience, an indiscriminate amalgam of dance, music, dialogue and other elements drawn from traditional and modern sources. Musinga has written and acted in *The Tragedy of Mr No-Balance*, *Night Marriages* and *Accountant Wawah*. The key feature of Musinga's dramaturgy is a certain sensitivity to the theatrical possibilities of the English language through creation of a range of registers for his characters.

Mustafa, Shubarna (1960–) Actor, Bangladesh. Mustafa's performance in the title role of Selim AL-DEEN's *Shakuntala* (with Raisul ASAD as Vishwamitra, Humayun FARIDI as Takkhak, directed by Nasiruddin YOUSUFF, 1978) earned her popularity and fame. Other important stage performances include the portrayal of Banasribala in Al-Deen's *Kittan Khola* (*The Fair of Kittan Khola*, with Shimul YOUSUFF as Dalimon, Faridi as Chhayaranjan and Asad as Bayati, set design by Jamil AHMED, directed by Nasiruddin Yousuff, 1981) and Paree in Al-Deen's *Jaibati Kanyar Mon* (*The Soul of the Virtuous Maiden*, with Shimul Yousuff as Kalindi, directed by Nasiruddin Yousuff, 1993). A versatile actor capable of delving into the depths of intense emotion, Shubarna Mustafa is also popular in film and on television. She is an active member of Dhaka Theatre (a leading theatre group in Bangladesh).

Muthusamy, Na (l940–) Director and dramatist, India. Muthusamy's major contribution to Tamil Theatre is his revival of Therukoothu and its vocabulary of gesture and movement (*adavus*) in his productions. He founded Koothu-p-pattarai, a theatre group in Madras and its training centre in the village of Purisai. Muthusamy's productions are often described as abstract: he believes in 'total theatre'. Muthusamy's notable productions are Molière's *Dom Juan*, Ionesco's *Beckett*, Bharathy's *Panchali Sabadam*, Bhasa's *Dutha Katotkaja*, his own *The last five seconds of Mahatma Gandhi* and Camus's *Caligula*. His own plays, including *England*, *Thana Terinjikanuum* (*You Should Know Yourself*) and *Suvarottikal* (*Posters*), are like extended poems without scene divisions or narratives, mirroring his production ethos which values the actor's body over the written text.

Mytnyts'ky, Eduard (1931–) Director, Ukraine. Mytnyts'ky trained at the Karpenko-Kary Institute for the Art of the Theatre, Kiev, and joined the teaching staff of the Institute in 1981. He has created his own school of directing. The young famous directors Dmytro Bohomazov, Iurii Odynoky, Dmytro Lazorko and Andrii Krytenko are among his pupils. From 1963–6 he worked at the theatres of Riazan' (Russia), and between 1965–73 and 1993–4 at the Lesia Ukrainka Russian Drama Theatre, Kiev. In 1978 he founded the Theatre of Drama and Comedy, Kiev. He has staged over 120 productions, including Zorin's *Varshavskaia melodiia* (*The Warsaw Melody*, Kiev, 1968), *Hamlet* (Kiev, 1984), Dudarev's *Vecher* (*Evening*, Kiev, 1985), *The Fiddler on the Roof* after Shalom-Aleichem (Odessa, 1987; Riga, Latvia, 1988; Germany, 1992), Gogol's *Revizor* (*The Government Inspector*, Germany, 1992), *Piat' pudov liubvi* (*The Five Pounds of Love*) after Chekhov's *Cajka* (*The Seagull*, 1993), Ivan Franko's *Ukradene shchastia* (*A Stolen Happiness*, Vilnus, Lithuania, 1996), and Tolstoi's *Zhivoi trup* (*Living Corpse*, 1997).

N

Naghiu, Iosif (1932–) Dramatist, poet, Romania. Naghiu trained at the Fine Arts Institute, Department of Graphic Arts, Bucharest, and started to publish poetry in 1967. In 1968 his first play, *Celluloid*, was published. *Absenta* (*The Absence*) was produced at the Bulandra Theatre under a different title and then forbidden by the communist censorship. Further plays include *Misterul Agamemnon* (*The Agamemnon Mystery*), *Valiza cu fluturi* (*A Suitcase with Butterflies*) and *Spitalui Special* (*The Special Hospital*). In his plays, Naghiu voices his social disappointment behind a mask of caricature, using metaphor, the grotesque and the absurd.

Nagy, András (1956–) Dramatist, Hungary. After studying Hungarian and Popular Education at the Budapest Eötvös Loránd University, Nagy was an assistant at the University's Department of Twentieth-Century Hungarian Literary History. Between 1982–90 he served as an editor in a publishing house. Winner of several literary scholarships, his effective, theatrical plays are searching secrets of contradictory literary and historical figures, striving to clarify contemporary existential and moral dilemmas. They include *Báthory Erzsébet* (*Elisabeth Báthory*, 1985), *Anna Karenina pályudvar* (*Anna Karenina Station*, 1990), *Magyar három nővér* (*Hungarian Three Sisters*, 1991) and *A csábító naplója* (*Diary of the Seducer*, 1992). His adaptation of Stendhal's *Le Rouge et le Noire* (*The Red and the Black*) was performed in 1995 in Györ. His most recent plays, *Mi, hárman* (*Us three*) and *Alma*, were produced in the 1995/96 season.

Naharin, Ohad (1952–) Choreographer and dancer, Israel. After training with Martha Graham and at the Juillard School in New York, Naharin danced with Graham's company and then with Maurice Béjart as well as with the Israeli Bat Dor Company. She started to choreograph in 1980 and worked in Israel, USA, Italy, The Netherlands and Sweden. After establishing an independent group in Israel, and in 1980 Naharin was appointed as artistic director of the Israeli Bat Sheva company. Since then he has led this company to international fame, combining choreography with live music, visual arts, theatre and singing in works like *Tabula Rasa* (1987), *Kyr* (1990), *Anaphase* (1993), *Z/Na* (1995) and *Jag* (1996).

Nakamura Ganjirô III (1931–) Kabuki actor, Japan. The son of Nakamura Ganjirô II, he first played O-hatsu in *Sonezaki Shinjû* (*The Love Suicide at Sonezaki*) by Monzaemon Chikamatsu (1653–1724) as an *onnagata* (female impersonator) opposite his father's Tokubei, *tachiyaku* (a leading male role) in 1953 when his stage name was still Nakamura Senjaku II. After his father's death, Tokubei's part has been taken over by his son and Ganjirô III has performed the same role over 1,000 times. He succeeded to the present stage name in 1990. He formed the Chikamatsu-za Theatre Company in 1981 to stage exclusively Chikamatsu's plays, and the CTC has been keeping its initial commitment. Ganjirô III plays both *onnagata* and *tachiyaku* in the artistic tradition of *wagoto* (domestic style) of *kamigata kabuki*. He has performed in Russia, Canada, the USA and Mexico on kabuki overseas tours since 1987.

Nakamura Kankurô V (1955–) Kabuki actor, Japan. The first son of Nakamura Kanzabuô XVII and the grandson of Onoe Kikugorô VI, he was given this stage name in 1959 in his first stage appearance, when he played Momotarô in the old Japanese folk tale *Momotarô*. He has mounted full productions of some *ki-zewamono* plays dedicated to the depiction of the poor, the wretched and the underworld, such as *Yotsuya Kaidan* (*Yotsuya Ghost Story*) by Namboku Tauruya, and *Shiranami Gonin Otoko* (*The Five Robbers*, 1995) by Mokuami Kawatake. His representative roles includes Shinza in *Tsuyukosode Mukashi Hachijo* (*The Hairdresser Shinza*, 1989) by Mokuami, Benten Kozo in *Shiranami Gonin Otoko* and Shunkan in *Heike Nyogo no Shima* (*Shunkan*) by Monzaemon Chikamatsu. He plays both *onnagata* (a female impersonator) and *tachiyaku* (a leading male role). He acts especially well in *tachiyaku* in *sewamano* (domestic style) plays of the late Edo kabuki with his crisp pronunciation of the Edo accent and excellent movements.

Napier, John (1944–) Designer, Great Britain. Napier studied at Hornsey College of Art, and from 1967–8 he designed at the Phoenix in Leicester. His London debut was in 1968. On Broadway he designed *Equus* in 1974, following design

for the same play for the National Theatre in 1972. From 1974 onwards he worked with the Royal Shakespeare Company, culminating in complex sets for David EDGAR's adaptation of *Nicholas Nickleby* there in 1980. Subsequently he has worked with Trevor NUNN, designing successful musicals such as *Starlight Express* and *Les Miserables*, but has continued designing for the theatre, such as a revival of Edward ALBEE's *Who's Afraid of Virginia Woolf?* at the Almeida in London (1996, with Diana RIGG, directed by Howard DAVIES), and most recently Nunn's production of Ibsen's *En Folkefiende* (*An Enemy of the People*, with Ian MCKELLEN) at the Royal National Theatre.

Navarra, Gilda (1921–) Director, mime and actor, Puerto Rico. Gilda Navarra began her career as a dancer before studying with Jacques LeCoq in Paris and earning a Certificat from the Ecole de Mime in 1964. She returned to Puerto Rico, where she taught courses in pantomime and commedia dell'arte at the University of Puerto Rico for twenty-eight years. During the 1980s, she founded and operated a mime troupe, Taller de Histriones (Actors' Workshop), which also presented commedia material. In 1989 she directed the anonymous commedia work *Three Cuckolds* at the University of Puerto Rico. Also an actor, Navarra appeared as Nanny alongside Lucy BOSCANA, Sharon Riley and Idalia PÉREZ GARAY in Paul Zindel's *The Effect of Gamma Rays on Man-in-the-Moon Marigolds* (directed by Dean ZAYAS, Teatro del Sesenta, 1971), and as Lucky in Julio BIAGGI's production of Beckett's *Waiting for Godot*, in a version translated by Francisco Prado (Proscenio, 1974).

Ndao, Cheik Sidi Ahmed (1933–) Dramatist, Senegal. Ndao has written seven plays, five in French and two in English, which deal mostly with the resistance of the African aristocracy to French and

European colonial conquest in the nineteenth century. His plays combine song, dance and movement to produce spectacular and colourful theatre images, and this is an attribute which he shares with other French African dramatists such as Nicole WEREWERE-LIKING (Cameroon), Zadi ZAOUROU (Ivory Coast) and Guillaume OYONO-MBIA (Cameroon). Another special quality of Ndao's plays, especially *L'Exil d'Albouri* (*Albouri's Exile*, 1967), is their epic conception and the huge canvas on which large crowds move across vast open spaces and the splendid battle scenes that are often filled with magnificently clad armies. His other plays are *Le Fils de L'Almany* (*The Son of the Almamy*, 1973), *La Case de l'homme* (*The Hut of Manhood*, 1973), *L'île de Bahila* (*The Island of Bahila*, 1975), *Tears for Tears* (1977), *Love But Educate* (1978) and *Du Sang pour un Trone* (*Blood for a Throne*, 1983).

Nelligan, Kate (1951–) Actor, USA. Nelligan trained at the Central School of Speech and Drama in London, leading to her professional debut in 1972 at the Bristol Old Vic. She appeared with the National Theatre (Ellie Dunn in Shaw's *Heartbreak House*, 1975) and the Royal Shakespeare Company (Rosalind in *As You Like It*, 1977). Since 1978 she has appeared mainly in the USA, making her Broadway debut in 1983 as Susan Traherne in David HARE's *Plenty*, followed in 1985 by the title role in Edna O'Brien's *Virginia*. More recently she played Maria Callas in Terrence MCNALLY's *Master Class* (1996) and appeared in Wasserstein's *An American Daughter* (1997, opposite Hal HOLBROOK). Critics have often noted the delicate combination of intelligence and vulnerability that she brings to her work.

Nelson, Richard (1938–) Designer, USA. Nelson graduated from High School of Performing Arts in New York City and began his distinguished and busy career as a lighting designer in 1958 on a production of *Hamlet at Stepney Green*. From 1963–82 he worked as production manager and technical director for the Seattle Repertory Theatre. He also lit musicals such as *Sunday in the Park with George* on Broadway, avant-garde theatre (e.g. Robert WILSON's *The King of Spain*, 1969), and modern dance (for example, for Merce Cunningham). Winner of numerous awards, his lighting for *Sunday in the Park* truly enhanced the Seurat-styled setting.

Neto, José Possi (1947–) Director, dramatist and designer, Brazil. A graduate from the School of Communication and Arts, University of São Paulo, Neto conducted research on avant-garde dance and theatre in New York (1976–88) under the Fullbright Foundation programme. His directing credits include *Three Tall Women* by Edward ALBEE, Shaw's *Saint Joan*, Maria Adelaide Amaral's *De Bracos Abertos*, Harold PINTER's *Betrayal* and several of his own plays, which fall under the category of 'dance theatre', using dancers as actors. For such productions, Neto also designed costumes, lighting and sometimes sets.

Neuenfels, Hans (1941–) Director, Germany. After training at the Max Reinhardt Seminar in Vienna, Neuenfels directed in Lucerne, Trier, Krefeld and Heidelberg (1968–1970, productions including Büchner's *Danton's Tod* (*Danton's Death*) and Strindberg's *Fröken Julie* (*Miss Julie*)). From 1972–6 he joined Peter Palitzsch in Frankfurt. Between 1986–90 he was artistic director of the Volksbühne, Berlin, where productions included Edward BOND's *Saved* and Sophocles's *Elektra*. His attempt to regenerate this stage with a young company and a daring repertory failed, due to financial and political reasons. Since then he has worked freelance, productions including Edward ALBEE's *Who's Afraid of Virginia Woolf?* (Vienna, 1991), and *A Midsummer*

Night's Dream at the Schiller-Theater, Berlin (in 1993, with Bernard Minetti as Puck). More recent work includes Genet's *Les bonnes* (*The Maids*, 1996), Horvath's *Geschichten aus dem Wiener Wald* (*Tales from the Vienna Wood*, 1996), and Williams's *The Rose Tatoo*, all at the Bayerisches Staatsschauspiel in Munich. 'Neuenfels rejects simple psychological explanations, always tracing the deeply hidden subtext. His best productions become images in thought, the highest form theatre can achieve.'

Nevin, Robyn (1942–) Actor and director, Australia. Nevin trained at the National Institute of Dramatic Art, Sydney. Recently she has been concentrating more on directing, and is now artistic director of the Queensland State Theatre. Her 1995 Melbourne Theatre Company production of the Australian classic, LAWLER's *The Summer of the Seventeenth Doll*, for the play's fortieth anniversary, toured most of Australia. Nevin cites director Rex Cramphorn as a seminal figure in her acting career, which includes Blanche in *Streetcar Named Desire* by Tennessee Williams, and Lavinia in O'Neill's *Mourning Becomes Electra* (Old Tote, Sydney, 1975). David WILLIAMSON wrote major roles for Nevin in *The Perfectionist*, *Emerald City* and *Money and Friends*. Nevin is still very much associated with tragic or strong women in crisis roles, such as Barbara in Katherine Thomson's *Diving for Pearls 1*, AYCKBOURN's *Woman in Mind* and Shasta in the critically acclaimed television series *Water Under the Bridge* (1980). One of her most remembered roles is the well-meaning but terrifying Miss Docker in Patrick White's *A Cheery Soul*. Less conventionally, Nevin played Mark Antony as a woman character in the MTC's 1996 modern dress production of *Julius Caesar*, directed by Simon PHILLIPS.

Newton, Christopher (1936–) Actor and director, Canada. Born in Britain, Newton toured Canada in *Julius Caesar* and Shaw's *Saint Joan* (1961–2). Newton was artistic director of several Canadian theatres and at the Shaw festival, where he balanced an inherited $600,000 deficit within four years and transformed the Festival from a summer repertory theatre to a company of international stature. The Shaw Festival now attracts some of Canada's best actors, and Newton has also expanded the Festival to include plays by Shaw's contemporaries. Some of his most celebrated productions, including Feydeau's *A Flea in Her Ear* and Rostand's *Cyrano de Bergerac*, are not of Shaw's work. But Newton continues to produce Shaw's plays and to invest them with a contemporary relevance, an immense theatricality and a tremendous sense of humour.

Neyolova, Marina (1947–) Actor, Russia. After graduating from the Leningrad State Institute for Theatre, Music and Film, Neyolova joined the Leningrad Film Studio in 1968. She then moved to Moscow and in 1971 joined the Mossovet Theatre Company. Since 1974 she has been with the Sovremennik Theatre, Moscow, where major work includes *Twelfth Night* (directed by Peter BROOK) Martha in ALBEE's *Who's Afraid of Virginia Woolf?* (1985) and Masha in Chekhov's *Tri sestry* (*Three Sisters*, 1982). Neyolova brought to the contemporary Russian stage a certain feeling of poignancy and despair. In her acting, grace, beauty and sex appeal are combined with real dramatic feeling and psychological depth. In Ginzburg's *A Steep Route* (1989, about a Stalin labour camp prisoner) she proved to be a mature tragic actor. During American tours of the Sovremennik theatre (1990, 1996) she was highly acclaimed by the press. Neyolova now lives in France, the wife of a diplomat. Each month she travels to Russia to perform at Sovremennik.

Ng, Karley (1957–) Dramatist and director, China (Hong Kong SAR). His pseudonym is Mok Hei. Ng has been active in the local theatre scene since 1972 and started his professional career in the early 1980s. He founded the Exploration Theatre in 1982 and has, as its artistic director, presented over sixty productions since, directing many himself, and mounted a performing tour in Vancouver. A leading figure in promoting original works, Ng's reputation as a playwright has included no less than three script awards. His major works as both playwright and director include *Between You and Me* (1985), *Curtain Up* (1988), *The Invincible Ladies* (1992) and *Dragon's Legend* (1996). An infusion of social issues characterized his *Close to My Heart* (1996). Ng's realistically set and socially provocative plays also include *Equality Index* (1998) and *Additive Friends* (1999). His recent introduction of interactive theatre in the local theatre scene is also widely acknowledged.

Ngema, Mbongeni (1955–) Dramatist, actor, director and musician, South Africa. Ngema first came to international attention with his very powerful performance in the 1980s in *Woza Albert!*, a play which also featured Percy MTWA (with directing and improvisation contribution from Barney SIMON). *Woza Albert!* carries on the tradition of the workshop play set by *Sizwe Bansi is Dead* by John KANI, Winston NTSHONA and Athol FUGARD, but unlike *Sizwe Bansi* the characters in the latter are many and cover a spectrum of South African society. This of course makes enormous demands on the acting abilities of Ngema and his co-actor Mtwa, who have to mutate into different characters. Much of Ngeni's theatre art draws upon traditions of Zulu music and dance, which he then blends, using his experience as a township actor in the musicals of Gibson KENTE. His first acting role was in Lucky Mavundla's *Isigiro* and later in Kessie Govender's *Working Class Hero*, before joining Kente's theatre company and getting a character role in *Mama and the Load*.

Niermeyer, Amélie (1965–) Director, Germany. Following two years as assistant director with Rudolf Noelte, Peter PALITZSCH and Peter Eschberg in Bonn, Niermeyer travelled to Southeast Asia and worked as an assistant director at the New Theatre, Sydney. From 1986–9 she studied German literature in Bonn and Munich, and continued her apprenticeship with Franz Xaver KROETZ and David MOUCHTAR-SAMORAI. Since 1990 she has been a resident director with the Bayerisches Staatsschauspiel in Munich, apart from one season as director with the theatre in Dortmund and freelance work in Weimar, Hamburg and Frankfurt. Productions include Bettina Fless's *Memmingen* (1991), Wedekind's *Frühlings Erwachen* (*Spring Awakening*, 1992), Aristophanes's *Lysistrata* (1993), Ibsen's *Hedda Gabler* (1995), Lessing's *Miss Sarah Sampson* (1996), Goethe's *Stella* (1997, and in 1999 in Frankfurt am Main), Kleist's *Der Zerbrochene Krug* (*The Broken Jug*, 1997) and *Romeo and Juliet* (1998). According to critical opinion, 'Niermeyer shows a set of basic skills that suggests future developments of her style towards the imaginary, symbolic or even visionary'.

Nieva, Francisco (1927–) Designer, dramatist and director, Spain. Nieva studied Fine Arts before leaving the conservative climate of Francoist Spain for France, where he associated with key figures of the avant-garde and absurdist movements. It was for the Théâtre National Populaire that Nieva undertook his first job as designer, *La Place Royal*, directed by Georges Wilson. Returning to Spain in 1964 he worked regularly in Madrid as a designer with the most prominent directors of the age, Miguel Narros, Adolfo MARSILLACH and José Luis Alonso. His designs moved away from the realism prevalent at the time, playfully interrogating the accepted myths, conventions and icons of Hispanic life and culture. Although he had been writing plays since the early 1950s, these grotesque, surreal and wildly funny works were not professionally produced until after Franco's death. Widespread recognition came with the productions in 1976 of *El combate de Opalos y Tasia* (*The Battle of Opalos and Tasia*) and *La carrota de plomo candente* (*The Carriage of White-Hot Lead*), erotic intertextual pieces touched with an anarchic sense of humour. During the 1980s and 1990s he has increasingly directed and designed his own plays and enjoyed high-profile productions of key works in France.

Nijholt, Willem (1934–) Actor, The Netherlands. Willem Nijholt was born in the former Dutch East Indies. After his family's return he went to the Drama School in Amsterdam (1957–60). He started his rich and chequered career with the Rotterdams Toneel, playing many repertory parts up to 1967. An excellent singer and showman, he performed many parts in cabaret, musical and entertainment from 1967 to 1980, including shows with top entertainer Wim Sonneveld and musicals by Annie M.G. Schmidt like *Wat een planeet* (*What a Planet*) and *Foxtrot*. He became a celebrity in these years, in part also because of his work for television. Nijholt is a highly skilled, conventional actor with a lot of charm, although he is always critical of colleagues with little interest in the handicraft of acting. In 1980 he returned to playing repertory parts, with the Haagse Comedie. He starred in Molière's *Tartuffe*, Pommerance's *The Elephant Man*, Medoff's *Children of a Lesser God* and many other plays. In 1985 he made a solo show and developed a taste for directing (for example, SHAFFER's *Amadeus*, in which he also acted twice, 1991). In recent years Nijholt directed three plays by Noël Coward, including. *The Marquise* (with Anne-Wil BLANKERS, 1992) and appeared in

musicals again, in *You're The Top* (about Cole Porter, 1995) and as The Engineer in *Miss Saigon* (1996).

Nilu, Kamaluddin (1955–) Director and actor, Bangladesh. Nilu trained at the National School of Drama (1978–81). His directorial credits include translations of *Oidipus tyrannos* (*King Oedipus*) by Sophocles (set design by Jamil AHMED, 1981), *The Sultan's Dilemma* by Taufique Al-Hakim (set design by Qamruzzaman Runu CHOWDHURY, 1991), Ibsen's *Gengangere* (*Ghosts*, 1996) and an adaptation of Molière's *L'avare* (*The Miser*, with Tariq KHAN in the title role and set design by Jamil Ahmed, 1983). These productions earned him considerable reputation as a director who seeks subtle balance between the text and the visual. He is the general secretary of the Centre for Asian Theatre and associate professor of theatre at the University of Chittagong. Nilu has travelled abroad extensively, attending seminars and conferences.

Ninagawa Yukio (1935–) Director, Japan. Ninagawa began his career in theatre with Gekidan Seihai (the Seihai Theatre Company). In 1969 he co-founded Gendaijin Gekijô (the Contemporary People's Theatre). He staged SHIMIZU Kunio's *Shinjô Afururu Keihakusa* (*The Hearty Frivolity*, 1969), which reflected the feelings of the youth at that time. This became the start of his long-standing collaboration with Shimizu on, for example, *Karasuyo Oretachi wa Tama o Komeru* (*Ravens! We Load Guns*, 1972), and *Tango Fuyu no Owarini* (*Tango at the End of Winter*, 1984). He began directing for the commercial theatre company, Tôhô with a production of *Romeo and Juliet* in 1974. His work with Tôhô includes *Chikamatsu Shinjû Monogatari* (*Chikamatsu Love Suicide Story*) by AKIMOTO Matsuyo (1979), *Ninagawa Macbeth* (1980), Euripides's *Medeia* (1983) and *The Tempest* (1987). Many of his productions have toured abroad. An English adaptation of

Tango at the End of Winter was staged at the Royal National Theatre in London in 1991, and *Shintoku-Maru* (*The Boy Shintoku*) by Shuji Terayama and *Hamlet* were performed at the Barbican Centre in 1997 and 1998. He formed Gekisha Ninagawa Studio (the present Ninagawa Company) in 1984 and the company continues experiments in its studio.

Nityanandam, Nirupama (1963–) Actor, France (born in India). Nityanandam trained with the Indian company of Bharatanatyam, Dhananjayan, between 1969–72, advancing to professor and choreographer at the school of Dhananjayan in 1984. In 1987 she came to France and joined Ariane MNOUCHKINE's Théâtre du Soleil, where she became one of the major actors. She played the leading role, Dina Jinnah (daughter of Jinnah) in CIXOUS's *The Indiad or the India of Their Dreams* (1987), Iphigenia in Euripides's *Iphigenia at Aulis* (1990), Cassandra in Aeschylus's *Agamemnon* (1990), Electra in Aeschylus's *The Libation Bearers* (1991), one of the Erinyes in Cixous's *La ville parjure ou le réveil des Erinyes* (1994) and Elmire in Molière's *Tartuffe* (1995). Since the creation of the Théâtre du Soleil, Ariane Mnouchkine has striven to unite Western and Oriental theatre traditions and dramaturgies, seeking out this combination in actors. On stage, Nityanandam's body movements and facial expression are inspired by traditional Indian theatre and dance.

Nitzan, Omri (1950–) Director, Israel. Nitzan studied directing at the Drama Centre in London. He has directed a large number of Shakespeare plays like *Twelfth Night*, *A Midsummer Night's Dream* and *The Merchant of Venice*, stressing the contemporary and the local perspectives. He has also directed many plays by Israeli playwrights like Hillel MITTELPUNKT and Yehoshua SOBOL, Edna MAZIA and Hanoch LEVIN. Nitzan has held most of the central managerial positions in Israeli theatre, through which he has been able to introduce new playwrights and directors. He has been the artistic director of the Haifa municipal theatre, the Habima national theatre, the Israel Festival and, since 1995, the Cameri Tel Aviv municipal theatre. As a director as well as in his managerial positions, Nitzan has had an enormous influence on Israeli mainstream theatre, which he sees as an expression of secular culture in a country where the religious influences have steadily been growing.

Nkosi, Lewis Dramatist and actor, South Africa. Nkosi was a member of the African Theatre Workshop, a group of black South African theatre artists who were closely associated with Athol Fugard and his wife Sheila in the 1950s and who eventually provided the bulk of actors who performed Fugard's *No-Good Friday* in Johannesburg in 1958. Included in this group were such notable South African acting talents as Bloke MODISANE and Zakes MOKAE. Nkosi took over the role of the white Father Higgins from Fugard when *No-Good Friday* went to the Brooke Theatre, an all-white venue in Johannesburg where a mixed race cast was forbidden. Nkosi is known more for his critical work, but his one published play, *The Rhythm of Violence* (1964), a play that explores apartheid South Africa, is well known and has been widely performed in many countries in Africa. He has spent years teaching, writing and presenting African theatre in exile in Europe and America.

Noble, Adrian (1950–) Director, Great Britain. Noble trained at Drama Centre and worked as an associate director at the Bristol Old Vic (1976–9). He joined the Royal Shakespeare Company in 1980, was an associate director between 1982–90, and took over as artistic director from Trevor NUNN and Terry HANDS in 1991. He has directed mainstream Shakespeare, such as *Hamlet* with Kenneth BRANAGH and Jane LAPOTAIRE (1992), Chekhov (such as *Tri sestry* (*Three Sisters*), 1990, and *Visnevyi sad* (*The Cherry Orchard*), 1994), contemporary plays (such as a revival of STOPPARD's *Travesties* with Anthony SHER, 1993), and presented cycles of plays such as *The Plantagenets*, based on Shakespeare's history plays, and *The Thebans*, based on Sophocles. His signature style has been described as 'bold, imaginative conception, narrative clarity, inventive visual texture and richly theatrical effects'.

Noda Hideki (1955–) Dramatist, director and actor, Japan. Noda began his career in Yume no Yûmin-sha (Dream Theatre Company), which had developed from his university drama society. His first play performed outside the university, *Hashire Merusu* (*Run Merusu*, 1976) was written for the competition of young theatre groups sponsored by VAN 99 Hall Theatre, Tokyo. His plays include *Shônen Gari* (*Hunting Boys*, 1979), *Zenda-jô no Toriko* (*The Capture in Zenda Castle*, 1981) and *Hanshin* (*The Half-God*, 1990). His theatre represents the major trend of the 1980s contemporary Japanese theatre, which is 'larger than human size'. It involves an athletic and dynamic style of acting, spacious and spectacular design and complicated plots and subplots from both Eastern and Western novels and classics. Yume no Yûmin-sha has been invited to Edinburgh International Festival in 1987 and to the New York International Art Festival in 1988. The company was dissolved in 1992. Since then Noda has extended his theatrical ideas by working freelance for various theatre productions.

Noesen, Philippe (1944–) Actor and director, Luxembourg. After his training at the Conservatoire National Supérieur de Paris, Noesen joined the Comédie Française as a resident actor. On his return to Luxembourg in 1974, he founded the Théâtre du Centaure and was its artistic

director for the next eighteen years. He directed some forty plays, commissioned new writing by Luxembourg authors, and played the title roles of Molière's *Dom Juan*, *The Miser* and *Tartuffe*. In 1992, Noesen became artistic director of the Théâtre d'Esch, until then a repertory theatre, and established regular in-house productions as part of their programme. Meanwhile, he played George in ALBEE's *Who's Afraid of Virginia Woolf?* (Théâtre du Centaure, 1992, with Marja-Leena JUNKER and Myriam MULLER, designed by Jeanny KRATOSCHWILL) and won great acclaim for his solo performance in Kafka's *Bericht für eine Akademie* (*Report to an Academy*, 1994, Théâtre d'Esch, presented at the Avignon Theatre Festival).

Nomura Mansaku II (1931–) Nôgaku kyôgen actor, Japan. The second son of Nomura Manzô VI, and trained under his father, he is a member of Izumi School of kyôgen. His first stage appearance was in the role of the monkey in *Utsubozaru* (*Utusbo Monkey*) in 1934. He succeeded to the present stage name when he performed *Sanbasô* (*Sanbaso: the Abundant Harvest*) in 1950. His representative performances include in *Tsuri Gitsune* (*Fox Hunting*, 1956), *Hanago* (1960) and *Makura Monogurui* (*A Pillow Talk*, 1991). He endorses the new repertoire of kyôgen and also works in modern theatre. *Gaki Kuyô* (*Memorial Service for a Hungry Ghost*, 1976) and *Shigosen no Matsuri* (*Requiem on the Meridian*, 1979) by KINOSHITA are the examples of his adventurous work. As kyôgen is the form of comedy of the mediaeval times, kyôgen actors basically play roles which are silly and funny to a certain degree. Mansaku wins the audience's laughter from the moment he enters the stage.

Noor, Asaduzzaman (1946–) Actor, Bangladesh. An ardent political–cultural activist in his student life, Noor attained fame as a stage actor in early 1980s. His most memorable performances include the title role in a translation of Zuckmayer's *Der Hauptmann von Köpenick* (*The Captain of Köpenick*, designed by Mansuruddin AHMED and directed by Aly ZAKER, 1981), Abbas in Syed HUQ's *Nooraldeener Sarajeeban* (*Nooraldeen: A Life*, with Aly Zaker in the title role, Sarah ZAKER as Lizbeth, Ataur RAHMAN as Goodlad, set design by Mansuruddin Ahmed, directed by Aly Zaker, 1981), Estragon in a translation of Beckett's *Waiting For Godot* (with Abdul HAYAT as Pozzo, directed by Ataur Rahman, 1984) and the Doctor in an adaptation of Dorfman's *Death and the Maiden* (with Hayat as the Lawyer and directed by Sarah Zaker, 1993). The captivating power of Noor's performance lies in his dexterous portrayal of the essence in detail, subtle interplay of emotion and mastery over speech.

Nordby, Terje (1949–) Dramatist, Norway. Nordby considers his ten years with Tramteatret, which he co-founded in 1976 and where he combined work as director, actor and administrator, as his fundamental theatre training. For Tramteatret, he wrote seven musical revues with a politically radical flare, including *Hven er Redd for Froken Lunde* (*Who is Afraid of Miss Lunde*) and *Det Enkleste er Pistol* (*The Simplest Thing is a Gun*). In his later plays for theatre, Nordby takes up storytelling traditions and suffused them with a modern consciousness. He has developed a growing interest for existential problems, seeking roots in the ancient past (mythology, folklore), but nevertheless relating to the concrete and social reality we live in.

Norman, Marsha (1947–) Dramatist, USA. From 1969–71 Norman worked with disturbed children at Kentucky Central State Hospital, an experience which influenced her plays. *Getting Out* (1978) deals with the problems of a woman just released from jail. 'Two actors simultaneously portray her former, criminal, and her current, reformed selves.' The Pulitzer Prize winning *'night Mother* (1983) is an equally powerful play, about a young woman's decision to commit suicide. Later plays include *Winter Shaker* (1987), the book and lyrics for a musical adaptation of *The Secret Garden* (1991), and *Loving Daniel Boone* (1993). *'night Mother* also helped solidify the career of Kathy BATES, who won numerous awards for her powerful performance.

Nowra, Louis (1950–) Dramatist, Australia. Nowra has written plays, film scripts (*Map of the Human Heart*), radio plays, novels and opera libretti. He has also translated plays and adapted Xavier Herbert's *Capricornia* (1988) for the stage. His early plays, the best-known of which is *The Golden Age* (1985), show a self-conscious interest in language, culture, insiders and outsiders and the downright bizarre. Several of these plays use an historical moment as their creative departure point. Initially Nowra often set his plays outside Australia, but more recently his plays have focused on dissecting Australian society. Nowra's most recent plays have been less anti-illusionistic and more conventional in their subject matter, particularly targeting corruption and politics (*The Temple*, 1993, *The Incorruptible*, 1995) and have been very successful with subscriber audiences. Several plays offer roles for Aboriginal actors, especially *Radiance* (1993) and *Crow* (1994). Autobiographical plays are *Summer of the Aliens* (1992, when Nowra himself played the role of the narrator, Lewis, for the Melbourne Theatre Company production) and *Cosi* (1992, later filmed).

Ntshona, Winston Zola (1941–) Actor, South Africa. Not much is known internationally about Winston Ntshona except that he was co-actor and co-devisor with John KANI and Athol Fugard on the internationally acclaimed *Sizwe Bansi is Dead* (first performed at The Space, Cape Town, October 8, 1972) and *The Island*.

Ntshona's acting abilities were in his very powerful portrayal of the central character Sizwe Bansi/Robert Zwelinzima and one of the Robben Island prisoners in *The Island*. It was felt that it was Ntshona's acting which brought home to the world the trauma and psychic dislocations which black people were experiencing under the infamous apartheid pass and employment laws. He gave this role a strong dose of emotional intensity and sincerity which moved all who saw it on the many stages and theatres of the world where it was performed.

Nunes, Celso (1941–) Director, Brazil. Nunes took a performing art course at the School of Dramatic Arts in São Paulo, and a theatre director's course at the Sorbonne in Paris. His obtained his doctorate at the School for Communication and Arts at São Paulo University. Practical training continued with Stanislavski method studies under Eugenio Kusnet, a period as assistant director with Antunes FILHO, and training periods with Grotowski, Eugenio BARBA, Jean Villar and Bernard Dort. Major productions include *Die Ermittlung* (*The Investigation*) by Peter Weiss, *Coriolanus* and *King Lear*, Peter SHAFFER's *Equus*, *Groß und Klein* (*Large and Small*) by Botho STRAUSS, and Brecht's *Leben des Galilei* (*Life of Galileo*). Founder of the Theatre Centre of the Universidade Estadual de Campinas and representative in Brazil for the International Theatre Institute, Nunes is working on the Rolfing therapy area for future establishment of a link between actors and Rolfing movement practices.

Nunn, Trevor (1940–) Director, Great Britain. Following two years at Belgrade Theatre, Coventry, where he also trained, Nunn became associate director at the Royal Shakespeare Company in 1964, artistic director between 1968–78 and joint artistic director with Terry HANDS from 1978–91. Among his many productions of Shakespeare, *Macbeth* (1975 with

Ian MCKELLEN and Judi DENCH) is noteworthy. 'His vision of Shakespeare at the Royal Shakespeare Company involved focusing on the private person rather than public issues.' In the early 1980s Nunn directed commercially successful musicals, *Cats* and *Starlight Express* (1981 and 1984), has directed opera and, more recently, a successful revival of Shaw's *Heartbreak House* (1992) and STOPPARD's *Arcadia* (1993, with Felicity KENDAL). In 1997 he succeeded Richard EYRE as director of the Royal National Theatre, choosing Christopher HAMPTON's version of Ibsen's *En Folkefiende* (*An Enemy of the People*) as first his production (starring Ian McKellen, set design by John NAPIER), followed by a revival of PINTER's *Betrayal*, *Mutabilitie* by Frank MCGUINNESS and the musical *Oklahoma!*.

Nwabueze, Emeka Patrick (1948–) Dramatist, Nigeria. Nwabueze played the role of Dr Ezenagu (as a member of Ebony Players) in the American premiere of his *Spokesman for the Oracle* in 1983. His other significant play is *Guardian of the Cosmos* (1990), almost a dramatized version of Chinua Achebe's famous novel, *Arrow of God*, already adapted for the stage successfully as *A Harvest for Ants* by Kalu UKA in 1977. Most of Nwabueze's plays are concerned with the psychological exploration of characters, and they are fairly realistic portrayals of both character and scenery: there is not much experimentation with dramatic form and staging technique. In *Guardian of the Cosmos*, traditional theatre media of dance and songs are used to add local colour.

Nwoko, Demas (1939–) Designer and director, Nigeria. Nwoko studied fine arts at Zaria (1956–61) and scenic design at the Centre Français du Théâtre in Paris (1962–3). His designs for the stage include Wole SOYINKA's *A Dance of the Forests* (also costume design), and Brecht's *Der Kaukasische Kreidekreis* (*The Caucasian Chalk Circle*). Directing credits include an

Mbari Theatre production of J.P. CLARK-BEKEDEREMO's *The Masquerade*, which featured among others the talented and versatile Wale OGUNYEMI. The production of Jarry's *Ubu Roi* (*King Ubu*), which also featured Ogunyemi, was influenced by Nwoko's wide knowledge of Oriental theatre styles and techniques and his expertise and skill of scenic and costume design. He later set up New Culture Studios, his own fully professional studio that designed theatres and furnitures, and published for a while a journal of cultural studies as well as offering in-house training and consultancy in the plastic and performing arts. His views on theatre and design arts have contributed immensely in the development of performing arts in Nigeria and Africa as a whole.

O

Obafemi, Olu (1951–) Dramatist, actor and director, Nigeria. Obafemi is the founder-director of Ajon Players, a University of Ilorin-based theatre group which tours the villages as a means of taking literary theatre to the people. Obafemi belongs to the second generation of radical Nigerian playwrights who are concerned with developing a 'revolutionary theatre aesthetic' capable of engaging with contemporary social realities of their Nigerian socio-political context (others in the group are Femi OSOFISAN, Bode SOWANDE, Kole OMOTOSO and Tunde FATUNDE). Like most of the other playwrights of his generation, he taps into the myths, folklore, dances, music and mime traditions of his Yoruba culture; however, these are radically subverted so that old values and assumptions are completely turned upside down and new insights gained.

Obileye, Yomi Actor, Nigeria. Yomi Obileye has been a very long standing member of Wole SOYINKA's Orisun Theatre along with other notable Nigerian actors such as Wale OGUNYEMI, Yewande Johnson, Tunji OYELANA and Segun SOFOWOTE. He has featured consistently in Soyinka's productions, including his most recent, *The Beatification of Area Boy*, which premiered at the West Yorkshire Playhouse on October 25, 1995. Significant roles in the theatre include his triple roles of Vandor/MC/Mother of the Day in *Area Boy*, and doubling up as Director of Security and Wing Commander in *From Zia with Love* (another Soyinka play) which premiered in Sienna, Italy in 1992. Other stage roles include the memorable performance with Ogunyemi and Femi Johnson in the opera *The Love Potion* (1967), as Boyfriend in *Childe Internationale* (written and directed by Soyinka, opposite Ogunyemi's Politician and Bettie OKOTIE's Wife, 1965). A versatile performer who can move comfortably between the tragic and the comic modes, he has appeared in many other roles and is well-respected as one of the leading actors of the Nigerian stage.

Oduneye, Bayo Director, Nigeria. Bayo Oduneye worked as a theatre technician at the School Drama at Ibadan University before going on to study theatre arts in the USA. He has been actively involved in directing for the stage and for film, serving as director of the Nigerian Film Corporation. One of his memorable productions was his *Hassan* for the Ibadan Theatre on Wheels in 1972, which featured Wale OGUNYEMI in the title role of Hassan. Oduneye's style of directing is influenced by his belief that acting is a physically demanding craft, and he therefore drills his actors the way a physical training instructor would in order to help them to achieve and maintain suppleness, flexibility and a strength of body needed to carry their roles through a punishing schedule of performances.

Özakman, Turgut (1930–) Dramatist, Turkey. Özakman attended the Institute of Theatre Studies at the University of Köln, Germany. On his return to Turkey he worked in many positions related to the theatre, including as dramaturge at the Ankara State Theatre and as the head of the Ankara Radio Performance Broadcasting Department. At Turkish Radio – Television Organisation (TRT), he institutionalized radio broadcasting to train the first broadcasting generation (1962–9). Between 1983–7 he became the general director of the Turkish State Theatres. Currently, he is an instructor at the Theatre Department of the Faculty of Letters, University of Ankara. He wrote his first play, *Masum Katiller* (*The Innocent Murderers*) in 1947. Since then he has written numerous plays, including *Pembe Evin Kaderi* (*The Fate of the Pink House*, 1951), *Güneşte On Kişi* (*Ten People on the Sun*, 1955), *Tufan* (*Deluge*, 1957), *Duvarların Ötesi* (*Beyond the Walls*, 1958), *Komsularımız* (*Our Neighbours*, 1967) and *Deliler* (*The Lunatics*, 1987). He explores Turkish issues, showing that world issues are not any different from those at home.

Ogunsola, Isola Actor-manager, Nigeria. Isola Ogunsola is one of those breed of actor-managers that make up the popular Yoruba Travelling theatre and operatic tradition: others are the late Hubert Ogunde, Moses Olaiya ADEJUMO (Baba Sala), Oyin ADEJOBI and Ade AFOLAYAN. Ogunsola represents a good example of a successful marriage between the Nigerian literary tradition and the Yoruba operatic tradition. His theatre company, which he controls totally – he is producer, director, chief drummer and theatre manager – has successfully adapted novels and several set literature texts for secondary schools for the stage. The most successful is the

adaptation for television of *Aja lo l'eru*, a Yoruba novel by Oladejo Okediji. His blend of popular and literary traditions and techniques has ensured that his productions are well attended: 14,000 spectators watched his *Efunsetan Aniwura* at the Liberty Stadium in Ibadan.

Ogunyemi, Wale (1939–) Actor, director, dramatist and designer, Nigeria. Trained as a typist, Ogunyemi received informal training in traditional arts and culture, and attended a few theatre training workshops. He was a pioneer member of the University of Ibadan School of Drama Acting Company, and through his membership of Wole SOYINKA's Orisun Theatre he became fully integrated into theatrical professionalism, research and writing. Apart from his playwriting, Ogunyemi has worked as director, stage manager, technical director, set and costume designer, choreographer, musician and theatre manager. However, his main forte is in the area of acting/performance for stage, radio, television and film, in both English and his native Yoruba. Major roles include the title role in *Hassan* (1972, directed by Bayo ODUNEYE), Man in *Sizwe Bansi is Dead* (1976, by Athol Fugard, John KANI and Winston NTSHONA, with Jimi SOLANKE as Buntu/Styles), Goyi in Soyinka's *Madmen and Specialists* and Bottom in *A Midsummer Night's Dream*. His published plays include *The Vow*, *Obaluaye*, *Langbodo* (directed by Dapo ADELUGBA for FESTAC 77), *Partners in Business*, *Kiriji* and *Ijaye War*.

Oh Hyun-Kyung (1936–) Actor and director, Korea. Oh graduated from Yonsei University and trained at the Drama Centre (later the Seoul Institute of Arts). He created a new concept in Korean theatre by mixing two contrasting elements, intellectual and comic. His rather slapstick acting style made him the most popular supporting actor in the Korean theatre. His major performances were as the Officer in *Je Sipchil Poro Sooyongso* (*The 17th Concentration Camp*, 1959), Juno in O'Casey's *Juno and the Paycock* (1960), Willy Loman in Arthur MILLER's *Death of a Salesman* (1962), the title role in *Heo-Saengjeon* (*The Story of Heo-Saeng*, 1966), the title role in Oh Young-Jin's *Maengjinsadak Gyeongsa* (*Maeng's Family's Happy Day*), Joo-Mong in LEE Gung-Sam's *Ilyoileui Boolcheonggaek* (*The Unwelcome Visitor on Sunday*, 1974), Father in LEE Gang-Baek's *Bomnal* (*One Spring Day*, 1984) and Dae-Boo in Lee Gun-Sam's *Makchatan Donggi Dong-chang* (*The Enemies Meet on the Last Train*, 1991). Since the late 1960s, Oh has gained major acclaim for his television productions and films. In 1996, Oh made his debut as a director with YOUN Dai-Sung's *Neodo Meokgo Moolreonara* (*Drink It and Go Away*).

Oh Oun-Hee (1965–) Dramatist, Korea. Oh studied Chinese Literature at Pusan University, Pusan, Korea and trained at the Korea Playwrighting Workshop. She is mainly known for her musical scripts, *Dongsoongdong Yeonga* (*Love Song on Dongsoong-Dong*, 1993), *Beondegi* (*Chrysalis*, 1994), *Gyeolhon Ilgi* (*Married Life*, 1994), *Byeolgeotdo Aningeosi* (*Nothing Special!*, 1996) and *Jisangeseo Boorunun Majimak Norae* (*The Last Song from the Earth*, 1997), all for the Maekto Theatre Company. Oh also wrote *Sarangun Birul Tago* (*Rainbow* (1995) and *Show Comedy* (1996) for the Seoul Musical Company. She developed her themes from contemporary Korean life, which she feels is the most effective way to appeal to a Korean audience.

Oh Tae-Seok (1940–) Dramatist and director, Korea. In his early days, Oh was known as a dramatist of the Korea style of absurd drama, writing and directing *Hwanjeolgi* (*Turning Point of the Season*, 1968) and *Yoodayeo Dalgi Woolgijeone* (*Before a Rooster Crows, Judas*, 1969). Since the 1970s, he has written experi-

mental performances such as *Choboon* (*Grass Tomb*, 1973), *Tae* (*The Navel Cord*, 1974) and *Choonpoongeui Cheo* (*Choon-Poong's Wife*, 1976). These are examples of the theatricality of the primitive human being. Influenced by seeing East European theatre in New York in 1979, Oh discovered the theatrical power of traditional Korean performances. He organized Oh's Division, later the Mokhwa Theatre Company, in order to realize his intercultural acting methods. He wrote and directed several masterpieces such as *Sachoogi* (*Adult at Puberty*, 1979 with JANG Min-Ho in the cast), *Jajeongeo* (*Bicycle*, 1983, revived in 1986), *Boojayoochin* (*The Struggle between the King and the Crown Prince as Father and Son*, 1987), *Simcheonginun Wae Indangsooe Doobeon Momul Deonjeotnunga?* (*Why did Shimcheong Throw Herself into the Indangsoo Sea twice?*, 1990), *Doraji* (*Ballon Flower*, 1992), *Baekmagang Dalbame* (*Moonlight of the River Baekma*, 1993) and *Cheonnyeoneui Sooin* (*A Prisoner for Thousands of Years*, 1998). In 1994, at a specially organized Theatre Festival in Seoul dedicated to Oh, his plays were presented over a two-month period.

Oida Yoshi (1933–) Actor and director, Japan. Oida first became a member of the Bungaku-za Theatre Company and moved to the Shiki Theatre Company. Whilst he had training in modern Japanese theatre, he studied nô, kyôgen, gidayû and kabuki dance. He then was invited to join Peter BROOK's International Centre for Theatre Research in 1968. He has acted in most of Brook's productions, including *The Tempest* (1968), *The Ik* (1975), *The Conference of Birds* (1979), *The Mahabharata* (1985) and *The Man Who* (1994). His recent directing credits are Brian FRIEL's *Molly Sweeny* in Holland and Mishima's *Hanjo* in Berlin in 1997. In the latter he experimented with theatrical variation in three styles of nô, kyôgen and shingeki or modern theatre. Oida's experiences in both Japanese and international theatre contribute to the establishment of the depth and the distinctiveness in his performances.

Oka, Ida Bagus (1957–) Designer, Indonesia. From a famous family of dancers (his grandfather was Ida Bagus Gagelug, a legendary performer in the early part of this century), Oka took a different path and began carving in his early teens. He worked for about four years under the tutelage of his uncle, the highly respected sculptor Tilem, before he struck out on his own. Always an innovator, he was the first of the Balinese woodcarvers to make African-style masks and has explored a number of other genres. However, Oka has never been satisfied to simply copy the work of others, but uses existing styles as inspiration for his own creations. He has created original designs for a number of theatre and dance companies throughout the world and the scope of his work is considerable. For example, for the Javanese choreographer Sardono, he created masks based on traditional Indonesian and Native American models, but he has also created original designs for TOM theatre of Japan's production of *The Magic Flute*. He has designed and made masks for companies in Europe and North and South America and still occasionally makes traditional Topeng masks for performers in Bali.

Okotie, Betty Actor and director, Nigeria. Betty Okotie (now Mrs Edewor) was one of the original members of the Orisun Theatre Company founded by Wole SOYINKA and Bola Ige. She has featured significantly and very memorably in many of Soyinka plays. Her major roles include the fine performance as Sidi in Soyinka's 1964 production of *The Lion and the Jewel*; she was Wife in *Childe Internationale* opposite other Orisun players such Wale OGUNYEMI (Politician), and Yomi OBILEYE (Boyfriend) in 1965; she played Segi in the 1965 production of *Kongi's*

Harvest with Dapo ADELUGBA as Daodu; and she played the chatterbox Amope in a 1966 production of *The Trials of Brother Jero* with Ogunyemi as Chume. She has since directed or choreographed other productions including Samuel Beckett's *Act Without Words* (1967) in which Ogunyemi and other Orisun players took part.

Olinger, Marc (1946–) Actor and director, Luxembourg. Olinger graduated from the Sorbonne in Paris with a Ph.D. in philosophy and French literature and received his grounding in theatre at the Cours René Simon (Paris), at the Conservatoire de Luxembourg and as the assistant to a number of productions in Paris. Together with Claudine PELLETIER, he founded the Théâtre Ouvert Luxembourg for which he acted in and directed some fifty productions from 1973–85. That year he assumed artistic directorship of the Théâtre des Capucins, the only producing house to be entirely funded by the Luxembourg city council, where he regularly stages plays, both in the classical and the contemporary repertory. He also appeared in many movies and directed a number of films for television.

Omar, Nasser (1961–) Actor and dramatist, Jordan. Omar was a member of the University Theatre Troupe, of Al-Fawanees Theatre Troupe, and founder of the Experimental Mawal Theatre Troupe. In addition to acting on stage and for television, he has written his own plays and performed in them, such as *Forbidden to Laugh*, *Insane Thoughts from Hamlet's Diary* and *And the Man Died*. He has been described as an actor who perpetually analyses and interprets difficult parts from a unique artistic vision always shocking, fresh and controversial, for example as Vladimir in Beckett's *Waiting for Godot*. Other appearances include HUSSEINI's *Lights of Jericho*. He gets involved emotionally in the roles he plays to the extent that they become the only truth for him, making theatre rather a dangerous game.

Omotoso, Kole (1943–) Dramatist and actor, Nigeria. Omotoso is one of the generation of Nigerian dramatists with a committed socialist ideology and desire to evolve a revolutionary aesthetic for the theatre, capable of articulating and championing the views of the working classes and peasants. His plays include the satiric and absurdist *The Curse* (1976), in which he explores the use and abuse of power, and *Shadows in the Horizon* (1977). His theatre is about his Nigerian society suffering under the weight of a decadent and selfish political elite. His sense of shock and disappointment at the failure of African political systems to deliver good government and a more egalitarian society is always evident in his work. Omotoso was also a member of the production team for the Ife premiere of Wole SOYINKA's *Requiem for a Futurologist* with a cast that included Jimi SOLANKE in role of Rev. Godspeak in 1983.

Ôno Kazuo (1906–) Butoh dancer, Japan. After graduation from Nihon Taiiku (Physical Education) University, he studied modern dance with Baku Ishii and Takaya Eguchi, who had studied dance in Germany with Mary Wigman. His first performances were *Kinjiki* (*Forbidden Colours*), *Tango* and *Rilke-Bodaiju* (*Rilke and a Linden Tree*) in 1949. His collaboration with Tatsumi Hjikata (1928–86) began in 1961 when he participated in the Hijikata Tatsumi Dance Experience. *Bara Iro Dance* (*Rose Colour Dance*, 1965), and *Anma* (*The Masseur*, 1963) are the works with Hijikata. Their new dance movement was soon named ankoku butoh (dance of the darkness), a postmodernist Japanese dance form free from the constraints of both Western-style modern dance and traditional Japanese dance. It is a provocative form of social criticism and strongly influenced the *angura* (underground) theatre movement in the

1960s. Ôno amazed the dance world by his solo performance of *La Argentina Sho* (*Celebrating la Argentina*, 1977) when he was seventy-one. The dance created an extraordinary situation in which Argentina, the dead, and Ôno, the living, communicated with each other through love. Further representative dances are *Watashi no Okasan* (*My Mother*, 1981) and *Suiren* (*Waterlilies*, 1987).

Onwueme, Tess (1955–) Dramatist, Nigeria. With Ama Ata AIDOO, Micere MUGO, Rose MBOWA and Nicole WERE-WERE-LIKING, Onwueme is among the few African women dramatists. Her plays are usually characterized by bold experiments with dramatic form, language and theatre technique. Notable among her published works are *A Hen Too Soon* (1983), *The Broken Calabash* (1984), her prize-winning *Desert Encroaches* (1985), *The Reign of Wazobia* (1988), *Legacies* (1988) and *Cattle Egret Versus Nama* (1989). Her themes and style range from the realistic domestic style of the earlier plays to the linguistically audacious and ambitious allegorical style of *Ban Empty Barn* and the ferocious satirical mode of *Cattle Egret Versus Nama*. Onwueme is a playwright with a highly politicized consciousness and sensibility who uses her theatre to engage with the socio-political and economic realities of her Nigerian society.

Orsini, Umberto (1934–) Actor, Italy. Umberto Orsini started working in the theatre with Giorgio De Lullo, Rossella FALK, Anna Maria GUARNIERI and Romolo Valli at the Compagnia dei Giovani in the late 1950s. A charismatic and versatile actor, Orsini has time and again enchanted Italian audiences in performances such as Harold PINTER's *Old Times* (1973), directed by Luchino Visconti, Schiller's *Die Räuber* (*The Robbers*, 1981), Ben Jonson's *Volpone* (1987) and Luigi Pirandello's *Il gioco delle parti* (*The Game of Roles*, 1996) directed by

Gabriele LAVIA. Orsini, who is also a television and film actor, rose to international fame in the late 1960s by appearing in films such as Luchino Visconti's *La caduta degli dei* (*The Damned*, 1969), Sergio Sollima's *Città violenta* (*Violent City*, 1970) and *La famiglia* (*The Family*, 1970). Whether on stage or on the screen, Orsini has been a reliable and yet at the same time innovative and eclectic interpreter of strong lead roles.

Ortiz, Rafael (1938–) Puppeteer, educator, dramatist and director, Puerto Rico. Rafael Ortiz is a key figure in the educational experiences of many of Puerto Rico's theatre professionals. After earning a BSc in pedagogy (University of Puerto Rico, 1960), he attended the University of Miami before returning to Puerto Rico to finish his MA in drama and education in 1972. He supervised the Theatre Program of the Department of Public Instruction from 1968–82 and served as that agency's executive director from 1982–6, after which he offered courses in puppetry at the University of Puerto Rico. Ortiz wrote several political satires in the late 1970s before founding the award-winning puppetry company El mundo de los Muñecos (Puppet World) in 1978, around which most of his present activities revolve. His adaptations of children's classics as well as his original folkloric material are renowned for their strong sense of cultural identity. He currently produces both radio and television programmes, and has participated with the Puppetry in Practice Program at Brooklyn College.

Oskarson, Peter (1951–) Director, actor, Sweden. He trained as an actor at the State Drama School in Stockholm, and has been artistic director of the Folkteatern Gaevleborg (1982–90 and again from 1997), artistic director for the Helsingegerden foundation for artistic study and research (1990–), and artistic director of Orion theatre, Stockholm (1993–). A member of the Swedish Theatre Academy

since 1994 and an honorary member of the Chinese Peking Opera Association, Oskarson has directed opera at Drottningholm Theatre as well as Stockholm, Malmoe, Stuttgart and Bonn. He has taught at the theatre high schools in Stockholm, Gothenburg and Malmoe. Some of his productions for the theatre include *A Midsummer Night's Dream*, *Hamlet*, *King Lear*, Brecht's *Leben des Galilei* (*Life of Galileo*) and *Der Gute Mensch von Sezuan* (*The Good Person of Sezuan*), Strindberg's *Ett Drömspel* (*A Dream Play*) and *Tri sestry* (*Three Sisters*) by Chekhov.

Osofisan, Babafemi Adeyemi (1946–) Dramatist, actor and director, Nigeria. With Bode SOWANDE, Olu OBAFEMI, Tunde FATUNDE and Kole OMOTOSO, he belongs to the second generation of Nigerian writers and critics who advocate a more radical role for the theatre in direct opposition to the perceived traditionalist aesthetics of Wole SOYINKA, John Pepper CLARK-BEKEDEREMO and the early Ola ROTIMI. Their works strive to be easily accessible to their audiences and directly relevant to the social and political conditions of Africa. Osofisan's plays are often open-ended, calling upon the audience to involve itself in the action, take sides and in some cases offer resolutions to the dilemmas posed in them. His theatre borrows directly from his Yoruba folk traditions, but subjects them to creative radicalization and interrogation. He has written close to twenty plays, including *A Restless Run of Locusts* (1975), *Red is the Freedom Road* (1982), *The Oriki of a Grasshopper* (1986) and *Another Raft* (1990).

Ôta Shôgo (1939–) Dramatist and director, Japan. Ôta first joined Hakken no Kai (the Discovery Theatre Company), and then became a founder member of Tenkei Gekijô (the Tenkei Theatre Company) in 1968, where he continued his major theatrical work until the company was dissolved in 1988. His *Komachi Fûden (A Man)*, was based on a nô play and used the nô stage. His trilogy of plays without dialogues – *Mizu no Eki (The Water Station)* in 1981, *Chi no Eki (The Earth Station)* in 1985 and *Kaze no Eki (The Wind Station)* in 1986 – have been performed in Japan, Europe and the USA. *The Water Station* was performed as part of the New York International Festival of Arts in 1988. *Sarachi (Vacant Lot,* 1992) has been performed both in Japan and overseas. Óta's main interest lies in exploring the power of language and that of silence in relation to the presence of actors' bodies. His theatrical concept is close to the idea of the anti-theatre.

Outinen, Kati Anna Katriina (1961–) Actor, Finland. Kati Outinen was only a teenager when her talent was recognized in school drama clubs. Soon she got her first film role, and after that trained at the Theatre Acdemy of Finland. Since 1994 she has worked in theatre KOM, appearing mainly in new Finnish drama, but also as Irina in Chekhov's *Tri sestry (Three Sisters)*, Girl in *Roberto Zucco* by Koltès, and Kyllikki in KYLÄTASKU's *Runar ja Kyllikki (Runar and Kyllikki)* at the Helsinki City Theatre in 1996. In addition, Outinen has starred in many films by Aki Kaurismäki. She excels in portraying fragile characters, deprived yet struggling in hard circumstances. The freezingly cruel Ina Terre in Oliver Bukowski's *Bis Denver* in Ryhmäteatteri (1999) is one example of her strong stylized acting. In addition, she has appeard in musicals (*West Side Story*) and music comedies.

Ouzounian, Richard (1950–) Director and dramatist, Canada. Ouzounian was brought up in New York and was theatre resident at Simon Fraser University. Here he directed many shows, straight theatre, musicals and his own plays. From 1978 onwards he has been (artistic) director of several theatres, including Festival Len-noxville (1978–80) and the Manitoba Theatre Centre (1980–84), where he developed a reputation for extravagant productions. In 1999, the Stratford Festival presented a musical version of *Dracula*, for which Ouzounian wrote the book and lyrics.

Owusu, Martin (1943–) Dramatist and actor, Ghana. Owusu's debt to his rich Ghanaian tradition includes the *anansesegoro* storytelling techniques of his *The Story Ananse Told*. He likes experimenting with African traditional forms of song, dance, folklore and myth in order to make these forms relevant to contemporary realities. His major plays include *The Sudden Return, The Mightier Sword, The Pot of Okro Soup, Anane* and *A Bird Called 'Go-Back-for-the-Answer'*. Among Owusu's acting credits is the major role of Fenyinka in a production of Joe de Graft's *Through a Film Darkly.*

Oyelana, Tunji Actor, Nigeria. Oyelana learned his acting skills through his membership of Wole SOYINKA's 1960 Masks and later Orisun Theatre. He has remained a key figure in many of Soyinka's productions, including acting and technical work in the premiere of *The Beatification of Area Boy* at the West Yorkshire Playhouse in 1995. Other roles include Uncle Dima Licasi alongside Wale OGUNYEMI's Friend Pe in Pirandello's *The Jar,* directed by Soyinka in 1970, and the triple role of Minister/Sebe/Second Trusty in *From Zia With Love* (Sienna, Italy in 1992, written and directed by Soyinka, with notable Orisun old hands such as Yomi OBILEYE, Ogunyemi, Segun SOFOWOTE and Yewande Johnson). Oyelana has contributed immensely to the Nigerian stage over the past three and a half decades. Like Ogunyemi, he can move quite easily between the comic and the tragic and still keep control of his audience. He also was a member of the team for the Ibadan premiere of Femi

OSOFISAN's *Midnight Hotel* in 1982, which included Sunmbo MARINHO.

Oyono-Mbia, Guillaume (1939–) Dramatist, Cameroon. Oyono-Mbia is a bilingual playwright working in French and English, whose plays have been widely produced in Cameroon. *Until Further Notice* and *Our Daughter will not Get Married* won drama competitions in England and France, respectively. He is, however, still best known for his very popular 'village comedy' *Three Suitors...One Husband* (1964). His fourth play, *His Excellency's Special Train* appeared in 1978. The central concern of most of Mbia's works is the disruptive influence of modernity on traditional values, and this he explores in a dramatic mode that is essentially comic. His strength as a dramatist is his ability to manipulate language, whether French or English, to achieve comic effect. He also exploits the inherent comic possibilities of stock characterization, slapstick, the occasional farce and mime for hilarious dramatic entertainment.

P

Padrissa, Carlos (1959–) Director, Spain. Padrissa is founder member of La Fura dels Baus, the influential Catalan theatre company whose interdisciplinary approach to performance has effectively juggled a recuperation of past cultural traditions and an innovative reforging of new artistic discourses. Padrissa played a seminal role in creating the provocative dissonant spectacles which characterize La Fura's performance aesthetic. With *Accions* (*Actions*, 1983), *SuzioSuz* (1985) and *Tier mon* (1988), all widely toured throughout Western Europe, the company's visceral energy, acrobatic skills, reinvention of performer–audience boundaries and appropriation of urban spaces for their site-specific performances have been in clear evidence. During the 1990s Padrissa and fellow *furero* Alex Ollé have diversified the company's interests, moving into musical theatre and opera where their productions of Manuel de Falla's *Atlándida* (1996) and Debussy's *Martyrdom of Saint Sebastian* (1997) have been much admired for their audacity and imaginative energy. Their version of Faust, *F@ust, Version 3.0* (1998) re-envisaged Goethe's morality play for the technological age with an array of images taken from media, advertising and the internet, and marked the company's adoption of text-based work for their strongly visual projects.

Paimo, Lere Actor-manager, Nigeria. Paimo began his theatre apprenticeship as a member of the well-known and successful Duro Ladipo Theatre Company. There he popularized the role of Iku in *Eda*, a piece inspired by Ulli Beier's adaptation of a fifteenth-century version of *Everyman*. Paimo brought a comic dimension to the often serious theatre of Ladipo: his wit endears Paimo to his audiences, and it was he who introduced comedy into the Yoruba Travelling Theatre tradition. He formed his own theatre company in 1971. One of his notable productions is *Gbangba d'Ekun.*

Pannikar, Kavalam Narayana (1928–) Director and dramatist, India. Pannikar is one of the few directors who promotes Sanskrit theatre without losing sight of developments in contemporary world theatre. Especially in productions of the plays of Bhasa, he fuses modern interpretation with the traditional theatre form of Kutiyattam and the martial art of Kalari. Founder of the Thiruvarangu theatre group, Pannikar organized the Bhasa Mahotasavam festival in 1987, 1988 and 1993, where the Sanskrit plays of Bhasa were performed by different groups; he now runs Sopanam Theatre Institute in Trivandrum (Thiruvananthapuram). He has written nineteen plays in Malayalam, some of which have become popular all over the world. They include *Ottayan*

(*The Lone Tusker*), *Karimkutty*, *Koyoma* and *Arani*, a Malayalam version of Aeschylus' *Prometheus Bound*. Among the productions he has directed are *Dootavakyam*, *Urubhangam* and *Sopanavasavadattam*. For him, the processes of transformation from actor to character and from character to actor are rituals.

Park Dong-Woo (1962–) Designer, Korea. Park trained at The School of Design, Hong-Ik University. Since 1987, Park has achieved fame as 'the designer of a new generation' for his stage design for *Goomhanul* (*The Heaven in a Dream*, 1987, directed by KIM Suk-Man for the Korean National Theatre), Jeong Bok-Gun's *Silbimyeong* (*Lost Epitaph*, 1989), *Bongsoonga Gotmool* (*Touch Me Not Manicure*, 1991), *A Day in the Life of a Chinaman Living in New York* (1991), KIM Kwang-Lim's *Jip* (*House*, 1994), and *Saeduldo Sesangul Tunungoona* (*Even the Birds are Leaving*, 1997, directed by Kim Suk-Man), in which he attempted to harmonize contemporary Western and Eastern culture. Since 1995, Park has worked for the Muchon Theatre Company of ARA Kim. Park designed stages using metallic materials, which he saw as the equivalent of the mental imbalance of the contemporary human being, in Jang Jeong-Il's *Oedipuswaeui Yeohaeng* (*The Journey with Oedipus*, 1995), Peter SHAFFER's *Equus* (1997) and LEE Kang-Baek's *Naema* (1998).

Park Jung-Ja (1942–) Actor, Korea. Park studied at Ewha Women's University, trained with the Jayoo Theatre Group and since the 1960s has worked as a voice actor in several radio dramas. In the theatre, she played Ondal's mother in CHOI In-Hoon's *Eodiseo Mooeosi Doieo Dasi Mannarya* (*When, Where to Meet Again as What*, 1970), and performed in Ionesco's *La cantatrice chauve* (*The Bald Soprano*), in *Baekyangseomeui Yokmang* (*Desire of the Baekyang Islanders*), played the mother of the bridegroom in Lorca's

Bodas de sangre (*Blood Wedding*), the title role in Marsha NORMAN's *'night Mother*, 1989), in *Nae Sarang Hiroshima* (*My Love Hiroshima*) and the title roles in *Moonyeodo* (*A Portrait of a Shaman*, 1994) and *Gu Yeoja Eokcheok Eomeom* (*That Woman Mother Courage*, 1997, written and directed by Kim Jeong-Ok). Park is known as a most powerful and charismatic actor, who can control the whole stage with her immense voice and energy.

Parker, Lynne (1961–) Director, Ireland. As co-founder (in 1984) and artistic director of arguably Ireland's most successful independent touring company, the Rough Magic Theatre Company, she has produced a repertoire of classical European as well as premières of new Irish plays with the company. The Rough Magic Theatre Company is considered to be the precursor of a 'new wave' in Irish theatre with an emphasis on 'mise-enscène' and high production values. Parker's strong, bold, visual style has earned her a large and young following. She has also directed outside the company, at the Almeida and Bush theatres in London and the Abbey and Gate theatres in Dublin. Notable productions include Brendan Kennelly's version of Euripedes's *Troades* (*The Trojan Woman*, 1993) and Synge's *The Playboy of the Western World* (1994). In 1995 she directed a sensitively naturalistic production of *Pentecost* by her late uncle Stewart Parker.

Parks, Suzan-Lori (1963–) Dramatist, USA. Parks trained at the Drama Studio in London and has held various teaching positions at American universities, as well as grants from the National Endowment for the Arts and the Rockefeller Foundation. Language provides the subject and theme of her plays, which do not have stage directions. They include *Imperceptible Mutabilities in the Third Kingdom* (1989), *The Sinner's Place* (1984) and *Devotees in the Garden of Love*. She seized upon the assassination of Abraham Lincoln for *The American Play* (1993), using a traditional music structure of theme and variation as her pattern of plot development.

Parthasarathy, Renganathan (1930–) Dramatist, India. A major dramatist in Tamil, Parthasarathy questioned some of the values of Tamil Pandits through his plays and novels. His *Nandan Kathai* (*The Story of Nandan*), a trendsetter for plays dealing with the problems of 'scheduled caste' (Dalit) communities, was considered a play that questioned not only the existing forms of Tamil theatre, but also the socio-political situation in Tamilnadu. Similarly, his *Kongai Thee*, an adaptation from Elango's *Silappathikaram* (*The Ankle Bracelet*), is a bold attempt at portrayal of the two female protagonists of the Tamil epic, Kannagai and Madhavi, from a psychological point of view. His *Eruthi Attam* is an adaptation of Shakespeare's *King Lear* after the fashion of Beckett's *Endgame*. His plays have been produced by major directors like RAMA-NUJAM and RAMASWAMY. He is a winner of the Sahitya Academy Award, the highest literary award in the country.

Pasqual, Lluís (1951–) Director and actor, Spain. Pasqual worked first as an actor and then as a director with La Tartana. During the 1970s he taught at the Institut del Teatre and the Escola de Teatre de Sants where he directed his first major production, *La setmana tragica* (*The Tragc Week*), devised in collaboration with the dramaturg Guillem Jordi Graells and the designer Fabià Puigserver. With Puigserver and Pere Planella, he founded the Teatre Lliure in 1976. Their inaugural production, *Cami de nit 1854* (*Path of Night 1854*, 1976) redefined political theatre in the aftermath of the Franco regime. After working at the National Theatre of Warsaw and Milan's Piccolo Theatre with Strehler in the late 1970s, Pasqual returned to Barcelona where,

with Puigserver as designer, his stylish, actor-centred Catalan language productions of European classics gained him wide admiration and in 1983 the artistic directorship of Madrid's Centro Dramático Nacional, where he remained until 1989. Here and subsequently at the Odéon Théâtre de l'Europe, where he succeeded Strehler in 1990, Pasqual realized much lauded productions of rarely staged Spanish plays. He succeeded actor Lluís HOMAR as artistic director of the Teatre Lliure in 1998. Pasqual also works regularly in opera.

Pathak, Dina (1923–) Actor, India. Pathak trained under Gurus Shanti Bardhan and Rasiklal Parik. She was a founder member of IPTA (Indian People's Theatre Association), Bombay and performed in all the major productions of IPTA. Major roles include Nora in Ibsen's *Et Dukkehjem* (*A Doll's House*, in Gujarati), and Padmini in Girish KARNAD's *Hayavadana* (in Hindi); she is especially known for her outstanding performance in *Mena Gujari*, an operatic play directed by Parik. She has been promoting the traditional Bhavai, a folk form of Gujarat, appeared in *Abhiman*, a popular play in the Bhavai form, and played the role of Puck in a production of *A Midsummer Night's Dream* in the Bhavai style. A veteran actor who has seen the dawn of independence and fervent nationalism, she is still active today, both on stage and in film.

Patroni Griffi, Giuseppe (1921–) Director and dramatist, Italy. Known internationally for the artistic collaboration with film directors Francesco Rosi, Alberto Lattuada and Valerio Zurlini, Giuseppe Patroni Griffi made his directorial debut in the theatre in 1962 with his *Il mare* (*The Sea*) in which he explored dramatic form in a cinematic way. In his work, Patroni Griffi echoes themes of contemporary Italian society in a mixture of romanticism and crude realism which is particularly manifest in his representation of the middle classes. His major pieces are *D'amore si muore* (*One Can Die for Love*, 1958), *Anima nera* (*Black Soul*, 1960), *In memoria di una signora amica* (*In Memory of a Lady Friend*, 1963), *Metti una sera a cena* (*Someone is Coming to Dinner*, 1967) and *Prima del silenzio* (*Before Silence*, 1982). Patroni Griffi has also directed a number of memorable films such as *Tis a Pity She's a Whore* (1973) with Charlotte Rampling, *The Driver's Seat* (1975) with Elizabeth Taylor and Andy Warhol, and *Divine Nymph* (1979) with Marcello Mastroianni.

Paulin, Eva (1955–) Designer and director, Luxembourg. A graduate in Latin and Oriental studies from the University of Graz, the Austrian-born Paulin studied stage design at the Hochschule für Musik und Darstellende Kunst. Since 1990, she has worked as a designer and director in Luxembourg at the festival of Steinfort, at the Kasemattentheater and at the Théâtre des Capucins. Her revival of André Duschcher's vaudeville comedy *D'Vilia Fina* (*Villa Fina*, 1995, Festival of Steinfort) was admired for the speed and precision of delivery. She also collaborates closely with Jean-Paul MAES, and directed and designed his play *Péiténg* (*Pétange*, 1995, Théâtre d'Esch), successfully combining the modern tone of the play with elements of Greek tragedy. Other unusual plays produced under her directorship are Marlene Steeruwitz's *Waikiki Beach* and Tankred DORST's *Ich Feuerbach* (*I Feuerbach*, both 1993, Kasemattentheater), Oliver Czeslik's *Rattenmenschen* (*Rat People*, 1996, Festival of Steinfort), and the trilingual epic *Hexensabbat* (*Witches' Sabbath*) by Maes, Pierre Pelot and Peter Höner (1995 Luxembourg European Cultural City). These have established Paulin as one of the country's most consistent and original theatre artists.

Pedrero, Paloma (1957–) Actor, dramatist and director, Spain. Pedrero studied theatre arts in Madrid and became strongly associated with the independent theatre movement of the 1980s, which challenged the dominant traditions of the mainstream stage through a presentation of intimate, limited cast, small-scale productions with subject matters of direct relevance to a new generation of Spaniards. Major credits include *En el corazón del teatro* (*In the Heart of the Theatre*, 1983) and Lorca's *La casa de Bernarda Alba* (*The House of Bernarda Alba*, 1982). She gained widespread acclaim for her first published play, *La llamada de Lauren* (*Lauren's Call*, 1985), in which she also performed. Her most popular works include *El color de agosto* (*The Colour of August*, 1988) and *Invierno de luna alegre* (*Winter of Happy Moon*, 1989), witty, idiomatic, metatheatrical plays which skilfully deconstruct the pains, fears and intricacies of contemporary relationships. Over the past five years Pedrero has increasingly directed her own work. Her recent plays include *Una estrella* (*First Star*), which opened in 1998 at Murcia's Teatro Romea and is reminiscent of much of her writing in its focus on gender politics, the fractured nature of identity and the psychological legacy of family ghosts. A number of her poems have been published in the daily newspaper *ABC*.

Pedro Leal, Odile (1964–) Actor, director and dramatist, France and Guyane. A childhood active in the performing arts led Pedro Leal to professional training at the Conservatoire National and a degree in applied languages from the University of Bordeaux, with her professional debut in the part of Vertu in Genet's *Les nègres* (*The Blacks*, 1989). After several parts for radio, television and film, she played her first stage lead as Camille in Debauche's *Flandrin-Acteur* (1993), gaining professional confidence under MESGUICH's direction. Citing several small parts in U'Tamsi's *Le Destin Glorieux du Maréchal Nnikon Nniku* (*The Glorious Fate of Field Marshal Nnikon Nniku* 1989, Paris) and the role of Elisa Valéry in Depestre's *Mât de Cocagne* (*Greasy Pole*, 1995) as deepening her sense of black identity, her *La Chanson de Philibert ou les Gens Simples* (*Philibert's Song or The Simple Folk*, 1996), is set in Guyane and turns on an interracial love affair. In 1997, she completed her doctorate in theatre studies from the Sorbonne. Her production of STEPHENSON's controversial *D'chmbo, la dernière surprise de l'amour* (*D'chimbo, Love's Last Surprise*) was included in the TOMA programme at Avignon in 1998 before touring in the Caribbean.

Pelletier Claudine (1942–) Actor and director, Luxembourg. The French-born actor Pelletier completed her studies of dramatic arts, among others, at the Cours René Simon in Paris with the Prix François Perier. She toured extensively with Gabrielle Robinne of the Comédie Française and appeared at the festivals of Guérande and Loches. In 1970, she settled in Luxembourg where, as well as working in television, she founded the Théâtre Ouvert Luxembourg with Marc OLINGER. With the company she appeared in many productions, in classical and contemporary repertory, mostly playing leading roles. From 1972–6, Pelletier held formation classes for aspiring actors at the TOL. Her directorial work, at the TOL and Théâtre des Capucins, was equally well received, particularly Molière's *Dom Juan*, Haim's *La peau d'un fruit* (*The Skin of a Fruit*) and Feyder's *Emballage perdu* (*Non-returnable Packaging*). Since 1989, she has taught dramatic arts at the Conservatoire d'Esch.

Pellicena, José Lluis (1933–) Actor, Spain. Pellicena abandoned his medical studies to join the repertory Lope de Vega theatre company, specializing in classical Spanish plays. In 1966 he moved to the Compañia de Teatro Español where he remained until 1971, playing central roles in classics like José Zorilla's *Don Juan Tenorio* (1969). He was a key member of Nuria

ESPERT's company for Víctor García's ground-breaking production of García Lorca's *Yerma* (1971), remaining with it until 1974 following extensive tours in Europe and the Americas. During the 1980s and 1990s Pellicena has remained a seminal performer within the established theatre network, enjoying major roles in Lluís PASQUAL's staging of Marlowe/Brecht's *Edward II* in 1983, Adolfo MARSILLACH's lively production of Lope de Vega's *Los locos de Valencia* (*The Fools of Valencia*, 1986) and José Carlos PLAZA's epic production of Valle-Inclán's *Comedias bárbaras* (*Savage Plays*) in 1992. More recently he has appeared in Argentinian writer Julio Cortázar's *No se preocupe de mi vida* (*Do not Worry About My Life*, 1996). His imposing presence, resonant voice, chiseled features and dynamic physicality have rendered him an attractive performer who has made an easy transition from romantic leads to more versatile authoritarian roles. Pellicena has also worked extensively in film and television.

Pennington, Michael (1943–) Actor, Great Britain. Pennington was a member of the Royal Shakespeare Company between 1964–6, 1974–81, and has returned for individual seasons since. Roles include the Duke in *Measure for Measure* (1978), the title role in *Hamlet*, directed by John BARTON (1980), POLIAKOFF's *Playing with Trains* (1989) and SHAFFER's *The Gift of the Gorgon* (1992, directed by Peter HALL). He also played for a season with the National Theatre, starring in Ottway's *Venice Preserved* (1984), and in the West End (in Harwood's *Taking Sides*, 1995). Between 1986–94 he acted and directed for the English Shakespeare Company, which he had co-founded with Michael BOGDANOV. In 1997 he joined Peter Hall's company at the Old Vic in London, appearing in *Waste* by Granville-Barker and as Trigorin in Chekhov's *Cajka* (*The Seagull*), both directed by Hall. Pennington convinces through his depth of portrayal, in which he is greatly assisted by his rich voice.

Pennont, Elie (1961–) Actor, storyteller, director and author, France and Martinique. Pennont's early training was with the SERMAC theatre workshop in Fort-de-France, where he was selected for a drama scholarship in France, later playing leading roles such as Caliban in Aimé Césaire's *Une tempête* (*A Tempest*, 1982) and gaining experience in local versions of major dramatic texts, Sophocles, Shakespeare, Kleist and SOYINKA's *Trials of Brother Jero*, initially directed by the author. He appeared in Paris as Lumumba in Aimé Césaire's *Une Saison au Congo* (*A Season in the Congo*, 1988). A powerful performer with expressive features seldom long in repose, Pennont has also specialised in storytelling, developing in partnership with Alfred Fantone a new kind of tale, drawing on Creole styles, wit and traditions but expressed mainly in French, hence accessible to international audiences. Between 1990–7 Pennont headed the Centre Dramatique Régional in Martinique, putting on seasons which ranged from his version of Sophocles, *Pè Filoktèt* (*Papa Philocetes*, 1990), to Creole farces. In 1998 he worked with Serge Quaknine on a virtuoso Creole *Othello*, taking all roles except Desdemona. His interest in a wide range of local and international drama has promoted greater professionalism and many opportunities for Caribbean talent.

Pennoyer, John (1949–) Designer, Canada. Pennoyer began work for the Stratford Festival as a property apprentice. After some time in Britain and the USA, he returned as design assistant before taking responsibility for his own productions. He designed costumes, among others, for *Hamlet* (1976), *Julius Caesar* (1982) and *Love's Labour's Lost* (1984), and sets for *Beauty and the Beast* (1981), Sheridan's *School for Wives* (1983) and Molière's *L'avare* (*The Miser*, 1985). Pennoyer has

worked for many years at the Stratford Festival (Canada), where his costumes and sets have garnered a reputation for simple elegance. In 1996–7, he was production designer for *The Taming of the Shrew* at Edmonton's Citadel Theatre.

Perceval, Luk (1957–) Director and actor, Belgium. Perceval graduated as an actor from the Royal Conservatory in Antwerp. After a few years at the Koninklijke Nederlandse Schouwburg (in Antwerp, one of Flanders's biggest theatres) Perceval founded his own group in 1984, Blauwe Maandag Compagnie, which he is still leading. Perceval works not only as a director and actor but also as a lighting designer, writer and teacher. He became especially well-known as a director. Characteristics of his productions are their variety of forms and their unpredictability. In 1986 he staged *Othello* as a very personal statement, not at all following traditional readings of the play. The performance meant a breakthrough for his company. It was followed by a remarkable series of productions, including Chekhov's *Cajka* (*The Seagull*) and Strindberg's *Fadren* (*The Father*). Perceval staged several plays by Arne SIERENS, whom he invited to work as a writer-in-residence at Blauwe Maandag Compagnie. Among the results were *Boste*, *De Drumleraar* (*Drummers*) and *Juffrouw Tania* (*Miss Tania*). Since 1996 Perceval has been working with author Tom LANOYE on *Ten Oorlog* (*To War!*), an adaptation of Shakespeare's history plays. The eight plays were be performed together as part of a grand project during the 1997–8 season.

Pérez de la Fuente, Juan Carlos (1959–) Director, Spain. In 1980 Pérez de la Fuente founded a fringe theatre company with whom he staged a variety of works by contemporary Spanish and English-language dramatists. After leaving Madrid's Real Escuela Superior de Arte Dramático in 1985, he continued to work with his own company before becoming artistic director of the School of Theatre of the Cultural Centre of Las Rozas. During the 1990s, he consolidated his reputation as a director working largely within the repertoire of the twentieth century, where his meticulous collaboration with actors and the clarity of his production style have brought new audiences to largely unknown plays such as Alejandro Casona's *La dama del alma* (*The Lady of the Dawn*, 1991). Following his acclaimed production of Eduardo GALÁN's *Mujeres frente al espejo* (*Women in Front of a Mirror*) at Madrid's Teatro Alcázar, Pérez de la Fuente was named artistic director of Spain's National Theatre, El Centro Dramático Nacional. Here his adventurous programming has allocated a primary role to contemporary works, and his own visceral productions of Francisco NIEVA's *Pelo de tormenta* (*Hair of Torment*, 1997) and Antonio Buero Vallejo's *La Fundación* (*The Foundation*, 1999) have succeeded in luring a new generation of audiences to the dramaturgy of two of Spain's most eminent playwrights.

Pérez Garay, Idalia (1945–) Actor and director, Puerto Rico. Idalia Pérez Garay is a leading lady renowned for characters who display grace and charm under emotional duress. She has won the Critics Circle Award for Best Actor on numerous occasions, including Shen Te in Brecht's *Der Gute Mensch von Sezuan* (*The Good Person of Sezuan*, Teatro de Sesenta, 1973), María Felix in Carlos Fuentes's *Orquídeas a la luz de la luna* (*Orchids in the Moonlight*, 1996) and Juana in Manuel Méndez Ballester's *Tiempo Muerto* (*Dead Times*, Candilejas, 1974), in which she appeared with Lucy BOSCANA and José Luis MARRERO. She has performed the principal roles in Peter Weiss's *Marat-Sade* (Teatro del Sesenta, 1974), Ibsen's *Hedda Gabler* (Corral de la Cruz, 1983), Gabriel García Marquez's *Erendira* (1994) and Luis Rafael Sanchez's *Quíntu-*

ples (*Quintuplets*, Teatro de la Comedia, 1984). Pérez Garay has also directed adaptations of works by Neruda, Pavlovsky and Bocaccio, as well as Luis Rafael Sánchez's *La pasión según Antígona Pérez* (*The Passion According to Antigone Perez*, Centro de Bellas Artes, 1991). She is currently a member and departmental chair of the drama faculty at the University of Puerto Rico.

Perlini, Memè (1940–) Director and performer, Italy. After working as a cartoonist and an actor in the Teatro La Fede, Memè Perlini founded the theatre company La Maschera in 1973 where he worked with the painter and set designer Antonello Aglioti and the composer Alvin Curran. He became established on the experimental scene with the production of *Pirandello: chi?* (*Pirandello: Who?*, 1973), which was the first of a series of highly influential conceptual events in which Perlini explored the use of actors as signs, part of a fragmented narrative incorporating evocative visual components and new technologies. Perlini unconventionally uses 'environmental' site-specific performance in which the protagonists' everyday-ness is constantly invaded by quotations from the worlds of painting and film. In productions such as *Yellow Whiteness (with Sounds of the Sea)* (1975), *Landscape 5* (1975) and *La partenza dell'astronauta* (*The Sailing of the Astronaut*, 1976), he provocatively used simultaneous action.

Peterson, Eric (1946–) Actor, Canada. Peterson studied acting at the University of Saskatchewan and worked in Britain as a stage manager. Returning to Vancouver in 1970, he studied for a year at the University of British Columbia and then co-founded Tamahnous Theatre. The collective work of this company paved his way to join Théâtre Passe Muraille, Toronto (1974). In 1981, Peterson starred in the musical *Billy Bishop goes to War*, followed by another tour de force in the one-man show *Der Kontrabaß* (*The Double Bass*) by Patrick Süskind (1985). Peterson co-starred in the popular CBC series drama *Street Legal* in the early 1990s. Peterson is a fine character actor with superb comic timing, who must also be credited for creating lead roles in premieres of major Candian plays like *Billy Bishop* and Rick Salutin's *Les Canadiens*.

Petrushevskaya, Liudmila (1938–) Dramatist, Russia. Petrushevskaya graduated from the journalism faculty of the Moscow State University and is now a principal figure in contemporary Russian drama. Her sphere is the privacy of human life, conflicts and relations, which were not welcome on the Soviet stage. She found unhappy divorced women, outrageous men, alcoholics and moral wrecks behind the facade of the happy Soviet officialdom. Her attempt to to bring street slang to the stage was strongly criticized by the purists. Her sombre and even striking plays – *Uroki muzyki* (*Lessons of Music*), *Moskovskii khor* (*The Moscow Choir*) and *Tri devushki v golubom* (*Three Girls in Blue*) – were full of compassion for those unhappy or broken lives. Because of the political climate in the USSR, her first plays were premiered in Poland. Only later did productions in Moscow follow: Mark ZAKHAROV at the Lenkom theatre successfully directed *The Three Girls in Blue* (1982), and the Moscow Art Theatre has shown *The Moscow Choir* (1989), a family history from Stalin's time up to now; the Moscow Yermolova Theatre has shown *Cinzano*, and the Mayakovsky theatre has shown *Lessons of Music*.

Peymann, Claus (1936–) Director, Germany. Peymann began as a director with several productions of new plays by Peter Handke at Theater am Turm in Frankfurt. From 1970–4 he worked with Peter STEIN at the Schaubühne in Berlin, and after that until 1979 in Stuttgart (among

his productions there were Schiller's *Die Räuber* (*The Robbers*), Kleist's *Das Käthchen von Heilbronn*, Goethe's *Faust I, II* and Chekhov's *Tri sestry* (*Three Sisters*). From 1979–84 he was artistic director of the theatre in Bochum, and since 1986 he has maintained his position of artistic director of the Burgtheater in Vienna in the middle of intrigues and political attacks. Recently he has tended to concentrate, although not exclusively, on the direction of world premieres by authors such as TURRINI and JELINEK. In 1999 he left his position at the Burgtheater in Vienna, moving on to run the Berliner Ensemble.

Phillips, Simon (1958–) Director, Australia. Phillips graduated from Auckland University and moved to Australia in the mid-1980s. The boldness of his directorial vision has resulted in several productions which have proved enduringly popular: his 1991 *Julius Caesar* for the State Theatre Company of South Australia (designed by Shaun GURTON) featured computers, videos, riot shields, paper shredders, tanks; Mark Antony, Casca and several other characters became power dressed women; the crowd became the pack of press and flashlight-wielding photographers; Mark Antony's forum speech was addressed to a bank of microphones and relayed across rows of television monitors. This production was then revived by the Melbourne Theatre Company (1996) and the Queensland Theatre Company (1997) with Robyn NEVIN as Mark Antony. Similarly, Phillips's Magritte-inspired *Comedy of Errors* (STCSA 1990) has been revived by the Sydney Theatre Company and the MTC in 1997. Phillips has also directed new Australian plays (he directed the MTC premiere of Jill SHEARER's *Shimada*) and musicals; he has choreographed (*Slave of Rhythm* for the Australian Dance Company) and acted, standing in in an emergency for Geoffrey RUSH in Phillips's *Aubrey*

Beardsley-inspired *The Importance of Being Earnest* for the MTC in 1989.

Piccolo, Ottavia (1949–) Actor, Italy. Ottavia Piccolo made her debut in the theatre in 1960 when, at the age of eleven, she acted in William Gibson's *The Miracle Worker* directed by Luigi SQUARZINA. In 1964–5 she worked with Giorgio Strehler in Goldoni's *Le baruffe Chiozzotte* (*The Chioggian Squabbles*, 1964), Luchino Visconti in Chekhov's *Visnevyi sad* (*The Cherry Orchard*, 1966) and Goethe's *Egmont* (1968), Luca RONCONI in *Orlando Furioso* (1969) and, again with Strehler, as the fool in *King Lear* (1972). Piccolo's acting is characterized by versatility and charisma, and an ongoing exploration of dramatic form and performance practice. Known internationally for her films, such as Visconti's *Il Gattopardo* (*The Leopard*, 1963), Mauro Bolognini's *Metello* (1970) and Ettore Scola's *La famiglia* (*The Family*, 1987), Piccolo is one of Italy's most popular actors.

Pillai, Kochugovinda Narayana (1917–) Actor, India. Pillai learnt Kathakali, a form of theatre in Kerala, at an early age from the great gurus Chathanur Velu Pillai, Kochu Pillai Panikker and Kurichi Kunjan Panikker. Today, he is recognized as one of the great exponents of Kathakali; his repertory comprises the traditional roles of Kathakali, including Hamsam, Pushkaran, Rugmangadan, Karna and Krishna. He has been teaching this art for sixty years; most of his students are now established performers. Pillai founded the theatre group Rangaprabhat to promote children's theatre. The group has staged more than thirty productions, with themes taken from Malayalam literature. In addition, workshops and festivals are organized every year.

Pinsent, Gordon (1930–) Actor and dramatist, Canada. Pinsent has had an illustrious career as an actor on stage, radio, television and film. In 1976, he adapted his novel *John and the Missus* for the stage and starred in the Neptune Theatre production. In 1986, his play *A Gift to Last* was produced at Gryphon Theatre in Barrie, Ontario. His work is characterized by a pervasive romanticism and an interest in Canada's rich and varied history. In 1989, his play *Brass Rubbings* was produced at the Factory Theatre in Toronto, directed by Jackie Maxwell. In 1990, he won the John Drainie Award for his lifetime contribution to Canadian broadcasting. Pinsent continues to be a popular television performer, with recent appearances in *The Red Green Show* and *Due South*.

Pinter, Harold (1930–) Dramatist, director and actor, Great Britain. Pinter trained at the Royal Academy of Dramatic Art and Central, and toured in Ireland in the 1950s. In his dramatic work, he thus has the actor's sensibility of what works. His breakthrough as a dramatist came with *The Caretaker* (1960), and since then he has been one of the most eminent contemporary British playwrights. His surreal, nightmarish, disturbing plays have been called 'comedy of menace'. The crafty, verbal surface appears formalist, but strips down psychological motivation and rationalizations, revealing drives and instincts. In the course of his career, his agenda has become increasingly political. Pinter also wrote screenplays, and has directed for the stage many of his own plays, those of Simon GRAY (most recently *Life Support*, starring Alan BATES) and Harwood's *Taking Sides* (1995, with Michael PENNINGTON and Daniel Massey).

Pitínský, Jan Antenna (1955–) Dramatist and director, Czech Republic. In 1985, Pitínský founded the Amateur Circle group in Brno. It became famous for the productions of his plays *Ananas* (*The Pineapple*, 1987) and *Matka* (*Mother*, 1988), directed by himself: they represent the first expression of post-modernism in

Czech drama. *The Pineapple* is an associative montage of heterogeneous motifs, while the compositionally more compact *Mother*, an ironic paraphrase of social naturalistic and pseudo-naturalistic drama, is written in a deformed language combining slang, dialect and political newspeak. Their central themes – the struggle for supremacy in the family, the manipulation of man – develop in subsequent work: *Park* (*The Park*, 1992, The Goose on a String (Husa na provázku) Theatre in Brno), *Pokojíček* (*The Little Room*, 1993, directed by Petr LÉBL at the Theatre on the Balustrade (Na zábradlí)) and *Buldočina* (*Bulldog Blues*, 1995). PITÍNSKÝ also works as a director, often presenting his own dramas and text montages, such as *Sestra Úzkost* (*Sister Anguish*) from the prose of Jan Cep and Jakub Deml (1995, Prague pocket theatre Dejvické divadlo).

Planchon, Roger (1931–) Director, France. Planchon made his debut as a director in Lyon in 1949, and became associated with theatre in that town and area for a long time. He founded the Théâtre de la Comédie Lyon in 1953, and the Théâtre Municipal Villeurbanne in 1957. In 1973 this became the Théâtre National Populaire. Planchon is especially known for his Brechtian approach to the classics. He also directed work by new French dramatists, however, such as VINAVER's *Les Coréen* (*The Koreans*). In recent years he has concentrated more on his film career.

Plashenko, Tamara (1955–) Actor, Ukraine. Plashenko trained at the Karpenko-Kary Institute for the Art of the Theatre, Kiev. Between 1977–9 she worked at the Maria Zan'kovets'ka Ukrainian Drama Theatre, L'viv, and since 1979 has been an actor at the Theatre on the Podil with a series of major parts, including Hippolita-Titania in *A Midsummer Night Dream* (1980), Maria Volkonska in Radzinskii's *Lunin ili smert' zhaka, zapisan-*

naia v prisutstvii Mastera (*Lunin or the Death of Jack, Recorded in the Presence of the Master*, 1987), Ottavia in MROZEK's *Portret* (*Portrait*, 1992), Shypenko's *Dama s kameliiami ili kogda my voidem v gorod* (*Dames with Camellias or When We Enter the City*, 1992), Molly Bloom in *Ulysses* by Joyce (directed by Oleg LIPTSYN, Theatre Club, 1995) and Popova in Chekhov's *Medved'* (*The Bear*, 1996). An actor of a delicate inner organization and bright individuality, Plashenko was twice a recipient of the Kievs'ka Pectoral' award (1993 and 1995). She has performed in many international festivals, including Edinburgh and Torun'.

Platel, Alain (1956–) Director and choreographer, Belgium. Platel started working as a dancer with Canadian Barbara Pearce in 1980. In 1984, he founded the ironically titled Les Ballets Contemporains de la Belgique, later abbreviated to Les Ballets C. de la B., with whom he created productions such as *Bonjour Madame...* (1993) and *La Tristeza Complice*. With Arne SIERENS, he directed the internationally acclaimed Victoria productions *Moeder & Kind* (*Mother and Child*, 1995) and *Bernadetje* (1996). All of Platel's work is the result of an open process in which the actors or dancers tell their own stories. Often, Platel shows a preference for a mixed cast of professional and inexperienced actors (sometimes children). The result is a kind of movement theatre, which, due to the democratic input of every performer, reflects his social awareness.

Plaza, José Carlos (1943–) Actor and director, Spain. Plaza began his career in theatre as director of the independent theatre group TEI. He established contact with William Layton and soon became one of the most fervent advocates of Stanislavski's writings in post-Franco Spain. During the 1980s he established his reputation as a careful director who paid close attention to the text, enjoying productive working relationships with a range of actors. Acclaimed productions of a series of twentieth-century Spanish works served to categorize him as a director keen to promote Spanish dramaturgy. These included Jardiel Poncela's *Eloisa esta debajo de un almendro* (*Eloisa is Under an Almond Tree*, 1984), García Lorca's *La casa de Bernarda Alba* (*The House of Bernarda Alba*, 1986) and Antonio Gala's *Carmen, Carmen* (1987) written especially for the popular actor Concha Velasco. From 1989–94 he served as artistic director of the Centro Dramático Nacional, where his high-profile productions included *Hamlet* (1989), Aeschylus's *Oresteia* (1990) set in a converted space in near Madrid's Atocha station, and the epic version of Valle-Inclan's trilogy *Comedias bárbaras* (*Savage Plays*) in 1991. He has also worked regularly in opera.

Plummer, Christopher (1929–) Actor, Canada. Plummer studied under Iris Warren and C. Herbertcasari and began his career with the Canadian Repertory Theatre in Ottawa. He has become one of the leading Canadian actors, on stage, film and television. Major parts in the theatre include Benedick in *Much Ado About Nothing*, both in Stratford, Ontario, and with the Royal Shakespeare Company, title roles in *Cyrano de Bergerac* (1962), *Macbeth* (1962), Brecht's *Der Aufhaltsame Austieg des Arturo Ui* (*The Resistable Rise of Arturo Ui*, 1963), Pizzarro in SHAFFER's *The Royal Hunt of the Sun* (1965), Henry V, Iago in *Othello* and Danton in Büchner's *Danton's Tod* (*Danton's Death*). Plummer's latest success is in the one-man show *Barrymore*, which opened on Broadway in 1997. His performances are characterized by a splendid voice and by a tremendous concentration and stage presence.

Podrug-Kokotović, Milka (1930–) Actor, Croatia. Podrug-Kokotović trained at the Acting School in Sarajevo. Since 1954 she has been working at the Theatre Marin Držić; in Dubrovnik. She created notable roles in plays of the most important Dubrovnik playwrights, such as Laura in M. Držić's *Dundo Maroje* (*Uncle Maroje*, 1964) and Jele in *Ekvinocijo* (*The Equinox*, 1970), and of other Croatian dramatists including Klara in Krleža's *Leda* (1962), Giga Barić in Begović's *Bez trećeg* (*Without the Third*, 1963) and the title role in V. Stulić's *Kate Kapuralica* (1973). Major examples of her international repertory include Mrs. Smith in Ionesco's *La cantatrice chauve* (*The Bald Soprano*, 1964), the Nurse in *Romeo and Juliet* and Gertrude in *Hamlet*. The drama of the character she plays does not come out through the words but reveals itself in her eyes. Sometimes her glances go against the words, sometimes they are in accordance with them. Her every gesture and movement are carefully controlled and balanced, making her the most Brechtian of all Croatian actors. She does not like masks, wigs and costumes; she would rather act in her everyday clothes, believing that the actor's face is enough if one knows how to use it.

Pohl, Klaus (1952–) Dramatist, actor and director, Germany. Pohl trained as an actor at the Max Reinhardt Seminar in Berlin, and initially worked as an actor only, in Berlin, Hamburg and Zürich. In Rotterdam he added directing to his career (1980–3), and returned to acting in Köln (1983–5). His breakthrough as a dramatist came in 1984 with *Das Alte Land* (*The Old Country*), first produced at the Burgtheater in Vienna. *Karate Billy kehrt Zurück* (*Karate Billy Returns*, 1991, Hamburg) was called the most energetic and precise analysis of the new situation in post-reunion Germany. On the other hand, it was criticized as not doing justice to GDR reality, one reason why it is still not performed in former GDR theatres. *Die Schöne Fremde* (*The Beautiful Stranger*) opened at Münchner Kammerspiele in 1992, directed by Helmut GRIEM, and

1995 saw the premiere of *Wartesaal Deutschland 1995 Stimmenreich* (*Waiting Room Germany 1995 Multiple Voices*) at the Deutsches Theater, Berlin.

Polack, Yossi (1944–) Actor and director Israel. Polack trained at Beit Zvi theatre school in Israel and began his acing career at the Habima national theatre in *Doda Liza* (*Aunt Liza*) by Nissim Aloni. He has played Othello twice, a play he has also directed at the Haifa Municipal theatre. His other roles include Marlowe's Doctor Faustus and the Captain in Strindberg's *Fadren* (*The Father*). Polack has also appeared in several films and is known for his distinct, sometimes even provocative individuality.

Poliakoff, Stephen (1952–) Dramatist and director, Great Britain. Poliakoff started writing while he was still a teenager. His major breakthrough came in 1975 with *Hitting Town* and *City Sugar*. Later plays include *Strawberry Fields* (1977), *Shout Across the River* (1978), *Breaking the Silence* (1984, with Juliet STEVENSON), *Coming in to Land* (1987) and *Playing with Trains* (1989, with Michael PENNINGTON). In the 1990s he turned mainly to writing film scripts, returning to the stage with *Talk of the City* (Royal Shakespeare Company, 1998), which also marks his debut as director. His plays tend to have a surface political concern informed by subtle emotion of the characters involved.

Polívka, Boleslav (1949–) Actor and mime, Czech Republic. Having studied acting at the Brno Academy of Performing Arts, Polívka worked from 1972–89 in the experimental theatre ensemble Goose on a String (Husa na provázku) in Brno, where he also performed evening-length pantomime clown-shows with his own scripts: *Am a Ea* (*Am and Ea*, 1973), *Pépe* (1974), *Pezza versus Čorba* (1975), *Trosecník* (*Castaway*, 1977), *Seance* (1987), and *Šašek a královna* (*The Fool*

and the Queen, 1983, filmed by Vìra Chytilová in 1988). With his tragicomic depiction of the contemporary world, he makes use of his extraordinary mime talents, his sense of the gag and his inspiration by film grotesque and circus clowns.

Pollock, Sharon (1936–) Dramatist, director and actor, Canada. Sharon Pollock studied at the University of New Brunswick. Although she has a distinguished and varied career as (artistic) director of several theatres, her main reputation is as a dramatist. Initially, her plays concerned large issues such as racism and class injustice (*Walsh*, 1973; *The Komagata Maru Incident*, 1976; *One Tiger to a Hill*, 1980). She has developed towards an emphasis on individuals and their conflicts. The beginning of this development is *Blood Relations*, and it continues with *Doc* (1984) and *Fair Liberty's Call* (1993). Pollock is currently artistic director of her own theatre, the Garry, in Calgary.

Popescu, Dumitru Radu (1935–) Dramatist, Romania. Popescu started to publish short stories and novels and made his debut as a playwright in 1966 with *Vara imposibilei iubiri* (*Summer of the Impossible Love*). To date he has written more than twenty plays, which were produced in almost all the theatres in Romania. Many of his plays were also translated, published and produced in Tokyo, Moskow, Kiev, Beijing, Istanbul, Sofia, Novi Sad, Budapest, Babi, Milano, Warsaw, Paris and Los Angeles. Among them are *These Sad Angels*, *Cezar*, *Măscăriciul Piratilor* (*Caesar, the Pirates' Jester*), *Pisica în noaptea anutui nou* (*The Cat on New Year's Eve*) and *Paznicul de la depozitul de nisip* (*The Guardian of the Sand Storehouse*). Popescu received many awards, has published thirty volumes of prose, many of them translated and published also outside Romania, and has written film scripts which were produced in Romania. Many of the productions of his plays were toured abroad. Popescu writes in a highly personal style, non-traditional, in a free construction, blending together the real and unreal, mythic inspiration and folklore, the ironical and the tragical view on the world, moral parables and grotesque fantasies with a poetical touch.

Popescu, Tudor (1930–) Dramatist, Romania. Popescu began his career as a journalist and a prose writer, edited journals of humour, then a department of the Film Studio Bucharest. He was director of the State Theatre in Sibiu and runs a publishing house. Since 1976 he has written over fifty plays, most of them comedies, and numerous sketches for television. Among the comedies most successful are *Concurs de frumusete* (*Beauty Contest*), *Jolly Joker*, *Paradis de Ocazie* (*Second Hand Paradise*), and *Sarpele Monetar* (*The Monetary Snake*). More serious plays include *Scaunul* (*The Chair*) and *Infernul Blând* (*Mild Hell*). Because of the satirical approach of his plays, he had frequent problems with communist censorship. His plays were staged by notable directors, both in Romania and abroad, including Silviu PURCĂRETE.

Porat, Orna (1924–) Actress and theatre director, Israel. Born in Germany and trained in Cologne, where she started her acting career prior to emigrating to Israel in 1948, Porat joined the Cameri Tel Aviv municipal theatre where she has played a large number of leading roles, like Shen Te in Brecht's *Der Gute Mensch von Sezuan* (*The Good Person of Sezuan*), Juliet in *Romeo and Juliet*, the title role and Elizabeth in Schiller's *Maria Stuart*, and the title roles in Aristophanes's *Lysistrate* and Euripides's *Elektra*. By founding the Theatre for Youth and Children, under the auspices of the Ministry of Education, and leading this theatre for its first twenty years, Porat has also made

and important contribution to the education of a new generation of theatregoers.

Pourveur, Paul (1952–) Dramatist, Belgium. Pourveur studied film editing in Brussels and worked first as a scriptwriter for film and television, but halfway through the 1980s he also started writing for the theatre. He has shown himself to be a startlingly productive and highly versatile dramatist, writing in both Dutch and French. From his position as a bilingual writer, Pourveur views language in a very specific way; he does not use it only as a medium, but it also becomes the most important theme in his work. By turning resolutely away from classical dramaturgy, Pourveur, together with a number of his contemporaries such as Arne SIERENS and Willy THOMAS, set in motion the 'new Flemish dramaturgy', which was born in Flanders in the early 1980s in the wake of a generation of theatre artists who broke away from the politically committed theatre of the 1970s and the traditional repertoire of the established theatres. Some of his main plays are *Le Diable au Corps* (*The Devil in the Body*, 1986), *Congo* (1989), *La minute anacoustique* (1994) and *White-out* (1995).

Prasanna, R.P. (1951–) Director and dramatist, India. Trained at the National School of Drama, Prasanna belongs to the class of contemporary directors who generate a debate every time they stage a play. He refused to compromise with the powers that be, the decision makers in the arts scene like the Sangeet Natak Akademi. His production of Girish KARNAD's *Tughlag* was considered a radical production in the contemporary political context, and he was branded an 'angry young man'. He has also directed Brecht's *Galileo*, Chekhov's *Tri sestry* (*Three Sisters*) and *Macbeth*. His production of *Uttara Rama Charitram* is an honest attempt to understand the epic hero Rama at a time when religious fundamentalists are misusing Rama's name. Similarly, his own new play *Gandhi* also aims at revisiting Mahatma Gandhi as a human being: 'It is a celebration of Gandhi, after all'. In all his productions, form is never predetermined. Prasanna developed and ran the important street-theatre group Samudaya in Karnataka from 1975 to the mid-1980s.

Proskurnia, Serhii (1957–) Director, Ukraine. Proskurnia trained at the Karpenko-Kary Institute for the Art of the Theatre and the Ivan Franko Ukrainian Drama Theatre, Kiev. He directed seventeen theatre productions, a number of productions for radio, video productions and television programmes. He was the organizer and director of five youth festivals in the Ukraine and Poland, and producer of seven international theatre projects. He published a number of articles on art in the Ukrainian and Russian press. His art exhibitions (collages, scenery, polygraph, photographic portraits) were held in Kiev (1993) and Augsburg (1995). Proskurnia took part in international theatre festivals in Germany, Great Britain, Italy, Poland and Switzerland. Main productions are *Pisnia pro brativ Neazovs'kykh* (*Song about Neazovs'ky Brothers*) after Lina Kostenko (Theatr-Studio Bud'mo!, 1990), the musical collage *Kraisler Imperial*, (L'viv Opera Theatre, 1992) and *Oderzhyma* (*One Possessed*) after Lesia Ukrainka (international project Ukraine-Germany, 1994–5). Proskurnia closely collaborated with the designer Volodymyr KARASHEVS'KY on the production of *Druzhe Li Bo, brate Du Fu* (*Friend Li Bo, brother Du Fu*), which was staged in two versions; it was shown fifty-seven times from 1992–5, took part in four international festivals, and toured in the Ukraine, Poland, Slovakia, the Czech Republic, Germany and Switzerland. Proskutnia is artistic director of the International Theatre Festival Laboratory Arts Berezillia in Kiev.

Puigcorbé, Juanjo (1955–) Actor and director, Spain. A former physics student, he trained at Barcelona's Institut del Teatre. He was one of the most dynamic young actors of his generation, securing a range of impressive roles with the leading directors of the time including Jorge LAVELLI in the 1984 production of *The Tempest*, Pere Planella in Offenbach's *La Belle Helene* (*The Beautiful Helena*, 1979), Fabià Puigserver in *Titus Andronicus* (1979) and Mario GAS in Dürrenmatt's *Frank V* (1989). Despite an appearance in Natalie Sarraute's *Per un si, per un no* (*For One Yes Or For One No*) at the Poliorama Theatre in 1989, the last ten years have seen Puigcorbé work increasingly in film where he has established himself as one of the best known comedy performers in Spain. Although perhaps most admired for his work in films like La Cuadrilla's *Justino: un asesino de la tercera edad* (*Justino: A Senior Citizen Serial Killer*, 1994) and Manuel Gómez Pereira's *El amor perjudica seriamente la salud* (*Love can Seriously Damage your Health*, 1996), his impressive range both in theatre and film encompasses comedy, farce, classical tragedy and contemporary drama. A well-built physique, roguish good looks and impeccable timing have ensured that he remains much in demand.

Purcărete, Silviu (1950–) Director, Romania. A graduate of the Bucharest Academy of Theatre and Film (1974), Purcărete worked with the Teatrul Tineretului – Youth Theatre – in Piatra Neamtz (*Romeo and Juliet*), and then with the Drama Theatre in Constantza, where he directed *Atrides Legend* after Aeschylus, Sophocles and Euripides and *Hecuba* by Euripides (an open air production). In 1978 he joined the Teatrul Mic – Little Theatre in Bucharest, where he directed Giraudoux's *La folle de Chaillot* (*The Madwoman of Chaillot*), *Richard III* and Caragiale's *Lost Letter*. In 1989 he joined the National Theatre in Craiova where he achieved his most important productions, including Dumitru Radu POPESCU's *Piticul din grădina de vară* (*The Dwarf in the*

Summer Garden), *Titus Andronicus, The Tempest* (at the National Theatre in Porto Portugal and at the Nottingham Playhouse) and the *Oresteia* after Aeschylus at the Centre Dramatique in Limoges (1996). All these productions were toured to many countries of the world and met with critical acclaim. Purcărete practices an intensely visual, imagistic theatre, with large, dynamic, metaphorical displays of crowds.

Q

Quartucci, Carlo (1938–) Director and dramatist, Italy. One of the signatories of a collective manifesto (1965) urging a theoretical reflection upon the new avant-gardes in Italian theatre, Carlo Quartucci has always been at the centre of Italian experimental theatre, both in his theory and practice. After working with Teatro Gruppo, Quartucci founded the company La Zattera di Babele (1981) which has produced performances and installations in venues such as the Biennale in Venice, the Castello di Rivoli in Turin, Dokumenta in Kassel and the Mickery Theatre in Amsterdam. Known for his subversive use of space, Quartucci produces striking visual theatre events, drawing from both classical texts and conceptual art. Among his most notable productions are Beckett's *Waiting for Godot* (1959), Marina Abramovic and Uwe Laysiepen's *Modus Vivendi* (1983), Henning Christiansen and Per Kirkeby's *Simone del deserto* (1983) and *Immagini di Passione (Images of Passion*, 1986), a project by Quartucci and Rudy Fuchs with installations by Jan Dibbets, Luciano Fabro, Jörg Immendorff, Per Kirkeby, Mario Merz, Hermann Nitsch, Giulio Paolini, David Salle and others. More recently, Quartucci also directed a fascinating re-interpretation of Aurelio Res' adaptation of *Medea* (1997) with his long-term collaborator Carla Tatò in the lead role.

Quatli, Walid (1939–) Director, Syria. Quatli received Stanislavski-based training in Bulgaria, but later tended to favour the ideas of Meyerhold. In Syria, he initially directed amateur groups, later taking up a teaching position at the Academy of Dramatic Arts. Productions include Edward ALBEE's *Zoo Story* (1978), Peter Handke's *Kaspar Hauser* (1991), Gogol's *Zapiski Sumasshedshego* (*The Diary of a Madman*, 1995), and a play without words in the tradition of physical theatre, *Bila Kalam* (*Without Words*, 1996). Occasionally, he was unable to make the desired impact upon his audience because of excessive experimentation. Although he aimed at physical theatre throughout, his training had not equipped him sufficiently to realise his ambitions; his theoretical background, however, proved sufficient to gain respect from many actors working with him.

Qudssia, Zeinati (1945–) Actor and director, Syria. Born in Jordan, but based since his early youth in Damascus, Qudssia began as an amateur university student actor, and then turned professional and joined the Damascus National Theatre. He has performed with most Syrian directors, including Asaad FUDDA, Mohamed Al-Tayeb, Walid QUATLI and Mahmoud KHADOUR. He also appeared in Edward ALBEE's *The Zoo Story*. Qudssia became a director and launched three one-man shows in the 1980s, all written by Mam-doub ADWAN: *Ahwalu'l-Dunya* (*How Life Is*), *Al-Qeyama* (*The Resurrection*) and *Al-Zabbal* (*The Rubbish Collector*). He has directed plays by Tunisian dramatists and other young Arab playwrights, and also starred in television serials, mostly written by himself.

Quintanar, Isabel Actor, Mexico. Quinta-nar graduated from the Dramatic Art School of The National Institute of Fine Arts. Since then she has appeared in eight films and 300 plays, ranging from musi-cals and comedy to serious drama. As well as theatre, she has developed her work in radio and television and has offered numerous theatre workshops for children and adults. Along with her acting career, Isabel Quintanar has had an active role in promoting new theatre talents nationally and internationally. She is the International Secretary of the Interna-tional Theatre Institute, UNESCO, and is involved in various international theatre projects. She is director of the Mexican Theatre Centre and edits the *Theatre Review* magazine of the ITI-UNESCO.

R

Rabe, David (1940–) Dramatist, USA. Rabe's breakthrough came in 1971 when five early plays were staged together at the New York Shakespeare Festival. Rabe is best-known for a trilogy on the Vietnam war: *Sticks and Bones* (1969), *The Basic Training of Pavlo Hummel* (1971) and *Streamers* (1976). In *Hurlyburly* (1984), which deals with three male outsiders, he takes his inspiration for the title from *Macbeth*. 'Grotesque comedy, fantasy and bitter satire' are combined in his work. More recently, he wrote *A Question of Mercy*, dealing with AIDS from the doctor's perspective.

Rabe, Pamela (1959–) Actor, Australia. Rabe emigrated from Vancouver, Canada in 1983. She has played leading roles in a wide variety of plays, particularly for the Melbourne Theatre Company, and has won Green Room awards for her performances in *A Room of One's Own* (adapted from Virginia Woolf's novel), Louis NOWRA's *Cosi*, Neil SIMON's *Lost in Yonkers* and Win Wills's *Gertrude Stein and a Companion*. As Alice B. Toklas in *Gertrude Stein* she was compelling, summoning up intensity, nervous energy, vulnerability and humour at the same time as towering over Miriam Margolyes's Gertrude Stein (Rabe is 188 cm tall). Other notable appearances have included Vittoria in Webster's *The White Devil*, Angelica in Aphra Behn's *The Rover*, Kate in *The Taming of the Shrew*, a punk Rosalind in *As You Like It*, Beatrice in *Much Ado About Nothing*, Amanda in Noel Coward's *Private Lives*, Josie in O'Neill's *A Moon for the Misbegotten* and the Wicked Witch of the West in *The Wizard of Oz*. Rabe is a very striking woman who can readily emanate strength and confidence, and so the casting of her as the girl/anima in Neil ARMFIELD's 1989 production of Patrick White *The Ham Funeral* was a surprise but extremely successful.

Radziwilowicz, Jerzy (1950–) Actor, Poland. Radziwilowicz graduated from the State Theatre Academy of Warsaw in 1972. Recipient of many prestigious awards and a well-known actor on television and in films by WAJDA, Godard and Kieslowski, his major stage credits include Raskolnikov in Dostoyevsky's *Prestuplenie I nakazanie* (*Crime and Punishment*, 1984), Henryk in Gombrowicz's *Slub* (*The Wedding*, 1991), the title roles in Koltès's *Roberto Zucco* (1991) and Molière's *Dom Juan* (1994 and 1996), Johnson in Hopkins's *This Story of Yours* (1992) and Konrad in *Dziady* (*Forefathers' Eve*) by Adam Mickiewicz (1995). He represents a highly intellectual acting, with a sharpened sense of form and an inclination towards innovative and daring experiments. A master of speech, the multiple patterns of his characteristic, tense behaviour usually convey a broad spectrum of shades and meanings.

Rahman, Ataur (1941–) Director and actor, Bangladesh. Rahman began his much acclaimed career as a director in 1972. Some of his notable productions include translations of Beckett's *Waiting For Godot* (with Abdul HAYAT as Pozzo and Asaduzzaman NOOR as Estragon in 1984), Brecht's *Leben des Galilei* (*Life of Galileo*, with Aly ZAKER in the title role, Noor as Barberini and set design by Mansuruddin AHMED, 1988) and *Irsha* by Syed HUQ (with Sarah ZAKER as Jubati, set design by Mansuruddin Ahmed). Ataur Rahman's directorial strength lies in drawing the best from his performers and arranging these faithfully to meet the demand of the text. He is a stage, radio and television actor of considerable reputation and also teaches theatre. He has jointly translated and adapted Sartre's *Huis clos* (*No Exit*), Gogol's *Zenit'ba* (*The Marriage*) and Molnar's *Liliom* with Zia HYDER and Noor, and has publications on theatre to his credit.

Raina, M. K. (1948–) Actor and director, India. Raina trained at the National School of Drama, New Delhi and studied with Ebrahim ALKAZI. Though his initial theatre training was in Western theatre, he later came to grips with Indian and folk theatre forms, leading workshops throughout the country. He has acted in more than a hundred productions and later added directing to his credits; he also formed the Delhi company Prayog. Major productions include BHARATI's *Andha Yug* which was performed at the Festival of India in the USSR and in Berlin in the 1960s, and Brecht's *The Mother*.

Rajmont Ivan (1945–) Director, Czech Republic. Rajmont studied directing at the Prague Academy of Performing Arts. From 1975–86 he was a director and head of the Činoherní Studio in Ústí nad Labem, where he directed Kundera's adaptation of *Jacob the Fatalist* (1975), *Troilus and Cressida* (1979, set design Jaroslav MALINA), Chekhov's *Tri sestry* (*Three Sisters*, 1982), Büchner's *Danton's Tod* (*Danton's Death*, 1983) and also the grotesque tragifarce by Karel STEIGERWALD, *Dobové tance* (*Period Dance*, 1980). His productions are marked by dynamic and striking comic approaches, hyperbolic detail and sharp transitions from the comic to tragic, all adding to the profile of this non-conformist ensemble. Among his other work at various venues, his markedly tragicomic interpretations of Steigerwald's original plays stand out – *Neapolská choroba* (*The Neapolitan Disease*, 1988, Žižkov Theatre, Prague), and *Tatarská pout'* (*Tartar Pilgrimage*, 1988, Theatre on the Balustrade (Na zábradlí), Prague) – reflecting the disintegration of the socialist utopia. In 1990, he became artistic director of the National Theatre drama department in Prague, where his direction has updated pieces from the classic repertoire, *As You Like It* (1991), Euripides's *Medeia* (1992), *Cymbeline* (1995) and *Othello* (1998).

Raju, Rajappa (1952–) Actor, India. Raju trained at the National School of Drama, New Delhi, began his career in children's theatre, and even now is popular with many children's theatre groups in Tamil Nadu. He has acted in more than fifty plays. Some of his significant achievements are in effecting a kind of Brechtian alienation in *Hamlet*, PARTHASARATHY's *Nandan Kathai*, *Kongai Thee* and *Aurangazeeb*, and in Molière's *L'avare* (*The Miser*). Influenced by Ebrahim ALKAZI, Raju attempts to achieve a kind of theatre language in his acting style which is close to a ritual. He believes in acting as a kind of resonance and his utmost concern today is to develop gestures which are not merely theatrical, but authentic. He tries to use trance as a source of energy in his acting. Currently, Raju is teaching theatre at the School of Performing Arts, Pondicherry University.

Ramamoorthi, Parasuram (1949–) Director and dramatist, India. Ramamoorthi
has directed many Indian and Western
plays, and all his productions are marked
by a sense of ritual, the use of paintings,
music and collage, and striking influences
of postmodernism. His production of
Macbeth demonstrates his intercultural
stance, Mahesh Elkunchwar's *Prathi-
bimba (Reflection)* is an example of his
anti-absurd theatre, and an adaptation of
The Adventures of Tom Sawyer exemplifies his vision of play as poetry. Ramamoorthi's production of Eugene O'Neill's
Before Breakfast can be seen as only one
instance of his feminist theatre: he has
also written and directed *En Kappalukku
Nane Captain (I'm the Captain of My
Ship)*, a feminist play and the first play in
Tamil where a woman plays the role of
Sutradhari (actor/stage-manager). In 1997
he directed Girish KARNAD's *Hayavadana*
in London for the Bharatiya Vidya Bhavan. His play *It's All a Game of Dice* was
shortlisted for the British Council International Playwrighting Award.

Ramanujam, Seshan (1930–) Director, India. Ramanujam trained at the National
School of Drama, New Delhi, and Ebrahim ALKAZI and G. Sankara Pillai are the
two major influences in his career. His
first major success was his production of
Sankara Pillai's *Crime No. 27*, followed
by the same author's *Karutha Theivam
(Black Goddess)* and *Saketham*, Indira
Parthasarathy's *Kala Endiram (Time Machine)*, and MUTHUSWAMY's *Narkalikarar-
kal*. Rhythms of the village are at the
centre of his productions, which tend to
create sepulchral images. He is also noted
for his contribution to the Tamil stage in
popularizing Brecht, Molière, Synge and
O'Neill.

Ramaswamy, Mu (1951–) Actor, director
and dramatist, India. Trained in Therukoothu under Purisai Kannappa THAM-
BIRAN, Ramaswamy founded the Nija
Nataka Iyakkam (Real Theatre Move-

ment). He is known for his skilful use of
folk theatre forms and Therukoothu in
modern Tamil plays. His performance in
his play *Thurkira Avalam*, an adaptation
of Sophocles's *Antigone*, was praised for
its attempt to relate Koothu and Greek
theatre. His recent interpretation of As-
wathama in BHARATI's *Andha Yug* has
been praised as a landmark in Tamil
theatre; the production used actors, puppets and slides to present images of
nuclear war. He has also performed the
traditional roles of Kichaka and Ducha-
sana in Therukoothu, and conducted
theatre workshops in Tamilnadu.

Rame, Franca (1929–) Performer and
dramatist, Italy. Franca Rame began her
acting career by working in her father's
travelling theatre company. In the early
1950s she started a lifelong partnership
and artistic collaboration with Dario FO,
with whom with she set up the theatre co-
operatives Nuova Scena (1968) and La
Comune (1970). Rame created the roles
of most of Fo's female parts for television,
film, radio and the theatre. She also co-
wrote with Fo *Tutta casa, letto e chiesa
(All Home Bed and Church*, 1977), *Cop-
pia Aperta (Open Couple*, 1983) and
Parti femminili (Female Parts, 1986).
Throughout her career Rame successfully
combined the roles of artist and political
activist. Aiming to encourage self-aware-
ness amongst her audience, Rame created
a witty and intriguing series of female
parts which represent a challenging political commentary on the female condition.
Her talent and generosity, both as a
performer and a feminist activist, have
inspired many practitioners of subsequent
generations.

Ramos-Escobar, José Luis (1950–) Dramatist and director, Puerto Rico. Along
with Roberto RAMOS-PEREA, José Luis
Ramos-Escobar is one of the New Puerto
Rican Playwrights, a term applied to
the socially and politically active dramatists of his generation. As a director,

Ramos-Escobar's preference is for the European avant-garde and Latin American contemporary theatre, and includes productions of Genet's *Le balcon* (*The Balcony*, 1992), several of Ionesco's 'Jacques' plays (*The Future is in Eggs* and *The Submission*), and *La pasión según Antígona Pérez* (*The Passion According to Antigone Perez*, 1975). From 1971–8, Ramos-Escobar worked with Anamú and Moriví, two guerrilla theatre groups devoted to collective creation. From 1991 to the present, he has served as director for the group Artemisa in Ponce, Puerto Rico. Ramos-Escobar's plays include *Mascarada* (*Masquerade*, 1985), *Indocumentados: El otro merengue* (*Undocumented: The Other Merengue*, 1989), and *El Olor de Popcorn* (*The Smell of Popcorn*, 1996), a play which in less than two years has received performances at thirteen international theatre festivals worldwide.

Ramos-Perea, Roberto (1959–) Dramatist, director, actor and critic, Puerto Rico. Roberto Ramos-Perea is known inside Puerto Rico as a total 'man of the theatre', although outside he is known primarily as a dramatist. Ramos-Perea studied theatre at Mexico's Instituto Nacional de Bellas Artes (National Institute of Fine Arts) before returning to the University of Puerto Rico for further study in Drama and Hispanic Studies. In 1992, Ramos-Perea received Spain's esteemed Tirso de Molina Prize for his play *Miénteme Más* (*Lie to Me Again*). He has also received the René Marqués Prize for *Módulo 104* (*Module 104*, 1982) and *Cueva de Ladrones* (*Thieves' Cave*, 1983). Other works include *Malasangre* (*Bad Blood*, 1987) and *Morir de Noche* (*To Die by Night*, 1992). As a principal playwright of the 'nueva dramaturgía puertorriqueña' (New Puertorican Dramaturgy) generation, Ramos-Perea's plays are characterized by social, economic and political critique set in intensely personal situations. As a critic and journalist, Ramos-Perea has written articles and

reviews for the newspapers *El Reportero, El Mundo* and *El Vocero* as well as a book of critical essays on the 'New Puerto Rican Dramaturgy' (*Perspectiva de la Nueva Dramaturgía Puertorriqueña*, Ateneo Puertorriqueño, 1989). He is currently the executive director of the Ateneo Puertorriqueño, a national arts research institution.

Ranzi, Galatea (1967–) Actor, Italy. While studying at the Accademia d'Arte Drammatica in Rome, Galatea Ranzi founded with Mira and Marco Andriolo the theatre company Machine de Theatre in 1986, for which her most notable performances have been in Christoph Gluck's *Orpheus and Eurydice* (1987) and Cesare Pavese's *Dialoghi con Leuco* (*Dialogues with Leuco*, 1988), both directed by Marco Andriolo. Ranzi subsequently worked with Massimo CASTRI in Euripides's *Electra* (1993) and Luca RONCONI in Vittorio Alfieri's *Mirra* (1988), Eugene O'Neal's *Strange Interlude* (1990) and Karl Kraus's *Die Letzten Tage der Menschheit* (*The Last Days of Humanity*, 1990), and has appeared in a number of films, most famously Paolo and Vittorio Taviani's *Fiorile* (1993). Her acting is characterized by commitment to the reinterpretation of classical female roles and a capacity, both on stage and on the screen, to offer passionate and evocative solo and ensemble performances.

Rashid, Mamunur (1948–) Dramatist, actor and director, Bangladesh. Rashid has a number of highly successful plays to his credit. These include *Ora Kadam Aly* (*The Oppressed*, 1977, also translated into German and performed in Berlin, 1989), *Iblish* (*The Devil*, 1981), *Ekhane Nongor* (*The Anchor is Here*, 1982) and *Manush* (*Humankind*, 1991). He also directed and acted in all the above productions. 'Mamunur Rashid's plays are generally concerned with class conflicts and the socio-economic exploitation of the poor, especially the rural poor, by rich landlords, scheming middlemen, corrupt government officials and unprincipled politicians.' This concern motivated him to organize the Mukta Natak movement, which sought to promote improvised performances of real-life tales of the oppression of rural people who do not own any land. He is the founder general secretary of Aranyak (a leading theatre group in Bangladesh), former chairman of Bangladesh Group Theatre Federation and founder of Bangla Theatre (a professional theatre company).

Ratto, Gianni (1916–) Designer and director, Brazil. Born in Italy, he studied architecture at Milan Polytechnic. Apart from that he is basically self-taught; he owes his education to the influence of people like Giorgio Strehler, a meeting with Gordon Craig, and daily contact with numerous artisans, stage hands, artists, architects and painters. Productions in Italy include *Richard III*, *The Tempest* and *Hamlet*. At La Scala in Milan, his designs for opera include Berg's *Wozzeck* and Mozart's *Entführung aus dem Serail* (*The Abduction from the Seralgio*). Moving to Brazil, Ratto added directing theatre and opera and teaching to his credits. His permanent aim is a technically and formally high-ranked theatre based on the authors and on the potential of a national dramaturgy.

Rayson, Hannie (1959–) Dramatist, Australia. Rayson studied at the Victorian College of the Arts as a performer. She is a founder member of Theatreworks, a company known for its adventurous approach to theatre. Theatreworks performed several of Rayson's early plays, most notably *Mary* (1982), which looks at Greek experience in Australia, and *Room to Move* (1985), a farce with a wry feminist outlook. Rayson now often writes plays focusing on women who are juggling careers and facing up to moral dilemmas; she is renowned for a combination of witty dialogue and effective rea-

lism. *Hotel Sorrento* deals with three sisters trying to reconcile themselves to a troubled past when one sister writes a Booker Prize-winning novel based on their shared experiences. *Falling from Grace* focuses on three successful career women. *Competitive Tenderness* is a farce about local government, featuring the outrageous machinations of Dawn Snow, a woman determined to get to the top. In 1995 Rayson co-wrote *Scenes from a Separation* with Andrew Bovell; this play presents the breakup of a marriage from the differing perspectives of the man and woman involved. Rayson's plays are distinguished by wit, observation and friendly feminism.

Rea, Stephen (1949–) Actor and director, Ireland. Rea trained at the Abbey Theatre School. In 1980 Rea established Field Day Theatre Company in Derry with playwright Brian FRIEL. A versatile and compelling actor, Rea contributed to the high performance standards which became a hallmark of all Field Day productions. His roles with Field Day included Owen in *Translations* by Friel (1980), Bracken and Joyce in KILROY's *Double Cross* (1986), Lenny in Stewart Parker's *Pentecost* (1987) and Vanya in Frank MCGUINNESS's adaptation of Chekhov's *Djadja Vanja* (*Uncle Vanya*) directed by Peter GILL (1995). Other roles include Edward in McGuinness's *Someone Who'll Watch Over Me*, directed by Robin Lefevre for the Hampstead Theatre, London (1992), and Devlin in PINTER's *Ashes to Ashes* at the Royal Court Theatre, London (1996) and the Pinter Festival at the Gate Theatre, Dublin (1997). In 1998 Rea made an exciting return to Field Day Theatre Company to direct *Northern Star* by Stewart Parker for the 1998 Belfast Theatre Festival, a co-production with Tinderbox Theatre Company. Films include *The Crying Game* and *Michael Collins* directed by Neil Jordan, and *Trojan Eddie* directed by Gillies Mackinnon. Television work includes *Hedda Gabler* directed by Deborah Warner for BBC 2.

Reaney, James (1926–) Dramatist, Canada. Reaney obtained the degrees of BA, MA and Ph.D. from University College, Toronto and served as professor of English at the University of Western Ontario until 1992. His early plays were to a large extent directed at a young audience, and even his plays for adults have been described as 'permeated by a sense of childhood innocence, usually in conflict with the forces of corrupted experience'. Later in his career, Reaney placed more emphasis on local history (*The Donnelly Trilogy*, 1973–5), and myth. His adaptation *Alice Through the Looking Glass* (1994) was produced at the Stratford (Canada) Festival, directed by Marti Maraden.

Rebengiuc, Victor (1933–) Actor, Romania. Rebengiuc trained at the Theatre and Film Institute in Bucharest (1956) and, after a year at the National Theatre in Craiova, joined the Bulandra Theatre in Bucharest where he has worked permanently as a main actor, collaborating occasionally also with Teatrul Mic. Between 1990–6 he was director of the Theatre and Film Academy in Bucharest. Rebengiuc is an actor of a powerful personality and of a special capacity to incarnate with truthfulness very different characters in serious drama and in comedy alike. He has worked with major directors, such as Liviu CIULEI, Cătălina BUZOIANU, Andrei SERBAN and others. Rebengiuc played major parts in plays by Shakespeare (Orlando in *As You Like It*, the title role in *Richard II*, Brutus in *Julius Caesar*, Caliban in *The Tempest*, Bottom in *A Midsummer Night's Dream*), O'Neill (*A Long Day's Journey into Night*, James in *A Moon for the Misbegotten*), Tennessee Williams (Stanley in *A Streetcar Named Desire*), Arthur MILLER (Biff in *Death of a Salesman*), Oscar Wilde (Jack in *The Importance of Being Earnest*), Gibson (Jerry in *Two for a*

Seesaw), Farquhar (*The Recruiting Officer*), Ibsen (the title role in *Rosmersholm*, Bernick in *Samfundets Støtter* (*The Pillars of Society*)), Chekhov (Astrov in *Djadja Vanja* (*Uncle Vanya*)) and in Romanian plays. Rebengiuc also appeared successfully in many films and on television.

Redgrave, Vanessa (1937–) Actor, Great Britain. Vanessa Redgrave is one of a large family of actors. She trained at Central School of Speech and Drama, and has enjoyed a notable career since her debut in 1957, both on the stage and on film. In the 1980s and 1990s, some striking performances include Arkadina in Chekhov's *Cajka* (*The Seagull*), Nora Melody in O'Neill's *A Touch of the Poet*, directed by David THACKER, and Shaw's *Heartbreak House* (1992), directed by Trevor NUNN. In 1996, she played Ella in Richard EYRE's Royal National Theatre production of Ibsen's *John Gabriel Borkman* with Paul SCOFIELD in the title role.

Régina, Jocelyn (1963–) Author, director and actor, France and Martinique. Régina has a great love of words; initially he was influenced by the poetic work of Aimé Césaire, and wrote poetry and serious drama in French. However, comic repartee and verbal invention in Creole is enjoyed by a much larger public, and in 1987 Régina founded the group Balan, performing sketches live and on television. He developed a number of comedies in Creole which have enjoyed wide success, since 1990 usually in co-production with the Centre Dramatique Régional. Subjects have included scandals in the divorce court in *Bakannal o tribunal* (*Trouble in the Divorce Court*, 1991), loosely based on Cervantes, and unbuttoned folk humour in plays such as *Le dorlis de ces dames* (*An Incubus Visits the Ladies*, 1990) and *Dis maman où est papa?* (*Ma, Where's Pa?*, 1991). Several shorter works are based on a double act, Philibert and Kumba, exploiting contrasts in age or class. An inventive and genial comedian, Régina's relaxed enjoyment of popular theatre and prolific production continue.

Reid, Christina (1942–) Dramatist, Ireland. Protestant working-class Belfast culture is represented in her plays which prominently feature the plight of women against a backdrop of patriarchal sectarianism. *Tea in A China Cup* (1983) was produced at the Lyric Theatre, Belfast, where she was writer-in-residence (1983–4). Her most successful play, *Joyriders* (1986), directed by Pip Broughton of Paines Plough, The Writers' Company, featured a liberal middle-class Protestant woman working in a youth work experience scheme in Catholic working-class West Belfast. It is a compassionate bridge of class and sectarian divides in a society whose endemic violence precludes easy solutions and happy endings. Ten years later, Reid revisited her *Joyriders* in *Clowns* (1996) on the eve of the IRA ceasefire. In *The Belle of the Belfast City* (1989), three generations of women of the one Belfast Protestant family take on the intransigent patriarchy of their loyalist heritage. Other plays for the theatre include *Did You Hear the One About the Irishman...?* (1985) and *My Name, Shall I Tell You My Name?* (1987). She has also written extensively for radio and television.

Reid, Fiona (1951–) Actor, Canada. Born in Britain, Reid became popular in the television comedy series *The King of Kensington* between 1975–8 and subsequently devoted more time to her stage career. She has performed at the Stratford Festival and, between 1983–5 and 1989–92, was a member of the Shaw Festival. Her parts include the title role in Ibsen's *Hedda Gabler* and Amanda in Coward's *Private Lives*. She is a recipient of two Dora Awards and of the Actra Radio Award for best performance by an actor (1986). She is a beautiful actor with a wonderful facility for comedy, but Reid

has also proven herself more than capable of playing tragic heroines. She has said of her work, 'If easy success was all I wanted, I could have stayed in television.' And, 'I could have been a 50 per center had I not been challenged by people who made me feel what I did was never enough'.

Reid, Graham (1945–) Dramatist, Ireland. Reid is best known for his television trilogy *Billy* (1982), starring Bríd BRENNAN and a young Kenneth BRANAGH, which focused on a working-class Protestant family struggling against a backdrop of sectarian violence. An equally compelling sequel, *Lorna*, featuring Brennan, followed in 1987. The same grim terrain was featured in his earlier stage plays, *The Death of Humpty-Dumpty* (1979), *The Closed Door* (1980) and *Dorothy* (1980). His stage play *The Hidden Curriculum* (1982) further explored entrenched sectarianism, and *Remembrance* (1984), first staged at the Lyric Theatre, Belfast, featured two middle-aged lovers, Bert and Theresa, from opposite sides of the sectarian divide meeting in a cemetery.

Reinshagen, Gerlind (1925–) Dramatist, Germany. Reinshagen attend the Hochschule der Künste in Berlin. Since 1956 she has worked freelance as a journalist and author, initially writing for children and radio. Many of her stage plays, including *Doppelkopf*, 1968) and *Eisenherz* (1982, directed by Andrea BRETH) deal critically but poetically with white-collar workers, their monotonous work and their careers. *Die Clownin* (1986) takes up the same topic in the arts world. Her most recent play, *Die Grüne Tür, oder Medea Bleibt* (*The Green Door, or, Medea Stays*), opened in Dresden in 1999.

Rendra, W.S. (1935–) Dramatist and director, Indonesia. Rendra trained at the American Academy of Dramatic Art, New York. One of the most important figures in modern Indonesian theatre, he was founder and artistic director of Bengkel Theatre of Yogyakarta, where he directed his own plays and adaptations of Schiller, Shakespeare and Sophocles. Published plays include *Selamatkan Anak Cucu Suleiman, Mastodon Dan Burung Kondor, Kisah Perjuangan Suku Naga, Sekda* and *Panembahan Reso*. A significant figure on the international literary scene, he has been an outspoken critic of economic exploitation and government corruption and has suffered censorship and arrest. During recent political upheavals in Indonesia, Rendra has been at the forefront of the Reformation Movement. His work is bold and uncompromising and is a significant influence on all theatre and literature in contemporary Indonesia.

Renée (1929–) Dramatist, New Zealand. She began writing for the stage at the age of fifty after completing a BA at Auckland University, though she had earlier experience of teaching, journalism and community theatre. She is interested in writing good roles for women of everyday life, which has often meant the wives and daughters of working men. Amongst her successful plays are *Setting the Table* (1982) and the trilogy *Wednesday to Come* (1984), *Pass It On* (1986) and *Jeannie Once* (1990), which shows how workers' strikes and other problems impinge on women of the same family over four generations, as well as highlighting the women's own political contribution.

Revuelta, Vicente (1929–) Director, Cuba. Revuelta started his artistic career as an actor in 1946. He has founded different centres and academies of actor training. In 1958 he founded the theatre group Teatro Estudio (together with Raquel Revuelta, Sergio Corrieri and other artists) where he still works as an actor and artistic director. Notable productions include O'Neill's *A Long Day's Journey into Night*, Lope de Vega's *Fuente Ovejuna*, and Brecht's *Der Gute Mensch von Se-*

zuan (*The Good Person of Sezuan*) and *Leben des Galilei* (*Life of Galileo*). In Bulgaria and in Mexico he directed Carlos Felipe's *El Travieso Jimmy* (*Fidgety Jimmy*) and Virgilio Piñera's *El No* (*The No*). Today Revuelta is considered one of the most prestigious directors in Latin America. He has participated in seminars and workshops at the Escuela Internacional de Teatro (EITALC), and has been part of the jury in several theatre competitions. He has attended conferences in more than fifteen countries in America and Europe. Tours have led him to Uruguay, Spain, Argentina, Brazil and Mexico.

Rézaire, Eugénie (1950–) Actor and director, France and Guyane. After a degree in languages at Tours and Paris University, Rézaire completed a masters degree at Mount Holyoke and returned home to teach English. The lack of professional theatre in Guyane lends importance to her efforts in high schools and through the Association of Friends of Léon Damas (founded 1978) to create dramatic works, often based on poetic texts by local authors and the black diaspora, and including a strong multicultural performance element (*Coeur de manioc* (*Heart of Cassava*), 1981; *Fleuves* (*Rivers*), 1995–6). Increasingly interested in film writing and deeply committed to developing opportunities in Guyane, Rézaire is a commanding performer and cultural activist. In 1997 she was elected to the Regional Council.

Riantiarno, Nano (1949–) Dramatist, performer and director, Indonesia. He is the husband of Ratna Riantiarno. He trained at the Indonesian National Theatre Academy (ATNI), Jakarta and studied at the Dreyar Kara Advanced School of Philosophy, Jakarta. As actor and assistant director in Teguh Rarya's drama company Teater Populer, he established his own Teater Koma in 1977. Interest in both traditional and Western theatre forms has influenced his style, and he has created a number of adaptations including *Opera Ikan Asin*, 1983, a version of Brecht's *Die Dreigroschenoper* (*The Threepenny Opera*). In the 1980s he wrote a quartet of plays following the same group of characters: *Bom Waktu* (Time Bomb), *Opera Kecoa*, *Opera Julini* and *Banci Gugat* (Transvestites Accuse). In May 1989 his adaptation of a Chinese opera, *Sam Pek Eng Tay*, was banned, as was his satire *Suksesi* (Sucession) in 1990. When the revival of *Opera Kecoa* was also banned, protests from the artistic community followed and Riantiarno temporarily withdrew from the theatre. However, he and the company have since produced *Rumah Sakit Jiwa* (Insane Asylum) and *Ular Putih* (another adaptation based on the Chinese opera *Lady White Snake*) in 1994, and in 1995 *Semar Gugat* about the god/clown of the Javanese, Wayang Kulit.

Ricalde, Mario Espinoza (1958–) Director, Mexico. Ricalde studied theatre at the University Theatre Centre at the National Autonomous University of Mexico. With a scholarship of the International Theatre Institute, he went to the theatres in Köln and Esslingen, Germany, and a British Council scholarship enabled him to study theatre administration in London, Leicester and Glasgow. Following some years as an assistant director, he directed his first play in 1986, Joe Orton's *Loot*. Other productions include Kaiser's *Von Morgens bis Mitternachts* (*From Morn to Midnight*) and Max Frisch's *Don Giovanni oder Die Liebe zur Geometrie* (*Don Giovanni or Love for Geometry*), as well as several operas.

Richmond, Brian (1947–) Director, Canada. Richmond was the founding artistic director of Persephone Theatre in 1975. In 1981–2, he worked as dramaturg for the Montréal Playwright's Workshop. He has since served as artistic director of several theatres, including Magnus Thea-

tre (1983–7) and Théâtre Passe Muraille (1988–91). Richmond has also been a guest teacher at several university drama departments and at the National Theatre School in Montréal. His best work, which includes the direction of smash hit premieres like *Cruel Tears and Fire*, is solidly based in strong stage movement and physicalization.

Rickman, Alan (1946–) Actor, Great Britain. After attending the Royal College of Art and working as a graphic designer, Rickman received a scholarship to train at the Royal Academy of Dramatic Art (1972–4). His stage career has been associated mainly with the Royal Shakespeare Company, where he has performed regularly since 1978. His semi-detached, casual, laidback, take-it-or-leave it approach was ideal for his parts as Jacques in *As You Like It* (1985), the Gustaf Gründgens-based Henrik Höfgen in Ariane MNOUCHKINE's adaptation of Klaus Mann's novel *Mephisto* (1985), and an insolently seductive Valmont in *Les Liaisons Dangereuses* (1985, directed by Howard DAVIES). He also played Hamlet in a production directed by Robert Sturua (1992), portraying Hamlet as a dangerous, unlikable man. In 1988 he launched an internationally successful film career, returning to the stage in 1998 as Antony in *Antony and Cleopatra* at the Royal National Theatre.

Rigg, Diana (1938–) Actor, Great Britain. Rigg trained at the Royal Academy of Dramatic Art, and scored a major early success as Cordelia in Peter BROOK's production of *King Lear* (with Paul SCOFIELD) for the Royal Shakespeare Company. She became well-known for her portrayal of Emma Peel in the television series *The Avengers*, but continued her stage career, with roles including STOPPARD's *Jumpers* (1972) and *Night and Day* (1978), Shaw's *Heartbreak House* (1983), *Berlin Bertie* by Howard BRENTON (1992), an award-winning performance in the title roles of Euripides's *Medeia* (1992 onwards, also Broadway), Brecht's *Mutter Courage und ihre Kinder* (*Mother Courage and her Children*, Royal National Theatre) and Racine's *Phèdre* (Almeida, 1998). She starred in Edward ALBEE's *Who's Afraid of Virginia Woolf?* at the Almeida (1996), directed by Howard DAVIES.

Rijnders, Gerardjan (1949–) Director and dramatist, The Netherlands. Rijnders read law and Norwegian, and later trained as a director at the Amsterdam Theatre School. His debut as a director was *La Dame aux Camélias* by Dumas fils in 1975, and as an author with the acclaimed *Schreber* (1976). In 1977 he became the leader of the Globe company in Eindhoven, where he raised a stir with his daring interpretations of the classics and his own camp comedies (such as *Troilus and Cressida* and Chekhov's *Tri sestry* (*Three Sisters*)). Influenced by Elizabeth LECOMPTE, Rijnders made many so-called 'montage-pieces', continuing after leaving Globe in 1985. In 1987 he took up his second big position as director of Toneelgroep Amsterdam. Work there includes successful productions of *Hamlet* and *Richard III* (with Pierre BOKMA in the lead), plays by Thomas Bernhard, and montages. Rijnders's work is clever, provocative and tends towards minimalism. His black comedies of misunderstanding that make up the *Silicone* trilogy (see Cas ENKLAAR and Marlies HEUER) have been translated into English, as has *Amateur*. The prolific Rijnders also acts and writes for television. He is considered a brilliant innovator of Dutch theatre. He has also directed at the Deutsches Theater in Berlin.

Ritter, Erika (1948–) Dramatist, Canada. Ritter received an MA in arts and drama from the University of Toronto. The themes of male–female relationships and the creating of art are recurrent in her plays, *A Visitor from Charleston* (1975),

The Splits (1975), *The Automatic Pilot* (1980) and *Murder at McQueens* (1986). 'Ritter's plays are all written in the style and tradition of the Comedy of Manners, where her shrewd eye for modern "yuppie" attitudes and ear for ways of talking are captured in often brilliant verbal wit'. The hugely popular *Automatic Pilot* deals with a young urban woman negotiating her way through a series of relationships and commenting on those relationships in a stand-up routine at a local comedy club. She has said of her work, 'If there is a common theme among [my] characters, it's the desire to have a kind of integrity. They make choices that run against the grain. If all the encouragement is towards selling out, towards making things easy, towards going for the bucks, there's something in these characters that wants to go the other way.'

Ritter, Ilse (1944–) Actor, Germany. Ritter trained at the Hochschule für Musik und Theater in Hannover, and was employed in Darmstadt, Wuppertal, Hamburg and Düsseldorf before joining Peter STEIN's Schaubühne (1973–7). She played Gertrude in Peter ZADEK's production of *Hamlet* (1977), Lady Macbeth with Luc BONDY, Celia in *As You Like It* (1986, directed by Zadek), and Queen Elizabeth in Schiller's *Maria Stuart* (1990, directed by Michael BOGDANOV). Recent roles include Chekhov's *Visnevyi sad* (*The Cherry Orchard*) and Susanne Amatosero's *Asylanten* (Hamburg, 1998, in a production directed by Kazuko WATANABE). Ritter has been described as 'a virtuoso performer without putting on an act, an expert of transformation but always recognizable, no classical heroine of tragedy but a fighter lost in dreams or a tough and thoughtful loser'.

Rodríguez, Gladys (1943–) Actor, Puerto Rico. Gladys Rodríguez earned a BA in theatre from the University of Puerto Rico, and since then has worked regularly as an actor, often under the direction of

Dean ZAYAS. Rodríguez's principal roles include the female leads in Bernard Slade's *Same Time Next Year* (1980), Bill Manhoff's *The Owl and the Pussycat* (1981) and D.H. Lawrence's *The Fox* (1983), as well as the only character in *Letter from an Unknown Wife*, adapted from the novel by Stephan Zweig. Rodríguez won particular praise for her sensuous and spirited portrayal of Blanche in Williams' *A Streetcar Named Desire* (El Otro Grupo, 1977, opposite Miguel Ángel SUÁREZ's Stanley on a set designed by Julio BIAGGI). Her films include *Desvío al paraíso* (*Shortcut to Paradise*, 1994, as Lona) and *Lo que le pasó a Santiago* (*Santiago, The Story of His New Life*, nominated for an Oscar for Best Foreign Language Film in 1989). Rodríguez has a reputation as a 'director's dream' for her discipline and versatility.

Rogovtseva, Ada (1937–) Actor, Ukraine. Rogovtseva graduated from the Karpenko-Kary Institute for the Art of the Theatre, Kiev, in 1950. She is an actor of bright individuality and great charm. Her repertoire is wide and varied. As a leading actor of the Lesia Ukrainka Russian Drama Theatre, Kiev (1959–94), she starred as Helen in Zorin's *Varshavskaia melodiia* (*The Warsaw Melody*, 1968), Lika Mizinova in Maliuhina's *Nasmeshlivoe moe schast'e* (*My Mocking Love*), Ranevskaya in Chekhov's *Visnevyi sad* (*The Cherry Orchard*, 1980, set designer Daniil LIDER) and Arkadina in *Cajka* (*The Seagull*, 1993), and Paola in Rattigan's *The Lady without Camelias*. She is well known to audiences for the role of Martha (with Bohdan STUPKA as her partner) in *Ne boius' siroho vovka* (*I am not Afraid of the Gray Wolf*) after *Who's Afraid of Virginia Woolf?* by Edward ALBEE (1995) written by the young Kievan experimenters Andrii Zholdak and Myroslav Hrynyshyn. She has also starred in numerous films.

Ronconi, Luca (1933–) Director and actor, Italy. After receiving a diploma from the National Academy of Dramatic Art, Ronconi worked as an actor with directors such as Luigi SQUARZINA. He started directing in 1963 and rose to international fame in 1969 with a dramatisation of Ludovico Ariosto's Renaissance epic poem *Orlando Furioso*, which he adapted with the poet Edoardo Sanguineti for theatre, television and film. In this piece, Ronconi subverted dramatic conventions related to the use of time and space by using mobile stages which encouraged spectators to follow the dramatic action from a number of locations. In 1977, Ronconi founded an experimental research group in Prato. Over the last thirty years he has become one of the most stimulating and influential practitioners in Italian theatre. His ongoing challenge to dramatic conventions and his exploration of the boundaries of dramatic form have offered material for debate to practitioners, academics, critics and theatregoers. Among his most notable productions are Goldoni's *La buona moglie* (*The Good Wife*, 1963), *Measure for Measure* (1967), Giordano Bruno's *Il Candelaio* (*The Candlemaker*, 1968), Kraus's *Die Letzten Tage der Menschheit* (*The Last Days of Humanity*, 1990) and O'Neill's *Mourning Becomes Elektra* (1997).

Ronen, Ilan (1947–) Director, Israel. Ronen trained at the Beit Zvi theatre school in Tel Aviv and began his professional work as an assistant to Mike Alfreds at the Khan Jerusalem municipal theatre, where he later became the artistic director. Ronen directed his own adaptations of Joseph Heller's *Catch 22* and Dostoyevsky's *Idiot* (*The Idiot*) as well as plays like Ben Jonson's *Volpone*. Ronen has directed a bilingual, Hebrew–Arabic production of Beckett's *Waiting for Godot*, and while serving as the artistic director at the Cameri Tel Aviv municipal theatre he directed plays like Motti LERNER's *Kastner*, Brecht's *Mutter Courage und ihre Kinder* (*Mother Courage and her Children*) and his own adaptation of von Kleist's *Michael Kohlhaas*. His productions mix theatrical spectacle with a strong ideological commitment.

Roofthooft, Dirk (1958–) Actor, Belgium. Following his training at the Studio Herman Teirlinck in Antwerp, Roofthooft became a member of the Nederlands Toneel Ghent (one of Flanders's biggest theatres) in 1983. Two years later, he left the company and decided to become a freelance actor. Since then, he has been playing in productions of most of the leading companies in Flanders and The Netherlands. He worked amongst others with Lucas VANDERVOST (De Tijd) in Schiller's *Don Carlos* (1988), Jan LAUWERS (Needcompany) in *Julius Caesar* (1990), Guy CASSIERS in *Het Liegen in Ontbinding* (*Lying in Decay*, Kaaitheater, 1993) and Theu BOERMANS (De Trust) in Chekhov's *Tri sestry* (*Three Sisters*). He also works for film and television. Roofthooft is praised as a versatile, ironic, exuberant and astonishing actor, who succeeds in making difficult texts accessible to his audience.

Rose, Jürgen (1937–) Designer, Germany. Rose became an assistant to set designer Franz Mertz at the theatre in Darmstadt. He studied at the Akademie der Bildenden Künste in Berlin, as well as at the acting school of Marlise Ludwig. Since 1961 he has worked with the Münchner Kammerspiele, as well as with other major theatres in Germany and Austria. Set designer Rosalie, one of his students, wrote: 'On the one hand, he unlike anyone else loves beautiful images, colours, landscapes, arrangements – on the other hand he always tries to find, in all his works, a connection with real situations and everyday life: "That is a beautiful image! – But where is the connection to today?"'

Rošič, Neva (1935–) Actor, Croatia. Rošič trained at the Academy of Dramatic Art in Zagreb. From 1956–68 she worked with the Zagreb Theatre Gavella where she stayed for twelve years, moving on to the HNK (Croatian National Theatre) in Zagreb. Since 1979 she has been working as a professor of acting at the Academy of Dramatic Art (the first woman professor). She was a very successful Rosaura in Goldoni's *La vedova scaltra* (*The Cunning Widow*). At the HNK she played three most complex and demanding characters of Croatian drama: Laura in Krleža's *U agoniji* (*In Agony*, 1969), Klara in *Leda* (1972) and Baroness Castelli in *Gospoda Glembajevi* (*The Glembays*, 1974). Further credits include Portia in *Julius Caesar* (1970), Gertrude in *Hamlet* (1975) and Arkadina in Chekhov's *Cajka* (*The Seagull*, 1976). In 1975 she played the title role in Matković's monodrama *Klitemnestra* (*Clytemnestra*), and gave a brilliant portrait of Sarah Bernhardt in Murell/Willson's *Sarah and the Scream of the Lobster*. The moment she steps on the stage she makes a direct contact with the audience. It is said that she represents the eternal feminine principle on the stage. Her acting is intertwined with intellect and sensuality, trying to reconcile these opposites.

Ross, Andrew (1947–) Director, Australia. Ross worked extensively in fringe and university theatre in Melbourne, but he is best known for his Perth-based work involving Aboriginal writers and theatre workers. He directed the premiere productions of Jack DAVIS's plays *Kullark* (1979), *The Dreamers* (1982), *No Sugar* (1985) and *Barungin* (1988), and he directed the latter three plays presented together as *The First Born* trilogy in 1988, thus offering a counter-statement to the celebrations of the Bicentennial year. Other Aboriginal works Ross has directed include Jimmy Chi's musical *Bran Nu Dae* (1990) and Sally Morgan's *Sistergirl* (1992). Ross was founding artistic director of the

Swan River Stage Company, Perth in 1982; he was also founding artistic director of the Black Swan Theatre Company, Perth, in 1991.

Rotimi, Ola (1938–) Dramatist and director, Nigeria. Rotimi's plays include *The Gods Are Not To Blame* (an adaptation of Sophocles's *Oidipus tyrannos* (*King Oedipus*), *Our Husband Has Gone Mad Again, Kurunmi, Holding Talks, If...* and *Hopes of the Living Dead*. Rotimi's plays are characterized by his bold experiments with dramatic form, staging techniques and manipulation of language. As a director, Rotimi is especially known for his abilitiy to move many characters in and through space. His directing credits include all his own plays and *King Christophe* by Aimé Césaire, *The Curse* by Kole OMOTOSO, *Sizwe Bansi is Dead* by Athol Fugard, Winston NTSHONA and John KANI, *The Emperor Jones* by Eugene O'Neill and *Behold My Redeemer* by Rasheed Gbadamosi.

Roxburgh, Richard (1961–) Actor, Australia. Trained at the National Institute of Dramatic Art, Sydney, Roxburgh has a successful career in film (for example, *Children of the Revolution*) and television, as well as theatre, but it was in theatre that he has had one of his most highly acclaimed successes as Hamlet, directed by Neil ARMFIELD (1994 and 1995). What appealed most about this Hamlet was his energy, his anger, his damaged innocence and his complex relation with Horatio (Geoffrey RUSH). Roxburgh created the absolute antithesis of the melancholic, inactive prince. Roxburgh was also an intriguing Trigorin in Armfield's 1997 *Seagull*, generating a powerful sense of a man unable to take control of anything in his life, touchingly excited and hopeful of what could come of his relationship with Nina.

Roy, Amitava (1947–) Actor, India. Roy has become known for his outstanding contribution to Theatre of the Absurd in India by playing roles such as Pozzo in Beckett's *Waiting for Godot*, and Jerry in ALBEE's *Zoo Story*. Additional roles include Julius Caesar, Macbeth and Thomas Beckett (in the play by Anouilh) in some remarkable Bengali productions. He has worked with Hansgünther HEYME, Günter Grass and Georg TABORI. Brecht wrote a play based on Roy's ancestor, *Calcutta 4th May*, which Roy directed in Calcutta in 1987.

Rudkin, (James) David (1936–) Dramatist, Great Britain. The Royal Shakespeare Company staged his first play *Afore Night Come* in 1962, as part of an 'experimental season'. Without violating its social realist form, the play suggests destructive and creative cosmologies and rites lurking beneath the superficial civilization of the English Black Country. *Cries from Casement as his Bones are Brought to Dublin* (1971), broadcast by BBC radio and staged by the RSC, develops a dramatic grappling with Anglo-Irish relations and sexual identity (Rudkin is himself half-Irish), pursued in more microscopic form in *Ashes* (1973). His major plays, *The Sons of Light* (1975), *The Triumph of Death* (1981) and *The Saxon Shore* (1986), are troubling, complexly romantic, mythic explorations of identity in social crisis, with characteristic reference to imperialism, religion, the animal savagery of instinct and the darkest recesses of sexuality. The experiences of his Promethean protagonists testify to Rudkin's sense that hope lies in the imaginative abilities of each individual to recreate myth in their own individual terms. While he has maintained a consistent level of activity with radio drama and television and cinema screenplays, including work as translator and adaptor, a reappraisal of his continuingly daring original work for the stage is overdue.

Ruganda, John (1941–) Dramatist, actor and director, Uganda. Ruganda was a member of the Makerere Free Travelling Theatre, a founder-member of the Makonde Theatre Group in Uganda and founder-member of the Nairobi Travelling Theatre in Kenya. His greatest strength as a playwright is his highly evocative and almost poetic prose which lends a certain elegiac dignity and beauty to some of his major characters. *The Floods* is a passionate extended elegy on Idi Amin's dictatorial regime in Uganda. Other plays include *The Burdens, Music Without Tears* (another play about the Idi Amin period, 1982), *Black Mamba* (1973), *The Covenant of Death* (1973) and *Echoes of Silence* (1986). Ruganda is also an accomplished actor and director He now lives and works in exile in Kenya, but his themes are still the ills plaguing his native Uganda.

Ruscitadewi, Anak Agung Mas (1965–) Director, dramatist and performer, Indonesia. Ruscitadewi studied Archaeology at Udayana University, Bali. She began writing theatre pieces and short stories in high school and, in 1985 her script *Laki-Laki Serumah,* was selected as the best new play in Bali. In 1990 she was assistant director of *Sumpah Palapa Gaja Mada* for the Bali Arts Festival, and in 1991 she wrote and directed *Mahkota Raja,* performed at the Arts Centre in Denpasar. The following year she directed a group of American university students in *A Midsummer Night's Dream* at STSI (Academy of Performing Arts), and in 1993 wrote and directed *Sang Puteri,* again for Denpasar Arts Centre. In 1994, her theatre company performed *Sang Pemburu* in Taiwan. She also wrote and directed *Lawa-Lawa,* which has toured schools and universities throughout Bali and was televised by TVRI Denpasar. Her theatre work is moving away from word-based productions to a performance style with more use of movement and voice; she says she seeks a theatre out of the ordinary, like holy sacrificial ceremony. She has published poetry, short stories and dramas and is a journalist for the *Bali Post.*

Rush, Geoffrey (1951–) Actor and director, Australia. Rush worked in Queensland Theatre company productions before training at the Lecoq school in Paris and as a director in London. After a period with the Adelaide Lighthouse ensemble, Rush has frequently been associated with the work of director Neil ARMFIELD, for whom Rush has played roles as diverse as Subtle in Ben Jonson's *The Alchemist,* where Rush's ability to transform himself from character to character was brilliantly displayed; a Horatio through whose eyes the action of *Hamlet* was seen; and Proposhkin in Gogol's *Zapiski sumasshedshego* (*Diary of a Madman*) in a production which received great acclaim. Rush's direction of the farcical pub-style entertainment *The Popular Mechanicals* and its sequel *Pop Mechs 2,* based on characters from *A Midsummer Night's Dream,* was a popular hit. Rush has appeared in several films but is best known for his Oscar-winning performance in *Shine.* Rush's greatest strength is his versatility and his ability to transform himself radically.

Ruszt, József (1937–) Director, Hungary. Ruszt first worked as a director of amateur actors at the Budapest University Theatre. By 1963 he had completed his training at the Academy of Theatre and Film Art. Between 1963–74 he was a member of the Csokonai Theatre in Debrecen. Since then he held various posts as artistic director (1974–8, Katona József Theatre of Kecskemét; 1978–82, Budapest Népszínház; 1982–7, artistic director, Hevesi Sándor Theatre of Zalaegerszeg; 1988–90, National Theatre of Szeged). With actors who had left the Szeged company, he founded the Independent Theatre which operated in Budapest between 1991–4. Since 1994, Ruszt has been a leading member of the Budapest Chamber Theatre. Major productions include Madách's *Az ember tragédiá* (*The Tragedy of Man*), *Romeo and Juliet* (several productions), *Troilus and Cressida*, *Othello*, Lessing's *Nathan der Weise* (*Nathan the Sage*), Goethe's *Egmont*, Chekhov's *Tri sestry* (*Three Sisters*), Marlowe's *Edward II*, Arthur MILLER's *The Price* and Strindberg's *Dödsdansen* (*Dance of Death*). Ruszt is one of the most interesting directors of contemporary Hungarian theatre, a constant experimenter and re-inventor. He specializes in modern adaptations of Hungarian classics and inspired new versions of the canon.

Rylance, Mark Actor, Great Britain. After training at the Royal Academy of Dramatic Art, Rylance appeared in Edward BOND's *Lear* at the Royal Shakespeare Company in 1982, where he later returned to play Hamlet (1989) as a vulnerable, pitiful invalid, and Romeo (1989). For the National Theatre, he appeared in Michelene Wandor and Mike Alfreds's *The Wandering Jew* (1987) and Goldoni's *Villeggiatura* (*Countrymania*, adapted by Mike Alfreds, 1987). He played Benedick in Matthew WARCHUS's West End production of *Much Ado About Nothing*, and has directed and acted in Shakespeare at the new Globe on the South Bank of London, of which he was made artistic director in 1995.

S

Sabban, Rafik (1933–) Director and scriptwriter, Syria. Sabban's work as a director was heavily influenced by Jean Villar (under whom he trained), and Jean-Louis Barrault. In Damascus, Sabban introduced Shakespeare and Molière to a Syrian audience accustomed to low comedies. From 1960 onwards he was the dominant force in the newly founded National Theatre, and later with Syrian State Television. With an average of twelve new productions a year, major credits include Sophocles *Antigone* and *Electra*, El-Hakim's *Al-Sultan'l-Ha'er* (*The Sultan's Dilemma*), *The Merchant of Venice*, *Twelfth Night*, *Macbeth*, *Much Ado About Nothing*, Molière's *Tartuffe* and Calderón's *La vida es sueño* (*Life is a Dream*). In the 1970s he emigrated to Egypt, taking up a professorship in drama and cinema while pursuing an active career as scriptwriter for film and television. He is still considered by many as the true founder of the National Theatre in Damascus, and certainly the first director to establish the public's appreciation of the classics, bringing innovative spirit of modern theatre with him from France.

Sa'ed, Jihad (1953–) Actor, director, Syria. Sa'ed was trained in Egypt. On his return, he started as a theatre actor in Georges Schehade's *The Emmigrant of Brisbane*. His breakthrough as actor was first on the television mini-series, *The Artist and Love*, written and directed by Riad ISMAT. His debut as stage director was with an acclaimed production of Albert Camus's *Caligula* (1986, revived in 1996). He adapted, acted and directed *Jason and Medea* from the famous Greek tragedy. His play *Awacs* (1995) was a forward step in experimental theatre, both as a dramatist, director and actor. The play was made of fragmented scenes about the need for freedom in a world of suppression and persecution by local and international forces. He was appointed artistic director for Damascus National Theatre in the 1990s. His latest production is Mohamed El-Magout's *Kharej'l-Serb* (*Astray from the Flock*, 1998).

Saez, Gloria (1949–) Designer, Puerto Rico. Gloria Saez was born in Asturia, Spain and studied at the Escuela de Bellas Artes in Salamanca (1968–9) before continuing her studies in Art and Design in Belgium. After arriving in Puerto Rico, she began her career as a professional costume designer for the television station WPR. A passionate theatre artist, Saez is particularly noted for her detailed period costumes in works by Shakespeare, García Lorca and the dramatists of Golden Age Spain, as well as more recent designs for works by Puerto Rican and Latin American authors such as Rene Marqués, Premier Maldonado and Luis Rechani Agrait. She also designed costumes for the world premiere production of García Lorca's *El Público* under the direction of Victoria ESPINOSA (1978). Recent work includes costume designs for Lope de Vega's *Fuente Ovejuna* (University of Puerto Rico, 1998), Moliere's *Tartuffe* (Teatro Tapia, 1998) and Verdi's opera *Il Trovatori* (*The Troubadours*, Centro de Bellas Artes, 1998).

Sağiroğlu, Duygu (1932–) Designer and director, Turkey. Educated at the Faculty of Architecture, University of İstanbul, Sağiroğlu joined the State Theatre in 1956 as a designer. From 1959–76, he worked in the film industry as a director, artistic director and scriptwriter. In 1979, he started to work as an instructor at the Institute of Cinema and Television, Academy of Fine Arts in İstanbul. Theatre design work includes Ben Elton's *Take a Deep Breath* (1991–2), Gogol's *Zapiski Sumasshedshego* (*The Diary of a Madman*, 1992–3), *İnsanlarım* (*My People*, a collage of the poetry of Nazim Hikmet, 1994–5) and Ronald Duncan's *Abelard and Heloise* (1996–7). As a designer, he does not work independently from the playtext, aiming at a creation that translates the playtext rather than overwhelming the production. At present, he is working an an instructor at the Faculty of Fine Arts, Cinema-Television Department of Mimar Sinan University, İstanbul.

Sagoe, Abeiku (1957–) Actor, dramatist and director, Ghana. Among the roles Sagoe has played are Mlanga in *Chaka, the Zulu*, Dubois in *The Trial of Kwame Nkrumah*, Mambo in *Mambo* and White Oppressor in *Struggling Black Race*. He has also written and directed some very successful plays/productions including *Samori*, *The President's Wife*, *Tale of Aids*, *Hand of God* and *Devil's Influence*. Sagoe has been involved in numerous films as an actor and as director, including *Son of the Thundergod*, *Avengers*, *Not Again* and *Passionate Woman*. He is the director of the theatre company Living Echoes

Drama. Sagoe's theatre is highly sociopolitical as it attempts to engage with contemporary issues of Ghanaian society.

Saint-Eloy, Luc (1955–) Actor, director and author, France and Guadeloupe. Saint-Eloy came to Paris and studied drama at the Studio Charpentier, and film at the University of Paris VIII. In 1982 his first play *Le Prix de la Terre* (*The Price of the Earth*) achieved favourable notice, and he has continued to compose fiction and drama. His early acting experience was with Jules-Rosette's Théâtre Noir, and his own work with his group Théâtre de l'Air Nouveau, founded 1983, shows a similar orientation towards imaginative texts. In addition to adaptations and poetic 'montages', often with a strong musical component, such as *Bwa brilé* (*Burnt Wood*, 1996), a tribute to Eugène Mona. He had a particular success with his prizewinning drama of urban alienation, *Trottoir Chagrin* (*Pavement of Sorrows*, 1991), starring Mylène Wagram. *Chemin d'école* (*School Days*, 1997) is based on Patrick Chamoiseau's bittersweet memoir. Since 1994, Saint-Eloy has been active in Yasmina HO-YOU-FAT's 'Pitt a Pawol', which organizes regular encounters with French Caribbean writers through dramatic readings and discussion of new work, and has worked in film and television.

Sakate Yôji (1962–) Dramatist and director, Japan. Sakate first joined the theatre Group Teni 21 and then formed Rinkô-gun Theatre Company with members of the theatre research group of Keiô University in 1982. All the productions of the Rinkôgun TC were written and directed by Sakate. His plays include *Tokyo Saiban* (*Tokyo Trial*, 1988), *Come Out* (1989), *Breathless* (1990), *Kujira no Bohyô* (*The Epitaph for the Whales*) and *Kamigami no Kuni no Shuto* (*The Capital of the Gods' Country*, 1993). The latter toured in Europe in 1994 and 1996. An English adaptation of *The Epitaph for the Whales* was staged at the Gate Theatre, London in 1998. Sakate writes political and social plays in the mixed style of fantasy and absurdist theatre. He focuses on such controversial issues as whale hunting, cult religions, the Emperor system and the problem of waste.

Salibur, Lucette (1955–) Actor, dramatist and director, France and Martinique. Born of Guadeloupean parents in France, where she studied psychology, Salibur 'discovered' theatre in Martinique through the SERMAC theatre workshop, acting in several of their inaugural productions as well as working with Existence, Théâtre de La Soif Nouvelle and the founders of Poutyi pa teyat. Subsequent roles include Emilia in *Othello* (1983, Limoges Festival de la Francophonie), Léna in Fugard's *Boesman and Lena* (1984), parts in SOYINKA's *The Trials of Brother Jéro* (1984) and several television productions. The credibility of her portrayal of Madame Léonce in the film *Black Shack Alley* (1983) betrays the determination behind her 1984 directing debut and her 1989 founding of Nowtéat, a group including many unemployed from the SERMAC theatre workshops. Initially producing educational and children's theatre, and adaptations of literary and poetic texts, Nowtéat aims at financially independent professionalism. The success of *Boum et Aïda rencontra Mutant* (*Boom and Aida meets Mutant*, 1991), her allegorical satire on international politics, *Masters of the Dew* (1992), and her interest in collaboration, reflect her commitment to breaking new ground in Martinican theatre.

Salminen, Esko Kullervo (1940–) Actor, Finland. Salminen trained at the Theatre School of Finland, and has worked as an actor with the Finnish National Theatre (1961–9 and since 1992), Helsinki City Theatre (1969–71 and 1977–92) and Turku City Theatre (1971–7). Apart from work for film and television, major stage

roles include Lopakhin in Chekhov's *Visnevyi sad* (*The Cherry Orchard*), Danton in Büchner's *Danton's Tod* (*Danton's Death*), Trigorin in Chekhov's *Cajka* (*The Seagull*), the title roles in Ibsen's *Peer Gynt*, *Othello* and *Macbeth*, and Eddie Carbone in Arthur MILLER's *A View from the Bridge*. 'The dominant feature of Esko Salminen's work is that he questions traditional interpretations, giving them complexity and inner conflict which increases their believability and somehow brings them closer to the audience. But at the same time he has preserved the curious, captivating twinkle in the corner of his eye of the young man who is seeking his own way and assessing the state of the world.'

Samel, Udo (1953–) Actor, Germany. Samel trained in Frankfurt am Main. After seasons in Darmstadt and Düsseldorf, he was a member of the Schaubühne in Berlin from 1978–92. Samel is a master of transformation, who is at home equally with cunning or foolish characters in comedy and as a split, brooding hero in tragedy. Important roles include Kalldewey in *Kalldewey Farce* by Botho STRAUSS (1982, directed by Luc BONDY), Trofimov in Chekhov's *Visnevyi sad* (*The Cherry Orchard* 1989, directed by Peter STEIN) and Sosias in Kleist's *Amphitryon* (1991, directed by Klaus Michael GRÜBER).

Sánchez-Gijón, Aitana (1969–) Actor, Spain. Sánchez-Gijón studied acting at the RESAD, the Drama School of Madrid. Although she is perhaps most recognized for her work in film, she remains an accomplished theatre actor who has exercised wise restraint in her choice of roles. Her work in theatre includes Jacinto Benavente's *La malquerida* (*The Non-Wanted Woman*) in an acclaimed production by Miguel Narros in the mid-1980s and more recently a controversial high-profile staging of Tennessee Williams's *Cat on a Hot Tin Roof* directed by Mario GAS (1995). Her delicate, dark beauty, exquisite poise and steely presence have seen her work increasingly abroad. Like the generation that precedes her, including Antonio Banderas, Veronica Forqué, Cristina Marcos and Ana Belén, Aitana Sánchez-Gijón is as comfortable working within theatre as in film and indeed has forged parallel careers in both. In 1998 she replaced film director José Luis Borau as President of the Spanish Academy of Film.

Sanchís Sinisterra, José (1940–) Dramatist, Spain. Sanchís Sinisterra founded the important Aula de Teatre at the University of Valencia in 1964. In 1977 he created the theatre company El Teatro Fronterizo in Barcelona, and began a practical exploration of the relationship between narrative and theatre, through a series of projects using prose writers such as Kafka, Melville and Cortázar. His plays include *La leyenda de Gilgamesh* (*The Legend of Gilgamesh*) produced in 1978, followed by *Ñaque o de piojos y actors* (*Ñaque or Louses and Actors*) in 1980, *La primera de la clase* (*The Best in Class*) in 1984, and one of the most commercially successful plays of the new democratic Spain, *¡Ay, Carmela!* (1987). His work is marked by a prolific versatility which encompasses popular comedy, vaudeville, historical drama and mythology. In 1989, Sanchís Sinisterra founded the Sala Beckett in Barcelona, which has evolved into a space facilitating ongoing research into performance and dramaturgy. Here he has nurtured a whole new generation of dramatists including Sergi BELBEL. His most recent plays include *Pervertimento* (*Perversion*, 1988), *Pérdida en los Apalaches* (*Lost in the Apalaches*, 1990) and *El cerco de Leningrado* (*The Leningrad Siege*, 1994). He lectures at the Institut del Teatre of Barcelona.

Sander, Otto (1941–) Actor and director, Germany. Sander trained at the Otto Falckenberg Schule in Munich. After seasons in Düsseldorf, Heidelberg and with the Freie Volksbühne in Berlin, he was a member of the Schaubühne in Berlin from 1970–81, returning in later years for guest performances. At home in both tragedy and comedy, he excels equally with passive, depressive and cynical characters and completely intolerable philistines. Major parts include the Dovre Master in Peter STEIN's production of Ibsen's *Peer Gynt* (1971), Suslov in Gorki's *Dacniki* (*Sommergäste*, 1974, directed by Stein), Vershinin in Chekhov's *Tri sestry* (*Three Sisters*, 1984, dircted by Stein) and the title role in Kleist's *Amphitryon* (1991, directed by Klaus Michael GRÜBER. Sander has also directed and pursued a career in film.

Santagata, Alfonso (1947–) Director, dramatist and performer, Italy. After training at the Civica Scuola D'Arte Drammatica in Milan, Alfonso Santagata worked with Dario FO, Luca RONCONI and Carlo CECCHI. In 1979, together with Claudio Morganti, he founded the theatre company Katzenmacher. Influenced by Antonin Artaud, Santagata developed a challenging politicized practice focused around the notion of alienation. Often working with found objects, Santagata has reinterpreted a number of classical texts in the light of what could be described as romantic neorealism. Among his most interesting productions with Morganti are *Katzenmacher* (1979), *Büchner Mon Amour* (1981), *Hauser/ Hauser* (1986), *Dopo* (*After*, 1987), Beckett's *Endgame* (1990), Manlio Sgalambro's *Schopenhauer Song* (1995) and *King Lear* (1996).

Santiago Lavandero, Leopoldo (1912–) Director, Puerto Rico. Leopoldo Santiago Lavandero is considered by most theatre professionals in Puerto Rico to have been the primary force behind the proliferation of modern theatrical activity there. He pursued postgraduate study in theatre at Yale University in the late 1930s, eventually earning an MA in 1948. Don

Leopoldo (as he is known among his students and collaborators) founded the group Areyto with Emilio Belaval in 1940, and the Department of Drama at the University of Puerto Rico in 1941, both of which were aimed toward the creation of a theatre with uniquely 'Puerto Rican' character. Together with Rafael Cruz Eméric, he instituted the Teatro Rodante de Puerto Rico (Puerto Rican Travelling Theatre) in 1946, a group composed of professional actors as well as scholarship students, which brought classics of world theatre to the people of Puerto Rico, using a truck which was converted on location into a stage (a practice which Joseph Papp adapted for some of his productions in New York some years later). He retired from the theatre in 1972 and is currently living in Florida.

Santos, Carles (1940–) Director, composer, performer and musician, Spain. Trained as a pianist at Barcelona's Conservatoire, Santos made his reputation as a concert pianist before moving on to specialize in contemporary music in the early 1970s. Since 1978 he has been associated almost exclusively with his own compositions. *La Pantera Imperial* (*The Imperial Panther*, 1998), forged from the music of Bach, is a marked exception, and it has been a search for a visual performance language for music which moves beyond the parameters of concert recitals or operatic rendition which has fuelled Santos's own evolution from pianist to choreographer of opulent, elegant spectacles infused with a raucous sensuality. His trajectory has been marked by a resistance to reductive or conclusive categorizations and the need, in his own words, to 'make music visible'. Working closely with choreographer Montserrat Colomé, he has created a company which has questioned the very parameters of music theatre. The exuberant theatricality of his non-plot driven productions, like the imaginative *Figasantos-Fagotrop*

(1996) and the gorgeously baroque *L'esplèndida vergonya del fet mal fet* (*The Splendid Shame of the Deed Badly Done*), both hinging on the process of physicalizing the aural, has secured his company a pivotal position within Catalunya's artistic scene.

Sarabhai, Mallika (1953–) Dancer, actor and theatre activist, India. Having achieved renown as a classical dancer and film actor, (including the role of Draupadi in Peter BROOK's *The Mahabharata*), Mallika Sarabhai's more recent co-written, co-directed and performed work includes multimedia and dance–theatre collaborations on sociopolitical issues. *Shakti: The Power of Woman* (1989), *Sita's Daughters* (1990) and *V for...* (1996) deal with images and roles of women in India and with the nature and causes of violence. These rank her among leading women practitioners in the contemporary performance scene, both in India and abroad, where her work has been consistently well-received. Co-director of Darpana Academy of Performing Arts, Ahmedabad, she has also developed extensive programmes using performance as social outreach in schools and rural communities. Her work is characterized by cross-border experimentation both formally and thematically.

Sarkola, Lauri Asko (1945–) Actor, Finland. Sarkola trained in the Swedish language at the Theatre School of Finland and worked as an actor at Lille Teatern (Little Swedish Theatre). For several years he also served as the theatre's artistic director. Since 1997 he has been artistic director of the Helsinki City Theatre. Major parts include Harpagon in Molière's *L'avare* (*The Miser*), Hamlet and numerous plays that demonstrated his talent as a comic actor. His work in light comedies and farces has attracted big audiences. Asko Sarkola acts both in Swedish and Finnish. At the Little Swedish Theatre, a play is often first rehearsed and played in Swedish and then, with almost the same cast, rehearsed and put on agan in Finnish.

Satô Makoto (1943–) Director, Japan. Satô attended Haiyû-za (Actors' Theatre) Drama School, then founded Jiyû Gekijô (the Freedom Theatre Company) with his course mates from the ATDS in 1966. He began staging a series of five plays, *Nezumi-kozô Jirokichi* (*Nezumi-kozô the Robber*) with the Engeki Centre 68 Theatre Group, which toured in a big black tent. He questioned the Shôwa era by his trilogy *Kigeki – Abesada no Inu* (*Abesada's Dog*), *Kinema to Kaijin* (*Cinema and a Monster*) and *Buranki Goroshi* (*Murder of Buranki*) – from 1973–5. Sato also directs for the marionette theatre company, Yûki-za in collaboration with Magosaburô Yuki; *The Virgin's Mask* by KARA (1975) was their first production. More recently, his *Heiwa no tame no Salome Dance* (*Salome Dance for the Peace*) was produced in Hong Kong (1992). His plays hold the political concerns or messages against the Establishment behind the dialogues.

Saunders, Justine (1953–) Actor, Australia. Trained at the National Institute of Dramatic Art, Sydney in 1980, Saunders is one of the best-known and most successful Aboriginal actors and one of the first to make a career in film, television and mainstream Australian theatre. Saunders has played leads in several Aboriginal authored plays, including *The Cake Man* by Robert Merritt and Jack DAVIS's *No Sugar* and *Honeyspot*. She played the lead role in an episode of *Women of the Sun* (1981), a series of four television dramas focusing on Aboriginal women. In 1988 she toured a one-woman recital of Aboriginal writing in the USA. In white authored plays, Saunders has played in Thomas Keneally's *Bullie's House* and Louis NOWRA's *Capricornia*. In 1991–2 Saunders played Tituba in a Sydney Theatre Company production of Arthur MILLER's *The Crucible* and for Q Theatre played the male white part of Samuel Simile in the nineteenth-century musical play *The Currency Lass*. Given the central joke of this play – Simile expects a Currency (i.e., Australian native free-born) lass to be black – this action was appropriately subversive.

Savary, Jérôme (1942–) Actor, director and dramatist, France. Born in Argentina, Savary grew up in France and New York, where he was influenced by jazz music. In 1965 he founded his own theatre company, which in 1968 became the Grand Magic Circus. His extravagant productions for the company soon became notorious; he later applied his spectacle approach to the classics: Büchner's *Leonce und Lena* at the Schauspielhaus in Hamburg, *'Tis Pity She's a Whore*, and most recently Brecht's *Mutter Courage und ihre Kinder* (*Mother Courage and her Children*) with Katharina THALBACH in the title role.

Sawamura Tôjûrô II (1943–) Kabuki actor, Japan. The second son of Sawamura Sôjûrô VIII and the younger brother of Sawamura Sôjûrô IX, he succeeded to the present stage name in 1976. In recent years, Tôjûrô has been working for a revival of the Konpira Ô-kabuki at the Kanamaru-za Theatre, one of the original kabuki theatres of the 1830s. He has also been working for a revival of the O-kuni Kabuki of the Izumo Shrine where kabuki originated in the late sixteenth century. Tôjûrô is a talented *onnagata* actor (a female impersonator) and plays a wide variety of female characters from a beautiful lady to a comical battered middle-class wife. He is good in *sewamono* (domestic style) kabuki. His representative roles are Chidori in *Heuke Nyogo no Shima* (*Shunkan*) by Monzaemon Chikamatsu, Otomi in *Yowanasake Ukina no Yokogushi* (*O-Tomi*) by Mokuami Kawatake, Chobei's wife in Ninjo *Banashi Bunshichi Mottoi* (*Bunshichi*), originally written by Sanyutei Encho I. Sawamura has performed in Canada, the USA (1986) and Egypt (1988) on kabuki overseas tours.

Schade, Doris (1924–) Actor, Germany. After growing up in the Soviet Union and Japan, Schade trained at the Altes Theater in Leipzig. After working in Osnabrück, Bremen, Nürnberg and Frankfurt, she joined the Münchner Kammerspiele in 1961, and from 1972–7 she was with the Deutsches Schauspielhaus Hamburg, returning to the Münchner Kammerspiele in 1977. Her parts range from bigotted, tyrannical mothers to worldly-wise, active servants: Desdemona, Julia in ALBEE's *A Delicate Balance*, Isabella in *Measure for Measure*, Merteuil in Heiner Müller's *Quartett*, Gunhild in Ibsen's *John Gabriel Borkman*, Mother in Thomas Bernhard's *Am Ziel* (*At the Goal*, 1993) and, most recently, in Martin McDonagh's *Beuaty Queen of Leenane* (1998).

Schäffer, Judit (1931–) Designer, Hungary. Schäffer studied at the Budapest Applied Arts College and joined the József Attila Theatre in 1957. Between 1966–87 she was the chief designer of the Budapest National Theatre, from 1987–91 at the Hungarian State Opera, and since 1991 she has been a member of the Budapest Chamber Theatre. She taught for four years at the Applied Arts College and took an important part in forming the Hungarian school of costume design in the 1960s and 1970s. She has designed costumes for several Hungarian theatres, open air stages and foreign opera houses, and has taken part in several exhibitions at home and abroad. Major productions include Chekhov's *Ivanov*, *A Comedy of Errors*, *The Tempest*, *The Merchant of Venice*, *Twelfth Night*, *The Taming of The Shrew*, *Othello*, Molière's *Les femmes savantes* (*Bluestockings*), ALBEE's *Three Tall Women*, Marlowe's *Edward II* and Wilde's *The Importance of Being Earnest*. In opera, productions include

Verdi's *La Traviata* and *Nabucco* and Bartók's *Bluebeard's Castle*. Her art is characterized by elegant formal culture, tasteful use of different styles and motifs, affinity to characterization, inventiveness and humour.

Scherhaufer, Peter (1942–) Director, Czech Republic. Scherhaufer graduated from the Brno Academy of Performing Arts. A co-founder and resident director of the Brno experimental theatre group Goose on a String (Husa na provázku) (1968), the group became significant as a centre of protest against the regime in the 1970s and 1980s. Influenced by the aesthetics of epic theatre (Brecht) and by folkloric principles, he mostly directs his own plays and adaptations (*Commedia del'arte*, 1974, Dostoyevsky's *Brat'ia Karamazovy* (*The Karamazov Brothers*), 1981, *Labyrint svìta a ráj srdce* (*The Labyrinth of the World and the Paradise of the Heart*), 1983, the three-part *Shakespearomania*, 1988–92). His productions synthesize different genres and are held in untraditional spaces, using a different acting surface and seating arrangement each time. He has also contributed to joint alternative theatre projects (*Cesty* (*Paths*), 1984, and *Mir Caravane*, 1989).

Schleef, Einar (1944–) Director, designer and author, Germany. Schleef studied at the Kunsthochschule Berlin-Weißensee and drew attention to his work as set designer and co-director of several productions at the Berliner Ensemble, including Wedekind's *Frühlings Erwachen* (*Spring Awakening*, 1973–4) and Strindberg's *Fröken Julie* (*Miss Julie*). In 1976 he moved to West Berlin and worked mainly as a novelist until, in 1986, he was invited to Frankfurt to direct his own project, *Mütter* (*Mothers*). The production was highly controversial, as were many of the following, characterized by strong images, loud staccato speeches, speaking or screaming chorus and multiple characters. Most reent work includes

Brecht's *Herr Puntila und sein Knecht Matti* (*Mr Puntila and his Servant Matti*) at the Berliner Ensemble (1996), Wilde's *Salome* in Düsseldorf (1997), and Elfriede JELINEK's *Ein Sportstück* (*A Piece of Sports*) in Vienna (1998).

Schmid, Jan (1936–) Director and dramatist, Czech Republic. Schmid studied at the College of Fine Arts in Prague and in 1963 founded the Studio Ypsilon in Liberec (which moved to Prague in 1979), where he works to this day. He directs unconventional plays (Picasso's *Desire Grabbed by the Tail*, 1969; Allen's *God*, 1990) and dramatizations (Ilf-Petrov's *Twelve Chairs*, 1973; Kafka's *America*, 1989). In addition to the many dramatizations, he has written several original plays for his ensemble, using cut montages, all aimed at exploring the Czech national character, including *Trináct vùní* (*Thirteen Fragrances*, 1975) and *Voni sou hodnej chlapec* (*You're a Good Lad*, 1984, based on the life of Czech writer Jaroslav Hašek) and the role of the artist in society (*Michelangelo Buonarotti*, 1974, and *Mozart in Prague*, 1991). His original style links factual theatre, cabaret, musical theatre and the fine arts with collective improvisation as a method of preparing the performance.

Schneider, Eric (1961–) Actor and director, Luxembourg. Schneider attended the University of Wales, Aberystwyth and the Whitechapel Academy of Dramatic Arts. He collaborated as an actor, co-director and actor's trainer with tag poetry's production of Movements of the Mouth, double-billing Ernst Jandl's *Die Humanisten* (*The Humanists*) and *Aus der Fremde* (*From the Distance*, 1991, The Octagon, London, directed by Thomas Gruber). The same year he played Starhemberg in the world premiere of Howard BARKER's *The Europeans* (Theatr Y Castell, Aberystwyth, directed by John O'Brien and David Ian Rabey). He has translated into Luxembourgeois and directed two of Barker's plays, *The Castle* (1990, Sprangfal Theatre Company, Escher Schluechthaus arts centre) and *The Europeans* (1995, Théâtre d'Esch, commissioned by the theatre and Luxembourg European Cultural City). He is a founder member of the Lurking Truth and played in the world premiere of David Ian Rabey's *The Back of Beyond* (1996). In 1998, he dramatised and directed Bulgakov's *Heart of a Dog* at the Théâtre d'Esch. He is also a writer of poetry and short stories.

Schroeter, Werner (1946–) Director, Germany. Schroeter studied psychology before embarking on his career, initially mainly in film. Since 1972 he has also directed in the theatre, where his work has proved as controversial as his films. He pushes his performers to extremes. Productions for the stage include Wilde's *Salome* (1973), Schiller's *Don Carlos* (1982), Euripides's *Medeia* (Düsseldorf, 1989), *King Lear* (Düsseldorf, 1990, with Hermann LAUSE in the title role), Aeschylus's *Persai* (*The Persians*, Köln, 1995), Marlowe's *Edward II* at the Berliner Ensemble (1996), and Croatian dramatist Slobodan SNAJDER's *Windsbraut* (*Bride of the Wind*, Bochum, 1998).

Schwab, Martin (1937–) Actor, Germany. Schwab trained for the stage at the Max Reinhardt Schule in Berlin and Max Reinhardt Seminar in Vienna. After Neuwied, Oldenburg (1963–8), and Ulm (1968–72), he joined Claus PEYMANN's company in Stuttgart (1972–9), Bochum (1979–82), and Burgtheater Vienna (since 1987), where roles include Orest in Goethe's *Iphigenie in Tauris* (1977), the title role in Büchner's *Woyzeck* (1989), and the Father in Pirandello's *Sei personaggi in cerca d'autore* (*Six Characters in Search of an Author*). More recently he appeared in Ionesco's *La cantatrice chauve* (*The Bald Soprano*) and *La leçon* (*The Lesson*, Burgtheater Vienna, 1997), and Marlowe's *Edward II*. Perhaps not a star, 'he has been called one of the most exciting German-speaking actors, especially because of his ability to very convincingly portray an extremely wide range of different characters'.

Schwarz, Elisabeth (1938–) Actor, Germany. Schwarz trained at the Otto Falckenberg Schule in Munich. From 1964–72 she worked with the Staatstheater Stuttgart, after that mainly with the theatre in Frankfurt, as well as the Münchner Kammerspiele, the Deutsches Schauspielhaus in Hamburg and the Freie Volksbühne Berlin, in productions by Peter Palitzsch, Luc BONDY, Frank-Patrick STECKEL, Dieter DORN, Hans NEUENFELS and Jürgen GOSCH. In 1985 she joined Jürgen Flimm at the Thalia Theatre in Hamburg, where roles include Herzeloide in DORST/WILSON's *Parzival* (1987), Anna Petrowna in Chekhov's *Platonov* (1989, directed by Flimm) and Laura in Strindberg's *Fadren* (*The Father*). She uses her highly differentiated means as an actor to engage with her characters in a thoughtful, reflexive exchange.

Schwarz, Libgart (1941–) Actor, Austria. Schwarz trained at the Mozarteum in Salzburg and the Max Reinhardt Seminar in Vienna. After seasons in Graz, she joined the Düsseldorfer Schauspielhaus; later she appeared with the Freie Volksbühne in Berlin, the Theater am Turm in Frankfurt am Main and the Staatstheater Stuttgart. Major parts early on in her career include Gretchen in Goethe's *Urfaust*, Desdemona, Ophelia and Anya in Chekhov's *Visnevyi sad* (*The Cherry Orchard*). Since the mid-1970s, Libgart Schwarz has been associated with the Schaubühne in Berlin, appearing in productions directed by Peter STEIN, Luc BONDY, Andrea BRETH and Klaus Michael GRÜBER, developing a uniquely remarkable style in both classical and modern parts.

Scofield, Paul (1922–) Actor, Great Britain. Scofield attended Croydon Repertory Theatre School and London Mask Theatre School. Since his debut in 1940 he has become one of the most renowned actors in Britain, frequently mentioned with Gielgud and Olivier. He was a notable Hamlet for Peter BROOK, and created the part of Sir Thomas More in Robert Bolt's *A Man for All Seasons*, a role he later repeated on film. For Brook he played the title role in *King Lear* (1962). In 1979 he scored another major success as Salieri in Peter SHAFFER's *Amadeus* (National Theatre, directed by Peter HALL, with Simon CALLOW as Mozart and Felicity KENDAL as Constanze). For the National Theatre he also played Othello (1980, also directed by Hall, with Kendal as Desdemona), Don Quixote and Oberon (1982). In 1992 he was Captain Shotover in *Heartbreak House* (directed by Trevor NUNN, with Vanessa REDGRAVE and Felicity Kendal). His portrayal of the title role in Ibsen's *John Gabriel Borkman* (Royal National Theatre, starring Vanessa Redgrave and directed by Richard EYRE, 1996) was called one of the great performances of this century and won the Evening Standard Award for best actor.

Scott-Mitchell, Michael (1960–) Designer, Australia. Scott-Mitchell graduated from the National Institute of Dramatic Art, Sydney in 1983. His design projects have ranged over theatre, operas, films, musical, architecture and interior design (D4 Design). He has designed several times for John BELL's Bell Shakespeare Company, including the controversial *Merchant of Venice* directed by Carol Woodrow, which set the opening scene of the play in a men's sauna. Scott-Mitchell's set for Richard WHERRETT's production of Brecht's *Leben des Galilei* (*Life of Galileo*, Sydney Theatre Company, 1996) combined revolves, flickering computer screens, astronomical instruments and a grand screen projecting images (including some of the space probe Galileo) for the finale. This design was provocative, interventionist, grand in scale, busy and a visual feast. Scott-Mitchell's skills in interior design as well as theatre design came to the fore in his conversion of the interior of Paddington (Sydney) Town Hall for *Pageant*, the drag beauty pageant show.

Seciu, Valeria (1939–) Actor, Romania. A graduate of the Theatre and Film Institute in Bucharest, Seciu gave her debut with the part of Veronica Micle in *Eminescu* by Mircea Stefănescu at the National Theatre in Bucharest. Among the numerous leading roles performed at the National Theatre were Camille in Musset's *On ne badine pas avec l'amour* (*Don't Joke about Love*), Honey in Edward ALBEE's *Who's Afraid of Virginia Woolf?* and other leading roles in plays by Josif NAGHIU and D.R. POPESCU. In 1978 she joined Teatrul Mic (The Little Theatre) where she appeared in many successful roles, most of all under the direction of Cătălina BUZOIANU, proving an extreme and charming sensitivity guided by a highly professional technique. In 1991 she founded the private theatre Levant, where she produced plays by VIŞNIEC and Ariel Dorfman. Valeria Seciu has received many awards for her work on both stage and film.

Seet, Khiam Keong (1957–) Director and critic, Singapore. Seet is the person behind several landmark productions in Singapore theatre's annals: he directed *The Eye of History* (1992) which featured Singapore's former prime minister and current senior minister as a principal character, and he also directed *Details Cannot Body Wants* (1992), the first Singapore play given an R(A) rating (entry restricted to those above the age of eighteen). As producer, he was responsible for the Asian premiere of a Beijing opera sung in English, Guan Hanqing's *Yuan zaju* (*Freed by a Flirt*, 1995) and the first full-length Kabuki presented in the English language, *Sukeroku: Flower of Edo* (1998). He currently heads the first and only degree-granting programme in theatre studies, at the National University of Singapore, and is instrumental in grooming new generations of thespians. As an Arts Advisor to the National Arts Council of Singapore, he sits on the Drama Advisory Committee (for which he assesses and evaluates local playscripts) as well as chairs the Grants Committee for Theatre, which administers and disburses various grants to Singapore's theatre groups and arts agencies. Recipient of a Fulbright Fellowship and two British Council fellowships, Seet holds a Ph.D. from the University of Exeter as well as degrees from the Universities of Toronto, Singapore and London.

Segda, Dorota (1966–) Actor, Poland. Segda graduated from the State Theatre Academy of Cracow. With her beautiful appearance of an angelic, innocent blonde, she created a series of roles in which the girl's inner tranquility is dramatically challenged, with characters on the verge of a nervous and mental breakdown urged to explore manifold and dark layers of their own femininity. Stage credits, all at Stary Teatr of Cracow, include Ophelia (1989), Sonya in Dostoyevsky's *Prestuplenie I nakazanie* (*Crime and Punishment*, 1989), Sasha in Chekhov's *Platonov* (1989), the title role in Gozzi's *Turandot* (1991), Albertynka in Gombrowicz's *Operetta*, Manka in Gombrowicz's *Slub* (*The Wedding*, 1991), and Hermia in *A Midsummer Night's Dream* (1992). On television, she played the title roles in Schiller's *Maria Stuart* (1994) and Strindberg's *Kristina* (1995), as well as Lady Macbeth (1996) and Gretchen in Goethe's *Faust* (1997).

Sella, Maini Marjatta (1936–) Actor, Finland. Sella trained at the Theatre School of Finland and worked at the Hämeenlinna City Theatre (1959–61), Turku City Theatre (1961–5), Intimiteatteri (1965–71), Radio Theatre (1971–7) and the Finnish National Theatre since 1990. Major roles include Hermia (*A Midsummer Night's Dream*), Eva in Brecht's *Herr*

Puntila und sein Knecht Matti (*Mr Puntila and his Servant Matti*), Hilkka in KYLÄTASKU's *Runar ja Kyllikki* (*Runar and Kyllikki*) and the title role in Arnold WESKER's *Annie Wobbler*. She is technically well equipped, especially in terms of her beautifully expressive voice. She has won audience acclaim both in tragic roles and as a sparkling comedienne. She is always looking for new challenges, working not only at the National Theatre but also with new experimental groups like the female theatre Raivoisat Ruusut (Raging Roses).

Sellars, Peter (1957–) Director, USA. While a student at Harvard, Sellars directed more than forty experimental productions of plays and opera, and his trademark soon became using contemporary settings for classical material. He worked as artistic director for several companies. 'Sellar's work has been labelled "postmodern" because of his disinterest in historical reproduction, his mixed time frames, his use of a visual text different from the literal one, and his layering of imagery in any given moment of the work. His work, however, is rooted in the theories of such modern theorists as Wagner, Meyerhold and Brecht. What he has accomplished so far in his directing career is to extend the theories of the moderns with a multicultural approach. Thus, he has helped to break down the ethnocentricity of the Western classic canon and has created a postmodern vision of theatre.' Among his most famous productions are *The Mikado* (1983) for the Lyric Opera of Chicago, and Aeschylus's *Persai* (*The Persians*, 1993) for the Salzburg Festival.

Sen, Tapas (1924–) Designer, India. A pioneer of modern lighting on the Indian stage, Sen started from scratch, using tin cans with apertures cut in them substituting for spots. He has since come to employ sophisticated computerized lighting technology. Sen has designed lighting for over 400 productions and worked

with celebrities like Sombu MITRA, Shyamanand Jalan, Mrinalini Sarabhai and international directors like Fritz Bennewitz. His lighting for ALKAZI's production of Osborne's *Look Back in Anger* and of van Itallies' *America Hurrah* are remarkable for lighting as characterizsation. Sen is India's leading lighting designer.

Şengezer, Osman (1941–) Designer, Turkey. In 1960, Şengezer joined the Ankara State Theatre as a designer. In 1974 he joined the İstanbul State Theatre as a costume and stage designer, and has designed costumes and theatre settings for numerous theatre companies in Ankara, İstanbul and other provinces of Turkey. His elaborate but not exaggerated designs, in which he is much concerned with the coordination of colours, are internationally known in countries such as Germany, Britain, France, Russia, Poland, Denmark, Holland and Cyprus. In 1967, he visited the Royal Ballet Company on a British Council grant arranged by Dame Ninette de Valois. In 1981, he visited USA by invitation of the International Communication Agency, and in 1983 he went on a research tour to Hungary by invitation of the Hungarian International Theatre Institute. Apart from his signatures on more than 350 productions, he has two books published in 1989 and 1993, respectively. At present, he is working as a designer for the İstanbul State Opera and Ballet in İstanbul. He is most famous for his collaborative manner of creating his designs without losing his individualistic spirit.

Şensoy, Ferhan (1951–) Actor, director, dramatist and film scriptwriter, Turkey. After attending Ecole Superieure d'Art Dramatique in Strasbourg in 1972, Şensoy became an actor-assistant to Jérôme SAVARY in Strasbourg in 1973. In 1974, he became an actor-assistant to André Perinetti at Théâtre National de Strasbourg. In the same year he performed in his own musical *Harem Qui Rit* (*The Laughing*

Harem) at the Théâtre de Quatre-Sous in Montreal. His play *Ce Fou de Gogol* (*That Crazy Gogol*) was staged by Théâtre Patriote in Montreal. In 1976, he directed and acted for Ali Poyrazoglu Theatre, Türk Yazarlari Theatre, and Nisa Serezli-Tolga Askiner Theatre in İstanbul. Since 1978, he has established several of his own companies. Plays include *İdi Amin* (1978), *Bizim Sınıf* (*Our Class*, 1978), *Şahları da Vururlar* (*They Kill Shahs Too*, 1980), *Anna'nın Yedi Ana Günahi* (*Anna's Seven Main Sins*, 1984, based on Brecht), *İçinden Tramvay Geçen Şarkı* (*The Tram Passing Through a Song*, 1986, based on the life and the short plays of Karl Valentin), and *Yorgun Matador* (*The Tired Matador*, 1990). Other productions include Dürrenmatt's *Romulus der Große* (*Romulus the Great*, 1982, and Aristophanes's *Sphekes* (*Wasps*). In 1994, he transformed a ship into a theatre and directed and acted in plays on this sailing stage at the Bosphorus in İstanbul.

Serban, Andrei (1943–) Director, Romania. Serban graduated from the Bucharest Theatre and Film Institute. In his early career, he distinguished himself with notable productions of Romanian plays and world repertory, including Brecht's *Der Gute Mensch von Sezuan* (*The Good Person of Sezuan*). Since 1970, Serban has regularly worked in the USA. For La MaMa, he directed a trilogy of Greek plays: Sophocles's *Electra* and Euripides's *Troades* (*The Trojan Women*) and *Medeia*. The productions were presented in ancient Greek language, thus putting into practice Serban's theory of the magic power of sound. He also worked at the Lincoln Centre (Chekhov's *Visnevyi sad* (*The Cherry Orchard*) with Meryl Streep, and Aeschylus's *Agamemnon*), and has directed many opera productions. Back in Romania in 1990, he became director general of the National Theatre in Bucharest and directed *The Ancient Trilogy*, Chekhov's *Visnevyi sad* and Timberlake WERTENBAKER's *Our Country's Good*. Ser-

ban is always in search of communication with audiences through the full exploration of the theatrical resources of sound, movement and visual imagery, discovering new unconventional theatrical spaces on rocks and mountains, in caves and castles.

Sewell, Stephen (1953–) Dramatist, Australia. Sewell worked in fringe theatre and began writing plays. His work is always serious and overtly political, with a left-wing commitment which makes his analyses of Australian life scathing. His plays are often grand in scale, needing large casts, and nervous commercial managements tend to be wary of them, even though Sewell has won much critical acclaim. His most produced play is *Traitors* (1979), which views the Stalinist takeover of the Russian revolution primarily through the consciousness of a powerfully characterized woman, Anna. *Dreams in an Empty City* (1986) provides an analysis of the corruption of innocence under capitalism. *Hate* (1988) focuses on a self-destructing family, and the two-hander *Sisters* (1991) dissects the relationship between two sisters. Between 1991–4, Sewell worked on an ambitious project, *The Garden of Earthly Delights Trilogy*, involving a collaboration between the State Theatre Company of South Australia and students from the Centre for Performing Arts, Adelaide.

Sha Ye Xin (1939–) Dramatist, China. Sha graduated in 1961 from the English Department, East China Normal University and attended Shanghai Academy's Advanced Programme on Chinese Traditional Dramaturgy from 1961–3. He has written some of the most sensational plays in the 1980s, including *Jia Ru Wo Shi Zhen De* (*What if I Were What I Claim to Be*, 1980), *Chen Yi Shi Zhang* (*Mayor Chen Yi*, 1981), *Xun Zhao Nan Zi Han* (*In Search of Real Man*, 1986), *Jidu, Kongzi, Pitoushi Lienong* (*Jesus, Confucius and John Lennon*, 1988) and *Dong Jing De Yue Liang* (*Moon over*

Tokyo, 1993). His works, mostly comedies, are characterized by a formal innovativeness.

Shaffer, Peter (1926–) Dramatist, Great Britain. Shaffer's breakthrough as a dramatist came in 1958 with *Five Finger Exercise*. He is mainly known for his major trilogy of plays, *The Royal Hunt of the Sun* (1964), *Equus* (1973, with Alec MCCOWEN) and *Amadeus* (1979, directed by Peter HALL, with Paul SCOFIELD, Felicity KENDAL and Simon CALLOW), all first produced at the National Theatre; these share the motif of the search for and destruction of God, although in different shapes. This clash of Apollonian and Dionysian forces is also evident in the less successful *Yonadab* (National Theatre, 1985, directed by Hall, with Alan BATES in the title role), the comedy *Lettice and Lovage* (with Maggie SMITH, directed by Michael BLAKEMORE, 1987) and *The Gift of the Gorgon* (1992, directed by Hall, with Judi DENCH and Michael PENNINGTON).

Shah, Naseeruddin (1950–) Actor and director, India. Shah trained at the National School of Drama and the Film and Television Institute at Pune. One of the celebrated actors of the Bombay stage, he worked for Satyadev DUBEY's Theatre Unit and Om Puri's Majma, two leading Bombay theatre groups. He started his own theatre group, Motley, in 1979. Since then, his acting and directing credits include Beckett's *Waiting for Godot*, Neil SIMON's *The Odd Couple* and *The Caine Mutiny Court Martial*; he has recently performed in *Gandhi* for Tara Arts (1996). His style is essentially Western, and he does not believe in exaggeration. He is also a popular film actor and has won many awards.

Sharma, Haresh (1965–) Dramatist, Singapore. One of the most prolific dramatists in Singapore, Sharma has written over thirty plays in the thirteen years of his writing career. A founder of a Singapore Theatre company, The Necessary Stage, Sharma has collaborated extensively with fellow director Alvin TAN to bring a new voice to Singapore theatre. Sharma's writings have sought to give voice to the disempowered in Singapore and more often to bring about opportunities for discussion of social issues in Singapore. His plays are varied in themes and approaches, from a Brechtian approach to a play on mental health (*Off Centre*, 1993) to ensemble playing (*Lanterns Never Go Out*, 1989; *This Chord and Others*, 1992) and more recently, the postmodern bricolage (*Pillars*, 1997; *Sea*, 1997; *Galileo: I Feel the Earth Move*, 1997). The resident playwright of the Necessary Stage, Sharma was the recipient of the Young Artist Award in 1997 and has also been conferred a Master of Arts (Playwriting) from the University of Birmingham.

Sharman, Jim (1945–) Director, Australia. Sharman graduated from the National Institute of Dramatic Art, Sydney, but his first training in showmanship was at home; Sharman's family ran a boxing sideshow which toured Australia from 1911–71. Sharman is still best known for co-creating the cult musical *The Rocky Horror Show*, which he first directed in London in 1973 before taking the show on to Sydney, New York, Los Angeles and finally film. Previous to this he had directed *Hair* in Australia, Japan and Boston, and *Jesus Christ Superstar* in Sydney and London. Sharman's directorial style is big, bold and very visual. Apart from his dazzling international box office success in musicals, Sharman was also responsible for first encouraging Patrick White back into the theatre after White's disenchantment in the early 1960s. While he ran the Lighthouse Company in Adelaide, Sharman also encouraged the work of director Neil ARMFIELD and playwrights Louis NOWRA and Stephen SEWELL. Sharman wrote and directed *The*

Burning Piano (1993) a television tribute to Patrick White.

Shaw, Fiona (1958–) Actor, Ireland. Shaw trained at the Royal Academy of Dramatic Art, London, and joined the National Theatre, London, playing Julia in Sheridan's *The Rivals*. She spent the next four years with the Royal Shakespeare Company playing many leading roles in Stratford and London, including Tatyana in Gorky's *Mescane* (*Philistines*), Celia in *As You Like It* and Kate in *The Taming of the Shrew*, directed by Jonathan MILLER (1987–8). She played Rosalind in *As You Like It* at the Old Vic, and the title roles in Brecht's *Der Gute Mensch von Sezuan* (*The Good Person of Sezuan*, Royal National Theatre) and Sophocles's *Electra* (Royal Shakespeare Company, 1988), the latter two directed by Deborah WARNER. She has only appeared in two productions in Ireland, first as Hedda Gabler (also directed by Warner) at the Abbey Theatre (1991), playing depression as action rather than inaction, and in her one-woman dramatization of Eliot's *The Waste Land* (1995). Sometimes using method acting and at others her own brand of emotional and poetic experimentation, Shaw breaks down texts and spaces to help theatre move forward. Examples of this include her role in Stephen DALDRY's production of Sophie Treadwell's *Machinal* (1993) and her cross-dressed *Richard II* (1995) both at the Royal National Theatre, London.

Shearer, Jill (1936–) Dramatist, Australia. Queensland-based Shearer has been writing plays for many years but has only recently gained national attention with her first fully professional production *Shimada* (1986), a play focusing on Australian–Japanese relations and the tensions that ensue when a Japanese company offers to buy up a Queensland bicycle company which was founded by two survivors of a Japanese POW camp. The play's successful Melbourne Theatre production was followed by a Broadway production in 1992. In 1994 Shearer reflected on Queensland's traumatic investigations into police corruption in *The Family*, a compelling examination of a policewoman confronting the possibility that her policeman father is implicated in widespread police corruption. Shearer's focus is often Queensland and that state's particular moral dilemmas. Another focus is women; for example, *Catherine* (1977) has a contemporary theatre group rehearsing a play about the convict woman who was the mother of one of the founding fathers of Australia, William Charles Wentworth.

Sheintsis, Oleg (1949–) Designer and director, Russia. He trained at Odessa (Ukraine) Theatre College and at the Moscow Art Theatre Studio (Faculty of Stage Design). He is the chief designer at Mark ZAKHAROV's Theatre Lenkom. Among his principal designs for this company were Arbuzov's *Zhestokiye igry* (*The Cruel Games*, 1979), PETRUSHEVS-KAYA's *Tri devushki v golubom* (*The Three Girls in Blue*, 1982), Ostrovsky's *Moudretz* (*The Wiseman*, 1989), all productions directed by Zakharov, as well as *Hamlet* and Beaumarchais's *Le mariage de Figaro* (*The Marriage of Figaro*) in the early 1990s. Sheintsis turned Russian scenography from the illustration of the director's ideas to a new role. His set always focuses the interpretation, serving as a lens or a prism. He does not want the spectators to identify themselves with the actors on stage. In certain scenes he develops an alienation effect and makes the action on the stage look like myth or fairy tale achieving the effect of a 'distant life'. In 1994, he co-directed Chekhov's *Cajka* (*The Seagull*) with Mark Zakharov.

Shepard, Sam (1943–) Dramatist and actor, USA. Shepard has written more than forty plays so far, in which he concentrates on the American West or the American Dream. His characters search for their roots, and often his plays tackle stereotypes. Most important plays include *The Curse of the Starving Class* (1978), *Buried Child* (1978), *True West* (1980), *Fool for Love* (1979) and, more recently, *The States of Shock* (1991) and *Simpatico* (1994). His deep interest in music, particularly jazz, has had a substantial impact on his works. Critics have often remarked that his long, lyrical speeches have the quality of musical improvisation.

Sher, Anthony (1949–) Actor, Great Britain. Born in South Africa, Sher trained at Webber Douglas, played in repertoire in Liverpool, Manchester and Nottingham, and had his major breakthrough in 1981 in *True West* by Sam SHEPARD at the National Theatre. In 1982 he was the Fool in *King Lear* for the Royal Shakespeare Company, followed, in the 1980s and 1990s, by the title roles in Molière's *Tartuffe* (1983 RSC, directed by Bill ALEXANDER, with Mark RYLANCE in the cast), *Richard III* (RSC, 1985), Brecht's *Der Aufhaltsame Aufstieg des Arturo Ui* (*The resistible Rise of Arturo Ui*, National Theatre, 1991), *Titus Andronicus* (National Theatre, 1995), British painter Stanley Spencer in Pam GEMS's *Stanley* (National Theatre, 1996), and he appeared in Terry JOHNSON's production of Johnson's *Cleo, Camping Emanuelle and Dick* (National Theatre, 1998). Sher brings to all his parts an unequalled intensity and attention to detail. He has written novels and created drawings, which accounts for the strikingly visual realization of his portrayal of Richard III. In preparing for the part, he studied the movements of disabled people, and developed the idea of becoming the most mobile character on stage through his crutches. They were used as legs, which, together with the special shape of the cloak, could make him appear like a spider, or they could be used as a weapon. The rehearsal process is documented in Sher's book *The Year of the King*.

Shiafkalis, Nikos (1934–) Director, Cyprus. Shiafkalis trained at the Guildhall School of Music and Drama in London. Vladimiros Kafkarides and Shiafkalis were the first two resident directors at the official state theatre in Cyprus, THOK (founded in 1971). There, his many production include *Sei personaggi in cerca d'autore* (*Six Characters in Search of an Author*) by Pirandello, *Gengangere* (*Ghosts*) by Ibsen, Arnold Wesker's *Roots*, Arthur MILLER's *The Crucible*, Shaw's *The Devil's Disciple*, Hellman's *Watch on the Rhine* and Aristophanes's *Lysistrata*. He has a realistic approach to directing, and insists on the interpretation of characters according to the dramatists' intentions, avoiding effects and rhetorical acting.

Shimizu Kunio (1936–) Dramatist and director, Japan. Shimizu was commissioned to write *Anohitachi* (*In Those Days*) by Gekidan Seihai (the Seihai Theatre Company) in 1966. There he met NINAGAWA and decided to write plays for Gendaijin Gekijô (the Contemporary People's Theatre). His plays directed by Ninagawa include *Shinjô Afururu Keihakusa* (*The Hearty Frivolity*, 1969), *Karasuyo Oretachi wa Tama o Komeru* (*Ravens! We Load Guns*, 1972), *Ame no Natsu Sanjûnin no Juliet ga Yattekita* (*Thirty Juliets Returned in the Rainy Summer*, 1982) and *Tango Fuyu no Owarini* (*Tango at the End of Winter*, 1984). Shimizu is one of the leading playwrights of the anti-*shingeki* movement in the 1960s. His plays best represent the feelings of the youth at that time. He keeps this tendency and writes plays on the relevant issues of his generation.

Shin, Sun-Hi (1945–) Scenographer, Korea. Shin trained at the University of Hawaii (MA, Drama and Theatre) and studied drawing and painting at the Rocky Mountain School of Arts in Denver, Colorado. She spent a further two years with the Art Students' League, New York, before working freelance in Theatre

Arts in New York. Since returning to Korea in 1983, Shin has been involved in many landmark productions such as OH Tae-Seok's *Jajeongeo* (*Bicycle*, 1983), CHOI In-Hoon's *Yennal Yetjeoge Hwei Hwei* (*Shoo Shoo Once Upon a Time*, 1985), YOUN Dai-Seong's *Koomgoonun Byeoldul* (*Dreaming Stars*, 1986), LEE Kang-Baek's *Biong Saong* (1986, directed by LEE Sung-Gyu), Shaw's *Androcles and the Lion*, 1988), Kim Eui-Kyung's *Gil Deonanun Gajok* (*A Family on the Road*, 1992, directed by LEE Yoon-Taek) and *Iboda Deo Naboolsoon Eopda* (*It Can't be Worse Than This*, 1998). Shin introduced the concept of the positive function of stage design to the Korean theatre, which sets the tone of the performance through a flexible visual impression.

Shiraishi Kayoko (1941–) Actor, Japan. Shiraishi became a member of Waseda Shô Gekijô (Wasesa Small Theatre) in 1967, founded by SUZUKI Tadashi, BET-SUYAKU Minoru and some other graduates of Waseda University in 1966. She played the role of Kasugano in *Shôjo Kamen* (*Virgin's Mask*) by KARA Jûrô in 1969. She acted in *Gekitekinaru Mono I, II and III* (*Dramatic Passions I, II and III*) in 1969, 1970 and 1975, directed by Suzuki. Shiraishi was his leading actor of that time, and acted in his adaptations of Greek tragedies, Euripides's *Troades* (*The Trojan Women*, 1974) and *Bakchai* (The Bacchae, 1978). Shiraishi also played Titania in NINAGAWA's production of *A Midsummer Night's Dream*, which toured in Europe in 1996, and appeared in *Shintoku Maru* (*The Boy Shitoku*) by Terayama Shuji at the Barbican, London, in 1997. She began a storytelling one-woman performance, *Shiraishi Kayoko Hyaku Monogatari* (*Shiraishi Kayoko's One Hundred Stories*), based on short stories from the traditional to the contemporary, in 1993. Her ability to understand the norms or the meanings of dialogue astonishes and inspires her audience with a new scope of intelligence.

Sibenke, Ben (1945–) Actor and dramatist, Zimbabwe. Ben Sibenke was one of the key figures to emerge from the various church organizations that helped during the colonial era to organize theatrical activities and drama festivals in Zimbabwe (then Rhodesia). He was a founder-member of the People's Company, one of the few indigenous theatre groups in Zimbabwe. He writes in both Shona and English. Among his published works are *Chidembo Chanhuwa* (*The Polecat Stank*) and *My Uncle Grey Bhonzo* (a comedy about the necessity to accept one's culture and roots, and of the need for the stabilising influence of traditional values in a rapidly urbanizing environment). Apart from his published plays, Sibenke in 1985 collaborated with Dominic Kanaventi and Walter Muparutsa in the Zimbabwe Arts Production's impressive stagings of *Sizwe Bansi is Dead* and *The Island* by Athol Fugard, John KANI and Winston NTSHONA, and Andrew Whaley's *Platform Five* (a play about tramps on the streets of Harare).

Sicardo, Mercedes (1927–) Actor, Puerto Rico. Mercedes Sicardo's family fled to Puerto Rico from Spain during the Civil War. Initially self-educated as an actor, she studied at the Ateneo Puertorriqueño early in her career, and later earned some recognition as a classical actor in plays by Shakespeare, Lope de Vega and Calderón. Like her husband, actor José Luis MAR-RERO, Sicardo is known for her versatility, appearing with him in numerous *zarzuelas* (light musical comedies). In the 1940s and 1950s she wrote scripts for radio soap operas, and also portrayed the female protagonists in many of them. Besides the classics, her notable roles include Bernarda in Lorca's *La casa de Bernarda Alba* (*The House of Bernarda Alba*) and

Ethel in Ernest Thompson's *On Golden Pond*.

Sierens, Arne (1959–) Dramatist and director, Belgium. Following studies in Brussels, Sierens founded De Sluipende Armoede (Creeping Poverty), a small company which focused on his activities as a director and writer. From 1992–4, he was writer-in-residence of the Blauwe Maandag Compagnie in Ghent, for whom he wrote the award-winning *Boste* (1992) and *De Drumleraar* (*Drummers*, 1994). His other pieces include *De Soldaat-Facteur en Rachel* (*The Postman-Soldier and Rachel*, 1986) and *Mouchette* (1990). With Alain PLATEL, he wrote and directed the internationally acclaimed Victoria productions *Moeder & Kind* (*Mother and Child*, 1995) and *Bernadetje* (1996). The world of Sierens is that of ordinary people, who draw vital strength from their harsh conditions of living. The dialect which is spoken in Ghent is his inspiration for a highly physical language, which is both folksy and artificial.

Silver, Philip (1943–) Designer, Canada. Silver studied theatre design at the National Theatre School, Montreal. After a year in the USA, he returned to Edmonton and worked for Citadel Theatre, where his designs include *Much Ado About Nothing* (1973) and Williams's *Night of the Iguana* (1978). For many years, Silver worked in Stratford, Ontario. The designs for Edna O'Brien's *Virginia* (with Maggie SMITH) exemplifies his personal style: 'to achieve a design shaped to embody the spirit and intention of the text, a design that was sculptured – as opposed to pictorial – in feel and inspiration'.

Simon, Barney (1933–) Director, South Africa. After working backstage for Joan Littlewood's Theatre (1957), Simon joined Athol Fugard at the African Music and Drama Association where they produced Fugard's *The Blood Knot*. He has directed plays in America and Britain, but apart from directing existing texts, he enjoys creating plays through workshops: collectively devised work with actors include *People*, *Storytime*, *Call Me Woman*, *Cincinatti*, *Woza Albert!* (he assisted Peter BROOK on his French production of the play) and *Born in the R.S.A.* He founded and managed several theatre companies in South Africa, most notably the The Market Theatre. The fact that The Market Theatre was for a long time during the apartheid era South Africa's only racially integrated theatre clearly shows Simon to be a politically committed theatre artist who utilizes the medium of theatre to examine the human condition and dilemma in a racially repressive society.

Simon, Neil (1927–) Dramatist, USA. After initially writing for radio and television, Simon's breakthrough in the theatre came in the 1960s with *Barefoot in the Park*, *The Odd Couple*, *The Star-Spangled Girl* and the musical *Sweet Charity*. Further plays include *California Suite* (1976), *Chapter Two* (1977) and several autobiographical plays in the 1980s and 1990s, including *Brighton Beach Memoirs* (1983) and *Lost In Yonkers* (1991), which brought literary acclaim (the Pulitzer Prize) in addition to commercial success. Arguably the most successful American playwright of the last forty years, he continues to produce new plays. *Laughter on the 23rd Floor* (1997) explored his days as a comic writer for television, mixing broad humor with shrewd observations about 1950s censorship and blacklisting.

Simons, Johan (1946–) Director, the Netherlands. Johan Simons originally trained as a dancer at the Rotterdam Dance Academy, a career which led him to star in the Dutch production of *Hair*, but no further. He then trained as an actor/director at the Maastricht Drama Academy from 1972–6. In 1982 he co-founded the Regio-theatre, a company set up to bring drama to the less urbanized areas of North-Holland. This was the predecessor to Simons' own company Hollandia, based on the same principle. There, together with co-director Paul Koek, he has created a distinctive body of work, including Greek tragedies in a formal style such as Aeschylus's *Prometheus desmotes* (*Prometheus Bound*, 1988) and *Persai* (*The Persians*, 1994), and modern German plays (by Herbert ACHTERNBUSCH, Franz Xaver KROETZ and others), full of pent-up emotions. Simons nearly always stages his plays outside theatres, in empty factories, churches and warehouses. There 'ordinary' people come to watch the fate of 'ordinary' people in the plays, reflecting Simons's interest in the natural over the 'arty'. Several excellent actors work within Hollandia, such as Betty Schuurman, Frieda PITTOORS, Elsie de Brauw and male lead Jeroen WILLEMS.

Sircar, Badal (1925–) Director and dramatist, India. Since 1956 Sircar has written over thirty plays in Bengali, including *Evam Indrajit* (*I'm Indrajit*), *Michil* (*Procession*), *Bhoma* and *Bhaki Ithihas* (*The Other Side of History*). All these plays are based on political and social issues of modern India. Sircar developed the concept of Third Theatre from his earlier concept of Free Theatre. Third Theatre is an alternative to folk theatre and the urban-based middle-class theatre. Sircar does not depend on sets, costume and music, and focuses on the performer's body and its relationship with the spectators. He abandoned the proscenium and worked in the streets, creating authentic street theatre. His group Satabdi takes plays to villages in and around Calcutta. Sircar has been an important influence through workshops on other leading Indian directors and companies, for example in Manipur (ARAMBAM, THIYAM).

Sirchadjiev, Joseph (1945–) Actor, Bulgaria. Sirchadjiev trained at the National Academy for Theatre and Film Arts in Sofia and has played many parts covering a wide range of styles, including Mercutio in *Romeo and Juliet*, Macduff in *Macbeth*, the King in *Love's Labour's Lost*, Wurm in Schiller's *Kabale und Liebe* (*Intrigue and Love*), the title role in Chekhov's *Ivanov*, Hjalmar in Ibsen's *Vildanden* (*The Wild Duck*), Vladimir in Beckett's *Waiting for Godot* and Tom in *The Glass Menagerie* by Tennessee Williams.

Sitarenos, Mary (1959–) Actor, Australia. Sitarenos studied at the Victorian College of the Arts, Melbourne. She has played in both mainstream and fringe theatre, particularly for Theatreworks and for Jean-Pierre Mignon's Anthill, Melbourne. At Anthill, Sitarenos was especially memorable in Mignon's series of Chekhovs in 1987, producing an insufferable Natasha in Chekhov's *Tri sestry* (*Three Sisters*). Sitarenos is associated particularly with the bilingual (Greek/ English) plays of Tes Lyssiotis, which chart the experiences of women negotiating Greek and Australian identities; she created the role of Eleftheria in Tes Lyssiotis's *The Forty Lounge Cafe* (1990) and has also appeared in Lyssiotis's *A White Sportscoat* and *Blood Moon*. Sitarenos has also worked with Jenny KEMP (*The White Hotel* and *The Black Sequin Dress*). She has often worked in collaboration with her partner, the director Robert Draffin, and their most recent success has been *The Last Supper* (1994–6) a celebration of rituals of eating and cooking. Sitarenos is a versatile performer but is particularly remarkable for her ability to confront big emotions at full throttle.

Slabolepszy, Paul (1948–) Dramatist, South Africa. Slabolepszy holds a performer's diploma from the University of Cape Town. He is regarded as one of South Africa's most prolific playwrights, with about sixteen plays performed and/ or published between 1980–93. These include *The Defloration of Miles Koekemoer* (1980), *Karoo Grand* (1983), *Under* the Oaks (1984), *Over the Hill* (1985), *Making Like America* (1986), *Travelling Shots* (1988), *Smallholding* (1989), *One for the High Jump* (1990), *Braait Laaities* (1991), *Mooi Street Moves* (1992), *Pale Natives* (1993) and *Victoria Almost Falls* (1993). Some of his plays have been translated into Swedish, Hebrew and German. Slabolepszy's vision and style are a comic one which avoids direct reference to the politics which suffuses his plays but still manages to deal with the tragedy and psychic destruction caused by apartheid politics. His plays are also marked by his fine handling of language, especially the unique idiosyncratic language of poor white characters. He is equally popular because of his comic treatment of 'apartheid's children'.

Slobodzianek, Tadeusz (1955–) Dramatist and director, Poland. He graduated in theatre studies from the Jagiellonski University of Cracow, co-founded the Theatre Association Wierszalin, and wrote this theatre's two most important plays, *Turlajgroszek* (*Roll-a-pea*) and *Merlin*. His productions and plays are often defined as an epitaph to the twentieth century: he sets traditional Christian values against contemporary socio-political experiments, posing universal questions about the human existence in an epoch dominated by various experiments of making everybody happy. Although most of his plays take place somewhere in the backwoods, this only intensifies their universal appeal, reinforcing the grotesque qualities and absurdity of the protagonists and the language in which they try to communicate.

Smith, Maggie (1934–) Actor, Great Britain. Smith trained at the Oxford Playhouse School. Early on in her career she joined the National Theatre company at the Old Vic, appearing as Desdemona opposite Olivier's Othello, as Hilde Wangel in Ibsen's *Bygmester Solness* (*The Master Builder*), and as Beatrice in *Much

Ado About Nothing*. At Stratford, Ontario, she played Masha in Chekhov's *Tri sestry* (*Three Sisters*), Rosalind in *As You Like It* and created the role of Virginia Woolf in Edna O'Brien's *Virginia*. She is equally at home in comedy, for example in Peter SHAFFER's *Lettice and Lovage* (1987) and as Lady Bracknell in Wilde's *The Importance of Being Earnest*. More recently she appeared in ALBEE's *Three Tall Women* (1993) and as Claire in Albee's *A Delicate Balance* (1997).

Smoček, Ladislav (1932–) Director and dramatist, Czech Republic. After studying direction at the Prague Academy of Performing Arts, Smoček worked in provincial theatres and in the Prague Magic Lantern. In 1965, he took part in founding a small venue in Prague, the Činoherní Club, where he still works as a resident director and where he has directed most of his original plays, such as *Piknik* (*The Picnic*, 1965) *Bludiště* (*The Maze*, 1966 and 1990), *Podivné odpoledne dotora Zvonka Burkeho* (*The Strange Afternoon of Dr Zvonek Burke*, 1966 and 1990), *Kosmické jaro* (*Cosmic Spring*, 1970 and 1996) and *Smycka* (*The Noose*, 1980). Other productions include O'Neill's *A Long Day's Journey into Night* (1978), HAMPTON's *Les Liaisons Dangereuses* (1988, at the National Theatre with Jana HLAVÁČOVÁ as Madame de Merteuil), and Schnitzler's *Das Weite Land* (*Undiscovered Country*, 1992, at the Vinohrady Theatre). As a dramatist, he is interested in the behaviour of people in extreme and often grotesquely exaggerated situations. His directorial style is characterized by precise co-operating with his actors: he stresses the physical side of the actor's expression, which leads to grotesque exaggeration. He has often worked in the Tyl Theatre in Plzeò, where he presented his latest play, *Nejlepší den* (*The Best Day*, 1995).

Šnajder, Slobodan (1948–) Dramatist, Croatia. A graduate in philosophy and

English language and literature from the Faculty of Philosophy in Zagreb, he is one of the founders of the theatre review *Prolog* (Prologue), where he published his first plays. They immediately drew the public's attention, revealing his tendency towards politically committed theatre and an influence of Brecht and Krleža. His next group of plays includes the so-called biographical plays like *Kamov. Smrtopis* (*Kamov. Thanatography*, 1977), *Držićev san* (*The Dream of Marin Držić*, 1979), *Hrvatski Faust* (*The Croatian Faust*, 1981) and *Gamllet* (1987). In the 1990s plays (staged mostly in the German speaking area of Frankfurt an der Oder, Tübingen, Frankfurt am Main, Vienna and Mülheim) he focuses on the problem of war, mass rape, concentration camps and genocide. He advocates a leftist political and cultural programme underlined by strong negation of any opposite view. Up to the 1990s he was considered as one of the most important contemporary playwrights in Croatia, but in the last few years he has been more prominent as public figure and columnist. There have been no productions of his plays in Croatian professional theatres since the late 1980s.

Snir, Hanan (1943–) Director, Israel. Snir trained at the Royal Academy of Dramatic Art in London, where he also directed his first productions. Holding a degree in councelling psychology from Boston University, Snir is also a specialist of psychodrama. He began his career as a director at the Beer Sheva municipal theatre with productions of *Twelfth Night* and Chekhov's *Cajka* (*The Seagull*). At the Habima national theatre he has directed plays like Chekhov's *Djadja Vanja* (*Uncle Vanya*), Strindberg's *Fadren* (*The Father*), Lorca's *Bodas de sangre* (*Blood Wedding*), Ibsen's *Gengangere* (*Ghosts*) and Gilead EVRON's plays *Yehu* and *Har lo zaz* (*A Mountain Doesn't Move*, 1996). He was the artistic director of Habimah for one year. In 1995 he directed *The*

Merchant of Venice in Weimar, Germany, staged as a play-within-a-play performed at a Nazi concentration camp. Snir teaches acting at the Kibbutz seminar and at Tel Aviv University and works as a psychodramatist.

Sobol, Yehoshua (1939–) Dramatist and director, Israel. After obtaining a Ph.D. in philosophy from the Sorbonne in Paris, Sobol worked as a journalist and started to write for the theatre for Nola CHILTON's documentary performances at the Haifa municipal theatre. His first major success as a playwright, *Night of the Twentieth* (1976), was also based on documentary materials, depicting a group of youngsters establishing a kibbutz in the 1920s. Since then Sobol has written more than thirty plays and has become internationally the most well-known Israeli playwright, mainly for his play *Ghetto*, which has been produced in more than fifty theatres all over the world. *The War of the Jews* (1981, later developed into *The Jerusalem Syndrome*, 1988), depicting the Jewish revolt against the Romans, *The Soul of a Jew* (1982) about Otto Weininger, 'The Ghetto Triptych' (*Ghetto, Adam* and *Underground*, 1983–8), depicting different aspects of life in the Vilna ghetto during the Nazi occupation, *Solo* (1991) about Baruch Spinoza, and *Alma Apassionata* (1996) about the life of Alma Mahler, are all based on historical materials. In *Village*, produced by the Geshertheatre (1996), the historical background in the village where Sobol grew up in Mandatory Palestine is presented in a poetic light. *Shooting Magda* (*The Palestinian Woman*, 1985) deals with the complex relations between Israelis and Palestinians. Sobol was the co-director of the Haifa municipal theatre between 1984–8.

Sofowote, Segun Actor and director, Nigeria. Sofowote was one of the initial members of Orisun Theatre who learned and perfected their acting techniques through participation in the many and pioneering productions of Wole SOYINKA (the other Orisun 'boys' were Wale OGUNYEMI, Yomi OBILEYE and Tunji OYELANA). A versatile actor and director, Sofowote has remained a regular feature of Soyinka's theatre activities beginning with the 1960 production of *A Dance of the Forests* in which he played the role of Murete, the brilliant Orisun performances of the revue *Before the Blackout* in 1965, *The Lion and the Jewel* (directed by Dapo ADELUGBA and choreographed by Betty OKOTIE) to the 1992 production of *From Zia with Love* in Italy, in which he played Third Trusty and Student Novice. Other memorable roles are as the Bear in *The Bear* by Chekhov directed by Segun Olusola for Theatre Express in 1966, featuring Ogunyemi.

Sohn Jin-Chaek (1947–) Director, Korea. Sohn trained at the Seorabeol College of Art and with the Sanha Theatre Company. Sohn has shown a special interest in the Korean working classes which he believed to be the central figures in history. He directed Og Young-Jin's *Hanneeui Sungcheon* (*Ascension of Hanne* (1975, 1976, 1979, 1983), Jeong Bok-Gun's *Jikimi* (*The Keeper*, 1987), YOUN Dai-Sung's *Namsadangeui Hanul* (*The Sky of Namsadang the Wandering Troupe*, 1993) and CHOI In-Hoon's *Doong Doong Nakrang Dong* (*Dom Dom the Drumrall of Nangrang*, 1996). Sohn has also sought to revitalize the spirit and methods of traditional Korean theatre in a modern context. He established Madang-Guk, a new type of performance which combines a static and flexible plot and the acting methods of traditional Korean performances with the dynamic spectacle of European theatre. As a Madang-Guk director, he has adapted and reconstructed classic Korean novels every year since 1981, including *Heo-Saengjeon* (*The Story of Heo-Saeng*, 1981), *Nolboojeon* (*The Story of Nolboo*, 1983), *Simcheonjeon* (*The Story of Sim-*

Cheong, 1988), *Sinpan Yi Choon-Poong-jeon* (*New Version of Lee Choon-Poong Story*, 1992), *Choon-Hyangjeon* (*The Story of Choon-Hyang*, 1995) and *Cheon-myeong* (*Heaven's Decree*, 1998).

Sohn Sook (1944–) Actor, Korea. Having performed for many on the amateur stage, sohn' professional debut was in the title role of O'Neill's *Mourning Becomes Electra* (1968). After joining the Korean National Theatre in 1971, she played Gretchen in Goethe's *Faust* (1979, 1984), and appeared in Cha Beom-Seok's *San Bool* (*Mountain Fire*), Ibsen's *Vildanden* (*The Wild Duck*) and Ro Gyeong-Sik's *Chimmookeui Bada* (*The Sea of Silence*, 1987). After leaving the Korean National Theatre in 1993, she performed in many feminist theatre productions including John Pielmeier's *Agnes of God* (1993), *Dambae Piwoonun Yeoja* (*Smoking Woman*, 1997) and Marsha NORMAN's *'night Mother* (1998). Sohn is an actor who gives a self-controlled and measured performance.

Solanke, Jimi Actor, Nigeria. Originally a member of the '1960 Masks', he is currently a member of the Obafemi Awolowo University Theatre in Ile-Ife. Jimi Solanke has been described by Femi OSOFISAN as perhaps the best actor that the Nigerian theatre in English has produced. Most of Wole SOYINKA's Ogunian/Protean individuals were written with Solanke in mind. He has acted in excerpts from *A Dance of the Forests* (with Osofisan and Alton Kumalo and directed by Soyinka at a festival of Théâtre des Nations in France). Other acting credits include the revue *Before the Blackout* and the Rev. Dr Godspeak in Soyinka's *Requiem for a Futurologist* (1983–4). In 1978 he played a very memorable Styles/Buntu opposite OGUNYEMI's Sizwe Bansi in Athol FUGARD, John KANI and Winston NTSHONA's *Sizwe Bansi is Dead*.

Solorzano, Carlos (1922–) Dramatist, Mexico. Soloranzo, who obtained doctorates from the National University of Mexico and the Sorbonne in Paris, is an expressionist. His plays have been translated into several languages and performed not only in Mexico but also in the USA, France and Spain. His best-known plays are *Las manos de Dios*, *Los fantoches* and *El crucificado*, all of which deal with popular themes of Mexican reality in symbolic terms, conserving indigenous images of Mexico but making them accessible to a wide range of audiences.

Somr, Josef (1934–) Actor, Czech Republic. After studying at the Brno Academy of Performing Arts, Somr worked in several ensembles outside Prague before joining the newly-founded Činoherní Club in Prague in 1965. There he quickly made his name through his interpretations of sundry forms of aggression, ranging from Porphyry in Dostoyevsky's *Prestuplenie I nakazanie* (*Crime and Punishment*, 1966) to Goldberg in PINTER's *The Birthday Party* (1972). His restrained but flexible expression, his sense for the paradoxical and the critical reflection on his characters, as if from the outside, have made him into one of the leading representatives of modern Czech acting. A member of the National Theatre since 1978, he has performed his mature work in Czech and world drama: Claudius in *Hamlet* (1982), the lead in Brecht's *Leben des Galilei* (*Life of Galileo*, 1984), Edgar in Strindberg's *Dödsdansen* (*Dance of Death*, 1993), and Kája in Máša's *Podivní ptáci* (*The Strange Birds*, 1996).

Song Young-Chang (1958–) Actor, Korea. Song trained at Joong-Ang University, obtaining a BA and an MFA in theatre arts. Having performed in two Beckett plays, *Catastrophe* (1986) and *A Piece of Monologue* (1987), Song played important supporting roles as Producer in *Cinders* (1987, directed by KIM Ara), Jeong

Bok-Gun's *Silbimyeong* (*Lost Epitaph*, 1989), the Police Officer in Dario FO's *Morte accidentale di un anarchico* (*Accidental Death of an Anarchist*, 1990), and played the main role in YOON Dae-Seong's *Saeui Chanmi* (*Praise of Death*, 1990) and OH Oun-Hee's *Show Comedy* (1996). Since 1990 he has extended his range by performing all four roles in Beckett's *Waiting For Godot* (1990, 1995, in Seoul, Dublin and Warsaw), and acted in OH Tae-Seok's monodrama *A Tumbling Doll on Rollerskates*, 1993.

Sorrah, Renata (1948–) Actor, Brazil. A graduate in psychology (Pontificia Universidade Católica, São Paulo), Sorrah took a drama course in California as well as workshops with MNOUCHKINE and BOAL. Apart from a career in television, major stage roles include Nina in Chekhov's *Cajka* (*The Seagull*), the title character in Fassbinder's *Die bitteren Tränen der Petra von Kant* (*The Bitter Tears of Petra von Kant*), Lotte in *Groß und Klein* (*Large and Small*) by Botho STRAUSS, Shirley in Willy Russell's *Shirley Valentine*, the title role in Schiller's *Maria Stuart* and Aline in MROZEK's *Tango*.

Sowande, Bode (1948–) Dramatist, actor, director and novelist Nigeria. Sowande belongs to the second generation of dramatists who espouse a materialistic and revolutionary aesthetic for the Nigerian theatre (this group also includes Femi OSOFISAN, Tunde FATUNDE, Olu OBAFEMI and Kole OMOTOSO). A resident playwright for the Orisun Theatre, Lagos from 1968–71, in 1972 he founded the Odu Themes which later became Odu Themes Meridian, the professional company which Sowande now manages since his retirement in 1990 as a lecturer in theatre arts at the University of Ibadan. His drama places the individual at the centre of the historical process and sees society as progressing to better and better states. His plays include *The Night Before*, *Flamingo*, *Afamako* and *Tornadoes*

Full of Dreams (1990). His acting roles include Baba Fakunle in Ola ROTIMI's *The Gods Are Not to Blame* (1968), Bello in *Afamako, The Workhorse* (1978), and Moniran in both *Farewell to Babylon* (1978) and *Flamingo* (1982).

Soyinka Akinwande Oluwole (Wole) (1934–) Dramatist, director, actor and poet, Nigeria. After a season as a playreader at the Royal Court Theatre, London, Soyinka returned to Nigeria and founded the '1960 Masks' (to become the fully professional Orisun Theatre Company in 1962) which produced the first generation of famous Nigerian actors, directors and scriptwriters (notably, Wale OGUNYEMI, Tunji OYELANA, Yewande Johnson (nee Akinbo), Yomi OBILEYE, Ralph Opara, Olga Adeniyi-Jones, Elizabeth Osisioma, Betty OKOTIE, Yemi Lijadu, Dapo ADELUGBA and Bode SOWANDE). To date, Soyinka has written close to forty plays and revues, most of which he has directed himself. He has also directed plays by Shakespeare, Brecht, Synge, Chekhov, Ogunyemi and J.P. CLARK-BEKEDEREMO. The key themes which run through Soyinka's plays are death, the contradiction of creativity and destruction, and human stupidity and violence. He has aimed to create a theatre that is uniquely African by going back to his Yoruba roots and enriching his writing and practice with its beliefs and rituals, its dances and songs. He now lives in exile because of his opposition to the military dictatorship in Nigeria. In 1986 he received the Nobel Prize for Literature.

Spiró, György (1946–) Dramatist, Hungary. Spiró studied Hungarian, Russian and Serbo-Croatian at the Budapest Eötvös Loránd University. He worked as a journalist for Hungarian Radio and as a publishing house editor, and served as dramaturg at the Cisky Gergely Theatre of Kaposvár between 1986–92. From 1992–5 he was general director of the Szolnok Szigligeti Theatre. His first plays

are historical-philosophical parables, such as *A nyulak Margitja* (*Margaret of the Rabbits*) and *Hannibal*. His breakthrough came with Gábor ZSÁMBÉKI's production of *Csirkefej* (*Chicken Head*) at the Katona József Theatre. Other plays include *Ahogy tesszük* (*As We Do It*), *A békecsászár* (*The Impostor*), *Dobardan* and *Vircsaft Muddle*. They are characterized by sensitivity to everyday problems and a satirical, typically Eastern European grotesque style.

Sprung, Guy (1947–) Director, Canada. Sprung worked as Assistant Director at the Schillertheater, West Berlin, and in 1971 he co-founded the Half Moon Theatre, a fringe venue in London. In Canada, he worked freelance between 1976–81, directing the popular *Paper Wheat* at 25th Street Theatre in Saskatoon. Subsequently, he has been (joint) artistic director at several theatres in Canada (including co-founder and artistic director of the Canadian Stage Co). Sprung's productions cover a wide range of plays, both classical and modern, not restricted to Canadian dramatists; he is equally at home with comedy and tragedy, and his style ranges from naturalistic detail to non-naturalistic experiment. He has directed celebrated premieres of Rick Salutin's *Les Canadiens*, David FENNARIO's *Balconville* and Sharon POLLOCK's *Doc*.

Squarzina, Luigi (1922–) Director, dramatist, actor and producer, Italy. After graduating in law and training at the National Academy of Dramatic Art in Rome, Luigi Squarzina started his dramatic career with a production of Arthur MILLER's *All My Sons* (1947). In 1952, together with Vittorio GASSMAN, he founded the Teatro dell'Arte, which moved away from declamatory styles of acting and focused on the characters' psychology. In the period between the late 1940s and the early 1970s, Squarzina's theatre represented a brave attempt to denounce the horrifying irrationalism that characterized the fascist period and offer a critical representation of contemporary Italian society. From 1962–76 he was artistic director of the Teatro Stabile in Genoa, and from 1976–83 of the Teatro Stabile in Rome. Since the late 1940s Squarzina has been directing both classical and contemporary plays and operas. Apart from saving Gabriele D'Annunzio's work from postwar neglect, he also became known for revivals of plays by Shakespeare, Pirandello and Goldoni. Among his most notable productions are *Esposizione Universale* (*Universal Exposition*, 1947), *Tre quarti di luna* (*Three Quarters of the Moon*, 1953), *Romagnola* (*Romagnese*, 1959) and *Rosa Luxemburg* (1976) and, more recently, Goldoni's *La Guerra* (*The War*, 1998).

Stafford-Clark, Max (1941–) Director, Great Britain. Stafford-Clark was associate director at the Traverse Theatre Company in Edinburgh and associate director, later artistic director, at the Royal Court in London (1971–93). Since then he has run his own company, Out of Joint, and is also a director in residence at the Royal Shakespeare Company.

Stănescu, Carmen (1925–) Actor, Romania. Stănescu trained at the Royal Academy of Music and Drama in Bucharest, as a pupil of the great actor Mahoara Voiculescu. Noted already as a student, she became a member of the National Theatre Company in Bucharest for about fifty years, performing major parts in Romanian and world drama and infectious the audience's sympathy by her infectious charm. She was a noble Maria the Lady in the Romanian historic play *Apus de soare* (*Sunset*), Amanda in *The Glass Menagerie* by Tennessee Williams, and a passionate Jocasta in *La Machine Infernale* (*The Infernal Machine*) by Jean Cocteau. Her most important success, however, was in comedy, from Caragiale (Mitza Baston in *D'ale Camavaiului* (*Car-*

nival Scenes) and Zoe in *O Scrisoare Pierduta* (*The Lost Letter*)) to Molière (Dorina in *Tartuffe* and Toinette in *Le malade imaginaire* (*The Imaginary Invalid*)), reaching a true record with the role of Lydia Ivanovna in Arbuzov's *Old Fashioned Comedy* (1,100 performances). Also successful in musicals, on television and in film, Carmen Stănescu has an extraordinary theatrical presence.

Stanford, Alan (1949–) Actor and director, Ireland. Born in Great Britain, Stanford trained at the Guildhall School of Music and Drama, London. After a brief period in repertory theatre and television drama in England, he moved to Ireland in 1969 where he has had a very extensive and successful career. Early work in Ireland included the ITC (national touring theatre of Ireland) playing such roles as Aston in Thomas KILROY's adaptation of Chekhov's *Cajka* (*The Seagull*), Broadbent in Shaw's *John Bull's Other Island*, and Malvolio in *Twelfth Night*. He was director of theatre at the Project Arts Centre in Dublin (1972–5), but is probably best known for his work at the Gate Theatre, Dublin, where over the past nineteen years he has appeared regularly in the leading roles of the major classics of the Western stage, particularly in the plays of Shaw, Wilde and Ibsen, winning a Harveys' Theatre Award in 1983. He gained international recognition for his portrayal of Herod in Wilde's *Salomé* at the Gate (1988–9) and two roles in the Gate's Beckett Festival (1992): Pozzo in *Waiting for Godot* and Hamm in *Endgame*. His career as a director has been centred principally at the Gate Theatre, where most recently he directed Rostand's *Cyrano de Bergerac* (1998) and also with the Dublin-based Second Age company with whom he has directed many plays by Shakespeare, productions which, for many Irish schoolchildren, will have been their first live experience of a Shakespeare play. Stanford was also responsible for founding the Dublin Theatre School and is noted as having taught many of Ireland's younger leading actors.

Steckel, Frank-Patrick (1943–) Director, Germany. Steckel worked as director with the Schaubühne in Berlin, and at theatres in Frankfurt, Munich and Bremen. From 1986–95 he was artistic director of the theatre in Bochum. Among his important productions are Kleist's *Penthesilea* (1978), Pirandello's *I giganti della montagna* (*Mountain Giants*, 1986), *Timon of Athens* (1990), Brecht's *Der Gute Mensch von Sezuan* (*The Good Person of Sezuan*, 1993) and *Hamlet* (1995). After leaving Bochum he has worked freelance, including Heiner Müller's *Germania 3* (1996) and Brecht's *Die Heilige Johanna der Schlachthöfe* (*St Joan*, 1997) at the Burgtheater in Vienna (1996), as well as *Love's Labour's Lost* (1998) in Köln. His productions are oriented towards the philosophical–political discourse of the text.

Steigerwald, Karel (1945–) Dramatist, Czech Republic. After studying screenplay-writing at the Prague Film Academy, Steigerwald started working in the Barrandov Film Studio. In the 1980s, he worked with director Ivan RAJMONT and the Činoherní Studio in stí n.L., for whom he wrote *Dobové tance* (*Period Dance*, 1980), and *Fox-trot* (1982). Two other plays were initially banned: *Tatarská pout'* (*Tartar Pilgrimage*, written 1979, premiered 1988 in the Theatre on the Balustrade (Na zábradlí), directed by Rajmont) and *Neapolská choroba* (*Neapolitan Disease*, 1988 at the Žižkov theatre, directed by Rajmont). This loose tetralogy maps the shape of the political and civic conformism and behaviour of the 'little' Czech in 'big' history. Bitter grotesques also run through his recent play *Nobel* (1994 at the National Theatre Prague, directed by Ivan Rajmont), satirically reflecting Czech society in the first years of the post-communist era.

Stein, Gisela (1935–) Actor, Germany. Stein trained for the stage at Wiesbadener Schauspielschule. After working in Koblenz, Krefeld-Mönchengladbach and Essen, she joined the company of the Staatliche Schauspielbühnen Berlin in 1960. She played, among others, the title role in Hebbel's *Maria Magdalena* (1966, directed by Fritz Kortner), Ranevskaja in Chekhov's *Visnevyi sad* (*The Cherry Orchard*, 1979) and Emma in PINTER's *Betrayal* (1979). Since 1979 she has been a member of the Münchner Kammerspiele, where her most recent roles include Atossa in Aeschylus's *Persai* (*The Persians*, 1993) and Ariel in *The Tempest*. She is considered one of the best actors today, especially in tragedy. 'She approaches her parts not intuitively, but creates the characters newly by analysing them and piecing them together again. This method allows her to show the ambiguities of her characters.'

Stein, Peter (1937–) Director, Germany. Stein began his theatre career as assistant dramaturg and assistant director with Fritz Kortner at Münchner Kammerspiele, where he directed his first production, Edward BOND's *Saved* in 1967. Important stages in his career were Bremen and Zürich. In 1970 he became artistic co-director of the Schaubühne am Halleschen Ufer (which moved to a new building at Lehniner Platz in 1981). One of the major results of an increasing institutional and artistic political awareness, this theatre was run as a an ensemble theatre, implying the cast and crew's thorough preparation for each production, continuous discussion of administrative and artistic matters, and keeping minutes of all processes and decisions. Stein left the Schaubühne in 1984–5, but continued directing there until 1992. From 1992–7 he was artistic director of the Salzburg Festival. His productions are characterized by elements he took over from Kortner and developed further: insistence on exact acting rich in nuances, suggestive techniques of representation and a tendency to forced gesture and diction.

Stembridge, Gerard (1958–) Dramatist and director, Ireland. A brilliant satirist, Stembridge has written for theatre, film, radio, television and opera. He worked with youth theatre from 1986–92 and believes strongly in collaborating and workshopping with actors. His plays staged at the Project Arts Centre, Dublin, include *Lovechild* (1993) and *The Gay Detective* (1996), which toured nationally and to the Tricycle, London. His work with the innovative Barabbas...The Company includes a version of *Macbeth* (1994) and the highly successful production of *The Whiteheaded Boy* by Lennox Robinson in 1997 and 1998. In August 1998 Stembridge's commitment to youth theatre was reaffirmed by the production of his new play *Sudden Death* by the recently established Limerick Youth Theatre. Stembridge worked for five years as a producer/director with RTE (Radio Telefis Eireann) where he wrote and directed *The Truth about Claire*, a two-hour drama about the vagaries of Ireland's controversial abortion law and its implications. He also co-wrote and directed a popular satirical comedy for RTE radio, *Scrap Saturday*, and the feature film *Guiltrip*.

Stephenson, Elie (1944–) Author, director and actor, France and Guyane. Stephenson studied economics at Paris-Nanterre, while also taking part in drama (Med Hondo's production of BOUKMAN's *West-Indies*) and continuing to write. Back in Cayenne as a teacher he composed some dozen plays, most of which he directed for productions by the Troupe Angela Davis or Les Jeunes de Mirza, notably *Un Rien de pays* (*A No Place*, 1976), *Les Voyageurs* (*The Travellers*, 1976), critical of the state of underdevelopment of Guyane, *O Mayouri* (*Working Together*, published 1988) inspired by Roumain's *Gouverneurs de la Rosée* (*Masters of the Dew*), and works re-evaluating local history such as *La nouvelle légende de D'Chimbo* (*The New Legend of D'Chimbo*, 1984). A versatile performer who also sang with a small group, Stephenson's intense nationalism sustains his production, despite administrative responsibilities as director of the Association Régionale de Développement Culturel (ARDEC) since 1994.

Stevenson, Juliet (1956–) Actor, Great Britain. Stevenson trained at the Royal Academy of Dramatic Art and soon afterwards joined the Royal Shakespeare Company with a series of major parts, including Isabella in *Measure for Measure* and Rosalind in *As You Like It*. In the first production of Christopher HAMPTON's *Les Liaisons Dangereuses* she played Mme de Tourvelle. For the National Theatre, she played the title roles in Lorca's *Yerma* (1987) and *Hedda Gabler* by Ibsen (directed by Howard DAVIES, 1990). With John MALKOVICH she starred in the London production of Lanford WILSON's *Burn This*, and created the part of Paulina in Ariel Dorfmann's *Death and the Maiden* (1991). In 1996 she played Grusha in Brecht's *Der Kaukasische Kreidekreis* (*The Caucasian Chalk Circle*) at the Royal National Theatre, London, returned for a season to the RSC to appear in Katie MITCHELL's production of *Beckett Shorts* (1997), and starred as Amanda in Noel Coward's *Private Lives* at the Royal National Theatre (1999). Stevenson is an actor of immense stage presence and emotional intensity with a striking, earthy, deep voice. Assisted by her method acting technique, she creates passionate, open, strong but vulnerable, immensely feminine characters. Since the late 1980s Stevenson has also gained major praise for her films.

Stonins, Ivars (1971–) Actor, Latvia. After graduating from the Theatre Department of the Latvian Music Academy in 1993, Stonins has worked with the Latvian National Theatre, appearing as Mozart in

SHAFFER's *Amadeus*, in the title role of Büchner's *Woyzek* and as Gregers Werle in Ibsen's *Wild Duck*. Critics agree that he lives up to the various roles, so far mainly in modern drama. Personally, he is working on the challenge of changing between rehearsals for one role during the day and playing a different role in the evening.

Stoppard, Tom (1937–) Dramatist, Great Britain. Initially, Stoppard worked as a journalist. In *The Real Inspector Hound*, Stoppard turned the traditional who-dun-nit inside out, beginning his practice of cross-fertilization of apparently unrelated areas or levels of reality. In *After Marguerite*, surrealist events are later intellectually explained. His breakthrough as a dramatist came in 1966 with *Rosencrantz and Guildenstern are Dead*, focusing on the dilemmas of the two characters in *Hamlet*. *Jumpers* (1972), combining philosophy and gymnastics, and *Travesties* (1974) were equally successful. Many critics felt that the works of the years that followed were somewhat shallow, with some adaptations of plays by Schnitzler and Nestroy. The original plays, such as *The Real Thing* (1982) and *Hapgood* (1988), at best divided critical opinion. Yet *Arcadia* (1993), *Indian Ink* (1994) and *The Invention of Love* (Royal National Theatre, 1997) refuted this view and (re-)established Stoppard as a dramatist who is able to successfully merge highly sophisticated subject matter and entertainment.

Storey, David (1933–) Dramatist and novelist, Great Britain. Storey studied at the Slade School of Art in London. He began as a novelist, scoring a major success with *This Sporting Life* (1963). In 1967, his first play was performed, *The Restoration of Arnold Middleton* (about an eccentric schoolteacher cracking up). *Home* (1970) starred Ralph Richardson and John GIELGUD, and Ralph Richardson played the lead in *Early Days* (1980, National Theatre). The National Theatre also staged

The March on Russia (1989) and *Stages* (1992). Rather than displaying intellectual ingenuity, like the characters in plays by STOPPARD, Storey's characters and his plays have to be intuitively apprehended, a fact which might, in Storey's own opinion, contribute to the fact that they are comparatively underrated in the theatre.

Stratiev, Stanislav (1941–) Dramatist, Bulgaria. In plays such as *The Roman Bath*, *The Bus*, *Buckskin Jacket* and *The Maximalist*, Stratiev examines ugly and socially dangerous individuals who prefer to make life dogmatic and senseless. His plays are full of paradoxes as he attempts to understand social and psychological deformation, especially as they apply to bureaucrats, demagogues and consumers. For Stratiev, the counterpoint to such depravity is found in the moral stability of creative life, uncompromising and implacable.

Stratton, Alan (1951–) Dramatist, Canada. Stratton's first play, *The Rusting Heart*, was produced at James REANEY's Alpha Centre in 1968. In his enormously successful *Nurse Jane Goes To Hawaii* (1980, Phoenix Theatre), Stratton juxtaposes the conventions of the modern sex farce and the cliches of pulp romantic fiction. *Rexy* (1981, Phoenix Theatre) explores the life of Canadian Prime Minister MacKenzie King with warmth and charm; it won the Chalmers Award, the Dora Mavor Moore Award, and the Canadian Authors' Association Award. He has also written *Joggers* (1982), *Papers* (1985), *The 101 Miracles of Hope Chance* (1988) and *A Flush of Tories* (1991). He has said of his writing, 'You write plays the way you view life. I don't set out to write "a comedy". I just see life that way. If the humour in *Nurse Jane* is light and fluffy, then the humour in *Rexy!* is detached and ironic, and in *Joggers* it's dark and disturbing'.

Strauß, Botho (1944–) Dramatist, Germany. Between 1967–70 Strauß was a theatre critic and editor in the German theatre monthly *Theater Heute*. In 1970 he became dramaturg with Peter STEIN's Schaubühne in Berlin, working on Kleist's *Prinz Friedrich Homburg* (1971), Ibsen's *Peer Gynt* (1971) and Gorki's *Dacniki* (*Sommergäste*). Subsequently he has written his own plays, mostly premiered at the Schaubühne, such as *Trilogie des Wiedersehens* (*Trilogy of Meeting Again*, 1977), *Der Park* (*The Park*), a contemporary version of *A Midsummer Night's Dream*, and *Die Fremdenführerin* (*The Tourist Guide*, 1988), *Das Gleichgewicht* (*Balance*, 1993, directed by Luc BONDY) and *Jeffers Akt I und II* (1998, directed by Edith CLEVER). His recurring theme is to show how an inability to communicate and fear of personal closeness destroy human longing for relationships.

Strijards, Frans (1952–) Director and dramatist, the Netherlands. Strijards started his theatrical career as an 'angry young man' in Eindhoven, at first in the student scene, which was to be the subject of his first play, *Ondergang voor beginners* (*A Beginner's Guide to Destruction*, 1976). Strijards has always combined writing and directing, at first with his own company Projekttheater (1974–82) and then from 1985 until the present with his company, Art and Pro. As a director he has shown affinity with plays by Ibsen (for example, *Rosmersholm* (1984), *Hedda Gabler* (1990) and a wonderfully moving *Wild Duck* in 1996), Chekhov (*Visnevyi sad* (*The Cherry Orchard*), *Djadja Vanja* (*Uncle Vanya*)) and Peter HANDKE. He uses a hectic, expressionist kind of acting to bring out unexpected meaning in the plays. The most successful of Strijards's own plays were *Hitchcocks Driesprong* (*Hitchcock's Junction*, 1987), *The Stendhal Syndrome* (1989) and *Gesprekken over G.* (*Conversations about G.*, 1991). They are available in German. Strijards's plays are often based on a 'whodunit?' type plot, but the investigation is usually more into what moves human beings in general, and always winds up in a frantic disillusion.

Stryhun, Fedir (1939–) Actor and director, Ukraine. Stryhun trained at the Karpenko-Kary Institute for the Art of the Theatre, Kiev, and joined the Maria Zan'kovets'ka Ukrainian Drama Theatre, Lviv, in 1965, serving as its chief director. The spontaneous Ukrainian emotionality, carriage and daring have been embodied in Sryhun's work. He usually appears in plays of predominantly heroic-dramatic and national character, and has become well known for the roles of Mykola Sadovskyi in Riabokliacha's *Maria Zan'kovets'ka* (1977), the title role in *Othello* (1986) and Kozak Iarema in Taras Shevchenko's *Haidamaky* (1988). Taisia Lytvynenko and Bohdan KOZAK were his partners in the plays he directed, *Marusia Churai* after Lina Kostenko (1989), *Narodnyi Malakhii* by Mykola Kulish (1990) and the trilogy *Mazepa* by Bohdan Lepkyi (1991–2).

Stückl, Christian (1961–) Director, Germany. Stückl began directing with amateurs in 1979. From 1981–4 he trained as a wood sculptor and became an assistant director to Dieter DORN at the Münchner Kammerspiele, which he joined as a director in residence in 1991. Productions include *Much Ado About Nothing* (1992), Marlowe's *Edward II* (1993), *Quai West* by Koltès (1994), Reza's *Art* in Bonn (1997) and JELINEK's *Raststätte oder Sie machens alle* (*Inn, or They All Do It*), Bonn, 1999.

Stuhr, Jerzy (1947–) Actor and director, Poland. Stuhr obtained a degree in Polish philology from the Jagiellonski University of Cracow and studied acting at the State Theatre Academy of Cracow, which he joined as a member of staff in 1972, becoming its president in 1990. His main theatre credits, with Stary Teatr of Cracow, include Belzebub in *Dziady* (*Fore-fathers' Eve*) by Mickiewicz, Wysocki in Wyspianski's *Noc Listopadowa* (*November Night*), Horondniczy in Gogol's *Revizor* (*The Government Inspector*), the contrabassist in Süßkind's *Der Kontrabaß* (*The Double Bass*) and the title roles in *Hamlet* and Dürrenmatt's *Romulus der Große* (*Romulus the Great*). He excelled in the characteristic type of a shameless career-maker, merciless and cynical, but still shaken by uncertainty and constantly fighting for his life. Stuhr also possesses outstanding comic skills, carrying away large audiences in his numerous roles of witty, mischievous and yet sympathetic fellows. His main directing credits include Süßkind's *Der Kontrabaß* as well as *The Taming of the Shrew* and *Macbeth*.

Stumbre, Lelde (1952–) Dramatist, Latvia. Even before he had graduated from the Dramaturgy Department of the Moscow Institute of Literature in 1983, Stumbre's double bill *Andersons and Millers* was produced at the Daile Theatre, Riga (1981). Other plays include *Zimejumi Smiltis* (*Drawings in the Sand*), *Kugitis Migla* (*A Ship in the Fog*) and *Svesinieki Seit* (*Strangers Here*, 1995). In content, she attempts to reflect the complex world of personal relationships. In form she is still experimenting, struggling between a traditional and non-traditional approach. Calling herself a 'woman of letters', she places much emphasis on language and style, and would rather see her plays published than presented on stage.

Stupka, Bohdan (1941–) Actor, Ukraine. Stupka trained at the Drama Studio of the Maria Zan'kovets'ka Ukrainian Drama Theatre, L'viv and at the Karpenko-Kary Institute for the Art of the Theatre, Kiev. Since 1978 Stupka has been a leading actor of the Ivan Franko Ukrainian Drama Theatre, Kiev. Nervousness and witticism are Stupkaís gifts as an actor, as well as a plastic expressiveness of his performance. One of the most famous

Ukrainian actors, Stupka has a complete command of different dramatic genres. Major parts in Serhii DANCHENKO's productions include the title role in *Richard III* (1974), Mykola Zadorozhny in Ivan Franko's *Ukradene shchastia* (*The Stolen Happiness*, 1977, 1979), Don Juan in Lesia Ukrainka's *Kam'ianyi hospodar* (*The Stone Host*, 1971, 1988), Ui in Brecht's *Der Aufhaltsame Aufstieg des Arturo Ui* (*The Resistible Rise of Arturo Ui* 1985), Master in *Master and Margarita* after Bulhakov (1987), Tevie in *Tevie-Tevel'* (*Tevie the Milkman*) after Shalom-Aleichem (1989), Rosmer in Ibsen's (*Rosmersholm*, 1994) and the title role in *King Lear* (1998).

Su Le Ce (1945–) Director, China. In 1967 Su graduated from the directing department of the Shanghai Academy of Drama, where he is now a professor. His main productions include Zong Fu Xian's *Yu Wu Sheng Chu* (*Out of Silence*, 1978), *Wu Wai You Re Liu* (*A Warm Flow Outside the House*) by Ma Zhong Jun and Jia Hong Yuan (1979), Zong Fu Xian's *Xue Zong Shi Re De* (*Blood is Warm*, 1981), *Lu* (*The Road*) by Ma Zhong Jun and Jia Hong Yuan (1982), Wang Jian Ping's *Da Xi Yang Dian Hua* (*Atlantic Phone Calls*, 1989), *Henry IV* (1994) and Sun Zu Ping's *Xu Hu Shi Fu* (*Master Xu Hu*, 1996). He is noted chiefly for his impact on the post-Mao Shanghai theatrical scene.

Suárez, Miguel Ángel (1939–) Actor, Puerto Rico. One of Puerto Rico's finest actors, and one of the few actors in Puerto Rico to have mastered the four major performance media (radio, television, theatre and film), Miguel Ángel Suárez began his professional career as a child actor on local radio programmes. Married to Nana Hudo (teacher, dancer and choreographer), he has worked in the Puerto Rican theatre since his teens. Suárez is an appealing and likable actor whose power nevertheless often verges on the violent. He has been noted for his powerful and multi-layered portrayals as Stockman in Ibsen's *En Folkefiende, (An Enemy of the People* (1978) and Stanley in Williams's *A Streetcar Named Desire* (1977), both directed by Dean ZAYAS. Together with his portrayal of The Angel in Ugo Betti's *Crime on Goat Island* (Teatro del Sesenta, 1972), these productions afforded him the opportunity to collaborate with José Luis MARRERO, Ernesto CONCEPCIÓN and Gladys RODRÍGUEZ. He also appeared as César in Walter Rodríguez's *La descomposición de César Sánchez (The Decomposition of César Sánchez*, 1973).

Subbanna, K.V. (1932–) Director, India. A founder member of Ninasam, a theatre school with an attached repertory company based in a village in Karnataka, Subbanna has directed many plays including Shudraka's *Mrcchakatika (The Little Clay Cart)*, Bhasa's *Urubhanga*, Vijay TENDULKAR's *Ghashiram Kotwal* and *Hamlet*. Subbanna received the Ramon Megasaysay Award as 'a social worker active in culture, someone who is trying to change the community in the cultural context through theatre'. A confirmed Gandhian who believes that genuine theatre begins with intimate communication, he advocates going back to one's roots: his theatre at Ninasam is built of mud, while the acoustics are provided by gunny bags. Tirugata, his repertory company, travels to villages in Karnataka with its productions, and the recent production of *Yagna Phala* was embellished with features of the traditional Karnataka folk form Yakshagana.

Subotić, Nada (1931–) Actor, Croatia. While training at the Academy of Dramatic Art in Zagreb, Subotić joined Zagreb Theatre Gavella where she acted for the next thirty years. At the age of twenty-eight she scored a major success when she played the part of eighty-year-old Terese Brown in Greene's *The Living Room*. Her next notable performances were Alice in Strindberg's *Dödsdansen (Dance of Death*, 1965) and the award-winning portrayal of prostitute Rahela in Arden's *Live like Pigs*. In 1978 she played Winnie in Beckett's *Happy Days*. She was awarded for the portrayal of supporting characters such as Eve's Mother in Krleža's *Vučjak* (1977) and the Duchess of York in *Richard II* (1981). She does not concentrate solely on her parts but likes to participate actively in the creation of the performance as a whole: for the production of Murell and Willson's play *Sarah and the Scream of the Lobster*, she suggested the cast list. Neva ROŠIĆ starred as Sarah Bernhardt and Subotič gave a splendid performance in the male role of the secretary Georges Pitou. In 1984 she celebrated thirty years of acting in monodrama *Tajna Barunice Castelli... (The Secret of Baroness Castelli...)*, based on Krleža's text. She played several roles on film and radio and she is an appreciated reciter.

Sueki Toshifumi (1939–) Director and translator, Japan. Sueki founded Te no Kai (the Hand Theatre Company) with BETSUYAKU Minoru and YAMAZAKI Masakazu in 1972. He also directs plays for the Kiyama Office, a theatre agency run by theatre producer, Kiyama Kiyoshi. Directing credits include a number of plays by Betsuyaku, such as *Machi to Hikôsen (A Town and a Zeppelin*, 1970), *Isu to Densetsu (The Chair and the Legend*, 1974) and *Kono Michi wa Itsuka Kita Michi (I Have Walked Down This Way Once*, 1995), and Yamazaki's *Zeami* when it was chosen for the production by Shingeki-dan Kyôkai (the Association of Shingeki theatre companies) in 1987, in which MATSUMOTO Kôshirô played the part of Zeami; the production toured in the USA in 1988. Sueki also translated and staged plays by Duras and Adamov. His apporach is straughtforward and intellectual, aiming to do justice to a dramatist's intention and trying to materialise what a play expresses in its original context.

Sundquist, Björn (1948–) Actor, Norway. Sundquist trained at the Norwegian State Theatre High School, and has become one of the leading actors of his generation. He is mainly known for his parts in the classical tragic repertoire and modern realistic plays, including Hamlet, Mercutio in *Romeo and Juliet*, Iago in *Othello*, the title role in Ibsen's *Brand*, Hjalmar Ekdal in *Vildanden* (*The Wild Duck*), Dr. Stockmann in *En Folkefiende* (*An Enemy of the People*) and Merlin in Tankred DORST's *Das Wüste Land* (*The Waste Land*). In January 1997 he began work on a one-man-show called *The Comical Tragedy*, hoping to develop his talents in comedy.

Suzuki Tadashi (1939–) Director, Japan. With BETSUYAKU Minoru and others, Suzuki founded Gekidan Jiyû Butai (the Freedom Stage Theatre Company) in 1962, renamed Waseda Shô Gekijô (the Wasesa Small Theatre) in 1966. He directed Betsuyaku's *Mattchi Uri no Shôjo* (*The Match Girl*, 1967) and KARA Jûrô's *Shojo Kamen* (Virgin's Mask, 1969). In his productions of *Gekitekinaru Mono I, II* and *III* (*Dramatic Passions I, II* and *III*) in 1969, 1970 and 1975, he examined and established his theatrical style, 'Footwork'. In 1976 he founded the Suzuki Company of Toga (SCOT). He also founded the Japan Performing Arts Centre, which organizes the Toga International Arts Festival and the International Actor Training Programme. Major productions include Euripides's *Troades* (*The Trojan Women*, 1974) and *Bakchae* (The Bacchae, 1978), Chekhov's *Tri sestry* (*Three Sisters*) and *Visnevyi sad* (*The Cherry Orchard*, 1987), and *King Lear* (1988). All have toured abroad. He held the Saratoga International Theatre Festival with Anne BOGART in Saratoga Springs in New York since 1992. Suzuki

has taught his training method both in Japan and overseas.

Svoboda, Josef (1920–) Designer and architect, Czech Republic. Svoboda has worked on many world stages, such as Chekhov's *Tri sestry* (*Three Sisters*, 1967), at the Old Vic, London, directed by Laurence Olivier, and Goethe's *Faust II* (1991), at the Piccolo Teatro di Milano, directed by Giorgio Strehler. By means of kinetic and light designs, he activates the stage space, which he understands as a dramatic component contributing to the action. He also makes use of stage vehicles (Kundera's *Majitelé klícu* (*The Owner of the Keys*), National Theatre Prague, 1962), and suspended architectural elements (*Romeo and Juliet*, National Theatre Prague, 1963). With light he creates dematerialised objects (Wagner's *Tristan and Isolde*, Grand Opéra Geneve, 1978) and imaginary spaces. He uses mirrors to reflect and outline the stage action as well as the public many times over (Pirandello's *I giganti della montagna* (*The Mountain Giants*), Theatre Beyond the Gate II (Za Branou II), Prague, 1994), and various projection techniques on multiple and moving spaces, television cameras allowing instant reproduction of shots on the stage itself (Nono's *Intoleranza*, The Opera Group, Boston, 1965), or holography and laser beams (Mozart's *Die Zauberflöte* (*The Magic Flute*), Munich, 1970). He is a true wizard of the stage, casting his spell by means of modern science and technology.

Szajna, Józef (1922–) Designer, director and dramatist, Poland. A graduate of the Academy of Fine Arts in Cracow, Szajna was imprisoned in the concentration camps of Auschwitz and Buchenwald during the Second World War. This experience has influenced his imagination since. From 1955–63 he was a designer, then stage director and managing director of the avant-garde Teatr Ludowy in Cracow. Later he worked with, among others, Stary Teatr Cracow, Teatr Slaski in Katowice, Teatr Wspólczesny in Wroclaw and Teatr Polski in Warsaw, as well as abroad. From 1971–82 he held a professorship in scenography at the Academy of Fine Arts in Warsaw. His main credits as designer include Gozzi's *Turandot*, *A Midsummer Night's Dream* and Sophocles's *Antigone*. Directing credits include Gogol's *Revizor* (*The Government Inspector*), Goethe's *Faust* and O'Casey's *Purple Dust*. He also wrote his own plays. Szajna treats stage design as an environment installation, theatre as an art of action. His chief medium is the moving image. As an artist, he draws from surrealism, emballage, assemblage and happening; as a director, he draws from the futurists, the Bauhaus and Witkacy theories. He often uses ready made objects, such as rugs, tyres, dirt, boots, wooden soles and deformed bodies in his productions. His theatre expresses the destruction of the inhuman world with people struggling for hope. Szajna shows both the tragedy and the dignity of human beings.

Szakács, Györgyi (1951–) Designer, Hungary. Szakács studied architecture at the Budapest Technical University, but turned to costume design in 1975. Stages in her career are Kecskemét, Katona József Theatre (1976–9), Miskolc, National Theatre (1979–88), and Budapest National Theatre (1989–91). Since 1994 she has been designer of the Budapest Új Theatre. She also regularly works as a guest at several theatres of the country. Major productions include Verdi's *Un ballo in maschera*, Chekhov's *Visnevyi sad* (*The Cherry Orchard*), Gogol's *Revizor* (*The Government Inspector*), Molière's *L'avare* (*The Miser*) and *Dom Juan*, *Hamlet*, *Julius Caesar*, *Coriolanus*, BARKER's *Scenes from an Execution*, STOPPARD's *Rosencrantz and Guildenstern Are Dead*, Ibsen's *Rosmersholm*, Dürrenmatt's *Der Besuch der Alten Dame* (*The Visit*) and Werner Schwab's *Die Präsidentinnen* (*The Presidents*). A renewer of Hungarian

costume design, her work can be connected to modern theatrical workshops and directors. Depending on the concept of the performance, her costumes are sometimes 'unnoticeable', at other times indicators of the age, atmosphere or character; but they are always very original.

Szakonyi, Károly (1931–) Dramatist, Hungary. After studying Hungarian and popular education at the Eötvös Loránd University, Szakonyi worked as dramaturg at the Budapest National Theatre (1963–6), the Miskolec National Theatre (1974–9), the Pécs National Theatre (1988–93) and as artistic consultant at the Debrecen Coskonai Theatre. Plays include *Zsóka*, *Életem* (*My Life*), *Hongkongi paróka* (*Hong Kong Wig*), *Apák és fiúk* (*Fathers and Sons*), *Égi kávéház* (*Heavenly Café*) and most recently *A pénz komédiája* (*The Comedy of Money*, 1995). These 'family dramas' are tragi-comedies presenting the perils hidden in the macro-cosmos through conflicts within micro-society.

Székely, László (1932–) Designer, Hungary. Székely studied at the Budapest Applied Arts College and began his career at the Eger Gárdonyi Géza Theatre. After seasons at the Szeged National Theatre (1965–71), the Szolnok Szigligeti Theatre (1971–9), the Budapest National Theatre (1979–83) and the Budapest Katona József Theatre (1983–90), he is now working freelance for several theatres of the capital, the country and also foreign countries. Since 1978 he has also taught in the Set and Costume Design Department at the Applied Arts College in Budapest, where he is currently head of department. Major productions include Molière's *Le malade imaginaire* (*The Imaginary Invalid*), *Georges Dandin*, Chekhov's *Tri sestry* (*Three Sisters*), *Timon of Athens*, *Troilus and Cressida*, *Coriolanus*, Büchner's *Dantons Tod* (*Danton's Death*), Wilde's *The Importance of Being Earnest*, Ibsen's *En Folkefiende* (*An Enemy of the*

People), Strindberg's *Fadren* (*The Father*) and Arthur MILLER's *The Price*. His set designs are characterized by thorough knowledge of style and drama history, original use of modem scenic technology, and a rich combination of elements and good taste.

T

Tabakov, Oleg (1935–) Actor and director, Russia. Tabakov graduated from the Moscow Art Theatre Studio in 1957 and started his theatre and film career as a performer in Russian classics: Nikolai Rostov in the film of *Vojna I Mir* (*War and Peace*, 1964), Aduyev in Goncharov's *Obyknovennaya istoriya* (*Ordinary Story*, at the Sovremennik theatre, 1966) and contemporary non-conformist drama such as plays by Viktor Rozov. In 1970 he became the director of the Sovremennik Theatre, which he left in 1983 left for the Moscow Art Theatre with Oleg YEFRE-MOV as artistic director. In the course of his career he turned to various character parts, such as Balalaikin in Shedrin's *Balalaikin I Kompaniya* (*Balalaikin and Co*, 1973). In the 1990s at the Moscow Art Theatre he played Famussov in Griboyedov's *Gore ot uma* (*Wit Works Woe*) and Salieri in Peter SHAFFERS' *Amadeus*. In the 1980s he added actor training to his credits, and is now rector of the Moscow Art Theatre Studio. At the same time he ran a theatre studio of his own (Tabakov Studio) which soon became one of the highest rating in Moscow. He also organized the American Studio of the Moscow Art Theatre, training future actors from the USA in Moscow.

Tabori, George (1914–) Actor, director and dramatist. Tabori was born in Budapest, emigrated to Britain in 1936 and is a British citizen. During the Second World War he was member of the Intelligence Office of the British Army, and from 1943–5 he worked for the BBC. While in the USA he met Bertolt Brecht in Hollywood, and his interest in theatre was kindled. After some film work in Italy and France, he lived in New York until 1971, writing and directing his own plays and screenplays. Since 1971 he has been living and working in Germany, closely working with the Münchner Kammerspiele and freelancing. Since 1990 he has been working with the Burgtheater in Vienna. His own plays, with *Mein Kampf* (1987) arguably the most successful one, deal mainly with the history of Germans and Jews. Tabori claims that every expression is therapeutic. On the stage one can enact the destructive (*ausagieren*), and only when it has been released is something constructive created.

Takemoto Sumitayû VII (1924–) Gidayû reciter and singer, Japan. The son of Tsuruzawa Tomokichi, he trained in gidayû (narrative music of Bunraku puppet theatre) under Toyotake Kôtsubodayû II, Takemoto Tsunatayû VIII and others, succeeding to this stage name in 1985. The role of a gidayû reciter is to read stage directions, to speak for the puppets, to explain the situation the characters are in and to express their feelings clearly to the audience. Sumitayû's recitation is especially good in expressing puppet characters' emotions in *sewamono* (domestic plays). His representative pieces are *Sakaya* (*Liquor Shop*), *Ueda-mura* (*Ueda Village*) and *Nozaki-mura* (*Nozaki Village*). He is a member of the Sanwa-kai group of the Bunraku association.

Tan, Alvin Cheong Kheng (1963–) Director, Singapore. Founder and Artistic Director of The Necessary Stage, Alvin Tan is considered one of the leading young voices in Singapore theatre. He founded the Necessary Stage while he was an undergraduate at the National University of Singapore and, together with resident playwright Haresh SHARMA, sought to forge an authentic Singapore identity and idiom in Singapore theatre with his directorial efforts, which included *Lanterns Never Go Out* (1989), *Still Building* (1992), *Off Centre* (1993) and *Pillars* (1997). Tan advocates what he terms 'intra-cultural' performances where he primarily deals with the interaction of the cultures within Singapore and contextualized by Singapore. The works of Brecht, Boal and more recently postmodernist aesthetics heavily influence his direction. Winner of the Singapore Young Artist Award in 1998, Alvin Tan has been awarded a M.Phil. (Arts) degree from the University of Birmingham in the UK.

Tan, Tarn How (1960–) Dramatist, Singapore. Currently the head scriptwriter at Television Corporation of Singapore's English Drama unit, Tan is attributed to be the writer of the first political satire in Singapore, *The Lady of Soul and her Ultimate 'S' Machine* (1992). The play dealt with the sensitive issue of Singapore's relentless search for 'Soul', and was not allowed to be performed as it depicted civil servants in an unflattering light. The play was subsequently passed. His next play, *Undercover* (1993), was a controversial discussion on the powers of the Internal Security Act in Singapore. The play oscillated between paranoia and

conspiracy and questioned the very relevance of arts censorship. His other more controversial play, *Six of the Best* (1996), was a dramatization of the Michael Fay incident but set in an office of local and expatriate workers. The play teased out racial, ethnic and sexual tensions in a modern working environment. Tan received a Fulbright fellowship in 1993 at Boston University.

Tandefelt, Liisi Kaarina (1936–) Actor and designer, Finland. Tandefelt trained at the Finnish Theatre School as well as at the Academy of Performing Arts in Bratislava. In the course of her career she has worked in television, at TTT Theatre in Tampere, Helsinki City Theatre and Turku City Theatre. Since 1976 she has run her own theatre, Avoiment Ovet, which tours Europe and performs in Finnish and German. Major costume designs include *The Tempest*, *My Fair Lady* and Brecht's *Leben des Galilei* (*Life of Galileo*). Major acting credits are Hedwig in Ibsen's *Vildanden* (*The Wild Duck*), and a remarkable series of monologues on famous women such as Käthe Kollwitz and Charlotte von Stein, *Jacke wie Hose* by Manfred KARGE and plays by Finnish poets Märta Tikkanen, Eeva Kilpi and Solveig von Schoultz. 'The citics and audiences alike were impressed by the intelligence and self-irony through which Tandefelt interprets the texts. As a stage and costume designer she uses the austerity for which Finnish design is known.'

Tanvir, Habib (1929–) Dramatist and director, India. One of the pioneers in revitalising the folk forms of Indian theatre, Tanvir began his career with IPTA in Bombay in the early 1940s. He moved to Delhi in 1954, where his first major play *Agra Bazaar* marks the beginning of popular culture in India, and received the prestigious Sangeet Natak Akademi award. He used folk tunes and songs to dovetail episodes and poems from the life of Urdu poet Nazir Akbarabadi. In his next play, *Mitti Ka Gadi*, an adaptation of Sudraka's *The Little Clay Cart*, he drew on training received at the Bristol Old Vic under Duncan Ross, particularly the importance of 'flow'. Tanvir also attended the Royal Academy of Dramatic Art, London, for a year which served paradoxically to renew his focus on his own indigenous tradition. His major achievement, *Charandas Chor*, is a blend of Chattisgarhi folk form and contemporary sensibility, using a folk tale to interrogate status, political power and honesty through the figure of a thief; it received a Fringe First at Edinburgh in 1982. Tanvir's group, Naya Theatre Company, is one of the few professional companies where actors receive a regular salary. Tanvir uses the verbal and physical language of the people but combines this with the intellect of a contemporary thinker. At present he is director of the Bharat Bhavan in Bhopal, a centre for Indian arts and culture.

Tassopoulou, Leda (1955–) Actor, Greece. Trained in music (flute and violin), movement (classical dance, Martha Graham method and jazz), and for the stage at the Drama School of the National Theatre of Greece, Tassopoulou co-founded the Amphi-Theatre and has played many leading roles there, in plays by Aeschylus, Sophocles, Euripides, Aristophanes, Menander, Shakespeare, Molière, Büchner, Strindberg, Brecht and others. In 1982 she followed an invitation of the American centre of the International Theatre Institute to teach monologues from ancient Greek drama at ten universities and theatre schools throughout the USA.

Távora, Salvador (1940–) Director, Spain. Távora likes to introduce himself as a former carpenter, flamenco singer and professional bull-fighter, but is now recognized as one of the most significant figures in Andalusian theatre culture. His career in theatre began with *Oratorio*

(*Oratory*, 1969) directed by Juan Bernabé for the Teatro Estudio Lebriano, a new play for which he composed the music and performed as *cantaor* (singer). In 1971 he co-founded the company La Cuadra de Sevilla and has remained its director. Moving away from text-based theatre in indoor spaces, Távora has looked to flamenco song for the material of his stage work. Machinery, song, dance, bulls and darkness became the company's discernable trademarks. A series of productions beginning with *Quejío* (*Lament*, 1972) were seen at Jack Lang's Nancy Festival and secured the company further international dates. The 1980s saw Távora turn to Lorca and Picasso with *Nana de espinas* (*Thorny Lullaby*, 1982) and *Picasso o la muerte del Minotauro* (*Picasso or The Death of the Minotaur*, 1991). Since the late 1980s, the company has looked increasingly to the classics for dramatic material, reworking Euripides's *Bakchai* (*The Bacchae*, 1987) and *Carmen* in 1996.

Tavori, Doron (1952–) Actor, Israel. Tavori is among the group of young actors who co-founded the Beer Sheva municipal theatre. His major roles are Otto Weininger in SOBOL's *The Soul of a Jew*, the Nazi officer Kittel in Sobol's *Ghetto* and Lucky (Beckett's *Waiting for Godot*) at the Haifa municipal theatre. His one-man show of the *Oresteia* as well as his interpretation of Shakespeare's Hamlet in a production directed by Stephen BERKOFF have demonstrated his virtuosity as an actor. In the Sternheim project at the Habima theatre, for which he was the producer as well as an actor, he showed his interest in expressionistic dramaturgy and acting style.

Tayeb, Mohamed (1952–) Director and actor, Syria. Tayeb trained in Egypt. On returning to Syria, he joined the National Theatre in Damascus where he directed many classics, including Shaw's *The Devil's Disciple* (1964), Arthur MILLER's

Death of a Salesman, Beaumarchais's *The Marriage of Figaro*, Ali Salem's *Ughniya Ala'l-Mamar* (*A Song on the Passage*), Riad ISMAT's *Sinbad*, Nouman Ashour's *Al-Qeyama* (*The Tower of Al-Madabegh*) and Alfred Farag's *Zawaj Ala Warket Talaq* (*A Marriage on a Divorce's Paper*). He played a number of supporting roles on television and taught voice and speech at the Academy of Dramatic Arts for some years. He refrained from working as director, maybe sensing that his dated traditional approach has been transcended and such lavish productions as his had become outdated.

Tekindor, Çetin (1945–) Actor, Turkey. Tekindor graduated from the theatre department of the Ankara State Conservatory in 1970, and in the same year started his acting career at the Ankara State Theatre. He also taught theatre students at the Ankara State Conservatory and Faculty of Music and Fine Arts at Bilkent University. He acted in famous plays such as ALBEE's *Who's Afraid of Virginia Woolf?*, Orhan Asena's *Hürrem Sultan*, Willy Russell's *Educating Rita* and Mehmet BAYDUR's *Cumhuriyet Kızı* (*The Daughter of the Republic*). He received the best actor award of the Arts Institution and the Ministry of Cultural Affairs. Tekindor's outstanding characteristic is his powerful voice: the delivery of his lines becomes the major means of expressing the interpretation of the part.

Ten Bruggencate, Catherine (1955–) Actor, The Netherlands. After training at the Drama School in Arnhem, where she graduated in 1977, Catherine Ten Bruggencate joined De Appel, a company in The Hague. She played many parts there, until she started an independent career from 1981–7, starring in plays as diverse as Thomas Bernhard's *Der Präsident* (*The President*, with Cas ENKLAAR), Strindberg's *Fröken Julie* (*Miss Julie*) and Brecht's *Mahagonny*. Strong-minded, lank, a beautiful mover and ladylike with a

twinkle in her brown eyes, Ten Bruggencate has built up an impressive career playing both strong women (Hermione in Racine's *Andromaque*) and slightly addled characters (Harper in Tony Kushner's *Angels in America*). She was with Gerardjan RIJNDERS's company from 1987–93 and is now freelancing again, apprearing in Guy CASSIERS's stage adaptation of Marguerite Duras's *Hiroshima Mon Amour*.

Ten Cate, Ritsaert (1938–) Producer and manager, The Netherlands. After a year at Bristol University and working in film production, Ritsaert Ten Cate started the Mickery Theatre in 1965, which made him renowned throughout the international theatre community. Mickery, first based in a farmhouse outside Amsterdam, and from 1972 in a disued cinema in the city itself, became a point of focus for new theatre. Ten Cate brought many groups, including La MaMa, Traverse, The Wooster Group (led by Elizabeth LECOMPTE) and the Pip Simmons Group to Holland. Thus he not only introduced the Dutch audience to innovative theatre, but also supported and stimulated the work of many experimental theatre companies throughout the world. Ten Cate became a well-known figure in the IETM (Informal European Theatre Meeting). He also directed and wrote his own plays. After Ten Cate closed Mickery in 1991, he was asked to set up DasArts, a post graduate department for drama and choreography. He is currently serving as its director.

Tendulkar, Vijay Dhondopant (1928–) Dramatist, India. Tendulkar came to be known as a dramatist of importance through his major play *Shantata! Court Chalu Ahe* (*Silence! The Court is in Session*) in 1968; Satyadev DUBEY directed the Hindi version, with Shulaba DESHPANDE in the lead role. The BBC broadcast the play in English. *The Vultures* (1971) and *Sakharam Binder* followed the first success. *Ghashiram Kotwal* turned out to be most controversial of his works: it was opposed by Shiva Sena, a group of Hindu fundamentalists who considered it anti-Brahminical, but received much acclaim at the Berlin Folk Theatre Festival in 1981. Justifiably, Tendulkar's later plays *Baby*, *Kamala* and *Kanyadan* have been less well received. Like Antonin Artaud, he believes in theatrical violence as a means of affecting the audience (physical – a forced abortion – in *Vulture*, psychological aggression in *Shantata*).

Terlecki, Wladyslaw (1933–) Dramatist, Poland. Most of Terlecki's plays for the stage, for television and radio are historical. The main protagonists are authentic people whose role and importance in Polish history is documented. For Terlecki, the history of Poland, especially the nineteenth century, is a very good lesson for our own times. It shows the perseverance of a nation ruled by the three partitioning powers. The language in plays such as *Dwie Glowy Ptaka* (*Two Heads of A Bird*, 1982), *Krotka Noc* (*Short Night*, 1987), *Zabij Cara* (*Kill the Tzar*, 1994) and *Mateczka* (*Mother*, 1995) is contemporaray.

Terzopoulos, Theodoros (1945–) Director, Greece. Terzopoulos trained at the Drama School of K. Michailidis and with the Berliner Ensemble in Germany. In 1981 he became director of the Drama School of the State Theatre of Northern Greece. In 1986 he founded Attis Theatre Group, for which he directed *Bakchai* (*Bacchae*) by Euripides, *Medea Material Landschaft mit Argonauten* (*Medea Material Landscape with Argonauts*) and *Quartet* by Heiner Müller, and *Persai* (*The Persians*) and *Prometheus Desmotes* (*Prometheus Bound*) by Aeschylus. Earlier productions include Lorca's *Yerma* and Brecht's *Mutter Courage und ihre Kinder* (*Mother Courage and her Children*). Since August 1993, Terzopoulos has been chairman of the International Committee of

Theatre Olympics, in charge for the Theatre Olympics of 1995 (Greece) and 1998 (Japan).

Thacker, David (1950–) Director, Great Britain. Thacker joined the Theatre Royal in York initially as assistant stage manager, and from 1975 was assistant director. In 1978 he founded Rolling Stock Company, and became artistic director of the Duke's Playhouse in Lancaster in 1980. He was artistic director of the Young Vic between 1984–93, where he directed numerous productions, Shakespeare and modern classics, some of which transferred to the West End (among them O'Neill's *A Touch of the Poet*, with Vanessa REDGRAVE, 1987). He has directed some London premieres of Arthur MILLER's recent plays, such as *The Last Yankee* (1993) and *Broken Glass* (1994). Since leaving the Young Vic, Thacker has directed freelance and with the Royal Shakespeare Company.

Thalbach, Katharina (1954–) Actor and director Germany. The daughter of actor Sabine Thalbach and director Benno Besson, Thalbach played children on stage as well as for film and television. Later she trained with the Berliner Ensemble, where she also made her debut. From 1972–6 she worked with the Volksbühne, East Berlin, playing Desdemona in KARGE/LANGHOFF's production of *Othello*. In 1976 she left the GDR for West Germany together with her partner, dramatist Thomas Brasch. Important parts include the title roles in Kleist's *Das Käthchen von Heilbronn* (Köln, 1979, directed by Jürgen FLIMM), Kleist's *Penthesilea* (1981, directed by Hans NEUENFELS), Frau John in Hauptmann's *Die Ratten* (*The Rats*, Maxim Gorky Theater, Berlin, 1997), Johanna Dark in Brecht's *Die Heilige Johanna der Schlachthöfe* (Zürich, 1998) and the title role in Brecht's *Der Gute Mensch von Sezuan* (*The Good Person of Sezuan*, 1998, Maxim Gorky Theater, Berlin). She has also directed, including

Macbeth (1987), Brasch's *Liebe Macht Tod* (*Love, Power, Death*, 1990), *As You Like It* and Molière's *Dom Juan* (Maxim Gorky Theatre, Berlin, 1996).

Thambiran, Purissai Kannappa (1915–) Actor, India. The grand old man of the Therukoothu tradition in Tamilnadu, Thambiran is a fourth-generation performer who learnt Koothu from his father Duraiswamy Thambiran and his uncle Raghava Thambiran. He taught Koothu at the National School of Drama, where his students included Mu RAMASWAMY and Na MUTHUSAMY. His celebrated production of Subramanya Bharathi's *Panchali Sabatham* is an instance of how the relevance of Koothu could be demonstrated by applying it to modern literature.

Thiyam, Ratan (1948–) Director and dramatist, India. Active in the theatre from his youth, Thiyam trained at the National School of Drama, New Delhi and later was the director of the School. He established the Chorus Repertory Theatre in Imphal, a tribal area. Drawing upon the traditional forms of Manipuri music, dance, recitation and martial arts, Ratan Thiyam has developed a distinctive contemporary style of his own. Among his major productions are Bhasa's *Urubhagam* and Sophocles's *Antigone*. His own play *Chakravyuha*, drawn from *The Mahabharata*, achieves a powerful blend of theme and form. Thiyam is widely known for his contribution to actor-training methodology and his workshops are popular in India and Europe.

Thomas, Gerald (1954–) Director and dramatist, Brazil. Productions include Heiner Müller's *Quartett*, Chekhov's *Cajka* (*The Seagull*), *Don Juan* by Otavio Frias and his own *Unglauber*, as well as operas such as *Tristan und Isolde*. Thomas has been the subject of a two-hour documentary by Brazilian State TV (in collaboration with the BBC), and his

plays have been televised in Austria and Germany. German television also recorded a fifteen-minute profile on Thomas's work in New York. Several publications in Brazil and the USA are in preparation. 'His work depends heavily on living images. In creating them he is greatly assisted both by his skill as a lighting designer and by the scenographer Daniela Thomas. Most of his productions also have sound scores not directly tied to the texts but with their own significance. Thomas works with professionally trained actors, a choice that contributes to the precision and quality of his productions.'

Thomas, Willy (1959–) Actor and dramatist, Belgium. Thomas studied at the Royal Conservatory in Brussels. In 1985, he co-founded the Dito'Dito company. Dito'Dito chose, by degrees, to work with their own textual material, which was intended to examine acting as well as every other aspect of a theatrical performance. A first step in this direction was *Duiven en Schoenen* (*Pigeons and Shoes*, 1988), which was written by the Dito'Dito company collectively. Since then Willy Thomas has emerged as a dramatist. By resolutely rejecting classical dramaturgy, Thomas, together with a number of his contemporaries such as Arne SIERENS and Paul POURVEUR, set in motion the 'new Flemish dramaturgy', which was born in Flanders in the early 1980s in the wake of a generation of theatre artists who broke away from the politically committed theatre of the 1970s and the traditional repertoire of the established theatres. His main plays are *B is A in Bubbels* (1990) and *Kleine Bezetting* (*Small Cast*, 1995).

Thompson, Judith (1954–) Dramatist and director, Canada. Thompson trained at the National Theatre School. Her plays, such as *The Crackwalker* (1980), *White Biting Dog* (1984), *I am Yours* (1987) and *Lion in the Streets* (1990), 'blend naturalism and surrealism in a portrayal of the complex struggle between the conscious and the unconscious mind'. The rich, psychologically complex texture of Thompson's work is augmented by her 'superb control of regional speech rhythms and voice, as well as by her manipulation of theatrical space'. She is particularly adept at exploring the (often animalistic) behaviour of marginalised characters: the disabled, the poverty-stricken, the mentally challenged. In recent years Thompson has freelanced as a director, including Ibsen's *Hedda Gabler* at the Shaw Festival (1991). She has also written several radio dramas, including *Tornado* (1988) and *Yellow Canaries*. In 1990, she won the Governor General's Award for *The Other Side of the Dark*.

Thomson, Brian (1946–) Designer, Australia. After training as an architect, Thomson moved into theatre via happenings and pop art, working initially with Jim SHARMAN. Thomson went on to design *Hair, Jesus Christ Superstar* and *The Rocky Horror Picture Show* for Sharman, productions which brought international success and recognition. Thomson also designed for Sharman's Patrick White productions. Thomson's designs are always audacious, sensational and radical; they are never literal or naturalistic. For example, Thomson's 1971 *As You Like It* consisted of a gift box set, which the cast then unwrapped, revealing a white steel and perspex set, lit from below. The forest of Arden was created by dragging green silk over the heads of the audience while a pop up book forest appeared. Thomson has designed for most major theatres in Australia as well as for opera, film, television, rock videos and for Barry Humphries's Edna Everage production *Housewife Superstar!* He won a Tony for his design for *The King and I*, which transferred to Broadway in 1996.

Thomson, R.H. (1947–) Actor, Canada. Thomson trained at the National Theatre School and the London Academy of Music and Dramatic Arts. While in Britain, he made a decision: 'I am a Canadian. Why shouldn't I be telling Canadian stories?' Since 1973, he has thus pursued his career in Canada, developing 'from being a rising young star to one of Canada's most praised and respected actors', working in many of the country's major theatres, including the Canadian Stage, Théâtre Passe Muraille, the Stratford Festival, the Tarragon Theatre and Theatre New Brunswick. His performances are marked by an unerring sense of truth and an intense inner life. He was named director of the Harbourfront World Theatre Festival in 1991

Tiezzi, Federico (1951–) Director and dramatist, Italy. While studying art history at the University of Florence, Federico Tiezzi founded the theatre company il Carrozzone, later called Magazzini Criminali and then, simply, Magazzini, where he worked with the performers Marion d'Amburgo and Sandro Lombardi. Tiezzi produces highly formal conceptual theatre events which use fragmented narratives and play with meta-textual points of reference which span from Antonin Artaud, Joseph Beuys, Marcel Duchamp, Gina Pane, Marina Abramovic and Ulay, to Jean Genet, Samuel Beckett and Pier Paolo Pasolini. Using elements from both minimalist theatre and rock music, as well as dance theatre and performance art, Tiezzi creates stunning and provocative pictorial performances which lucidly and radically challenge the boundaries of performance practice. Among Tiezzi's most interesting productions are *Vedute di Porto Said* (*Sights from Port Said*, 1978), *Ebdòmero* (1979, devised by the company, and later filmed by Rainer Werner Fassbinder), as well as his own plays *Crollo nervoso* (*Nervous Breakdown*, 1980), *Genet a Tangeri* (*Genet in Tangier*, 1984) and *Ritratto d'un attore da giovane* (*Portrait of the Actor as a Young Man*, 1985), Brecht's *Im Dickicht der Städte* (*In the Jungle of the Cities*, 1997) and Mario

Luzi's *Scene di Amleto* (*Scenes from Hamlet*, 1998). Tiezzi, who, throughout the last twenty years has been working in theatres and opera houses all over the world, is one of Italy's most interesting and innovative theatre directors.

Tillinger, John (1939–) Director, actor and dramatist, USA. Born and raised in Great Britain, Tillinger trained at the Bristol Old Vic School. Following his stage debut at the Nottingham Playhouse Theatre in 1960, he first appeared on Broadway in 1966. Apart from some work as an actor, Tillinger's main emphasis became directing. Among his productions are Orton's *Entertaining Mr Sloane* (1981) and *Loot* (1986), Arthur MILLER's *After the Fall* (1984) and HAMPTON's *Total Eclipse* (1984). More recently, he directed Miller's *Last Yankee* (1993), *Broken Glass* (1994), Guerney's *Sylvia* (1997), Neil SIMON's *The Sunshine Boys* (1997), Noel Coward's *Blithe Spirit* (1999) and Emlyn Williams's *Night Must Fall* (1999). Although he has worked in a wide variety of genres, his productions have a consistent intelligence and focus on clear story telling.

Tilly, Grant (1937–) Actor, designer and director, New Zealand. Tilly trained as an arts and crafts teacher before making the theatre the centre of his career, exploiting his teaching skills as a tutor at the New Zealand Drama School for fourteen years. In 1961 he attended the Central School of Speech and Drama, London, but became a freelance actor in Wellington only in the late 1960s. From 1970–3 he was associate artistic director at Downstage Theatre, but left to become a co-founder of Circa Theatre, with which he has since been associated. Not a personality actor, he is renowned for the distinctive individuality he brings to every role. He has been especially successful in New Zealand plays, as Colin in Roger HALL's *Middle Age Spread* (1977), Tupper in Greg McGee's *Foreskin's Lament* (1981), Dad

in Robert Lord's *Joyful and Triumphant* (1992) and Dickie Hart in Roger Hall's solo piece *C'mon Black* (1996).

Tindberg, Svein (1953–) Actor, Norway. Trained at the Norwegian State Theatre High School, Tindberg has worked for Television Theatre and Trøndelag Teater in Trondheim. For a number of years he was in the company of Det Norske Teatret, where roles include Figaro in Beaumarchais's *Le mariage de Figaro* (*The Marriage of Figaro*), Osvald in Ibsen's *Gengangere* (*Ghosts*) and the lead in Molière's *Tartuffe* (directed by Jacques Lasalle). Tindberg is now a member of the Nationaltheatret, where he has played Gregers Werle in Ibsen's *Vildanden* (*The Wild Duck*) and Lord Goring in Wilde's *An Ideal Husband*. In 1995 he appeared for 217 performances of his one-man show *The Gospel According to St Mark*, directed by Kjetil BANG-HANSEN.

Tipton, Jennifer (1937–) Designer, USA. Tipton created the lighting design for numerous productions in mainstream theatre, ballet and opera, both in the USA and abroad. In addition, she has been a professor at Yale University School of Drama since 1981. Tipton has a preference for abstract forms of theatre, and has thus worked with Robert WILSON, JoAnne AKALAITIS, Peter SELLARS and the Wooster Group.

Tisnu, Tjokorda Raka (1947–) Performer and director, Indonesia. Tisnu trained at ASTI (Akademi Seni Tingii Indonesia), Denpasar. He began dancing at the age of ten, and has performed in a number of traditional Balinese dance/drama genres including Kecak and Topeng. As a performer and teacher, his skilled command of traditional choreography puts him very much in demand. As a director, he has found innovation within the context of traditional forms and has created startling new work which is transforming Indonesian dance-drama. He has toured with the

STSI Denpasar Kecak ensemble to Australia and Japan and has trained Kecak performers in Tokyo and in Bali. He also teaches at STSI (Academy of Performing Arts) in Denpasar.

To, Raymond (1946–) Dramatist, China (Hong Kong SAR). To's first play was *Ball* (1979), which was nominated the most outstanding stage play in the Hong Kong Repertory Theatre's (HK Rep) original script project. In the same year, he was invited by the HK Rep to adapt Lao She's *The Rickshaw-Puller Camel Cheung* (1979), and this marked the beginning of his playwriting career. Since 1993, To has become the playwright-in-residence of the HK Rep. In the years between 1979–99 he has written more than thirty stage plays, which include *Tin Hau* (*Goddess of the Sea*, 1990, staged at the Istropolitana Festival in Czechoslovakia), *The Legend of the Mad Phoenix* (directed by KO Tin-lung, 1993 and 1995), *Love a la Zen* (1996 and 1998, directed by Daniel Yang) and *Sentimental Journey* (1999, directed by CHUNG King-fai). To's *I Have a Date with Spring* (1992), a sentimental drama about the friendships of four female singers working at a nightclub during the 1960s, was regarded as one of the most popular stage plays of the 1990s and won the Hong Kong Drama Awards for best script. In recent years, many of his enormous stage hits have been made into films, among which were *I Have a Date with Spring* (1994) and *The Mad Phoenix* (1997).

Törőcsik, Mari (1935–) Actor and director, Hungary. Törőcsik started filming during her training at the Academy of Theatre and Film Art. After graduating in 1958 she immediately joined the company of the National Theatre. In 1979 she became artistic director of the Kisfaludy Theatre at Györ, and in 1980 joined the company of the Hungarian Film Studios. Between 1990–2 she was a member of the Szigligeti Theatre in Szolnok, then director of the Budapest Arizona Theatre, which later changed its name to Mûvész Theatre and stayed under her direction until 1993. Since 1989 she has been a teacher at the Academy of Theatre and Film, and from the same year to 1992 president of the Hungarian Actors' Chamber. In 1995 she worked for a year in Moscow, with VASSILYEV. Major roles include Shakespeare (Viola, *Twelfth Night*, and Cordelia, *King Lear*), Brecht (Sen Te, Sui Ta in *Der Gute Mensch von Sezuan* (*The Good Person of Sezuan*), the title role in *Mutter Couraage und ihre Kinder* (*Mother Courage and her Children*) and Mrs Peachum in *Die Dreigroschenoper* (*The Threepenny Opera*)), and Beatrice Bryan in Arnold Wesker's *The Kitchen*. Törőcsik is one of the most important personalities of the Hungarian theatre, excellent as tragic heroine, comedienne or operetta prima donna.

Tóibín, Niall (1929–) Actor, Ireland. Tóibín gained his first acting experience in amateur drama while working in the civil service. He began working as a professional actor in the early 1950s, spending fourteen years as a member of the Radio Eireann Players, and has played a wide variety of roles in the course of his career. Tóibín appeared in the first productions of Brian FRIEL's *Lovers* at the Gate Theatre, Dublin (1967), Brendan Behan's *Borstal Boy* at the Abbey Theatre, Dublin (1967), a work with which Tóibín has become particularly associated, and Tom MURPHY's *Famine* at the Peacock Theatre, Dublin (1968). He played The Bull McCabe in the revised version of *The Field* by John B. KEANE, directed by Ben BARNES at the Abbey Theatre (1987), and Archbishop Lombard in Brian Friel's *Making History*, produced by Field Day Theatre Company (1988). In 1998 Tóibín played ageing band leader Sylvie Tansey in *The Salvage Shop* by Jim Nolan, directed by Ben Barnes and produced by Red Kettle Theatre Company, Waterford. Television work includes BBC's *Ballykissangel*

(1995–), and his many film credits include *The Ballroom of Romance* directed by Pat O'Connor (1979) and *The Nephew* directed by Eugene Brady (1996).

Tolnay, Klári (1914–) Actor, Hungary. After her graduation, Tolnay was first spotted by the Vígszínház, where she played until 1946. Then she joined the Müvész Theatre. In 1948–9 she was one of the three directors of the Vígszínház, and from 1950 she was a member of the Madách Theatre. From 1934 she played several film roles and was one of the most important Hungarian film stars of the 1930s and 1940s. In 1994 Hungarian Television presented a series of her films, and an exhibition documenting her career was also organized. Recently she has taken up translating (for example, the stage adaptation of Graham Greene's *Travels With My Aunt*). In 1993 she directed one of her old successes (Devals' *Soubrette*). Major roles include Eurydike (Anouilh's *Eurydike*), Sonya (Dostoyevsky's *Prestuplenie I nakazanie* (*Crime and Punishment*)), Juliet (*Romeo and Juliet*), Nora (Ibsen's *Et Dukkehjem* (*A Doll's House*)), The Queen (Hugo's *Ruy Blas*), Blanche (Williams's *A Streetcar Named Desire*), Julika (Molnár's *Liliom*), Irina (Chekhov's *Tri sestry* (*Three Sisters*)), Arkadina (Chekhov's *Cajka* (*The Seagull*)), Maude (Higgins's *Harold and Maude*) and Mrs Gibbs (Wilder's *Our Town*). Her acting is spontaneous, colourful and playful. She has become the grande dame of Hungarian theatre.

Tomelty, Frances Actor, Ireland. As the daughter of actor/playwright Joseph Tomelty, Frances Tomelty has had a lifelong involvement in drama. She has worked extensively in film, television and radio, but remains a strong force in contemporary Irish and British theatre. She played Kate in the first production of FRIEL's *Dancing at Lughnasa* produced by the Abbey Theatre (1990) and directed by Patrick MASON, and has recently appeared at the Abbey Theatre as Gráinne Fitzmaurice in Brian Friel's *Give Me Your Answer, Do!* (1997, directed by the playwright). Roles at the Royal Shakespeare Company include Portia in *The Merchant of Venice*, directed by John CAIRD, and Queen Elizabeth in *Richard III*, directed by Bill ALEXANDER. Other roles include La Paiva in *Les Grandes Horizontales* at the Royal National Theatre (1993) and Harriet in *The Maiden Stone* at Hampstead Theatre (1995). Tomelty has played many roles on film and television, including the Widow in the film version of *The Field* directed by Jim Sheridan, Mrs Carter in *Monk Dawson* directed by Tom Waller, and Monagh in *Catchpenny Twist* for BBC Play For Today, directed by Rob Knights.

Tompa, Gábor (1957–) Director, Romania. While studying at the Bucharest Institute of Theatre and Film, Tompa directed Beckett's *Happy Days*, *Woyzeck* by Büchner and *Tango* by MROZEK. After graduating in 1981 he joined the State Magyar Theatre in Cluj-Napoca, of whom he became the leader after a few years. He directed many productions there and at the National Theatre in Târgu-Mures (Magyar Section), at the Bulandra Theatre in Bucharest, at the Craiova National Theatre and also in Yugoslavia, Hungary, the USA, France and elsewhere. Among his major productions are *Hamlet*, Caragiale's *O Noapte furtunoasa* (*A Stormy Night*), ALBEE's *The Sandbox* and *The Zoo Story*, *As You Like It*, *A Midsummer Night's Dream*, a highly praised production both in Romania and abroad of Ionesco's *La cantatrice chauve* (*The Bald Soprano*), *Waiting for Godot* by Beckett, *Molière* by Bulgakov and *The Innocent* by Dehel Gábor. Winner of many prizes, Tompa is also a poet and an essayist. His productions provide a deep insight into the world of the plays and a capacity for various scenic styles.

Toms, Carl (1927–) Designer, Great Britain. Toms was educated at Mansfield College of Art, attended the Royal College of Art and the Old Vic School, and began designing in London in 1957. He has designed extensively in the London West End, the Edinburgh and Chichester Festivals, and the National Theatre. Productions include Tom STOPPARD's *On The Razzle* (1981), *The Real Thing* (1982), *Rough Crossing* (1984) and *Jumpers* (1985 revival), and ALBEE's *Three Tall Women* (1994, with Maggie SMITH and Frances DE LA TOUR).

Topol, Josef (1935–) Dramatist, Czech Republic. Topol drew attention to himself with his first play, *Půlnoční vítr* (*Midnight Wind*, 1955), a poetic drama from the beginnings of Czech history. His next plays, *Jejich den* (*Their Day*, 1959) and *Konec masopustu* (*The End of the Carnival*, 1963 in Olomouc) were written for director Otomar KREJČA, with whom he founded the Theatre Beyond the Gate (Za branou) in Prague in 1965. Topol was its author in residence. Apart from the one-act chamber plays *Kočka na kolejích* (*Cat on the Rails*, 1965) and *Hodina lásky* (*An Hour of Love*, 1968), he also wrote the absurdist *Slavík k večeri* (*Nightingale for Dinner*, 1967) and a symbolic depiction of the Russian invasion, *Dvì noci s dívkou* (*Two Nights with the Girl*, 1972). After the official dissolution of the theatre, all his plays were banned until 1988. His subsequent work includes *Sbohem, Sokrate!* (*Farewell, Socrates!*, written 1976, premiered 1991 at the National Theatre Prague, directed by Jan KAČER), and *Hlasy ptáků* (*The Voices of the Birds*, 1989). His heterogeneous work is marked by poetically figurative language, multi-layered nature of the dramatically central dialogue and thematic interconnections: basic existential questions pervade the private stories (love, death, search for the self, uncertainty and so on).

Toren, Roni (1955–) Designer, Israel. Toren trained at Tel Aviv University where he also teaches design. His sets for productions like Hanoch LEVIN's *Neshot Troja* (*Women of Troy*) and *Hayeled Cholem* (*Dreaming Child*), LERNER's *Castner* directed by Ilan RONEN, Lorca's *Bodas de sangre* (*Blood Wedding*), directed by SNIR and Ibsen's *Fruen fra Havet* (*The Lady from the Sea*) directed by YZRAELI, have earned him a reputation as a versatile and imaginative designer for the stage. Toren has made the design for many operas in Israel as well as abroad which have earned him an international reputation.

Torriente, Alberto Pedro (1954–) Actor and dramatist, Cuba. Torriente trained at the Escuela Nacional de Arte de la Habana. As an actor, he has worked both in the theatre and in film. He has written several plays: *Temas para Verónica* (*Themes for Veronica*, 1979), *Lo que Sube* (*What it Goes Up*, 1980), *Fin de semana en Bahia* (*Weekend in Bahía*, 1985), *Pasión Malinche* (*Malinche Passion*, 1991), *Desamparados* (*No Shelter*, 1992), *Mestiza* (*Half-Caste*, 1993), *Delirio Habanero* (*Delirium in Habana*, 1995) and *Caballo Negro* (*Black Horse*, 1996). His plays have been staged at various European and American festivals. He has been in charge of theatre workshops at the university department of radio, film and television studies in La Habana (1992), the Real Escuela Superior de Artes Dramaticas in Madrid (1985–6) and the University of Toronto (1984).

Towb, Harry (1929–) Actor and writer, Ireland. Harry Towb began his professional acting career in Derry in 1947. The following year he moved to England to begin a very successful fifty-year career, first in repertory theatres and then in the West End and on television. He has made regular appearances on the stages of the Royal National Theatre, London, in such roles as Lieutenant Branigan in *Guys and*

Dolls (1981), and Jack in Neil SIMON's *Brighton Beach Memoirs* (1985). Recent roles at the Abbey Theatre, Dublin, include the Rabbi (*inter alia*) in Kushner's *Angels in America Part 1* (1995) and S.B. O'Donnell in FRIEL's *Philadelphia Here I Come!* (1995), all directed by Patrick MASON. At the Old Vic in London he played Stephen Pearse in Sebastian BAR-RY's *The Prayers of Sherkin* (1997) directed by John Dove, and in 1998 he appeared in Barry's *Our Lady of Sligo* directed by Max STAFFORD-CLARK at the Royal National Theatre London. His diverse television acting roles stretch from *The Professionals* to *The Camomile Lawn*, and are matched by a writing career which includes many short stories and radio plays such as *The Debt Collector* and *The Righteous Gentile* (BBC).

Tremblay, Michel (1942–) Dramatist, Canada. Tremblay is considered the major Québec playwright. His first plays, such as *Les Belles Soeurs* (translated as *The Good Sisters*, 1968), *A toi, pour toujours, ta Marie-Lou* (*Forever Yours, Marie-Lou*, 1971), *Hosanna* (1973) and *Damnée Manon, Sacrée Sandra* (*Damned Manon, Holy Sandra*, 1977), depict the misery of the Montréal proletariat, focusing on marginalized characters in a marginalized Québecois society. With the election of the separatist Parti Québecois in 1976 came a shift of emphasis. Like other Québec dramatists, Tremblay turned to middle-class concerns (*L'impromptu D'Outremont* (*The Impromptu of Outremont*), 1980), or universal topics such as aging (in *Albertine, en cinq temps* (*Albertine in Five Times*), 1984). In addition, Tremblay turned to adaptations of foreign works and to opera in the 1990s, and has become an important Québec novelist. His recent plays *Marcel poursui par les chiens* (*Marcel Pursued by the Hounds*, National Arts Centre, 1992) and *Encore une fois, si vous le permettez* (*For the Pleasure of Seeing You Again*, Théâtre du Rideau Vert, 1998) were both directed in their premieres by Tremblay's longstanding collaborator Andre Brassard.

Triffit, Nigel (1949–) Designer, director and writer, Australia. Triffit was thrown out of the National Institute of Dramatic Art, Sydney and the Drama Centre, London. He does not separate the activities of designing, directing and writing, and although he has designed and directed texts written by others (for example his full frontal nudity *Samson and Delilah* for the Victorian State Opera in 1983), he has more often devised his own texts and exerts enormous control over all aspects of his productions. Triffitt has had international successes with *Momma's Little Horror Show* (1978, restaged 1981), and *Secrets* (1983–7). *Outer Sink* (1985) was a co-production with Los Trios Ringbarkus; *Wild Stars* (1979) was a dance spectacular. Triffitt devised and directed *The Fall of Singapore* in 1987, and in 1990 he staged *Moby Dick*. He has also designed sets for tours by Ice House and Men at Work, and has designed several festival openings. More recently Triffitt designed and directed the international smash hit *Tap Dogs*. Triffitt's distinctive style includes the use of puppets, grotesque masks, multimedia and music which overwhelms the audience. He believes that 'theatre is about making the impossible possible'.

Tripp, Tony (1940–) Designer, Australia. Tripp has been associated with the Melbourne Theatre Company for much of his career although he also worked in Perth for much of the 1970s, where he designed for the world premiere of Dorothy HE-WETT's *The Man from Mukinupin* in 1979. At the MTC Tripp has designed classics (*The Tempest*, Chekhov's *Visnevyi sad* (*The Cherry Orchard*), *The Taming of the Shrew*), modern hits (Christopher HAMPTON's *Les Liaisons Dangereuses*), and Australian plays (Ray LAWLOR's *The Summer of the Seventeenth Doll*). One of his most noteworthy designs was for

Arthur MILLER's *The Crucible* in 1991, a set which created a powerful sense of the isolation and claustrophobia of the Salem community by the use of tall, brooding pine trees encroaching on the actors' space. Tripp does not like overbearing visual statements, and claims his strong point is a flexible naturalism. He avoids abstract designs and is happy to be seen as a craftsman. He often works with lighting designer Jamieson Lewis.

Trissenaar, Elisabeth (1944–) Actor, Austria. Trissenaar career is closely linked with that of her husband, Hans NEUENFELS, whom she met while training at the Max Reinhardt Seminar, Vienna. She worked for several seasons each in Bern, Krefeld/Mönchengladbach, Heidelberg, Bochum, Stuttgart, Frankfurt and Berlin (Staatliche Schauspielbühnen and Freie Volksbühne). She is considered as one of the most expressive and intensive actors of her generation, excelling particularly in classical tragedy. Apart from Neuenfels, she has worked with Peter PALITZSCH and Jürgen FLIMM. Major roles include Alkmene in Kleist's *Amphitryon*, Lady Macbeth, the title role in Strindberg's *Fröken Julie* (*Miss Julie*), Warja in Chekhov's *Visnevyi sad* (*The Cherry Orchard*), Nora in Ibsen's *Et Dukkehjem* (*A Doll's House*), the title roles in Kleist's *Penthesilea*, Irma in Genet's *Le balcon* (*The Balcony*), Euripides's *Electra*, Martha in ALBEE's *Who's Afraid of Virginia Woolf?* and Valerie in Horvath's *Geschichten aus dem Wiener Wald* (*Tales from the Vienna Wood*).

Tse Kwan-ho (1963–) Actor, China (Hong Kong SAR). After graduating from the Hong Kong Academy for Performing Arts in 1989, Tse began his acting career with the Hong Kong Repertory Theatre. From 1994–7, Tse was the principle actor and performed in more than fifty productions. He played Father Ubu in Alfred Jarry's *Ubu roi* (*King Ubu*, 1990) and Miller in Peter SHAFFER's *Black Comedy* (1991).

Tse did not achieve prominent success, however, until he played the leading role in Raymond TO's *The Legend of the Mad Phoenix* (1993, directed by KO Tin-lung). A film adaptation was produced in 1994 in which he played the same role, winning the 34th Taiwan Golden Horse Film Awards for best actor. In 1997, Tse joined the Spring-time Stage Productions, where he played the title role in Raymond To's *The Magic is the Moonlight* (HKAPA Lyric Theatre, 1997). He starred in To's *Sentimental Journey* (directed by Chung King-fai, 1999), in which he played the role of Tang Dick-san, the famous Cantonese opera playwright of the 1960s.

Tsujimura Jusaburô (1933–) Puppet maker, art and costume designer, script writer, actor and director, Japan. Tsujimura first trained as a puppeteer when he was with the Ningyô-za theatre company in 1956, then worked for the stage properties maker Kodôgu Fujinami until 1958. He began making costumes for puppets at that time. His breakthrough came when his puppet, Yaoya O-shichi, inspired by a kabuki play, won an award in the Contemporary Doll Exhibition in 1961. Jusaburô created puppets for the NHK (Japan Broadcasting Association) TV's serial puppet drama, *Shin-Hakkenden* (*The New Story of Eight Dogs*) which was on air from 1973–5. He worked as an art director on the costumes, make-up and the properties for NINAGAWA's production of Euripides's *Medeia* in 1978, and for Ninagawa's *Chikamatsu Shinjû Monogatari* (*Chikamatsu's Love Suicide Story*, 1979), an adaptation of Chikamatsu's plays by AKIMOTO Matsuyo. He created a puppet for the role of Umekawa and manipulated it on stage with human actors. *Chikamatsu Shinjû Monogatari* was performed in London and Brussels in 1989. In 1982 he performed puppet productions, *Katsushika Sunago*, *Bird Woman*, and *Villa of the Sea God* at the theatre festivals in Asti, Florence and Avignon. Tsujimura's puppets have enchanting expressions resulting from his characterization of the puppets' roles, and they immediately succeed in communicating with audiences. He combines old and new kimono fabric to establish the sense of the time in which the play was written.

Tsypin, George (1954–) Designer, USA. Born in the former USSR, Tsypin obtained a BFA at the Institute of Architecture, Moscow (1977). After his emigration to the USA in 1979, he studied with John CONKLIN at New York University (MFA 1984). His set designs include *The Power and the Glory* (1984), *Measure for Measure* (1986) and *Henry IV Parts I and II* (1991), as well as opera, mainly working with director Peter SELLARS. Aronson comments: 'The sets show a strong constructivist influence and often use metal, moving parts and an overlay of projected images; images from contemporary culture mingle with references to classical architecture and theatre'.

Tudorache, Olga (1929–) Actor, Romania. Tudorache made her debut in the part of Veta in Caragiale's *O Noapte furtunoasa* (*A Stormy Night*) while studying at the Theatre and Film Institute in Bucharest. Here she displayed a strong scenic temperament, but later she also displayed a vein for tragic and dramatic characters. She has become mainly associated with Teatrul Mic (Little Theatre), where she remained for thirty years, appearing as a guest star at the Craiova National Theatre, the Bucharest National Theatre and the Nottara Theatre. Major roles include the title role in Shaw's *Mrs Warren's Profession*, Cleopatra in *Antony and Cleopatra*, Kate Keller in William Gibson's *The Miracle Worker*, and the role of Sarah Bernardt in *Memoirs* by John MURRELL. In her distinguished career, Tudorache has worked with notable directors such as Silviu PURCĂRETE and Cătălina BUZOIANU. She has served as professor of acting at the Theatre and Film Academy

in Bucharest, and sometimes her students become her partners on the stage.

Tukur, Ulrich (1957–) Actor, Germany. After training at the Hochschule für Darstellende Kunst und Musik in Stuttgart, he has worked in Heidelberg, Berlin and Zürich, and joined Deutsches Schauspielhaus in Hamburg in 1985. Roles include Orlando in *As You Like It*, Mark Anthony in *Julius Caesar*, and title roles in *Hamlet*, *Macbeth* and Ibsen's *Peer Gynt*. Among the contemporary repertory, he appeared in Reza's *Art* (1996). Critics have commented that Tukur's particular strength is his voice: 'never obtrusive but used with precision even when expressing extreme emotions, it becomes an instrument for the actor, like a piano'.

Turkka, Jouko Veli (1942–) Director and dramatist, Finland. Turkka trained at the Finnish Theatre School and was theatre director at the City Theatres of Seinäjoki (1967–8), Joensuu (1968–72), Kotka (1973–5) and Helsinki (1975–82). From 1981–8 he taught at the Theatre Academy of Finland, serving as its principal between 1982–5. Since 1989 he has held a state grant for artists (fifteen years). Major productions include Jussi KYLÄTASKU's *Runar ja Kyllikki* (*Runar and Kyllikki*), Hannu Salama's *Siinä Näkijä Missä Tekijä* (*Where There is a Deed, there is a Witness*) and Maiju Lassila's *Viisas neitsyt* (*Wise Virgin*). His own plays include *Hypnoosi* (*Hypnosis*) and *Valheita* (*Lies*). 'Thought is the most violent element in Turkka's theatre. Its energy made flesh, concrete and forceful. It feels as if blood is flying and bones are crushing when Turkka rethinks the world and the theatre.'

Turrini, Peter (1944–) Dramatist, Austria. After working at odd jobs, Turrini has been a freelance dramatist, resident in Vienna, since 1971. Although violent images dominate his plays, Turrini claims that he is looking for beauty, harmony and belonging: 'I never reach these paradises if I invent something beautiful. The beautiful, the harmonious, is always betrayal, fake. One has to invent the dreadful to overcome it...If you talk and write about the negative, then that is the positive'. Recent plays include *Tod und Teufel* (*Death and Devil*, 1991), *Alpenglühen* (*Glowing Alps*, 1993) and *Die Schlacht um Vienna* (*The Battle for Vienna*, 1995), all directed by Claus PEYMANN at the Burgtheater in Vienna.

U

Udvaros, Dorottya (1954–) Actor, Hungary. After training at the Academy of Theatre and Film Art, Udvaros joined the Szigligeti Theatre of Szolnok in 1978, the National Theatre in 1981, the József Theatre in 1982, and the Új Theatre in 1994. Also a popular film and television actor, she recorded an album of songs in 1985. Major roles include Ala (MROZEK's *Tango*), Cressida (*Troilus and Cressida*), Polly (Brecht/Weill's *Die Dreigroschenoper* (*The Threepenny Opera*)), Natasha (Chekhov's *Tri sestry* (*Three Sisters*)), Sofya Egorovna (Chekhov's *Platonov*), Celimène (Molière's *Le misanthrope* (*The Misanthropist*)), Alkmene (Kleist's *Amphitryon*), Lulu (Wedekind's *Lulu*), Isabelle Glass (HARE's *The Secret Rapture*) and Hyppolita-Titania (*A Midsummer Night's Dream*). Udvaros is an important personality of the Hungarian theatre, the ideal modern woman. Her characteristics are passionate, sometimes grotesque, detailed stage acting.

Uka, Kalu Director and dramatist, Nigeria. Uka is a very inspiring director, one who can tease fine performances from his actors while retaining a firm grip on the entire production process. He has directed numerous plays some of which are Sonny OTI's *The Old Masters* (1977 with a cast which included Toni DURUAKU as Okereke) and *A Harvest for Ants* (1976, his adaptation of Chinua Achebe's *Arrow of God*). Uka is also a successful poet and playwright; his published play is *Ikhanma* which ran successfully at Nsukka and Enugu in 1981. But it is as a director-producer that Uka has contributed to and will be remembered in Nigerian theatre.

Ukala, Sam C. (1948–) Dramatist, director and actor, Nigeria. Ukala is interested in using traditional Nigerian theatrical forms to create a viable contemporary Nigerian theatre capable of appealing to a wider audience. His first play, written while he was still an undergraduate student at Nsukka, is *Whiteness is Barrenness*. His other plays include *The Slave Wife*, *The Log in Your Eye* (1986), *Akpakaland* (1989) *Break a Boil* (1992), *The Trials of Obiamaka Elema* (1992), *The Placenta of Death* and *The Last Heroes* (1997). Ukala's major strength as a dramatist is his sensitivity to the nuances of language and its ability to be an index to character; his plays thus attempt to capture the different registers of English in use within his Nigerian setting. He directs all his plays and has acted in his own and other plays including the roles of Gidi in *Break a Boil*, Ofume in *The Trials of Obiamaka Elema*, Narrator in *There's Darkness There*, Nwankwo in *Whiteness is Barrenness*, Prophet Moses in *Gateway to Heaven* and Narrator in *The Placenta Soup*. Other roles include Igwezu in SOYINKA's *The Swamp Dwellers*, Diribi in

CLARK-BEKEDEREMO's *The Masquerade*, John in J.C. de Graft's *Through a Film Darkly*, Kojo Tabi in Martin OWUSU's *The Sudden Return* and Egonwanne in Kalu UKA's *A Harvest for Ants*.

Ularu, Nicolae (1953–) Designer, Romania. Ularu graduated in scenography from the Arts Academy of Bucharest in 1980 and worked as scenographer in Romanian Television and then at the National Theatre in Bucharest, the Little Theatre, Nottara Theatre, Odeon and other theatres in the country. Productions include *Hamlet*, *Rosenkrantz and Guildenstern are Dead* by Tom STOPPARD, *The Prince of the Darkness* by Iris Murdoch, *Turandot* by Gozzi, *Uriel Acosta* by Karl Gutzkov (at the State Jewish Theatre in Bucharest) and Romanian plays by Horia Lovinescu, Teodor Mazifu, Romulus Guga, Ecaterina Oproiu and others. He also worked in Belfast, Gothenborg and Minnesota. As a visiting professor he taught courses in stage and costume design in Germany, Sweden, London, Italy, the USA, Denmark and Hong Kong. Since 1994 he has been chairman of the Scenography Department of the Fine Arts Union of Romania

Ursan, Ali Oqla (1941–) Dramatist and director, Syria. Trained at Egypt's Academy of Dramatic Art and in France, he was active as a director in the 1960s and 1970s, with major productions of Sophocles's *Oidipus tyrannos* (*King Oedipus*), *King Lear*, Dürrenmatt's *Der Besuch der Alten Dame* (*The Visit*) and Anouilh's *Antigone*. His ten plays include *Al-Shaykh Wa'l-Tareeq* (*The Old Man and the Road*, 1971), *Al-Falastinyat* (*The Palestinian Woman*, 1971), *Al-Ghuraba'a* (*The Strangers*, 1974), *Rida Qaysar* (*Caesar's Satisfaction*, 1975) and *Al-Aqni'a* (*The Masks*, 1982). Ursan's major themes are the Arab–Israeli conflict, seeking freedom and defending moral issues that are in decline. In 1982 he became chairman of the Writers' Union, and gave up directing and concentrated on scholarship instead. He had already published his controversial *The Theatrical Phenomena of the Arabs* (1981), in which he was critical of his own influence by European theatre, arguing that forms of theatre different from the Western traditions flourished in ancient Arabia. In 1987 he published the equally controversial *Politics in Drama*.

V

Väänänen, Kari Kyösti (1953–) Actor, Finland. Väänänen trained at the Theatre Academy of Finland and worked as an actor with the Vaasa City Theatre (1977–79), Helsinki City Theatre (1979–81) and Ryhmäteatteri (Group Theatre, 1981–9). Since 1992 he has been professor of acting at the Theatre Academy of Finland. Major roles inlude Oberon in *A Midsummer Night's Dream* and the title role in *Othello*. He has also starred in several films by Aki and Mika Kaurismäki. Kari Väänänen is considered the leading actor of his generation in Finland. His characters have a strong personal impact, they are deep in emotions but at the same time skillfully controlled by the actor's technique.

Vacis, Gabriele (1955–) Director and dramatist, Italy. After graduating in architecture Gabriele Vacis founded, with Laura CURINO, Mariella Fabbris, Roberto Tarasco and others, the Cooperativa Teatro Settimo (1979). Working mostly on devised pieces, often set in unconventional theatrical spaces, Vacis is known for the creation of highly formalized and stylized environmental theatre performances. Centred around the lyrical and choral aspects of storytelling, often intensified by the use of strong physical theatre and the employment of alternative and even made-up languages, Vacis's visually striking and politically aware theatre practice constitutes a refreshing and challenging voice in contemporary Italian theatre. Among his most notable productions with Teatro Settimo are the company-devised *Signorine* (1982), *Esercizi sulla tavola di Mendeleev* (*Exercises on the Mendeleyev Table*, 1984), *Elementi di struttura del sentimento* (*Structural Elements of Feeling*, 1985), *Stabat Mater* (1989) and *La storia di Romeo e Giulietta* (*The Story of Romeo and Juliet*, 1991), and Alessandro Bariccoís *Novecento* (*The 1900s*, 1994).

Vágó, Nelly (1937–) Designer, Hungary. After training at the Budapest Applied Arts College as a student of Judit SCHÄFFER, Vágó began her career in 1962–3 in the Szigligeti Theatre of Szolnok. At the same time she was a member of the Budapest National Theatre. She has worked as a guest in almost every Hungarian theatre, the Opera House and open air venues. A designer of numerous films and television movies, she also worked for the Graz and West Berlin Operas and for the Tbilisi National Theatre. Major productions include Shakespeare – *King Lear*, *Timon of Athens*, *Richard II*, *Henry IV*, *Othello* and *As You Like It* – Madách's *Az ember tragédiá* (*The Tragedy of Man*), Bulgakov's *Molière*, Peter Weiss's *Marat/Sade*, Chekhov's *Tri sestry* (*Three Sisters*), Büchner's *Dantons Tod* (*Danton's Death*), Brecht and Weill's *Die Dreigroschenoper* (*The Threepenny Opera*), Molières'

Tartuffe and Schiller's *Maria Stuart*. Vágó is an outstanding member of the Hungarian school of designers. Expressive, colourful and various costume creations are her characteristics. Her works are often connected to the most modern, and significant theatrical workshops and directors.

Valdez, Luis (1940–) Director and dramatist, USA. Valdez travelled to Cuba, and joined San Francisco Mime Troupe. In 1965 he founded Teatro Campesino, initially a troupe of striking farm workers who worked under his direction to create brief sketches (*actos*) about the need for a farm workers' union. Many similar troupes emerged, adopting the *acto*-style and dealing with Chicano and Mexican experience in the USA. Valdez later shifted his emphasis from *acto* to *mito* (myth), exploring the 'theatre of the sphere, which integrated the physical dynamism of the human body with the emotional power of the human spirit to engender a balanced universal vision of humanity'.

Van Hove, Ivo (1958–) Director, Belgium. Van Hove trained as a director in Brussels. Van Hove's artistic career coincides to a large extent with that of scenographer Jan VERSWEYVELD. In 1981 they co-founded the company Akt, which in 1988 fused with Het Gezelschap van de Witte Kraai and became a new company, De Tijd. Van Hove became director, together with Lucas VANDERVOST. Only two years later he left for Het Zuidelijk Toneel in Eindhoven, of which he is still the director. From 1981–8, van Hove staged mainly texts of his own; since 1988 he has chosen to stage only plays from the world repertoire. By means of a radical use of theatrical signs and by demanding from his actors a very physical style of acting, he shows the plays in their bare essence. Important productions include *Macbeth* (1988), Wedekind's *Lulu* (1990), Sophocles's *Ajax/Antigone*, O'Neill's *De-*

sire Under the Elms (1992), and Camus's *Caligula* (1996). As a visiting director, van Hove staged *Bakchai* (Euripides) at the Schauspielhaus Hamburg (1993), and O'Neill's *Desire under the Elms* at the Staatstheater in Stuttgart. In 1997 he directed his first film.

Van Veldhuizen, Matin (1948–) Dramatist and director, The Netherlands. Self-made woman Matin van Veldhuizen got involved with the theatre through catering for the Onafhankelijk Toneel (see Jan Joris LAMERS) in the 1970s. She participated in several productions (for example, *Andy Warhol*, 1979) and in 1983 decided to write, direct and act. With two other actors she made *Jane*, about author Jane Bowles. The way in which she divided the character over different actors gained acclaim and remains a feature of her work. She is considered a feminist, 'though one with a sense of humour'. She herself sees no incompatibility between the two. Van Veldhuizen continued to write and direct with various companies (*Een kwestie van twee* (*Matter for Two*, 1985), *Dorothy Parker, You Might as Well Live*, (1987), until she became director of Carrousel together with Marlies HEUER (1992). There she has continued her investigation into the difference between the male and the female perception of the world in productions like *The Interview* (by Nathalia Ginzburg, 1992), *The Picture of Dorian Grey*, (1994, with Cas ENKLAAR), and Williams's *A Streetcar named Desire* (1997). Her play *Eten* (1991) has been translated as *Eat*.

Van Warmerdam, Alex (1952–) Dramatist, director, designer and actor, The Netherlands. Coming from a theatre clan (his father a technician, his brothers composer and actor/producer), Alex van Warmerdam was destined for the theatre. At first, however, he trained as an artist at the Rietveld Academy in Amsterdam (1969–74). This background still shows in the sets and posters he designs for his productions. During his academy years van Warmerdam started a company for music and theatre, Hauser Orkater. Shows like *Het vermoeden* (*The Suspicion*, 1977) and *Zie de mannen vallen* (*Watch the Men Fall*, 1979) were immensely popular with a young audience. Van Warmerdam continued this line of work in De Mexicaanse Hond, which he started in 1980. Main successes were *Broers* (*Brothers*, 1981), *Graniet* (*Granite*, 1982) and *De wet van Luisman* (*Luisman's Law*, 1984). The company also toured these shows in the USA, the UK, France and other countries; French and English texts are available. Recently van Warmerdam has been making films (*Abel* (1985) and *The Dress* (1995)). His wry, black humour was described by *Le Monde* as 'Buster Keaton meeting Samuel Beckett'. Van Warmerdam has managed to translate the boredom of life in the Holland of the 1950s into drama. His most recent theatre show was *Kleine Teun* (1996), which he turned into a film (1998).

Vančura, Jan (1940–) Designer, Czech Republic. Originally a glass designer, Vančura started working for theatre in 1976. He first drew attention to himself with the costumes for Čapek's *Ze zivota hmyzu* (*Insect Play*, 1978, Šalda Theatre in Liberec), created out of authentic plastic objects. In his work, principles of painting precedes the architectural design of the space. He returned the system of Baroque wings to the stages (Händel's *Rodelinda*, Brno State Theatre, 1985), but keeps an ironic distance. He designs mainly for opera, where his preference for historical artistic styles is well applied. His 'archaic' designs have embellished productions of contemporary plays as well, such as HAVEL's *Asanace* (*Slum Clearance*, Šalda Theatre, Liberec, 1990), and TOPOL's *Dvì noci s dívkou* (*Two Nights with the Girl*, Šalda Theatre, 1995).

Vandervost, Lucas (1957–) Director and actor, Belgium. Vandervost trained as an actor at the Royal Conservatory of Antwerp, then founded Het Gezelschap van de Witte Kraai (White Crow Company) with his colleague Sam Bogaerts. In 1987, a new company was born out of a fusion with Ivo VAN HOVE's Akt-Vertikaal, the Antwerp-based De Tijd (The Time). After van Hove left in 1990, Vandervost remained as sole artistic leader. Amongst his most remarkable productions are his stage version of Robert Musil's *Die Fantasten* (1993) and the monologue *Der Untergang der Titanic* (*The Sinking of the Titanic*, 1994) by Hans Magnus Enzensberger, which he performed himself. As a director, Vandervost has a preference for highly literary texts, and specializes in a sober, epic theatre.

Vanek, Joe (1948–) Designer, Ireland. Born in Great Britian, Vanek is best known in Ireland for his work with director Patrick MASON, being director of design at the Abbey Theatre, Dublin, and undoubtedly the most innovative of designers working in Ireland. He trained at the Universities of Sussex and Manchester in art education and theatre design, respectively. His early career included work with several regional English repertory companies, and he was head of design with Michael Attenborough at the Palace Theatre, Watford (1980–4). Although he has worked extensively for the Gate Theatre, Dublin, and with many Irish and UK opera companies, his design is most closely associated with the recent plays of Brian FRIEL, including *Dancing at Lughnasa* (1990), *Wonderful Tenessee* (1993) and *Molly Sweeney* (1994). Recent design work at the Abbey includes Kushner's *Angels in America* (1995), *Macbeth* (1996), KILROY's *The Secret Fall of Constance Wilde* (1997), Shaw's *Saint Joan* (1998) and a haunting expressionistic set for MCGUINNESS's *Observe the Sons of Ulster Marching Towards the Somme* (1994), all directed by Patrick Mason.

Vassilyev, Anatoly (1942–) Director, Russia. After training at the State Institute of Theatre Art, Vassilyev made his debut in 1973 at the Moscow Art Theatre with Zagradnik's *Solo dlya chasov s boem* (*Solo for a Clock with Chime*). From 1977–80 he worked at the Moscow Stanislavski Drama Theatre, where he directed the first version of Gorky's *Vassa Zheleznova* and Slavkin's *Vzroslaya doch molodogo cheloveka* (*Adult Daughter of a Young Man*). Both productions were informed by nostalgic mood and humanism. He followed the path of psychological theatre, having renovated the very notion of naturality of acting. For Vassilyev, acting is a process which has no start and no ending: in his theatre (The School of Dramatic Art, founded in 1986) actors stay at the theatre living in a community for the whole rehearsal period. The production of Slavkin's *Cepco – Serso* (*Cerceau*, Moscow Taganka Theatre, 1986) reinforced his image as non-conformist and thoroughly analytic. His production of Pirandello's *Sei personaggi in cerca d'autore* (*Six Characters in Search of an Author*, 1987) was a great success in Italy. More recent productions include Lermontov's *Maskarad* (*Maskerade*, 1991,- at Comédie Française) and *Plach Ieremei* (*Jeremiah's Cry*, 1996, based on the Bible).

Verma, Jatinder (1954–) Director, Great Britain. In 1977 Verma founded Tara Arts, which has established itself as the leading Asian company in Great Britain. It rose to national renown when Verma directed a multinational cast in Moliere's *Tartuffe* (1990), and in *The Little Clay Cart* (1991), a classical Sanskrit play, at the National Theatre. In 1995, an adaptation of *Cyrano de Bergerac* followed, also at the National Theatre. Other productions by Verma/Tara Arts include Büchner's *Danton's Tod* (*Danton's Death*), *Troilus and Cressida*, Gogol's *Revizor* (*The Government Inspector*), *A Midsummer Night's Dream* and various productions from the Indian repertoire such as

Heer Ranjha and *The Broken Thigh* (by Bhasa, a classical Sanskrit dramatist). In all his productions, Verma has used both Asian and Western performers and has been able to successfully blend story, dance and song.

Versweyveld, Jan (1958–) Designer, Belgium. Versweyveld studied design at the Royal Academy in Antwerp. His artistic career coincides to a large extent with that of director Ivo VAN HOVE. In 1981 they co-founded the company Akt, which seven years later fused with Het Gezelschap van de Witte Kraai and became a new company, De Tijd. Ivo van Hove became director, together with Lucas VANDERVOST. Versweyveld worked as a stage designer for both directors. In 1990 Versweyveld left De Tijd together with Ivo van Hove for Het Zuidelijk Toneel in Eindhoven, where they are still working now. Versweyveld's interest in stage design originated in a fundamental interest in light and lighting. He creates the atmosphere and draws theatrical space by means of light. Since 1981 he has designed the set, lighting and costumes for every production Ivo van Hove directed. He also works with other directors. In 1995 he created the lighting design for *Amor Constante mas alla de la muerte*, a choreography by Anne Teresa De Keersmaeker.

Villoresi Pogany, Pamela (1957–) Actor and director, Italy. After training at the Teatrostudio del Metastasio, Pamela Villoresi made her theatrical debut in 1972. She became known to the wider public after working with Giorgio Strehler in Gotthold Lessing's *Minna von Barnhelm* (1983-4), Goldoni's *Il Campiello* (*The Campiello*, 1976-7) and *Arlecchino, servitore di due padroni* (*Harlequin, The Servant of Two Masters*, 1978). Villoresi also worked with Antonio CALENDA in Christopher HAMPTON's *Les Liaison Dangereuses* (1988). She is known as an adventurous interpreter of classical female roles. Apart from working in film and television, Villoresi also directs her own work, such as in the acclaimed *Diotima o la vendetta di Eros (Diotima or Eros's Revenge*, 1990) written by Bebetta Campetti.

Vinaver, Michel (1927–) Dramatist, France. Vinaver studied English and American literature at Wesleyan University, USA. His dramatic work is mainly associated with the concept of *théâtre du quotidien*, everyday theatre, a new realism influenced by Brecht, and similar to that of KROETZ, Fassbinder or ACHTERNBUSCH in Germany. *Les coréen (The Koreans*, 1955) is an anti-war play, *Les huissiers* deals with the Algeria crisis, and *Iphigénie Hotel* uses a Greek subtext for political events of the day. Much of his later work was influenced by his work as a business executive (*Les Travaux et les Jours*), and more recently he has moved to psychological drama (*Portrait of a Woman*).

Violić, Božidar (1931–) Director, Croatia. After graduation from the Academy of Dramatic Art in Zagreb Violić worked as an assistant director and dramaturg with Radio Zagreb. From 1959–72 he served as a resident director at the Zagreb Theatre Gavella. He was a part-time professor of acting (1958–72) and professor of directing (1972–9) at the Academy of Dramatic Art in Zagreb. In 1979 he became a resident director and dramaturg in the ZKM (Zagreb Youth Theatre). He directed over seventy plays and operas by Croatian and foreign writers and composers. Early credits include Marinković's *Zagrljaji (Embraces*), and Šenoa's *Ljubica* (1963). Violić established Ivo BREŠAN as a playwright with the production of his *Predstava Hamleta u selu Mrduša Donja* (*The Performance of Hamlet in Central Dalmatia*, 1971, &TD Theatre). In 1974 he directed the stage adaptation of Novak's novel *Mirisi, zlato, tamjan* (*The Fragrance, Gold and Incense*). This was followed by Jonson's *Volpone* (1977), *Richard III* (1979) and Molière's *Dom Juan* (1983). He also directed opera, radio

dramas and television adaptations of his own theatre productions. He adapts and dramatizes prose texts for the stage and writes original film and television scripts for both short and feature films. In 1989 he published his book on theatre, *Lica i sjene (Faces and Shadows*).

Vişniec, Matei (1956–) Dramatist and poet, Romania and France. Vişniec studied philosophy in Bucharest and worked as a teacher for some years. During this time he also began publishing poetry. Since 1987 he has lived in France, where he works as a journalist at the Radio France Internationale in Paris. *Angajare de clown (Clown to Hire*) was his first play to be produced in Romania in 1990. Other plays include *Caii fa fereastră* (*Horses at the Window*), and *Buzunarul cu pâine (The Pocket Full of Bread*). He became the most produced contemporary author in Romania, and in 1996 the Timişoara National Theatre organized an international festival dedicated to his works. His plays have been produced in France, Germany, Finland, the USA, Poland and The Netherlands. The Avignon International Festival has reserved a major place to his plays, showing productions of *Horses at the Window, Clown to Hire* and *Ultimul Godot (The Last Godot*) and presenting fourteen other plays in public readings. Vişniec's plays remind one of Beckett, Ionesco and Jarry with their absurd appearance, but they have a truly personal sound.

Viswanathan, Poornam (1920–) Actor, India. Viswanathan joined the All India Radio as a news reader. He began his career in traditional fashion as a singing artist in female attire, and has acted in more than 200 stage plays. His strength now, in contrast to most Tamil acting, is underplaying: 'To him acting is an experience of reliving'. Some of his notable performances include the title roles in Sujata's *Singaram Iyengar Peran (Singaram Iyengar's Grandson*) and *Dr Narendranin*

Vinotha Vazhaku (*The Strange Trial of Dr Narendran* Savi's *Washintonil Thirumanam* (*Marriage in Washington*) and *Policekaran Makal* (*Policeman's Daughter*). Viswanathan also pursues an active career in television.

Vitti, Monica (1931–) Actor, Italy. After training at the National Academy of Dramatic Art in Rome, Monica Vitti began her career as a stage actor. In 1960 she came to international fame with the film *L'avventura* directed by Michelangelo Antonioni, who also directed her in *La notte* (*The Night*, 1961), *L'eclissi* (*The Eclipse*, 1962) and *Il Deserto rosso* (*The Red Desert*, 1965). Vitti also worked with Joseph Losey in *Modesty Blaise* (1966), Luis Buñuel in *The Phantom of Liberty* (1974) and Alberto Sordi in *Io so che tu sai che io so* (*I Know That You Know That I Know*, 1982). Both on stage and on the screen Vitti has a compelling casual acting style, which she often exploits for the tragicomic exploration of modern restless female characters.

Voss, Gert (1941–) Actor, Germany. Voss trained with Ellen Mahlke in Munich. After working in Konstanz and Munich, he joined Claus PEYMANN in Stuttgart (1972–9), playing, among others, the title role in Büchner's *Woyzeck* (1975), Karl Moor in Schiller's *Die Räuber* (*The Robbers*, 1975) and Puck in *A Midsummer Night's Dream* (1977). He followed Peymann to Bochum and Vienna. In 1993–4 he joined the Berliner Ensemble in Berlin. In 1992, when Voss received the Kortner Prize, George TABORI praised his 'obsession to give himself, to give as only great lovers can, without shame, without the bourgeois virtues of decency, and without mixing up mendacity with the demands of art. He is a dangerous, naked actor, an eerie clown, a wild bull'. More recent work includes Beckett's *Endgame* (Vienna, 1998) and Horvath's *Figaro Läßt sich Scheiden* (*Figaro gets Divorced*, 1999, Vienna, directed by Luc BONDY).

W

wa Mirii, Ngugi (1951–) Dramatist and theatre activist, Kenya. It was while working for the University of Nairobi's Institute of Development Studies that Ngugi wa Mirii became involved with the peasants and workers of Kamiriithu, a contact that was to influence his subsequent work in the theatre, both in Kenya and now in exile in Zimbabwe. He was the coordinating director of the Kamiriithu Community Education and Culture Centre, in which others like Ngugi WA THIONG'O and Kimami Gecau participated and which produced politically explosive plays such as *Ngaahika Ndeenda* (*I'll Marry When I Want*) and *Maitu Gitayi* (*Mother, Sing to Me*). These plays were so successful in articulating the feelings, aspirations and anger of the peasants and workers that they were banned by the government and the intellectuals such as the two Ngugis were either detained or forced into exile. In Zimbabwe, wa Mirii, together with Kimami Gecau and with official help and support from Steve CHIFUNYISE, has been indefatigable in his commitment to the cause of the peasants and workers and he has been helping to set up rural cultural centres in Zimbabwe.

wa Thiong'o, Ngugi (1938–) Dramatist and director, Kenya. Although better known for his very successful novels, Ngugi wa Thiong'o has also had considerable impact in contemporary theatre in Kenya and Africa. His plays include *The Black Hermit, This Time Tomorrow* and *The Trial of Dedan Kimathi*, which he co-wrote with Micere Githae MUGO. The Kamiriithu theatre projects with Ngugi WA MIRII and the Kamiriithu community resulted in the very successful plays *Ngaahika Ndeenda* (*I'll Marry When I Want*, 1982) and *Maitu Gitayi* (*Mother, Sing for Me*, 1986). Ngugi's theatre style is characterized by an active engagement with the political and social realities of neo-colonial Kenya. This is carried out progressively at a collective level and in the Gikuyu language. Without being firmly within the mould of theatre-for-development, Ngugi's Kamiriithu work is solidly part of the new aesthetics of the theatre in Africa in which theatre is transformed into a tool and context for communal exploration and expression.

Wajda, Andrzej (1926–) Director, Poland. Wajda studied at the Academy of Fine Arts in Cracow and graduated from the State Film, Theatre and Television Academy in Łódź. He has directed dozens of plays for the stage and television, in addition to a distinguished career in film. From 1972–83 he was artistic director of the film company X, from 1978–83, chairman of the Polish Film-makers Association, and from 1989–91 a senator for Solidarity. In his works in all genres,

Wajda shows his attachment to national traditions: he often touches upon current socio-political issues. At the same time, being a painter, he takes great care of the visual concept of his productions, and for some he designs the sets himself.

Walcott, Derek (1930–) Dramatist, St Lucia. Walcott has written some thirty-eight plays and published more than fifteen volumes of poetry. He attended the University College of the West Indies in Jamaica and studied theatre in the USA with a Rockefeller Foundation fellowship (1958–9). In Trinidad he founded the Trinidad Theatre Workshop, which he ran for seventeen years. Since 1981 he has held a professorship at the University of Boston, and in 1992 he was awarded the Nobel Prize for Literature. In his plays he has integrated postcolonial views of local issues and a typically European theatrical form, developing from verse drama via exuberance and colour of folk material to a more introverted mode. His plays include *Dreams and Colours* (1958), *Dream on Monkey Mountain* (1967), *Pantomime* (1978), *Haitian Earth* (1984) and the musical *Steel* (1991). In 1992 the Royal Shakespeare Company produced his adaptation of the *Odyssey*.

Walker, George F. (1947–) Dramatist and director, Canada. Walker is considered the foremost Canadian author of black comedy. His plays have been linked to surrealism because they defy linear structures. They often take popular culture as a point of departure, such as romantic comedy, detective novels or movies, and through 'confrontational scenes between two characters' allow the discussion of 'Walker's obsessions: power politics, the nature of evil, impending chaos, the restorative power of laughter, obsession itself'. Walker has won Governor General's Awards for his plays *Criminals in Love* (1986) and *Nothing Sacred* (1989). In 1998, he co-directed his own six-play cycle *Suburban Motel* at the Factory Theatre in Toronto.

Walker, Kerry (1948–) Actor, Australia. Trained at the National Institute of Dramatic Art, Sydney, Walker is an actor of enormous versatility and who transformed herself almost unrecognizably in a huge range of roles: an androgynous Feste in Neil ARMFIELD's *Twelfth Night* (filmed), a mesmerizing and scintillating Edith Sitwell in her own *Knuckledusters – the Jewels of Edith Sitwell* and a comic cameo in Jane Campion's *The Piano*. Walker has been particularly associated with roles in plays by her friend Patrick White, creating roles in *Netherwood*, *Signal Driver* and *Shepherd on the Rocks* as well as enacting a powerful and predatory Mrs Lusty in Armfield's acclaimed 1989 revival of White's *The Ham Funeral* and a threatening, leather-clad, bizarre young woman in the extraordinary film *The Night the Prowler*, scripted by White and directed by Jim SHARMAN. Walker was a foundation member of the Hunter Valley Theatre Company in Newcastle, NSW, worked with the Adelaide Lighthouse Company (1982–3) and then was very much involved in the establishment of the Belvoir St Theatre in Sydney. Walker is a chameleon performer but always compellingly charismatic onstage.

Walton, Tony (1934–) Designer, USA. Born in Britain, Walton trained at the Slade School of Fine Arts. In 1955 he began his career in Wimbledon, and moved to New York in 1957. He has created set and/or costume designs for musicals (*Guys and Dolls*, 1992), and straight theatre such as STOPPARD's *The Real Thing* (1984), Herb Gardner's *I'm Not Rappaport* (1985), *Conversations with My Father*, starring Judd HIRSCH (1992), Dorfman's *Death and the Maiden*, Neil SIMON's *Laughter on the 23rd Floor* (1997) and the musicals *1776* (1997), and *Annie Get Your Gun* (1999). He has designed in London, and films include

Equus (based on SHAFFER's play, 1977). His highly detailed and fanciful designs for contemporary musicals and comedies have been particularly successful, earning him numerous awards.

Wang Gui (1932–) Director, China. Without either a university education or training for the theatre, Wang is the leading director in the Spoke Drama Troupe affiliated with the political department of the air force, where he used to be the director. His main productions include Ding Yi San's *Jiu Yi San Shi Jian* (*September 13 Incident*), Wang Pei Gong's *Zhou Lang Bai Shuai* (*Young Marshal Zhou*), Han Jing Ping's *Kai Xuan Zai Zi Ye* (*The Midnight Triumph*), Ye Zi's *Tian Di Ren* (*Heaven, Earth and Man*), Zhang Li Li's *Xue Ran De Feng Cai* (*Gory Glory*), LI Long Yun's *Sa Man Yue Guang De Huang Yuan* (*Moon-lit Wasteland*), Beckett's *Waiting for Godot*, Wang Jian's *Da Mo Zhi Hun* (*Soul of the Desert*), Mo Ji Dong's *Hai Xia Qing Ji* (*Cross-Strait Emotions*) and Liu Jin Yuan's *Quan Shi Beijing Ren* (*We Are all Beijingers*) His later works, in his own description, are 'playful plays'. He aims for what he describes as Chinese, modern, non-realistic theatre.

Wang Xiao Ying (1957–) Director, China. Wang studied directing at the Central Academy of Drama in two periods, from 1980–4 and from 1992–5, obtaining a doctoral degree. In 1984 he became a director at the China Youth Theatre. His productions include *Gua Zai Qiang Shang De Lao B* (*Old B on the Wall*) by Sun Hui Zhu and Zhang Ma Li, Tao Jun's *Mo Fang*, Xu Yan's *Ah, Nu Ren Men* (*Oh, Women...*) ZHAO Yao Min's *Ben Shi Ji Zui Hou De Meng* (*Last Dream of the Century*), Cao Yu's *Lei Yu* (*Thunderstorm*), Wu Yu Zhong's *Qing Gan Cao Liang* (*A Sentimental Exercise*), Wu Shuang's *Chun Qiu Hun* (*The Spirit of the Warring States Period*) and Du Cun's *Ai Qing Pao Pao* (*Amorous Bubbles*). He

aims at a more externalized and stylized expression of emotions.

Warchus, Matthew (1967?–) Director, Great Britain. Warchus has been one of the most promising young directors to emerge during the 1990s. Following first experiences as a director in London Fringe venues, he was assistant director for Adrian NOBLE's *The Thebans* for the Royal Shakespeare Company in 1992. His production of *Much Ado About Nothing* with Mark RYLANCE was very successful in the West End (1993), as was the revival of Sam SHEPARD's *True West* at the Donmar Warehouse (1994). For the RSC, Warchus directed *Henry V*, *The Devil is an Ass* (1994), a controversial, drastically cut *Hamlet* (1997) for the Royal National Theatre, and Ben Jonson's *Volpone* (1995), with Michael GAMBON and Simon Russell BEALE. In 1996, Warchus scored another success with his production of *Art* by Yasmina Reza (starring Albert FINNEY in the original cast), whose earlier play *The Unexpected Man* (starring Michael GAMBON) he directed for the RSC in 1998.

Warner, Deborah (1959–) Director, Great Britain. Warner studied stage management at the Central School of Speech and Drama. She founded Kick Theatre Company in 1980 and was its artistic director until 1986. From 1987–9 she was a resident director with the Royal Shakespeare Company. Her production of *King John* sculpted a form out of the formless chronicle, making it into a series of alliances formed and betrayed. Strong narrative drive was characteristic of her production of *Titus Andronicus*. Following a successful production of Brecht's *Der Gute Mensch von Sezuan* (*The Good Person of Sezuan*, with Fiona SHAW in the title role) at the Royal National Theatre in 1989, she has been an associate director there in 1990, directing amongst others *King Lear* (1990, with Brian COX as Lear and Ian MCKELLEN as Kent). She has directed opera (*Don Giovanni*, Glyndebourne) and at the Salzburg Festival (*Coriolanus*, 1993, with Bruno Ganz), and resumed her collaboration with Fiona Shaw in *Electra*, Ibsen's *Hedda Gabler*, Beckett's *Footfalls* and T.S. Eliot's *The Waste Land* (for television).

Warning, Marc (1955–) Designer, The Netherlands. Although he studied briefly at the Gerrit Rietveld Academy in Amsterdam, Marc Warning was formed mainly through his apprenticeship with Jan Joris LAMERS's company Onafhankelijk Toneel in the early 1980s. He also appeared in several productions, such as *Style*. Warning's work is stylish, antirealistic and completely original, both in his use of everyday material and his scenic solutions. He has designed many sets for director Matin VAN VELDHUIZEN, especially with her company Carrousel, including an adaptation of Wilde's *The Picture of Dorian Gray* (with Cas ENKLAAR) and Shaw's *Mrs Warren's Profession* (with Marlies HEUER, both 1995). The main part of Warning's work however, has been with the reborn Onafhankelijk Toneel (OT) as a collective in which dance, acting and art take equal place. With Gerrit Timmers, Warning created *On Wings of Art* (1988), about two artists stuck in a villa in Egypt. He also designed Chekhov's *Platonov* and several dance productions, both inside and outside OT. Warning is also a graphic designer, well-known for his eye-catching posters.

Wassef, Muna (1942–) Actress, Syria. Wassef began her career with a minor company, where she worked in commercial comedies. She joined the National Theatre in the early 1960s and became one of the ensemble's top stars. Her breakthrough was in Molière's *Tartuffe*, directed by Rafik SABBAN. Under his direction she played several further major roles including Calderón's *La vida es sueño* (*Life is a Dream*). She appeared in

Rashomon directed by Mohamed TAYEB, in several plays written and directed by Ali Oqla URSAN, Al-Tayeb Al-Ulj's *Al-Sa'ed* (*The Good Luck*) and Sudqi Ismail's *Ayam Salamon* (*The Days of Salamon*) both directed by Asaad FUDDA. She starred in the American film *The Message*, directed by Moustapha Akkad. Her many roles on television made her one of the most popular stars in the Arab world as well as a public figure with a social role and responsibility.

Watanabe Kazuko Designer and director, Germany. Born in Japan, Watanabe came to Vienna with her husband, and studied costume design at the Hochschule für angewandte Kunst. In the early 1970s, she assisted Moidele BICKEL at the Salzburg Festival, and was invited to work at the Schaubühne am Halleschen Ufer. She designed costumes for productions by Wilfried MINKS and Peter PALITZSCH. Since 1978, she has also designed sets for TABORI, B.K. Tragelehn and David MOUCHTAR-SAMORAI. She recalls that because 'she had to be present at rehearsals anyway, she might as well direct'. Her chance for this came in 1988 when she joined the theatre in Bonn. Since then she has often directed and designed her own productions, such as Wedekind's *Frühlings Erwachen* (*Spring Awakening*, 1988, Bonn), Edward BOND's *Summer* (1992, Karlsruhe), Lorca's *La casa de Bernarda Alba* (*The House of Bernarda Alba*, 1993, Düsseldorf), Elfriede JELINEK's *Stecken Stab und Stangl* (Leipzig, 1997) and Susanne Amatosero's *Asylanten* (Hamburg, 1998). 'She resists pressure to create large, elaborate, costly designs in favour of simple but highly imaginative impressive creations.'

Weaving, Hugo (1960–) Actor, Australia. Weaving graduated from the National Institute of Dramatic Art, Sydney in 1981. Although probably best known internationally for his appearance in the film *The Adventures of Priscilla, Queen*

of the Desert, Weaving has been able to sustain a high profile theatre career alongside his many successful film appearances. His ability to exude sexual intensity on stage is compelling and this has stood him in good stead as Valmont in Christopher HAMPTON's *Les Liaisons Dangereuses* for Nimrod, Sydney and as a sexy James Dean lookalike Petruchio in *The Taming of the Shrew* for the Melbourne Theatre Company. By contrast, as Face in Ben Jonson's *The Alchemist* (1996) to Geoffrey RUSH's Subtle, Weaving delivered a performance which was by turns sleazy, swashbuckling, energetic, suave and ingratiating, and full of the enjoyment of self-confessed theatricality.

Wellman, Mac (1945–) Dramatist, USA. Wellman has been a playwright in residence with several universities (New York, Yale, Princeton). Focusing on the American language, his plays, including *Harm's Way* (1985), *Sincerity Forever* (1990), *A Murder of Crows* (1991), *The Land of Fog and Whistles* (1993) and *tigertigertiger* (1997) have rebelled in form and content against mainstream playwrighting.

Werewere-Liking, Nicole (1950–) Dramatist, director and musician, Cameroon. Nicole Werewere-Liking is one of the few women dramatists in francophone West Africa. In her plays she is mainly concerned with exploring for the stage most of the myths, rituals, songs and dances that were very much part of her childhood and early experience of theatrical performance, because in a family of musicians, she was exposed to traditional styles and practices of performance. What is remarkable about Werewere-Liking's dramaturgy is her radical departure from the prevalent styles and practices of much francophone theatre of West Africa. She structures theatre as a ritual experience capable of completely transforming the spectator–participant. Her best-known works are *The Devil's Tail* (also known

in her home country as *Ngonga* and in France as *Les Batards*), *A New Land* (1980), *Of the Unjust Sleep* (1980), *Hands Have Meaning* (1987) and *The Rainbow Measles* (1987).

Wertenbaker, Timberlake Dramatist, Great Britain. In 1983 Wertenbaker was an Arts Council Resident Writer with the theatre company Shared Experience. Her plays tend to focus on human relationships, with a wide range of issues from domestic to mythic. Major successful plays include *The Grace of Mary Traverse* (1985), *Our Country's Good* (1988), *The Love of the Nightingale* (1989), *Three Birds Alighting on a Field* (1992), *The Break of Day* (1995) and *After Darwin* (1998). She also gained reputation as a translator and adapter, notably *The Theban Plays* for the Royal Shakespeare Company (1991, directed by Adrian NOBLE), for which she adapted the two *Oedipus* plays and *Antigone*.

Wherrett, Richard (1940–) Director, Australia. After working as co-artistic director of Nimrod, Sydney 1974–9 and associate director of the Old Tote, Sydney 1970–2, Wherrett became director and chief executive at the Sydney Theatre Company 1979–90, creating a stylish and financially successful profile for the company and overseeing the opening of the new Wharf theatre. Wherrett's range is enormous and encompasses Brecht (*Mahoganny, Galileo*) classics (a dance party version of *A Midsummer Night's Dream*), musicals (an arena *Jesus Christ Superstar*), opera, modern Australian plays, kitsch (*Pageant*, Sydney 1997) and film. One career highlight was his production of *The Elocution of Benjamin Franklin* (1976), a monologue by a transvestite homosexual, performed originally by Gordon Chater. This production won an off-Broadway Obie for direction, toured the world and has been revived several times. Wherrett's production of Arthur MILLER's *The Crucible* was also much acclaimed and revived. Wherrett was artistic director for the Melbourne International Festival of Arts for 1992 and 1993. His productions are renowned for their stylishness.

Wiest, Diane (1948–) Actor, USA. Originally trained as a ballet dancer, Wiest appeared in Thornton Wilder's *Our Town* and *Inherit the Wind*. She played the title role in Ibsen's *Hedda Gabler* (1981), Nora in Ibsen's *Et Dukkehjem* (*A Doll's House*, 1982), Masha in Chekhov's *Tri sestry* (*Three Sisters*, 1982), Desdemona (1982), Deborah in PINTER's *Other Places* (1984), and appeared in Arthur MILLER's *After the Fall* (1984) and *Square One* by Steve Tesich (1990). In 1985 she directed Stephen MacDonald's *Not About Heroes* off-Broadway. Her film career began in 1982, culminating in an Academy Award for Best Supporting Actor for Woody Allen's *Hannah and her Sisters* (1986). Although much of her stage work has been in classic dramatic roles, her films have shown a great comic skill. This was particularly evident in her award-winning performance in Woody Allen's recent *Bullets Over Broadway* (1996).

Willems, Jeroen (1962–) Actor, The Netherlands. After graduating from the Drama Academy in Maastricht in 1987, Jeroen Willems appeared with different companies, but his quiet rise to fame has come about mainly with Hollandia (see Johan SIMONS). There he used his great formal techniques, musicality and sense of language in creating moving yokels and simpletons in plays by Franz Xaver KROETZ, such as *Bauern sterben* (*Farmers Dying*, 1989) and *Stallerhof* (1991). Willems was equally impressive in his stylized handling of Greek tragedies, as Jason in Euripides's *Medeia* (1991), in Aeschylus's *Persai* (*The Persians*, 1995) and as Cassio in *Othello* and 'the man' in Duras' *La Musica II*. Willems has an unostentatious but very concentrated way of acting. He has fine, almost aquiline features, and a charming but never fawning presence. On television and film, his realistic abilities come out. Willems is typical of a generation of intelligent young actors who are more interested in work than fame.

Williams, Eugene F. (1952–) Director, Jamaica. Williams studied at the City University of New York, Brooklyn College, and Jamaica School of Drama, where he now serves as director of studies. Major productions he directed include Chekhov's *Visnevyi sad* (*The Cherry Orchard*), Williams's *A Streetcar Named Desire* and Beckett's *Waiting for Godot*. One of his aims in directing is to help actors to find creative approaches to the characters. He activates directorial imagery theatrically in a variety of production styles. In arriving at his dynamic concepts for productions, he his guided by using Brecht's method. As a teacher of drama, he strives to identify a clear methodology of the acting process and instrumental training, particularly for arriving at internal reality and active projection of the role.

Williamson, David (1942–) Dramatist, Australia. Williamson graduated in mechanical engineering from Monash University, Melbourne. He has an international profile; many of his plays have been filmed and he is the most consistent box office draw in Australian theatre. Williamson dissects the pretensions and dilemmas of the Australian middle classes with great wit, writing predominantly realistically. Williamson's early work was associated with the alternative Melbourne theatre scene; his powerful early play *The Removalists* (1971) premiered at La MaMa, Carlton, and *Don's Party* (1971) premiered at the Australian Performing Group's Pram Factory. Later Williamson plays feature characters who are wealthier and more successful careerists. Williamson is a master at generating controversy and regularly engages in high-profile disputes with his critics in the newspapers. His attack on academia, *Dead White Males* (1995), purports to contribute to the debate on political correctness. Williamson's life history is recounted in exhaustive detail by Brian Kiernan.

Wilson, August (1945–) Dramatist, USA. One of the best known African American dramatists, Wilson's aim is to provide a cycle of plays of African American life in each decade of the twentieth century, showing the African American characters often as victims of racism and economic oppression. *Joe Turner's Come and Gone* (1986) is set in 1911, *Ma Rainey's Black Bottom* (1984) in 1927. The 1930s are covered in *The Piano Lesson* (1987). *Fences* (1985) is set in 1957, and *Two Trains Running*, written in 1990, brings the cycle to the 1960s. The latest play, *Seven Guitars* (1996) is set in Pittsburgh in the 1940s. His language has been described as 'rich and casually revealing'.

Wilson, Lanford (1937–) Dramatist and director, USA. In Wilson's plays, including the trilogy *5th of July* (1978), *Talley's Folly* (1979) and *Talley and Son* (1981) and also *Angels Fall* (1982), *Burn This* (1987), *The Moonshot Tape* (1990), *Redwood Curtain* (1992) and *Sympathetic Magic* (1999), primary values are 'honesty, love of friends, family and home, set within a conflict between traditional values of the past and the pressures of modern life'.

Wilson, Robert (1941–) Director, dramatist, performer, choreographer, designer, sculptor and painter, USA. Wilson trained as an architect, studied visual arts and worked as a movement therapist for mentally disturbed people. Some of his patients participated in his early productions, in which Wilson dramatized 'an unstable, decentered self, and explored the role of language in structuring the self. In later stages of his career, when he turned his eye to classic texts, Wilson used many strategies to decentre the self

and dramatise the inner world of schizophrenia. In his production of Ibsen's *Når vi Dode Vågner* (*When We Dead Awaken*, American Repertory Theatre, 1990), for instance, he divided the part of Irene between a white and an African-American actor. Through autistic movements without any apparent relation to the text; by dividing the lines between the actors (at times in mid-sentence); and by having them occasionally speak together – sometimes in unison, sometimes out of sync – Wilson fragmented Ibsen's heroine into schizophrenic multiple selves waging war against themselves.'

Wilson, Susan (1945–) Director and actor, New Zealand. Wilson studied at Victoria University of Wellington and trained as a teacher, but soon took up freelance acting on stage and radio and later on television. Her early 'light and twinkling talent' suited soubrette roles, but she has also had heavier parts like Paula Tanqueray in Pinero's *The Second Mrs Tanqueray* (1979) and Mrs Alving in Ibsen's *Gengangere* (*Ghosts*, 1985). She is especially connected with Circa Theatre, Wellington, of which she was a co-founder, and more recently has developed into an important director. An early success at the Circa was Terry JOHNSON's *Insignificance* (1984), and she has championed Robert Lord's plays, directing, for example, *Bert and Maisy* (1986) and *Joyful and Triumphant* (1992). She also directed notable productionsof Kushner's *Angels in America* (1994) and STOPPARD's *Arcadia* (1995). Circa is an actors' co-operative theatre, and Wilson has always avoided ostentatious directing, aiming instead to find the rhythm of each scene and to provide room for characters to grow.

Winge, Stein (1940–) Director and actor, Norway. Winge trained as an actor at the Norwegian State Theatre High School, but soon shifted to directing. He now has over 100 productions to his credit, covering a wide range of the repertory:

Shakespeare (*Hamlet*, *Richard II*, *Richard III*, *King Lear* and *Othello*), Goethe's *Faust*, Chekhov's *Tri sestry* (*Three Sisters*) and *Djadja Vanja* (*Uncle Vanya*), Greek tragedy and most of Ibsen's plays, as well as DORST's *Merlin oder Das Wüste Land* (*Merlin or The Waste Land*, with Björn SUNDQUIST), Botho STRAUSS's *Die Zeit und das Zimmer* (*The Time and the Room*) and Dorfman's *Death and the Maiden*). In addition to all of the Norwegian theatres, Winge has also worked abroad and has established himself as a leading director of opera over the last few years.

Wisniak, Kazimierz (1931–) Designer, Poland. A graduate of the Academy of Fine Arts, Cracow, Wisniak has created the designs for more than 200 productions. He has worked closely with the Pantomime Theatre of Wroclaw since its beginning in 1956. From 1981–6 he was director of the Teatr Bagatela in Cracow, and since 1971 he has worked with Stary Teatr in Cracow and Teatr Dramatyczny in Warsaw. He gained his best artistic achievements while working with three directors, Henryk Tomaszewski, Jerzy Jarocki and Konrad Swinarski. Wisniak usually divides the stage area into two. The downstage area, close to the audience, is dominated by the actors and is realistic, limited in colour. The upstage area is visible only at moments. It is symbolic, metaphysical and sometimes gives an ironic commentary on the action.

Wistari, Christina (1945–) Performer, Indonesia. Wistari was born in Italy. Having first trained in mime at Quelli di Grok in Milan, she studied mask carving in Sri Lanka and Bali and Kathakali in India with the renowned Guru Gopinath. She returned to Bali in 1983 and began to study Balinese Topeng with I Made DJIMAT, Joged Pingitan (a rarely seen woman's solo narrative dance) with his mother Ni Ketut Cenik, and Balinese singing with Ni Nyoman Candri. She has

since become perhaps the only non-Indonesian master of Balinese dance and has given lectures, demonstrations and performances in Italy, Holland, France, Denmark and Australia. In 1991 she appeared in SARDONO's *Dongeng dari Dirah* in Jakarta. In 1993 she began the Gambuh Preservation Project with the help of the Ford Foundation. The project seeks to document and preserve this ancient classical dance theatre and presents performances twice monthly in Batuan. In 1995 and 1996 she and Djimat worked with Eugenio BARBA and the International School of Theatre Anthropology (ISTA). While continuing to teach and perform both in Bali and internationally, Wistari is preparing a monograph on the Gambuh under the auspices of the Ford Foundation.

Wolfe, George C. (1954–) Dramatist and director, USA. Wolfe obtained an MFA from New York University. Since 1993 he has been artistic director of the New York Shakespeare Festival. *The Colored Museum* (1986) is a collection of eleven satirical sketches, museum exhibits, on contemporary African American life. Other plays are *Spunk* (1989) and *Jelly's Last* (1992). In 1993 Wolfe directed an acclaimed production of Kushner's *Angels in America*. His productions reflect a vivid theatrical imagination and great sense of musicality in their finely detailed stagecraft.

Wonder, Erich (1944–) Designer, Austria. After studying at the Kunstgewerbeschule Graz and the Akademie der Bildenden Künste, Vienna, Wonder began his career as assistant to Wilfried MINKS in Bremen (1968–71). He has worked with most important directors, including Jürgen FLIMM, Peter PALITZSCH, Hans NEUENFELS and Luc BONDY, and has also designed for opera (including *Tristan und Isolde* in Bayreuth, 1993, directed by Heiner Müller). He considers himself as a cameraman who builds spaces. 'His spaces are magical; spaces from light which keep their secrets and create meaningful associations in the spectator.' Since 1978 he has held a professorship at the Akademie für Bildende Künste in Vienna.

Wong, Eleanor Siew Yin (1962–) Dramatist, Singapore. A trained lawyer, Wong is an acclaimed playwright in Singapore whose plays are philosophical and intelligent. Her most acclaimed play, *Mergers and Accusations* (1992), and its sequel, *Wills And Successions* (1995), dealt sensitively with the issue of alternative sexuality in Singapore. The main character, a lesbian, deals with the pressures of marriage, religion and family in the two plays. Naturalistic in approach, Wong's craft is in her wit and her irony. Her plays are comical but also provide commentary on the social situation in Singapore. Among her more politically oriented plays are *Peter's Passionate Pursuit* (1985), *Jackson on a Jaunt* (1987), which was an AIDS play, *Exit* (1990) and *Joust* (1991).

Woudstra, Karst (1947–) Dramatist, director, The Netherlands. Woudstra's father wrote and directed plays, and his mother did not like this. Family conflicts have haunted Woudstra from his early youth, and have been at the centre of everything he wrote. He studied Swedish and has introduced the plays of Lars Norén, a friend with a similar taste for the psychoanalytical, to The Netherlands. Woudstra's debut was *Hofscènes* (*Scenes at Court*, 1981), about the relation between King Philip II of Spain and his son Carlos. Directed by Gerardjan RIJNDERS it was an enormous success. Feeling rejected by his colleagues, Woudstra did not continue writing until 1989, after which he released a steady flow of plays, including

Een hond begraven (*To Bury a Dog*, 1989), *De linkerhand van Meyerhold* (*Meyerhold's Left Hand*, 1990) and the much acclaimed *Een zwarte Pool* (*A Black Pole*, 1992, also in German). The play tackles the uncertainties of two couples, successful at first glance but tied up in their past. As a director, Woudstra has had more success abroad, especially in Belgium, than in Holland. However, he managed the repertory theatre in Amsterdam briefly in the mid-1980s, directing a wonderful *Night, Mother of the Day* by Lars Norén (1985).

Wuttke, Martin Actor, Germany. After training at the Schauspielschule Bochum, Wuttke's first employment was in Frankfurt, as a member of critic turned artistic director Günther Rühle's company, where he became one of the chief protagonists of controversial director Einar SCHLEEF. In 1991 he joined Jürgen FLIMM's Thalia Theater in Hamburg. Early in 1996 he became artistic director of the Berliner Ensemble, resigning towards the end of the year in a controversy involving Schleef. 'What fascinates him about theatre is the transformation of literature into language: from the voice of a single dramatist to the voices of many performers on the stage.' Important credits include the title role in Brecht's *Der Aufhaltsame Aufstueg des Arturo Ui* (*The Resistable Rise of Arturo Ui*, 1995, directed by Heiner Müller), Danton in Büchner's *Danton's Tod* (*Danton's Death*, 1998, directed by Robert WILSON in a co-production of the Salzburg festival and the Berliner Ensemble) and Titus Andronicus in Heiner Müller's *Anatomie Titus Fall of Rome* (*Anatomy Titus Fall of Rome*, 1999).

X

Xi Mei Juan (1956–) Actor, China. Xi graduated in 1976 from the diploma course on acting at the Shanghai Academy of Drama. She has played leading roles in Zhao Guo Qing's *Jiu Jiu Ta* (*Please Save Her*, 1977), Zong Fu Xian's *Yu Wu Sheng Chu* (*Out of Silence*, 1978), *Romeo and Juliet* (1981), *The Taming of the Shrew* (1983), SHA Ye Xin's *Xun Zhao Nan Zi Han* (*In Search of Real Man*, 1986), Sun Hui Zhu's *Zhong Guo Meng* (*China Dream*, 1987), Peter SHAFFER's *Equus* (1988), Yue Mei Qin's *Liu Shou Nu Shi* (*The Waiting Wife*, 1991) and Amy Tan's *Joy Luck Club* (1993).

Xu Fan (1967–) Actor, China. Xu trained at the Central Academy of Drama from 1987–91 and became a member of Beijing People's Art Theatre upon graduation. Her major roles include Su Fang in Cao Yu's *Beijing Ren* (*Peking Characters*), Nina in Chekhov's *Cajka* (*The Seagull*), Liu Chun Yan in Bei Po's *Wu Tai Shang de Zhen Gu Shi* (*True Story on Stage*), Xiao Zhen in Wei Min's *Hong Bai Xi Shi* (*Weddings and Funerals*), Xiao Xia in GUO Shi Xing's *Niao Ren* (*The Bird Master*), Gertrude in *Hamlet* and Liu Xiao Yan in Guo She Xing's *Yu Ren* (*The Angling Master*). Her most well-known part is probably the eponymous heroine in Liu Jing Yun's *Ruan Ling Yue*, about the famous Shanghai film star in the thirties. She has appeared in many quality films and soap operas. Xu has created a number of young melancholic women on stage. She is known for her understated style as well as refined diction.

Xu Xiao Zhong (1928–) Director, China. From 1948–60 Xu studied at the Nanking National Academy of Drama, North China University and Moscow Lunarcharski School of Drama. He has taught for forty years at the Central Academy of Drama. As the reigning director, he adheres to the policy of teaching, creating and researching. The principle he set for the Academy is 'to maintain and develop the realistic aesthetics, draw on Chinese indigenous traditions, and critically absorb the accomplishments of theatres abroad'. He stresses the importance of a self-centred attitude towards borrowing Chinese and foreign heritage. His main productions include Vsevelod Vishnevski's *Optemisticheskaya Tragedia* (*The Optimistic Tragedy*), *Macbeth*, LI Long Yun's *Sa Man Yue Guang De Huang Yuan* (*Moon-lit Wilderness*), Chekhov's *Visnevyi sad* (*The Cherry Orchard*) and Wu Shuang's *Chun Qiu Hun* (*Spirit of the Warring States*).

Xue Dian Jie (1937–) Designer, China. Xue graduated from the Hochschule fur Bildende Kunst in Dresden. His main works include designs for Brecht's *Leben des Galilei* (*Life of Galileo*, 1979), Chen

Bai Chen's *A Qu Zheng Zhuan* (*Anecdotal History of A Q*, 1980), LIU Shu Gang's *Shi Wu Zhuang Li Huen An De Diao Cha Fen Xi* (*Fifteen Divorce Cases Analyzed*, 1984), ZHANG Xiao Feng's *Heshi Bi* (*He's Jade*, 1986), Cao Yu's *Beijing Ren* (*Peking Characters*, 1989), an adaptation of Goethe's *Faust* (1994) directed by LIN Zhao Hua, Tan Zhi Xiang's *Ying Xiong Zhuang Zhi Shao Nian Lang* (*Heroic Youth*, 1994), directed by CHEN Rong, Sartre's *Mort sans Sepulcure* (*Dead without Burial*, 1997) and Brecht's *Die Dreigroschenoper* (*The Threepenny Opera*, 1998). He tries to combine old traditions with new trends.

Y

Yadin, Jossi (1920–) Actor, Israel. Yadin trained at the Habima studio and was one of the co-founders of the Cameri Tel Aviv municipal theatre. Among his most memorable roles are Lenni (Steinbeck's *Of Mice and Men*), Falstaff, the father in Hanoch LEVIN's *Shitz* and Willi Loman in Arthur MILLER's *Death of a Salesman*. More recently he has appeared in *The Comedy of Errors* and Levin's *Peore Pe (Mouth Open)* and *Retsach (Murder)*. His one-man performance of HOROWITZ's *Hadod Artur (Uncle Arthur)* was a virtual tour-de-force. Yadin has also played in many films and received the Israel prize in 1991.

Yamaguchi Akira (1948–) Costume researcher, restorer and designer, Japan. Yamaguchi specializes in reproducing the textile for the original nô costumes. He began his research on the nô costumes of the Edo era (1603–1867) in 1978 and started reproducing the textile by using the *sorahikibata* or *sorahiki* method of weaving in 1983. The reproductions of the nô costumes were shown in the national museums of Northern European countries such as Sweden and Denmark. In 1985, he founded the Yamaguchi Nô Costume Research Centre in Shiga, Japan. He reproduced the nô costumes of Chûson-ji (the Temple Chûson) and opened the Asai Shiryô-kan (The Asai Institute of Nô Material) in Shiga in 1993. From 1993–4 he took the reproductions to the exhibitions to Germany, Italy and the USA. Some of his nô costumes are kept in museums of Japan and abroad.

Yamazaki Masakazu (1934–) Dramatist and translator, Japan. Yamazaki wrote *Zeami* and received the Kishida Play Award in 1963. *Zeami* was translated into English and was performed in Italy in 1971. *Fune wa Hosen yo (The Boat is a Sailboat)* was written for Te no Kai (the Hand Theatre Group) when it was formed by Yamazaki with playwright BETSUYAKU Minoru and director SUEKI Toshifumi in 1972. *Mokuzô Haritsuke (Rikyû Crucified*, 1978) was also staged by Sueki. Yamazaki studied (1965) and taught (1967) at the Yale University in the USA. In 1987 *Zeami* was staged by Shingeki-dan Kyôkai (the Association of the Theatre Companies of Shingeki) under Sueki's direction, with MATSUMOTO Kôshirô as Zeami. Yamazaki often uses famous artists in Japanese history as heroes of his plays focusing on on the conflict between the art and politics, personified in the artists and the rulers of the time.

Yang, Daniel (1936–) Director, USA and China. Formerly the producing artistic director of the Colorado Shakespeare Festival from 1976–82 and 1985–90, Yang joined the Hong Kong Repertory

Theatre (HK Rep) in 1990 and has been the artistic director ever since. He directed over sixty modern and classical productions, in both English and Chinese. Some of his most acclaimed directions are *Love's Labour's Lost* (1980) and *The Merchant of Venice* (starring RSC actor Tony Church as Shylock, 1987). With the HK Rep, Yang's major directing credits include *King Lear* (1993), with two casts of Cantonese and Mandarin, Raymond TO's musical *Tales of the Walled City* (third run in 1997), and He Ji-ping's *De Ling and Empress Dowager Ci Xi* for the opening performance of the Second Chinese Drama Festival (1998, Hong Kong). Under his leadership, the HK Rep has seen marked development in promoting original productions and in launching numerous overseas tours. Jerry Sterner's *Other People's Money* (1995) at the Shanghai People's Art Theatre, Peter SHAFFER's *Equus* (1994) and Ray Cooney's *Whose Wife is It Anyway?* (1999) at the National Theatre of Taiwan are Yang's recently successful overseas productions.

Yefremov, Oleg (1927–) Director and actor, Russia. After completing his training at the Moscow Art Theatre Studio in 1949, Yefremov was an actor at the Theatre for Children in Moscow. He founded the Sovremennik Theatre Studio (1956) to generate aesthetics. For the opening he chose Rozov's *Vechno zhivyie* (*Always Alive*). His main productions at the Sovremennik were documentary plays, dealing with crucial periods of Russian history (Shatrov's *Bolsheviki* (*The Bolsheviks*), 1967), or classics (Chekhov's *Cajka* (*The Seagull*), 1970). His direct position, interest in sharp moral and social conflict, and disapproval of political collaborationism soon brought him sympathy of the public, but not of the authorities. He was moved to the Moscow Art Theatre, where he established a successful combination of Russian classics and modern plays, thus restoring its position as a leading theatre.

A cycle of Chekhov's plays was begun in 1980. Yefremov's keen eye on Russian history and politics led to quite unusual version of Pushkin's *Boris Godunov* (1994), in which he also played the title part, as a tragic figure. Since 1950, Yefremov has been a professor of Moscow Art Theatre Studio. During the last years Yefremov has been taking part in the study and editing of Stanislavski's works.

Yenersu, Işik (1942–) Actor, Turkey. After graduating from the Ankara State Conservatory, Yenersu joined the Ankara State Theatre in 1963. When the French director, Roger PLANCHON visited Turkey, she became his asistant (1968–9). Between 1969–70 she worked as an assistant for the Drama Programmes Office de Radiodiffusion-Television Française (ORTF). She has acted in famous plays like Shaw's *Caesar and Cleopatra* (1963), Arthur MILLER's *All My Sons* (1967), *The Taming of the Shrew* (1985), Alan AYCKBOURN's *Woman in Mind* (1987) and Dorfman's *Death and the Maiden* (1991). She has received various awards in her acting career, and she also took part in many radio and television programmes as well as in films. At present she is working at the İstanbul State Theatre. As her name (Işik, light) suggests, as soon as she enters the stages she brings along with her a sphere of light which illuminates the hearts and minds of the spectators.

Yeo, Robert Cheng Guan (1940–) Dramatist, Singapore. Yeo is a seminal figure in Singapore English-language theatre. His trilogy – *Are You There, Singapore* (1974), *One Year Back Home* (1980) and *Changi* (1996) – provided a strong and pertinent political voice in Singapore theatre. These plays explicitly attacked the hegemonic impulses of government policies and were highly critical of the one-party political system in Singapore. Having served on both the Drama Advisory Committee and the Drama Review

Committee, Yeo is a staunch advocate for indigenous Singapore dramatic writing. His other plays include *Eye of History* (1992), a fantasia where Sir Stamford Raffles meets Mr Lee Kuan Yew, and *Second Chance* (1988), a play about beauty and morality. Educated at the University of Singapore and the University of London, Yeo is currently an associate professor at the National Institute of Education. He also won the Public Service Medal in 1991.

Yerushalmi, Rina (1939–) Director, Israel. Yerushalmi began her training as a dancer and later as an actor at the Royal Academy of Dramatic Art in London. She has directed at La MaMa in New York and is affiliated to New York University. After directing several conventional productions at different Israeli theatres, Yerushalmi founded the more experimental ITIM theatre where she has directed Büchner's *Woyzeck*, *Hamlet* and *Romeo and Juliet*, and later a performance project based on Bible texts. The originality of the Bible production has been recognized both in Israel and abroad and has earned her and the group an international reputation.

Yi Li Ming (1963–) Designer, China. Yi graduated in 1985 from the Central Academy of Drama. His lighting works include Cao Yu's *Beijing Ren* (*Peking Characters*, 1989, in collaboration with the stage designer XUE Dian Jie), GUO Shi Xing's *Niao Ren* (*Bird Master*, directed by LIN Zhao Hua) and Wang Zi Fu's *Hong He Gu* (*Red River Valley*, 1996). He designed Lin Zhao Hua's 1990 production of *Hamlet*, his 1994 production of Goethe's *Faust* and Guo Shi Xing's *Qi Ren* (*The Go Master*). Generally considered a major designer in that flagship of the mainstream theatre, Beijing People's Art Theatre, he also designed the works of the experimentalist MO Sen, including the latter's *Ling Dang An* (*File Zero*, 1994), *Yu Ai Zi You Guan* (*Aids, Aids*, 1994) and *Gu Xiang Tian Xia Huang*

Hua (*Chrysanthemums in My Home Town*, 1995). His most recent work is for Lin Zhao Hua's 1998 production of *Three Sisters Waiting for Godot*, a collage piece executed by Lin that combines Beckett and Chekhov. Characterized by primal colors and exact positioning, his lighting works stress intensity and taste, although it also has considerable warmth and sensitivity underlying the overwhelming impact. His stage designs have caught critical attention for their experimental daring and sophistication.

Ying Ruo Cheng (1929–) Actor, China. Ying graduated from the department of European languages of the prestigious Qing Hua University in 1946 and later became a member of Beijing People's Art Theatre. He created a series of memorable parts in Lo She's plays *Long Xu Gou* (*Dragon Whiskers Gutter*), *Luo Tuo Xiang Zi* (*Camel Son*) and *Cha Guan* (*Tea House*), which helped the company establish its house style. A fluent speaker of both English and French, he is well-versed in European literature and drama. He played Willy Loman in Arthur MILLER's *Death of Salesman*. He has also played leading roles in a number of internationally known films including *Dr Norman Bethune*, *The Last Emperor*, *Marco Polo* and *Little Buddha*. He has translated Stanislavski's *Othello Plan*, *Measure for Measure* and Arthur Miller's *Death of Salesman*.

Yirenkyi, Mary E. (1938–) Actor and choreographer, Ghana. A very good singer and dancer, Yirenkyi provided some of the music and dance sequences for the 1990 Leeds Workshop Theatre premiere of Olu OBAFEMI's *Naira Has No Gender*, in which she also performed the role of mother of the bride alongside other UK-based African theatre artists such as Kemi Ilori as groom, Sam Kasule as Papa, Osi Okagbue as Chief Awandu, and the African American Anita Franklin in the role of Abeke. She also put in a distinguished performance as one of the dancing and gyrating bacchantes in Wole SOYINKA's *The Bacchae of Euripides*, directed by Amanda Price at the Workshop Theatre, Leeds in 1989. She currently lectures in theatre and performance at the University of Ghana at Legon.

Yoon Ju-Sang (1952–) Actor, Korea. Yoon trained at Seorabeol College of Art and soon afterwards joined the Gagyo, Sanha Theatre Company where he had a series of major parts including the title roles in Goethe's *Faust* and *Othello*, and Shylock in *The Merchant of Venice*, Emperor Chin in Max Frisch's *Die Chinesche Mauer* (*The Chinese Wall*, 1996), Creon in Sophocles's *Antigone*, Willy Loman in Arthur MILLER's *Death of a Salesman* Teach in David MAMET's *American Buffalo*, Professor Frank in Willy Russell's *Educating Rita* and Lee in Sam SHEPARD's *True West*. In Korean originals, he played the Chief of the village in LEE Gang-Baek's *Chilsanri* (*The Town of Chilsanli*, 1989), the Thief in Jeong Bok-Gun's *Sanneomeo Gogaeneomeo* (*Over the Hill Over the Mountain*, a Railway Officer in Youn Dae-Sung *Choolbal* (*Departure*) and the main role in LEE Gun-Sam's *Acasia Gotipun Barame Naligo* (*Wind Spread Acacia Flowers*, 1998). Yoon is known as an actor who can naturally portray both the comic and serious sides of one character. Since the 1980s, he has worked for the Minjoong Theatre Company, now joined with the In-Chon Yu Repertory Theatre Company.

Yoon Suk-Hwa (1956–) Actor, Korea. Yoon trained at The City College of New York and Harvard Drama Institute. During the 1970s, she played the title role in *Cinderella* (1976) and main roles in *West Side Story* (1977) and *You Can't Take It With You* (1979). Returning to Korea from her three-year stay in the USA, her first stage performance was in John Pielmeier's *Agnes of God* (1983, with PARK Jung-Ja in the cast) which she translated

and in which she played the title role. This became the longest running production in Korean theatre history. After producing and playing the main roles in *Annie* (1986) and *Song and Dance* (1986), her reputation as the most popular actor in Korea was confirmed. She has since played star roles in the musicals *Guys and Dolls* (1987), *Myeong-Seong Hwanghoo* (*Empress Myeongseong*, 1995), Jeong Bok-Gun's *Na Kim Soo-Im* (*Me, Soo-Im Kim*, 1997, with HAN Myung-Gu in the cast) and Terence MCNALLY's *Master Class* (1998). Yoon has also performed in the so-called theatre for women such as in Kempinski's *Duet for One* (1989) and Cocteau's *La Voix Humaine* (1990), in which she fully revealed her talent in expressing delicate female psychology.

Yoshida Tamao (1919–) Bunraku puppeteer, Japan. Trained under Yoshida Eiza, Yoshida Tamajiro and Yoshida Tamasuke, Yoshida Tamao is a member of the Chinami-kai Group of the Bunraku association. The way Yoshda manipulates puppets is elegant and upright. The movements of his puppets are strictly based on his characterization of the roles, and he succeeds in engaging his audience in the puppet characters. He has been in charge of Ningyô Kowari (casting of puppeteers) since 1964. His representative roles includes Tomomori, Mitsuhide, Genta and Motome, which are *tachiyaku* (the leading male part). He is especially good in *sewamono* (domestic plays) by Chikamatsu Monzaemon and has manipulated the puppet of Tokubei in Chikamatsu's *Sonezaki Shinju* (*Love Suicide at Sonazaki*) more than one thousand times.

Youn Dai-Sung (1939–) Dramatist, Korea. Youn trained at the Seoul Institute of Arts. Since writing his first play *Choolbal* (*Departure*, 1972), Youn has focused in his later works on the systematic violence of modern society, particularly the mass media. They include *Nobimoonseo*

(*Document of a Slave*, 1974), *Choolsegi* (*The Success Story*, 1974), *Sinhwa 1900* (*The Myth 1900*, 1982), *Saeui Chanmi* (*Praise of Death*, 1988), *Doo Namja Doo Yeoja* (*Two Men and Two Women*, 1992), *Namsadangeui Hanul* (*The Sky of Namsadang, The Wandering Troupe*, 1993) and *Choolsegi 2* (*The Success Story 2*, 1998). He is also known for his trilogy for teenagers, highly acclaimed by teenagers and adults alike, *Banghwanghanun Byeoldul* (*The Wandering Stars*, 1985), *Goomgoonun Byeoldul* (*The Dreaming Stars*, 1987) and *Booltanun Byeoldul* (*The Burning Stars*, 1989), which deal with up to the minute issues in a semimusical form.

Youn So-Jung (1944–) Actor, Korea. Youn had no official theatre training, but as the daughter of famous film director Youn Bong-Choon, she was accustomed to the artistic life and trained with her family. Her major parts have been as Gui-Deok in Cha Beom-Seok's *Sanbool* (*Mountain Fire*, 1974), OH Tae-Seok's *Choboon* (*Grass Tomb*, 1974), as Na-Young in Oh Tae-Seok's *Hwanjeolgi* (*The Turning Point of the Season*, 1975), Dr Livingston in John Pielmeier's *Agnes of God* (1983, with YOON Suk-Hwa and PARK Jung-Ja in the cast) and *Cello* (1994). Youn is an actor of emotional tension, who can naturally create an uncomfortable mood and express internal discord.

Yousuff, Nasiruddin (1950–) Director, Bangladesh. Beginning his directorial career in 1972, Yousuff has seventeen productions to his credit, of which the following have been specially acclaimed for their artistic merit: Selim AL-DEEN's *Shakuntala* (with Shubarna MUSTAFA in the title role and Raisul ASAD as Vishwamitra, 1978), Al-Deen's *Kittan Khola* (*The Fair of Kittan Khola*, with Shubarna Mustafa as Banasribala, Shimul YOUSUFF as Dalimon, Humayan FARIDI as Chhayaranjan and Asad as Bayati, designed by Jamil AHMED, 1981) and Al-Deen's *Kera-*

mat Mangal (*The Epic of Keramat*, with Shimul Yousuff as Shamala and Faridi as Keramat, designed by Jamil Ahmed, 1985). These productions have earned him the distinction of being recognized as a director capable of deftly handling ensemble acting and producing poetically rich visual metaphors. Yousuff is the founder artistic director of Dhaka Theatre (a leading theatre group in Bangladesh), executive member of the Cultural Identity and Development Committee of the International Theatre Institute and chairman of Bangladesh Group Theatre Federation. Yousuff has also conducted workshops abroad and presented papers in international conferences.

Yousuff, Shimul (1957–) Actor and composer, Bangladesh. Yousuff trained as a vocalist, and has seventeen stage productions to her credit. These include Dalimon in Salim AL-DEEN's *Kittan Khola* (*The Fair of Kittan Khola*, 1981), Shamala in Al-Deen's *Keramat Mangal* (*The Epic of Keramat*, with Humayun FARIDI as Keramat, directed by Nasiruddin YOUSUFF and designed by Jamil AHMED, 1985), Chhukkuni in Al-Deen's *Hat Hadai* (*The Seven Voyages*, with Raisul ASAD as Anarbhandari, directed by Nasiruddin Yousuff, 1989) and the Narrator in Al-Deen's *Chaka* (*The Wheel*, with Asad as the Oxcart Driver, directed and designed by Jamil Ahmed, 1991). She also composed the original music score for all these productions. Combining her musical talent with acting, Shimul Yousuff is at her best with indigenous theatrical elements where she captivates her spectators with delicate charm and vibrant energy. She is a renowned vocalist on radio and television and is an active member of Dhaka Theatre (a leading theatre group of Bangladesh).

Yu In-Chon (1951–) Actor, Korea. Yu was educated at Joongang University (BA and MA in Theatre Arts). After having first staged *Othello*, 1971), Yu has mainly worked in television drama and won nationwide fame. He has been involved in only a limited number of performances, including *Hamlet* (1981), *The Merchant of Venice* (1983), and in musicals such as *Jesus Christ Superstar* (1984 and 1990), Oh Young-Jin's *Hanneui Sungcheon* (*Ascension of Hanne*, 1994) and von Trapp in *The Sound of Music*, 1994). In 1995, he founded the In-Chon Yu Repertory Theatre Company in order to produce forgotten masterpieces. He produced and performed the title role in *Moonjejeok Ingan Yeonsan* (*King Yeonsan-A Controversial Figure*, 1995, written and directed by LEE Youn-Taek, designed by SHIN Sun-Hee). Additional appearances include the part of Mephistopheles in Goethe's *Faust*, 1996, with YOON Ju-Sang in the cast), and *Iboda Deo Naboolsoon Eopda* (*It Can't be Worse Than This*, 1998, designed by Sun-Hi Shin). Yu is an objective actor with perfectly controlled and emotional intensity.

Yu, Ovidia (1961–) Dramatist, Singapore. Yu holds a BA (Hons) in English from the National University of Singapore and is undoubtedly one of the strongest feminist voices in Singapore. Her plays deal primarily with social stereotypes of women and the effective dismantling of these cultural constructs. Her plays are biting and satirical. One of her more celebrated works, *Three Fat Virgins Unassembled* (1992), is a glib pastiche of the Singapore woman's dilemma in a materialist context. Yu redefines the oppressed woman as a 'Fat Virgin' and discusses the making and the breaking of a fat virgin in her play. Another play, *The Woman in a Tree on the Hill*, cleverly juxtaposes the western patriarchal myths of Noah with the Chinese myth of origins in the story of Nu-Wa to offer a new perspective on the relationship between men and women. Yu continues to explore other aspects of the woman in her later plays, but has also moved on to experiment with other genres like musicals (*A Twist of Fate*, 1997)

and stand-up routines (*Kumar: A Life ALIVE*, 1998). Yu received both the Japanese Chamber of Commerce and Industry's Culture Award and the National Young Artist Award in 1996.

Yu Shi Zhi (1927–) Actor, China. Yu studied French at Peking University in the 1940s, and established his position at Beijing People's Art Theatre in 1951 when he created the role of Crazy Cheng in Lao She's *Long Xu Gou* (*Dragon Whiskers Gutter*). He played major parts in Tian Han's *Guan Han Qing*, Cao Yu's *Lei Yu* (*Thunderstorm*), Tian Han's *Ming You Zhi Si* (*Death of a Famous Opera-singer*) and Lao She's *Luo Tuo Xiang Zi* (*Camel Son*). He created the definitive Mr Wang, the proprietor of Lao She's *Cha Guan* (*Tea House*). He also played the Duke in the Chinese premiere of *Measure for Measure*. He collaborated with Cao Yu and Mei Qian in composing the history play *Dan Jian Pian*. He is now the deputy director of Beijing People's Art Theatre.

Yudane, Wayan Gde (1964–) Designer, Indonesia. Having trained as a performer at STSI Denpasar (Academy of Performing Arts), Yudane has become a sound and scenic designer as well as composer. He designed sets for the Puspita Jaya *Kecak* at Singapore Arts Festival 1997; IKARANAGARA's *Ritus Topeng*, the 1994 international tour of the Paris-based company La Temp Fort, and the Asian Collective Performing Art Festival in Kumamoto, Japan, 1989. He is also the official composer and designer for the City of Denpasar. His innovative and original designs transform traditional motifs to create something wholly new, yet subtly familiar.

Yuliarsa, Ketut (1960–) Dramatist, performer and designer, Indonesia. Yuliarsa studied music at Saraswati School, Denpasar, journalism in Yogyakarta, Java, and English at Sydney College, Australia. He received his training in drama working with Abu BAKAR's Teater Poliklinik, Denpasar. Actor, musician, designer and now principally a dramatist, he has performed in Melbourne (Melbourne Theatre Company), Sydney (Belvoir Street Theatre) and Tokyo. He has also designed contemporary theatre productions for the Bali Arts Festival including Putu Wijaya's *Aum* in 1995. His latest play, *The Coffin*, premiered at the 1997 Festival. He writes skillfully in both English and Indonesian with a sensibility which encompasses values and viewpoints of both East and West.

Yzraeli, Yossi (1939–) Director, Israel. Yzraeli trained at the Royal Academy of Dramatic Art in London and at Bristol University, and obtand a Ph.D. from the Carnegie Mellon Institute in Pittsburgh. Yizraeli has directed classics like Beckett's *Waiting for Godot*, Ibsen's *Peer Gynt* and *Fruen fra Havet* (*The Lady from the Sea*), and *The Merchant of Venice*, but is best known for his stage adaptatations of Jewish sources and narrative materials such as several of S.J. Agnon's novels and short stories and An-Ski's *The Dybbuk*. Yizraeli teaches at Tel Aviv University and has been the director of the Habima national theatre (1975–7) and the Khan Jerusalem municipal theatre (1984–7). He has also directed in the USA and England.

Z

Zachwatowicz-Wajda, Krystyna (1930–) Designer, Poland. After graduating in Art History from the Jagiellonski University in Cracow and in scenography at the Fine Arts Academy in Cracow, Zachwatowicz-Wajda began her career at the end of the 1950s in the theatre of Cracow and the Silesian region of Poland. In her long and distinguished career, she has worked with many of the most important Polish and foreign directors, including Jorge LAVELLI, Andrzej WAJDA, Jerzy Jarocki and Konrad Swinarski. Productions include works after Dostoyevsky (*The Brothers Karamasov, Besy* (The Possessed), *Idiot* (*The Idiot*) and *Prestuplenie I nakazanie* (*Crime and Punishment*)), Wyspianski (*Noc Listopadowa* (*November Night*) and *Wesele* (*The Wedding*)), Genet's *Les bonnes* (*The Maids*), *Hamlet* and Strindberg's *Spöksonaten* (*The Ghost Sonata*).

Zadek, Peter (1926–) Director, Germany. Zadek's family emigrated to Britain in 1933, where he trained at the Old Vic School in London with Tyrone Guthrie. At the Old Vic he directed a double bill of Wilde's *Salome* and Eliot's *Sweeney Agonistes*. In the 1950s he worked for the BBC and throughout Britain, culminating in a major success with Genet's *Le balcon* (*The Balcony*, 1957) at the Arts Theatre Club in London. In 1958 he returned to Germany, carrying with him his love for Shakespeare, his love for boulevard and

his preference for topical provocation. In 1960 he joined Kurt Hübner in Ulm, and stayed with him in Bremen (1962–7). He was artistic director in Bochum (1972–7), and later in Hamburg (Deutsches Schauspielhaus, 1985–9) and Berliner Ensemble (1993–6), where he frequently worked with Ulrich Wildgruber, Rosl ZECH, Eva MATTES and Ilse RITTER. In the 1960s and 1970s, many of his productions caused scandals. However, today his interpretations of Shakespeare are regarded as seminal for the reception of the classics on the German stage. 'There may be much shocking chaos, but there are also quiet, unpretentious productions which show Zadek as a master of psychological characterization.'

Zaker, Aly (1944–) Director and actor, Bangladesh. Aly Zaker holds a BA in sociology from the University of Dhaka (1966). Important in his directorial career are Badal Sircar's *Baki Itihas* (*The Other Side of History*, with Abdul HAYAT as Sitanath, Sarah ZAKER as Kona and Ataur RAHMAN as Saradindu, 1973), Tagore's *Achalayatan* (set and lighting design by Jamil AHMED, 1980), Syed HUQ's *Nooraldeener Sarajeeban* (*Nooraldeen: A Life*, 1981) and an adaptation of Zuckmayer's *Der Hauptmann von Köpenick* (*The Captain of Köpenick*, 1981). His acting career includes male lead roles in a translation of Brecht's *Leben des Galilei* (*The Life of*

Galileo, 1988) and an adaptation of Brecht's *Herr Puntila und sein Knecht Matti* (*Mr Puntila and his Servant Matti*, with Hayat as Matti, directed by Asaduzzaman NOOR, 1977). Aly Zaker's acting is distinct for the vibrant energy he infuses into his characters. As a director he is committed to the performers and the text: he deftly handles them to uncover unexpected layers of meaning in the text. He has toured abroad with his productions and has also adapted a number of plays. Zaker is the president of Nagorik Natya Sampradaya (a leading theatre group in Bangladesh), vice president of the International Theatre Institute, Bangladesh Centre and a communication consultant by profession.

Zaker, Sarah (1954–) Actor and director, Bangladesh. Zaker trained at the British Theatre Institute (1981). With over a thousand appearances on stage, Sarah Zaker's important performances include Kona in Badal Sircar's *Baki Itihas* (*The Other Side of History*, 1973), Shen Te/ Shui Ta in an adaptation of Brecht's *Der Gute Mensch von Sezuan* (*The Good Person of Sezuan* with Asaduzzaman NOOR as Yang Sun and Abdul HAYAT as Wang, directed by Aly ZAKER, 1976) and Jubati in Syed Huq's *Irsha* (*Jealousy*, directed by Ataur RAHMAN, set design by Mansuruddin AHMED, 1991). Her portrayal of characters is distinct because of their razor's edge which sends resonances of subterranean torment and violence. She has also directed the much-acclaimed production of *Mukhosh* (an adaptation of Ariel Dorfman's *Death and the Maiden*, with Hayat as the Lawyer and Noor as the Doctor, 1993). A well-known television actor, Sarah Zaker is an active member of Nagorik Natya Sampradaya (a leading theatre group in Bangladesh). She has toured abroad with her performances and is professionally engaged in market research management.

Zakharov, Mark (1933–) Director, Russia. Zakharov started his career as a satirical poet and actor and has no professional background as a stage director. Since 1973 he has been artistic director of the Lenkom theatre, Moscow. Five years before that his production of Ostrovsky's *Na vsyakogo moudretza dovol'no prostoty* (*Diary of a Scoundrel*) at the Satire Theatre, Moscow, was forbidden because of the censor's dissapproval. Zakharov is among the first Russian directors to perform musicals on the dramatic stage. His productions are usually well-shaped, full of humor and acute allusions, and contain musical interventions, dance scenes and so on. He combines different genres and usually modernizes a well-known story. Principal productions include Chekhov's *Ivanov* (1975), PETRUSHEVSKAYA's *Tri devushki v golubom* (*Three Girls in Blue*, 1982), Ostrovsky's *Moudretz* (*The Wiseman*, 1989) and *Le mariage de Figaro* (*The Marriage of Figaro*) by Beaumarchais (1993). Zakharov is also professor of Russian Academy of Theatre Art (where he has taught many excellent actors of the contemporary Russian stage, including some who are working at his theatre and have won international publicity, such as Inna Churikova and Oleg Yankovsky). Zakharov serves as the Russian President's Adviser in the field of culture.

Zaks, Jerry (1946–) Director and actor, USA. Born in Germany, Zaks grew up in the USA. He began his professional career as an actor, adding directing to his credits when he had a chance to direct Christopher Durang's *Sister Mary Ignatius Explains it All for You* (1979). Since then, Zaks has specialized in contemporary comedy, often the work of Durang and John GUARE, and musicals. More recent work includes *Guys and Dolls* (1997), and Martin McDonagh's *The Cripple of Inishmaan* (1999). 'Zaks's directorial style shows a close rapport with actors, a commitment to the playwright's vision as expressed through dialogue and action, and the importance of building an ensemble'.

Zaourou, Bernard Zadi (1938–) Dramatist, Ivory Coast. Zaourou is a leading left-wing thinker on and experimenter with dramatic form, theatre styles and staging techniques, informed by a desire to develop a radical theatre aesthetic that is rooted in his country's traditional performing art forms. His *L' Oeil* (*The Eye*, 1974), an agit-prop style play, was censored for its perceived intentional incitement to class hatred and violence. But as a piece of theatre it was remarkable and well-appreciated for its successful experiments with both dialogue in words, drum language, silence and mime. *Les Sofas* (*The Sofas*, 1975) was a more traditional history play. In *La Termitière* (*The Termites' Nest*, 1981), the experiments are pushed even further in an initiation-cum-ritual play steeped in deep mysticism, symbolism and surrealist poetry. His other plays are *Sory Lambre* (1968), *Les Tignasses* (*The Mane*, 1984), *L'Oeuf de pierre* (*The Stone Egg*) and *Le Secret des dieux* (*The Secret of the Gods*, 1984). Most of these plays were the result of Zaourou's experiments into and with the traditional *didiga*, an artistic traditional form which is centred around the concept of the unthinkable and in which the familiar is set in juxtaposition to the strange and the irrational in order to shock the audience into a new awareness. He is the founder-director of Digida, a multiplex performing company formed in 1980 and dedicated to researching into and employing traditional forms and styles in its dramatic presentations.

Zayas, Dean (1939–) Director, Puerto Rico. One of Puerto Rico's most prolific directors, Dean Zayas earned an MA in theatre education/directing from New York University (1963) after earning his BA in theatre from the University of Puerto Rico, where he is currently pursuing a doctorate in Hispanic Studies as a member of the drama faculty. Zayas achieved notoriety in the 1960s as co-founder of Teatro de Sesenta (Sixties Theatre) and Teatro Sylvia Rexach, although he continued to work with other groups such as El Otro Grupo (The Other Group) and Candilejas (Candlelight). Zayas prefers to stage classics of the world theatre, particularly modern American drama. Notable productions include Williams's *The Glass Menagerie* (1973), Ibsen's *En folkefiende* (*An Enemy of the People*, 1978) and Lorca's *La casa de Bernarda Alba* (*The House of Bernarda Alba*, 1978). More recent productions include HWANG's *M. Butterfly* (Centro de Bellas Artes, 1990) and HAMPTON's *Les Liaisons Dangereuses* (Teatro Tapia, 1993). As director of the University's Traveling Theatre, Zayas has also directed works by Shakespeare, Tirso de Molina, Goldoni, and Calderón. From 1980–6, Zayas served as both chair of the University of Puerto Rico's Department of Drama and as director of the Institute of Puerto Rican Culture's Theatre Division.

Zech, Rosel (1942–) Actor, Germany. Zech left her training at Max Reinhardt School in Berlin to take up her first employment in Landshut (1962–5). After working in Wuppertal (1965–70) and Stuttgart (1970–2), she joined Peter ZADEK's company in Bochum, where her many parts included Polonius/Osrick in *Hamlet* (1977) and the title role in Ibsen's *Hedda Gabler* (1977). After that, she has worked mainly freelance with major theatres in Germany. More recently, she played Elisabeth in Schiller's *Maria Stuart* (Munich, 1991) Ranevskaya in Chekhov's *Visnevyi sad* (*The Cherry Orchard*, Vienna, 1992), Anne in Bernhard's *Über allen Gipfeln ist Ruh* (*Silence beyond all Mountain Peaks*, Münchner Kammerspiele, 1993, directed by Alexander LANG), Genet's *Les bonnes* (*The Maids*, 1996) and Marthe Rull in Kleist's *Der Zerbrochene Krug* (*The Broken Jug* 1997, both at the Bayerisches Staatsschauspiel in Munich). She has been described as very precise, lacking vanity. Her clear diction and her unvarying discipline in acting have been praised.

Zhao Yao Min (1956–) Dramatist, China. Zhao studied dramatic literature at the Shanghai Drama Academy and Chinese at Nanking University. He has written *Tian Cai He Feng Zi* (*Genius and Maniac*, 1985, original name *A Grim Romance*), *Qin Sheng You Qi* (*That Music Again*, 1987) *Qin Ai De Ni Shi Ge Mi* (*My Dear, You are an Enigma*, 1989), *Ben Shi Ji Zui Hou De Meng Xiang* (*Last Dream of the Century*, 1990), *Nao Zhong* (*Alarm Clock*, 1992), *Wu Ye Xin Qing* (*Midnight Feelings*, 1994) and *Ge Xing Yu Xing Xing* (*The Gorilla and the Pop Star*) designed by HAN Sheng. He writes about the absurd conditions of marginalized people with a touch of black humor.

Zheng Rong (1924–) Actor, China. Zheng studied Western style painting at the Peking National School of Fine Arts. From the 1950s to 1980s he played major 'old man' roles in many important plays with Beijing People's Art Theatre, including including Lao She's *Long Xu Gou* (*Dragon Whiskers Gutter*, 1950), Cao Yu's *Lei Yu* (*Thunderstorm*, 1954), Guo Mo Ruo's *Hu Fu* (*Tiger Tally*, 1957), Lao She's *Cha Guan* (*Tea House*, 1958), Zhao Qi Yang's *Zhi Qu Wei Hu Shan* (*Take the Tiger Mountain by Stratagem*), a dramatization of an excerpt from Qu Bo's novel *Lin Hai Xue Yuan*, Guo Mo Ruo's *Cai Wen Ji*, Guo Mo Ruo's *Wu Ze Tian* (*Empress Wu Ze Tian*), Su Shu Yang's *Dan Xin Pu* (*Devoted Heart*, 1978) and Liang Bing Kun's *Bing Tang Hu Lu* (*Toffee Haw*, 1996). He is known for his forceful portrayals and a touch of character acting.

Zhu Lin (1923–) Actor, China. Zhu neither attended university nor received any training for the theatre. She is a member of Beijing People's Art Theatre, where she played leading female roles from the 1950s to the 1980s in such plays as Gogol's *Revizor* (*The Government Inspector*), Cao Yu's *Lei Yu* (*Thunderstorm*), Guo Mo Ruo's *Hu Fu* (*Tiger Tally*), Guo Mo Ruo's *Wu Ze Tian* (*Empress Wu Ze Tian*), *Dan Xin Pu* (*Devoted Heart*), Dürrenmatt's *Der Besuch der Alten Dame* (*The Visit*) and Arthur MILL-ER's *Death of Salesman*. Many Chinese theorists seeking the 'sinasation' of Western spoken drama see her as an example of their aesthetic ideal, as she has sought to introduce elements of Chinese operatic tradition in her acting and speech.

Zinsou, Senouvo (1946–) Dramatist, Togo. Zinsou has always been a pioneer of theatre and performance in Togo, having helped to establish while still at college an inter-secondary school dramatic society, L'Entente Scolaire pour le Théâtre et le Folklore. On his return from Paris and subsequent appointment to the Culture Ministry, he founded the Togoese National Company for the Performing Arts and was its director until 1992. Zinsou's theatre is remarkable for the way he exploits the traditional and contemporary popular theatre and folk forms of Togo in his plays and staging technique. He wrote his first play, *L'amour d'un sauvage* (*The Love of a Savage*), in 1968. His published plays include *On joue la comédie* (*Let's Play the Play*, 1975) which won the first prize in the Inter-African Radio competition and was his country's entry for FESTAC 77 (Black and African Festival of Arts and Culture held in Lagos, Nigeria), *Le Club* (*The Club*, 1983); *La Tortue qui chante* (*The Singing Tortoise*, 1987), *La Femme du blanchisseur* (*The Laundryman's Wife*, 1987) and *Yevi au pays des monstres* (*Yevi in the Land of the Monsters*, 1987).

Zobda, France (1958–) Actor, France and Martinique. After university studies in English and Business, Zobda studied drama at the Cours Florent (with Francis Huster). Some stage roles include Mariette in Laou's *Ne m'appelez jamais nègre* (*Don't Ever Call Me Nigger*, 1983) and Lady Teazle in an adaptation of Sheridan's *School for Scandal* (1984). These led to a busy screen career, attracting critical praise for her role in Michel Drach's *Sauve-toi, Lola* (*Save Yourself, Lola*, 1986), and starring among others in Diop's *Mamy Wata* (*River Mother*) and Deslauriers's *L'Exil de Bèhanzin* (*King Behanzin's Exile*), where her energy and charm as a mulatto laundress reinvigorate the exiled king. Although in much demand for French television drama, she has continued to be loyal to the less commercial Caribbean work of Juiius Amédée LAOU, appearing in his hommage to Joseph Zobel (1996).

Zohar, Miriam (1928–) Actor, Israel. Zohar was born in Romania and began her career on the Yiddish stage, later joining the Habima national theatre in 1951 where she has played many major roles like Solveig in Ibsen's *Peer Gynt*, Cordelia (*King Lear*), Martha (Edward ALBEE's *Who's Afraid of Virginia Wolf?*) and Euripides's *Medeia*. She has played the mother in all the three parts in the trilogy by Shmuel HASPARI. She received the Israel Prize in 1986.

Zsámbéki, Gábor (1943–) Director, Hungary. After graduating from the Academy of Theatre and Film Art in 1968 Zsámbéki immediately joined the company of the Csiky Gergely Theatre in Kaposvár. In 1978 he became artistic director of the Budapest National Theatre, and in 1982 of the Katona József Theatre, serving as it general director since 1989. Since 1978 he has also taught acting and directing at the Academy of Theatre and Film Art, and since 1989 he has been a member of the Founding Committee of the European Theatre Union. He has worked in Helsinki, several times in Stuttgart, in Frankfurt and at the Düsseldorfer Schauspielhaus. Major productions include PINTER's *The Caretaker*, Chekhov's *Cajka* (*The Seagull* and *Ivanov*; *As You Like It*, *Hamlet*, *Twelfth Night*, Wesker's *The Kitchen*, Mihály Kornis's *Halleluja*, Jarry's *Ubu Roi* (*King Ubu*), György SPIRÓS' *Csirkefej* (*Chicken Head*) and Molière's *L'avare* (*The Miser*). He works in different styles, depending on the material and his own vision, often stripping off every convention associated with the plays.